AN EMPIRICAL
BASIS FOR CHANGE
IN EDUCATION

Edited by
Wesley C. Becker
Professor of Special Education
College of Education
University of Oregon

AN EMPIRICAL BASIS FOR CHANGE IN EDUCATION

Selections on Behavioral Psychology for Teachers

S R A

SCIENCE RESEARCH ASSOCIATES, INC.
Chicago, Palo Alto
Toronto, Henley-on-Thames, Sydney

A Subsidiary of IBM

To
Sidney W. Bijou
Donald M. Baer
and
Montrose M. Wolf

Karl Schmidt
Sponsoring Editor

Lynn Peacock
Project Editor

Judith Olson
Designer

Table of Contents

Part III. Programing Educational Sequences

Editor's Preface

The impact of B. F. Skinner and his students on the understanding of human behavior and human institutions is accelerating at a rate that seemed impossible seven years ago. At that time I was fighting with others to bring Skinner's views into training programs in clinical psychology. The resistance by those trained in the concepts of phenomenology, existentialism, psychoanalysis, and personality theory of a variety of sorts was often discouraging. In a matter of six or seven years, however, the functional behavioral approach has won acceptance, at least as an alternative, in most educational circles.

In my opinion, forces for change have been set in motion that will not stop. These forces consist of—

1. an empirical body of evidence showing how behavior can be built and changed;
2. a methodology applicable to research in the animal laboratory, the clinic, the school, or the hospital; and
3. a cadre of applied-research workers who day by day are gathering strong evidence that operant learning principles and behavior analysis methods can be used in all sorts of settings to deal with all sorts of problems.

The movement of behavior analysis from the laboratory to clinics, homes, classrooms, and hospitals has had many contributors. However, an investigation of the training origins and sources of professional influence of the contributors to this volume reveals an overwhelming impact of three people who found themselves working together at the University of Washington several years ago— namely, Montrose M. Wolf, Donald M. Baer, and Sidney W. Bijou. The majority of the selections in this volume came directly from these three persons and their students.

I consider myself to be indirectly trained by them, through their writings as well as through personal contact. Their demonstrations with nursery school children, retarded children, and emotionally disturbed children were the first to make it clear to many in psychology and education that Skinner's methods and principles really worked with people.

This collection has been selected to assist in the training of teachers in the use of behavior modification procedures. The readings are not expected to stand alone as a teaching device, but were originally designed to supplement a text entitled *Teaching: A Course in Applied Psychology*. These readings can contribute to a variety of education and psychology courses such as Educational Psychology, Mental Health in the Schools, Behavior Modification for Teachers, Child Development, Special Education of the Disadvantaged, Special Education of the Retarded, Special Education of the Emotionally Disturbed, and so forth.

While this book focuses to a large extent on methods for motivating children and changing behavior problems, the reader should keep in mind that the basic principles of operant learning provide a strong basis for curriculum development and change. A sampling of readings on instructional applications is provided in part III.

The references for the selections have been left substantially as they appeared in the original.

The editor is indebted to the contributing authors and publishers who have made this volume possible.

WESLEY C. BECKER
Eugene, Oregon

Acknowledgments

"What Psychology Has to Offer Education—Now" by Sidney W. Bijou. From *Journal of Applied Behavior Analysis*, Vol. 3, No. 1, 1971, 65–71. Copyright 1971 by the Society for the Experimental Analysis of Behavior, Inc. Reprinted with permission of the author and publisher.

"The First Encounter" by Philip H. Wickersham. Reprinted by permission of the author.

"Who's Responsible: Teacher or Learner?" From *Carnegie Quarterly*, Vol. 15, No. 4 (Fall 1967) and Vol. 16, No. 1 (Winter 1968). © Carnegie Corporation of New York Quarterly.

"The Technology of Teaching" by B. F. Skinner. From *Proceedings of the Royal Society*, B, Vol. 162, 1965. Copyright 1965, The Royal Society. Reprinted by permission of the author and the Council of the Royal Society.

"Special Education for the Mildly Retarded—Is Much of It Justifiable?" by Lloyd M. Dunn. From *Exceptional Children*, Vol. 35, September 1968, 5–22. © 1968, Council for Exceptional Children, Arlington, Va. Reprinted with permission of the author and The Council for Exceptional Children.

"The Educational Technology Game: A Tragedy in Two Acts" by William A. Deterline. Reprinted with permission from *Educational Technology Magazine*, September 15, 1968. © Educational Technology Publications, 1968.

"Are Operant Principles Tautological?" by Robert L. Burgess and Ronald L. Akers. From *The Psychological Record*, Vol. 16, 1966, 305–12. © 1966, The Psychological Record. Reprinted with permission of the authors and publisher.

"Strong Inference" by John R. Platt. From *Science*, Vol. 146, # 3642, October 16, 1964, 347–52. © 1964 by the American Association for the Advancement of Science. Reprinted by permission of the author and publisher.

"A Method to Integrate Descriptive and Experimental Field Studies at the Level of Data and Empirical Concepts" by Sidney W. Bijou, Robert F. Peterson, and Marion H. Ault. From *Journal of Applied Behavior Analysis*, Vol. 1, No. 2, 1968, 175–91. Copyright 1968 by the Society for the Experimental Analysis of Behavior, Inc. Reprinted with permission of the authors and publisher.

For permission to reprint or adapt material in "Reducing Behavior Problems: An Operant Conditioning Guide for Teachers" by Wesley C. Becker, Don R. Thomas, and Douglas Carnine, the following are acknowledged:

"Effect of Contingent and Non-Contingent Social Reinforcement on the Cooperative Play of a Preschool Child" by Betty M. Hart, Nancy J. Reynolds, Donald M. Baer, Eleanor R. Brawley, and Florence R. Harris. From *Journal of Applied Behavior Analysis*, Vol. 1, No. 1, 1968, 75. Copyright 1968 by the Society for the Experimental Analysis of Behavior, Inc.

"Remedial Use of the Reinforcement Contingency" by Donald M. Baer. Paper presented at the Annual Convention of the American Psychological Association, Chicago, Illinois, 1966.

"The Contingent Use of Teacher Attention and Praise in Reducing Classroom Behavior Problems" by Wesley C. Becker, Charles H. Madsen, Jr., Carole Arnold, and Don R. Thomas. From *The Journal of Special Education*, Vol. 1, No. 3, 1967. © 1967, Buttonwood Farms, Inc.

"Rules, Praise, and Ignoring: Elements of Elementary Classroom Control" by Charles H. Madsen, Wesley C. Becker, and Don R. Thomas. From *Journal of Applied Behavior Analysis*, Vol. 1, 1968, 146. Copyright 1968 by the Society for the Experimental Analysis of Behavior, Inc.

"Production and Elimination of Disruptive Classroom Behavior by Systematically Varying Teacher's Behavior" by Don R. Thomas, Wesley C. Becker, and Marianne Armstrong. From *Journal of Applied Behavior Analysis*, Vol. 1, 1968, 39. Copyright 1968 by the Society for the Experimental Analysis of Behavior, Inc.

"The Effects of Direct and 'Vicarious' Reinforcement on the Behavior of Problem Boys in an Elementary School Classroom" by Douglas Carnine, Wesley C. Becker, Don R. Thomas, Meredith Poe, and Elaine Plager. Unpublished manuscript, Bureau of Educational Research, University of Illinois, 1968.

"Social Reinforcement and Remedial Instruction in the Elimination of a Classroom Behavior Problem" by Don R. Thomas, Loretta J. Nielson, David S. Kuypers, and Wesley C. Becker. From *Journal of Special Education*, Vol. 2, 1968. © 1968, Buttonwood Farms, Inc.

"Experiments with Token Reinforcement in a Remedial Classroom" by Montrose M. Wolf, Daniel K. Giles, and R. Vance Hall.

Part I

CONCEPTS, ISSUES, AND METHODS

Part I. *Concepts, Issues, and Methods*

Part I opens with a succinct statement by Bijou on what psychology has to offer teachers now. As a science dealing with generalizations about the ways in which stimulus events influence behavior, operant psychology is able to provide the teacher with practical procedures for using stimulus events to make learning happen. Bijou also outlines new roles for supporting school personnel such as psychologists and social workers. Finally, the requirements for the teacher who would use what psychology can offer today are specified: a modest amount of specialized training and supervised practice.

"The First Encounter" provides a touch of satire on the current educational scene. "Who's Responsible: Teacher or Learner?" introduces the reader to Skinner's book *The Technology of Teaching*. Some of the key issues separating Skinner from other educators and psychologists are highlighted in this review. Do educators fear effective teaching? Is freedom jeopardized by the new technology? What about creativity?

Skinner's classic lecture "The Technology of Teaching," provides a direct statement on what teaching is about and also raises many questions. Do technological approaches lead to children being treated like animals? Are classrooms becoming so mechanized that the human element is neglected? Should children be given material rewards for learning?

Dunn raises a critical issue for education today: Are special classes justified? Have educators been trapped into using methods that do not best serve the needs of children? As the reader considers the need for change in education today, some perspectives on the problems to be solved are gained through the issues raised by Dunn.

In "The Educational Technology Game," we return to satire. Historically, satire has been a powerful way of criticizing the establishment under the guise of fun. The issues raised are serious ones.

The remaining selections in this section focus on technical issues of methodology in science. Burgess and Aker deal with a common criticism of operant psychology and outline basic definitions and principles for the reader. "Some Questions and Answers" and "Strong Inference" deal with the question "Are some methods better than others?" Platt states that simple models and careful analytical methods that isolate one variable at a time are really paying off in the physical and biological sciences, whereas complex interaction models and survey approaches are not. I believe that a comparison of Skinner's analytic methods with other approaches to research in psychology and education would yield the same result.

The last article in this section, by Bijou, Peterson, and Ault, provides basic procedures and rationales for doing experimental field research. The paper is a statement of a method for use in applied settings. This method is consistent with the methods of experimental analysis of behavior that have been found to be so revealing in the laboratory.

1

What Psychology Has to Offer Education – Now

Sidney W. Bijou
University of Illinois

Some day, the question, "What does psychology have to offer education – now?" addressed to any group of psychologists will result in approximately similar accounts. But right now, today, the answer depends almost entirely on the particular orientation of the psychologists to whom the question is put. As you know, psychologists differ greatly in the way they view the subject matter of psychology. Some say it is the domain of the mind, others, the interaction of the individual with environmental events. Psychologists also differ greatly in what they see as the task of psychology. Some say it is understanding and explanation, others prediction and control. Again, psychologists differ markedly in their notion of the basic research methodology. Some stress analysis of differences between groups, others, analysis of changes in the individual organism. Finally, psychologists differ greatly on their strategy for building a theory of psychology. Some follow the hypothetico-deductive procedure, others, the empirical-inductive method.

If the *great majority* of psychologists were asked what psychology has to offer education now, the answer would be something like this,

Invited address, Division of School Psychologists, American Psychological Association, 76th Annual Convention, September 1, 1968, San Francisco. The analysis presented was generated in large measure from research supported by the U.S. Office of Education, Division of Research, Bureau of Education for the Handicapped, Project No. 5-0961, Grant No. OEG-32-23-6002.

"Well, we offer a collection of ideas about the child and his growth and development, learning, teaching, and the socialization process, and we advocate a professional attitude which favors tentative ideas and actions because we know so very little about the educational process."

The offerings of this group are culled from many fields of study — psychology, sociology, anthropology, and medicine. They are based on a variety of theories, including psychoanalysis, cognitive theory, and social learning theory. And they have been generated from different research methods — correlational, clinical case studies, experimental, psychometric, and field observational. Consequently, they are vague, nonsystematic, and often contradictory. This group is eclectic in research methodology. In general, they believe that it is advisable to assess abilities and to obtain as many measures as possible. Since they consider teaching an intuitive art, their attitude would be that some of the thoughts and ideas they offer should help educators to evaluate their philosophy of education and to revise their curricula, and should acquaint classroom teachers with new, interesting, and appealing developments.

If, on the other hand, the *large minority* is asked the question, the reply would be of this sort: "We offer some tentative ideas about the nature of the child, strong convictions about the stages of cognitive growth, some theoretical formulations about the nature of learning, the will to learn, coping and defending, and a philosophy of science which stresses hypothetical causes of behavior."

Although these concepts are systematically related, they are vague and often refer to unobservable conditions and processes. The principles are autistic and will be found to vary widely from person to person in the group. Application is indirect and speculative. It either operates through a series of hypothetical variables or it depends on precepts to bring the research findings into the classroom. Research which consists mostly of comparing the products of learning aims at testing a theory or an hypothesis. Finally, the core theory encourages one to attribute school failures to something inside the child, as for example, lack of motivation, dyslexia, preceptual disability, or clinically inferred brain-damage.

Still another group of psychologists, the *small minority* responding to the same query, would in all likelihood reply, "We offer a set of concepts and principles derived from an experimental analysis of behavior, a definite procedure for the application of these concepts and principles to education, a research method which concentrates on the individual child, and a philosophy of science which encourages a search for observable causes."

Faced with a complex state of affairs, a house of psychology divided on what it has to offer education, I must limit myself and focus on the offer of the last-mentioned group, the mini-minority, and expound on its exciting promise. I shall also point out the influence it would have on the role of the school psychologist, and finally, I shall suggest what you, as educators, must do to pick up the option of this offer.

The Offer of the Small Minority

The offer by the small minority will be considered in terms of the nature of the concepts and principles, the procedure for their application to education, the research method, and the philosophy of science.

The Concepts and Principles

The concepts are *empirical.* They are based on observable interactions between stimulating events and behavior. The concepts are also *functional.* Stimuli are defined in terms of their effects on an individual's behavior, and an individual's behavior is defined in terms of its effects on the environment. For example, a reinforcing stimulus is a consequent stimulus which strengthens the operant behavior of an individual under specific circumstances. Note that a reinforcing property of a stimulus is defined by its effects on an individual; it is tailored to fit the individual under specified conditions.

The principles are statements of *demonstrated relationships* between environmental events and behavior, or stimuli and responses. Here is a statement of this sort: "The longer the interval between an operant response and its reinforcing stimulus the less the strengthening effect on responses of the same class." These statements are the *facts* of the science of psychology as generated by an experimental analysis of behavior. They have been accumulating gradually over the past sixty years, despite the distractions from a continuous parade of fads and fashions in concepts and theoretical models over the same time span.

Application to Education

The concepts and principles are applied *directly* to the teaching situation, that is, to the behavior of the pupil as he interacts with instructions, the materials presented, and the reinforcement contingencies. The process is clearly spelled out by Skinner in his new book, *The Technology of Teaching* (1968). Therefore, application of the concepts and principles is not in the form of speculations about which conditions in the classroom coordinate with which concepts of a theory, nor is the application in the form of a set of precepts.

The teaching process is analyzed as a complex situation (compared to the laboratory in which most experimental studies are performed) in which the teacher arranges the contingencies of reinforcement to expedite learning by the child. The teacher is the *arranger,* and since she generally works in the classroom by herself, we may think of her as the "Lone Arranger."

For the most part, the teacher arranges contingencies to eliminate behaviors which compete with the desired academic and social behaviors in the class. She also arranges contingencies to strengthen appropriate study behavior—attending and work habits—and hopefully she arranges them so that this behavior becomes part of a child's way of dealing with future study tasks. Finally, the teacher arranges contingencies by programming the subject matter of both the visible (formal academic subjects) and the invisible (manners and moral behavior) curricula in such a way that learning is accomplished with minumum errors and the child makes progress at his own pace.

Two comments about arranging the educational environment are appropriate at this point—one pertains to programming the contingencies of reinforcement; the other, to programming the stimulus material. The fact that academic and social behaviors are operants, and hence sensitive to consequent stimulation, has led many teachers and researchers to use indiscriminately contrived contingencies such as tokens, M & Ms, points, stars, etc. Such contrived reinforcers are not always necessary, and in many instances in which they have been used, they have not been meaningful to the child. That is to say, the child's behavior was not strengthened by directly dispensing M & Ms to him, or by whatever else he received when he exchanged a collection of tokens or a sum of points for it. Contrived reinforcers are appropriate only when the reinforcers available to a teacher (confirmation, indications of progress, approval, and the like) are not functional for a child. Furthermore, when contrived reinforcers are considered necessary, they should be programmed so that they are gradually eliminated and replaced by the reinforcers which evolve from the activity learned. These are called by Ferster (1967) "natural," "intrinsic," or "automatic" reinforcers. As Skinner (1968) has pointed out, the critical task in most teaching situations is not the incorporation of new reinforcers but the effective utilization of those currently available to the teacher.

Let us turn to the programming of stimulus materials. The fact that a school task can be learned with a minimum of frustration and on the basis of positive reinforcement via a program of differential reinforcement of successive approximations to the ultimate form of a response (skill), or the desired expression in the proper situation (knowledge), has led to an over-emphasis on the role of teaching machines, and a misconception about which school subjects can be properly programmed. Teaching machines, from the most primitive to the most elaborate, are of value in an educational setting only in so far as they assist the teacher in arranging contingencies to expedite learning. The programming procedure, which can be used for any school subject that can be specified, is straight-forward: (1) state in objective terms the desired terminal or goal behavior, (2) assess the child's behavioral repertory relevant to the task, (3) arrange stimulus material or behavioral criteria for reinforcement in sequence, (4) start the child on the unit in the sequence that he can respond to correctly 90 per cent of the time or better, (5) manage contingencies of reinforcement to strengthen successive approximations to the terminal behavior and to build conditioned reinforcers that are intrinsic to the task learned, and (6) keep records of the child's progress and modify the program accordingly.

On the basis of the research to date, it is clear that the behavioral concepts and principles developed thus far can be applied to the teaching situation and can produce gratifying results. They work! With further advances in basic and technological research they are expected to work even better.

Research

The reference to research brings us to the third feature of an applied behavior analysis. Research, whether it is aimed at exploring a functional relationship or at assessing a practical application, is centered on the individual child in relation to the conditions and processes that change his behavior. The research is not geared to test a theory of learning or an hypothesis but to demonstrate a functional relationship or the feasibility of a practical application. It follows that the strategy of research in the technology of teaching does not consist of asking whether Method A is better than Method B to teach Subject Matter C. Rather, it consists of engineering an educational environment that works for each child in the group *and then* comparing the achievement of the children in that situation with that of children in some other situation based on a different set of principles, or on "traditional methods."

The Philosophy of Science

We turn now to the fourth and final feature of this approach: the assumptions or philosophy of science of an experimental analysis of behavior. The philosophy of science of an approach is worth examining because it influences the kinds of problems studied, the basic method of gathering data, the form of the data collected, and the interpretations of findings. I shall, for the purpose of this paper, limit myself to a discussion of three of the assumptions.

1. The interactions between a child and environmental events are *lawful*. Given a child with a unique biological endowment, changes in his behavior are a function of his interactional history and the current situation in which he is behaving. Behavior is determined by environmental events — past and present, external and internal. Buckminister Fuller has recently remarked, "I have stopped trying to reform men, I an devoting my life to reforming the environment." It follows from this proposition that successes and failures in school learning are attributed to successes and failures in the way the teacher arranges the environment. Hypothetical internal causes are ruled out.

2. As in all science, the subject matter of psychology exists in *continuities,* not in dichotomies. Continuities are assumed to exist in the stages of development, in the patterns of development—normal, retarded, accelerated, etc. in the problems and procedures of basic and applied research, and in the analysis of psychological interactions from raw data to theoretical formulation.

3. A psychological theory and technology based on a behavior analysis is an *open system.* A new concept, principle, or technique may be added to the list at any time, provided it can display the proper credentials: that it is tied firmly to observable events; that it is functional, and that it does not overlap with those concepts, principles or techniques already catalogued.

Implications for the School Psychologist

Now let us look at the offer from the mini-minority of psychologists in terms of its implications for the school psychologist. Let us suppose that we have a school in which all the teachers are happily applying behavioral principles to all aspects of the educational process. In such a situation the school psychologist would be the person who would be called upon to perform at least four significant duties.

First, he would devote a great deal of his time to kindergarten and first grade teachers, helping children make a smooth transition from the home to the classroom, aiming at the *prevention* of school retardation and associated behavior problems. Specifically, the psychologist would help these teachers to assess all entering children on an individual basis (personal inventories), would help them to identify the particular difficulties of individual children which hinder progress in the tool subjects, and would help them to arrange appropriate individual tutorial work. He would also work with teachers and auxiliary teachers in assessing and modifying the tutorial procedures and programs.

Second, he would work with counselors, teachers, school social workers, and parents on mitigating or eliminating problem behavior in children at any grade level. His analyses and courses of action would be based on the same set of concepts and principles that are applied to teaching. He would be engaging in behavior modification or *action counseling* as described by Krumboltz and his colleagues (1966).

Third, the school psychologist would help teachers with problems of classroom management and subject matter programming. His efforts with respect to classroom management would be very much like the work of Becker and his colleagues (1968). On request from the teacher, he would observe the behavior of a problem child or group of children in the classroom situation, and on the basis of data (usually in the form of frequency of occurrences) he would analyze the situation, work out a course of action with the teacher, try it, and evaluate it. If necessary, he would repeat this procedure until a satisfactory solution was found. His function in regard to helping the teacher program her formal subjects would consist of analyzing the daily progress data on each child and arriving at modifications in procedures and in the sequencing of materials. And with respect to assisting the teacher to program informal subjects, such as paying attention, it would be similar to the procedures described by Hall, Lund, and Jackson (1968).

Fourth, and finally, he would conduct in-service training programs to prepare those who would help the teacher. In many instances they would be clerks, like the IPI clerks in the University of Pittsburgh type of programming; or they may be teachers' aides who assist in individual tutorials and small group instruction. The psychologist would also be the person who, through in-service training would keep the teaching staff informed on advances in the technology of teaching.

It should be apparent from this description that the school psychologist would not be a junior psychiatrist, would not be a part-time clinical psychologist, would not be an administrator of group tests, would not be a psychometrician and writer of mysteriously worded reports; rather he would be a person well-informed and well-skilled in the application of behavior principles to the teaching process as it applies to the normal and deviant pupil at all levels of education.

Requirements for Those in Education Who Wish to Accept the Offer

Now I should like to suggest what educators must do if they think that this offer is an attractive one and they wish to avail themselves of it.

First, they must learn with precision the specifics of the approach. A thorough grounding is necessary because the approach does not offer a touchstone. It is necessary because the approach has an apparent simplicity which can be deceptive. It is necessary because the approach has alluring features which can be misleading. Lastly, it is necessary because effective application of these concepts and principles requires a minute analysis of behavior of the learner and the teaching situation as well as a certain ingenuity in arranging the environments so as to eliminate problems and to expedite the establishment and maintenance of the desired behavior. It is therefore essential that the practitioner learn from *first sources:* (1) the nature of the concepts and principles and the supporting data, (2) the procedure of application and the literature on the technology of teaching, (3) the research methodology, and (4) the details of the philosophy of science and its implications.

Second, the practitioners must obtain experience in applying these principles. That is to say, those who would use this approach must take it upon themselves to observe demonstrations of the use of these concepts and principles in actual educational settings. In addition, they must avail themselves of opportunities to apply the principles under supervision. Only in this way can they face and deal with the special problems of contingency management and stimulus control programming, and only in this way can they hope also to be reinforced by seeing their efforts come to fruition. If there are no preschool or elementary school demonstration classes within easy reach, educators can apply these principles to their college classes. I did exactly that last year and I found out how exciting teaching can be – one of the most exciting things that has happened to me during my 23 years of college teaching.

Summary and Conclusions

A small but rapidly growing group of psychologists have to offer educators, now, a set of concepts and principles derived from the experimental analysis of behavior, a procedure for practical application, a research method that concentrates on individual behavior, and a philosophy of science which says, "Look for the observable causes of behavior."

Application of behavioral principles to education would require the classroom teacher to become facile in managing the contingencies of reinforcement and in programming her explicit and implicit curricula. Application would also change the style of research in education from comparing the products of teaching to analyzing the conditions and processes involved in modifying the behavior of a child. Finally, application of these principles would change the role of the school psychologist. He would be an expert in the technology of teaching. As such, he would work with kindergarten and first grade children to prevent school problems and to remediate difficulties at their inception. He would also serve as a participating consultant on problems of classroom management and programming, and through in-service classes would train those aides who would work with the teacher.

To accept this offer from the small minority of psychologists educators are advised to learn the details of this approach from primary sources. In addition, they must have experience in applying it. They must experience its application first-hand, and participate in the problems, solutions, and reinforcements that evolve from its applications.

What would result from an acceptance of this offer? It is difficult to outline the details but certain broad indications are clear. First, the teacher would derive new satisfactions from teaching. Certainly, this would not come about because I dubbed her the "Lone Arranger." (Some may think I am making her out to be some sort of an intellectual cowboy.) I believe she would gain new satisfactions from teaching because she would be participating in a situation in which she can see concretely the progress of each child, and she would know what to do when a child is not advancing. In addition, she would gain new confidence in herself as a teacher because she would know *what* she is doing for each child and *why* she is doing it. Furthermore, she would be secure in knowing that her practices are based on demonstrated principles, and that she can readily refine and extend her methods in accordance with new findings. Finally, she would have opportunities to embark on new ways of teaching old subjects, and to explore the possibilities of programming new subjects.

Second, accepting this offer and putting it into operation would provide a common basis for the discussion of problems among those working with the teacher — the principal, the psychologist, the counselor, and the school social worker. It would make no differences whether the problem were the persistent descriptive behavior of a single child, difficulties with a segment of the curriculum, a disorderly classroom, an uncooperative parent, or the behavior of children in large groups in the dining room or on the playground. A common empirical approach to analysis of behavior and the teaching process can not help but advance the whole profession of teaching.

Third, systematic application of behavior principles would reduce the number of children who reach the fourth grade without learning to read at a functional level. Present estimates range from 20% to 40% of the school population. In terms of numbers, this is a staggering figure. It is not unrealistic to think that that percentage can be made to approach zero. Furthermore, it would reverse the trend of the need for ever-increasing remedial services. Remember, the program offered here is preventitive and remedial, with the greatest emphasis on the kindergarten and first grade child.

Fourth, the ultimate result, of course, would be a better educated community — the first requisite in the preparation of a society to utilize the advances of science and technology for *human goals*.

REFERENCES

Ferster, C. B. Arbitrary and natural reinforcement. *Psychological Record*, 1967, 17, 341–347.

Hall, R. V., Lund, Diane, and Jackson, Deloris. Effects of teacher attention on study behavior. *Journal of Applied Behavior Analysis*, 1968, 1, 1–12.

Krumboltz, J., (Ed.). *Revolution in Counseling*. New York: Houghton Mifflin, 1966.

Skinner, B. F. *The Technology of Teaching*. New York: Appleton-Century-Crofts, 1968.

Thomas, D. R., Becker, W. C., and Armstrong, Marianne. Production and elimination of disruptive classroom behavior by systematically varying teacher's behavior. *Journal of Applied Behavior Analysis*, 1968, 1, 35–45.

The First Encounter

Philip H. Wickersham
Slippery Rock State College

Did you ever wonder why it is that:

— professors who lecture to you about learning theory, never use that theory themselves?

— students are engaged in the grand game of telling professors what they want to hear?

— the assumption is made that if you know something, you can teach it to others?

— students haven't the backbone to walk out of classes that are neither stimulating nor informative?

— the lecture system, instituted in Medieval times when books were relatively scarce so that teachers had to disseminate and interpret for students, is the primary technique used in the twentieth century?

— if students were given a choice between required courses and areas of interest, many classrooms would be empty?

— professors who decry educating for an elite group are hell bent on making either the Ph.D. degree or the Ed.D. degree (depending on which they hold) the more prestigious?

News of Pi Chapter (Phi Delta Kappa), University of Illinois, Urbana, December 11, 1968, P. H. Wickersham, T. A. Auger, R. Grandchamp, editors, vol. 33, no. 2.

— teachers administer tests and children submit to them, each knowing full well the perpetration of fraud. If you don't believe it, try giving a test without announcing it in advance. We both know what the results will be. We also know what would happen if the same test were given six months hence.

— those who write profusely on innovation in the schools do so little of it themselves?

— with all of the knowledge we have about the effect of child rearing practices, the matter is still left largely to chance? Is this knowledge any less important or crucial than how to solve quadratic equations?

— your *fear* of the grade prevents you from enrolling in courses in areas that would broaden, not confine, your interests?

— something happens to that curiosity and wonder so natural in the early grades? Observe those same children in college preparatory programs.

— the skills needed to get you through college are not congruent with those needed to function as a competent practitioner?

— qualifying examinations, don't?

— the following expression is held to be true?

teaching = understanding = lecturing = testing

— there is manifest unrest among students today? Perhaps we ought to be listening to what they have to say—or is that unreasonable?

Who's Responsible: Teacher or Learner?

"William James argued that there was nothing wrong with the American school system which could not be corrected by 'impregnating it with geniuses.' He was right, but we shall have to find a more realistic remedy."

In The *Technology of Teaching* (Appleton-Century-Crofts, 1968) B. F. Skinner of Harvard University makes clear wherein he thinks the remedy lies: basing instruction on certain theories about human behavior and using modern technology—as well as teachers—to apply them. The preparation of his book was supported primarily by the Ford Foundation and the federal government, with some help from Carnegie Corporation. It includes several essays which had been published earlier, including the famous "The Science of Learning and the Art of Teaching," plus new chapters written especially for the present book.

Those who are not already familiar with the Skinnerian thesis— that behavior can be shaped by the appropriate use of appropriate reinforcements—are referred to the book for two reasons. One is that Mr. Skinner lays forth his theories more clearly and more simply than anyone else could do; there is nothing to be gained by paraphrasing him (which is more than can be said about many people who write

From *Carnegie Quarterly* (Carnegie Corporation of New York), vol. 15, no. 4 (Fall 1967) and vol. 16, no. 1 (Winter 1968).

on pedagogy). The other reason is to draw primary attention to the devastating criticisms he makes of education as it is now practiced. These have been largely obscured by the controversy surrounding his own theory of learning. One may or may not accept that theory. But it is no answer to the profound questions Mr. Skinner raises to say "he did his research on pigeons" (which is only a very partial truth anyway). It is easier to take this line of offense, however, than to mount a successful defense of much that goes on in the name of education. Besides, Mr. Skinner has few natural allies (though he may gain some among readers of his book), because almost everybody has his own sacred cow and Mr. Skinner makes wounding attacks on every one of them: the "discovery" method as well as the "cane" method, teaching "thinking" as well as teaching "citizenship." Still, readers who are able to approach the book with anything like an open mind will be inclined to think again, perhaps even twice, about some educational practices and goals which have gained wide acceptance largely, perhaps, because they have a nice warm sound to them.

In his essays, Mr. Skinner stresses that there is a vast difference between learning something on one's own and being taught it.

"The school of experience is no school at all, not because no one learns in it but because no one teaches. Teaching is the expediting of learning; a person who is taught learns more quickly than one who is not." Everyone agrees with that, of course; that is why we have education.

But, Mr. Skinner would say, much learning that does go on in classrooms today is in fact accidental, and often no learning whatsoever is going on, or only one or two students are learning, or they are learning different things from what the teacher intended. This is for two reasons which are related. One has to do with the lack of definition of what is to be taught; the other is lack of technique.

"The teacher who has been told that he is to 'impart information' or 'strengthen rational powers' or 'improve the student's mind' does not really know what he is to do, and he will never know whether he has done it."

Furthermore, even if a teacher should know precisely what kind of behavior he wants to elicit, he seldom knows how to produce it. And "Eventually, weakness of technique emerges in the disguise of a reformulation of the aims of education. Skills are minimized in favor of vague achievements — educating for democracy, educating the whole child, educating for life, and so on. And there the matter ends; for, unfortunately, these philosophies do not in turn suggest improvements in techniques."

What Mr. Skinner calls "aversive control" still plays a large, though unacknowledged, role in educational technique. Few masters nowadays beat their students, at least in this country, but what reinforcements the student gets are still mainly negative: the displeasure of the teacher, ridicule or criticism from classmates, low marks, and so on. These produce undesirable by-products such as anxiety, boredom, and aggression, and they lead to attempts to escape, of which there are many forms to choose among: truancy, daydreaming, overt defiance, plain inaction. "One of the easiest forms of escape is simply to forget all one has learned," Mr. Skinner points out, "and no one has discovered a form of control to prevent this ultimate break for freedom."

Those who lean toward a more "permissive" form of education will be applauding Mr. Skinner so far, but they are likely to fall silent as they read on. "Natural learning," to be brought about by non-coercive "telling and showing" on the part of the teacher, unfortunately does not work either. In a hilarious passage, Mr. Skinner describes the experience of one of Rousseau's disciples who tried to apply the technique with his own flesh-and-blood son. "His diary is one of the most pathetic documents in the history of education," Mr. Skinner notes, and in a footnote on the same page he tells of another of Rousseau's followers who died, "a martyr to Reason and Nature," from a kick by a horse he was trying to break according to the master's principles.

Surely if it were possible to get and keep the student's attention, "showing and telling" would work, some reason. And so all sorts of what might be called advance reinforcements are employed: books printed in four colors, attractive schools and classrooms, films, and so on. All of these may improve the student's attitude toward school, thus providing a favorable setting for instruction, but "they do not teach what students are in school to learn." Mr. Skinner takes the same view toward many efforts to make classes exciting. "Many ways of stimulating a class are as foolproof as tickling a baby—and as useless." He thinks exhilaration can be a good thing in itself, but it does not necessarily result in learning the second law of thermodynamics.

Since material, no matter how attractive or interesting or excitingly presented, often is not learned, "many educational theorists have concluded that the teacher cannot really teach at all but can only help the student learn." In this conception, the teacher is seen as a sort of midwife who creates the environment in which the student discovers knowledge for himself. (Mr. Skinner says that this method is designed "to absolve the teacher from a sense of failure by making instruction unnecessary.") While human beings do learn without being taught, and while it is a particularly pleasurable way of learning, "it is unlikely that anyone alive today has discovered agriculture or the controlled use of fire for himself," and a good thing it is, too, Mr. Skinner would say. "Great thinkers build upon the past, they do not waste time in rediscovering it."

Apart from the major objections—"a culture is no stronger than its capacity to transmit itself"—there are other problems with the discovery method. In the classroom, a few good students usually make all the discoveries, and the other students not only miss the thrills but "are left to learn material presented in a slow and particularly confusing way." Furthermore, the teacher's role is ambiguous and likely to lead to strain between him and his students, since he must either pretend not to know, or teach only what he truly does not know, or simply refuse to tell what he clearly does know. (In the discovery method, of course, the teacher is not supposed to teach the students anything directly, though he probably does. Mr. Skinner points out the same problem with efforts to teach creativity: "The teacher steers a delicate course between two great fears — on the one hand that he may not teach and on the other that he may tell the student something.")

Thinking and Creating

A chapter each is devoted to the teaching of thinking and to creativity. Many critics of programmed instruction, of which Mr. Skinner is of course one of the granddaddies, charge that it is these indubitably valuable processes that programming ignores or, in fact, would suppress. There will be no attempt here to summarize the chapters but simply to set forth some of the Skinnerian criticisms of our present efforts to teach thinking and foster creativity, criticisms which, again, have to do largely with lack of definition.

"Traditional formulations of human behavior not only fail to explain freedom, individuality, and creativity, they brand them as basically inexplicable. Free, idiosyncratic, and creative acts are admired, perhaps in the hope that they will become more common, but when upon occasion the admiration seems to work, no one knows why."

Of the teaching of thinking, Mr. Skinner says of the teacher: "Possessing no clear-cut description of the behavior he is to set up . . . he is forced back upon the notion of exercise." Thus problems are set to be solved, and the student is reinforced if he solves them. This, says Mr. Skinner, is no more than a sink-or-swim technique.

"If we throw a lot of children into a pool, some of them will manage to get to the edge and climb out. We may claim to have taught them to swim, though most of them swim badly. Others go to the bottom, and we rescue them. We do not see those who go to the bottom when we teach thinking, and many of those who survive think badly. The method does not teach; it simply selects those who learn without being taught." Later, he says "To make the student solve the problem of learning is to refuse to solve the problem of teaching."

And of the mystical view which we take toward creativity, Mr. Skinner says: "The teacher who believes that a student creates a work of art by exercising some inner, capricious faculty will not look for the conditions under which he does in fact do creative work. He will be also less able to explain such work when it occurs and less likely to induce students to behave creatively."

Regimentation or Freedom?

When Mr. Skinner refers to a "technology" of teaching he does not mean merely teaching machines and programmed instruction, though he believes great use should be made of these techniques. Just as programs, he would say, should be based upon the findings to date of the experimental analysis of behavior and upon new ones as they are made, so teachers should be taught to apply these findings in their dealings with students. Some of the knowledge is now at hand, and more soon will be, which would enable us to teach effectively what we wanted to teach.

This is precisely what frightens people — including, Mr. Skinner says, many of those charged with the improvement of education, who continue to discuss learning and teaching in a way that is analogous to what the situation would be if those concerned with improving medicine and public health were to "talk about disease as a lack of balance among the humors." We fear the regimentation that could result from effective teaching, but Mr. Skinner says we must not beg the question in that fashion. Nothing could be more regimented, in principle, than education as it now stands, with state authorities and school authorities prescribing what students are to learn year by year, universities insisting on requirements which presumably are to be met by all entrants, the administering of standard examinations, and so on.

"We do not worry about all this," says Mr. Skinner, "because we know that students never learn what they are required to learn."

But does it make sense to tolerate a system not despite, but because of, its ineffectiveness?

"We fear effective teaching," Mr. Skinner says, "as we fear all effective means of changing human behavior. Power not only corrupts, it frightens; and absolute power frightens absolutely. We take another — and very long — look at educational policy when we conceive of teaching which really works."

We should take that long look now, Mr. Skinner says. He acknowledges that a technology of teaching could be very unwisely used — that it could destroy initiative and creativity and make men all alike, and not necessarily alike in nice ways. Or, he says, it could make the individual "as skillful, competent, and informed as possible; it could build the greatest diversity of interests; it could lead him to make the greatest possible contribution to the survival and development of his culture. Which of these futures lies before us will not be determined by the mere availability of effective instruction. The use to which a technology of teaching is to be put will depend upon other matters. We cannot avoid the decisions which now face us by refusing to make use of the technology which inevitably flows from such a science."

The Technology of Teaching

B. F. Skinner
Department of Psychology
Harvard University

More than 60 years ago, in his *Talks to teachers on psychology,*
William James (1899) said: 'You make a great, a very great mistake,
if you think that psychology, being the science of the mind's laws,
is something from which you can deduce definite programs and
schemes and methods of instruction for immediate schoolroom use.
Psychology is a science, and teaching is an art; and sciences never
generate arts directly out of themselves. An intermediary inventive
mind must make the application, by using its originality.' In the years
which followed, educational psychology and the experimental psychology of learning did little to prove him wrong. As late as 1962, an
American critic, Jacques Barzun (1962), asserted that James's book
still contained 'nearly all that anyone need know of educational
method.'

Speaking for the psychology of his time James was probably right,
but Barzun was clearly wrong. A special branch of psychology, the
so-called experimental analysis of behaviour, has produced if not an
art at least a technology of teaching from which one can indeed 'deduce programs and schemes and methods of instruction.' The public
is aware of this technology through two of its products, teaching
machines and programmed instruction. Their rise has been mete-
oric. Within a single decade hundreds of instructional programmes

Lecture delivered November 19, 1964. Reprinted from *Proceedings of the Royal Society*, B, vol. 162 (1965), 427–43.

have been published, many different kinds of teaching machines have been offered for sale, and societies for programmed instruction have been founded in a dozen countries. Unfortunately, much of the technology has lost contact with its basic science.

Teaching machines are widely misunderstood. It is often supposed that they are simply devices which mechanize functions once served by human teachers. Testing is an example. The teacher must discover what the student has learned and can do so with the help of machines; the scoring of multiple-choice tests by machine is now common. Nearly 40 years ago Sidney Pressey (1926) pointed out that a student learned something when told whether his answers are right or wrong and that a *self*-scoring machine could therefore teach. Pressey assumed that the student had studied a subject before coming to the testing machine, but some modern versions also present the material on which the student is to be tested. They thus imitate, and could presumably replace, the teacher. But holding a student responsible for assigned material is not teaching, even though it is a large part of modern school and university practice. It is simply a way of inducing the student to learn without being taught.

Some so-called teaching machines serve another conspicuous function of the teacher: they are designed primarily to attract and hold attention. The television screen is praised for its hypnotic powers. A machine has recently been advertised which holds the student's head between earphones and his face a few inches from a brightly lit text. It is intended that he will read a few lines, then listen to his recorded voice as he reads them over again—all in the name of 'concentration.' Machines also have the energy and patience needed for simple exercise or drill. Many language laboratories take the student over the same material again and again, as only a dedicated private tutor could do, on some theory of 'automaticity.'

These are all functions which should never have been served by teachers in the first place, and mechanizing them is small gain.

The programming of instruction has also been widely misunderstood. The first programmes emerging from an experimental analysis of behaviour were copied only in certain superficial aspects. Educational theorists could assimilate the principles they appeared to exemplify to earlier philosophies. Programmed instruction, for example, has been called Socratic. The archetypal pattern is the famous scene in the *Meno* in which Socrates takes the slave boy through Pythagoras's theorem on doubling the square. It is one of the great frauds in the history of education. Socrates asks the boy a long series of leading questions and, although the boy makes no response which has not been carefully prepared, insists that he has told him nothing. In any case the boy has learned nothing; he could not have gone through the proof by himself afterwards, and Socrates says as much later in the dialogue. Even if the boy had contributed something to the proof by way of a modest original discovery, it would still be wrong to argue that his behaviour in doing so under Socrates's careful guidance resembled Pythagoras's original unguided achievement.

Other supposed principles of programming have been found in the writings of Comenius in the seventeenth century—for example, that the student should not be asked to take a step he cannot take—and in the work of the American psychologist, E. L. Thorndike, who more than 50 years ago pointed to the value of making sure that the student understood one page of a text before moving on to the next. A good programme does lead the student step by step, each step is within his range, and he usually understands it before moving on; but programming is much more than this. What it is, and how it is related to teaching machines, can be made clear only by returning to the experimental analysis of behaviour which gave rise to the movement.

An important process in human behaviour is attributed, none too accurately, to 'reward and punishment.' Thorndike described it in his Law of Effect. It is now commonly referred to as 'operant conditioning'—not to be confused with the conditioned reflexes of Pavlov. The essentials may be seen in a typical experimental arrangement. Figure 1, plate 50, shows a hungry rat in an experimental space which contains a food dispenser. A horizontal bar at the end of a lever projects from one wall. Depression of the lever operates a switch. When the switch is connected with the food dispenser, any behaviour on the part of the rat which depresses the lever is, as we say, 'reinforced with food.' The apparatus simply makes the appearance of food *contingent upon* the occurrence of an arbitrary bit of behaviour. Under such circumstances the probability that a response to the lever will occur again is increased (Skinner 1938).

The basic contingency between an act and its consequences has been studied over a fairly wide range of species. Pigeons have been reinforced for pecking at transilluminated disks (figure 2, plate 51), monkeys for operating toggle switches which were first designed for that more advanced primate, man, and so on. Reinforcers which have been studied include water, sexual contact, the opportunity to act aggressively, and—with human subjects—approval of one's fellow men and the universal generalized reinforcer, money.

The relation between a response and its consequences may be simple, and the change in probability of the response is not surprising. It may therefore appear that research of this sort is simply proving the obvious. A critic has recently said that King Solomon must have known all about operant conditioning because he used rewards and punishment. In the same sense his archers must have known all about Hooke's Law because they used bows and arrows. What is technologically useful in operant conditioning is our increasing knowledge of the extraordinarily subtle and complex properties of behaviour which may be traced to subtle and complex

Fig. 1. Rat pressing a horizontal bar attached to a lever projecting through the wall. The circular aperture below and to the right is a food dispenser.

features of the contingencies of reinforcement which prevail in the environment.

We may arrange matters, for example, so that the rat will receive food only when it depresses the lever with a given force. Weaker responses then disappear, and exceptionally forceful responses begin to occur and can be selected through further differential reinforcement. Reinforcement may also be made contingent upon the presence of stimuli: depression of the lever operates the food dispenser, for example, only when a tone of a given pitch is sounding. As a result the rat is much more likely to respond when a tone of that pitch is sounding. Responses may also be reinforced only intermittently. Some common schedules of reinforcement are the subject of probability theory. Gambling devices often provide for the reinforcement of varying numbers of responses in an unpredictable sequence. Comparable schedules are programmed in the laboratory by interposing counters between the operandum and the reinforcing device. The extensive literature on schedules of reinforcement (see, for example, Ferster & Skinner 1957) also covers intermittent reinforcement arranged by clocks and speedometers.

A more complex experimental space contains two operanda—two levers to be pressed, for example, or two disks to be pecked. Some of the resulting contingencies are the subject of decision-making theory. Responses may also be chained together, so that responding in one way produces the opportunity to respond in another. A still more complex experimental space contains two organisms with their respective operanda and with interlocking schedules of reinforcement. Game theory is concerned with contingencies of this sort. The study of operant behaviour, however, goes beyond an analysis of possible contingencies to the behaviour generated.

The application of operant conditioning to education is simple and direct. Teaching is the arrangement of contingencies of reinforcement under which students learn. They learn without teaching in their natural environments, but teachers arrange special contingencies which expedite learning, hastening the appearance of behaviour which would otherwise be acquired slowly or making sure of the appearance of behaviour which might otherwise never occur.

A teaching machine is simply any device which arranges contingencies of reinforcement. There are as many different kinds of machines as there are different kinds of contingencies. In this sense the apparatuses developed for the experimental analysis of behaviour were the first teaching machines. They remain much more complex and subtle than the devices currently available in education—a state of affairs to be regretted by anyone who is concerned with making education as effective as possible. Both the basic analysis and its technological applications require instrumental aid. Early experimenters manipulated stimuli and reinforcers and recorded responses by hand, but current research without the help of extensive apparatus is unthinkable. The teacher needs similar instrumental support, for it is impossible to arrange many of the contingencies of reinforcement which expedite learning without it. Adequate apparatus has not eliminated the researcher, and teaching machines will not eliminate the teacher. But both teacher and researcher must have such equipment if they are to work effectively.

Programmed instruction also made its first appearance in the laboratory in the form of programmed contingencies of reinforcement. The almost miraculous power to change behaviour which frequently emerges is perhaps the most conspicuous contribution to date of an experimental analysis of behaviour. There are at least four different kinds of programming. One is concerned with generating new and complex patterns or 'topographies' of behaviour. It is in the nature of operant conditioning that a response cannot be reinforced until it has occurred. For experimental purposes a response is chosen which presents no problem (a rat is likely to press a sensitive lever within

Fig. 2. Pigeon pecking a translucent disk. The square aperture below contains a food dispenser.

a short time), but we could easily specify responses which never occur in this way. Can they then never be reinforced?

The programming of a rare topography of response is sometimes demonstrated in the classroom in the following way. A hungry pigeon is placed in an enclosed space where it is visible to the class. A food dispenser can be operated with a handswitch held by the demonstrator. The pigeon has learned to eat from the food dispenser without being disturbed by its operation, but it has not been conditioned in any other way. The class is asked to specify a response which is

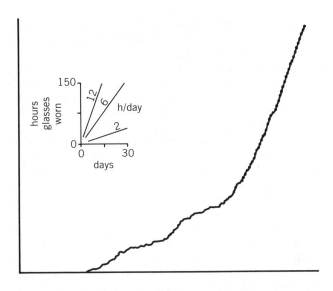

Fig. 3. Curve showing the number of hours per day during which glasses were worn, plotted cumulatively. The final slope is about twelve hours per day.

not part of the current repertoire of the pigeon. Suppose, for example, it is decided that the pigeon is to pace a figure eight. The demonstrator cannot simply wait for this response to occur and then reinforce it. Instead he reinforces any current response which may contribute to the final pattern — possibly simply turning the head or taking a step in, say, a clockwise direction. The reinforced response will quickly be repeated (one can actually see learning take place under these circumstances), and reinforcement is then withheld until a more marked movement in the same direction is made. Eventually only a complete turn is reinforced. Similar responses in a counterclockwise direction are then strengthened, the clockwise movement suffering partial 'extinction.' When a complete counterclockwise movement has thus been 'shaped,' the clockwise turn is reinstated, and eventually the pigeon makes both turns in succession and is reinforced. The whole pattern is then quickly repeated. Q.E.D. The process of 'shaping' a response of this complexity should take no more than five or ten minutes. The demonstrator's only contact with the pigeon is by way of the handswitch, which permits him to determine the exact moment of operation of the food dispenser. By selecting responses to be reinforced he improvises a programme of contingencies, at each stage of which a response is reinforced which makes it possible to move on to a more demanding stage. The contingencies gradually approach those which generate the final specified response.

This method of shaping a topography of response has been used by Wolf, Mees & Risley (1964) to solve a difficult behaviour problem. A boy was born blind with cataracts. Before he was of an age at which an operation was feasible, he had begun to display severe temper tantrums, and after the operation he remained unmanageable. It was impossible to get him to wear the glasses without which he would soon become permanently blind. His tantrums included serious self-destructive behaviour, and he was admitted to a hospital with a diagnosis of 'child schizophrenia.' Two principles of operant conditioning were applied. The temper tantrums were extinguished by making sure that they were never followed by reinforcing consequences. A programme of contingencies of reinforcement was then designed to shape the desired behaviour of wearing glasses. It was necessary to allow the child to go hungry so that food could be used as an effective reinforcer. Empty glasses frames were placed about the room and any response which made contact with them was reinforced with food. Reinforcement was then made contingent on picking up the frames, carrying them about, and so on, in a programmed sequence. Some difficulty was encountered in shaping the response of putting the frames on the face in the proper position. When this was eventually achieved, the prescription lenses were put in the frames. Wolf *et al.* publish a cumulative curve (figure 3) showing the number of hours per day the glasses were worn. The final slope represents essentially all the child's waking hours.

Operant techniques were first applied to psychotic subjects in the pioneering work of Lindsley (1960). Azrin and others have programmed contingencies of reinforcement to solve certain management problems in institutions for the psychotic (Ayllon & Azrin 1965). The techniques are not designed to cure psychoses but to generate trouble-free behaviour. In one experiment a whole ward was placed on an economic basis. Patients were reinforced with tokens when they behaved in ways which made for simpler management, and in turn paid for services received, such as meals or consultations with psychiatrists. Such an economic system, like any economic system in the world at large, represents a special set of terminal contingencies which in neither system guarantee appropriate behaviour. The contingencies must be made effective by appropriate programmes.

A second kind of programming is used to alter temporal or intensive properties of behaviour. By differentially reinforcing only the more vigorous instances in which a pigeon pecks a disk and by advancing the minimum requirement very slowly, a pigeon can be induced to peck so energetically that the base of its beak becomes inflamed. If one were to begin with this terminal contingency, the behaviour would never develop. There is nothing new about the necessary programming. An athletic coach may train a high jumper simply by moving the bar higher by small increments, each setting permitting some successful jumps to occur. But many intensive and temporal contingencies — such as those seen in the arts, crafts, and music — are very subtle and must be carefully analysed if they are to be properly programmed.

Another kind of programming is concerned with bringing behaviour under the control of stimuli. We could determine a rat's sensitivity to tones of different pitches by reinforcing responses made when one tone is sounding and extinguishing all responses made when other tones are sounding. We may wish to avoid extinction, however; the organism is to acquire the discrimination without making any 'errors.' An effective procedure has been analysed by Terrace (1963). Suppose we are to condition a pigeon to peck a red disk but not a green. If we simply reinforce it for pecking the red disk, it will almost certainly peck the green as well and these 'errors' must be extinguished. Terrace begins with disks which are as different as possible. One is illuminated by a red light, but the other is dark. Although reinforced for pecking the red disk, the pigeon is not likely to peck the dark disk, at least during a period of a few seconds. When the disk again becomes red, a response is immediately made. It is possible to extend the length of time the disk remains dark. Eventually the pigeon pecks the red disk instantly, but does not peck the dark disk no matter how long it remains dark. The important point is that it has never pecked the dark disk at any time.

A faint green light is then added to the dark disk. Over a period of time the green light becomes brighter and eventually is as bright as the red. The pigeon now responds instantly to the red disk but not to the green *and has never responded to the green.*

A second and more difficult discrimination can then be taught without errors by transferring control from the red and green disks. Let us say that the pigeon is to respond to a white vertical bar projected on a black disk but not to a horizontal. These patterns are first superimposed upon red and green backgrounds, and the pigeon is reinforced when it responds to red-vertical but not to green-horizontal. The intensity of the colour is then slowly reduced. Eventually the pigeon responds to the black and white vertical bar, does not respond to the black and white horizontal bar, *and has never done so.* The result could perhaps be achieved more rapidly by permitting errors to occur and extinguishing them, but other issues may need to be taken into account. When extinction is used, the pigeon shows powerful emotional responses to the wrong stimulus; when the Terrace technique is used it remains quite indifferent. It is, so to speak, 'not afraid of making a mistake.' The difference is relevant to education, where the anxiety generated by current methods constitutes a serious problem. There are those who would defend a certain amount of anxiety as a good thing, but we may still envy the occasionally happy man who readily responds when the occasion is appropriate but is otherwise both emotionally and intellectually

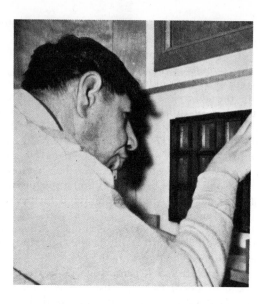

Fig. 4. Microcephalic idiot, 40 years old, operating a complex apparatus used in teaching form
discrimination.

disengaged. The important point is that the terminal contingencies
controlling the behaviour of both anxious and nonanxious students
are the same; the difference is to be traced to the programme by way
of which the terminal behaviour has been reached.

The discriminative capacities of lower organisms have been investigated with methods which require very skilful programming.
Blough (1956), for example, has developed a technique in which a
pigeon maintains a spot of light at an intensity at which it can just
be seen. By using a range of monochromatic lights he has shown
that the spectral sensitivity of the pigeon is very close to that of man.
Several other techniques are available which make it possible to use
lower organisms as sensitive psychophysical observers. They are
available, however, only to those who understand the principles of
programming.

Some current work by Murray Sidman provides a dramatic example of programming a subtle discrimination in a microcephalic
idiot. At the start of the experiment Sidman's subject (figure 4, plate
51) was 40 years old. He was said to have a mental age of about 18
months. He was partially toilet trained and dressed himself with
help. To judge from the brain of his sister, now available for post-
mortem study, his brain is probably about one-third the normal size.
Sidman investigated his ability to discriminate circular forms pro-

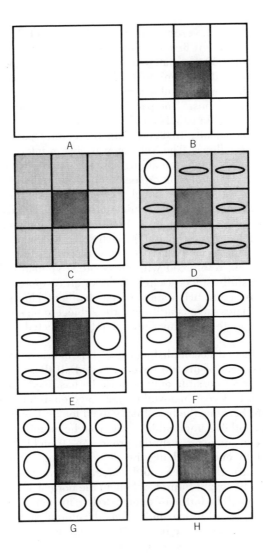

Fig. 5. A programme designed to teach subtle form discrimination. Reinforcement was contingent on: (A) a response moving a large panel; (B) a response moving any one of the nine smaller panels (with the exception of the centre panel); (C) a response moving only the one panel on which a circle is projected; (D) as before except that flat ellipses appear faintly on the other panels; (E, F, G) a response to the panel bearing a circle, appearing in random position among ellipses the shorter axis of which is progressively lengthening; (H) a response to the panel bearing a circle among ellipses closely approximating circles.

jected on translucent vertical panels. Small pieces of chocolate were used as reinforcers. At first any pressure against a single large vertical panel (figure 5A) operated the device which dropped a bit of chocolate into a cup within reach. Though showing relatively poor motor co-ordination, the subject eventually executed the required, rather delicate response. The panel was then subdivided into a three by three set of smaller panels (to be seen in figure 4, plate 51, and represented schematically in figure 5B), the central panel not being used in what follows. The subject was first reinforced when he pressed any of the eight remaining panels. A single panel was then lit at random, a circle being projected on it (figure 5C). The subject learned to press the lighted panel. Flat ellipses were then projected on the other panels at a low illumination (figure 5D). In subsequent settings the ellipses, now brightly illuminated, progressively approached circles (figure 5E to G). Each stage was maintained until the subject had formed the necessary discrimination, all correct responses being reinforced with chocolate. Eventually the subject could successfully select a circle from an array approximately like that shown in figure 5H. Using similar shaping techniques Sidman and his associates have conditioned the subject to pick up and use a pencil appropriately, tracing letters faintly projected on a sheet of paper.

The intellectual accomplishments of this microcephalic idiot in the forty-first year of his life have exceeded all those of his first 40 years. They were possible only because he has lived a few hours of each week of that year in a well programmed environment. No very bright future beckons (he has already lived longer than most people of his kind), and it is impossible to say what he might have achieved if he had been subject to a similar programme from birth, but he has contributed to our knowledge by demonstrating the power of a method of instruction which could scarcely be tested on a less promising case. (The bright futures belong to the normal and exceptional children who will be fortunate enough to live in environments which have been designed to maximize *their* development, and of whose potential achievements we have now scarcely any conception.)

A fourth kind of programming has to do with maintaining behaviour under infrequent reinforcement. A pigeon will continue to respond even though only one response in every hundred, say, is reinforced, but it will not do so unless the contingencies have been programmed. A fresh pigeon is no more likely to peck a disk a hundred times than to pace a figure eight. The behaviour is built up by reinforcing every response, then every other response, then every fifth response, and so on, waiting at each stage until the behaviour is reasonably stable. Under careful programming pigeons have continued to respond when only every ten-thousandth response has been reinforced, and this is certainly not the limit. An observer might say that the pigeon is 'greatly interested in his work,' 'industrious,' 'remarkably tolerant to frustration,' 'free from discouragement,' 'dedicated to his task,' and so on. These expressions are commonly applied to students who have had the benefit of similar programming, accidental or arranged.

The effective scheduling of reinforcement is an important element in educational design. Suppose we wish to teach a student to read 'good books'—books which, almost by definition, do not reinforce the reader sentence by sentence or even paragraph by paragraph but only when possibly hundreds of pages have prepared him for a convincing or moving dénouement. The student must be exposed to a programme of materials which build up a tendency to read in the absence of reinforcement. Such programmes are seldom constructed deliberately and seldom arise by accident, and it is therefore not surprising that few students even in good universities learn to read books of this sort and continue to do so for the rest of their lives. In their pride, schools are likely to arrange just the wrong conditions; they are likely to maintain so-called 'standards' under which books are forced upon students before they have had adequate preparation.

Other objectives in education need similar programming. The dedicated scientist who works for years in spite of repeated failures is often looked upon as a happy accident, but he may well be the product of a happy if accidental history of reinforcement. A programme in which exciting results were first common but became less and less frequent could generate the capacity to continue in the absence of reinforcement for long periods of time. Such programmes should arise naturally as scientists turn to more and more difficult areas. Perhaps not many effective programmes are to be expected for this reason, and they are only rarely designed by teachers of science. This may explain why there are so few dedicated scientists. Maintaining a high level of activity is one of the more important achievements of programming. Repeatedly, in its long history, education has resorted to aversive control to keep its students at work. A proper understanding of the scheduling of reinforcement may lead at long last to a better solution of this problem.

Let us look at these principles of programming at work in one or two traditional educational assignments. Instruction in handwriting will serve as one example. To say that a child is to learn 'how to write' tells us very little. The so-called signs of 'knowing how to write' provide a more useful set of behavioural specifications. The child is to form letters and words which are legible and graceful according to taste. He is to do this first in copying a model, then in writing to dictation (or self-dictation as he spells out words he would otherwise speak), and eventually in writing as a separate nonvocal form of verbal behaviour. A common method is to ask the child to copy letters or words and to approve or otherwise reinforce his approximations to good copy. More and more exact copies are demanded as the hand improves — in a crude sort of programming. The method is ineffective largely because the reinforcements are too long deferred. The parent or teacher comments upon or corrects the child's work long after it has been performed.

A possible solution is to teach the child to discriminate between good and bad form before he starts to write. Acceptable behaviour should then generate immediate, automatic self-reinforcement. This is seldom done. Another possibility is to make reinforcement immediately contingent upon successful responses. One method now being tested is to treat paper chemically so that the pen the child uses writes in dark blue when a response is correct and yellow when it is incorrect. The dark blue line is made automatically reinforcing through generous commendation. Under such contingencies the proper execution of a letter can be programmed; at first the child makes a very small contribution in completing a letter, but through progressive stages he approaches the point at which he composes the letter as a whole, the chemical response of the paper differentially reinforcing good form throughout. The model to be copied is then made progressively less important by separating it in both time and space from the child's work. Eventually words are written to dictation, letter by letter, in spelling dictated words, and in describing pictures. The same kind of differential reinforcement can be used to teach good form, proper spacing, and so on. The child is eventually forming letters skilfully under continuous automatic reinforcement. The method is directed as much toward motivation as toward good form. Even quite young children remain busily at work for long periods of time without coercion or threat, showing few signs of fatigue, nervousness, or other forms of escape.

As a second example we may consider the acquisition of a simple form of verbal behaviour. A behavioural specification is here likely to be especially strongly resisted. It is much more in line with traditional educational policy to say that the student is to 'know facts, understand principles, be able to put ideas into words, express meanings, or communicate information.' In *Verbal behaviour* (Skinner 1957) I tried to show how the behaviour exhibited in such activities could be formulated without reference to ideas, meanings, or information, and many of the principles currently used in programming verbal knowledge have been drawn from that analysis. The field is too large to be adequately covered here, but two examples may suggest the direction of the approach.

What happens when a student memorizes a poem? Let us say that he begins by reading the poem from a text. His behaviour is at that time under the control of the text, and it is to be accounted for by examining the process through which he has learned to read. When he eventually speaks the poem in the absence of a text, the same form of verbal behaviour has come under the control of other stimuli. He may begin to recite when asked to do so — he is then under control

Fig. 6. Caduceus

of an external verbal stimulus—but, as he continues to recite, his behaviour comes under the control of stimuli he himself is generating
(not necessarily in a crude word-by-word chaining of responses).
In the process of 'memorizing' the poem, control passes from one
kind of stimulus to another.

A classroom demonstration of the transfer of control from text to
self-generated stimuli illustrates the process. A short poem is projected on a screen or written on a chalkboard. A few unnecessary letters are omitted. The class reads the poem in chorus. A second slide
is then projected in which other letters are missing (or letters erased
from the chalkboard). The class could not have read the poem correctly if this form had been presented first, but because of its recent
history it is able to do so. (Some members undoubtedly receive help
from others in the process of choral reading.) In a third setting still
other letters are omitted, and after a series of five or six settings the
text has completely disappeared. The class is nevertheless able to
'read' the poem. Control has passed mainly to self-generated stimuli.

As another example, consider what a student learns when he con-
sults an illustrated dictionary. After looking at a labelled picture,
as in figure 6, we say that he knows something he did not know before. This is another of those vague expressions which have done so
much harm to education. The 'signs or symptoms of such knowledge'
are of two sorts. Shown the picture in figure 6 without the text the
student can say 'caduceus' (we say that he now knows what the object
pictured in the figure is called) or, shown the word *caduceus,* he can
now describe or reconstruct the picture (we say that he now knows
what the word *caduceus* means). But what has actually happened?

The basic process is similar to that of transferring discriminative
control in the Terrace experiment. To begin with, the student can

respond to the picture in various ways: he can describe it without naming it, he can find a similar picture in an array, he can draw a fair copy, and so on. He can also speak the name by reading the printed word. When he first looks at the picture and reads the word, his verbal response is primarily under the control of the text, but it must eventually be controlled by the picture. As in transferring the control exerted by red and green to vertical and horizontal lines, we can change the control efficiently by making the text gradually less important, covering part of it, removing some of the letters, or fogging it with a translucent mask. As the picture acquires control the student can speak the name with less and less help from the text. Eventually, when the picture exerts enough control, he 'knows the name of the pictured object.' The normal student can learn the name of one object so quickly that the 'vanishing' technique may not be needed, but it is a highly effective procedure in learning the names of a large number of objects. The good student learns how to make progressive reductions in the effectiveness of a text by himself: he may glance at the text out of the corner of his eye, uncover it bit by bit, and so on. In this way he improvises his own programme in making the text less and less important as the picture acquires control of the verbal response.

In teaching the student 'the meaning of the word *caduceus*' we could slowly obscure the picture, asking the student to respond to the name by completing a drawing or description or by finding a matching picture in an array. Eventually in answer to the question *What is a caduceus?* he describes the object, makes a crude sketch, or points to the picture of a caduceus. The skilful student uses techniques of this sort in studying unprogrammed material.

'Knowing what a caduceus is' or 'knowing the meaning of the word caduceus' is probably more than responding in these ways to picture or text. In other words, there are other 'signs of knowledge.' That is one reason why the concept of knowledge is so inadequate. But other relevant behaviour must be taught, if at all, in substantially the same way.

These examples do scant justice to the many hundreds of effective programmes now available or to the techniques which many of them use so effectively, but they must suffice as a basis for discussing a few general issues. An effective technology of teaching, derived not from philosophical principles but from a realistic analysis of human behaviour, has much to contribute, but as its nature has come to be clearly seen, strong opposition has arisen.

A common objection is that most of the early work responsible for the basic formulation of behaviour was done on so-called lower animals. It has been argued that the procedures are therefore appropriate only to animals and that to use them in education is to treat the student like an animal. So far as I know, no one argues that because something is true of a pigeon, it is therefore true of man. There are enormous differences in the topographies of the behaviours of man and pigeon and in the kinds of environmental events which are relevant to that behaviour — differences which, if anatomy and physiology were adequate to the task, we could probably compare with differences in the mediating substrata — but the basic processes in behaviour, as in neural tissue, show helpful similarities. Relatively simple organisms have many advantages in early stages of research, but they impose no limit on that research. Complex processes are met and dealt with as the analysis proceeds. Experiments on pigeons may not throw much light on the 'nature' of man, but they are extraordinarily helpful in enabling us to analyse man's environment more effectively. What is common to pigeon and man is a world in which certain contingencies of reinforcement prevail. The schedule of reinforcement which makes a pigeon a pathological gambler is to be found at race track and roulette table, where it has a comparable effect.

Another objection is to the use of contrived contingencies of reinforcement. In daily life one does not wear glasses in order to get food or point to circles in order to receive chocolate. Such reinforcers are not naturally contingent on the behaviour and there may seem to be something synthetic, spurious, or even fraudulent about them. The attack on contrived contingencies of reinforcement may be traced to Rousseau and his amazing book, *Émile*. Rousseau wanted to avoid the punitive systems of his day. Convinced as he was that civilization corrupts, he was also afraid of all social reinforcers. His plan was to make the student dependent upon *things* rather than people. John Dewey restated the principle by emphasizing real life experiences in the schoolroom. In American education it is commonly argued that a child must be taught nothing until he can reap natural benefits from knowing it. He is not to learn to write until he can take satisfaction in writing his name in his books, or notes to his friends. Producing a purple rather than a yellow line is irrelevant to handwriting. Unfortunately, the teacher who confines himself to natural reinforcers is often ineffective, particularly because only certain subjects can be taught through their use, and he eventually falls back upon some form of punishment. But aversive control is the most shameful of irrelevancies: it is only in school that one parses a Latin sentence to avoid the cane.

The objection to contrived reinforcers arises from a misunderstanding of the nature of teaching. The teacher expedites learning by arranging special contingencies of reinforcement, which may not resemble the contingencies under which the behaviour is eventually useful. Parents teach a baby to talk by reinforcing its first efforts with approval and affection, but these are not natural consequences of speech. The baby learns to say *mama, dada, spoon,* or *cup* months before he ever calls to his father or mother or identifies them to a passing stranger or asks for a spoon or cup or reports their presence to someone who cannot see them. The contrived reinforcement shapes the topography of verbal behaviour long before that behaviour can produce its normal consequences in a verbal community. In the same way a child reinforced for the proper formation of letters by a chemical reaction is prepared to write long before the natural consequences of effective writing take over. It was necessary to use a 'spurious' reinforcer to get the boy to wear glasses, but once the behaviour had been shaped and maintained for a period of time, the natural reinforcers which follow from improved vision could take over. The real issue is whether the teacher prepares the student for the natural reinforcers which are to replace the contrived reinforcers used in teaching. The behaviour which is expedited in the teaching process would be useless if it were not to be effective in the world at large in the absence of instructional contingencies.

Another objection to effective programmed instruction is that it does not teach certain important activities. When required to learn unprogrammed material for an impending examination the student learns how to study, how to clear up puzzling matters, how to work under puzzlement, and so on. These may be as important as the subject-matter itself. The same argument could have been raised with respect to a modern experimental analysis of learning when contrasted with early studies of that process. Almost all early investigators of learning constructed what we now call terminal contingencies of reinforcement to which an organism was immediately subjected. Thus, a rat was put into a maze, a cat was put into a puzzle box, and so on. The organism possessed little if any behaviour appropriate to such a 'problem,' but some responses were reinforced, and over a period of time an acceptable terminal performance might be reached. The procedure was called 'trial and error.' A programme of contingencies of reinforcement would have brought the organism to the same terminal performance much more rapidly and efficiently and without trial and error, but in doing so it could have been said to deprive the organism of the opportunity to learn how to try, how to explore – indeed, how to solve problems.

The educator who assigns material to be studied for an impending test presents the student with an opportunity to learn to examine the material in a special way which facilitates recall, to work industriously at something which is not currently reinforcing, and so on. It is true that a programme designed simply to impart knowledge of a subject-matter does not do any of this. It does not because it is not designed to do so. Programming undertakes to reach one goal at a time. Efficient ways of studying and thinking are separate goals. A crude parallel is offered by the current argument in favour of the cane or related aversive practices on the ground that they build character; they teach a boy to take punishment and to accept responsibility for his conduct. These are worthwhile goals, but they should not necessarily be taught at the same time as, say, Latin grammar or mathematics. Rousseau suggested a relevant form of programming through which a child could be taught to submit to aversive stimuli without alarm or panic. He pointed out that a baby dropped into a cold bath will probably be frightened and cry, but that if one begins with water at body temperature and cools it one degree per day, the baby will eventually not be disturbed by cold water. The programme must be carefully followed. (In his enthusiasm for the new science, Rousseau exclaimed 'Use a thermometer!') Similar programmes can teach a tolerance for painful stimuli, but caning a boy for idleness, forgetfulness, or bad spelling is an unlikely example. It only occasionally builds what the eighteenth century called 'bottom,' as it only occasionally eliminates idleness, forgetfulness, or bad spelling.

It is important to teach careful observation, exploration, and inquiry, but they are not well taught by submitting a student to material which he must observe and explore effectively or suffer the consequences. Better methods are available. There are two ways to teach a man to look before leaping: he may be severely punished when he leaps without looking or he may be positively reinforced (possibly 'spuriously') for looking before leaping. He may learn to look in both cases, but when simply punished for leaping without looking he must discover for himself the art of careful observation, and he is not likely to profit from the experience of others. When he is reinforced for looking, a suitable programme will transmit earlier discoveries in the art of observation. (Incidentally, the audiovisual devices mentioned earlier which undertake to attract attention do not teach careful observation. On the contrary, they are much more likely to deprive the student of the opportunity to learn such skills than effective programming of subject-matters.)

Learning how to study is another example. When a teacher simply tests students on assigned material, few ever learn to study well, and many never learn at all. One may read for the momentary effect and forget what one has read almost immediately; one obviously reads in a very different way for retention. As we have seen, many of the practices of the good student resemble those of the programmer. The student can in a sense programme material as he goes, rehearsing what he has learned, glancing at a text only as needed, and so on. These practices can be separately programmed as an important part of the student's education and can be much more effectively taught than by punishing the student for reading without remembering.

It would be pleasant to be able to say that punishing the student for not thinking is also not the only way to teach thinking. Some relevant behaviours have been analysed and can therefore be explicitly programmed. Algorithmic methods of problem-solving are examples. Simply leading the student through a solution in the traditional way is one kind of programming. Requiring him to solve a series of problems of graded difficulty is another. More effective programmes can certainly be prepared. Unfortunately, they would only emphasize the rather mechanical nature of algorithmic problem-solving. Real thinking seems to be something else. It is sometimes said to be a matter of 'heuristics.' But relevant practices can be formulated as techniques of solving the problem of solving problems. Once a heuristic device or practice is formulated and programmed, it cannot be distinguished in any important way from algorithmic problem-solving. The will-of-the-wisp of creative thinking still leads us on.

Human behaviour often assumes novel forms, some of which are valuable. The teaching of truly creative behaviour is, nevertheless, a contradiction in terms. Original discovery is seldom if ever guaranteed in the classroom. In Polya's little book, *How to solve it* (Polya, 1945), a few boys in a class eventually arrive at the formula for the diagonal of a parallelopiped. It is possible that the teacher did not tell them the formula, but it is unlikely that the course they followed under his guidance resembled that of the original discoverer. Efforts to teach creativity have sacrificed the teaching of subject-matter. The teacher steers a delicate course between two great fears — on the one hand that he may not teach and on the other that he may tell the student something. Until we know more about creative thinking, we may need to confine ourselves to making sure that the student is in full possession of the contributions of earlier thinkers, that he has been abundantly reinforced for careful observation and inquiry, that he has the interest and industry generated by a fortunate history of successes.

It has been said that an education is what survives when a man has forgotten all he has been taught. Certainly few students could pass their final examinations even a year or two after leaving school or the university. What has been learned of permanent value must therefore not be the facts and principles covered by examinations but certain other kinds of behaviour often ascribed to special abilities. Far from neglecting these kinds of behaviour, careful programming reveals the need to teach them as explicit educational objectives. For example, two programmes prepared with the help of the Committee on Programmed Instruction at Harvard — a programme in crystallography constructed by Bruce Chalmers and James G. Holland and a programme in neuroanatomy by Murray and Richard Sidman — both reveal the importance of special skills in three-dimensional thinking. As measured by available tests, these skills vary enormously even among scientists who presumably make special use of them. They can be taught with separate programmes or as part of crystallography or neuroanatomy when specifically recognized as relevant skills. It is possible that education will eventually concentrate on those forms of behaviour which 'survive when all one has learned has been forgotten.'

The argument that effective teaching is inimical to thinking, whether creative or not, raises a final point. We fear effective teaching, as we fear all effective means of changing human behaviour. Power not only corrupts, if frightens; and absolute power frightens absolutely. We take another—and very long—look at educational policy when we conceive of teaching which really works. It has been said that teaching machines and programmed instruction will mean regimentation (it is sometimes added that regimentation is the goal of those who propose such methods), but in principle nothing could be more regimented than education as it now stands. School and state authorities draw up syllabuses specifying what students are to learn year by year. Universities insist upon 'requirements' which are presumably to be met by all students applying for admission. Examinations are 'standard.' Certificates, diplomas, and honours testify to the completion of specified work. We do not worry about all this because we know that students never learn what they are required to learn, but some other safeguard must be found when education is effective.

It could well be that an effective technology of teaching will be unwisely used. It could destroy initiative and creativity, it could make men all alike (and not necessarily in being equally excellent), it could suppress the beneficial effect of accidents upon the development of the individual and upon the evolution of a culture. On the other hand, it could maximize the genetic endowment of each student, it could make him as skilful, competent, and informed as possible, it could build the greatest diversity of interests, it could lead him to make the greatest possible contribution to the survival and development of his culture. Which of these futures lies before us will not be determined by the mere availability of effective instruction. The use to which a technology of teaching is to be put will depend upon other matters. We cannot avoid the decisions which now face us by putting a stop to the scientific study of human behaviour or by refusing to make use of the technology which inevitably flows from such a science.

The experimental analysis of behaviour is a vigorous young science which will inevitably find practical applications. Important extensions have already been made in such fields as psychopharmacology and psychotherapy. Its bearing on economics, government, law, and even religion are beginning to attract attention. It is thus concerned with government in the broadest possible sense. In the government of the future the techniques we associate with education are most likely to prevail. That is why it is so important that this young science has begun by taking its most effective technological step in the development of a technology of teaching.

Preparation of this lecture has been supported by Grant K 6-MH-21,775-01 of the National Institute of Mental Health of the U.S. Public Health Service, and by the Human Ecology Fund.

REFERENCES

Ayllon, T., and Azrin, N. H. 1965 Measurement and reinforcement of behavior of psychotics, *J. Exp. Anal. Beh.*, 1965, **8**, 357–83.

Barzun, J. 1963 Review of Bruner, J. S. *Essays for the left hand, Science,* **25**, 323.

Blough, D. 1956 Dark adaptation in the pigeon. *J. Comp. Physiol. Psychol.* **49**, 425–430.

Ferster, C. B., and Skinner, B. F. 1957 *Schedules of reinforcement.* New York: Appleton-Century-Crofts.

James, W. 1889 *Talks to teachers on psychology.* New York: Henry Holt.

Lindsley, Ogden R. 1960 Characterization of the behavior of chronic psychotics as revealed by free operant conditioning methods. *Diseases of the Nervous System,* Monograph Supplement, **21**, 66–78.

Polya, G. 1945 *How to solve it.* Princeton, New Jersey: Princeton University Press.

Pressey, S. J. 1926 A simple apparatus which gives tests and scores—and teaches. *Sch. Soc.* **23**, 373–376.

Rousseau, J. J. 1762 *Émile ou de l'éducation.* Le Haye: Néaulme.

Skinner, B. F. 1938 *The behaviour of organisms.* New York: Appleton-Century-Crofts.

Skinner, B. F. 1957 *Verbal behaviour.* New York: Appleton-Century-Crofts.

Sidman, M. 1964 Personal communication.

Terrace, H. S. 1963 Errorless transfer of a discrimination across two continua. *J. Exp. Anal. Behav.* **6**, 223–232.

Wolf, M., Mees, H., and Risley, T. 1964 Application of operant conditioning procedures to the behaviour problems in the autistic child. *Behav. Res. Therapy,* **1**, 305–312.

5

Special Education for the Mildly Retarded – Is Much of It Justifiable?

Lloyd M. Dunn

A better education than special class placement is needed for socioculturally deprived children with mild learning problems who have been labeled educable mentally retarded. Over the years, the status of these pupils who come from poverty, broken and inadequate homes, and low status ethnic groups has been a checkered one. In the early days, these children were simply excluded from school. Then, as Hollingworth (1923) pointed out, with the advent of compulsory attendance laws, the schools and these children "were forced into a reluctant mutual recognition of each other." This resulted in the establishment of self contained special schools and classes as a method of transferring these "misfits" out of the regular grades. This practice continues to this day and, unless counterforces are set in motion now, it will probably become even more prevalent in the immediate future due in large measure to increased racial integration and militant teacher organizations. For example, a local affiliate of the National Education Association demanded of a local school board recently that more special classes be provided for dis-

From *Exceptional Children*, vol. 35 (September 1968). Lloyd M. Dunn has been Director, Institute on Mental Retardation and Intellectual Development, George Peabody College for Teachers, Nashville, Tennessee. An early version of this paper was presented as the Ray Graham Memorial Address at the 18th Annual Convention of the Illinois Council for Exceptional Children, Chicago, October 1967.

ruptive and slow learning children (Nashville *Tennessean*, December 18, 1967).

The number of special day classes for the retarded has been increasing by leaps and bounds. The most recent 1967–1968 statistics compiled by the US Office of Education now indicate that there are approximately 32,000 teachers of the retarded employed by local school systems — over one-third of all special educators in the nation. In my best judgment, about 60 to 80 percent of the pupils taught by these teachers are children from low status backgrounds — including Afro-Americans, American Indians, Mexicans, and Puerto Rican Americans; those from nonstandard English speaking, broken, disorganized, and inadequate homes; and children from other nonmiddle class environments. This expensive proliferation of self contained special schools and classes raises serious educational and civil rights issues which must be squarely faced. It is my thesis that we must stop labeling these deprived children as mentally retarded. Furthermore we must stop segregating them by placing them into our allegedly special programs.

The purpose of this article is twofold: first, to provide reasons for taking the position that a large proportion of this so called special education in its present form is obsolete and unjustifiable from the point of view of the pupils so placed; and second, to outline a blueprint for changing this major segment of education for exceptional children to make it more acceptable. We are not arguing that we do away with our special education programs for the moderately and severely retarded, for other types of more handicapped children, or for the multiply handicapped. The emphasis is on doing something better for slow learning children who live in slum conditions, although much of what is said should also have relevance for those children we are labeling emotionally disturbed, perceptually impaired, brain injured, and learning disordered. Furthermore, the emphasis of the article is on children, in that no attempt is made to suggest an adequate high school environment for adolescents still functioning as slow learners.

Reasons for Change

Regular teachers and administrators have sincerely felt they were doing these pupils a favor by removing them from the pressures of an unrealistic and inappropriate program of studies. Special educators have also fully believed that the children involved would make greater progress in special schools and classes. However, the overwhelming evidence is that our present and past practices have their major justification in removing pressures on regular teachers and pupils, at the expense of the socioculturally deprived slow learning pupils themselves. Some major arguments for this position are outlined below.

Homogeneous Grouping

Homogeneous groupings tend to work to the disadvantage of the slow learners and underprivileged. Apparently such pupils learn much from being in the same class with children from white middle class homes. Also, teachers seem to concentrate on the slower children to bring them up to standard. This principle was dramatically applied in the Judge J. Skelly Wright decision in the District of Columbia concerning the track system. Judge Wright ordered that tracks be abolished, contending they discriminated against the racially and/or economically disadvantaged and therefore were in violation of the Fifth Amendment of the Constitution of the United States. One may object to the Judge's making educational decisions based on legal considerations. However, Passow (1967), upon the completion of a study of the same school system, reached the same conclusion concerning tracking. The recent national study by Coleman, et al. (1966), provides supporting evidence in finding that academically disadvantaged Negro children in racially segregated schools made less progress than those of comparable ability in integrated schools. Furthermore, racial integration appeared to deter school progress very little for Caucasian and more academically able students.

What are the implications of Judge Wright's rulings for special education? Clearly special schools and classes are a form of homogeneous grouping and tracking. This fact was demonstrated in September, 1967, when the District of Columbia (as a result of the Wright decision) abolished Track 5, into which had been routed the slowest learning pupils in the District of Columbia schools. These pupils and their teachers were returned to the regular classrooms. Complaints followed from the regular teachers that these children were taking an inordinate amount of their time. A few parents observed that their slow learning children were frustrated by the more academic program and were rejected by the other students. Thus, there are efforts afoot to develop a special education program in D.C. which cannot be labeled a track. Self contained special classes will probably not be tolerated under the present court ruling but perhaps itinerant and resource room programs would be. What if the Supreme Court ruled against tracks, and all self contained special classes across the nation which serve primarily ethnically and/or economically disadvantaged children were forced to close down? Make no mistake—this could happen! If I were a Negro from the slums or a disadvantaged parent who had heard of the Judge Wright decision and knew what I know now about special classes for the educable mentally retarded, other things being equal, I would then go to court before allowing the schools to label my child as "mentally retarded" and place him in a "self contained special school or class."

Thus there is the real possibility that additional court actions will be forthcoming.[1]

Efficacy Studies

The findings of studies on the efficacy of special classes for the educable mentally retarded constitute another argument for change. These results are well known (Kirk, 1964) and suggest consistently that retarded pupils make as much or more progress in the regular grades as they do in special education. Recent studies such as those by Hoelke (1966) and Smith and Kennedy (1967) continue to provide similar evidence. Johnson (1962) has summarized the situation well:

It is indeed paradoxical that mentally handicapped children having teachers especially trained, having more money (per capita) spent on their education, and being designed to provide for their unique needs, should be accomplishing the objectives of their education at the same or at a lower level than similar mentally handicapped children who have not had these advantages and have been forced to remain in the regular grades [p. 66].

Efficacy studies on special day classes for other mildly handicapped children, including the emotionally handicapped, reveal the same results. For example, Rubin, Senison, and Betwee (1966) found that disturbed children did as well in the regular grades as in special classes, concluding that there is little or no evidence that special class programming is generally beneficial to emotionally disturbed children as a specific method of intervention and correction. Evidence such as this is another reason to find better ways of serving children with mild learning disorders than placing them in self contained special schools and classes.

Labeling Processes

Our past and present diagnostic procedures comprise another reason for change. These procedures have probably been doing more harm than good in that they have resulted in disability labels and in that they have grouped children homogeneously in school on the basis

---

1. Litigation has now occurred. According to an item in a June 8, 1968, issue of the *Los Angeles Times* received after this article was sent to the printer, the attorneys in the national office for the rights of the indigent filed a suit in behalf of the Mexican-American parents of the Santa Ana Unified School District asking for an injunction against the District's classes for the educable mentally retarded because the psychological examinations required prior to placement are unconstitutional since they have failed to use adequate evaluation techniques for children from different language and cultural backgrounds, and because parents have been denied the right of hearing to refute evidence for placement. Furthermore, the suit seeks to force the district to grant hearings on all children currently in such special classes to allow for the chance to remove the stigma of the label "mentally retarded" from school records of such pupils.

of these labels. Generally, these diagnostic practices have been conducted by one of two procedures. In rare cases, the workup has been provided by a multidisciplinary team, usually consisting of physicians, social workers, psychologists, speech and hearing specialists, and occasionally educators. The avowed goal of this approach has been to look at the complete child, but the outcome has been merely to label him mentally retarded, perceptually impaired, emotionally disturbed, minimally brain injured, or some other such term depending on the predispositions, idiosyncracies, and backgrounds of the team members. Too, the team usually has looked for causation, and diagnosis tends to stop when something has been found wrong with the child, when the why has either been found or conjectured, and when some justification has been found for recommending placement in a special education class.

In the second and more common case, the assessment of educational potential has been left to the school psychologist who generally administers — in an hour or so — a psychometric battery, at best consisting of individual tests of intelligence, achievement, and social and personal adjustment. Again the purpose has been to find out what is wrong with the child in order to label him and thus make him eligible for special education services. In large measure this has resulted in digging the educational graves of many racially and/or economically disadvantaged children by using a WISC or Binet IQ score to justify the label "mentally retarded." This term then becomes a destructive, self fulfilling prophecy.

What is the evidence against the continued use of these diagnostic practices and disability labels?

First, we must examine the effects of these disability labels on the attitudes and expectancies of teachers. Here we can extrapolate from studies by Rosenthal and Jacobson (1966) who set out to determine whether or not the expectancies of teachers influenced pupil progress. Working with elementary school teachers across the first six grades, they obtained pretest measures on pupils by using intelligence and achievement tests. A sample of pupils was randomly drawn and labeled "rapid learners" with hidden potential. Teachers were told that these children would show unusual intellectual gains and school progress during the year. All pupils were retested late in the school year. Not all differences were statistically significant, but the gains of the children who had been arbitrarily labeled rapid learners were generally significantly greater than those of the other pupils, with especially dramatic changes in the first and second grades. To extrapolate from this study, we must expect that labeling a child "handicapped" reduces the teacher's expectancy for him to succeed.

Second, we must examine the effects of these disability labels on the pupils themselves. Certainly none of these labels are badges of distinction. Separating a child from other children in his neighborhood—or removing him from the regular classroom for therapy or special class placement—probably has a serious debilitating effect upon his self image. Here again our research is limited but supportive of this contention. Goffman (1961) has described the stripping and mortification process that takes place when an individual is placed in a residential facility. Meyerowitz (1965) demonstrated that a group of educable mentally retarded pupils increased in feelings of self derogation after one year in special classes. More recent results indicate that special class placement, instead of helping such a pupil adjust to his neighborhood peers, actually hinders him (Meyerowitz, 1967). While much more research is needed, we cannot ignore the evidence that removing a handicapped child from the regular grades for special education probably contributes significantly to his feelings of inferiority and problems of acceptance.

Improvements in General Education

Another reason self contained special classes are less justifiable today than in the past is that regular school programs are now better able to deal with individual differences in pupils. No longer is the choice just between a self contained special class and a self contained regular elementary classroom. Although the impact of the American Revolution in Education is just beginning to be felt and is still more an ideal than a reality, special education should begin moving now to fit into a changing general education program and to assist in achieving the program's goals. Because of increased support at the local, state, and federal levels, four powerful forces are at work:

Changes in school organization. In place of self contained regular classrooms, there is increasingly more team teaching, ungraded primary departments, and flexible groupings. Radical departures in school organization are projected—educational parks in place of neighborhood schools, metropolitan school districts cutting across our inner cities and wealthy suburbs, and, perhaps most revolutionary of all, competing public school systems. Furthermore, and of great significance to those of us who have focused our careers on slow learning children, public kindergartens and nurseries are becoming more available for children of the poor.

Curricular changes. Instead of the standard diet of Look and Say readers, many new and exciting options for teaching reading are evolving. Contemporary mathematics programs teach in the primary grades concepts formerly reserved for high school. More programed textbooks and other materials are finding their way into the classroom. Ingenious procedures, such as those by Bereiter and Engelmann (1966), are being developed to teach oral language and reasoning to preschool disadvantaged children.

Changes in professional public school personnel. More ancillary personnel are now employed by the schools — i.e., psychologists, guidance workers, physical educators, remedial educators, teacher aides, and technicians. Furthermore, some teachers are functioning in different ways, serving as teacher coordinators, or cluster teachers who provide released time for other teachers to prepare lessons, etc. Too, regular classroom teachers are increasingly better trained to deal with individual differences — although much still remains to be done.

Hardware changes. Computerized teaching, teaching machines, feedback typewriters, ETV, videotapes, and other materials are making autoinstruction possible, as never before.

We must ask what the implications of this American Revolution in Education are for special educators. Mackie (1967), formerly of the US Office of Education, addressed herself to the question: "Is the modern school changing sufficiently to provide [adequate services in general education] for large numbers of pupils who have functional mental retardation due to environmental factors [p. 5]?" In her view, hundreds — perhaps even thousands — of so called retarded pupils may make satisfactory progress in schools with diversified programs of instruction and thus will never need placement in self contained special classes. With earlier, better, and more flexible regular school programs many of the children should not need to be relegated to the type of special education we have so often provided.

In my view, the above four reasons for change are cogent ones. Much of special education for the mildly retarded is becoming obsolete. Never in our history has there been a greater urgency to take stock and to search out new roles for a large number of today's special educators.

A Blueprint for Change

Two major suggestions which constitute my attempt at a blueprint for change are developed below. First, a fairly radical departure from conventional methods will be proposed in procedures for diagnosing, placing, and teaching children with mild learning difficulties. Second, a proposal for curriculum revision will be sketched out. These are intended as proposals which should be examined, studied, and tested. What is needed are programs based on scientific evidence of worth and not more of those founded on philosophy, tradition, and expediency.

A Clinical Approach

Existing diagnostic procedures should be replaced by expecting special educators, in large measure, to be responsible for their own diagnostic teaching and their clinical teaching. In this regard, it is suggested that we do away with many existing disability labels and the present practice of grouping children homogeneously by these labels into special classes. Instead, we should try keeping slow learning children more in the mainstream of education, with special educators serving as diagnostic, clinical, remedial, resource room, itinerant and/or team teachers, consultants, and developers of instructional materials and prescriptions for effective teaching.

***

A Thought

There is an important difference between regular educators talking us into trying to remediate or live with the learning difficulties of pupils with which they haven't been able to deal; versus striving to evolve a special education program that is either developmental in nature, wherein we assume responsibility for the total education of more severely handicapped children from an early age, or is supportive in nature, wherein general education would continue to have central responsibility for the vast majority of the children with mild learning disabilities—with us serving as resource teachers in devising effective prescriptions and in tutoring such pupils.

***

The accomplishment of the above *modus operandi* will require a revolution in much of special education. A moratorium needs to be placed on the proliferation (if not continuance) of self contained special classes which enroll primarily the ethnically and/or economically disadvantaged children we have been labeling educable mentally retarded. Such pupils should be left in (or returned to) the regular elementary grades until we are "tooled up" to do something better for them.

PRESCRIPTIVE TEACHING. In diagnosis one needs to know how much a child can learn, under what circumstances, and with what materials. To accomplish this, there are three administrative procedures possible. One would be for each large school system—or two or more small districts—to establish a "Special Education Diagnostic and Prescription Generating Center." Pupils with school learning problems would be enrolled in this center on a day and/or boarding school basis for a period of time—probably up to a month and hopefully until a successful prescription for effective teaching had been evolved. The core of the staff would be a variety of master teachers with different specialties—such as in motor development, perceptual training, language development, social and personality development, remedial education, and so forth. Noneducators such as physicians, psychologists, and social workers would be retained in a consultative role, or pupils would be referred out to such paraeducational professionals, as needed. A second procedure, in lieu of such centers with their cadres of educational specialists, would be for one generalist in diagnostic teaching to perform the diagnostic and prescription devising functions on her own. A third and even less desirable procedure would be for one person to combine the roles of prescriptive and clinical teacher which will be presented next. It is suggested that 15 to 20 percent of the most insightful special educators be prepared for and/or assigned to presecriptive teaching. One clear virtue of the center is that a skilled director could coordinate an inservice training program and the staff director could coordinate an inservice training program and the staff could learn through, and be stimulated by, one another. In fact, many special educators could rotate through this program.

Under any of these procedures, educators would be responsible for the administration and interpretation of individual and group psychoeducational tests on cognitive development (such as the WISC and Binet), on language development (such as the ITPA), and on social maturity (such as the Vineland Social Maturity Scale). However, these instruments — with the exception of the ITPA which yields a profile of abilities and disabilities — will be of little use except in providing baseline data on the level at which a child is functioning. In place of these psychometric tests which usually yield only global scores, diagnostic educators would need to rely heavily on a combination of the various tools of behavior shapers and clinical teachers. The first step would be to make a study of the child to find what behaviors he has acquired along the dimension being considered. Next, samples of a sequential program would be designed to move him forward from that point. In presenting the program, the utility of different reinforcers, administered under various conditions, would be investigated. Also, the method by which he can best be taught the material should be determined. Different modalities for reaching the child would also be tried. Thus, since the instructional program itself becomes the diagnostic device, this procedure can be called diagnostic teaching. Failures are program and instructor failures, not pupil failures. In large measure, we would be guided by Bruner's dictum (1967) that almost any child can be taught almost anything if it is programed correctly.[2]

This diagnostic procedure is viewed as the best available since it enables us to assess continuously the problem points of the instructional program against the assets of the child. After a successful and appropriate prescription has been devised, it would be communi-

---

2. By ignoring genetic influences on the behavioral characteristics of children with learning difficulties, we place responsibility on an inadequate society, inadequate parents, unmotivated pupils, and/or in this case inadequate teachers. Taking this extreme environmental approach could result in placing too much blame for failure on the teacher and too much pressure on the child. While we could set our level of aspiration too high, this has hardly been the direction of our error to date in special education of the handicapped. Perhaps the sustained push proposed in this paper may not succeed, but we will not know until we try it. Insightful teachers should be able to determine when the pressures on the pupil and system are too great.

cated to the teachers in the pupil's home school and they would continue the procedure as long as it is necessary and brings results. From time to time, the child may need to return to the center for reappraisal and redirection.

Clearly the above approach to special education diagnosis and treatment is highly clinical and intuitive. In fact, it is analogous to the rural doctor of the past who depended on his insights and a few diagnostic and treatment devices carried in his small, black bag. It may remain with us for some time to come. However, it will be improved upon by more standardized procedures. Perhaps the two most outstanding, pioneering efforts in this regard are now being made by Feuerstein (1968) in Israel, and by Kirk (1966) in the United States. Feuerstein has devised a *Learning Potential Assessment Device* for determining the degree of modifiability of the behavior of an individual pupil, the level at which he is functioning, the strategies by which he can best learn, and the areas in which he needs to be taught. Also, he is developing a variety of exercises for teaching children with specific learning difficulties. Kirk and his associates have not only given us the ITPA which yields a profile of abilities and disabilities in the psycholinguistic area, but they have also devised exercises for remediating specific psycholinguistic disabilities reflected by particular types of profiles (Kirk, 1966). Both of these scientists are structuring the assessment and remediation procedures to reduce clinical judgment, although it would be undesirable to formalize to too great a degree. Like the country doctor versus modern medicine, special education in the next fifty years will move from clinical intuition to a more precise science of clinical instruction based on diagnostic instruments which yield a profile of abilities and disabilities about a specific facet of behavior and which have incorporated within them measures of a child's ability to learn samples or units of materials at each of the points on the profile. If psychoeducational tests had these two characteristics, they would accomplish essentially the same thing as does the diagnostic approach described above—only under more standardized conditions.

ITINERANT AND RESOURCE ROOM TEACHING. It is proposed that a second echelon of special educators be itinerant or resource teachers. One or more resource teachers might be available to each sizable school, while an itinerant teacher would serve two or more smaller schools. General educators would refer their children with learning difficulties to these teachers. If possible, the clinical teacher would evolve an effective prescription for remediating the problem. If this is not possible, she would refer the child to the Special Education Diagnostic and Prescription Generating Center or to the more specialized prescriptive teacher who would study the child and work out an appropriate regimen of instruction for him. In either event, the key role of the resource room and itinerant clinical educators would be to develop instructional materials and lessons for implementing the prescription found effective for the child, and to consult and work with the other educators who serve the child. Thus, the job of special educators would be to work as members of the schools' instructional teams and to focus on children with mild to moderate school learning problems. Special educators would be available to all children in trouble (except the severely handicapped) regardless of whether they had, in the past, been labeled educable mentally retarded, minimally brain injured, educationally handicapped, or emotionally disturbed. Children would be regrouped continually throughout the school day. For specific help these children who had a learning problem might need to work with the itinerant or resource room special educator. But, for the remainder of the day, the special educator would probably be more effective in developing specific exercises which could be taught by others in consultation with her. Thus, the special educator would begin to function as a part of, and not apart from, general education. Clearly this proposed approach recognizes that all children have assets and deficits, not all of which are permanent. When a child was having trouble in one or more areas of learning, special educators would be available to devise a successful teaching approach for him and to tutor him when necessary. Perhaps as many as 20 to 35 percent of our present special educators are or could be prepared for this vital role.

TWO OTHER OBSERVATIONS. First, it is recognized that some of today's special educators — especially of the educable mentally retarded — are not prepared to serve the functions discussed. These teachers would need to either withdraw from special education or develop the needed competencies. Assuming an open door policy and playing the role of the expert educational diagnostician and the prescriptive and clinical educator would place us in the limelight. Only the best will succeed. But surely this is a responsibility we will not shirk. Our avowed *raison d'etre* has been to provide special education for children unable to make adequate progress in the regular grades. More would be lost than gained by assigning less than master teachers from self contained classes to the diagnostic and clinical educator roles. Ainsworth (1959) has already compared the relative effectiveness of the special class versus itinerant special educators of the retarded and found that neither group accomplished much in pupil progress. A virtue of these new roles for special education is that they are high status positions which should appeal to the best and therefore enhance the recruitment of master regular teachers who should be outstanding in these positions after having obtained specialized graduate training in behavior shaping, psychoeducational diagnostics, remedial education, and so forth.

Second, if one accepts these procedures for special education, the need for disability labels is reduced. In their stead we may need to substitute labels which describe the educational intervention needed.

We would thus talk of pupils who need special instruction in language or cognitive development, in sensory training, in personality development, in vocational training, and other areas. However, some labels may be needed for administrative reasons. If so, we need to find broad generic terms such as "school learning disorders."

New Curricular Approaches

Master teachers are at the heart of an effective school program for children with mild to moderate learning difficulties — master teachers skilled at educational diagnosis and creative in designing and carrying out interventions to remediate the problems that exist. But what should they teach? In my view, there has been too great an emphasis in special classes on practical arts and practical academics, to the exclusion of other ingredients. Let us be honest with ourselves. Our courses of study have tended to be watered down regular curriculum. If we are to move from the clinical stage to a science of instruction, we will need a rich array of validated prescriptive programs of instruction at our disposal. To assemble these programs will take time, talent, and money; teams of specialists including creative teachers, curriculum specialists, programers, and theoreticians will be needed to do the job.

What is proposed is a chain of Special Education Curriculum Development Centers across the nation. Perhaps these could best be affiliated with colleges and universities, but could also be attached to state and local school systems. For these centers to be successful, creative educators must be found. Only a few teachers are remarkably able to develop new materials. An analogy is that some people can play music adequately, if not brilliantly, but only a few people can compose it. Therefore, to move special education forward, some 15 to 20 percent of our most creative special educators need to be identified, freed from routine classroom instruction, and placed in a stimulating setting where they can be maximally productive in curriculum development. These creative teachers and their associates would concentrate on developing, field testing, and modifying programs of systematic sequences of exercises for developing specific facets of human endeavor. As never before, funds are now available from the US Office of Education under Titles III and VI of PL 89-10 to embark upon at least one such venture in each state. In fact, Title III was designed to support innovations in education and 15 percent of the funds were earmarked for special education. Furthermore, most of the money is now to be administered through state departments of education which could build these curriculum centers into their state plans.

The first step in establishing specialized programs of study would be to evolve conceptual models upon which to build our treatments. In this regard the creative teachers would need to join with the theoreticians, curriculum specialists, and other behavioral scientists. Even the identification of the broad areas will take time, effort, and thought. Each would require many subdivisions and extensive internal model building. A beginning taxonomy might include the following eight broad areas: (a) environmental modifications, (b) motor development, (c) sensory and perceptual training, (d) cognitive and language development including academic instruction, (e) speech and communication training, (f) connative (or personality) development, (g) social interaction training, and (h) vocational training. (Of course, under cognitive development alone we might evolve a model of intellect with some ninety plus facets such as that of Guilford [1967], and as many training programs.)

In the area of motor development we might, for example, involve creative special and physical educators, occupational and physical therapists, and experts in recreation and physical medicine, while in the area of language development a team of speech and hearing specialists, special educators, psychologists, linguists, and others would need to come together to evolve a conceptual model, to identify the parameters, and to develop the specialized programs of exercises. No attempt is made in this article to do more than provide an overview of the problem and the approach. Conceptualizing the specific working models would be the responsibility of cadres of experts in the various specialties.

ENVIRONMENTAL MODIFICATIONS. It would seem futile and rather unrealistic to believe we will be able to remediate the learning difficulties of children from ethnically and/or economically disadvantaged backgrounds when the schools are operating in a vacuum even though top flight special education instructional programs are used. Perhaps, if intensive around the clock and full calendar year instruction were provided beginning at the nursery school level, we might be able to counter appreciably the physiological weaknesses and inadequate home and community conditions of the child. However, the field of education would be enhanced in its chances of success if it became a part of a total ecological approach to improve the environments of these children. Thus special educators need to collaborate with others — social workers, public health officials, and other community specialists. Interventions in this category might include (a) foster home placement, (b) improved community conditions and out of school activities, (c) parent education, (d) public education, and (e) improved cultural exposures. For optimal pupil development, we should see that children are placed in a setting that is both supportive and stimulating. Therefore, we must participate in environmental manipulations and test their efficacy. We have made a slight beginning in measuring the effects of foster home placement and there is evidence that working with parents of the disadvantaged has paid off. The model cities programs would also seem to have promise. But much more human and financial effort must be invested in this area.

MOTOR DEVELOPMENT. Initial work has been done with psychomotor training programs by a number of persons including Delacato (1966), Oliver (1958), Cratty (1967), Lillie (1967), and others. But we still need sets of sequential daily activities built around an inclusive model. Under this category, we need to move from the early stages of psychomotor development to the development of fine and large movements required as vocational skills. Programs to develop improved motor skills are important for a variety of children with learning problems. In fact, one could argue that adequate psychomotor skills constitute the first link in the chain of learning.

SENSORY AND PERCEPTUAL TRAINING. Much of our early efforts in special education consisted of sensory and perceptual training applied to severe handicapping conditions such as blindness, deafness, and mental deficiency. Consequently, we have made a good beginning in outlining programs of instruction in the areas of auditory, visual, and tactual training. Now we must apply our emerging technology to work out the step by step sequence of activities needed for children with mild to moderate learning difficulties. In this regard, visual perceptual training has received growing emphasis, pioneered by Frostig (1964), but auditory perceptual training has been neglected. The latter is more important for school instruction than the visual channel. Much attention needs to be given to this second link in the chain of learning. Children with learning problems need to be systematically taught the perceptual processes: they need to be able to organize and convert bits of input from the various sense modalities into units of awareness which have meaning.

COGNITIVE AND LANGUAGE DEVELOPMENT INCLUDING ACADEMIC INSTRUCTION. This is the heart of special education for slow learning children. Our business is to facilitate their thinking processes. We should help them not only to acquire and store knowledge, but also to generate and evaluate it. Language development could largely be included under this caption—especially the integrative components—since there is much overlap between the development of oral language and verbal intelligence. However, much of receptive language training might be considered under sensory and perceptual training, while expressive language will be considered in the next topic.

A major fault of our present courses of study is failure to focus on the third link in the chain of learning—that of teaching our children systematically in the areas of cognitive development and concept formation. A major goal of our school program should be to increase the intellectual functioning of children we are now classifying as socioculturally retarded. For such children, perhaps as much as 25 percent of the school day in the early years should be devoted to this topic. Yet the author has not seen one curriculum guide for these children with a major emphasis on cognitive development—which is a sad state of affairs indeed!

Basic psychological research by Guilford (1959) has provided us with a useful model of intellect. However, little is yet known about the trainability of the various cognitive processes. Actually, Thurstone (1948) has contributed the one established set of materials for training primary mental abilities. Thus, much work lies ahead in developing programs of instruction for the training of intellect.

We are seeing more and more sets of programed materials in the academic areas, most of which have been designed for average children. The most exciting examples today are in the computer assisted instruction studies. Our major problem is to determine how these programed exercises need to be modified to be maximally effective for children with specific learning problems. Work will be especially needed in the classical areas of instruction including written language and mathematics. Hopefully, however, regular teachers will handle much of the instruction in science and social studies, while specialists would instruct in such areas as music and the fine arts. This will free special educators to focus on better ways of teaching the basic 3 R's, especially written language.

Speech and Communication Training. This area has received much attention, particularly from speech correctionists and teachers of the deaf. Corrective techniques for specific speech problems are probably more advanced than for any other area, yet essentially no carefully controlled research has been done on the efficacy of these programs. Speech correctionists have tended to be clinicians, not applied behavioral scientists. They often create the details of their corrective exercises while working with their clients in a one to one relationship. Thus, the programs have often been intuitive. Furthermore, public school speech therapists have been spread very thin, usually working with 75 to 100 children. Many have been convinced that only *they* could be effective in this work. But remarkable changes have recently occurred in the thinking of speech therapists; they are recognizing that total programs of oral language development go far beyond correcting articulation defects. Furthermore, some speech therapists believe they could be more productive in working with only the more severe speech handicaps and devoting much attention to the development and field testing of systematic exercises to stimulate overall language and to improve articulation, pitch, loudness, quality, duration, and other speech disorders of a mild to moderate nature. These exercises need to be programed to the point at which teachers, technicians, and perhaps teacher aides can use them. Goldman (1968) is now developing such a program of exercises to correct articulation defects. This seems to be a pioneering and heartening first step.

Connative (or Personality) Development. This emerging area requires careful attention. We must accept the position that much of a person's behavior is shaped by his environment. This applies to all aspects of human thought, including attitudes, beliefs, and mores. Research oriented clinical psychologists are providing useful information on motivation and personality development and before long we will see reports of research in shaping insights into self, the effects of others on self, and one's effects on others. It is not too early for teams of clinical psychologists, psychiatric social workers, creative special educators (especially for the so called emotionally disturbed), and others to begin developing programs of instruction in this complex field.

SOCIAL INTERACTION TRAINING. Again we have an emerging area which overlaps considerably with some of those already presented, particularly connative development. Special educators have long recognized that the ability of a handicapped individual to succeed in society depends, in large measure, on his skill to get along with his fellow man. Yet we have done little to develop his social living skills, a complex area of paramount importance. Training programs should be developed to facilitate development in this area of human behavior.

VOCATIONAL TRAINING. Closely tied to social interaction training is vocational training. Success on the job for persons that we have labeled educable mentally retarded has depended on good independent work habits, reliability, and social skills, rather than on academic skills. Consequently, early and continuing emphasis on developing these traits is necessary. In fact, it is likely to be even more important in the years ahead with few job opportunities and increasing family disintegration providing less shelter and support for the so called retarded. Therefore sophisticated programs of instruction are especially needed in this area. Even with our best efforts in this regard, it is likely that our pupils, upon reaching adolescence, will continue to need a variety of vocational services, including trade and technical schools, work study programs and, vocational training.

ANOTHER OBSERVATION. It seems to me to be a red herring to predict that special educators will use these hundreds of specialized instructional programs indiscriminately as cookbooks. Perhaps a few of the poor teachers will. But, the clinical teachers proposed in this article would be too sophisticated and competent to do this. They would use them as points of departure, modifying the lessons so that each child would make optimal progress. Therefore, it seems to me that this library of curriculum materials is necessary to move us from a clinical and intuitive approach to a more scientific basis for special education.

An Epilogue

The conscience of special educators needs to rub up against morality. In large measure we have been at the mercy of the general education establishment in that we accept problem pupils who have been referred out of the regular grades. In this way, we contribute to the delinquency of the general educations since we remove the pupils that are problems for them and thus reduce their need to deal with individual differences. The *entente* of mutual delusion between general and special education that special class placement will be advantageous to slow learning children of poor parents can no longer be tolerated. We must face the reality—we are asked to take children others cannot teach, and a large percentage of these are from ethnically and/or economically disadvantaged backgrounds. Thus much of special education will continue to be a sham of dreams unless we immerse ourselves into the total environment of our children from inadequate homes and backgrounds and insist on a comprehensive ecological push—with a quality educational program as part of it. This is hardly compatible with our prevalent practice of expediency in which we employ many untrained and less than master teachers to increase the number of special day classes in response to the pressures of waiting lists. Because of these pressures from the school system, we have been guilty of fostering quantity with little regard for quality of special education instruction. Our first responsibility is to have an abiding commitment to the less fortunate children we aim to serve. Our honor, integrity, and honesty should no longer be subverted and rationalized by what we hope and may believe we are doing for these children—hopes and beliefs which have little basis in reality.

Embarking on an American Revolution in Special Education will require strength of purpose. It is recognized that the structure of most, if not all, school programs becomes self perpetuating. Teachers and state and local directors and supervisors of special education have much at stake in terms of their jobs, their security, and their programs which they have built up over the years. But can we keep our self respect and continue to increase the numbers of these self contained special classes for the educable mentally retarded which are of questionable value for many of the children they are intended to serve? As Ray Graham said in his last article in 1960:

We can look at our accomplishments and be proud of the progress we have made; but satisfaction with the past does not assure progress in the future. New developments, ideas, and facts may show us that our past practices have become out-moded. A growing child cannot remain static—he either grows or dies. We cannot become satisfied with a job one-third done. We have a long way to go before we can rest assured that the desires of the parents and the educational needs of handicapped children are being fulfilled.

REFERENCES

Ainsworth, S. H. *An exploratory study of educational, social and emotional factors in the education of mentally retarded children in Georgia public schools.* US Office of Education Cooperative Research Project Report No. 171(6470). Athens, Ga.: University of Georgia, 1959.

Bereiter, C., and Engelmann, S. *Teaching disadvantaged children in the pre-school.* Englewood Cliffs, N.J.: Prentice-Hall, 1966.

Bruner, J. S., Olver, R. R., and Greenfield, P. M. *Studies in cognitive growth.* New York: Wiley, 1967.

Coleman, J. S., et al. *Equality of educational opportunity.* Washington, D.C.: USGPO, 1966.

Cratty, P. J. *Developmental sequences of perceptual motor tasks.* Freeport, Long Island, N.Y.: Educational Activities, 1967.

Delacato, C. H. (Ed.) *Neurological organization and reading problems.* Springfield, Ill.: Charles C Thomas, 1966.

Feuerstein, R. *The Learning Potential Assessment Device.* Jerusalem, Israel: Haddassa Wizo Canada Child Guidance Clinic and Research Unit, 1968.

Frostig, M., and Horne, D. *The Frostig program for the development of visual perception.* Chicago: Follett, 1964.

Graham, R. Special education for the sixties. *Illinois Educational Association Study Unit,* 1960, **23**, 1-4.

Goffman, E. *Asylums: Essays on the social situation of mental patients and other inmates.* Garden City, N.Y.: Anchor, 1961.

Goldman, R. *The phonemic-visual-oral association technique for modifying articulation disorders in young children.* Nashville, Tenn.: Bill Wilkerson Hearing and Speech Center, 1968.

Guilford, J. P. *The nature of human intelligence.* New York: McGraw-Hill, 1967.

Hoelke, G. M. *Effectiveness of special class placement for educable mentally retarded children.* Lincoln, Neb.: University of Nebraska, 1966.

Hollingworth, L. S. *The psychology of subnormal children.* New York: MacMillan, 1923.

Johnson, G. O. Special education for mentally handicapped—a paradox. *Exceptional Children,* 1962, **29**, 62-69.

Kirk, S. A. Research in education. In H. A. Stevens and R. Heber (Eds.), *Mental retardation.* Chicago, Ill.: University of Chicago Press, 1964.

Kirk, S. A. *The diagnosis and remediation of psycholinguistic disabilities.* Urbana, Ill.: University of Illinois Press, 1966.

Lillie, D. L. The development of motor proficiency of educable mentally retarded children. *Education and Training of the Mentally Retarded,* 1967, **2**, 29-32.

Mackie, R. P. *Functional handicaps among school children due to cultural or economic deprivation.* Paper presented at the First Congress of the International Association for the Scientific Study of Mental Deficiency, Montpellier, France, September, 1967.

Meyerowitz, J. H. Family background of educable mentally retarded children. In H. Goldstein, J. W. Moss and L. J. Jordan. *The efficacy of special education training on the development of mentally retarded children.* Urbana, Ill.: University of Illinois Institute for Research on Exceptional Children, 1965. Pp. 152-182.

Meyerowitz, J. H. Peer groups and special classes. *Mental Retardation,* 1967, **5**, 23-26.

Oliver, J. N. The effects of physical conditioning exercises and activities on the mental characteristics of educationally sub-normal boys. *British Journal of Educational Psychology,* 1958, **28**, 155-165.

Passow, A. H. *A summary of findings and recommendations of a study of the Washington, D.C. schools.* New York: Teachers College, Columbia University, 1967.

Rosenthal, R., and Jacobson, L. Teachers' expectancies: Determinants of pupils' IQ gains. *Psychological Reports*, 1966, **19**, 115-118.

Rubin, E. Z., Senison, C. B., and Betwee, M. C. *Emotionally handicapped children in the elementary school.* Detroit: Wayne State University Press, 1966.

Smith, H. W., and Kennedy, W. A. Effects of three educational programs on mentally retarded children. *Perceptual and Motor Skills*, 1967, **24**, 174.

Thurstone, T. G. *Learning to think series.* Chicago, Ill.: Science Research Associates, 1948.

Wright, Judge J. S. *Hobson vs Hansen: U.S. Court of Appeals decision on the District of Columbia's track system. Civil Action No. 82-66.* Washington, D.C.: US Court of Appeals, 1967.

The Educational Technology Game: A Tragedy in Two Acts

William A. Deterline

Act One

Time: *The present.*

Scene: *Office of the President, Well-Known Large Company.*

Cast: *President of Well-Known Large Company and visiting Instructional Technologist.*

Setting: *The Instructional Technologist (I. T.) has heard that the President (Pres.) has recently announced entry of his company into the field of instructional technology. Excited, the I. T. has come to see Pres. to find out what Well-Known Large Company plans to do.*

I. T.   Except for your major product line, I don't know very much about your company or about your recent announcement. Would you tell me what you have done, what you are doing, and how you are going about it?

PRES.   (Expansively) Happy to. First of all, since you are not a business man yourself, you probably don't realize how important it is to keep a finger on the pulse of the market place. You can sink or swim depending on whether you

From *Educational Technology*, September 15, 1968.

are on top of all developments or trailing along behind the herd too blinded by the dust of the trail to keep your eye on the ball and one jump ahead of the competition. Ever think of that?

I. T.   Not exactly in those terms, no.

PRES.   Well, it was obvious to me that we belong in the instructional technology business since we already have a division that sells instructional products.

I. T.   What was your first step?

PRES.   We changed the name of our Pedagogical Products Division to Instructional Systems Division.

I. T.   What will the new division do?

PRES.   The same thing the old division did.

I. T.   And what is that?

PRES.   Sell our hornbooks, magic lanterns, pencils, and student slates to education, industry and government.

I. T.   Oh. (*Pause*) Do you sell many?

PRES.   Well, on hornbooks alone, for example, our sales have jumped since we changed the name of the division.

I. T.   How much did they jump?

PRES.   We changed the name a month ago, and sales of hornbooks during the past month were exactly double the sale of all of 1966!

I. T.   In numbers, what did that involve?

PRES.   Last year—three; last month—six.

I. T.   Six million dollars?

PRES.   No. Six hornbooks.

I. T.   You attribute this growth to a new look and a new approach in the new division?

PRES.   What new approach? No, just the new name. It has sizzle; it's a grabber, it's *in* this year! It turns people *on*!

I. T.   Do you produce software, too?

PRES.   Software?

I. T.   The instructional materials themselves, containing information, providing instruction: textbooks, filmstrips, and so on.

PRES.   Well, the hornbooks are preprinted with the multiplication table and things like that. But in general the answer is no. We expect teachers to use our devices but prepare their own materials. Besides, teachers *want* to prepare their own materials. We like to think of our items as magic wands and magic carpets, which, in the hands of any teacher, can change the world for the students, transporting them effortlessly to new knowledge. That's what instructional technology *means!*

I. T.   (*Gagging slightly*) Er, yes. And tell me . . .

PRES.   Oh, let me interrupt for a second. I forgot that we do, in two other cases, have instructional materials with our devices.

I. T.   And what are the materials?

PRES.   Well, on our Plato model slate . . .

I. T.   Plato model?

PRES.   Yes, you see our first model was called—

I. T.   Don't tell me. Socrates.

PRES.   Ah, you're familiar with the line.

I. T.   And the third, I'll bet, is Aristotle.

PRES.   Right! You *are* familiar with our products. Well, our Plato model has the alphabet printed in four colors on the bottom edge of the wooden frame so the letters are right there to be copied.

I. T.   (*Softly*) Unbelievable.

PRES.   Startling concept, isn't it? Now that's my idea of the ingenuity required in instructional technology. Let me tell you what the Aristotle slate has on it.

I. T.   (*Stifling a whimper*) Please don't. Let me ask about the reason for the recent name change. Why did you pick "Instructional Systems" as the new name?

PRES.   We want to keep up to date, of course, and everybody in our business is doing it, you know.

I. T.   (*Heavily*) Yes, I know.

PRES.   Why, in the past year I counted 35 new instructional systems divisions in the electronics industry alone. The food machinery business has 14, and the cosmetics industry almost a dozen.

I. T.	(*With feeling*) It is almost too much to bear.
PRES.	We've also made significant changes in our own training. The training director reports directly to me, and he and I have completely revamped our training department.
I. T.	In what way?
PRES.	We renamed it the Instructional Technology Department.
I. T.	I see. Anything else?
PRES.	We changed all the job titles in the department.
I. T.	And job descriptions and procedures?
PRES.	Why would we want to do that? No, just the titles.
I. T.	(*Sighing*) For example?
PRES.	Well, our technical writers are now called Instructional Design Technologists. Their supervisors are called Senior Instructional Design Technologists.
I. T.	(*Very small voice*) And your instructors?
PRES.	Their title is now Instructional Implementation Technologist.
I. T.	(*Small voice, breaking slightly*) What do they do?
PRES.	The same things they've always done.
I. T.	(*Feebly*) In exactly the same way?
PRES.	Yes, we don't want to rock the boat, you know. One thing we thought of doing was have them read Mager's *Preparing Instructional Objectives*.
I. T.	(*With look of drowning man clutching at straw*) Yes, and . . .?
PRES.	Well, the training director—oops, Director of Applied Instructional Technology—and I read it and decided not to have the I. D. T.'s and I. I. T.'s read it.
I. T.	Why not?
PRES.	We decided that they wouldn't really understand it or really appreciate it—not in depth, anyway.
I. T.	Not the way you did, right?
PRES.	Right! And besides, I don't think they would gain anything from it. You see, that approach might work in some areas, but our training problems and our subjects are different. In fact, they're quite unique.

I. T.	(*To himself*) Aren't they all.
PRES.	Beg your pardon?
I. T.	(*Resigned*) Nothing. I was going to ask what else you are doing in the field of instructional technology.
PRES.	Well, we're thinking of offering to run a Job Corps Center.
I. T.	Oh?
PRES.	Considering our long history and experience — our first hornbook was produced in 1801, you know . . .
I. T.	No, I didn't know.
PRES.	Yes, the Socrates model hornbook was introduced that year. Notice that all models of all our items are named after education's big three.
I. T.	Education's big three?
PRES.	Yes. Socrates, Plato, and Aristotle. What's good and old is old and good, you know.
I. T.	Yes, of course. What's good and old is . . .
PRES.	Well, anyway, considering our experience, we would appear to be ideally qualified to pitch in, suit up, turn on — heh heh — and help win the war on poverty.
I. T.	I'm sure that the President will be speechless when you tell him.
PRES.	Well, whatever we can do we feel we should do.
I. T.	That's rather well put.
PRES.	Thank you. And we do have sort of an ulterior motive.
I. T.	Ulterior motive?
PRES.	Well yes, in a way, but a *selfless* ulterior motive.
I. T.	That's a thought-provoking concept.
PRES.	You see, we have a huge stock of our Socrates slates and we want to make them available for training of the disadvantaged. I feel that we should do everything we can to provide as many opportunities as possible for the poor people of the nation (tear appears in left eye), and besides, we want the opportunity to use government money to buy our inventory since we have so much invested.
I. T.	A selfless ulterior motive.
PRES.	Oh yes, because the slates are beautifully made, and I'm

	sure the Job Corpsmen would find them jolly fun.
I. T.	Jolly fun. You are apparently right in touch with the problems and needs of the present.
PRES.	Oh yes, and our plans for the education market are also quite exciting.
I. T.	Can you tell me about any of those plans?
PRES.	I suppose that because we are so far ahead of the competition I can go ahead and tell you about some of the things coming off the old drawing board. You must understand our philosophy in order to appreciate fully our approach.
I. T.	I think I do already. Doesn't it go "What is good and old . . .
PRES.	. . . is old and good." Right. We have devoted considerable time, effort, and money to solving one of the most critical and one of the oldest problems confronting teachers.
I. T.	You mean . . .
PRES.	Yes. We are designing powderless chalk, a chalk that absolutely will not leave white powder on the clothes of the teacher!
I. T.	I hardly know what to say.
PRES.	Now, that problem has been with us since the first piece of chalk was taken into the classroom. And nobody, the big companies, those smarty educators, or anyone else, solved it. Now, *our* approach you wouldn't believe.
I. T.	I'd believe.
PRES.	Really, you wouldn't believe it.
I. T.	Oh, yes indeed I would. But rather than take up any more of your time on that topic, let me ask what else you are developing.
PRES.	Oh, many things. Our magic wand line . . . Did you say something?
I. T.	No, not really. Go on.
PRES.	Our magic wand line will include all the latest in instructional technology things.
I. T.	Things?
PRES.	You know: desks, chairs, shelves, TV cameras, report cards, the backbone of instructional technology.
I. T.	You aren't going to design instruction?

PRES.   That's the teacher's job. Our job is providing the magic wands.

I. T.   Thank you very much. This has all been very inspiring.

PRES.   *(Turning to a cabinet behind his desk)* Here, let me give you one of our magic wand pointer, knuckle-rapper, and chalk holder combinations. It's the latest in our Instructional Technology line. *(Turning to the front again)* Hey, where'd he go? Probably hurried off to sit down somewhere and digest all this and contemplate with awe the contributions that the education industry is going to make to education. Young fellow did seem to be a bit overwhelmed.

Act Two

Scene: *Two hours later.*

Time: *The office of the Dean, School of Education, Well-Known University.*

Cast: *The Dean of the Well-Known School of Education and the same Instructional Technologist.*

Setting: *The I. T. we saw in Act One has recovered from his earlier experience and has come to see the Dean of the Well-known School of Education. The school has been receiving a lot of publicity from its research activities and new Learning Center. After exchanging greetings the Dean and the I. T. walk toward the Learning Center.*

DEAN.   I'm delighted to have the opportunity to show you what we have been doing. As I understand it, you call yourself an instructional technologist. I hope that that doesn't mean you are an audiovisual salesman *(laughing)*.

I. T.   *(Laughing)* No, of course not.

DEAN.   And I hope it doesn't mean that you write those little-step programmed textbooks that have proven to be such a bust?

I. T.   Ah, well, er, among other things I *do* develop programmed texts. What do you mean, "proven to be such a bust?"

DEAN.   *(Ignoring the question)* Glad to hear you say, "among other things." Those programs, in spite of all the rash promises made about them, can do only a very little, in only a few areas, for low-level skills, and low-level students.

I. T.   Did you see Schramm's report on the research on programmed instruction?

DEAN.   Yes, and he described one of my studies, done before I became a dean, in which I demonstrated that a ten-frame program is no better than a paragraph in a book.

I. T.   Ten frames. Did you ever look at longer programs, going beyond short-term memory effects?

DEAN.   No. Too many variables become confounded. The short programs give us a purer measure, and nothing revealed itself that would suggest that a program has any value. Quite the contrary, since the students took longer to do the ten frames than to read the paragraph. I was a bit irritated that Schramm ignored my data and concluded that programs do have value. Ah, here we are.

DEAN.   This is one of our individualized study centers. This is our pride and joy. Come over to one of these empty carrels. Notice that each carrel has a book shelf, writing area, and acoustical walls on three sides. On the front wall is a small TV monitor, a recessed tape playback unit, and a rear screen cartridge movie projector.

I. T.   Very impressive.

DEAN.   Notice the telephone-type dial. The student can dial any videotape or audiotape from our central control and it will be played through the TV monitor or the speaker over here. In addition, those shelves over there *(points)* contain other audio tapes, motion picture cartridges, filmstrips and special projectors for use in these carrels.

I. T.   The hardware is quite impressive. What about the materials?

DEAN.   We bought whatever we could afford. We also videotaped many of our classes, visiting speakers, and some of our seminars.

I. T.   Do you design any materials especially for these media?

DEAN.   Of course. Instructors put their lectures on audio tape, and we design lecture and demonstrations for videotape.

I. T.   How do you evaluate the materials?

DEAN.   By having committees check each tape or film for technical accuracy.

I. T.   No, I mean how do you evaluate instructional effectiveness?

DEAN.   *(Puzzled)* If it is technically accurate, it can't help but be effective.

I. T.   Oh? But some technically accurate presentations teach more than others, and . . .

DEAN.   Ah yes, and you have put your finger on the crux of a problem on which I suspect that you and I disagree.

I. T.   Oh, and what is that?

DEAN.   I believe that the difference to which you refer is a difference in how interesting a presentation is, compared to another presentation. A teacher knows his subject, of course, but if he doesn't make it interesting, the students must simply work a little harder, and the less motivated students aren't able to keep up. *That's* why some presentations are more effective than others: differences in student motivation, and some students can't be motivated.

I. T.   But how about objectives? Generally it appears that any presentation, including a lecture, is more effective if the objectives have been identified and specified, and if we systematically generate student interaction, and provide some form of continuous progress evaluation . . .

DEAN.   And, I know, test and revise the presentations, right?

I. T.   Well, yes.

DEAN.   Nonsense.

I. T.   Nonsense?

DEAN.   *(Firmly)* Nonsense. Teaching is communication. It requires inspiration and enthusiasm on the part of both teachers and students. Remember Horace Mann's statement that "The teacher who tries to teach without first inspiring the pupil with a desire to learn is hammering on cold iron."

I. T.   Of course, but interest and motivation are not enough.

DEAN.   Of course not, intelligence and stick-to-it-iveness are also needed. We don't need objectives, and we don't need any more than teachers who know their subject matter and can be interesting, and students who are bright, alert, motivated, and serious about learning.

I. T.   Don't you see *any* value to objectives and evaluating instruction for the purpose of improving it?

DEAN.   I am sure that industry and military training could profit from things like that, since they are dealing with low-level skills, but we are dealing with the highest kind of mental abilities, like creativity, and judgment, and insight, and appreciation, and knowledge. Things that are considered "bad" by you people who preach behavioral objectives.

I. T.   What! That isn't the case at all. We are concerned with the same kinds of goals, but we simply want to define the observable aspects of knowledge, and insight, and so on, so we have a better chance of producing it and identifying it when it has been achieved.

DEAN.   I never heard anything so demeaning, so de-humanizing in my life. You can't reduce Knowledge to observables, at least not at this college. Our goals are quite unique.

I. T.   (To himself) I heard that earlier today. (Louder but sadly) Well, perhaps we should go on. Tell me a bit more about the things that you have been doing.

DEAN.   We did a study comparing two ways of designing TV lectures. Each instructor first recorded a lecture using no notes, just his own intuitive skills and did it all extemporaneously. Then he wrote a script on the same topic and organized it all and then read it before the TV camera. We then had his colleagues evaluate each presentation. Almost everybody found the systematically prepared script reading to be more monotonous and without a spark or any value at all compared to the intuitive presentation. And several of the instructors who had prepared some of the pairs of presentations told me that they knew in advance that that is what would happen!

I. T.   Sounds a bit like the deck was stacked.

DEAN.   Of course it was. Intuition will always triumph over technology or any attempt to oversystematize instruction.

I. T.   You might have tried some other possibilities. Did you evaluate the intuitive presentation?

DEAN.   Oh yes, as I said, other instructors evaluated the presentations; and not only that, so did students, and they agreed that the scripted presentation was not as interesting.

I. T.   Did you evaluate either presentation to see how much the students learned?

DEAN.   No sir! We were getting too close to stepping on the academic freedom of the faculty members who participated even by going this far.

I. T.   (Puzzled) In what way?

DEAN.   A faculty member must be free to teach in his own way, and we rely on his own professionalism to teach what the students should learn, and on his own good judgment to avoid inappropriate subject matter. If we were to spy on him or attempt to evaluate what he does in the classroom, that would be a serious infringement of his academic freedom.

I. T.   But professionals in all professions are evaluated and their effectiveness determined every day, in everything they do, and their own professional peers or superiors do this for the good of the profession. Why should teaching be any different?

DEAN.   Because you can't evaluate the mystical properties of the teacher-student interaction.

I. T.   But you *can* evaluate the students if you have precise indications of what the students are to achieve and that is one way of evaluating instruction, and the teacher.

DEAN.   No. That tells about the intelligence and motivation of the students. What we *do* evaluate and use as a basis for promotions and salary increases are things like number of publications, research grants, number of majors, registration in each of his courses, and whether he is Our Kind of Faculty Member.

I. T.   Oh. Why do you use those criteria?

DEAN.   Simple enough. We evaluate our faculty on the basis of their expertise in their fields. Obviously publications, grants, and speeches at professional meetings are our best indicators. Number of majors and course registrations are important budgetary items and also tell us how well the students like a faculty member. These are all objective indicators.

I. T.   Have any of your faculty indicated that their main interest is in teaching, not research or publications?

DEAN.   Yes, and there is a place for them if the other indicators are high enough, but they really provide only intangible value.

I. T.   Intangible value! Don't you . . .

DEAN.   *(Firmly)* This door leads to our C. A. I. project.

I. T.   *(Hesitating, then, with a sigh)* Tell me about it.

DEAN.   We have it because it seems to be the thing to do, but frankly I am not very enthusiastic.

I. T.   Why not?

DEAN.   Because it seems to me to be only an automated pro-
           grammed instruction teaching machine, and as I told you,
           we know that that doesn't work.

I. T.   But wait a minute . . .

DEAN.   And besides, the course that we prepared and had pro-
           grammed into the computer doesn't work.

I. T.   Who programmed the course — who did the instructional
           programming?

DEAN.   Several of our faculty members.

I. T.   Who trained them?

DEAN.   The equipment manufacturer. It took only a day.

I. T.   One day?

DEAN.   Yes, and they said, and I agree, that subject matter exper-
           tise and experience in teaching is all that is needed. But
           some of the teachers felt that they needed to know more
           and receive more training.

I. T.   So what did you do?

DEAN.   Took them off the project, of course. The students don't
           like the course, by the way, and don't seem to learn very
           much.

I. T.   You *do* evaluate the course?

DEAN.   Yes, the computer has no academic freedom. *(Laughing)*

I. T.   How about the faculty members who prepared the course?

DEAN.   They did not *program* the course. They wrote a technically
           accurate course. They identified possible errors and pro-
           vided corrective information. All of the information was
           there for the computer to use as best it could. The course
           was then programmed for the computer. The failure is
           C. A. I.'s, not the writers'!

I. T.   I have difficulty seeing how that conclusion was reached.
           A computer can only use what it is given.

DEAN.   *(With some exasperation)* I suppose that you think that the
           message is more important than the medium. Let me give
           you some friendly advice. There is a lot of talk about soft-
           ware and hardware these days, and things like objectives,
           specifications, and quality control, as if education is the
           missile business. We are not dealing with tangibles here,

we are dealing with human minds, and only human minds can communicate with human minds. There is magic in communication and in education, and all of this silly talk about instructional technology is irrelevant.

I. T.   But . . .

DEAN.   We are keeping our minds open. We have the latest that the education equipment manufacturers have to offer us. And it doesn't do a thing that we can't do already, usually better and at less expense.

I. T.   But . . .

DEAN.   We will buy the equipment — some of it helps automate the library — but we won't buy your ideas.

I. T.   *(Desperately)* But the ideas are more important than the equipment.

DEAN.   Not here they aren't. Education is an art, and we practice that art as it should be practiced.

I. T.   *(Sadly)* Yes, I know.

DEAN.   *(Angrily)* Some of our faculty want to change, and they're as bad as some of the student agitators. But we'll keep them under control. *(Pauses, then, heartily)* But now I must go to a committee meeting. Come by again sometime and let's continue our discussion of your interesting views on education. By the way, why don't you drop in and see my brother-in-law. He's the president of Well-Known Large Company, which has recently decided to plunge into the instructional technology field. I think that you and he will find that you have a lot in common.

Are Operant Principles
Tautological?

Robert L. Burgess
Ronald L. Akers

Department of Sociology
University of Washington

In a scientific discourse, controversies are perhaps unavoidable. But to resolve intellectual controversies to the benefit of all, and this means essentially to the benefit of cumulative science, each side must be sensitive to, and respond in, a reasonable manner to the other. Lines of communication must remain open, for it does little good for those holding to one position to shrug off the other position as entirely wrong or simply irrelevant. If, in the behavioral sciences, powerful principles are discovered by those working in one discipline or sub-field, it is incumbent upon those in another to take note of them. But if they are to be accepted, objections to them must be examined, and an attempt made to see how validly the objections apply.[1] We, as sociologists, have been impressed by operant principles, developed by those toiling in other scientific soil, and have tried to adapt them to questions of interest to us. (Burgess & Akers, 1966) But in presenting these ideas to colleagues, two basic objections have been raised—reductionism and tautology. These may seem to be only minor points to the behavioral psychologists who have developed the principles, but they are major stumbling blocks to the acceptance of them by sociologists. In this paper we want to examine and propose an answer only to the question of tautology.

From *The Psychological Record* **16**, (1966) 305-312.

1. The point to be emphasized here is that the principles of one discipline need to be carefully examined before they are incorporated into another.

The Problem of Tautology

Propositions or theoretical statements about the world which can never be shown to be false, for which we cannot conceive or possibly devise conditions under which exceptions to them may be found, are not good scientific propositions. They cannot be tested, because they are *non-falsifiable*. Given the usual definition of operant behavior, some basic propositions can be charged with being tautologically true, that is, true by definition. Definitions are of necessity tautological, but if we propose statements about that which is defined which do no more than restate the definition, then we have a tautological proposition.

Let us briefly examine some definitions of operant behavior and then one kind of proposition about operant behavior to see if this charge can be maintained.

> Operant behavior . . . *operates* or acts upon the environment. (Reese, 1964, pp. 8-9)
>
> It [operant behavior] takes in all those movements of an organism that may at some time be said to *have an affect upon* or *do something* to his outside world. Operant behavior *operates* on this world . . . ." (Keller, 1954, p. 2)

These definitions taken from introductory explications of behavior theory are not satisfactory to most psychologists, although similar definitions are frequently given. For instance, at one point Skinner defines it as "behavior which has some effect upon the surrounding world . . . ." (1953, p. 59) This type of definition is unsatisfactory because it can also include respondent behavior; even respondents may operate upon or make some change in the organism's environment.

The kind of definition that would satisfy is one that states, in effect, operant behavior is a function of its environmental consequences. Or as Skinner says, "behavior which is shaped up by the environment." (1959, p. 101) In another place he states,

> The consequences of behavior may 'feed back' into the organism. When they do so, they may change the probability that the behavior which produced them will occur again. (Skinner, 1953, p. 59)

Consider, also, these definitions:

> . . . . operants are those responses which are controlled (strengthened or weakened) basically by the stimuli that follow them. (Bijou and Baer, 1961, p. 15)
>
> Behaviors which are best understood as functionally related to their consequences in the environment are called *operants*. (Bijou and Baer, 1961, p. 32)

Given this type of definition, what kinds of propositions can be made about operant behavior? One finds propositions similar to this:

> If the occurrence of an operant is followed by the presentation
> of a reinforcing stimulus, the strength is increased. (Skinner,
> 1938, p. 21)

This says, in essence, that behavior that is a function of its environmental consequences will be a function of its environmental consequences. For by adding certain auxiliary definitions this statement cannot help but be true, *by definition*. Reinforcing stimulus is defined as an environmental consequence that will increase an operant's frequency of occurrence, and the strength of an operant is defined as its frequency of occurrence. To reinforce means to strengthen and to strengthen means to increase in frequency. Thus, this proposition turns out to be: If the occurrence of an operant is followed by the presentation of a stimulus that will increase its frequency of occurrence, then its frequency of occurrence will increase.

This tendency to state definitions *as if* they were propositions is often repeated in the attempts to apply operant principles to sociology and social-psychology. This results in one's associates charging tautology — a response that has done nothing to increase the frequency of interaction between operant-oriented sociologists and social-psychologists and their colleagues.

A Suggested Solution

Does this mean, then, that operant principles are nothing but definitions? *We think not, indeed know not.* We submit that tautologies can be found in statements about operant behavior, not because of any intrinsic circularity in reasoning, but because too often the propositions have been only implicit, while definitions have been stated. The line between a definition and a proposition is thin enough that as long as they remain unarticulated there is room for stating one as the other. The two are not distinct enough that they automatically will not be confused. The experimental analysis of behavior has produced a relatively large and impressive body of demonstrated empirical relationships between behavior and the kinds of changes it produces in its environment. But a science is most efficient and productive when it takes the time to order its empirical propositions into a deductive system of general and derived principles that are empirically testable. We submit that operant principles are such that not only can testable deductions be drawn, but the general propositions themselves are testable directly. It may be suggested that this situation results from the fact that, as in the best tradition of the physical sciences, these principles were inductively arrived at. In any case, it is potentially the most powerful theory now available in behavioral science.

In Table 1 we have presented one way of ordering operant principles into a systematic scheme. From this it can readily be seen that these behavioral prcinciples constitute an integrated set of non-tautological and testable statements of general and derived propositions. Operant conditioners, of course, will immediately recognize nearly all of these, and this is as it should be. We are not suggesting a *new* theory, only a form of explicitly stating it that makes it clear when we are proposing definitions and when we are making propositions.

The general law of operant behavior is clearly non-tautological, for empirical exceptions can conceivably be found.[2] There is the possibility that behavior will produce events which have no effect upon its future occurrence, and we temporarily label these events neutral stimuli. (2.b in the table.) If, however, a neutral stimulus is posited for every case of non-effect, then the theory will be tautological. But if, after *extended and systematic analysis,* we find that the behavior in question is neither strengthened nor weakened by any event contingent upon it, then we say that it is an empirically established exception to the law.

One exception does not falsify the theory; a number (as yet unspecified) must be found. If the empirical exceptions accumulate to such an extent that they render the theory useless for explaining a large range of behavior, then we conclude that the theory is wrong in too many cases, and hence falsified. Then, other more general propositions which better explain the broader range of behavior could be sought and found. If several exceptions are found to be similar enough that they constitute a whole class of exceptions, then we may want to say that the theory explains all but that class, and try to find other law-like statements to explain this class of exceptions and incorporate them into the overall theory. We, of course, already know of an empirical class of exceptions for which all events produced by it are irrelevant to its future occurrence, namely that class called respondent behavior. And we also know something about the principles under which this class of behavior operates, although they are not presented here. Both classes are related through the basic assumption that behavior is a function of stimulus events.

---

2. Our proposed definitions of operant and respondent behaviors are similar to the classical distinction between voluntary and involuntary behaviors. There is some evidence, however, that this distinction between operants and respondents, in terms of the basic components of the nervous system, may not be as hard and fast as we would like. Nevertheless, it is much more useful and certainly more respectable logically to be able to define a phenomenon *independently* of the propositions that apply to that phenomenon. This same reasoning also applies to our definitions of reinforcers, punishers and neutral stimuli. Hopefully, in the near future we will be able to define these phenomena independently of their effects.

Discussion

Many operant conditioners would deny the usefulness of theory construction of this sort. They have been deliberately, even proudly, a-theoretical. This perspective has carried the field a long way, and in a relatively short period of time, in the analysis of behavior. In fact, the kind of ordered statement presented here would be impossible to construct *ad hoc* from the armchair: it could only have been inductively developed from firm empirical findings. But theory of this sort not only orders, sums up, and states general principles from accumulated empirical generalizations; it also points to lacunae in our knowledge, suggests further research, and makes explicit the relationship among established principles. An explicit theoretical stance may, of course, lead to unproductive quibbling over concepts, especially when the theorizing lacks a firm empirical base. But this has not been the case, historically, for inductively arrived at theories such as that under discussion.

The stimulus for bringing principles together into a unified statement at this point, however, derives not so much from these benefits as from the current efforts among some sociologists and others to utilize operant principles. A statement is needed that can help us all avoid unnecessary, aversive, and time-consuming debate with our colleagues or potential colleagues. By so doing, we can get on with the important work at hand, including the extension of these principles to more and more complex social situations.

TABLE 1
General and Derived Propositions and Definitions
of Modern Behavior Theory

Behavior is a function of stimulus events.
Def. 1: Those behaviors that are mediated by the autonomic nervous system are called *respondents.**

   1. *Law of Respondent Behavior: All respondents are a function of antecedent stimulus events.*

Def. 2: Those behaviors that are mediated by the somatic (central) nervous system are called *operants.*

   2. *Law of Operant Behavior: All operants have the potential to produce stimulus events which alter the behaviors' future occurrence.*

   2.a. *Law of Operant Reinforcement: All operants have the potential to produce events which will strengthen their future occurrence.*

Def. 3: Those stimulus events which will strengthen the future occurrence of operants are termed, reinforcing events.

   2.a.1. *Law of Positive Reinforcement:* Those events which will strengthen an operant's future occurrence include the presentation of stimuli.

Def. 4: Those stimuli whose presentation will strengthen an operant's

---

*The other laws of respondent behavior will not be presented here.

future occurrence are called positive reinforcers; the process, positive reinforcement.

2.a.2.   *Law of Negative Reinforcement:* Those events which will strengthen an operant's future occurrence include the removal of stimuli.

Def. 5:   Those stimuli whose removal will strengthen an operant's future occurrence are called negative reinforcers; the process, negative reinforcement.

Def. 6:   The strength of an operant before any known reinforcement is termed its *operant level.*

Def. 7:   The strengthening of an operant as a function of reinforcement is called *operant conditioning.*

Def. 8:   The response-contingencies that determine when reinforcement will be delivered are termed *schedules of reinforcement.*

Def. 9:   A schedule of reinforcement in which each operant is reinforced is called continuous reinforcement (CRF).

Def. 10:   Any schedule of reinforcement which does not provide reinforcement following each response is called *intermittent reinforcement.* The following are instances of intermittent reinforcement:

10.1)   Fixed-interval reinforcement (FI) is a schedule in which reinforcement is delivered following the first response after a constant period of time has elapsed since the last reinforcement.

10.2)   Fixed-ratio reinforcement (FR) is a schedule of reinforcement in which every n^{th} response is reinforced.

10.3)   Variable-interval reinforcement (VI) is an interval schedule of reinforcement in which the time intervals between reinforcement vary about a given mean.

10.4)   Variable-ratio reinforcement (VR) is a ratio schedule of reinforcement in which the number of responses between reinforcement varies about a given mean. (We could continue and define various kinds of multiple, mixed, tandem and differential-rate schedules of reinforcement.)

2.a.3.   Ratio reinforcement produces a higher rate of responding than interval reinforcement.

2.a.4.   Variable schedules produce more stable rates of responding than fixed schedules.

2.a.5.   The strength of an operant is a function of the amount of its reinforcement.

Def. 11:   We may call the number of reinforcements per given time period the frequency of reinforcement.

2.a.6.   The strength of an operant is a function of the frequency of its reinforcement.

Def. 12:   We may call the reciprocal of responses-per-reinforcement the probability of reinforcement.

2.a.7.   The strength of an operant is a function of the probability of its reinforcement.

Note: Because the emission of a ratio of responses requires a period of time, the rate of responding will indirectly determine the frequency of reinforcement.

2.a.8.   *Law of Extinction:* If an operant no longer produces its customary reinforcers, it will eventually return to its operant level.

Def. 13: Let us call the process whereby an operant returns to its operant level, extinction.

2.a.8$_1$ The amount of time elapsed between the onset of extinction and an operant's return to its operant level is a function of that operant's previous schedule of reinforcement.

2.a.8$_2$ The amount of time elapsed between the onset of extinction and an operant's return to its operant level is greater for an operant reinforced intermittently than continuously.

2.a.8$_3$ Ratio reinforcement produces a greater number of responses following the onset of extinction and an operant's return to its operant level than interval reinforcement.

2.a.8$_4$ The amount of time elapsed between the onset of extinction and an operant's return to its operant level is greater for interval reinforcement than for ratio reinforcement.

Def. 14: The strengthening of certain behaviors while others are being extinguished is termed *differential reinforcement*.

2.a.9. *Law of Differential Reinforcement:* Given a number of available operants, all of which produce the same reinforcer, that operant which produces the reinforcer in the greatest amount, frequency and probability will have the higher probability of occurrence.

2.a.10. *Law of Stimulus Discrimination:* Differential reinforcement increases the future probability of an operant to a greater extent in the presence of stimulus conditions the same as those that were present during previous reinforcement.

Def. 15: The process whereby an operant is emitted only in the presence of certain stimuli is called stimulus discrimination.

Def. 16: Those stimuli in whose presence the strength of an operant is increased are termed discriminative stimuli ($_sD_s$).

Def. 17: Those stimuli in whose presence an operant is less likely to occur than in their absence are termed S-deltas ($_s\Delta_s$)

2.a.11. *Law of Conditioned Reinforcement:* The same stimulus may function as an $_sD$, thereby determining the strength of the operant that prevails in the presence of that stimulus, and as a reinforcer (conditioned),† thereby determining the strength of the operant preceding that stimulus.

2.a.11$_1$ The establishment of stimulus as an S^D is not a necessary condition for the establishment of that stimulus as a reinforcer (conditioned).

2.a.12. *Law of Stimulus Satiation:* As a function of past reinforcement, a reinforcer will temporarily cease to strengthen the operant that produced it.

Def. 18: The process whereby a reinforcer temporarily ceases to strengthen an operant is termed satiation.

2.a.13. *Law of Stimulus Deprivation:* The reinforcing power of a stimulus will be restored by depriving the organism of it for a period of time.

Def. 19: The process whereby the reinforcing power of a stimulus is restored through the withholding of that stimulus is termed deprivation.

2.a.14. *Law of Stimulus Generalization Type I:* Whenever a stimulus acquires discriminative stimulus properties, then other stimuli will also take on discriminative properties for the same operant

---

†See: 2.b.1.

to the extent that they are similar to the original discriminative stimulus.

Def. 20:   The process whereby stimuli similar in nature acquire discriminative properties is termed stimulus generalization.

2.a.15.   *Law of Response Differentiation:* Differential reinforcement has the potential to alter some specific property of an operant such as its duration, intensity or topography.

Def. 21:   The process whereby reinforcement alters an operant's duration, intensity or topography is termed response differentiation.

2.b.   *Law of Neutral Stimuli:* All operants have the potential to produce events which will not alter their future occurrence.

Def. 22:   Those events which have no effect upon the strength of an operant are termed *neutral stimuli.*

2.b.1.   *Law of Conditioning:* A neutral stimulus may acquire reinforcing properties through temporal association with another reinforcer.

Def. 23:   Those stimuli which can function as reinforcers without any special history of conditioning are called *unconditioned reinforcers.*

Def. 24:   Those stimuli which can function as reinforcers only after a special history of conditioning are called, *conditioned reinforcers.*

2.b.1_I The conditioned reinforcing effectiveness of a previously neutral stimulus is a direct function of the amount, frequency and probability of reinforcement in its presence.

2.b.2.   *Law of Stimulus Generalization Type II:* Whenever a stimulus acquires conditioned reinforcing properties, then other stimuli will take on reinforcing properties to the extent that they are similar to the original conditioned reinforcer.

2.c.   *Law of Punishment:* All operants have the potential to produce events which will weaken their future occurrence.

Def. 25:   Those stimulus events whereby an operant's future occurrence is weakened are termed punishing events.

2.c.1.   *Law of Positive Punishment:* Those events which will weaken an operant's future occurrence include the presentation of stimuli.

Def. 26:   Those stimuli whose presentation will weaken an operant's future occurrence are called punishers; the process, positive punishment.

2.c.2.   *Law of Negative Punishment:* Those events which will weaken an operant's future occurrence include the removal of stimuli.

Def. 27:   Those stimuli whose removal will weaken an operant's future occurrence are called positive reinforcers; the process, negative punishment.

2.c.3.   *Law of Differential Punishment:* All the behavioral effects produced by punishers are analogous to those produced by reinforcers except that the direction of change in the strength of the operant is reversed.

Def. 28:   Those stimuli which can function as punishers without any special history of conditioning are called *unconditioned punishers.*

Def. 29:   Those stimuli (neutral and reinforcing) which can function as punishers only after a special history of conditioning are called *conditioned punishers.*

2.c.3_I The amount of operant suppression produced by an operant-contingent punisher is a function of the intensity of that punisher.

2.c.3$_3$ Smaller intensities of punishers will produce complete operant suppression if they are paired with positive reinforcement for an alternative and incompatible operant.

2.c.3$_3$ When a punisher is delivered during extinction, it will reduce the number of responses and the amount of time required before an operant will reach its operant level as a function of the intensity of that punisher.

2.c.3$_4$ If a punisher is repeatedly paired with positive reinforcement, and reinforcement is not available otherwise, the punisher will become an S^D for the operant which results in that reinforcement, as well as a conditioned reinforcer.

REFERENCES

Bijou, S. W., and Baer, D. M. 1961. *Child development*, Volume 1. New York: Appleton-Century-Crofts.

Burgess, R. L., and Akers, R. L. 1966. "A Differential Association-Reinforcement Theory of Criminal Behavior." *Social Problems*, Volume 14, No. 2, 128–47.

Keller, F. S. 1954. *Learning: reinforcement theory*. New York: Random House.

Reese, E. P. 1964. *Experiments in operant behavior*. New York: Appleton-Century-Crofts.

Skinner, B. F. 1938. *The behavior of organisms*. New York: Appleton-Century-Crofts.

Skinner, B. F. 1953. *Science and human behavior*. New York: Macmillan.

Skinner, B. F. 1959. *Cumulative record*. New York: Appleton-Century-Crofts.

Some Questions and Answers

1. Q. If a biologist (chemist, physicist, biochemist, etc.) were to study *experimental design*, where would he study it?

   A. Laboratory.

2. Q. If an educator (psychologist, sociologist, etc.) were to study experimental design, where would he study it?

   A. In the calculating room.

3. Q. If a biologist ran an experiment and got suggestive, but unclear results, what would he do?

   A. Refine procedure, vary things, try again with changes after such analysis.

4. Q. If a psychologist ran an experiment and got suggestive, but unclear results, what would he do?

   A. Increase the N.

5. Q. If the biologist mentioned refines his study adequately and runs it, how soon does he know the results?

   A. Within minutes or hours.

Stolen from Howard Sloane. He didn't say where he stole it.

6. Q. When the psychologist increases his N and reruns the study, how soon does he know the results?

   A. It takes a long time to analyze a seven way analysis of variance.

7. Q. Please discuss the above with relation to delay of reinforcement and the probability that one will continue in research.

   A. Well. . .

8. Q. If a scientist who got suggestive but inconclusive results reruns the experiment with a larger N, what does he learn from rerunning it that he did not already know (assume it turns out as expected)?

   A. How to publish?

9. Q. If a scientist who got suggestive but inconclusive results reruns it after "playing around" to find out what accounted for the variability and incorporating these findings in his rerun, what does he learn that he did not know at first?

   A. New independent variables.

Strong Inference

John R. Platt
University of Michigan

> Certain systematic methods of scientific thinking may produce
> much more rapid progress than others.

Scientists these days tend to keep up a polite fiction that all science
is equal. Except for the work of the misguided opponent whose
arguments we happen to be refuting at the time, we speak as though
every scientist's field and methods of study are as good as every
other scientist's, and perhaps a little better. This keeps us all cordial
when it comes to recommending each other for government grants.

But I think anyone who looks at the matter closely will agree that
some fields of science are moving forward very much faster than
others, perhaps by an order of magnitude, if numbers could be put
on such estimates. The discoveries leap from the headlines — and
they are real advances in complex and difficult subjects, like molecular biology and high-energy physics. As Alvin Weinberg says,
"Hardly a month goes by without a stunning success in molecular
biology being reported in the Proceedings of the National Academy
of Sciences."[1]

Why should there be such rapid advances in some fields and not
in others? I think the usual explanations that we tend to think of —
such as the tractability of the subject, or the quality of education of
the men drawn into it, or the size of research contracts — are important but inadequate. I have begun to believe that the primary factor
in scientific advance is an intellectual one. These rapidly moving

From *Science* 146, 3642 (16 October 1964).
1. A.M. Weinberg, *Minerva*, 159 (Winter 1963); *Phys. Today* 17, 42 (1964).

fields are fields where a particular method of doing scientific research is systematically used and taught, an accumulative method of inductive inference that is so effective that I think it should be given the name of "strong inference." I believe it is important to examine this method, its use and history and rationale, and to see whether other groups and individuals might learn to adopt it profitably in their own scientific and intellectual work.

In its separate elements, strong inference is just the simple and old-fashioned methods of inductive inference that goes back to Francis Bacon. The steps are familiar to every college student and are practiced, off and on, by every scientist. The difference comes in their systematic application. Strong inference consists of applying the following steps to every problem in science, formally and explicitly and regularly:

1. Devising alternative hypotheses;
2. Devising a crucial experiment (or several of them), with alternative possible outcomes, each of which will, as nearly as possible, exclude one or more of the hypotheses;
3. Carrying out the experiment so as to get a clean result;
4. Recycling the procedure, making subhypotheses or sequential hypotheses to refine the possibilities that remain; and so on.

It is like climbing a tree. At the first fork, we choose — or, in this case, "nature" or the experimental outcome chooses — to go to the right branch or the left; at the next fork, to go left or right; and so on. There are similar branch points in a "conditional computer program," where the next move depends on the result of the last calculation. And there is a "conditional inductive tree" or "logical tree" of this kind written out in detail in many first-year chemistry books, in the table of steps for qualitative analysis of an unknown sample, where the student is led through a real problem of consecutive inference: Add reagent A; if you get a red precipitate, it is sub-group alpha and you filter and add reagent B; if not, you add the other reagent B'; and so on.

On any new problem, of course, inductive inference is not as simple and certain as deduction, because it involves reaching out into the unknown. Steps 1 and 2 require intellectual inventions, which must be cleverly chosen so that hypotheses, experiment, outcome, and exclusion will be related in a rigorous syllogism; and the question of how to generate such inventions is one which has been extensively discussed elsewhere.[2,3] What the formal schema

2. G. Polya, *Mathematics and Plausible Reasoning* (Princeton Univ. Press, Princeton, N.J., 1954), vol. 1, *Induction and Analogy in Mathematics;* vol. 2, *Patterns of Plausible Inference.*

3. J. R. Platt, *The Excitement of Science* (Houghton Mifflin, Boston, 1962); see especially chapters 7 and 8.

reminds us to do is to try to make these inventions, to take the next step, to proceed to the next fork, without dawdling or getting tied up in irrelevancies.

It is clear why this makes for rapid and powerful progress. For exploring the unknown, there is no faster method; this is the minimum sequence of steps. Any conclusion that is not an exclusion is insecure and must be rechecked. Any delay in recycling to the next set of hypotheses is only a delay. Strong inference, and the logical tree it generates, are to inductive reasoning what the syllogism is to deductive reasoning, in that it offers a regular method for reaching firm inductive conclusions one after the other as rapidly as possible.

"But what is so novel about this?" someone will say. This is the method of science and always has been; why give it a special name? The reason is that many of us have almost forgotten it. Science is now an everyday business. Equipment, calculations, lectures become ends in themselves. How many of us write down our alternatives and crucial experiments every day, focusing on the *exclusion* of a hypotheses? We may write our scientific papers so that it looks as if we had steps 1, 2, and 3 in mind all along. But in between, we do busywork. We become "method-oriented" rather than "problem-oriented." We say we prefer to "feel our way" toward generalizations. We fail to teach our students how to sharpen up their inductive inferences. And we do not realize the added power that the regular and explicit use of alternative hypotheses and sharp exclusions could give us at every step of our research.

The difference between the average scientist's informal methods and the methods of the strong-inference users is somewhat like the difference between a gasoline engine that fires occasionally and one that fires in steady sequence. If our motorboat engines were as erratic as our deliberate intellectual efforts, most of us would not get home for supper.

Molecular Biology

The new molecular biology is a field where I think this systematic method of inference has become widespread and effective. It is a complex field; yet a succession of crucial experiments over the past decade has given us a surprisingly detailed understanding of hereditary mechanisms and the control of enzyme formation and protein synthesis.

The logical structure shows in every experiment. In 1953, James Watson and Francis Crick proposed that the DNA molecule — the "hereditary substance" in a cell — is a long two-stranded helical molecule.[4] This suggested a number of alternatives for crucial test. Do the two strands of the helix stay together when a cell divides,

---

4. J. D. Watson and F. H. C. Crick, *Nature* **171**, 737 (1953).

or do they separate? Matthew Meselson and Franklin Stahl used an ingenious isotope-density-labeling technique which showed that they separate.[5] Does the DNA helix always have two strands, or can it have three, as atomic models suggest? Alexander Rich showed it can have either, depending on the ionic concentration.[6] These are the kinds of experiments John Dalton would have liked, where the combining entities are not atoms but long macromolecular strands.

Or take a different sort of question: Is the "genetic map" — showing the statistical relationship of different genetic characteristics in recombination experiments — a one-dimensional map like the DNA molecule (that is, a linear map), as T. H. Morgan proposed in 1911, or does it have two-dimensional loops or branches? Seymour Benzer showed that his hundreds of fine macrogenetic experiments on bacteria would fit only the mathematical matrix for the one-dimensional case.[7]

But of course, selected crucial experiments of this kind can be found in every field. The real difference in molecular biology is that formal inductive inference is so systematically practiced and taught. On any given morning at the Laboratory of Molecular Biology in Cambridge, England, the blackboards of Francis Crick or Sidney Brenner will commonly be found covered with logical trees. On the top line will be the hot new result just up from the laboratory or just in by letter or rumor. On the next line will be two or three alternative explanations, or a little list of "What he did wrong." Underneath will be a series of suggested experiments or controls that can reduce the number of possibilities. And so on. The tree grows during the day as one man or another comes in and argues about why one of the experiments wouldn't work, or how it should be changed.

The strong-inference attitude is evident just in the style and language in which the papers are written. For example, in analyzing theories of antibody formation, Joshua Lederberg gives a list of nine propositions "subject to denial", discussing which ones would be "most vulnerable to experimental test."[8]

The papers of the French leaders Francois Jacob and Jacques Monod are also celebrated for their high "logical density," with paragraph after paragraph of linked "inductive syllogisms." But the style is widespread. Start with the first paper in the *Journal of Molecular Biology* for 1964,[9] and you immediately find: "Our con-

---

5. M. Meselson and F. Stahl, *Proc. Natl. Acad. Sci. U. S.* **44**, 671 (1958).

6. A. Rich, in *Biophysical Science: A Study Program*, J. L. Oncley et al., eds. (Wiley, New York, 1959), p. 191.

7. S. Benzer, *Proc. Natl. Acad. Sci. U. S.* **45**, 1607 (1959).

8. J. Lederberg, *Science* **129**, 1649 (1959).

9. P. F. Davison, D. Freifelder, B. W. Holloway, *J. Mol. Biol.* **8**, 1 (1964).

clusions . . . might be invalid if . . . . (i) . . . (ii) . . . or (iii) . . . . . We shall describe experiments which eliminate these alternatives." The average physicist or chemist or scientist in any field accustomed to less closely reasoned articles and less sharply stated inferences will find it a salutary experience to dip into that journal almost at random.

Resistance to Analytical Methodology

This analytical approach to biology has sometimes become almost a crusade, because it arouses so much resistance in many scientists who have grown up in a more relaxed and diffuse tradition. At the 1958 Conference on Biophysics, at Boulder, there was a dramatic confrontation between the two points of view. Leo Szilard said: "The problems of how enzymes are induced, of how proteins are synthesized, of how antibodies are formed, are closer to solution than is generally believed. If you do stupid experiments and finish one a year, it can take 50 years. But if you stop doing experiments for a little while and *think* how proteins can possibly be synthesized, there are only about 5 different ways, not 50! And it will take only a few experiments to distinguish these."

One of the young men added: "It is essentially the old question: How *small* and *elegant* an experiment can you perform?"

These comments upset a number of those present. An electron microscopist said, "Gentlemen, this is off the track. This is philosophy of science."

Szilard retorted, "I was not quarreling with third-rate scientists: I was quarreling with first-rate scientists."

A physical chemist hurriedly asked, "Are we going to take the official photograph before lunch or after lunch?"

But this did not deflect the dispute. A distinguished cell biologist rose and said, "No two cells give the same properties. Biology is the science of heterogeneous systems." And he added privately, "You know there are *scientists;* and there are people in science who are just working with these over-simplified model systems — DNA chains and in vitro systems — who are not doing science at all. We need their auxiliary work: they build apparatus, they make minor studies, but they are not scientists."

To which Cy Levinthal replied: "Well, there are two kinds of biologists, those who are looking to see if there is one thing that can be understood, and those who keep saying it is very complicated and that nothing can be understood. . . . You must study the *simplest* system you think has the properties you are interested in."

As they were leaving the meeting, one man could be heard muttering, "What does Szilard expect me to do — shoot myself?"

Any criticism or challenge to consider changing our methods strikes of course at all our ego-defenses. But in this case the analytical method offers the possibility of such great increases in effectiveness that it is unfortunate that it cannot be regarded more often as a challenge to learning rather than as a challenge to combat. Many of the recent triumphs in molecular biology have in fact been achieved on just such "oversimplified model systems," very much along the analytical lines laid down in the 1958 discussion. They have not fallen to the kind of men who justify themselves by saying, "No two cells are alike," regardless of how true that may ultimately be. The triumphs are in fact triumphs of a new way of thinking.

High-Energy Physics

This analytical thinking is rare, but it is by no means restricted to the new biology. High-energy physics is another field where the logic of exclusions is obvious, even in the newspaper accounts. For example, in the famous discovery of C. N. Yang and T. D. Lee, the question that was asked was: Do the fundamental particles conserve mirror-symmetry or "parity" in certain reactions, or do they not? The crucial experiments were suggested; within a few months they were done, and conservation of parity was found to be excluded. Richard Garwin, Leon Lederman, and Marcel Weinrich did one of the crucial experiments. It was thought of one evening at suppertime; by midnight they had rearranged the apparatus for it; and by 4 a.m. they had picked up the predicted pulses showing the nonconservation of parity.[10] The phenomena had just been waiting, so to speak, for the explicit formulation of the alternative hypotheses.

The theorists in this field take pride in trying to predict new properties or new particles explicitly enough so that if they are not found the theories will fall. As the biologist W. A. H. Rushton has said, "A theory which cannot be mortally endangered cannot be alive."[11] Murray Gell-Mann and Yuval Ne'eman recently used the particle grouping which they call "The Eightfold Way" to predict a missing particle, the Omega-Minus, which was then looked for and found.[12] But one alternative branch of the theory would predict a particle with one-third the usual electronic charge, and it was not found in the experiments, so this branch must be rejected.

The logical tree is so much a part of high-energy physics that some stages of it are commonly built, in fact, into the electronic coincidence circuits that detect the particles and trigger the bubble-chamber photographs. Each kind of particle should give a different kind of pattern in the electronic counters, and the circuits can be set to exclude or include whatever types of events are desired. If

---

10. R. L. Garwin, L. M. Lederman, M. Weinrich, *Phys. Rev.* **105**, 1415 (1957).

11. W. A. H. Rushton, personal communication.

12. See G. F. Chew, M. Gell-Mann, A. H. Rosenfeld, *Sci. Am.* **210**, 74 (Feb. 1964); ibid, **210**, 60 (Apr. 1964); ibid, **210**, 54 (June 1964).

the distinguishing criteria are sequential, they may even run through a complete logical tree in a microsecond or so. This electronic preliminary analysis, like human preliminary analysis of alternative outcomes, speeds up progress by sharpening the criteria. It eliminates hundreds of thousands of the irrelevant pictures that formerly had to be scanned, and when it is carried to its limit, a few output pulses, hours apart, may be enough to signal the existence of the antiproton or the fall of a theory.

I think the emphasis on strong inference in the two fields I have mentioned has been partly the result of personal leadership, such as that of the classical geneticists in molecular biology, or of Szilard with his "Midwest Chowder and Bacteria Society" at Chicago in 1948–50, or of Max Delbruck with his summer courses in phage genetics at Cold Spring Harbor. But it is also partly due to the nature of the fields themselves. Biology, with its vast informational detail and complexity, is a "high-information" field, where years and decades can easily be wasted on the usual type of "low-information" observations or experiments if one does not think carefully in advance about what the most important and conclusive experiments would be. And in high-energy physics, both the "information flux" of particles from the new accelerators and the million-dollar costs of operation have forced a similar analytical approach. It pays to have a top-notch group debate every experiment ahead of time; and the habit spreads throughout the field.

Induction and Multiple Hypotheses

Historically, I think, there have been two main contributions to the development of a satisfactory strong-inference method. The first is that of Francis Bacon.[13] He wanted a "surer method" of "finding out nature" than either the logic-chopping or all-inclusive theories of the time or the laudable but crude attempts to make inductions "by simple enumeration." He did not merely urge experiments, as some suppose; he showed the fruitfulness of interconnecting theory and experiment so that the one checked the other. Of the many inductive procedures he suggested, the most important, I think, was the conditional inductive tree, which proceeded from alternative hypotheses (possible "causes," as he calls them), through crucial experiments ("Instances of the Fingerpost"), to exclusion of some alternatives and adoption of what is left ("establishing axioms"). His Instances of the Fingerpost are explicitly at the forks in the logical tree, the term being borrowed "from the fingerposts which are set up where roads part, to indicate the several directions."

Many of his crucial experiments proposed in Book II of *The New*

---

13. F. Bacon, *The New Organon and Related Writings* (Liberal Arts Press, New York, 1960), especially pp. 98, 112, 151, 156, 196.

Organon are still fascinating. For example, in order to decide whether the weight of a body is due to its "inherent nature," as some had said, or is due to the attraction of the earth, which would decrease with distance, he proposes comparing the rate of a pendulum clock and a spring clock and then lifting them from the earth to the top of a tall steeple. He concludes that if the pendulum clock on the steeple "goes more slowly than it did on account of the diminished virtue of its weights . . . we may take the attraction of the mass of the earth as the cause of weight."

Here was a method that could separate off the empty theories!

Bacon said the inductive method could be learned by anybody, just like learning to "draw a straighter line or more perfect circle . . . with the help of a ruler or a pair of compasses." "My way of discovering sciences goes far to level men's wit and leaves but little to individual excellence, because it performs everything by the surest rules and demonstrations." Even occasional mistakes would not be fatal. "Truth will sooner come out from error than from confusion."

It is easy to see why young minds leaped to try it.

Nevertheless there is a difficulty with this method. As Bacon emphasizes, it is necessary to make "exclusions." He says, "The induction which is to be available for the discovery and demonstration of sciences and arts, must analyze nature by proper rejections and exclusions; and then, after a sufficient number of negatives, come to a conclusion on the affirmative instances." "(To man) it is granted only to proceed at first by negatives, and at last to end in affirmatives after exclusion has been exhausted."

Or, as the philosopher Karl Popper says today, there is no such thing as proof in science—because some later alternative explanation may be as good or better—so that science advances only by disproofs. There is no point in making hypotheses that are not falsifiable, because such hypotheses do not say anything; "it must be possible for an empirical scientific system to be refuted by experience."[14]

The difficulty is that disproof is a hard doctrine. If you have a hypothesis and I have another hypotheses, evidently one of them must be eliminated. The scientist seems to have no choice but to be either soft-headed or disputatious. Perhaps this is why so many tend to resist the strong analytical approach—and why some great scientists are so disputatious.

Fortunately, it seems to me, this difficulty can be removed by the use of a second great intellectual invention, the "method of multiple

14. K. R. Popper, *The Logic of Scientific Discovery* (Basic Books, New York, 1959), p. 41. A modified view is given by T. S. Kuhn, *The Structure of Scientific Revolutions* (Univ. of Chicago Press, Chicago, 1962), p. 146; it does not, I believe, invalidate any of these conclusions.

hypotheses," which is what was needed to round out the Baconian scheme. This is a method that was put forward by T. C. Chamberlin,[15] a geologist at Chicago at the turn of the century, who is best known for his contribution to the Chamberlin-Moulton hypothesis of the origin of the solar system.

Chamberlin says our trouble is that when we make a single hypothesis, we become attached to it.

"The moment one has offered an original explanation for a phenomenon which seems satisfactory, that moment affection for his intellectual child springs into existence, and as the explanation grows into a definite theory his parental affections cluster about his offspring and it grows more and more dear to him. . . . There springs up also unwittingly a pressing of the theory to make it fit the facts and a pressing of the facts to make them fit the theory. . . .

"To avoid this grave danger, the method of multiple working hypotheses is urged. It differs from the simple working hypothesis in that it distributes the effort and divides the affections. . . . Each hypothesis suggests its own criteria, its own means of proof, its own method of developing the truth, and if a group of hypotheses encompass the subject on all sides, the total outcome of means and of methods is full and rich."

Chamberlin thinks the method "leads to certain distinctive habits of mind" and is of prime value in education. "When faithfully followed for a sufficient time, it develops a mode of thought of its own kind which may be designated the habit of complex thought . . ."

This charming paper deserves to be reprinted in some more accessible journal today, where it could be required reading for every graduate student—and for every professor.

It seems to me that Chamberlin has hit on the explanation—and the cure—for many of our problems in the sciences. The conflict and exclusion of alternatives that is necessary to sharp inductive inference has been all too often a conflict between men, each with his single Ruling Theory. But whenever each man begins to have multiple working hypotheses, it becomes purely a conflict between ideas. It becomes much easier then for each of us to aim every day at conclusive disproofs—at *strong* inference—without either reluctance or combativeness. In fact, when there are multiple hypotheses which are not anyone's "personal property" and when there are crucial experiments to test them, the daily life in the laboratory takes on an interest and excitement it never had, and the students can hardly wait to get to work to see how the detective story will come out. It seems to me that this is the reason for the development of those "distinctive habits of mind" and the "complex thought" that

---

15. T. C. Chamberlin, *J. Geol.* **5**, 837 (1897). I am indebted to Professors Preston Cloud and Bryce Crawford, Jr., of the University of Minnesota for correspondence on this article and a classroom reprint of it.

Chamberlin described, the reason for the sharpness, the excitement, the zeal, the teamwork—yes, even international teamwork—in molecular biology and high-energy physics today. What else could be so effective?

When multiple hypotheses become coupled to strong inference, the scientific search becomes an emotional powerhouse as well as an intellectual one.

Unfortunately, I think, there are other areas of science today that are sick by comparison, because they have forgotten the necessity for alternative hypotheses and disproof. Each man has only one branch—or none—on the logical tree, and it twists at random without ever coming to the need for a crucial decision at any point. We can see from the external symptoms that there is something scientifically wrong. The Frozen Method. The Eternal Suveyor. The Never Finished. The Great Man With a Single Hypothesis. The Little Club of Dependents. The Vendetta. The All-Encompassing Theory Which Can Never Be Falsified.

Some cynics tell a story, which may be apocryphal, about the theoretical chemist who explained to his class, "And thus we see that the C-Cl bond is longer in the first compound than in the second because the percent of ionic character is smaller."

A voice from the back of the room said, "But Professor X, according to the Table, the C-Cl bond is shorter in the first compound."

To the extent that this kind of story is accurate, a "theory" of this sort is not a theory at all, because it does not exclude anything. It predicts everything, and therefore does not predict anything. It becomes simply a verbal formula which the graduate student repeats and believes because the professor has said it so often. This is not science, but faith; not theory, but theology. Whether it is hand-waving or number-waving or equation-waving, a theory is not a theory unless it can be disproved. That is, unless it can be falsified by some possible experimental outcome.

In chemistry, the resonance theorists will of course suppose that I am criticizing *them,* while the molecular-orbital theorists will suppose I am criticizing *them.* But their actions—our actions, for I include myself among them—speak for themselves. A failure to agree for 30 years is public advertisement of a failure to disprove.

My purpose here, however, is not to call names but rather to say that we are all sinners, and that in every field and in every laboratory we need to try to formulate multiple alternative hypotheses sharp enough to be capable of disproof.

Systematic Application

I think the work methods of a number of scientists have been testimony to the power of strong inference. Is success not due in many cases to systematic use of Bacon's "surest rules and demonstrations" as much as to rare and unattainable intellectual power? Faraday's famous diary,[16] or Fermi's notebooks,[17] show how these men believed in the effectiveness of daily steps in applying formal inductive methods to one problem after another.

Within 8 weeks after the discovery of x-rays, Roentgen had identified 17 of their major properties. Every student should read his first paper.[18] Each demonstration in it is a little jewel of inductive inference. How else could the proofs have gone so fast, except by a method of maximum effectiveness?

Organic chemistry has been the spiritual home of strong inference from the beginning. Do the bonds alternate in benzene or are they equivalent? If the first, there should be five disubstituted derivatives; if the second, three. And three it is.[19] This is a strong-inference test—not a matter of measurement, of whether there are grams or milligrams of the products, but a matter of logical alternatives. How else could the tetrahedral carbon atom or the hexagonal symmetry of benzene have been inferred 50 years before the inferences could be confirmed by x-ray and infrared measurement?

We realize that it was out of this kind of atmosphere that Pasteur came to the field of biology. Can anyone doubt that he brought with him a completely different method of reasoning? Every two or three years he moved to one biological problem after another, from optical activity to the fermentation of beet sugar, to the "diseases" of wine and beer, to the disease of silkworms, to the problem of "spontaneous generation," to the anthrax disease of sheep, to rabies. In each of these fields there were experts in Europe who knew a hundred times as much as Pasteur, yet each time he solved problems in a few months that they had not been able to solve. Obviously it was not encyclopedic knowledge that produced his success, and obviously it was not simply luck, when it was repeated over and over again; it can only have been the systematic power of a special method of exploration. Are bacteria falling in? Make the necks of the flasks S-shaped. Are bacteria sucked in by the partial vacuum? Put in a cotton plug. Week after week his crucial experiments build up the logical tree of exclusions. The drama of strong inference in molecular biology today is only a repetition of Pasteur's story.

The grand scientific syntheses, like those of Newton and Maxwell, are rare and individual achievements that stand outside any rule or method. Nevertheless it is interesting to note that several of the

---

16. M. Faraday, *Faraday's Diary 1820–62* (Bell, London, 1932–36).

17. H. L. Anderson and S. K. Allison, *Rev. Mod. Phys.* **27**, 273 (1955).

18. E. C. Watson (*Am. J. Phys.* **13**, 281 (1945)) gives an English translation of both of Roentgen's first papers on x-rays.

19. See G. W. Wheland, *Advanced Organic Chemistry* (Wiley, New York, 1949), chapter 4, for numerous such examples.

great synthesizers have also shown the strong-inference habit of thought in their other work, as Newton did in the inductive proofs of his *Opticks* and Maxwell did in his experimental proof that three and only three colors are needed in color vision.

A Yardstick of Effectiveness

I think the evident effectiveness of the systematic use of strong inference suddenly gives us a yardstick for thinking about the effectiveness of scientific methods in general. Surveys, taxonomy, design of equipment, systematic measurements and tables, theoretical computations—all have their proper and honored place, provided they are parts of a chain of precise induction of how nature works. Unfortunately, all too often they become ends in themselves, mere time-serving from the point of view of real scientific methodology that justifies itself as a lore of respectability.

We praise the "lifetime of study," but in dozens of cases, in every field, what was needed was not a lifetime but rather a few short months or weeks of analytical inductive inference. In any new area we should try, like Roentgen, to see how fast we can pass from the general survey to analytical inferences. We should try, like Pasteur, to see whether we can reach strong inferences that encyclopedism could not discern.

We speak piously of taking measurements and making small studies that will "add another brick to the temple of science." Most such bricks just lie around the brickyard.[20] Tables of constants have their place and value, but the study of one spectrum after another, if not frequently re-evaluated, may become a substitute for thinking, a sad waste of intelligence in a research laboratory, and a mistraining whose crippling effects may last a lifetime.

To paraphrase an old saying, Beware of the man of one method or one instrument, either experimental or theoretical. He tends to become method-oriented rather than problem-oriented. The method-oriented man is shackled; the problem-oriented man is at least reaching freely toward what is most important. Strong inference redirects a man to problem-orientation, but it requires him to be willing repeatedly to put aside his last methods and teach himself new ones.

The great value of mathematical formulation is that when an experiment agrees with a calculation to five decimal places, a great many alternative hypotheses are pretty well excluded (though the Bohr theory and the Schrodinger theory both predict exactly the same Rydberg constant!). But when the fit is only to two decimal places, or one, it may be a trap for the unwary; it may be no better

---

20. B. K. Forscher, *Science* 142, 339 (1963).

than any rule-of-thumb extrapolation, and some other kind of qualitative exclusion might be more rigorous for testing the assumptions and more important to scientific understanding than the quantitative fit.

I know that this is like saying that the emperor has no clothes. Today we preach that science is not science unless it is quantitative. We substitute correlations for causal studies, and physical equations for organic reasoning. Measurements and equations are supposed to sharpen thinking, but, in my observation, they more often tend to make the thinking noncausal and fuzzy. They tend to become the object of scientific manipulation instead of auxiliary tests of crucial inferences.

Many — perhaps most — of the great issues of science are qualitative, not quantitative, even in physics and chemistry. Equations and measurements are useful when and only when they are related to proof; but proof or disproof comes first and is in fact strongest when it is absolutely convincing without any quantitative measurement.

Or to say it another way, you can catch phenomena in a logical box or in a mathematical box. The logical box is coarse but strong. The mathematical box is fine-grained but flimsy. The mathematical box is a beautiful way of wrapping up a problem, but it will not hold the phenomena unless they have been caught in a logical box to begin with.

What I am saying is that, in numerous areas that we call science, we have come to like our habitual ways, and our studies that can be continued indefinitely. We measure, we define, we compute, we analyze, but we do not exclude. And this is not the way to use our minds most effectively or to make the fastest progress in solving scientific questions.

Of course it is easy — and all too common — for one scientist to call the others unscientific. My point is not that my particular conclusions here are necessarily correct, but that we have long needed some absolute standard of possible scientific effectiveness by which to measure how well we are succeeding in various areas — a standard that many could agree on and one that would be undistorted by the scientific pressures and fashions of the times and the vested interests and busywork that they develop. It is not public evaluation I am interested in so much as a private measure by which to compare one's own scientific performance with what it might be. I believe that strong inference provides this kind of standard of what the maximum possible scientific effectiveness could be — as well as a recipe for reaching it.

Aids to Strong Inference

How can we learn the method and teach it? It is not difficult. The most important thing is to keep in mind that this kind of thinking is not a lucky knack but a system that *can* be taught and learned. The molecular biologists today are living proof of it. The second thing is to be explicit and formal and regular about it, to devote a half hour or an hour to analytical thinking every day, writing out the logical tree and the alternatives and crucial experiments explicitly in a permanent notebook. I have discussed elsewhere[21] the value of Fermi's notebook method, the effect it had on his colleagues and students, and the testimony that it "can be adopted by anyone with profit."

It is true that it takes great courtesy to teach the method, especially to one's peers — or their students. The strong-inference point of view is so resolutely critical of methods of work and values in science that any attempt to compare specific cases is likely to sound both smug and destructive. Mainly one should try to teach it by example and by exhorting to self-analysis and self-improvement only in general terms, as I am doing here.

But I will mention one severe but useful private test — a touchstone of strong inference — that removes the necessity for third-person criticism, because it is a test that anyone can learn to carry with him for use as needed. It is our old friend the Baconian "exclusion," but I call it "The Question." Obviously it should be applied as much to one's own thinking as to others'. It consists of asking in your own mind, on hearing any scientific explanation or theory put forward, "But sir, what experiment could *dis*prove your hypotheses?"; or, on hearing a scientific experiment described, "But sir, what hypothesis does your experiment *dis*prove?"

This goes straight to the heart of the matter. It forces everyone to refocus on the central question of whether there is or is not a testable scientific step forward.

If such a question were asked aloud, many a supposedly great scientist would sputter and turn livid and would want to throw the questioner out, as a hostile witness! Such a man is less than he appears, for he is obviously not accustomed to think in terms of alternative hypotheses and crucial experiments for himself; and one might also wonder about the state of science in the field he is in. But who knows? — the question might educate him, and his field too!

On the other hand, I think that throughout most of molecular biology and nuclear physics the response to The Questions would be to outline immediately not one but several tests to disprove the hypothesis — and it would turn out that the speaker already had two or three graduate students working on them!

I almost think that government agencies could make use of this kind of touchstone. It is not true that all science is equal, or that we cannot justly compare the effectiveness of scientists by any method other than a mutual-recommendation system. The man to watch, the

---

21. J. R. Platt, *The Excitement of Science* (Houghton Mifflin, Boston, 1962); see especially chapters 7 and 8.

man to put your money on, is not the man who wants to make "a survey" or a "more detailed study" but the man with the notebook, the man with the alternative hypotheses and the crucial experiments, the man who knows how to answer your Question of disproof and is already working on it.

There are some really hard problems, some high-information problems, ahead of us in several fields, problems of photosynthesis, of cellular organization, of the molecular structure and organization of the nervous system, not to mention some of our social and international problems. It seems to me that the method of most rapid progress in such complex areas, the most effective way of using our brains, is going to be to set down explicitly at each step just what the question is, and what all the alternatives are, and then to set up crucial experiments to try to disprove some. Problems of this complexity, if they can be solved at all, can be solved only by men generating and excluding possibilities with maximum effectiveness, to obtain a high degree of information per unit time—men willing to work a little bit at thinking.

When whole groups of us begin to concentrate like that, I believe we may see the molecular-biology phenomenon repeated over and over again, with order-of-magnitude increases in the rate of scientific understanding in almost every field.

10

A Method to Integrate Descriptive and Experimental Field Studies at the Level of Data and Empirical Concepts

Sidney W. Bijou
Robert F. Peterson
Marion H. Ault

University of Illinois

It is the thesis of this paper that data from descriptive and experimental field studies can be interrelated at the level of data and empirical concepts if both sets are derived from frequency-of-occurrence measures. The methodology proposed for a descriptive field study is predicated on three assumptions: (1) The primary data of psychology are the observable interactions of a biological organism and environmental events, past and present. (2) Theoretical concepts and laws are derived from empirical concepts and laws, which in turn are derived from the raw data. (3) Descriptive field studies describe interactions between behavioral and environmental events; experimental field studies provide information on their functional relationships. The ingredients of a descriptive field investigation using frequency measures consist of: (1) specifying in objective terms the situation in which the study is conducted, (2) defining and recording behavioral and environmental events in observable terms, and (3) measuring observer reliability. Field descriptive studies following the procedures suggested here would reveal interesting new relationships in the usual ecological settings and would also provide provocative cues for experimental studies. On the other hand, field-experimental studies using frequency measures would probably yield findings that would suggest the need for describing new interactions in specific natural situations.

From *Journal of Applied Behavior Analysis* 1 (1968), 175–91.

Psychology, like the other natural sciences, depends for its advancement upon both descriptive accounts and functional analyses of its primary data. Descriptive studies answer the question "How?". They may, for example, report the manner in which a Bantu mother nurses her child, or the way in which the Yellow Shafted Flicker mates. Experimental studies, on the other hand, provide the "Why?". They might discuss the conditions which establish and maintain the relationships between the mother and infant, between the male and female birds.

It has been claimed that progress in the behavioral sciences would be enhanced by more emphasis on descriptive studies. This may be true, but one may wish to speculate on why descriptive accounts of behavior have been de-emphasized. One possibility is the difficulty of relating descriptive and experimental data. For example, a descriptive study of parent-child behavior in the home may have data in the form of ratings on a series of scales (Baldwin, Kalhorn, and Breese, 1949), while an experimental study on the same subject may have data in the form of frequencies of events (Hawkins, Peterson, Schweid, and Bijou, 1966). Findings from the first study cannot reasonably be integrated with the second at the level of data and empirical concepts. Anyone interested in relating the two must resort to imprecise theory or concepts like "permissive mother", "laissez-faire atmosphere", "controlling child", "negativism", *etc.* This practice is unacceptable to psychologists who believe that all concepts must be based on or linked to empirical events.

It is the thesis of this paper that descriptive field studies (which include cross-cultural, ecological, and normative investigations) and experimental field studies can be performed so that the data and empirical terms in each are continuous, interchangeable, and mutually interrelatable.

Barker and Wright (1955) state that one of the aims of their ecological investigations is to produce data that may be used by all investigators in child behavior and development. Their study of "Midwest" and its children (1955) is in part devoted to the development of a method which provides raw material (which they compared to objects stored in a museum) amenable to analyses from different theoretical points of view. There are two considerations which make this doubtful. First, their data consist of "running accounts of what a person is doing and his situation on the level of direct perception or immediate inference" with "minor interpretations in the form of statements *about* rather than descriptions *of* behavior or situations" (Wright, 1967). It would seem that the material they collect would be serviceable only to those who accept non-observables in the raw data defined according to their prescription. Investigators who prefer to define their hypothetical variables some other way or who wish to exclude non-observables will find it difficult to integrate their data with those in the Barker and Wright studies. Second, final data in the form of running narrations cannot readily be transformed into units describing interactions between behavioral and environmental events, such as duration, intensity, latency, or frequency. Any attempt to convert such verbal accounts into one or more of the interactional dimensions would require so many arbitrary decisions that it would be doubtful whether another investigator could even come close to producing the same operations and results.

If, however, frequency-of-occurrence measures of environmental and behavioral events were used in both descriptive and field experimental studies, data and empirical concepts could be made congruous. The measure of frequency is preferable to that of duration, intensity, and latency for several reasons (Skinner, 1953). First, this measure readily shows changes over short and long periods of observations. Second, it specifies the *amount* of behavior displayed (Honig, 1966). Finally, and perhaps most important, it is applicable to operant behaviors across species. Hence, a methodology based on frequency of events would be serviceable for both experimental and descriptive studies of both human and infra-human subjects. This versatility has been illustrated by Jensen and Bobbitt in a study on mother and infant relationships of the pigtailed macaques (Jensen and Bobbitt, 1967).

With the use of frequency measures, the work of the ecological psychologist and the experimental psychologist would both complement and supplement each other. Descriptive studies would reveal interesting relationships among the raw data that could provide provocative cues for experimental investigations. On the other hand, field experimental studies would probably yield worthwhile leads for descriptive investigations by pointing to the need for observing new combinations of behavioral classes in specified situations. Ecological psychologists would show in terms of frequency of events, the practices of a culture, subculture, or an institutional activity of a subculture; experimental investigators working with the same set of data terms and empirical concepts would attempt to demonstrate the conditions and processes which establish and maintain the interrelationships observed.

Before considering the procedures for conducting a descriptive study using frequency measures, it might be well to make explicit three basic assumptions. The first: for psychology as a natural science, the primary data are the observable interactions between a biological organism and environmental events, past and present. These interrelationships constitute the material to be recorded. This means that the method does not include accounts of behavior isolated from related stimulus events. ("Jimmy is a rejected child." "Johnny is a highly *autistic* child." "First Henry moved about by making swimming movements, later he crawled, now he can walk with support.") Furthermore, it means that it excludes statements of generalizations about behavior and environmental interactions.

("This is an extremely aggressive child who is always getting into trouble.") Finally, it means that it excludes accounts of interactions between behavioral and environmental events intertwined with hypothetical constructs. ("The preschool child makes errors in describing the water line in a jar because of his undeveloped cognitive structure.")

The second assumption: concepts and laws in psychology are derived from raw data. Theoretical concepts evolve from empirical concepts and empirical concepts from raw data; theoretical interactional laws are derived from empirical laws and empirical laws from relationships in the raw data.

The third assumption: descriptive studies provide information only on events and their occurrence. They do not provide information on the functional properties of the events or the functional relationships among the events. Experimental studies provide that kind of information.

We move on to consider the procedures involved in conducting a descriptive field investigation. They include: (1) specifications of the situation in which a study is conducted, (2) definitions of behavioral and environmental events in observable terms, (3) measurements of observer reliability, and (4) procedures for collecting, analyzing, and interpreting the data. We terminate the paper with a brief illustration of a study for the behavior of a 4-yr-old boy in a laboratory nursery school.

Specifying the Situation in which a Study is Conducted

We define the situation in which a study is conducted in terms of its physical and social setting and the *observable events* that occur within its bounds. The physical setting may be a part of the child's home, a hospital or residential institution, a store, or a playground in the city park. It may be a nursery school, a classroom in an elementary school, or a room in a child guidance clinic.

The specific part of the home selected as a setting may consist of the living room and kitchen if the design of the home precludes flexible observation (Hawkins, Peterson, Schweid, and Bijou, 1966). In a hospital it might be the child's bedroom, the dining room, or the day room (Wolf, Risley, and Mees, 1964). In a state school for the retarded, it may be a special academic classroom (Birnbrauer, Wolf, Kidder, and Tague, 1965); in a regular elementary school, a classroom (Becker, Madsen, Arnold, and Thomas, 1967); and in a nursery school, the schoolroom and the play yard (Harris, Wolf, and Baer, 1964).

During the course of a study, changes in the physical aspect of the situation may occur despite efforts to keep them constant. Some will be sufficiently drastic to prevent further study until restoration of the original conditions (*e.g.*, power failure for several days). Others will be within normal limits (*e.g.*, replacement of old chairs in the child's bedroom) and hence will not warrant disrupting the research.

The social aspect of the situation in a home might consist of the mother and the subject's younger sibling (Hawkins, *et al.*, 1966); in a child guidance clinic, the therapist and the other children in the therapy group. In a nursery school it might include the head teacher, the assistant teacher, and the children (Johnston, Kelley, Harris, and Wolf, 1966).

Sometimes the social situation changes according to routines and the investigator wishes to take records in the different situations created by the changes. For example, he may wish to describe the behavior of a preschool child as he engages in each of four activities in the morning hours of the nursery school: show and tell, music and games, snack, and preacademic exercises. Each would be described as a field situation and data would be taken in each as if it were a separate situation. The events recorded could be the same for all the activities (*e.g.*, frequency of social contacts), or they could be specific to each depending upon the nature of the activity. They could also be a combination of both (*e.g.*, frequency of social contacts and sum total of prolonged productive activity in each preacademic exercise).

Major variations in social composition in a home study that would be considered disruptive could include the presence of other members of the family, relatives, or friends. In a nursery school, it might be the absence of the head teacher, presence of the child's mother, or the absence of many of the children. These and other events like them would probably call a halt to data collection until the standard situation is returned.

Temporary social disruptions may take many forms. For example, in the home the phone may ring, a salesman may appear, a neighbor may visit; and in the nursery school it might be a holiday preparation, or a birthday party for a member of the group.

In summary, the physical and social conditions in which an ecological study is conducted is specified at the outset. Whether the variations occurring during the study are sufficient to disrupt data collection depends, in large measure on the interactions to be studied, practical considerations, and the investigator's experience in similar situations in the past. However, accounts of changes in physical and social conditions, whether major or minor, are described and noted on the data sheets.

Defining Behavioral and Stimulus Events in Observable Terms

In this method we derive definitions of behavioral and stimulus events from preliminary investigations in the actual setting. Such pilot investigations are also used to provide preliminary information on the frequencies of occurrences of the events of interest and the feasibility of the situation for study.

A miniature episode in the life of a preschool boy, Timmy, will serve as an example. We start with having the observer make a running description of Timmy's behavior in the play yard in the style she would use if she were a reporter for a magazine.

> Timmy is playing by himself in a sandbox in a play yard in which other children are playing. A teacher stands nearby. Timmy tires of the sandbox and walks over to climb the monkeybars. Timmy shouts at the teacher, saying, "Mrs. Simpson, watch me." Timmy climbs to the top of the apparatus and shouts again to the teacher, "Look how high I am. I'm higher than anybody." The teacher comments on Timmy's climbing ability with approval. Timmy then climbs down and runs over to a tree, again demanding that the teacher watch him. The teacher, however, ignores Timmy and walks back into the classroom. Disappointed, Timmy walks toward the sandbox instead of climbing the tree. A little girl nearby cries out in pain as she stumbles and scrapes her knee. Timmy ignores her and continues to walk to the sandbox.

To obtain a clearer impression of the time relationships among antecedent stimulus events, responses, and consequent stimulus events, the objective aspects of the narrative account are transcribed into a three-column form and each behavioral and stimulus event is numbered in consecutive order.

Setting: Timmy (T.) is playing alone in a sandbox in a play yard in which there are other children playing. T. is scooping sand into a bucket with a shovel, then dumping the sand onto a pile. A teacher, Mrs. Simpson (S.), stands approximately six feet away but does not attend to T.

Time	*Antecedent Event*	*Response*	*Consequent Social Event*
9:14		1. T. throws bucket and shovel into corner of sandbox.	
		2. . . . stands up.	
		3. . . . walks over to monkeybars and stops.	
		4. . . . turns toward teacher.	
		5. . . . says. "Mrs. Simpson, watch me."	
			6. Mrs. S. turns toward Timmy.
	6. Mrs. S. turns toward Timmy.	7. T. climbs to top of apparatus.	
		8. . . . looks toward teacher.	
		9. . . . says, "Look how high I am. I'm higher than anybody."	

Time	Antecedent Event	Response	Consequent Social Event
9:16			10. Mrs. S. says, "That's good, Tim. You're getting quite good at that."
	10. Mrs. S. says, "That's good, Tim. You're getting quite good at that."	11. T. climbs down.	
		12. . . . runs over to tree.	
		13. . . . says. "Watch me climb the tree, Mrs. Simpson."	
			14. Mrs. S. turns and walks toward classroom.
	14. Mrs. S. turns and walks toward classroom.	15. T. stands, looking toward Mrs. S.	
9:18	16. Girl nearby trips and falls, bumping knee.		
	17. Girl cries.		
		18. T. proceeds to sandbox.	
		19. . . . picks up bucket and shovel.	
		20. . . . resumes play with sand.	

Note that a response event (e.g., 5. . . . says, "Mrs. Simpson, watch me.") may be followed by a consequent social event (e.g., 6. Mrs. S. turns toward Timmy.) which may also be the antecedent event for the next response (e.g., 7. T. climbs to top of apparatus.). Note, too, that the three-column form retains the temporal relationships in the narration. Note, finally, that only the child's responses are described. Inferences about feelings, motives, and other presumed internal states are omitted. Even words like "ignores" and "disappointed" do not appear in the table.

On the basis of several such running accounts and analyses a tentative set of stimulus and response definitives are derived and criteria for their occurrence are specified. This material serves as a basis for a provisional code consisting of symbols and definitions. Observers are trained to use the code and are tested in a series of trial runs in the actual situation.

Consider now the problems involved in defining behavioral and stimulus terms, devising codes, and recording events. But first let us comment briefly on the pros and cons of two recording methods.

When discussing the definitions of events and assessing reliability of observers, we refer to observers who record with paper and pencil.

In each instance the same could be accomplished by electro-mechanical devices. The investigator must decide which procedure best suits his purpose. For example, Lovaas used instruments to record responses in studies on autistic behavior. He and his co-workers have developed apparatus and worked out procedures for recording as many as 12 responses in a setting. The following is a brief description of the apparatus and its operation (Lovaas, Freitag, Gold, and Kassorla, 1965b).

> The apparatus for quantifying behaviors involved two units: an Esterline-Angus 20-pen recorder and an operating panel with 12 buttons, each button mounted on a switch (Microswitch: "Typewriter pushbutton switch"). When depressed, these buttons activated a corresponding pen on the Esterline recorder. The buttons were arranged on a 7 by 14-in. panel in the configuration of the fingertips of an outstretched hand. Each button could be pressed independently of any of the others and with the amount of force similar to that required for an electric typewriter key (p. 109).

An electro-mechanical recording device has certain advantages over a paper-and-pencil system. It requires less attention, thus allowing the observer to devote more of his effort to watching for critical events. Furthermore, instruments of this sort make it possible to assess more carefully the temporal relationships between stimulus and response events, as well as to record a large number of responses within a given period. On the other hand, paper-and-pencil recording methods are more flexible. They can be used in any setting since they do not require special facilities, such as a power supply.

Defining and Recording Behavioral Events

The main problem in defining behavioral events is establishing a criterion or criteria in a way that two or more observers can agree on their occurrences. For example, if it is desired to record the number of times a child hits other children, the criteria of a hitting response must be clearly given so that the observer can discriminate hitting from patting or shoving responses. Or if it is desired to count the number of times a child says, "No," the criteria for the occurrence of "No" must be specified to discriminate it from other words the child utters, and from non-verbal forms of negative expressions. Sometimes definitions must include criteria of loudness and duration. For example in a study of crying behavior (Hart, et al., 1964), crying was defined to discriminate it from whining and screaming and it had to be (a) "loud enough to be heard at least 50 feet away, and (b) of 5-sec or more duration".

The definitions of complex behavioral events are treated the same way. Studies concerned with such intricate categories of behavior as isolate behavior, fantasy-play, aggressive behavior, and temper-tantrums must establish objective criteria for each class of responses included in the category. We shall elaborate on defining multiple response classes in the following discussion on recording behavioral events.

There are two styles of recording behavioral events in field situations: one consists of logging the incidences of responses (and in many situations, their durations); the other of registering the frequencies of occurrences and non-occurrences within a time interval. Sometimes frequencies and their durations are recorded (Lovaas, Freitag, Gold, and Kassorla, 1965b).

Recording the frequencies of occurrences and non-occurrences in a time interval requires the observer to make a mark (and only one mark) in each time interval in which the response occurred. It is apparent that in this procedure the maximum frequency of a response is determined by the size of the time unit selected. If a 5-sec interval were used, the maximum frequency would be 12 per min; if a 10-sec interval were employed, the maximal rate would be six responses per minute, and so on. Thus, in studies with a high frequency of behavioral episodes, small time intervals are employed to obtain high correspondence between the actual and recorded frequencies of occurrences.

There are several approaches to defining and recording single and multiple class responses. One method consists of developing a *specific observational code* for each problem studied. For example, in studies conducted at the Child Behavior Laboratory at the University of Illinois, codes were prepared for attending-to-work behavior, spontaneous speech, and tantruming. The attending-to-work or time-on-task code was employed with a distractible 7-yr-old boy. It included: (1) counting words, (2) looking at the words, and (3) writing numbers or letters. When any of these behaviors occurred at any time during a 20-sec interval, it was scored as an interval of work. In a second study involving a 6-yr-old boy with a similar problem, this code was used with one additional feature: in order for the observer to mark occurrence in the 20-sec interval, the child had to engage in relevant behavior for a minimum of 10 sec. The reliability on both codes averaged 90% for two observers over 12 sessions. (See Section 3 for our method of determining reliability.)

A code for spontaneous speech was developed for a 4-yr-old girl who rarely spoke. Incidences of speech were recorded whenever she uttered a word or words which were not preceded by a question or a prompt by a peer or teacher. Although this class of behavior was somewhat difficult to discriminate, reliability averaged 80% for two observers over 15 sessions.

Tantrum behaviors exhibited by a 6-yr-old boy were defined as including crying, whining, sobbing, and whimpering. The average reliability for this class of behavior was 80% for two observers over 11 sessions.

In contrast to this more or less vocal form of tantrum behavior, a code developed in another study on temper-tantrums centered around gross motor responses of an autistic child (Brawley, Harris, Allen, Fleming, and Peterson, 1968, in press). Here a tantrum was recorded whenever the child engaged in self-hitting in combination with any one of the following forms of behavior: (1) loud crying, (2) kicking, or (3) throwing himself or objects about.

Another method of defining and recording responses is to develop a *general observational code*, one that is inclusive enough to study many behaviors in a given field situation. An example of such a code is the one prepared by the nursery school staff at the University of Washington. In essence, verbal and motor responses are recorded in relation to physical and social events using a three or four track system. Tables 1 and 2 show sample lines from data sheets. Each box represents an interval of 15 sec.

TABLE 1

Sample Line from a Data Sheet of Nursery School Girl
Who Changed Activities with High Frequency

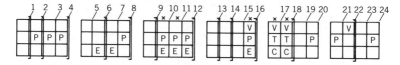

TABLE 2

Sample Line from a Data Sheet of Nursery School Boy
Displaying Aggressive Behaviors

1	2	3	4	5	6	7	8	9	10	11	12	13	14	15	16	17	18	19	20	21	22	23	24	25	26	27	28	29	30
V				V							(V)				V	V	V	V	V	(V)(V)							V		
P	P			P	P	P	P								P	P	(T)(T)	P		P	P	P	P	P	P	T	P		
C	C		C	C	C	C	C	C	C	A	A	A	A	A	A	A	A	A	A	A			A	A	C	C			
				B	B	B	B	B	B	B					B	B	B	B	B	B	B	B	B	B	B	B			

In Table 1, which is a segment of a data sheet for a nursery school girl who changed activities with high frequency, entries were made in the boxes in the top row to indicate occurrences of vocalizations (V). Entries were made in the middle row to show proximity (P) or physical contact (T) with another person, and in the bottom row to indicate contact with physical objects (E) or with children and whether the interaction was parallel play (A) or shared play (C). Other marks and symbols are added in accordance with the problem studied. For example, each single bracket in Table 1 indicates leaving of one activity and embarking on another. During the 6-min period in which records were taken (24 15-sec intervals), the child changed her activity 12 times. During that time the teacher gave approval five times contingent upon her verbal or proximity behavior as indicated by X's above the top line (10, 11, 16, 17, and 18). A tally of the data indicated that she spent most of the 6-min period alone or in close proximity to another child, sometimes on the same piece of play equipment. During three intervals (16, 17, and 18) she talked (V), touched (T), and engaged in physical interaction with another child (C). Even though rate of activity change, and not peer interaction, was the subject of the study, the other data on social behavior provided interesting information: decline in rate of activity change was related to an increase in rate of appropriate peer behavior.

This code can be readily modified to handle more complex interactions. For example, it was used to record the behavior of a nursery school boy who shouted epithets, kicked, and hit other children. Ordinarily these aggressive acts would appear in the record sheets undifferentiated from a non-aggressive interaction. To differentiate them from other behaviors the symbol letter was circled if the behavior met the criteria of an aggressive act. As shown in Table 2, intervals 13, 22, and 23 contain a "V" with a circle, $\textcircled{V}$, which indicates aggressive verbalizations, while intervals 19 and 20 contain a "T" with a circle, $\textcircled{T}$, which indicates physical "attack" (actual hitting, kicking, or pinching). Another bit of information was incorporated in the recording system. The letter "B" was entered in the fourth row to indicate that the child was playing with or being aggressive to a specific nursery school boy named Bill. This additional notation was made midway in the study when teachers observed that the subject and Bill usually behaved aggressively toward each other. Data collected before this change served as a baseline against which to judge the effects of changing social contingencies. Subsequently, teachers gave approval contingent on nonaggressive interactions between these boys as shown by the X's above intervals 6, 7, 8, 11, 12, 17, 18, 26, 27, and 29.

Another general observational code, tailored for analysis of pupils' behavior in the elementary school classroom, has been devised by Thomas and Becker (1967). Like the nursery school code, it consists of symbols and definitions designed to cover the range of interactions that may take place in the field situation defined by the classroom.

Defining and Recording Stimulus Events

The ease or difficulty of defining a stimulus class is related to its source. It has been pointed out (e.g., Bijou and Baer, 1961) that some stimuli originate in natural and man-made things, some in the biological make-up of the subject himself, and some in the behavior of people and other living organisms. Consider briefly each source in turn.

Defining stimuli from physical things does not pose a difficult problem since physical objects are usually available for all to see. All that is required is that these stimuli be described in the usual physical dimensions of space, time, size, velocity, color, texture, and the like.

Defining stimuli which originate in the biological make-up of the subject is beset with difficulty mostly because of their obscurity under any circumstance and particularly under field conditions. Consider what must be available to an observer if he is to record in objective terms the duration, intensity, or frequency of stimuli involved in a toothache, "butterflies" in the stomach, general bodily weakness, dizziness, and hunger-pangs. Instruments would be needed to make visible all sorts of internal biological events; and for the most part, these are not yet available in practical forms. It seems clear that at present, field methods of research, especially with human beings, are not appropriate for describing biologically anchored variables. Research on these variables must be postponed until it is practical to monitor physiological actions through cleverly designed telemetric devices. But it should be stressed that the exact role of specific biological variables *must* be studied at some time for a thorough functional analysis of psychological behavior (defined here as the interaction of a total functioning biological individual with environmental events).

Defining social stimuli, or stimuli which evolve from the action of people, ranges in difficulty between physical and biological events. This is so because social events, like physical and biological events, must in many instances be described in terms of their physical dimensions, and as is well known, the components of social stimuli can be terribly subtle and complex. For the reader interested in a further analysis of social events within the framework of a natural science, Skinner's discussion is recommended (1953, pp. 298–304).

In field studies, the procedure for defining and recording social stimuli is the same as that for defining and recording response events, since social events are treated as the responses of people in antecedent or consequent relationships to the behavior of the subject. Therefore, the entire previous section on defining and recording behavioral events pertains to defining and recording social events.

Some social stimuli, like response stimuli, may consist of a single class of behavior on the part of an adult or a child and may be recorded on the basis of frequency or its occurrence or nonoccurrence within a time interval. Examples of single-class antecedent stimuli are simple commands and requests, *e.g.*, "Start now," "Gather around in a circle," "Come, let's ride the trikes." Examples of single-class consequent stimuli are confirmations ("Right"), disconfirmations ("Wrong"), approval ("Good") and disapproval ("You play too rough").

Other social stimuli may be composed of several classes of behavior stemming from one person or several in concert. As in the case of defining multiple response classes, criteria for each subclass in the group may constitute a code. A specific observational code may be developed to describe social events in a specific situation for a specific study. For example, in a study of autistic behavior, adult attention was defined as: "(1) Touching the child; (2) being within two feet of and facing the child; (3) talking to, touching, assisting or going to the child" (Brawley, *et al.* 1968). With such criteria the investigator catalogued the types of behaviors which constituted social interaction involving attention and excluded other stimuli originating in the behavior of an adult in contact with the subject.

General observational codes for social events, like those for response events, have also been devised to study many problems in a general type of field setting. For example, Becker and Thomas (1967) have developed a comprehensive code for recording the teacher's behavior in an elementary classroom situation.

Which classes of behavior-environmental interactions will be selected for study will depend on the purpose of the investigation; the maximum number, however, will be limited by the practical considerations. Studies requiring detailed analyses of many response classes may be planned as a series. The first dealing with grossly defined classes and the others with more and more progressively refined categories. For example, the first study may be concerned with the frequency of social contacts with adults and peers, and the second with specific verbal and motor responses directed to specific adults (teachers and parents) and peers (boys and girls).

Assessing Observer Reliability

Disagreements between observers may be related to inadequacies in (1) the observational code, (2) the training of the observers, or (3) the method of calculating reliability.

The Observational Code

Problems of defining and recording behavioral and stimulus events have been discussed in Section 2. Observer reliability is directly related to the comprehensiveness and specificity of the definitions in the observational code. Generally it is advisable to devise codes with mutually exclusive event categories, each definition having criteria that do not occur in any other definition.

Training of Observers

Even when a code is completely serviceable, two observers may not necessarily record the occurrence of the same event at the same time unless each has been adequately trained in using the code and in controlling his behavior while observing and recording.

For example, training might begin by familiarizing the observer with the tools for recording, *e.g.*, the clipboard, stopwatch, and data sheets. This might be followed by an orientation to the code and exercises in recording behavioral events. A film or video tape of sequences similar to those in the actual situation might be used to provide supplementary experiences.

It is often helpful to have a second observer to record along with the first observer. During trial recordings the observers can indicate to each other the behaviors being scored and uncover misunderstandings regarding the nature of the code or ambiguities in the definition of particular responses. Such a procedure reduces interpretation on the part of the observer and can contribute to an improved code.

Since it is relatively easy for the observers to slip an interval in the course of a long recording session, they should be instructed to note the beginning of certain activities, e.g., story time, snack, nap, etc. This allows them to determine easily when they are out of phase with one another. Slips may also result from inaccurate stopwatches. Watches should be periodically tested by starting them simultaneously and checking them a few hours later.

After training on the proficient use of the code the observer might then be given instruction on how to conduct himself while observing and recording. Thus, he might be told how to refrain from interacting with the subject, e.g., ignore all questions, avoid eye-contact, and suppress reactions to the subject's activities as well as those associated with him. He might also be instructed in moving about to maintain a clear view of the subject yet not make it obvious that he is following him.

Method of Calculating Reliability

The reliability index is to some degree a function of how it is calculated. Suppose we have data from two observers showing the frequency of a class of events taken over 1 hr. Unless the sums obtained by each observer are equal, the smaller sum is divided by the larger to obtain a percentage of agreement. If the sums are identical the reliability index would be 100. This method is often used when the investigator is interested in frequencies per se, since the measure obtained gives only the amount of agreement over the total number of events observed. It does not indicate whether the two observers were recording the same event at exactly the same time. Thus, it might be possible that one observer was recording few behaviors during the first half hour and many during the second, while the second observer was doing just the opposite. To ascertain whether this is the case, one could divide the period of observation into small segments and calculate the reliability of each. Agreements over progressively smaller segments give confidence that the observers are scoring the same event at the same time. One may assess the agreement over brief intervals such as 5 or 10 sec. Reliability is calculated by scoring each interval as agree or disagree (match or mismatch) and dividing the total number of agreements by the number of agreements plus the number of disagreements. Note that one may score several agreements or disagreements in an interval if a number of events are being recorded simultaneously as shown in Tables 1 and 2. In this case the interval is broken down according to the number of different events recorded, with each event scored as a match or mismatch.

The reliability index may also be influenced by the frequency of response under study. When a behavior is displayed at a very low rate, the observer will record few instances of occurrence and many of nonoccurrence. In this situation the observers could disagree on the occurrence of the behavior yet still show high reliability due to their agreement on the large number of intervals where no behavior was recorded. A similar problem exists with regard to high-frequency behaviors. Here, however, the observers may disagree on the nonoccurrence of the behavior and agree on occurrence, because of the frequency of the latter. The problem may be resolved by computing not one but two reliability coefficients, one for occurrence and one for nonoccurrence.

In some cases the requirement of perfect matching of intervals may be relaxed slightly. Thus, behaviors recorded within one interval (especially if the interval is short) may also be considered as instances of agreement for reliability purposes. A technique of noncontinuous observing may also increase reliability (O'Leary, O'Leary, and Becker, 1967). In this procedure the observers record for shorter portions of time. For example, instead of taking continuous 10-sec observations, the observer might record for 10 out of every 15 sec, or for 20 out of every 30 sec. During the period in which the observer is not attending to the child, he should be recording the behaviors just observed.

The use of a second observer does not insure high reliability of recording; it is possible for both observers to agree on the scoring of certain events and at the same time be incorrect (Gewirtz and Gewirtz, 1964). Both observers might record some events which should not be noted and ignore others which should. Hence, a third observer might be used on occasion to determine if this possibility exists.

Collecting, Analyzing, and Interpreting Data

Data Collection

Final data collection is begun as soon as it is evident that the observers are adequately trained, the field situation is feasible, and the subject has adapted to the presence of the observers.

Whether the investigator collects data during all of the time available for observation or takes time samples will depend upon many factors, including the purpose of the study, the nature of the data, and the practical considerations. Regardless of the frequency with which observations are made, it is recommended that the data be plotted at regular intervals to provide a kind of progress chart. A visual account of the fluctuations and trends can help the investigator make important decisions, *e.g.*, setting up the time for the next reliability evaluation or establishing the termination time for a phase of the study.

Data Analysis

Up until now we discussed the investigators' activities in relation to the interactions between the observer and the field events. The investigator was viewed as a critic, watching the observer record the events in a natural ecology. Thus, in the data collection phase of a study the investigator's role is somewhat similar to that of a motion picture director evaluating what the camera is recording in relation to the scene as he sees it. In this section on data analysis and in the next on interpretation, we shall consider what the investigator does, not in relation to the recording equipment and field events, but in relation to the data collected.

Basically, in data analysis the investigator looks at the data collected to "see what is there." Usually he finds that making one or several transformations in the raw data helps him to see more clearly the relationships among the events observed. Transformational procedures might consist of converting the frequency counts into graphic, tabular, verbal, arithmetical, or statistical forms. Exactly which operations he performs on the data will depend on the purpose of the study, the nature of the data, and his theoretical assumptions about what can or cannot be demonstrated by a descriptive field study.

Usually, data analysis begins when data collection ends. However, as noted previously, an investigator might graph the data while the study is in progress. Under these circumstances data analysis might consist of revising and refining the graphs and making other transpositions to show the relationships among the subparts of the data.

Data collected in terms of rate are usually plotted in a graphic form with responses on the vertical axis and time on the horizontal axis. Points on the chart may represent either discrete or cumulative values. Discrete values are the sums or means for each successive session; cumulative values are the sums or means for all previous sessions. Therefore, curves with discrete values might go up, stay at the same level, or go down; cumulative curves might also go up or stay at the same level. Cumulative curves do not go down. A decrease in the frequency of a response is shown in the curve as a deceleration in rate (bends toward the horizontal axis); an increase in frequency as an acceleration (bends toward the vertical axis); a constant frequency as no change in rate; and a zero frequency as a horizontal line.

In most instances graphic presentations are made more meaningful when accompanied by percentage values. In addition, it is often advantageous to show percentages of occurrences in the different conditions and sub-conditions of the field situation.

Viewing the interactions in selected time periods (early morning, and late morning) or around certain events (before and after mealtime) as populations, statistical analyses may be made to assess the nature of and the reliability of differences observed.

Interpretation of Findings

Essentially, interpretation of findings consists of the investigator's statements on what is "seen" in the data together with his conception of their generality. Such statements are the *raison d'être* of an investigation.

Obviously, an investigator is free to interpret his findings in any way he chooses. The investigator who accepts the assumptions of a natural science approach to psychology seeks to limit his interpretations to empirical concepts and relationships consistent with his observations and the analytical operations made upon the products of his observations. Hence, in a descriptive field study his interpretations would usually consist of a discussion of what was found in the situation with comparisons to other findings obtained under functionally similar conditions. Conclusions on the similarities and differences between his findings and others would be incorporated in his argument for the generality of his findings. Interpretations in an experimental field study would depend on the number and type of manipulations employed and would usually be limited to describing the functional relationships obtained.

Illustrative Study

Using the procedures previously described, a study was undertaken to obtain a descriptive account of a boy in a laboratory nursery school at the University of Illinois. The nursery school curriculum and the practices of the teaching staff of this school were based on behavioral principles (Skinner, 1953, and Bijou and Baer, 1961).

Subject and Field Situation

The subject (Zachary) was typical of the children in the nursery school in the judgment of the teachers. He was 4.5 yr old, of high average intelligence (Peabody IQ 116) and from a middle socioeconomic class family. On the Wide Range Achievement Test he scored kindergarten 3 in reading, pre-kindergarten 5 in spelling, and kindergarten 6 in arithmetic.

The nursery school consisted of a large room, approximately 21 by 40 ft. Evenly spaced along one wall were three doors which led to three adjacent smaller rooms. One of these rooms was a lavatory, the second contained paints, papers, and other equipment, and the third a variety of toys. Nearby was a large table and several chairs used for art activities and snack. Opposite these rooms along the other wall were several tables separated by brightly colored, movable partitions. In these booths, the children worked on academic subjects.

The school was attended by 12 children, six boys and six girls, between 4 and 5 yr of age. The teaching staff consisted of a full-time teacher and an assistant teacher, and depending on the time of day, one to three undergraduates who assisted in administering new programs in reading, writing, and arithmetic.

In general, the morning program was as follows:

    9:00–10:00   Art, academic, and pre-academic work
  10:00–10:30   Free play
  10:30–11:00   Snack
  11:00–12:00   Academic work, show-and-tell, and storytime.

A typical morning might begin with art. At this time, 8 to 10 children sat around a large table working with various materials. During this activity each child in turn left the group for 10 to 20 min to work on writing or arithmetic. While engaged in writing or arithmetic the child worked with a teacher in one of the booths. After completing his assigned units of work he returned to his art activity and another child left the group to work on his units of writing or arithmetic. After all the children had participated in these academic subjects, the art period was terminated and was followed by play. During play, the children were free to move about, often spending much of the time in either of the smaller nursery school rooms playing with blocks or other toys. After approximately 30 min of play, the youngsters returned to the large table for a snack of juice and cookies. While eating and drinking they talked spontaneously and informally with their teachers and peers. Following snack time some of the children participated in reading while the others gathered for show-and-tell or storytime. During storytime the children sat on the floor in a group while the teacher read and discussed the story. In show-and-tell, instead of the teacher leading the group, each child had a chance to stand by the teacher in front of the group, and show an object he had brought from home and tell about it. As they did during the art period the children left the group one at a time for a period of reading. Because of variations in the amount of time a child spent on academic subjects, a child did not engage in all of these activities every day.

Behavioral and Stimulus Events Recorded

The behaviors recorded were of two general categories: social contacts and sustained activities. Social contacts included verbal interchanges and physical contacts with children and teachers. Sustained activities involved behaviors in relation to the school tasks. The specific observational code developed for the study is presented in Table 3.

Observation began 3.5 weeks after the start of the school year and covered a 3-hr period in the morning. The observations were taken on 28 school days. The observer sat a few feet from the subject and discretely followed him as he moved from one activity to another in the nursery school room. Every 10 sec the teacher recorded the occurrence or nonoccurrence of events defined in the code. The data sheet was similar to that shown in Table 1; however, only the first and second rows were used.

Observer Reliability

The reliability of observation and the adequacy of the behavioral code was evaluated several times throughout the study by having a second observer record stimulus and response events. Reliability was calculated by scoring each interval as a match or mismatch and dividing the total number of agreements by the number of agreements plus disagreements. Four checks on social contacts showed agreements of 75, 82, 85, and 87%. Three checks on sustained activity yielded agreements of 94, 95, and 97%. Thus, average agreement on social contacts exceeded 82% while average agreement of sustained activity exceeded 95%.

Analysis of Data

SOCIAL CONTACTS. Data were gathered on Zachary's social behaviors in informal activities of art, play, snack, storytime, and show-and-tell. They will be described and samples of the detailed accounts in art and snack will be presented in graphic form. The youngster's most dominant behavior during the art period shown in Fig. 1, was talking to others (14% of the time).

Teachers and peers talked with him about equally, an average of 8 and 7% respectively. Physical contacts between Zachary, teachers, and peers were low, around 1 to 2%.

The child's verbal behavior to peers during the play period was higher than in the art period. He talked to his friends on an average of 38%; they talked to him on an average of only 10%. Verbal exchanges with teachers were low (an average of 2.5%). Zachary touched other children 7% of the time on the average and they reciprocated on an average of 3%. Physical contacts with teachers were relatively infrequent.

118

TABLE 3

Observational Code for Describing the Behavior of a Boy in a
Laboratory Nursery School

Symbol	Definition
	First Row **(Social Contacts)** S verbalizes to himself. Any verbalization during which he does not look at an adult or child or does not use an adult's or child's name. Does not apply to a group situation.
	S verbalizes to adult. S must look at adult while verbalizing or use adult's name.
	S verbalizes to child. S must look at child while verbalizing or use child's name. If in a group situation, any verbalization is recorded as verbalization to a child.
S	Child verbalizes to S. Child must look at S while verbalizing or use S's name.
△	Adult verbalizes to S. Adult must look at S while verbalizing or use S's name.
∽	Adult gives general instruction to class or asks question of class, or makes general statement. Includes storytelling.
	S touches adult. Physical contact with adult.
	S touches child with part of body or object. Physical contact with child.
V	Adult touches S. Physical contact with adult.
T	Child touches S with part of body or object. Physical contact with child.

TABLE 3 *(Continued)*

Symbol	Definition
	Second Row (Sustained Activity)
⊡	*Sustained activity in art.* S must be sitting in the chair, facing the material and responding to the material or teacher within the 10-sec interval. Responding to the material includes using pencil, paint brush, chalk, crayons, string, scissors or paste or any implement on paper, or working with clay with hands on clay or hands on implement which is used with clay, or folding or tearing paper. Responding to the teacher includes following a command made by an adult to make a specific response. The behavior must be completed (child sitting in his chair again) within two minutes.
⊡	*Sustained activity in storytime.* S must be sitting, facing the material, or following a command given by the teacher or assistant. If the S initiates a verbalization to a peer, do not record sustained activity in the 10-sec interval.
⊡	*Sustained activity in show-and-tell.* S must be sitting, facing the material, or following a command given by the teacher. If the S initiates a verbalization to a peer, do not record sustained activity in that 10-sec interval.
⊡	*Sustained activity in reading.* S must be sitting in the chair, facing the material and responding to the material or the teacher within the 10-sec interval.
⊡	*Sustained activity in writing.* S must be sitting in the chair, facing the material and responding to the material or the teacher within the 10-sec interval. Responding to the material includes using the pencil (making a mark), or holding the paper or folder. Responding to the teacher includes responding verbally to a cue given by the teacher.
⊡	*Sustained activity in arithmetic.* S must be sitting in the chair, facing the material and responding to the material or the teacher within the 10-sec interval. Responding to the material or teacher includes using the pencil or eraser or holding the paper or folder or responding verbally to cue.
⧄	Sustained activity did not occur in interval.

120

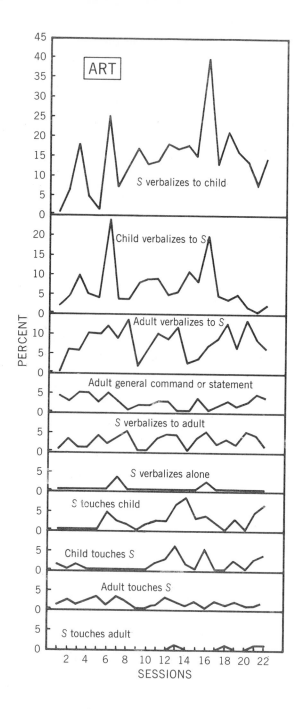

Fig. 1. Social contact during art

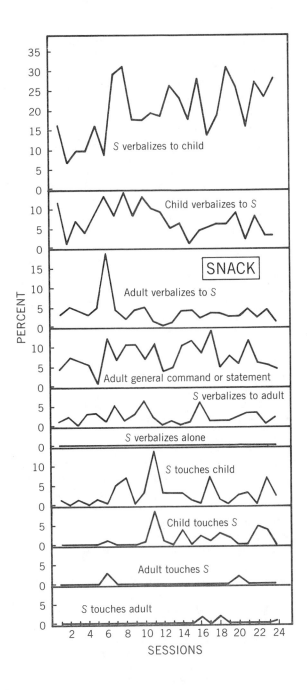

Fig. 2. Social interaction during snack

As in the art and play periods, Zachary's social interactions during snack time, shown in Fig. 2, consisted mostly of talking to his classmates, an average of 21%. They, in turn, talked to him only an average of 7%. During this period the teacher's general commands (instructions addressed to the group) were relatively high, averaging 7% in contrast to the 2% during art and play. Physical contacts with other children were low, as in art and play, about 3%.

Compared to the art, play, and snack periods, Zachary's verbalizations to peers and to teachers were low (8 and 4% respectively), and the number of times he touched children (10%), and children touched him were also relatively low (2%). Storytime had a high frequency of teacher's general commands and statements (average of 73%) since this category was scored when the teacher read and discussed the stories.

In show-and-tell, Zachary's social behavior was similar to that during storytime. He talked to other children 14% of the time and touched them 9% of the time. Zachary physically contacted teachers about 1% of the time and they reciprocated about 3% of the time.

In respect to Zachary's social behavior during the academic periods, these data clearly indicate that the teacher talked to Zachary a great deal during the reading (an average of 69%), writing (an average of 71%), and arithmetic periods (an average of 58%), and the child talked to the teacher with high frequency, particularly in reading (an average of 44%) and arithmetic (an average of 41%). In writing he talked to the teacher only 3% of the time. There were also a few instances in which the teacher touched Zachary and rare occasions in which Zachary interacted socially with other children. Figure 3 is a detailed graphic account of his social behavior during the writing period.

SUSTAINED ACTIVITY. For the observer to mark the occurrence of sustained activity, Zachary had to respond in a manner appropriate for a particular school activity. (See second part of Table 3.) For example, during art, the child had to be sitting in his chair, facing the art materials and manipulating them during each 10-sec interval. Similar definitions were used for other situations and periods. Given these definitions, the results show a generally high level of sustained activity in all phases of the morning program. Daily rates of sustained activities in art, storytime, and show-and-tell range between 70 and 99% with an average of 89% for art, 95% for storytime, and 88% for show-and-tell. See Fig. 4 for variations from session to session in Zachary's sustained behavior during art. Sustained activity in reading, writing, and arithmetic range from 90 to 100% over the days observed with an average of 97, 95, and 96% respectively. See Fig. 5 for variations in the child's sustained behavior in writing. Due to the limited availability of the observer, and the fact that not every activity occurred every day, the number of observations on each activity varied.

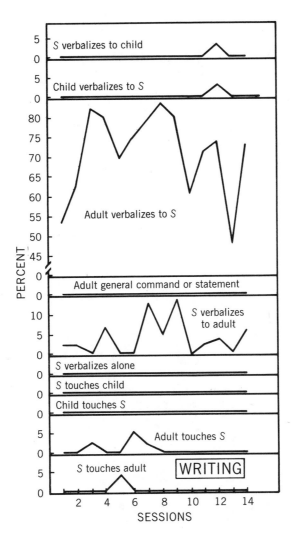

Fig. 3. Social behavior during writing

DISCUSSION

A descriptive account of the behaviors of a boy during the morning hours in a laboratory nursery school was obtained in terms of the frequency of occurrence of objectively defined stimulus and response events. The account shows rates of changes in social interactions (verbal and physical contacts) and sustained activities during eight periods of the school morning.

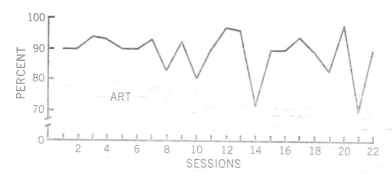

Fig. 4. Sustained activity during art

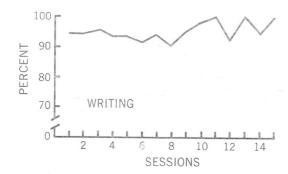

Fig. 5. Sustained activity during writing

In the informal activities of the nursery school in which the youngster performed on an individual basis, as in art, free play, and snack time, the subject talked to his peers and teachers to a moderate degree. His peers and teachers responded to him verbally to a lesser extent. He talked more than he listened and over the period of the study, his verbal output increased. Physical interactions with peers and teachers in these situations were at a relatively low level. Finally, the youngster's sustained activity in the art period was high (between 70 and 98%) and became more variable, on a day-to-day basis, during the second half of the study. In the other two informal activities, storytime and show-and-tell, the child participated as a member of a group in which the teacher's verbal behavior was prominent, especially during storytime. In these two situations the child talked to others less, but as in art, free play, and snack time, he talked more than he listened. In storytime and show-and-tell he engaged in some body contacts with peers and teachers, yet his sustained activity on nursery school tasks was high, with a range of 90 to 99% for the former and 70 to 95% for the latter.

In the more structured activities of reading, writing, and arithmetic the teacher's verbal behavior to the child was high and his verbal behavior to her was correspondingly high, particularly in reading and arithmetic. During academic exercises all other social interactions were zero or near zero, and the child's sustained activities were consistently high over days, ranging from 90 to 100% of the time.

The data gathered in this study can serve two main purposes. First, they can provide normative information on behavior in a laboratory preschool. Thus, it might be interesting to compare this child's rates of response obtained in this study after 3.5 weeks of school with his rates during the last month of the school year. It might also be interesting to compare this child's behavior with another child's in the same nursery school. Such a comparison might be especially valuable if someone claimed that the second child's behavior was deviant. In addition, it might be informative to compare this child's behavior with a comparable child in a community-operated nursery school. Second, the data suggest certain relationships between the behavior of the subject, the teacher, and other children. Thus, the investigator might use the data as a baseline for an experimental study in which conditions are manipulated to test for possible functional relationships.

References

Baldwin, A. L., Kalhorn, J., and Breese, F. H. The appraisal of parent behavior. *Psychological Monographs*, 1949, **63**, No. 299.

Barker, R. G., and Wright, H. F. *Midwest and its children: the psychological ecology of an American town.* New York: Harper & Row, 1955.

Becker, W. C., Madsen, C. H., Jr., Arnold, Carole R., and Thomas, D. R. The contingent use of teacher attention and praise in reducing classroom behavior problems. *Journal of Special Education*, 1967, **1**, 287–307.

Becker, W. C., and Thomas, D. R. A revision of the code for the analysis of a teacher's behavior in the classroom. Unpublished manuscript, 1967.

Bijou, S. W., and Baer, D. M. *Child development: a systematic and empirical theory.* Vol. 1, New York: Appleton-Century-Crofts, 1961.

Birnbrauer, J. S., Wolf, M. M., Kidder, J. D., and Tague, Cecilia. Classroom behavior of retarded pupils with token reinforcement. *Journal of Experimental Child Psychology*, 1965, **2**, 219–235.

Brawley, Eleanor R., Harris, Florence R., Allen, K. Eileen, Fleming, R. S., and Peterson, R. F. Behavior modification of an autistic child. *Behavioral Science*, 1969, **14**, 87–97.

Gewirtz, Hava, and Gewirtz, J. L. A method for assessing stimulation behaviors and caretaker-child interaction. Unpublished manuscript, 1964.

Harris, Florence R., Wolf, M. M., and Baer, D. M. Effects of adult social reinforcement on child behavior. *Young Children*, 1964, **20**, 8–17.

Hawkins, R. P., Peterson, R. F., Schweid, Edda, and Bijou, S. W. Behavior therapy in the home: Amelioration of problem parent-child relations with the parent in a therapeutic role. *Journal of Experimental Child Psychology,* 1966, **4**, 99–107.

Honig, W. K. Introductory remarks. In W. K. Honig (Ed.) *Operant behavior: areas of research and application.* New York: Appleton-Century-Crofts, 1966.

Jensen, G. D., and Bobbitt, Ruth A. Implications of primate research for understanding infant development. *The exceptional child,* Vol. 1, J. Hellmuth (Ed.), Special Child Publications, Seattle, Washington, 1967.

Johnston, Margaret S., Kelley, C. Susan, Harris, Florence R., and Wolf, M. M. An application of reinforcement principles to development of motor skills of a young child. *Child Development,* 1966, **37**, 379–387.

Lovaas, O. I., Freitag, G., Gold, Vivian J., and Kassorla, Irene C. Recording apparatus and procedure for observation of behaviors of children in free play settings. *Journal of Experimental Child Psychology,* 1965, **2**, 108–120. (*b*)

Lovaas, O. I., Freitag, G., Gold, Vivian J., and Kassorla, Irene C. Experimental studies in childhood schizophrenia: analysis of self-destructive behavior. *Journal of Experimental Child Psychology,* 1965, **2**, 67–84. (*a*)

O'Leary, K. D., O'Leary, Susan G., and Becker, W. C. Modification of a deviant sibling interaction pattern in the home. *Behaviour Research and Therapy,* 1967, **5**, 113–120.

Skinner, B. F. *Science and human behavior.* New York: Macmillan, 1953.

Wolf, M. M., Risley, T. R., and Mees, H. L. Application of operant conditioning procedures to the behavior problems of an autistic child. *Behaviour Research and Therapy,* 1964, **1**, 305–312.

Wright, H. F. *Recording and analyzing child behavior.* New York: Harper & Row, 1967.

PROGRAMING CONSEQUENCES To Reduce Behavior Problems and Motivate the Learner

A. Overview

Part II. *Programing Consequences to Reduce Behavior Problems and Motivate the Learner*

Consequences that are called reinforcers and punishers are the stimulus events that eventually determine what behavior occurs under what conditions. The teacher who has learned to use consequences effectively will find her job a pleasant and rewarding one. She will have the skills to produce a well-managed classroom of highly motivated students. Part II presents a series of studies showing just what it is that teachers need to do to reduce a variety of behavior problems.

Part II is organized into four subparts. Section A gives a summary of concepts and studies. Following this summary, based on some of the most up-to-date research available, we return to a 1934 paper by Willard Olson. This paper was brought to my attention by Sam Kirk. After I presented some of my recent research to Kirk's class, Kirk sent a copy of Olson's paper with a note: "We knew all that back in the 30s." Indeed, many of the basic procedures were well established, although the research methods of the day did not provide the convincing evidence that has been recently generated.

Section B provides the student with original research reports in which social reinforcers were used to modify behavior. The "Technical Glossary" should aid the student in interpreting the research findings.

Section C samples some of the many alternatives open to the teacher when the first approach (using social reinforcers) is not sufficient. This section could be extended indefinitely, with exciting studies coming from applied laboratories almost daily. The studies included have been selected to illustrate a variety of procedures and strategies for dealing with difficult educational problems.

The last section in part II is intended to convince teachers or student teachers that they too can do research in their classrooms, and to show them how to do it. The function of this research is not to make teachers into researchers, but to make them into better teachers. By learning to gather data on what is happening in the classroom and on attempts made to change problem behavior, teachers will find that they have the information upon which to base decisions concerning effective and ineffective procedures.

11

Reducing Behavior Problems:
An Operant Conditioning Guide
for Teachers

Wesley C. Becker
Don R. Thomas
Douglas Carnine

Introduction

Peter is a 4-year-old-boy. His mother was having great difficulty managing him and sought help. Peter often kicked objects or people, removed or tore his clothing, spoke rudely to people, bothered his younger sister, made various threats, hit himself, and was easily angered. He demanded constant attention. He had been evaluated at a clinic for retarded children and was found to have a borderline IQ (70–80). He was said to be hyperactive and possibly brain damaged.

Peter's behavior was observed in the home an hour a day for 16 days. During an hour Peter showed 25 to 112 behaviors which mother found objectionable. When Peter misbehaved, mother would often attend to him and try to explain why he should not do so and so. At times she would try to interest him in some new activity by offering toys or food. (This procedure is called the distraction method for dealing with problem behaviors.) Mother would sometimes punish Peter by taking away a toy or misused object, but Peter was usually able to persuade mother to return the item almost immediately. At times he was placed on a chair for short periods of time as a punishment. Considerable tantrum behavior usually followed such disci-

This paper was originally published in 1969 as a monograph by the ERIC Clearinghouse on Childhood Education, Urbana, Illinois.

pline. Mother responded to tantrums with additional arguments, attempting to persuade Peter to stop.

Peter's behavior was changed by the following procedure (Hawkins, Peterson, Schweid, & Bijou, 1966). An observer in the home would cue mother by raising one, two, or three fingers. One finger was raised when Peter showed an objectionable behavior. Mother was instructed that this meant that she was to tell Peter to stop what he was doing (a warning signal). If Peter did not stop, two fingers were raised. This meant that mother was to immediately place Peter in his room and shut the door (punishment). He had to stay there until he was quiet for a short period before he could come out. If Peter was playing in a nice way, three fingers were raised. This meant that mother was to go to Peter, give him attention, praise him, and be physically affectionate (reinforcement).

Peter's objectionable behavior dropped to near zero within a few days. Follow-up observations showed a continuing good interaction between Peter and mother and an absence of the objectionable behaviors. Peter was receiving more affection from mother and approaching mother in more affectionate ways. Mother was much more sure of herself, provided clear consequences for Peter's behavior, and no longer gave in after starting a correction procedure.

Psychologists who have worked with many children like Peter for years on end are often amazed by the convincing data presented to demonstrate that rapid change took place in Peter and mother. When we talk about Peter to teachers, they immediately see parallels to children with whom they are working and they wonder if similar procedures will help them handle management problems in their classrooms. The answer is YES.

In this review, we have attempted to outline some of the more recent research findings on applications of learning principles in elementary classrooms and pre-schools. *We have focused on what the teacher can do* to make it possible for her children to learn better. The first step toward better classroom management is knowing that *what the children do is a function of the teacher's behavior.* The teacher can change the behavior of her children by changing her behavior. Three procedures which can be followed by teachers in changing children's behavior are presented in some detail, along with supporting research, and evaluations of when each procedure might or might not be appropriately used.

A Selected Glossary

Contingency. A stimulus event which is made conditional upon a response. If response X occurs, then stimulus Y will be presented.

Contingent Reinforcement. A reinforcer is presented if, and only if, a specified response occurs.

Differential Reinforcement. Some specified responses are followed by reinforcers and other specified responses are not reinforced.

Extinction. A procedure whereby an accustomed reinforcer is withheld. The effect on behavior is first a slight increase in the strength of the behavior followed by a weakening of the behavior.

Incompatible Behavior. Behaviors that can't be performed at the same time. For example, a child cannot be seated and moving about the room, simultaneously. Therefore, by inference, one behavior is increased as the other is reduced.

Operant Behavior. Behaviors involving the voluntary muscle system which are strengthened or weakened by stimulus events which follow such behaviors. Operant behaviors operate on the environment.

Punisher. A stimulus presented following a response which weakens the probability of future occurrence of the response. The process of presenting stimuli following responses which weaken the responses is called punishment.

Reinforcer. A stimulus presented following a response which strengthens the probability of future occurrence of the response. The process of presenting stimuli following responses which strengthen responses is called reinforcement.

Respondent Behavior. Behavior usually involving smooth muscles and glands which is controlled by stimuli which precede it. Reflexive behavior.

Response. That part of behavior which is essential for reinforcement or punishment to occur. An operant response is always a member of a class of responses which have the same consequence.

Stimulus. An environmental event which does or can be made to influence behavior. The plural of stimulus is stimuli.

Operant Conditioning

In its simplest form, operant conditioning involves the systematic use of consequences to strengthen and weaken behaviors under specified stimulus conditions. Operant behavior is strengthened by some consequences called reinforcers, and weakened by other consequences called punishers. Withdrawal of reinforcing consequences will also weaken behavior. This procedure is called extinction.

The laws of operant behavior are generalizations drawn from the experimental analysis of behavior. They summarize which events influence behavior in what ways. Many persons seem shocked when first exposed to the idea that there are systematic ways of influencing the behavior of others (or one's own). They find it a difficult idea to accept; it smacks of *Brave New World*. Actually, the law of reinforcement is no more revolutionary today than the law of gravity. Capitalistic economic systems are built on such a law of behavior. How many of you would continue to teach if you were not paid for doing so? A paycheck is an important reinforcing consequence for most of us. For most teachers another important reinforcing consequence for teaching is seeing children learn. If all our teaching efforts failed, we would very likely quit teaching ("be extinguished for teaching"). The teacher does not have a choice in the question of whether or not her children will be influenced by reinforcing and punishing events. The only choices the teacher has are (1) to use reinforcement principles systematically to optimally help her children develop, (2) to blindly and haphazardly approach the training of her children, or (3) to leave the training to less competent sources of reinforcement and punishment, such as other children.

Another commonly raised objection to operant conditioning is that the approach is often associated with the use of tangible rewards for improvement in behavior or learning. "I want my children to love learning itself, not just learn in order to get something." Again, remember your paycheck. The children need a payoff, too. The fundamental question here is this: "Suppose the children right now do not work at learning for its own sake? What are you going to do about it?" It so happens that those using operant conditioning principles are able to teach children to work at learning for its own sake. They do this initially by using tangible reinforcers or social reinforcers which can be slowly faded out as task completion becomes reinforcing to children, or until sufficient skills are acquired so that reinforcers of various sorts can be gained from the learning task (e.g., reading a funny story).

To those who are concerned about issues of freedom and control over human behavior we say the issues are always there whether one makes use of available knowledge or not. There is available a technology of teaching and training which makes it possible to help children and adults live more effective and useful lives. Many children and adults who now populate our institutions for the retarded and the mentally ill, our special education classrooms, and the ghettos of our cities need not continue to do so. Is it morally right to foster stupidity, starvation, incompetence, and degradation when we could do otherwise?

While the present review will focus on the recently articulated implications of operant principles for the reduction of behavior problems with the teacher as the change agent, the reader should keep in mind that these principles have many other applications for the improvement of society. Just in public schools, however, it is our impression that as many as 80 to 90 percent of the children typically referred by the teacher to psychologists, social workers, or special education classes can be handled more effectively by the regular classroom teacher.

This review draws heavily on examples from the work of its authors (Becker, Thomas, and Carnine). The reader should recognize that parallel and related studies are being carried out in many other applied behavioral research centers from Oregon to Kansas to Michigan to Long Island.

In general, the research strategies used in the studies covered by this report have the following features:

1. Individuals are studied under specified experimental conditions, with the same individuals going through the various phases of the experiment. This approach leads more directly than others to knowledge of procedures which will or will not work with individual children.

2. Often the experimental procedure is withdrawn after being introduced to show more clearly the effect of experimental procedure. For example, when teacher praises more, on-task behavior increases; when teacher praises less, on-task behavior decreases.

3. The behaviors to be changed are defined in terms of observables, events which the teacher can see and do something about. Before the experiment starts, reliability of observations is established by checking the agreement among several observers. A review of field experimental research procedures may be found in Bijou, Peterson, and Ault (1968).

Change Procedure I: Presentation of Social Reinforcers Following Appropriate Behaviors and Withdrawal of Social Reinforcers Following Inappropriate Behaviors

Stimuli which are based on the behavior of people are called social stimuli. These include physical nearness, contact, verbal behavior, physical appearance (face, smiles, frowns). Social stimuli which function to strengthen behaviors which they follow are called social reinforcers. It is of extreme social importance that stimulus events most readily managed by the teacher (those stimulus events produced by her behavior) have been found to be the most influential in strengthening and maintaining the behavior of children. The following studies illustrate the range of behaviors found to be controlled by social reinforcers in a variety of settings.

Preschool Studies

Work in the experimental preschools at the University of Washington, University of Kansas, and University of Illinois by Wolf, Baer, Bijou, and their students laid the groundwork for extensions of operant procedures to public schools. Only a few examples of this research will be presented. The bibliography in this area is growing very rapidly. Hart, Reynolds, Baer, Brawley, and Harris (1968) carefully

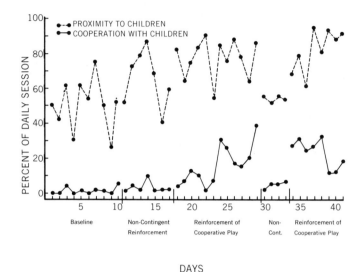

Fig. 1. Daily percentages of proximity and cooperative play over sequential experimental conditions

studied the consequences controlling the obnoxious behavior of a 5-year-old girl named Martha who was "balky, verbally insulting, occasionally foulmouthed, and prone to tell disjointed stories about violent accidents." The general results of the study are graphed in Figure 1.

For the first 10 days, Martha's teachers maintained their ongoing pattern of responding to her. This initial period is called the baseline and serves as a basis for comparing experimental effects. During baseline Martha was found to be near other children about 50 percent of the preschool time, but played cooperatively less than 5 percent. The teachers interacted with Martha about 10 percent of the available time intervals.

For the next 7 days, the teachers showered Martha with social reinforcement and desirable material goods. They attended closely to her, laughing, conversing, and showing admiration. Such attention was given about 80 percent of the available time. Some psychologists might have predicted that this "unconditional love" might lead Martha to be more cooperative. Cooperative play remained at less than 5 percent. This period is labelled noncontingent reinforcement on Figure 1 since events which usually function as reinforcers were presented on a random basis, rather than being contingent upon a class of behaviors.

In the third phase of the experiment, cooperative behavior was directly followed by attention, praise, and equipment or materials.

Martha was ignored if she showed her obnoxious behaviors. Ignored in this case simply means withdrawal of attention of all sorts from Martha and giving attention to another child. Cooperative play rose to 40 percent.

When noncontingent reinforcement was again introduced, cooperative behavior decreased. Finally, reinstatement of reinforcement for cooperative play increased such play.

The conclusion of the study was that social reinforcers from adults can serve to strengthen behaviors followed by such reinforcement. *Just being nice is not enough.* It is very likely that Martha's obnoxious behaviors were being maintained by the attention they received although the present study did not address itself to that question.

Consider two more examples. Harris, Johnston, Kelley, and Wolf (1964) studied a 3-year-old who spent 80 percent of the time crawling on the floor. When the teachers only gave attention for standing and walking, a normal walking pattern was established within a week. Switching attention back to crawling and not attending to standing reinstated regressive crawling for 80 percent of the time periods. Again switching back to attention for standing reinstated a normal pattern of upright behavior.

Buell, Stoddard, Harris, and Baer (1968) examined the effects of reinforcing play on outdoor equipment on the development of social skills. Polly was physically inactive and showed little social interaction with her peers. When physically active play was strengthened by using social reinforcement, it was found that other desirable behaviors appeared. There were more social contacts with peers in the form of talking and cooperative play, and there was less baby behavior.

Social reinforcement can also be used by peers. Wahler (1967) has demonstrated the profound effects of attention to or ignoring of behaviors by preschool peers. For example, in his study, Sally's doll play greatly diminished when peers were instructed to ignore such behavior. Play with other toys increased in the meantime. When the peers again reinforced doll play, its rate returned to the baseline level. Dick's aggressive behaviors were similarly controlled by the presence or absence of peer attention.

In his review of preschool studies, Baer (1966) concluded with the following appropriate comment:

> There have been a number of other studies, all of strikingly similar outcome, involving behaviors such as excessive dependency, wild and disruptive social play, extreme aggression, exclusive play with a single peer, inattentiveness, inarticulate use of language, and hyperactivity. The data of these studies are remarkably similar to the data already seen, despite differences in the personnel, the settings, the children, and the problem behaviors.

Elementary Classroom Studies

COMBINED EFFECTS OF RULES, IGNORE, AND PRAISE. Several studies have been conducted by Becker and his students to assess the possibility of extending the findings on preschool children to the elementary school setting.

In the first set of studies, two problem children were chosen from each of five classes (Becker, Madsen, Arnold, & Thomas, 1967). Categories of child behaviors were those which disrupted learning, which violated the teacher's rules, or which the teacher saw as undesirable, e.g., thumbsucking. These categories consisted of behaviors which were similar in some important way and were defined in terms of observables (inferences were not involved). The child behavior categories are summarized in Table 1.

TABLE 1

Coding Categories for Children with Teachers A, B, and C

Symbols	Class Label	Class Definitions
A. Behaviors Incompatible with Learning: General Categories		
X	Gross motor behaviors	Getting out of seat; standing up; running; hopping; skipping; jumping; walking around; rocking in chair; disruptive movement without noise; moving chair to neighbor.
N	Disruptive noise with objects	Tapping pencil or other objects; clapping; tapping feet; rattling or tearing paper. Be conservative, only rate if you can hear noise with eyes closed. Do not include accidental dropping of objects or noise made while performing X above.
A	Disturbing others directly and aggression	Grabbing objects or work; knocking neighbor's book off desk; destroying another's property; hitting; kicking; shoving; pinching; slapping; striking with object; throwing object at another person; poking with object; attempting to strike; biting; pulling hair.

O	Orienting responses	Turning head or head and body to look at another person; showing objects to another child; attending to another child. Must be of 4 seconds duration to be rated. Not rated unless seated.
!	Blurting out, commenting, and vocal noise	Answering teacher without raising hand or without being called on; making comments or calling out remarks when no question has been asked; calling teacher's name to get her attention; crying; screaming; singing; whistling; laughing loudly; coughing loudly. Must be undirected to another particular child, but may be directed to teacher.
T	Talking	Carrying on conversations with other children when it is not permitted. Must be directed to a particular child or children.
//	Other	Ignoring teacher's question or command; doing something different from that directed to do (includes minor motor behavior such as playing with pencil when supposed to be writing). To be rated only when other ratings not appropriate.

B. Special categories for children with teachers A, B, and C (to be rated only for children indicated)

+	Improper position Carole and Alice	Not sitting with body and head oriented toward the front with feet on the floor, e.g., sitting on feet; standing at desk rather than sitting; sitting with body sideways but head facing front. *Do not rate if chair is sideways but head and body both oriented toward the front with feet on the floor.*
S	Sucking Alice and Betty	Sucking fingers or other objects.

B	Bossing Carole	Reading story out loud to self or other children *(do not rate! in this case);* acting as teacher to other children, as showing flash cards.
//	Ignoring Charley	This category expanded to include playing with scissors, pencils, or crayons instead of doing something more constructive during free time.

C. Relevant Behavior

—	Relevant Behavior	Time on task, e.g., answers question, listening, raises hand, writing assignment. *Must include whole 20 seconds except for orienting responses of less than 4 seconds duration.*

Additional categories of behavior were to be recorded for children who frequently demonstrated the behaviors of improper seating position, sucking, bossing, and ignoring teacher's instructions.

Observations of teacher behaviors were made to determine if the experimental program was being carried out effectively and to record other behaviors which could possibly influence child behaviors. The teacher categories are summarized in Table 2.

TABLE 2

Teacher Coding Categories

Symbols	Class Label	Class Definitions
C	Positive Contact	Positive physical contact must be included—such behaviors as embracing, kissing, patting (on head), holding arm, taking hand, sitting on lap, etc.
P	Verbal Praise	This category includes paying attention to appropriate behavior with verbal comments indicating approval, commendations, or achievement such as: "That's good." "You're studying well." "Fine job." "I like you."

R	Recognition in Academic Sense	Calling on child when hand is raised. (Do not rate if child calls teacher's name or makes noises to get her attention.)
F	Facial Attention	Looking at child when smiling. (Teacher might nod her head or give other indication of approval— while smiling.)
A	Attention to Undesirable Behavior	This category includes the teacher's verbally calling attention to undesirable behavior and may be of high intensity (yelling, screaming, scolding, or raising the voice) or of low intensity ("Go to the office." "You know what you are supposed to be doing." etc.). Calling the child to the desk to talk things over should also be included, as well as threats of consequences. Score the following responses to deviant behavior separately:
L	Lights	Turning off the lights to achieve control.
W	Withdrawal of Positive Reinforcement	Keeping in for recess, sending to office, depriving child in the classroom.
PR	Physical Restraint	Includes holding the child, pulling out into hall, grabbing, hitting, pushing, shaking.

After a 5-week baseline the teachers were to begin the experimental program which had three components. The teacher's rules for classroom behavior were made explicit and repeated frequently. Teachers were also to show approval for appropriate behaviors (conducive to learning), and to ignore disruptive behaviors. If a child was hurting someone, appropriate punishment, preferably the withdrawal of some reinforcement, was permitted. Part of the instructions to teachers follows:

> In general, give praise for achievement, prosocial behavior, and following the group rules. Specifically, you can praise for concentrating on individual work, raising hand when appropriate, responding to questions, paying attention to directions

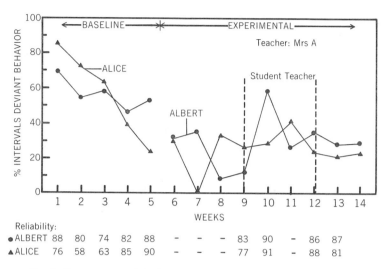

Fig. 2. Percentages of deviant behavior for two children in Class A

and following through, sitting in desk and studying, and sitting quietly if noise has been a problem. Try to use variety and expression in your comments. Stay away from sarcasm. Attempt to become spontaneous in your praise; smile when delivering praise. At first you will probably get the feeling that you are praising a great deal and it sounds a little phony to your ears. This is a typical reaction and it becomes more natural with the passage of time. Spread your praise and attention around. If comments sometimes might interfere with the ongoing class activities then use facial attention and smiles. Walk around the room during study time and pat or place your hand on the back of a child who is doing a good job. Praise, quietly spoken to the children, has been found effective in combination with some physical sign of approval.

In addition to the general instructions, the teachers were given specific instructions for each problem child. Teachers were also given daily feedback regarding their effectiveness in showing approval contingent on appropriate behavior and in ignoring inappropriate behavior.

The percentage of intervals of deviant behavior for the 10 children dropped from 62.13 percent of the time during baseline to 29.19 percent of the time during the experimental program when approval, ignore, and rules were introduced. Teacher A, speaking of one of the two problem children selected for the study, commented after using the experimental program in her class: "Albert has become a delightful child and an enthusiastic member of our class who feels his ideas are accepted and have merit." During baseline, Albert, a second

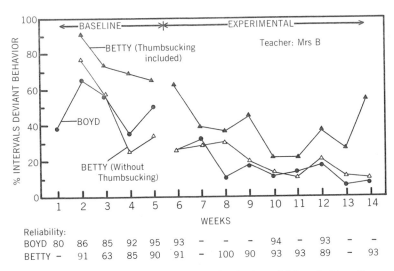

Reliability:													
BOYD 80	86	85	92	95	93	–	–	–	94	–	93	–	–
BETTY –	91	63	85	90	91	–	100	90	93	93	89	–	93

Fig. 3. Percentages of deviant behavior for two children in Class B

grader with a normal Stanford-Binet test score, was still on first grade material and talked, made other noises, did not attend to the teacher, and often got out of his seat. During the experimental phase he worked diligently without blurting out. His stuttering stopped and the percentage of time spent in deviant behavior dropped to about 20 percent. The data on Alice (the other problem child) is less clear since the average deviant behavior began declining during baseline; however, orienting, sucking, and other categories did decrease in frequency with the introduction of the experimental program.

Teacher B initially used sharp commands, physical punishment, and withholding privileges. However, she effectively followed the experimental program with Betty and Boyd. Betty initially pestered others, made noises, blurted out, and sucked her thumb. The experimental program brought Betty's problem behavior under control, particularly for the last 5 weeks. During the final week, however, the frequency of thumbsucking increased. Boyd, the second problem child in this class, was often out of his seat, and would not work alone. The experimental program increased the time he spent seated, a large portion of which was spent on academic work.

The two children in Teacher C's class required stronger measures than anticipated. Both bullied others and were often out of their seats. Carole talked incessantly and was very responsive to peer attention. A token system (token systems will be discussed in detail later) was instituted but was effective only sporadically with her; her deviant behavior ranged around 50 percent. Charley was more influenced by the approval and the tokens; he worked harder, and his

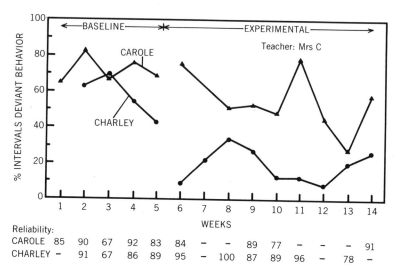

Fig. 4. Percentages of deviant behavior for two children in Class C

level of deviant behavior fell to around 15 to 20 percent, well below that of the baseline.

Teacher D had Danny and Don. Don was a boy of average IQ, who had been recommended for the Educable Mentally Handicapped placement 4 years earlier. He had a high frequency of moving about the room and talking during study time. He responded well to approval, and his level of deviant behavior fell from 40 percent to 20 percent. Danny, who had academic failings, responded well to teacher attention only after tutoring was begun (his case and tutoring in general will be considered in detail later).

Teacher E had relied mainly on shouting to maintain order in an "unruly class." The children showed much whistling, running around the room, yelling at other children, loud incessant talk, hitting, pushing, and shoving. In this class no special instructions were given to the teacher concerning the two children chosen for observation. Rather, the measurement of changes in their behavior would act as an indicator for the effects on the entire class. The average level of deviant behavior for the two boys fell from about 70 percent to about 25 percent, a drastic reduction.

These results indicate that quite different kinds of teachers can learn to systematically apply differential social reinforcement to modify the behavior of problem children.

Separate Effects of Rules, Ignore, and Praise. Madsen, Becker, and Thomas (1968) attempted to determine the relative effectiveness of the three components of the experimental program in the study just reviewed. After baseline, each of the three components of the experimental program (rules, ignore, and praise) were

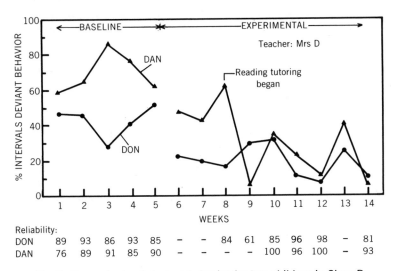

Reliability:

DON	89	93	86	93	85	–	–	84	61	85	96	98	–	81
DAN	76	89	91	85	90	–	–	–	–	100	96	100	–	93

Fig. 5. Percentages of deviant behavior for two children in Class D

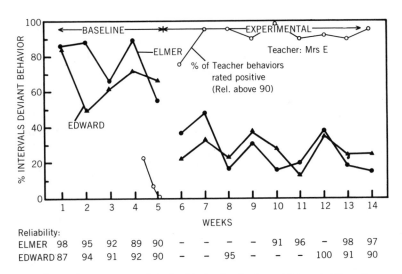

Reliability:

ELMER	98	95	92	89	90	–	–	–	–	91	96	–	98	97
EDWARD	87	94	91	92	90	–	–	95	–	–	–	100	91	90

Fig. 6. Percentages of deviant behavior for two children in Class E

introduced separately. After their effects had been determined, the teacher attempted to match her own baseline behavior to see if the problem behaviors would reappear. Finally, the three components of the experimental program were once again introduced.

The *rules* phase of the experiment consisted of the teacher forming four or five rules for classroom behavior and repeating them four to

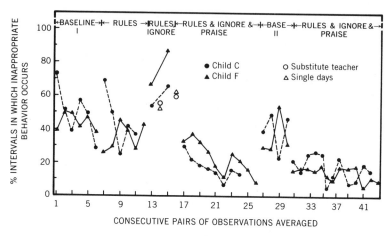

Fig. 7. Inappropriate behavior of two problem children as a function of experimental conditions

six times a day, e.g., "sit quietly while working," "walk," "raise hand," etc.

The *ignore* phase of the experiment consisted of the teacher attempting to not respond to disruptive behaviors with scolding or reprimands. She was to act as if such behavior did not happen. This part of the program was very difficult for the teacher to follow.

Finally, *praise* was added. Appropriate behaviors incompatible with deviant behaviors were to be given social approval. The teacher was to show approval of as many good behaviors as possible during the first few days. A prime rule was "Catch the children being good." Moreover, she was to give approval to improvements in behavior in order to shape the child's behavior. For example, a problem child who frequently wandered around the room would be given approval when found in his seat even if he was not working on a task. As the time spent in the seat increased, the teacher would begin to praise him only when he was both seated and working on a task. In each case the teacher would explicitly state what behaviors she approved of; e.g., "I like the way Tommy is sitting at his desk and filling out his workbook assignment."

The results indicate that the introduction of rules alone was not effective in modifying behavior. The procedure of ignoring inappropriate behavior was difficult for the teacher to hold to. She would ignore for a while and then scold as the children got out of hand. When praise for appropriate behavior was added, in conjunction with the ignoring of inappropriate behavior, deviant behavior fell from about a 70 percent level (during baseline) to 30 percent. Deviant behavior returned to the baseline level when the teacher approximated her behavior during baseline. Finally, when the experimental procedures were reinstated, the level of deviant behavior again fell.

This correspondence between the experimental changes in teacher's behavior and the level of deviant behavior points to the marked influence the teacher can have over classroom behavior.

THE REINFORCING EFFECT OF "SIT DOWN" COMMANDS. Often our attempts to correct children by telling them what not to do fail. Madsen, Becker, Thomas, Koser, and Plager (1968) obtained clear evidence to show that the more frequently first grade teachers asked their children to sit down, the more frequently they stood up. Only when the children were given praise for sitting and working did the frequency of standing up decline.

HOW TO MAKE A "BAD" CLASS OUT OF A GOOD ONE. The data presented in Figure 8 show that a teacher might, without intending it, produce a poor classroom with a high rate of disruptive behaviors (Thomas, Becker, and Armstrong, 1967). The data in Figure 8 are based on observing 10 children for 2 minutes each, each day. The children are bright second graders who are being observed during a morning reading time when most children are doing seat work and the rest are in a group with the teacher. Disruptive behavior was measured in a way similar to that reported earlier.

The first four experimental phases compare baseline conditions (1 and 3) with conditions where all praise is withdrawn (2 and 4). The effect of withdrawal of teacher's praise for appropriate behavior is to increase disruptive behavior from under 10 percent to approximately 28 percent. Teacher's praise is important in maintaining a well-functioning classroom.

During Phase 5 of the experiment (frequent disapproval), the teacher's critical comments were tripled so that they were occurring almost once a minute. Disruptive behaviors hit a new high. Teacher disapproval appears to be reinforcing disruptive behavior.

Phase 6 of the experiment simply returned to the No Approval condition again with a lower level of criticism. Little change resulted.

Finally, in Phase 7, the reinstatement of approval reactions by the teacher reduced disruptive behaviors to its original low level.

Moral. It is important how the teacher behaves. Teachers can learn to manage their own behavior in ways which can reduce problem behavior in the classroom.

DIRECT VERSUS INDIRECT REINFORCEMENT. Does it make any difference which children receive the praise? Carnine, Becker, Thomas, Poe, and Plager (unpublished) examined this question by having the teacher praise three children and not praise three others. The children were initially matched for age, academic level, and frequency of relevant (on-task) behavior. Figure 9 presents the data. During baseline no praise was used for any class members (with a few slips). During Experimental Phase I, Group 1 (top graph) received much praise from teacher and relevant behavior increased from 18.5 percent to 59.2 percent. Group 2 received no praise during this period and did not improve. During Experimental Phase II,

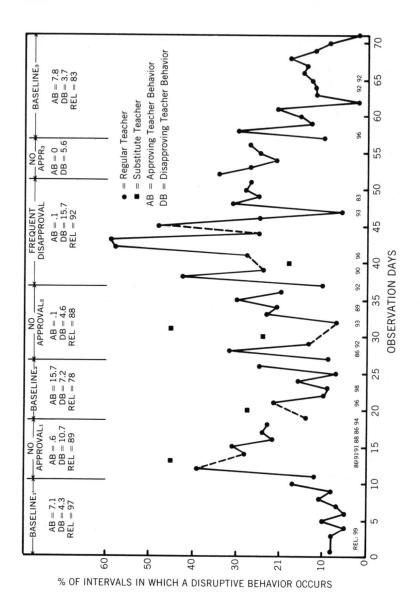

Fig. 8. Disruptive classroom behaviors as a function of nature of teacher behavior. Data points represent 2 minute samples on 10 children each day. Dotted lines cross observations where the regular teacher was absent due to a recurrent illness, including a 10 day hospitalization between days 39 and 41. The dotted line connecting days 44 and 45 represents the Easter vacation break. The data for day 26 were taken with the teacher out of the room.

147

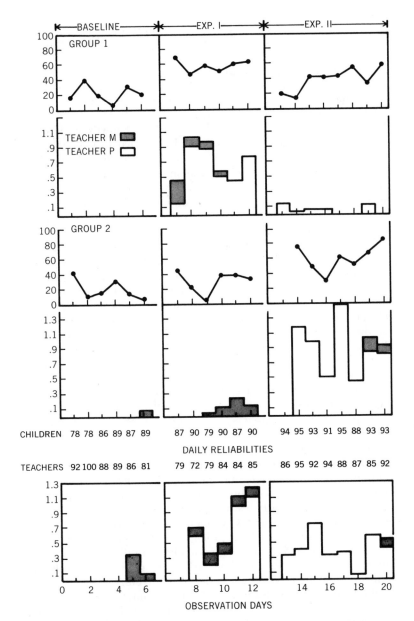

Fig. 9. Top Figures: Percentage of time intervals Group 1 boys show relevant behavior (line graph), and average number of approval statements per minute directed to Group 1 boys by teachers (bar graph).
Middle Figures: Percentages of time intervals Group 2 boys show relevant behavior (line graph), and average number of approval statements per minute directed to Group 2 boys by teachers (bar graph).
Bottom Figures: Average number of approval statements per minute directed by teachers to other members of the class.

Group 2 received the praise and Group 1 did not. Group 1 decreased some in relevant behavior (but not to baseline), and Group 2 now shows more on-task behavior.

The results are clear in indicating that it is not the total amount of praise given by the teacher which is important for good classroom management, but when and to whom the praise is given.

A PROGRAM TO PROVIDE ACADEMIC SUCCESS IS ALSO ESSENTIAL. Reinforcement procedures may be used to get rowdy children to quit messing around, to sit down, and to appear to pay attention. However, all this is to no avail if the academic program available to the child is not one in which he can succeed (learn). In a series of studies where the deviant child was behind the rest of the class in academic skills (reading being most central), we have explored some of the interactions of social reinforcement and special tutoring to help the children catch up in reading.

The first case of this sort was reported earlier in Figure 5. During baseline, Dan was off-task over 70 percent of the time. Three weeks of positive social reinforcement for work behaviors showed an initial improvement which was then lost. Remedial tutoring in reading was then started for 30 minutes a day. Marked improvements in *classroom relevant behavior* occurred very quickly and were sustained throughout the next 6 weeks. Within 4 weeks after the tutoring had begun Danny had dropped to an average of only 15 percent off-task behavior during his seatwork activities. He still showed deviant behaviors up to 50 percent of the time in his afternoon classes (where the teachers were not trained to use praise) and in morning periods requiring skills he did not have, such as English composition.

Thomas, Nielson, Kuypers, and Becker (1968) attempted to investigate the relative contributions of tutoring and social reinforcement in the elimination of a severe classroom behavior problem. The plan of the study was to introduce the social reinforcement procedures and the remedial tutoring one at a time and assess their effects on both classroom behavior and academic performance in order to more stringently test the program. Classroom behavior was assessed at a time of the day which did not involve the tutored behavior (reading). The subject, Rich, was a 6-year-old Negro boy whose behavior had grown progressively more disruptive throughout his first 6 months in school. Although intelligence tests had indicated that Rich was functioning in the average range (IQ = 93 on the Stanford-Binet, Form L-M) he had completed only three pre-primers in the Ginn basic reading series. Prior to the start of tutoring in mid-March, Rich scored 1.4 in reading on the Wide Range Achievement Test and had a total language age of 6 years and 4 months on the Illinois Test of Psycholinguistic Abilities. This would indicate only a mild educational retardation. However, the deficit might be expected to be cumulative unless appropriate interventions were made.

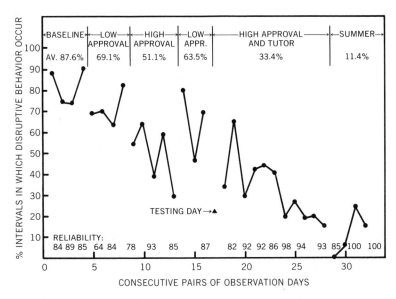

Fig. 10. Percentage of intervals in which disruptive behavior occurred as a function of experimental conditions

Social reinforcement procedures were somewhat difficult for this teacher to perform systematically, but with some aid from the experimenters she began to praise appropriate behaviors and approximations of appropriate behavior. She ignored deviant or disruptive behavior unless a child was being hurt, and she made a list of rules (positively worded) which the children learned. These techniques were effective in bringing the level of disruptive behavior down from an average of 87.6 percent during baseline to 51.1 percent prior to the tutoring (see Figure 10). When tutoring was used in conjunction with the program of differential reinforcement, Rich's disruptive behavior continued to decline. Some additional observations were obtained during the summer which indicated that Rich's gains were being maintained in a different classroom, with a different peer group and teacher.

The remedial tutoring program used with Rich was derived from the Staats and Butterfield (1965) procedures. The basic procedure was to start the tutoring materials well below the level at which Rich was working in class. Tokens (points) were given for correct responses during the tutoring session and for problems worked correctly in his workbook while he was studying in the classroom. During the tutoring session he was given points or tokens for learning new vocabulary words, for knowing words previously learned, for reading sentences, and for answering comprehension questions over the readings. In addition, the tutor paired social reinforcement with the earning of tokens throughout the tutoring sessions. Points could be exchanged periodically for candy and toys.

The remedial program was carried out by a university undergraduate who spent 21 hours tutoring Rich over a 6-week period. Test results after the tutoring program indicated that Rich had raised his scores on the Wide Range Achievement Test from 1.4 before tutoring to 2.0 after tutoring. Additionally, on the Illinois Test of Psycholinguistic Abilities his total language age increased from 6 years 4 months to 6 years 10 months, with gains of a year or more appearing on four of the subtests.

The effect of the combination of social reinforcement and tutoring should be carefully considered. A common report of teachers is that children who are being tutored learn to work well in a one-to-one situation, but still cannot function on their own in the classroom. This was not the case with Rich. In fact, there were occasions when he brought worksheets to the tutoring session which he claimed to have completed at home. Two procedures are thought to be responsible for this carry over. First, appropriate behavior in the classroom was strongly supported by the teacher's verbal praise; and second, work done in the classroom could earn points toward the prizes chosen in the tutoring session. The combination of procedures proved to be very effective.

A recently completed, and as yet unreported study, by Varna Garis and Becker, adds immeasurably to the interpretation of the above studies. Five second graders with low first grade reading skills were given tutoring using the Staats procedures outlined above. All of the children showed good reading gains. The variable of experimental concern, however, was on-task behavior in the classroom as determined by direct observation. Three of the children were in one class and two in another. The experimental phases were (a) baseline, classroom observations made with no interventions, (b) tutoring outside of the classroom, no changes in the classroom, (c) points given in tutoring session for completion of classroom workbook assignments in reading, and (d) instruction to teachers on how to praise in the classroom.

The children were off-task initially about 50 percent of the time. Tutoring alone produced a minor improvement in classroom behavior for only one of the five children. Points for completion of workbook exercises produced improvements in classroom behavior for two of the five children (both with the same teacher). Social reinforcement by the teacher produced clear effects for the teacher who was able to increase her level of praise. Teacher A was able to raise her level of praise from 2 percent to 22 percent of the time intervals and her three children showed only 18 percent off-task behavior. Teacher B was only able to raise her level of praise from .2 percent to 6 percent and her two children averaged 44 percent off-task.

None of the three studies covered in this last section provides clearly separated effects because of the practical difficulties in gaining control of some critical variables. However, taken together the studies suggest a need to carefully examine current procedures and beliefs about school practices. They raise questions like these:

1. Rich was described as very emotionally disturbed (unruly, tantrums, off-task 85 percent). We did not treat his emotional disturbance. We taught him to read and taught his teacher to praise him for good work. He no longer showed the behaviors which would lead one to label him as emotionally disturbed. Was he emotionally disturbed? Could emotional disturbance in any way account for his failure to perform in school?

2. Our remedial reading programs were carried out by persons with no technical training in remedial reading. Is it possible that with a detailing of procedures and the use of effective reinforcement systems technical level people could do jobs for which we now require Masters' degrees? Many school failures might be eliminated at a reasonable cost if this is so. Other studies by Staats with older children support this implication.

3. We often expect a child taught to perform in one situation to do so in another. In the present studies, relevant classroom behaviors occurred with high frequency only when (a) the program made it possible to make right responses, and (b) the child was reinforced for doing so. Teachers often talk as if children ought to like to learn for its own sake and the teachers shouldn't have to do anything special to get children to like learning. But suppose the children do not work on task? Do we just blame the child?

AN INDEPENDENT SET OF FINDINGS. Hall, Lund, and Jackson (1968) have reported a series of experiments further demonstrating the reinforcing effects of teacher attention in increasing study behavior. When the teacher was able to ignore disruptive behaviors and praise on-task behaviors, sharp increases in on-task behavior were found. In each of these studies following the first reinforcement period, the teacher returned to her old way of reacting (attending to disruptive behaviors). As a result, disruptive behavior increased and study behavior decreased. Reinstatement of reinforcement for study behavior again produced the expected change. Follow-up checks, made up to 14 weeks after the experimental procedure was completed, showed maintenance of a high level of study behavior.

Summary — Change Procedure I

Change Procedure I involves the simultaneous use of the principles of reinforcement and extinction. Social reinforcers are made to occur following behaviors you wish to strengthen and all reinforcement is withdrawn from behaviors you wish to weaken. In the studies examined, this change procedure was found to be effective with a variety of behaviors in nursery school and elementary school children. These behaviors are usually termed personality problems, e.g.

passivity, regressive crawling, aggressiveness, and withdrawal. For the elementary school teacher, use of this change procedure often involves providing appropriate academic tasks for the child so that relevant behavior can occur and be reinforced. In general, Change Procedure I follows the rule: *Reinforce behavior incompatible with that you wish to eliminate.* But a second rule is also important. *Select imcompatible behaviors to reinforce which will be most beneficial to the child's development.* A great economy of effort is achieved if one teaches important social and cognitive skills in the process of eliminating disruptive behaviors.

The various studies covered in this section have the following additional points to make:

1. Social reinforcement will not work with all children but will work with most. Additional procedures may be required.

2. Rules alone do little to influence behavior. They must be made important by providing reinforcement for behaving according to the rules.

3. Many kinds of verbal commands may appear to be effective in eliminating undesired behavior. However, appearances may be deceiving. While commands and critical comments may cue the child to stop a particular unwanted behavior (standing, talking, etc.), the attention given to that behavior by the persons making the command or critical comment may actually increase its future occurrence. "Sit down" commands and disapproving comments were both found to increase the frequency of behaviors they followed. They served as positive reinforcers for the behaviors they were attempting to eliminate. *Learning not to respond to disruptive behaviors* is important for effective teaching. "Ignore" is a key word.

4. If, in fact, the teacher, through the use of her verbal behavior can create "good" or "bad" classroom behaviors, and the controlling variables can be isolated and modified, there is little reason why all teachers can not be taught to be effective teachers. We can no longer blame the unchangeable personality of the teacher or the pupils for an undesired state of affairs.

5. Educational psychologists have often indicated that the good teacher is the one who is warm and positive with her children. The work reported here is consistent with such findings, but leads to a more specific recommendation. The frequency of use of positive social reinforcers (smiles, praise, etc.) is not related to improvement in behavior. It matters *when* the teacher praises *whom* and for *what behavior.*

Change Procedure II: Strengthen the Reinforcers

In our experience, 80 percent to 90 percent of the problem children in elementary classrooms will respond well to some variant of Change Procedure I. For some children, however, the usual methods of reinforcement for school behaviors do not work and it is necessary to devise more effective methods. The procedure generally involves finding effective reinforcers which can be used to strengthen currently ineffective reinforcers. In adopting systems which involve the use of stronger reinforcers, such as food, toys, special events, it has usually been advisable to use some kind of token reinforcement system along with the stronger reinforcers.

The principles guiding the design of token systems may be stated non-technically as follows:

1. Reinforcers given immediately are more effective than delayed reinforcers. Tokens should be rapidly and easily administered.

2. Tokens or points serve as *conditioned reinforcers* which can be backed up by *many* effective reinforcers. The variety of back-up reinforcers increases the probability that reinforcers will be present for different children.

3. In building new behaviors, frequent reinforcement is desired. After behaviors are established an intermittent schedule of reinforcement is more effective in maintaining behavior. The token system should permit continuous or intermittent presentation of tokens depending on the progress of the child.

4. To reduce the future need for a special reinforcement system, presentation of tokens should be paired with verbal reinforcements, such as "you're right," "good," completing a task, or just working on-task.

Token reinforcement systems have been used successfully, when other approaches have failed, with a variety of problem groups (e.g., Birnbrauer, Wolf, Kidder, and Taque, 1965; Girardeau and Spradlin, 1964; Haring and Lovitt, in press).

Applications in public schools have been entirely experimental to this point. Many promising procedures have been tested. A few of the better controlled studies will be summarized, and then other possibilities will be briefly discussed.

An After School Program for Potential Dropouts. A token system which has proven effective and which might be adaptable to the school setting was developed by Wolf, Giles, and Hall (1968). In this study 16 pupils, from two elementary schools located in the low income district of Kansas City, worked in a remedial program during the summer and after school hours during the regular school year. Evaluation of the program was made in terms of a control group who went to the regular school but was not involved in a remedial program.

The token reinforcement procedure was somewhat like a trading stamp plan. The students accumulated cards marked off into squares and checked by an instructor whenever a student had obtained a point. Each checked square was a token. When a child first joined the program, points were given for each problem which he worked correctly. As a higher response rate was attained by the student, the amount and difficulty of the work required to obtain points increased. The number of points given to a child for a particular bit of work was determined by the instructor alone or by negotiation with the child.

Pages filled with points were redeemable for a variety of goods and events, such as a circus, swimming, zoo, daily snacks, candy, toiletries, novelties; or long range goals, such as clothes or secondhand bicycles. A number of other contingencies were provided in the program. Their functions were not systematically analyzed. However, they did seem to operate as intended. In an effort to encourage effective instruction, a monetary contingency was arranged for the instructors which was linked to the productivity of their students. Also, in some instances, favorite subjects or popular activities could be attempted after completion of work in less favored areas. Additionally, an increasing bonus was given for longer periods of perfect attendance. A system for rewarding the behavior of the least disruptive child was set up using a kitchen timer which was set to go off at variable intervals during the remedial session. There was also a contingency for report card grades and improvement in grades. A party was given after each grading period for all students who had improved. The students also received bonus points for reports of good behavior from their teacher.

During each of the preceding 2 years the median gain by the experimental and control groups on the Stanford Achievement Test had been .6 years. The gain during the year of the remedial program for the token group was 1.5 years as compared to .8 years for the control group. Remedial group gains were significantly greater. Comments by the regular school teachers suggest that the remedial program benefited the regular school classroom as well. Not only were the program children helped, but their increased participation and changed attitudes increased the productivity of the other children in the classrooms.

The cost per child of the program averaged $225. Wolf has this to say about the cost:

> The cost of the program, which was substantial, must be contrasted with the long-term cost to society in terms of human as well as economic resources lost by not educating these children adequately. The cost could be reduced significantly by utilizing the potential reinforcers which exist in almost every educational setting. Properly used, such events as recess, movies, and athletic and social activities could be arranged as consequences for strengthening academic behavior (Wolf, Giles, and Hall, 1968, p. 64).

An In-School Program for an Adjustment Class. Most of the early experimental work on token programs have used at least one adult for each four or five children. O'Leary and Becker (1967) successfully devised a token program which could be used by one teacher with a classroom of 17 problem children. The children had been placed in a special class because of academic and behavioral deficiencies. They were from deprived homes. The children were 9-year-olds working on a beginning first grade curriculum. Eight of the more disturbed children averaged 76 percent deviant behavior during baseline observations. The teacher had a most difficult time carrying out any procedures which might be considered teaching. She would usually leave the classroom exhausted. The token program was in effect from 12:30 P.M. to 2:00 P.M. each day.

On the first day of the token program, the experimenter placed the class rules on the blackboard and explained the token procedures to the children. Small 10 cent notebooks were taped to each child's desk. The children were told that they would receive points in their notebooks each 15 minutes. At each rating period they could get from one to 10 points. A mark of 10 meant that they were following the rules very well, while a mark of one indicated that they were not doing their assigned tasks during the rating period. The points or ratings could be exchanged for small prizes, such as candy, comics, perfume, and kites. A variety of items was provided to maximize the probability that at least one of the items would be a reinforcer for a given child at a given time. The experimenter repeated the instructions each day for a week. It was the teacher, however, who provided ratings for the children. For the first 3 days the tokens were traded in at the end of the token period. During the next 4 days points were exchanged at the end of the token period on the second day. For 15 days, the children had to save tokens for 3 days; for the remaining 24 school days, they saved 4 days. During the 3- and 4-day delay periods tokens were exchanged at the end of school. The rating period was extended from 15 to 30 minutes after the first 3 days. The number of points required for a given level of prize was gradually increased.

The results are summarized in Figure 11. During baseline, the children averaged 76 percent disruptive behavior. This dropped to 10 percent during the token period. The gang atmosphere which had prevailed in the room was gone. It was possible now to begin to teach. The children readily came to respond to the teacher's praise which accompanied the giving of points. The class, considered the worst behaved, became the best behaved class in the school. The children readily learned to tolerate delays in exchanging tokens for prizes. Anecdotal records indicated that while the token procedure was in effect, the children behaved more appropriately, not only in other classroom activities when points were not given, but also during music and library periods. These additional gains are likely due to two procedures: (a) the systematic use of praise for good behavior throughout the day, and (b) the use of various privileges and activities as rewards for improved behavior. The rewards for the program cost $80.76 during the 8 weeks it was in effect. Rewards appear to be less expensive than psychologists! Token program benefits to the teacher were very noticeable in the classroom, and also outside of school hours. For instance, the teacher's roommate commented on how

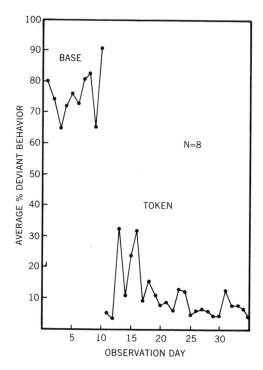

Fig. 11. Average percentage of deviant behavior during base and token periods

relaxed she (the teacher) was in the evening of the second day of the program.

Two additional studies of similar token systems were carried out to permit a better specification of the critical variables (Kuypers, Becker, and O'Leary, 1968; O'Leary, Becker, Evans, and Saudargas, 1969). Kuypers et al. instituted a program using the bare essentials of the point system used by O'Leary and Becker. The teacher was not trained in behavioral principles; she did not use praise or other reinforcement procedures throughout the day; and she gave praise and points for an absolute level of performance rather than rewarding improvement. Under these conditions, there was no generalization of effects from the token period to the nontoken periods. The effects on individuals were varied. Those who were initially better received prizes and showed improvement. Those who were initially more deviant received little reinforcement, did not meet the absolute standard, and were, in fact, punished by the system. They did not show improvement. The effect was like that produced by many current grading systems. The kids who need the reinforcement the most to keep them in school, are those who are given the least reinforcement. It is clear that a simplified token system, like that proposed by O'Leary and Becker, requires a procedure for shaping improvement and the use of other reinforcers (including social reinforcers) to bridge the periods when tokens are not being given. Explicit training in the principles of behavior theory may also be important in allowing the teacher to improvise special program variations as the need arises.

O'Leary, et al (1969) placed a token system similar to that under discussion into a second grade classroom with a nucleus of boys who were difficult to manage. During the study, observational data were collected through eight different conditions. The conditions in order were (a) baseline period, (b) classroom rules added to baseline conditions, (c) educational structure added to condition b, (d) praise for appropriate behavior and ignoring of disruptive behavior were added to condition c, (e) tokens and backup reinforcement (prizes) added to the previous conditions, (f) return to condition d (reversal), (g) repetition of condition e (i.e., tokens, etc.), and (h) shift from tokens and prizes to stars for good behavior, which were backed up once a week by candy.

An analysis of the obtained data indicated that the token reinforcement program was effective in reducing disruptive behavior. The results also showed that a token system based on prizes could be shifted to one based on more commonly used classroom rewards, i.e., stars. Introduction of classroom rules had no effect on disruptive behavior. Educational structure, which was defined as an ordered routine each day of one activity following another, had no effect. Also, praise was not effective with the problem children in this group.

COMMENTS. Special reinforcement systems will most likely be used with groups of children who are atypical in some way. They promise the special educational teacher powerful approaches to problems which have been highly resistant to change with traditional methods. The complexities of initiating and fading out of token systems are such that we could recommend they be used only under the supervision of someone well-versed in behavioral analysis. As training in basics becomes more available, we can expect extensive applications of these procedures in the near future.

MINITOKEN SYSTEMS (INFORMAL DATA). Many of us working with teachers and their problems on a day-to-day basis have had to devise more effective reinforcement systems for single children in the classroom. In this section, we just want to mention briefly some procedures which have been tried and appear to work, even though objective data has not been collected.

1. Jimmy was aggressive and did not complete class assignments. The teacher worked out a procedure with mother so that Jimmy brought a note home each day he worked hard and was cooperative. With a note Jimmy could watch TV for a specified period that evening; without a note he could not. The note was a token or ticket earned for good classroom behavior which could be exchanged for the privilege of doing something Jimmy liked to do.

2. Aaron was a fourth grade boy from a deprived background. He would not get down to work in class, preferring to dawdle or play with his friends. He was often reported to be aggressive with younger children coming to and from school. Aaron earned checkmarks on the board, one check for each 10 minutes of good working behavior. If he earned 10 checks, he could spend 30 minutes in the kindergarten supervising younger boys in the use of carpentry tools. The younger children could use the tools only when he was there. They appreciated his coming. Aaron learned to work in the classroom, and work cooperatively with younger children.

3. The problem was how to manage the rowdiness, fighting, running, etc., that accompanies leaving school. The solution found was to train the patrol boys to record names of children who were well-behaved leaving school, rather than having them play policeman. The class with the most names recorded that week got a pennant for its door.

4. Jack earned an "X" on the board for each half day he did not fight in class. Initially four "Xs" earned a party for the whole class, e.g., Jack passed out a candy treat to all. Later he worked for 10 "Xs," etc.

5. Sloane and Allen at the University of Utah have had a number of teachers using a program they devised to train a child to remain in his seat for longer periods of time. The same program can be used for increasing on-task behavior, decreasing thumbsucking, or any one of a variety of other behaviors. The teacher sets a kitchen timer according to a variable schedule specified by the program. When the bell rings the teacher looks at the child and determines whether reinforcement is due or not. If the child is showing the target behavior when the bell goes off, the teacher nods to the child to cue him to record a mark on the ladder chart on his desk. When the 50 steps of the ladder are filled, the child can spend the points for a preselected activity or prize (the list of reinforcers is made ahead of time to include activities or tangibles the child would work for). The program slowly increases the time between bells. Then step by step, the timer, the chart, the points, and eventually the special reinforcers fade out. Most teachers whom we have had use the program have reported that it works well.

6. A number of teachers we have worked with have had their class members earn recess by showing good working habits. The general procedure is to determine about how long the available work time is and divide that by an average recess duration. The whole class then works to earn recess each day. For each 5, 8, 10, or 15 minute period of good working, one or more minutes of recess is earned. The formula should be set so that improved working will earn a slightly longer recess than is currently vailable "free." Some of our teachers have found this procedure to be effective; whereas, the contrary procedures of counting black marks which led to losing re-

cess often failed. The points-for-recess procedure can also be used with a single child in the class.

7. Kenney was being sent to see the social worker every time he had a tantrum or fought in class. Tantrums and fighting seemed to increase. After a discussion with the teacher and the social worker, it was decided that Kenny would have to earn time with the social worker by showing progressively improved classroom behaviors. Tantrums and fighting decreased rapidly.

In general, there are all sorts of reinforcers available to the teacher every day which only require a little ingenuity to detect and use. Anything that children will engage in readily can be used to reinforce behavior. "You can lead the pledge because you raised your hand." "Mary's row is ready and quiet with coats all buttoned. You may line up first." "Jim's finished his assignment. He can help me pass out these papers from yesterday." "Tony really worked hard during reading. What game would you like the class to play at recess?" The list of possible contingency statements of this sort is endless.

Summary—Change Procedure II

When the usual methods for reinforcing behavior do not work, it is necessary to find effective reinforcers. Often this means going back to more primary reinforcers like food, but any effective reinforcer will do. Token systems attempt to provide effective reinforcers by allowing a choice of possible items or activities for which tokens can be exchanged. Most token systems, which have been devised for use with special problems groups, require more manpower to operate than is typically available. Often, however, the extra manpower is worth the cost in terms of the benefit to the children. Our attempts to provide a simplified token system which could be used in a public school classroom have met with some success. But, at this point, it is recommended that similar programs be instituted only when professional consultation is available to help adapt the procedures to a particular setting and group of children. A number of less elaborate ways of strengthening the reinforcing consequences available to a child were discussed.

Change Procedure III: Punishment of Inappropriate Behaviors Combined with Reinforcement of Appropriate Behaviors

Certain stimulus events which occur following operant behaviors will weaken such behavior. Stimulus events with such properties are termed punishing stimuli; the process is termed punishment.

There has been little systematic investigation of punishment procedures in the elementary school classroom. Thomas, Becker, and Armstrong (1968) investigated the effects of frequency of criticism and O'Leary and Becker (1969) explored the effects of intensity of verbal reprimands. In the study by Thomas and others, criticisms were found not to function as punishers, but as reinforcers for misbehavior. O'Leary found that quiet reprimands were more effective than loud reprimands in controlling misbehavior during a rest period. Carlson, Arnold, Becker, and Madsen (1968) describe a case study in which restraint by a teacher aid was used as part of a program to eliminate tantrums by an 8-year-old girl. Being held in her chair until the tantrums ceased probably functioned as a punishing stimulus. This punishment procedure, however, was accompanied by the use of several reinforcement procedures. Peers were given candy for not paying attention to the girl when she tantrumed. The girl could earn stars toward a class party for each half day without tantrums. The tantrums were eliminated in 3 weeks.

Under proper conditions, punishment can be very effective in controlling behavior. Generally, however, we prefer not to use punishment procedures except in those few cases where problem behavior is so frequent that we would have no behavior to reinforce unless the problem behavior was first punished, or so intense that one could not safely risk the behavior occurring for fear of danger to the child or others.

Punishment procedures can take two forms: (1) presenting stimulus events following a response (e.g., a spanking), and (2) terminating stimulus events following a response (e.g., preventing the child from access to reinforcers which are usually available). We generally avoid using punishment which involves presenting stimuli (physical punishment), not because it can't be made to work, but because of the undesired side effects it has. We learn to avoid and escape from sources of punishment. If children are taught to avoid and escape from adults responsible for their socialization, the adults in effect lose control over the children. Avoidance and escape behaviors often have names such as lying, hiding, truancy, cheating on exams, doing things behind one's back, etc. Accompanying such avoidance and escape behaviors are negative feelings for the persons who use punishment. For the most part, the teacher is wise to find other means of influencing children.

Punishment by terminating reinforcing stimuli has been given many names. Deprivation of privileges and isolation is close to the currently popular technical term: time out. Repeated studies with varieties of problem children have demonstrated time out to be an effective method for punishing frequent and/or intense deviant behaviors. Time out is short for "time out from positive reinforcement." The term is to be preferred over isolation simply because it cues the user concerning important characteristics of the procedure. Unless there is a reinforcing state of affairs present, there can be no time out from it. Simply isolating a child from an otherwise neutral environment could not be expected to function as a punishment. An effective time out procedure requires a currently reinforcing state of affairs which is effectively stopped. Some teachers send children to the office, or into the halls as a kind of time out. If the children receive more attention in time out than they will behave badly in order to have such procedures repeated. Time out becomes reinforcing. Unless the ground work has been carefully prepared so that proper procedures and facilities are available for time out, the teacher is better off to use no punishment at all and focus on reinforcing incompatible behaviors. Punishment that doesn't work is likely to be reinforcing problem behaviors.

One final point to be considered is that whenever punishment procedures are used and are effective, there remains a choice in procedures: (1) keep up the punishment day by day, or (2) reinforce incompatible behavior while the rate of the punished behavior is low. Punished behavior will return to its prepunishment rate if punishment is withdrawn and the behavior can still pay off. Since most of us do not like to punish (it's hard on the punisher, too), we should always consider the reinforcement of behavior, incompatible with that which led to punishment, an important part of any punishment procedure. If the child is aggressive, we reinforce cooperative efforts. If the child blurts out a lot, we reinforce by asking him to raise his hand and wait for a turn to be called on.

Summary — Change Procedure III

Change Procedure III is a real option for the teacher. However, punishment procedures are not used extensively because of their undesired side effects. Although they are not needed very often, intelligent and selective use of punishment may be just what is required for some problem behaviors.

Recap of Key Procedures for Classroom Management

1. Specify in a positive way the rules which are the basis for your reinforcement. Demonstrate the behaviors you desire by praising the children who are good examples of following the rules. Rules are made important to children by providing reinforcement for following the rules. Rules may be different for different work, study, or play periods. Keep the rules to five or less. As the children learn to follow the rules, repeat them less frequently, but continue to praise good classroom behaviors.
2. Relate the children's performance to the rules. Be specific about the behaviors children show which mean "paying attention" or "working hard." "That's right, you're a hard worker." "You

watched the board all the time I was presenting the example. That's paying attention." "That's a good answer. You listened very closely to my question." "Jimmy is really working hard. He'll get the answer. You'll see." "Gee, you got it. I didn't think you would. That's good working." Relax the rules between work periods. Don't be afraid to have fun with your children when the work period is over.

3. Catch the children being good. Reinforce behavior incompatible with that you wish to eliminate. Select incompatible behaviors to reinforce which will be most beneficial to the child's development. Focus on reinforcing tasks important for social and cognitive skills in the process of eliminating disruptive behaviors.

4. Ignore disruptive behaviors unless someone is getting hurt. Focus your attention on the children who are working well to prompt the correct behaviors in the children who are misbehaving. Reinforce improvement when it does occur.

5. When you see a persistent problem behavior, look for the reinforcing events. It may be your own behavior.

6. You can use as a reinforcer any activity the child likes to participate in, as well as social attention, praise, or more tangible reinforcers.

7. In looking for reinforcers to use to strengthen behaviors remember these:

reinforcers controlled by parents	being right
the social worker's attention	being first
games and puzzles	toys and edibles
honors and privileges	trinkets
helping teacher	a class party
playing teacher's role	art activities
recess	music
praise and attention	extra gym periods

8. Reinforcing events must immediately follow the behavior to be strengthened.

9. Social reinforcers do not work for all children. When necessary to get appropriate behavior going, strengthen the reinforcers being used.

10. If a point system backed up by tangibles or special activities is introduced, always accompany the points given with praise and words telling the children what they did well. These steps will help make praise alone effective as a reinforcer, as well as completing the tasks which are the basis for reinforcement. "You finished all of your arithmetic problems. That really pleases me.

I'm giving you nine points for that." Relate the payoff to what he did to earn it. "You earned this model airplane by working really hard on arithmetic and reading. I'm proud of your improvement." Slowly require the child to work for longer periods with less tangible payoffs, but give lots of praise and other forms of social reinforcement.

11. Seek special training or consultation if elaborate token systems seem to be the answer for you.

12. Punishment is most likely to be required when the unwanted behavior is very intense (so that there is potential danger to self or others) or very frequent (so that there is little positive behavior to work with).

13. If punishment is necessary, first try isolating the child in a room by himself with only a chair and a light. The child should remain in the time out room until he is quiet for several minutes. Give one warning prior to the use of time out, so that the warning signal can be used most of the time as a punishment without the need for time out.

14. Any use of punishment should be accompanied by the use of reinforcement of behaviors incompatible with the punished behaviors.

15. Hold consistently to your rules for reinforcement, extinction, or punishment. This means do not sometimes reinforce and sometimes punish the same behavior. Do not give in after deciding a behavior should not be reinforced. Only if you show consistent reactions to the children's behaviors can they learn what is reinforced and what is not.

The Future

In this review, we have focused mainly on *consequent* stimulus events and how the teacher can use them to motivate more effective classroom behaviors. One must also be very concerned with the academic program provided the child in order to achieve long-term improvements in classroom behavior. Academic programs mainly deal with stimulus events which precede operant behaviors. Generically, we call such stimuli *discriminative stimuli*. They involve such things as members of concept classes, cues and prompts, instructions, and questions. New strategies for concept teaching and the programming of effective instruction for every child are now under development and are being tested. Engelmann's (1969a, 1969b) recent publications in this area outline some exciting possibilities for the improvement of teaching techniques, and provide very practical suggestions *now* for the teacher wishing to do a better job of instruction.

References

Baer, D. M. Remedial use of the reinforcement contingency. Paper presented at the Annual Convention of the American Psychological Association, Chicago, Illinois, 1966.

Becker, W. C., Madsen, C. H. Jr., Arnold, Carole R., and Thomas, D. R. The contingent use of teacher attention and praise in reducing classroom behavior problems. *Journal of Special Education*, 1967, **1**, 287–307.

Bijou, S. W., Peterson, R. F., and Ault, M. H. A method to integrate descriptive and experimental field studies at the level of data and empirical concepts. *Journal of Applied Behavior Analysis*, 1968, **1**, 175–191.

Birnbrauer, J. S., Wolf, M. M., Kidder, J. D., and Tague, Cecilia E. Classroom behavior of retarded pupils with token reinforcement. *Journal of Experimental Child Psychology*, 1965, **2**, 219–235.

Buell, Joan, Stoddard, Patricia, Harris, Florence R., and Baer, D. M. Collateral social development accompanying reinforcement of outdoor play in a preschool child. *Journal of Applied Behavior Analysis*, 1968, **1**, 167–173.

Carlson, Constance S., Arnold, Carole R., Becker, W. C., and Madsen, C. H. The elimination of tantrum behavior of a child in an elementary classroom. *Behavior Research and Therapy*, 1968, **6**, 117–119.

Carnine, D., Becker, W. C., Thomas, D. R., Poe, Meridith, and Plager, Elaine. The effects of direct and "vicarious" reinforcement on the behavior of problem boys in an elementary school classroom. Unpublished manuscript, Bureau of Educational Research, University of Illinois, 1968.

Engelmann, Siegfried. *Preventing Failure in the Primary Grades*. Chicago: Science Research Associates, 1969a.

Engelmann, Siegfried. *Conceptual Learning*. San Rafael, California: Dimensions Publishing Co., 1969b.

Girardeau, F. L., and Spradlin, J. E. Token rewards in a cottage program. *Mental Retardation*, 1964, **2**, 345–351.

Hall, R., Lund, Diane, and Jackson, Deloris. Effects of teacher attention on study behavior. *Journal of Applied Behavior Analysis*, 1968, **1**, 1–12.

Haring, N. G., and Lovitt, T. C. Operant methodology and educational technology in special education. In N. G. Haring and R. Schiefelbusch (Eds.), *Methods in Special Education*. New York: McGraw Hill (in press).

Harris, Florence R., Johnston, Margaret K., Kelley, C. Susan, and Wolf, M. M. Effects of positive social reinforcement on regressed crawling of a nursery school child. *Journal of Educational Psychology*, 1964, **55**, 35–41.

Hart, Betty M., Reynolds, Nancy J., Baer, Donald M., Brawley, Eleanor R., and Harris, Florence R. Effect of contingent and non-contingent social reinforcement on the cooperative play of a preschool child. *Journal of Applied Behavior Analysis*, 1968, **1**, 73–76.

Hawkins, R. P., Peterson, R. F., Schweid, Edda, and Bijou, S. W. Behavior therapy in the home: Amelioration of problem parent-child relations with the parent in a therapeutic role. *Journal of Experimental Child Psychology*, 1966, **4**, 99–107.

Kuypers, D. S., Becker, W. C., and O'Leary, K. D. How to make a token system fail. *Exceptional Children*, 1968, **35**, 101–109.

Madsen, C. H. Jr., Becker, W. C., and Thomas, D. R. Rules, praise, and ignoring: Elements of elementary classroom control. *Journal of Applied Behavior Analysis*, 1968, **1**, 139–150.

Madsen, C. H. Jr., Becker, W. C., Thomas, D. R., Koser, Linda, and Plager, Elaine. An analysis of the reinforcing function of "sit down" commands. In Parker, R. K. (Ed.), *Readings in Educational Psychology*. Boston: Allyn and Bacon, 1968.

O'Leary, K. D., and Becker, W. C. Behavior modification of an adjustment class: A token reinforcement program. *Exceptional Children*, 1967, 34, 637–642.

O'Leary, K. D., and Becker, W. C. The effects of intensity of a teacher's reprimands on children's behavior. *Journal of School Psychology*, 1968, 7, 8–11.

O'Leary, K. D., Becker, W. C., Evans, M. B., and Saudargas, R. A token reinforcement program in a public school: A replication and a systematic analysis. *Journal of Applied Behavior Analysis*, 1969, 2(1), 3–13.

Staats, A. W., and Butterfield, W. H. Treatment of nonreading in a culturally-deprived juvenile delinquent: An application of reinforcement principles. *Child Development*, 1965, 36, 925–942.

Thomas, D. R., Becker, W. C., and Armstrong, Marianne. Production and elimination of disruptive classroom behavior by systematically varying teacher's behavior. *Journal of Applied Behavioral Analysis*, 1968, 1, 35–45.

Thomas, D. R., Nielson, Loretta J., Kuypers, D. S., and Becker, W. C. Social reinforcement and remedial instruction in the elimination of a classroom behavior problem. *Journal of Special Education*, 1968, 2, 291–305.

Thorne, G. L., Tharp, R. G., and Wetzel, R. J. Behavior modification techniques: New tools for probation officers. *Federal Probation*, June 1967, 21–27.

Varna Garis, Ann, and Becker, W. C. Effects of remedial tutoring and social reinforcement by teachers on classroom behavior problems. Unpublished manuscript, Bureau of Educational Research, University of Illinois, 1969.

Wahler, R. G. Child-child interactions in free field settings: Some experimental analyses. *Journal of Experimental Child Psychology*, 1967, 5, 278–293.

Wolf, M. M. Giles, D. K., and Hall, R. V. Experiments with token reinforcement in a remedial classroom. *Behavior Research and Therapy*, 1968, 6, 51–64.

12

The Diagnosis and Treatment of Behavior Disorders of Children

Willard C. Olson
University of Michigan

I. Objectives

Sufficient knowledge to diagnose, predict, and control behavior is an ideal goal for the classroom teacher, as well as for the technical student of psychology. Behavior, broadly defined to include overt expression and inward responses, embraces the whole range of the school program as it affects children. The intent of this section, however, is to use the term 'behavior' in its narrower sense as pertaining to the overt action and mental and physical correlates of action of children in fields not covered by measures of achievement in subject matter and skill. Behavior of this type is often discussed under the terms 'conduct,' 'attitudes,' 'character,' or 'personality,' with an inclusiveness in the order named.

The objectives of constructive, preventive, and remedial work in social and emotional adjustment are in a broad sense the goals of all education. More specifically, however, students of the process are concerned with the development of desirable human relations while enhancing the personal satisfactions gained from interactions in the social group. In general, clinical workers have been concerned with

From *Educational Diagnosis*, 34th Yearbook, National Society for Study of Education. Bloomington, Ill.: Public School Publishing Co., 1935.

extreme deviation and more commonly with deviation in the direction of inefficiency, discomfort, economic loss, and social stigma. As problems and methods have become clearer, there has emerged a philosophy of mental hygiene that envisages a constant planning for individual and social betterment for all. Teachers are rapidly coming to feel the desirability of an acquaintance with the general principles and methods of work that have evolved. . . .

V. General Principles of Treatment

1. Multiple Causation and Varied Approach

The problem presented by a given child is always unique. The multiple nature of causation in the field of behavior precludes the writing of any simple, uniform prescription for behavior disorders. Practice is still in the stage where frequently there is no precise agreement on the specific procedures to be recommended. Behavior problems do not emerge as isolated phenomena, and a specific maladjustment is likely to carry with it some degree of general maladjustment. For example, there is frequently a concomitant occurrence of inability to read and certain related emotional or behavior disturbances, and it is often difficult to determine which is antecedent and which is consequent. From the treatment point of view, if you can help any aspect of the total picture, you are likely to help all, particularly if the approach is fundamental and related to the causative framework. If the approach is not so related, the submergence of one disorder may simply be signalled by the appearance of another.

2. What is Symptomatic Treatment?

In general the formulation, "Treat causes, not symptoms," is sound, in that it tends to force a study of the factors behind the symptoms. There has appeared, however, from time to time, an uncritical condemnation of the treatment of symptoms in behavior problems—a condemnation based on mere analogy with organic disease or on a wholesale acceptance of theories of behavior causation that reject the formulations of the academic psychology of learning. If the symptom is the result of the repetition of some phase of behavior that has satisfying consequences, there is a clear analogy to the laws of learning as formulated in the acquisition of skill and information or through the experimentation with conditioned reflexes. If such is the case, the removal of the symptom through direct work on a learning basis is synonymous with cure. This view is, of course, heretical to many persons dominated by other systematic approaches.

Nursery schools and other schools are constantly demonstrating that behavior problems in normal children can be modified through the same direct attacks characteristic of learning in other fields. Whether such an attack is fundamental depends on whether contributory factors have been properly sought and accepted or rejected as the major source of the disturbance. It is futile, of course, to direct a training approach to a problem where an organic defect is the basic factor. It is equally futile to argue that social and emotional learnings have nothing in common with intellect and skill. Our expanding boundaries of knowledge should presently bring about a concurrence among the controversial issues involved. There is already a growing tendency in clinical practice to avoid carrying the level of analysis and treatment to a point beyond that needed to effect the desired changes. In many situations the teacher will find little success in a direct approach on a symptomatic basis. Effective work will usually require an indirect approach through multiple underlying etiological factors.

Some general principles for behavior management through environment will serve to suggest numerous applications to the thoughtful teacher. The procedures should not be considered solely as methods for solving behavior problems or for immediate control, since they are of broader application and carry with them the possibility of the modification, through learning, of the organism itself.

3. The Principle of the Graded Stimulus

Whenever a child meets what is to him a radically different situation, the possibility of inadequate response arises. The corollary is that adequate adjustment to new situations is fostered by a gradually increasing application of the given stimulus.

The general principle may be illustrated by what happens to young children upon first encountering the school environment. Table I, based on entering kindergarten children, shows the percentage who indicate some maladjustment by crying upon each of the five opening days of school. The percentages are often higher in nursery schools. Gradual adaptation to the new situation is indicated in the table. The experience of workers suggests that the situation is much improved by (1) spreading the introduction of children over a few days, (2) having the child and parent visit the school in advance, and (3) planning to avoid extraneous disturbances or lack of equipment incident to the opening of school. The detailed psychology of the process need not be discussed here.

Other examples are to be found in the gradual exclusion of light where a child has been conditioned to sleeping with a light, the gradual lengthening of the child-control period in the treatment of enuresis, and the gradual withdrawal of an adult from a setting where he has taken responsibility for some aspect of a child's behavior. In a general philosophy of development it is, of course, clear that the pertinence of the principle in given situations changes at different ages. The college orientation week represents a recognition of the same principle.

TABLE 1

The Adjustment of Kindergarten Children to the First Five Days of School
as Reflected in the Disappearance of Crying as a Symptom

Day	Boys (N = 82)		Girls (N = 77)		Total (N = 159)	
	Number	Percentage	Number	Percentage	Number	Percentage
First	8	9.8	4	5.2	12	7.5
Second	4	4.9	2	2.6	6	3.8
Third	3	3.7	1	1.3	4	2.5
Fourth	1	1.2	2	2.6	3	1.9
Fifth	1	1.2	1	1.3	2	1.3

4. The Principle of the Added Stimulus

Response does not occur in the absence of stimulus (external or internal). Modifications of the organism, apart from maturity, do not occur without stimulation. After an analysis of a situation, missing stimuli may be added for treatment purposes. We shall not pause here to consider the large changes in school and home regimen that are often recommended after analysis on the basis of this general principle.

> Let us borrow an actual illustration of a more subtle use of the formulation. John, upon entering the nursery school, withdrew from other members of the group, appeared insecure concerning his status, and was unable to establish contacts. After analysis of the situation, the teacher procured a toy that was entirely new and arranged the setting so that John was the first to secure it. The stimulus value of the toy, added to that of John himself, produced responses toward him on the part of other members of the group. The resultant enhancement of self feelings (ego) on the part of John was, subjectively at least, the beginning of an expanding process of socialization.

5. The Principle of the Subtracted Stimulus

Since behavior may be thought of as a release of energy set off by a stimulus, particular behavior may be controlled and gradually modified by the removal of stimuli conducive to undesirable or undesired responses. Thus, in the treatment of nervous, over-active children, a line of action may be based on the reduction of sensory bombardment through simplification of the environment. The same principle is applied in the relaxation and sleeping programs of some schools.

6. The Use of Language in the Control and Modification of Behavior

The universality of the use of language in human relations makes it a tool of large actual and potential importance in the control and modification of child behavior. Scattered studies on the use of praise and reproof, or on the effect of the simple formula, 'Right' and 'Wrong,' indicate the importance of a more conscious use of the tool.

> Some of the finer nuances in language control are now being studied by Wilker in the child development laboratories at the University of Michigan. She has experimented with the effect of variation in the language formula on the behavior elicited in a large number of situations. Experimental and control groups have been employed with various criteria on the efficacy of control. In general, she finds that effective response is secured in so far as the words used are directive and point to the desired goal. Words that block action rather than direct attention along the desired line are clearly to be avoided. 'Do' is more effective than 'Don't.' Words should be encouraging rather than discouraging and point to success rather than failure. Words must be selected that have some relation to the child's stage of learning, and they are more effective when accompanied by the postural, gestural, emotional, or material influences necessary to help the child respond to them.
>
> A study in progress by Olson and Wilkinson at the University of Michigan suggests that the effective teaching personality as a whole is indicated, at least in part, by the nature of the language used by the teacher in the control of behavior. Sheer quantity of verbalism seems to be relatively unimportant. The extent, however, to which the teacher is positive and constructive in her words used for behavior control is an item of some importance. The teachers with the most favorable general ratings avoid negative statements. Similarly, the effective teacher directs her statements to the person she wishes to reach and does not, from irritability, indulge in blanket responses to the class of children as a whole.

When one considers the cumulative effect over the years of the type of language control to which children are subjected, the possibilities of desirable and undesirable responses to the language influence of associates may readily be appreciated.

7. Manual Guidance as Treatment Technique

In general, in work with older children, a 'hands off' policy is indicated for behavior control and modification. Educational workers with children, however, do make use of manual control in securing behavior of desired types. It is usually necessary to affect a child's feelings, thoughts, and actions in order to secure desirable behavior outcomes. Guiding the thoughts and actions of a child through remote control does not always secure the desired result. The general laws of habit formation suggest that, if the outcome is a desirable one, the stimulus used must be attached to a desired response if the behavior is to be secured in the future in response to similar stimuli. Nursery-school teachers who employ the habit approach give manual assistance in the case of faulty food habits, toilet habits, or sleep habits. The efficacy of the procedure can easily be demonstrated, and the practice will probably be continued as long as no disputing evidence is forthcoming. It must be said, however, that giving manual guidance is a skilled performance and giving it firmly, unemotionally, and patiently comes only with extensive training. For the uninitiated, the technique may merge very easily into punishment and may then arouse anger responses in the recipient of the attention. Judgment and knowledge must also be exercised to determine whether the objective sought is desirable or necessary at the age of the child who is the subject of the teacher's attention.

8. Physical Punishment as Treatment Technique

Spanking and other forms of corporal punishment have largely disappeared as an element in the management of modern schools. Today it is considered a sign of inefficiency and incompetence for a teacher to resort to striking or pulling ears and hair, and such behavior is seldom encountered on the part of emotionally well-adjusted teachers. The shift away from physical punishment has in part been a deduction from the experimental studies of learning in animals and the accumulation of evidence that directive and rewarding methods are much more effective than punishment. Physical punishment also carries with it the possibilities of complications, such as sex stimulation, injury, or legal action. Most psychiatrists, psychologists, teachers, and social workers are agreed concerning the undesirability of physical punishment. It remains as a home practice, particularly with young children, for a large number of parents. As a rule, the better the education and social background of the parent, the less frequently is spanking adopted as the method of punishment. Physical punishment leading to submissiveness or revolt has no place in the philosophy of the modern school, which looks forward to coöperative activity.

9. The Isolation Technique in Treatment

In general, the careful teacher attempts to avoid situations in which a child is given the feeling of being cut off from a group. An occasional child, however, may 'go to pieces' so completely as to disrupt either the comfort or activities of his associates in a room. Nursery-school teachers, in particular, have found it highly advantageous to remove such a child from the group to a place where he may relax and acquire control without being a distracting influence or attracting the attention he may be seeking. In some instances special rooms have been set aside for this purpose. The isolation technique must be used skillfully in order to be an educational experience for the child, gradually modifying him in the direction of greater control. This goal may be defeated if the child regards the treatment simply as punishment and develops a feeling of antagonism toward the teacher.

The isolation technique in the simple sense of 'social distance' has also been used successfully in the management of eating and sleeping problems. The thoughtful teacher will make a careful study of the situation in order to promote the welfare of both the group and the individual. She should be ready to vary her technique sympathetically in terms of the developing situation.

10. The Equipment of the Playground and Room as Treatment Technique

Current investigations suggest that the selection and management of equipment is an important factor in the armament of the modern teacher in her development and control of behavior in the room. The simple addition of constructive play material on a playground has been shown to make a large increase in the coöperative activity that occurs and a marked reduction in the amount of fighting and quarreling. Similarly, certain types of equipment tend toward the practice of individualistic play, while other types lead to the promotion of group contact and extroverted activity. The teacher who is not familiar with the possibilities in this direction can be aided enormously by simple suggestions concerning the arrangement of centers of interest in the classroom or on the playground. Equipment can be managed to promote harmoniously both individual and group objectives.

B.

Examples of Studies Using Social Reinforcers

13

Technical Glossary

PHRASE TO BE USED IN RESEARCH REPORT	TRANSLATION
"It has long been known that . . ."	I haven't bothered to look up the original reference.
"While it has not been possible to provide definite answers to these questions . . ."	The experiments didn't work out, but I figured I could at least get publicity out of it.
"high purity" "very high purity" "extremely high purity"	Composition unknown except for the exaggerated claim of the supplier.
"accidentally stained during mounting"	Dropped on the floor.

From *The Scientist Speculates,* edited by Irving John Good, Alan James Mayne, and John Maynard Smith. New York: Basic Books, 1962.

"handled with extreme care throughout the experiments"

Not dropped on the floor.

"It is clear that much additional work will be required before a complete understanding . . ."

I don't understand it.

"Unfortunately, a quantitative theory to account for these effects has not been formulated."

Neither does anyone else.

"It is hoped that this work will stimulate further work in the field."

This paper isn't very good, but neither are any of the others on this miserable subject.

"of great theoretical and practical importance"

Interesting to me.

"Three of the samples were chosen for detailed study."

The results on the others didn't make sense and were ignored.

"These results will be reported at a later date."

I might possibly get around to this sometime.

"It might be argued that . . ."

I have such a good answer to this objection that I shall now raise it.

"Although some detail has been lost in reproduction, it is clear from the original micrograph that . . ."

It is impossible to tell from the micrograph.

"The most reliable values are those of Jones."

He was a student of mine.

"It is suggested . . ." "It is believed that . . ."

I think.

"It is generally believed that . . ."

A couple of other guys think so too.

14

Effects of Adult Social Reinforcement on Child Behavior

Florence R. Harris, *University of Washington*
Montrose M. Wolf, *University of Kansas*
Donald M. Baer, *University of Kansas*

There is general agreement among educators that one of the primary functions of a nursery school is to foster in each child social behaviors that contribute toward more pleasant and productive living for all. However, there is no similar consensus as to precisely how this objective is to be attained. Many writers subscribe to practices based on a combination of psychoanalytic theory and client-centered therapy principles, usually referred to as a mental hygiene approach. Yet there is considerable variation and vagueness in procedures recommended, particularly those dealing with such problem behaviors as the child's hitting people, breaking valuable things, or withdrawing from both people and things. Read (1955), for example, recommends accepting the child's feelings, verbalizing them for him, and draining them off through vigorous activities. Landreth (1942) advises keeping adult contacts with the child at a minimum based on his needs, backing up verbal suggestions by an implicit assumption that the suggestion will be carried out, and, when in doubt, doing nothing unless the child's physical safety is involved.

Reprinted from *The Young Child: Reviews of Research*, Willard W. Hartup and Nancy L. Smothergill (eds.), National Association for the Education of Young Children, 1967. These studies were supported in part by research grants from the National Institute of Mental Health (MH-02208-07) and the University of Washington Graduate School Research Fund (11-1873). The authors are also indebted to Sidney W. Bijou for his general counsel and assistance.

In addition to some of the above precepts, Taylor (1954) counsels parents and teachers to support both desirable and undesirable behaviors and to give nonemotional punishment. According to Standing (1959), Montessori advocates that teachers pursue a process of nonintervention, following careful preparation of a specified environment aimed at "Canalizing the energy" and developing "inner command." Nonintervention does not preclude the "minimum dose" of instruction and correction.

Using some combination of such guidance precepts, teachers have reported success in helping some nursery school children who showed problem behaviors, but sometimes adherence to the same teaching principles has not been helpful in modifying the behavior of concern. Indeed, it is usually not at all clear what conditions and principles may or may not have been operative. All of these precepts have in common the adult behaviors of approaching and attending to a child. Therefore, it seemed to the staff of the Laboratory Preschool at the University of Washington that a first step in developing possible explicit criteria for judging when and when not to attend was to study the precise effects that adult attention can have on some problem behaviors.

This paper presents an account of the procedures and results of five such studies. Two groups of normal nursery school children provided the subjects studied. One group enrolled 12 3-year-olds and the other, 16 4-year-olds. The two teachers of the younger group and the three teachers of the older group conducted the studies as they carried out their regular teaching duties. The general methodology of these studies was developed in the course of dealing with a particularly pressing problem behavior shown by one child at the beginning of the school year. It is worth considering this case before describing the procedures which evolved from it.

The study dealt with a 3-year-old girl who had regressed to an excessive amount of crawling (Harris, Johnston, Kelley, & Wolf, 1964). By "excessive" is meant that after three weeks of school she was spending most of her morning crawling or in a crouched position with her face hidden. The parents reported that for some months the behavior had been occurring whenever they took her to visit or when friends came to their home. The teachers had used the conventional techniques, as outlined above, for building the child's "security."

Observations recorded in the third week at school showed, however, that more than 80% of the child's time was spent in off-feet positions. The records also showed that the crawling behavior frequently drew the attention of teachers. On-feet behaviors, such as standing and walking, which occurred infrequently, seldom drew such notice.

A program was instituted in which the teachers no longer attended to the child whenever she was crawling or crouching, but gave her continuous warm attention as long as she was engaging in behavior in which she was standing, running, or walking. Initially the only upright behaviors that the teachers were able to attend to occurred when the child pulled herself almost to her feet in order to hang up or take down her coat from her locker and when she pulled herself up to wash her hands in the wash basin. Within a week of the initiation of the new attention-giving procedure, the child acquired a close-to-normal pattern of on-feet behavior.

In order to see whether the change from off- to on-feet behavior was related to the differential attention given by the teachers, they reversed their procedure, making attention once again contingent only upon crawling and other off-feet behavior. They waited for occasions of such off-feet behavior to "reinforce" with attention, while not attending to any on-feet behavior. By the second day the child had reverted to her old pattern of play and locomotion. The observational records showed the child was off her feet 80% of the class session.

To see whether on-feet behavior could be reestablished, the teachers again reversed their procedure, giving attention to the child only when she was engaging in behaviors involving upright positions. On-feet behavior rose markedly during the first session. By the fourth day, the child again spent about 62% of the time on her feet. Once the child was not spending the greater portion of her day crawling about, she quickly became a well-integrated member of the group. Evidently she already had well-developed social play skills. As a result of this demonstration that either walking or crawling could be maintained and that the child's responses depended largely upon the teachers' attending behaviors, the teachers began a series of further experimental analyses of the relationship between teacher attention and nursery school child behavior.

Procedures

A specified set of procedures common to the next studies was followed. First, a child showing problem behavior was selected and records were secured. An observer recorded all of the child's behavior, the environmental conditions under which it occurred, and its immediate consequences under conventional teacher guidance. This was done throughout the 2½-hour school session, daily, and for several days. The records gave detailed pictures of the behavior under study. In each case, it became apparent that the problem behavior almost always succeeded in attracting adult attention.

As soon as these records, technically termed "baseline" records, of the typical behavior of the child and teachers were obtained, teachers instituted a program of systematically giving differential attention to the child. When the undesired behavior occurred, they did not in any way attend to him, but remained absorbed in one of the many necessary activities of teachers with other children or with equipment. If the behavior occurred while a teacher was attending to the child, she at once turned to another child or task in a matter-of-fact and nonrejecting manner. Concurrently, teachers gave immediate attention to other behaviors of the child which were considered to be more desirable than the problem behavior. The net effect of these procedures was that the child could gain a great deal of adult attention if he refrained from engaging in "problem behavior." If under this regime of differential attention the problem behavior diminished to a stable low level at which it was no longer considered a problem, a second procedure was inaugurated to check out the functional relationship between changes in the child's behavior and the guidance procedures followed.

The second procedure was simply to reverse the first procedure. That is, when the problem behavior occurred, the teacher went immediately to the child and gave him her full, solicitous attention. If the behavior stopped, she turned to other children and tasks, remaining thus occupied until the behavior recurred. In effect, one sure way for the child to secure adult attention was to exhibit the problem behavior. This procedure was used to secure reasonably reliable information on whether the teachers' special program had indeed brought about the changes noted in the child's behavior. If adult attention was the critical factor in maintaining the behavior, the problem behavior should recur in stable form under these conditions. If it did so, this was evidence that adult attention was, technically speaking, a positive social reinforcer for the child's behavior.

The final stage of a study was, of course, to return to procedures in which attention was given at once and continuously for behaviors considered desirable. Concurrently, adult attention was again withheld or withdrawn as an immediate consequence of the problem behavior. As the problem disappeared and appropriate behaviors increased, the intense program of differential adult attention was gradually diminished until the child was receiving attention at times and in amounts normal for the teachers in the group. However, attention was given only on occasions of desirable behavior and never (or very seldom) for the undesirable behavior.

Crying and Whining

Following the above procedures, a study was conducted on a 4-year-old boy who cried a great deal after mild frustrations (Hart, Allen, Buell, Harris, & Wolf, 1964). This child averaged about eight full-fledged crying episodes each school morning. The baseline observa-

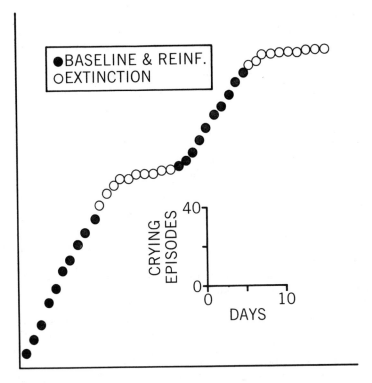

Fig. 1. Cumulative record of the daily number of crying episodes

tions showed that this crying behavior consistently brought attention from the teachers, in the form of going to him and showing solicitous concern. During the following days, this behavior was simply ignored.(The only exceptions to this were to have been incidents in which the child had hurt himself considerably and was judged to have genuine grounds for crying. Naturally, his hurts were to be attended to. Such incidents, however, did not occur.) Ten days of ignoring the outcries, but giving approving attention for verbal and self-help behaviors, produced a steady weakening of the crying response to a nearly zero level. In the final five days of the interval, only one crying response was recorded. The number of crying episodes on successive days is graphed in cumulative form in Fig. 1.

During the next 10 days, crying was again reinforced whenever it occurred, the teachers attending to the boy on these occasions without fail. At first, it was necessary to give attention for mere grimaces that might follow a bump. The daily crying episodes quickly rose to a rate almost as high as formerly. A second 10-day period of ignoring the outcries again produced a quick weakening of the response to a near-zero level, as is apparent in the figure. Crying remained at this low level thereafter, according to the informal judgment of the teachers.

The same procedures were used in another study of "operant crying" of a 4-year-old boy, with the same general results.

Isolate Play

Two studies involved children who exhibited markedly solitary play behavior. Extremely little of their morning at nursery school was spent in any interaction with other children. Instead, these children typically played alone in a quiet area of the school room or the play yard, or interacted only with the teachers. For present purposes, both of these response patterns will be called "isolate play." Systematic observation showed that isolate play usually attracted or maintained the attention of a teacher, whereas social play with other children did so comparatively seldom.

A plan was initiated in which the teacher was to attend regularly if the child approached other children and interacted with them. On the other hand, the teacher was not to attend to the child so long as he engaged in solitary play. To begin with, attention was given when the child merely stood nearby, watching other children; then when he played beside another child; and finally, only when he interacted with the other child. Teachers had to take special precautions that their attending behaviors did not result in drawing the child away from children and into interaction solely with the teacher. Two techniques were found particularly effective. The teacher directed her looks and comments to the other child or children, including the subject only as a participant in the play project. For example, "That's a big building you three boys are making; Bill and Tom and Jim (subject) are all working hard." Accessory materials were also kept at hand so that the teacher could bring a relevant item for the subject to add to the play: "Here's another plate for your tea party, Ann." In both isolate cases this new routine for giving adult attention produced the desired result. Isolate play declined markedly in strength while social play increased two- or three-fold.

After about a week of the above procedure, the consequences of nonisolate and isolate play were reversed. The teachers no longer attended to the child's interactions with other children, but instead gave continuous attention to the child when he was alone. Within a week, or less, isolate play became the dominant form of activity in both cases.

The former contingencies were then reinstated. The teachers attended to social interactions by the child and ignored isolate play as completely as they could. Again, isolate play declined sharply while social interaction increased as before. The results of one of

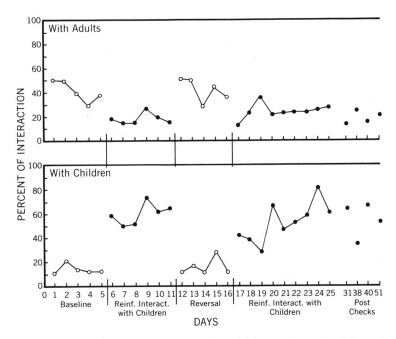

Fig. 2. Daily percentages of time spent in social interaction with adults and with children during approximately two hours of each morning session

these studies (Allen, Hart, Buell, Harris, & Wolf, 1964) are summarized in Fig. 2.

Figure 2 shows the changes in behavior of a 4½-year-old girl under the different guidance conditions. The graph shows the percentage of play time that she spent in interaction with other children and the percentage of time spent with an adult. The remainder of her time was spent alone. It is apparent that only about 15% of this child's play time was spent in social play as long as the teachers attended primarily to her solitary play. But interacting behaviors rose to about 60% of total play time when the teachers attended only to her social play. At the same time, her interactions solely with teachers, not being reinforced, fell from their usual 40% of the child's play time to about 20%. These were considered reasonable percentages for this nursery school child. During Days 17–25 the schedule of adult reinforcement of social play was gradually reduced to the usual amount of attention, given at the usual irregular intervals. Nevertheless the social behavior maintained its strength, evidently becoming largely self-maintaining.

After Day 25, the teachers took care not to attend too often to the child when she was alone, but otherwise planned no special contingencies for attending. Four checks were made at later dates to see if the pattern of social behavior persisted. It is apparent (Fig. 2, post-checks) that the change was durable, at least until Day 51. Further checks were not possible because of the termination of the school year.

A parallel study of a 3-year-old isolate boy (Johnston, Kelley, Harris, Wolf, & Baer, 1964) yielded similar results showing the same pattern of rapid behavioral change in response to changing contingencies of adult attention. In the case of this boy, post-checks were made on three days during the early months of the school year following the summer vacation period. The data showed that on those days his interaction with children averaged 55% of his play time. Apparently his social play was well established. Teachers reported that throughout the remainder of the year he continued to develop ease and skills in playing with his peers.

The immediate shifts in these children's play behavior may be partly due to the fact that they had already developed skills readily adapted to play with peers at school. Similar studies in progress have shown that, for some children, development of social play behaviors may require much longer periods of reinforcement.

Excessive Passivity

A fifth case (Johnston, Kelley, Harris, & Wolf, 1966) involved a boy noted for his thoroughgoing lack of any sort of vigorous play activity. The teachers reported that this child consistently stood quietly about the play yard while other children ran, rode tricycles, and climbed on special climbing frames, trees, fences, and playhouses. Teachers also reported that they frequently attempted to encourage him, through suggestions or invitations, to engage in the more vigorous forms of play available. Teachers expressed concern over his apparent lack of strength and motor skills. It was decided to select a particular form of active play to attempt to strengthen. A wooden frame with ladders and platforms, called a climbing frame, was chosen as the vehicle for establishing this activity. The teachers attended at first to the child's mere proximity to the frame. As he came closer, they progressed to attending only to his touching it, climbing up a little, and finally to extensive climbing. Technically, this was reinforcement of successive approximations to climbing behavior. Figure 3 shows the results of nine days of this procedure, compared to a baseline of the preceding nine days. In this figure, black bars represent climbing on the climbing frame, and white bars represent climbing on any other equipment in the play yard. The height of the bars shows the percentage of the child's play time spent in such activities. It is clear that during the baseline period less than 10% of the child's time was spent in any sort of climbing activity, but that during the course of reinforcement with pleased adult attention for climbing on the frame, this behavior greatly increased, finally exceeding 50% of

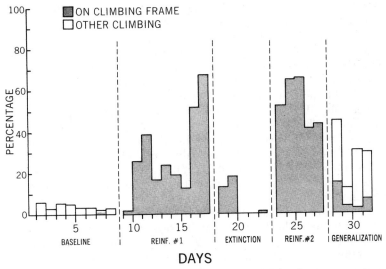

Fig. 3. Daily percentages of time spent in using climbing-frame apparatus. Open bars indicate time spent in climbing on other equipment.

the child's morning. (Climbing on other objects was not scored during this period.) There then followed five days during which the teachers ignored any climbing on the frame, but attended to all other appropriate activities. The rate of climbing on the frame promptly fell virtually to zero, though the child climbed on other apparatus and was consistently given attention for this. Another five days of reinforcement for use of the climbing frame immediately restored the climbing-frame behavior to a high stable level, always in excess of 40% of the boy's play time. After this, the teachers began an intermittent program of reinforcement for climbing on any other suitable objects, as well as vigorous active play of all sorts, in an effort to generalize the increased vigorous activity. Frame-climbing weakened considerably, being largely replaced by other climbing activities, which were now scored again as data. Activities such as tricycle-riding and running were not systematically recorded due to difficulties in reliably scoring them. It is clear from the data obtained, however, that climbing activities were thoroughly generalized by this final procedure. Checks made the following school year in another play yard indicated that vigorous climbing had become a stable part of his behavior repertoire.

Summary and Discussion

The above studies systematically examined effects of adult attention on some problem behaviors of normal preschool children. The findings in each case clearly indicated that for these children adult attention was a strong positive reinforcer. That is, the behavior that was immediately followed by a teacher's giving the child attention rose rapidly to a high rate, and the rate fell markedly when adult attention was withheld from that behavior and concurrently given to an incompatible behavior. While it seems reasonable that for most young children adult attention may be a positive reinforcer, it is also conceivable that for some children adult attention may be a negative reinforcer. That is, the rate of a behavior may decrease when it is immediately followed by the attention of an adult and rise again as soon as the adult withdraws. Actually, for a few children observed at the preschool, it has been thought that adult attention was a negative reinforcer. This seemed to be true, for instance, in the case of the climbing-frame child. Before the study was initiated, the teachers spent several weeks attempting to make themselves positively reinforcing to the child. This they did by staying at a little distance from him and avoiding attending directly to him until he came to them for something. At first, his approaches were only for routine help, such as buttoning his coat. On each of these occasions they took care to be smilingly friendly and helpful. In time, he began making approaches of other kinds, for instance, to show a toy. Finally, when a teacher approached him and commented with interest on what he was doing, he continued his play instead of stopping, hitting out, or running off. However, since his play remained lethargic and sedentary, it was decided that special measures were necessary to help him progress more rapidly. It was the use and effects of these special measures that constituted the study. Clearly, however, adult attention must be or become positively reinforcing to a child before it can be successfully used to help him achieve more desirably effective behaviors.

Studies such as those reported here seem to imply that teachers may help many children rapidly through systematic programming of their adult social reinforcements. However, further research in this area seems necessary. Some of our own studies now in progress suggest that guidance on the basis of reinforcement principles may perhaps bring rapidly into use only behaviors which are already available within the repertory of the child. If the desired behavior requires skills not yet in the child's repertory, then the process of developing those skills from such behaviors as the child has may require weeks or months. For example, a 4-year-old child who could verbalize but who very rarely spoke was helped to speak freely within several days. On the other hand, a child of the same age who had never verbalized required a lengthy shaping process that involved reinforcing first any vocalization, then gradually more appropriate sounds and combinations of sounds. The latter study was still incomplete at the close of a year of work. The time required to develop social behaviors in isolate children has likewise varied considerably, presumably for the same reasons.

Although the teachers conducted these studies in the course of carrying out their regular teaching duties, personnel in excess of the usual number were necessary. The laboratory school was staffed with one teacher to no more than six children, making it possible to assign to one teacher the role of principal "reinforcer teacher" in a study. This teacher was responsible for giving the child immediate attention whenever he behaved in specified ways. In addition, observers were hired and trained to record the behavior of each child studied. Each observer kept a record in 10-second intervals of his subject's behavior throughout each morning at school. Only with such staffing could reinforcement contingencies be precisely and consistently administered and their effects recorded.

Unless the effects are recorded, it is easy to make incorrect judgments about them. Two instances illustrate such fallibility. A boy in the laboratory preschool frequently pinched adults. Attempts by the teachers to ignore the behavior proved ineffective, since the pinches were hard enough to produce at least an involuntary startle. Teachers next decided to try to develop a substitute behavior. They selected patting as a logical substitute. Whenever the child reached toward a teacher, she attempted to forestall a pinch by saying, "Pat, Davey," sometimes adding, "Not pinch," and then strongly approving his patting, when it occurred. Patting behavior increased rapidly to a high level. The teachers agreed that they had indeed succeeded in reducing the pinching behavior through substituting patting. Then they were shown the recorded data. It showed clearly that although patting behavior was indeed high, pinching behavior continued at the previous level. Apparently, the teachers were so focused on the rise in patting behavior that, without the objective data, they would have erroneously concluded that development of a substitute behavior was in this case a successful technique. A second example illustrates a different, but equally undesirable, kind of erroneous assumption. A preschool child who had to wear glasses (Wolf, Risley, & Mees, 1964) developed a pattern of throwing them two or three times per day. Since this proved expensive, it was decided that the attendants should put him in his room for 10 minutes following each glasses-throw. When the attendants were asked a few days later how the procedure was working, they said that the glasses-throwing had not diminished at all. A check of the records, however, showed that there was actually a marked decrease. The throwing dropped to zero within five days. Presumably, the additional effort involved in carrying out the procedure had given the attendants an exaggerated impression of the rate of the behavior. Recorded data, therefore, seem essential to accurate objective assessments of what has occurred.

The findings in the studies presented here accord generally with results of laboratory research on social development reviewed by Horowitz (1963). The importance of social reinforcement was also noted by Bandura (1963) in his investigations of imitation. Gallwey (1964) has replicated the study of an isolate child discussed here, with results "clearly confirmatory of the effectiveness of the technique." Further studies in school situations that can combine the function of research with that of service seem highly desirable.

REFERENCES

Allen, K. Eileen, Henke, Lydia B., Reynolds, Nancy J., Harris, Florence R., and Baer, D. M. The control of hyperactivity by social reinforcement of attending behavior in a preschool child. *J. educ. Psychol., in press.*

Allen, K. Eileen and Harris, Florence R. Elimination of a child's excessive scratching by training the mother in reinforcement procedures. *Behav. Res. Ther.,* 1966.

Allen, K. Eileen, Hart, Betty M., Buell, Joan S., Harris, Florence R., and Wolf, M. M. Effects of social reinforcement on isolate behavior of a nursery school child. *Child Develpm.,* 1964, **35**, 511–518.

Brawley, Eleanor R., Harris, Florence R., Peterson, R. F., Allen, K. Eileen, and Fleming, R. E. Behavior modification of an autistic child. *Behavioral Science,* 1969, **14**, 87–97.

Bandura, A. The role of limitation in personality development. *J. nursery Ed.,* 1963, **18**, 207–215.

Gallwey, Mary. Washington State Univ., Pullman, Wash., 1964. Personal communication.

Harris, Florence R., Johnston, Margaret K., Kelley, C. Susan, and Wolf, M. M. Effects of positive social reinforcement on regressed crawling of a nursery school child. *J. educ. Psychol.,* 1964, **55**, 35–41.

Hart, Betty M., Allen, K. Eileen, Buell, Joan S., Harris, Florence R., and Wolf, M. M. Effects of social reinforcement on operant crying. *J. exp. child Psychol.,* 1964, **1**, 145–153.

Horowitz, Frances Degen. Social reinforcement effects on child behavior. *J. nursery Ed.,* 1963, **18**, 276–284.

Johnston, Margaret K., Kelley, C. Susan, Harris, Florence R., and Wolf, M. M. An application of reinforcement principles to development of motor skills of a young child. *Child Develpm.,* 1966, **37**, 379–383.

Johnston, Margaret K., Kelley, C. Susan, Harris, Florence R., Wolf, M. M., and Baer, D. M. Effects of positive social reinforcement on isolate behavior of a nursery school child. Unpublished manuscript, Univ. of Washington, 1964.

Landreth, Catherine. *Education of the Young Child.* New York: John Wiley, 1942.

Read, Katherine H. *The Nursery School* (2nd ed.). Philadelphia: Saunders, 1955.

Standing, E. M. *Maria Montessori, Her Life and Work.* Fresno: American Library Guild, 1959.

Taylor, Katherine W. *Parent Cooperative Nursery Schools.* New York: Teachers College, Columbia Univ., 1954.

Wolf, M. M., Risley, T. R., and Mees, H. L. Application of operant conditioning procedures to the behavior problems of an autistic child. *Behav. Res. Ther.,* 1964, **1**, 305–312.

15

Control of Aggression in a Nursery School Class

Paul Brown
Rogers Elliott

Dartmouth College

The rate of emission of aggressive responses of twenty-seven 3- and 4-year-old boys in a nursery school class was successfully manipulated by teachers systematically ignoring aggression and attending acts incompatible with aggression.

The aim of the present study was to add to the data of the field of social learning theory (Bandura and Walters, 1963), at several points. First, among the techniques of controlling operant social behavior, simple extinction (Williams, 1959), simple reinforcement (Azrin and Lindsley, 1956), or both of them in combination (Zimmerman and Zimmerman, 1962; Ayllon and Michael, 1960; Baer, Harris, and Wolf, 1963) have been employed frequently with children. Second, the use of explicit learning techniques has been shown effective in young nursery school subjects (Ss) in two recent papers (Baer *et al.*, 1963; Homme, de Baca, Devine, Steinhorst, and Rickert, 1963). Finally, antisocial acts of the assertive-aggressive kind are known

From *Journal of Experimental Child Psychology* 2 (1965), 103–107.

This is a report of work done by the first author, under the direction of the second, in partial fulfillment of the requirements of the senior courses in independent research at Dartmouth. The authors thank Edith Hazard, director, and the members of the staff of the Hanover Nursery School. Not only did they make this study possible, they made it very enjoyable.

to have operant components which are extinguishable (Williams, 1959) and reinforcible (Cowan and Walters, 1963).

With the above as background, we took seriously the following:

> Theorizing and experimentation on the inhibition of aggression have focused exclusively on the inhibitory influence of anxiety or guilt, on the assumption that response inhibition is necessarily a consequence of pairing responses with some form of aversive stimulation. The development of aggression inhibition through the strengthening of incompatible positive responses, on the other hand, has been entirely ignored, despite the fact that the social control of aggression is probably achieved to a greater extent on this basis than by means of aversive stimulation (Bandura and Walters, 1963, p. 130).

We set out to control the aggressive behavior of all of the boys in an entire nursery school class, by using as techniques the removal of positive generalized reinforcement (attention) for aggressive acts, while giving attention to cooperative acts.

Method

Subjects

The subjects were the 27 males in the younger (3- to 4-year-old) of the two groups at the Hanover Nursery School. Observation and teachers' reports made it clear that the younger boys were more aggressive than any other age-sex subgroup.

Ratings

Aggressive responses were defined by enumeration of the categories of the scale devised by Walters, Pearce, and Dahms (1957). The scale has two major subcategories—physical aggression and verbal aggression. Each of these is subdivided into more concrete categories; e.g., under physical aggression are categories labeled "pushes, pulls, holds"; "hits, strikes"; "annoys, teases, interferes"; and there are similar specific descriptions (e.g., "disparages"; "threatens") under the verbal category.

The observations of the behavior were made by two raters, both undergraduates at Dartmouth.[1] They were trained in the use of the scale, and given practice in observing the class during the free-play hour from 9:20 to 10:20 in the morning. Such observation was possible because the rater could stand in a large opening connecting the two spacious play areas. The rating scale had the categories of aggressive behavior as its rows, and 12 five-minute intervals as its

---

1. We thank James Miller and James Markworth for their assistance.

columns. The raters simply checked any occurrence of a defined behavior in the appropriate cell.

One rater observed on Monday, Wednesday, and Friday mornings, the other observed on Tuesday and Thursday. On two of the four observed Wednesday sessions, both raters observed, so that inter-rater reliability could be estimated. At the conclusion of the study, the raters were interviewed to determine what changes, if any, they had observed in the behavior of teachers and children, and whether they had surmised the research hypothesis.

Procedure

The pre-treatment period was simply a one-week set of observations of aggressive responses by the younger boys, to furnish a reference response rate. Two weeks later the first treatment period was initiated by the teachers and the first author (see below) and it lasted for two weeks. Ratings were taken during the second week of this period. The teachers were then told that the experiment was over, and that they were no longer constrained in their behavior toward aggressive acts. Three weeks after this another set of ratings was taken to assess the durability of the treatment effect. Finally, two weeks after this follow-up observation, the treatment was reinstituted for two weeks, and, again, observations were made in the second of these weeks.

The teachers were the agents of treatment (along with the first author) and they were instructed verbally, with reference to a typed handout, which read in part as follows:

> There are many theories which try to explain aggression in young children. Probably most are partly true and perhaps the simplest is the best. One simple one is that many fights, etc. occur because they bring with them a great deal of fuss and attention from some adult. If we remember that just 3 or 4 short years ago these children would have literally died if they were not able to command (usually by crying) attentive responses from some adult, we can see how just attending to a child could be rewarding. On the other hand, when a child is playing quietly most parents are thankful for the peace and leave well enough alone. Unfortunately, if attention and praise is really rewarding, the child is not rewarded when he should be. Thus, many parents unwittingly encourage aggressive, attention-getting behavior since this is the only way the child gets some form of reward. Of course this is an extreme example but it would be interesting to see if this matter of attention is really the issue, and the important issue especially in a setting where punishment of behavior is not a real option.
>
> At the school I have noticed that whenever it has been possible cooperative and non-aggressive acts are attended to and praised by teachers. During the intervening week we would

like to exaggerate this behavior and play down the attention given to aggressive acts. I hope to concentrate on the boys, but if a boy and girl are concerned that is perfectly all right.

Briefly, we will try to ignore aggression and reward cooperative and peaceful behavior. Of course if someone is using a hammer on another's head we would step in, but just to separate the two and leave. It will be difficult at first because we tend to watch and be quiet when nothing bad is happening, and now our attention will *as much as possible* be directed toward cooperative, or non-agressive behavior. It would be good to let the most aggressive boys see that the others are getting the attention if it is possible. A pat on the head, 'That's good Mike,' 'Hello Chris and Mark, how are you today?' 'Look what Eric made,' etc. may have more rewarding power than we think. On the other hand, it is just as important during this week to have no reprimands, no 'Say you're sorry,' 'Aren't you sorry?' Not that these aren't useful ways of teaching proper behavior, but they will only cloud the effects of our other manner of treatment. It would be best not even to look at a shove or small fight if we are sure no harm is being done; as I mentioned before, if it is necessary we should just separate the children and leave.

Results and Discussion

The Raters

The correlation between the raters of total aggressive responses checked in each of 24 five-minute periods was 0.97. This is higher than the average interrater correlation of 0.85 reported by Walters, *et al.* (1957), but their raters were working with a one-minute, rather than a five-minute observation period.

When interviewed, one rater said that the only change he saw in the children was in the two "most troublesome" boys, who at the end (the fourth-rating period) seemed less troublesome. The other noticed no change in any of the children, even though his ratings described the changes shown in Table 1. One rater had noticed, again during the fourth-rating period, that the first author was being "especially complimentary" to one of the troublesome boys, and the other rater did not notice any change in the behavior of any adult.

Aggressive Responses

Table 1 presents the average daily number of physical, verbal, and overall aggressive responses in each of the four periods of observation. Analyses of variance of the daily scores as a function of treatments yielded F ratios ($df = 3$, 16) of 6.16 for physical aggression ($p < 0.01$), 5.71 for verbal aggression ($p < 0.01$), and 25.43 for overall aggression.

TABLE 1
Average Number of Responses in the Various Rated
Categories of Aggression

Times of observation	Categories of Aggression		
	Physical	Verbal	Total
Pre-treatment	41.2	22.8	64.0
First treatment	26.0	17.4	43.4
Follow-up	37.8	13.8	51.6
Second treatment	21.0	4.6	25.6

There seems little doubt that ignoring aggressive responses and attending cooperative ones had reliable and significant effects upon the behavior of the children.

Verbal aggression did not recover after the first treatment, while physical aggression did. Since we were rating children, not teachers, we offer the following speculation with only casual evidence. We believe the teachers find it harder to ignore fighting than to ignore verbal threats or insults. It is certainly true that the teachers (all females) found aggression in any form fairly difficult to ignore. During treatment periods, they would frequently look to the first author as if asking whether they should step in and stop a fight, and they often had the expression and behavior of conflict when aggressive, especially physically aggressive behavior occurred — i.e., they would often, almost automatically, move slightly toward the disturbance, then check themselves, then look at the first author. The more raucous scenes were tense, with the teachers waiting, alert and ready for the first bit of calm and cooperative behavior to appear and allow them to administer attention. The teachers, incidentally, were skeptical of the success of the method when it was first proposed, though they came ultimately to be convinced of it. What made its success dramatic to them was the effect upon two very aggressive boys, both of whom became friendly and cooperative to a degree not thought possible. The most aggressive boys tended to be reinforced for cooperative acts on a lower variable ratio than the others, because teachers were especially watchful of any sign of cooperation on their parts.

Conclusion

As Allen, Hart, Buell, Harris, and Wolf (1964) have pointed out recently, the principles involved in the present application of controlling techniques are simple. What makes this and other demonstrations of them successful in a real-life setting is systematic observation, systematic application, and systematic evaluation.

REFERENCES

Allen, Eileen K., Hart, Betty, Buell, Joan S., Harris, Florence R., and Wolf, M. M. Effects of social reinforcement on the isolate behavior of a nursery school child. *Child Develpm.*, 1964, **35**, 511–518.

Ayllon, T., and Michael, J. The psychiatric nurse as a behavioral engineer. *J. exp. anal. Behav.*, 1959, **2**, 323–334.

Azrin, N. H., and Lindsley, O. R. The reinforcement of cooperation between children. *J. abnorm. soc. Psychol.*, 1956, **52**, 100–102.

Baer, D. M., Harris, Florence R., and Wolf, M. M. Control of nursery school children's behavior by programming social reinforcement from their teachers. *Amer. Psychologist*, 1963, **18**, 343. (Abstract.)

Bandura, A., and Walters, R. H. *Social learning and personality development.* New York: Holt, 1963.

Cowan, P. A., and Walters, R. H. Studies of reinforcement of aggression. I. Effects of scheduling. *Child Develpm.*, 1963, **34**, 543–551.

Homme, L. E., de Baca, P. C., Devine, J. V., Steinhorst, R., and Rickert, E. J. Use of the Premack principle in controlling the behavior of nursery school children. *J. exp. anal. Behav.*, 1963, **6**, 544.

Walters, J. C., Pearce, Doris, and Dahms, Lucille. Affectional and aggressive behavior of preschool children. *Child Develpm.*, 1957, **28**, 15–26.

Williams, C. D. The elimination of tantrum behavior by extinction procedures. *J. abnorm. soc. Psychol.*, 1959, **59**, 269.

Zimmerman, Elaine H., and Zimmerman, J. The alteration of behavior in a special classroom situation. *J. exp. anal. Behav.*, 1962, **5**, 59–60.

16

The Alteration of Behavior
in a Special Classroom Situation

Elaine H. Zimmerman
J. Zimmerman

Indiana University Medical Center

Unproductive classroom behavior was eliminated in two emotionally disturbed boys by removing social consequences of the
behavior. Behavior which was more adequate and efficient with
respect to social and scholastic adjustment was shaped and
maintained with social reinforcers.

The classroom behavior of two emotionally disturbed boys was
altered by arranging and manipulating its consequences.

The boys, in-patients in a residential treatment center (LaRue D.
Carter Memorial Hospital), attended the first author's English class
daily for 1 hr as part of an educational therapy program. There were
three boys in the class, each receiving individual attention.

Case I

Subject 1 (S-1) was 11 years old. He appeared to have no organic
disorder and was of normal intelligence. In early class sessions,
whenever S-1 was called upon to spell a word which had previously
been studied and drilled, he would pause for several seconds, screw

From *Journal of the Experimental Analysis of Behavior,* **5,** 1 (January 1962).

up his face, and mutter letters unrelated to the word. Following this, the instructor (E) consistently asked him to sound out the word, often giving him the first letter and other cues, encouraging him to spell the word correctly. Only after E had spent considerable time and attention would the boy emit a correct response. The procedure was inefficient and profitless for improving the boy's spelling behavior. In fact, it may have been maintaining the undesirable pattern, since over the first 10 or 15 class sessions, consistently more time and attention were required of E to obtain a correct spelling response.

While "studying" in class, S-1 would obtain sheets of paper, wrinkle them, and throw them away, laughing as he caught E's eye or that of one of the other students.

The Change in Approach

After several weeks in class, S-1 was quizzed via paper-and-pencil test on a lesson based on 10 spelling words, with time allotted for study and review. He handed in a paper with a muddled combination of barely legible letters. Immediately, E asked him to go to the blackboard. Her instructions were simply: "We will now have a quiz. I will read a word and you will spell it correctly on the board." She read the first word, and the subject misspelled it 10 or more times on the board. During this time, E sat at her desk, ignoring S-1, apparently busy reading or writing. Each time S-1 misspelled the word, he glanced at E; but she did not respond. The boy erased the word and tried again, several times repeating "I can't spell it," or "I can't remember how," etc. Although ignored, the boy made no effort to sit down or leave the room. After approximately 10 min, he spelled the word correctly; E looked up at him immediately, smiled, and said, "Good, now we can go on." She read a second word; and after a similar series of errors and verbal responses, S-1 spelled the word correctly. With each successive word (through 10 words), the number of inappropriate (unreinforced) responses decreased, as did the latency of the correct response. At the end of the quiz, E took the boy's spelling chart, wrote an "A" on it, and praised him. She then asked the subject to help her color some Easter baskets. They sat down together, and chatted and worked.

Thereafter, attention in the form of smiling, chatting, and physical proximity was given only immediately after the emission of desired classroom behavior or some approximation of it in the desired direction. Undesirable behavior was consistently ignored. As a result of a month of this treatment, the frequency of bizarre spelling responses and other undesirable responses declined to a level close to zero per class session. At the conclusion of this study, the boy was working more efficiently, and was making adequate academic progress.

Case II

Subject S-2 was an 11-year-old boy, who, like S-1, had no apparent organic disorder and was also of normal intelligence. In initial class Sessions, S-2 emitted behavior considered undesirable in the classroom context with high frequency. He displayed temper tantrums (kicking, screaming, etc.), spoke baby-talk, and incessantly made irrelevant comments or posed irrelevant questions.

Several times a week, attendents dragged this boy down the hall to one of his classes as the boy screamed and buckled his knees. On several of these occasions, the boy threw himself on the floor in front of a classroom door. A crowd of staff members inevitably gathered around him. The group usually watched and commented as the boy sat or lay on the floor, kicking and screaming. Some members of the group hypothesized that such behavior seemed to appear after the boy was teased or frustrated in some way. However, the only observable in the situation was the consistent consequence of the behavior in terms of the formation of a group of staff members around the boy.

Observing one such situation which occurred before *E*'s class, *E* asked the attendent to put the boy in the classroom at his desk and to leave the room. Then *E* closed the door. The boy sat at his desk, kicking and screaming; *E* proceeded to her desk and worked there, ignoring S-2. After 2 or 3 min, the boy, crying softly, looked up at *E*. Then *E* announced that she would be ready to work with him as soon as he indicated that he was ready to work. He continued to cry and scream with diminishing loudness for the next 4 or 5 min. Finally, he lifted his head and stated that he was ready. Immediately, *E* looked up at him, smiled, went to his desk, and said, "Good, now let's get to work." The boy worked quietly and cooperatively with *E* for the remainder of the class period.

The Handling of Tantrums, Irrelevant
Verbal Behavior, and Baby-talk

Each time a tantrum occurred, *E* consistently ignored S-2. When tantrum behavior was terminated, *E* conversed with the boy, placed herself in his proximity, or initiated an activity which was appealing to him. After several weeks, class tantrums disappeared entirely. Because the consequence of tantrum behavior varied in other situations, no generalization to situations outside the classroom has been observed.

Furthermore the frequency of irrelevant verbal behavior and of baby-talk declined almost to the point of elimination following the procedure of withholding attention after the emission of such behavior. On the other hand, when S-2 worked quietly or emitted desirable classroom behavior, *E* addressed him cordially and permitted some verbal interchange for several seconds. When a lesson was being presented to the class at large and S-2 listened attentively, E reinforced him by asking him a question he could answer or by looking at him, smiling at him, etc. The reinforcement was delivered intermittently rather than continuously because: (a) reinforcing every desired response of one student was impossible since E's time was parcelled out among several students; and (b) intermittent reinforcement would probably be more effective than continuous reinforcement in terms of later resistance of the desired behavior to extinction. Like S-1, at the conclusion of the study this boy was working more efficiently in class and was making good progress. His speech was more generally characterized by relevancy and maturity.

17

Reinforcement Therapy in the Classroom

Michael H. Ward
Bruce L. Baker

Harvard University

Teachers were trained in the systematic use of attention and praise to reduce the disruptive classroom behavior of four first-grade children. Observation measures showed a significant improvement from baseline to treatment for these children and no significant changes for same-class controls. While the amount of teacher attention to target children remained the same from baseline to treatment, the proportion of attention to task-relevant behavior of these children increased. Psychological tests revealed no adverse changes after treatment.

Reinforcement techniques have been demonstrated to be quite effective in altering behavior in the laboratory situation (Krasner and Ullmann, 1965), and recently there have been increasing at-

From *Journal of Applied Behavior Analysis*, 1968, 1 (4), 323–28. This research was supported in part by National Institute of Mental Health Grant 1-F1-MH-36, 634-01 (MTLH), and Harvard University Faculty Science Research Grant No. 33-493-68-1718. The authors wish to acknowledge the cooperation and assistance of Assistant Superintendent William Cannon of the Boston Public Schools, and Principal Gladys Wood and Assistant Principal Mary Lynch of the Aaron Davis School. Appreciation is expressed to the teachers, Carol Baumgardt, Sandra Napier, and Elaine Schivek, whose collaboration made this study possible. Our sincere thanks to Virginia Worcholick, Susan Hole, and Janet Ward, who served as observers, and to Sally Sanford, who did the testing. Reprints may be obtained from Michael H. Ward, Psychology Services, Menlo Park Division, Palo Alto VAH, Miranda Drive, Palo Alto, California 94306.

tempts to extend these methods to treatment in "real-life" situations. Of considerable importance is the potential usefulness of reinforcement therapy in the school classroom (*e.g.*, Clarizo and Yelon, 1967; Hall, Lund, and Jackson, 1968; Woody, 1966).

Zimmerman and Zimmerman (1962) eliminated disruptive classroom behavior in two emotionally disturbed boys by removing the social consequences of maladaptive behavior. Quay, Werry, McQueen, and Sprague (1966) reported on the use of conditioning techniques in a small special class with conduct problem children. A program in which public school teachers were trained to manage classroom behavior problems by the contingent use of teacher attention and praise has been described by Becker, Madsen, Arnold, and Thomas (1967).

While these applications of reinforcement methods are certainly encouraging, several legitimate questions are often raised by psychologists and teachers concerned with treating disruptive classroom behavior. One critical area of concern is the generalization of treatment effects. First, when a child's disruptive behavior is successfully reduced, what are the effects on other aspects of his observable behavior and on his psychological test functioning? Second, how are other pupils in the class affected when the teacher concentrates on treating deviant behavior in one or two specific children?

The present study further explored the effectiveness of the teacher as a therapeutic agent, but it also attempted to assess the generalized effects of reinforcement therapy. Thus, teachers were trained to eliminate deviant behavior by differentially reinforcing the target children's desirable and undesirable classroom behavior. Control procedures were instituted to ascertain the effects of the reinforcement therapy procedures on the psychological adjustment of target and non-target children.

Method

Subjects

Twelve first-grade Negro children in an urban public school were assigned to three groups.

The Experimental Group (Group E) consisted of four behavior problem children. Three boys presented a high frequency of disruptive classroom behaviors, such as inappropriate talking and running around; one girl was highly withdrawn and inattentive. These target children were selected from three separate classrooms, on the basis of teachers' referrals and direct observations.

Control Group CI (Group CI) consisted of four children, matched for sex with the Group E children and selected at random from the three teachers' class lists. Thus, for each target child, a control child in the same classroom was also studied.

Control Group CII (Group CII) consisted of three boys and one girl, selected randomly from the classroom of a fourth first-grade teacher. These pupils provided a baseline for test-retest changes in psychological test performance, independent of any experimental manipulations.

Apparatus

All treatment was carried out in the classroom. For two of the experimental subjects, two small (4-in.) electrically operated signal lights were used in six special-treatment sessions (after Patterson, 1965).

Procedure

For five weeks, the frequency of various deviant classroom behaviors of Group E and Group CI children was coded by trained observers. Deviant behavior was calculated as the percentage of 30-sec intervals in which the child exhibited any behavior which was not task-relevant. These observations constituted the baseline measure of deviant behavior.

At week six, the experimental treatment phase was instituted and continued for seven weeks (until the end of the school year). In the treatment phase, teachers systematically ignored deviant behavior and reinforced, with attention and praise, task-relevant productive behavior. Regular classroom observations of the Group E and Group CI children were continued throughout the study; the Group CII children were not observed at any time.

All three groups were administered a battery of psychological tests, both during baseline and at the conclusion of the seven-week experimental treatment phase.

OBSERVERS AND OBSERVATIONS. Three female undergraduates were trained to observe and record classroom behavior. The observers sat in the rear of the classroom; they did not interact with or respond to the children. Each Group E child was observed for four 15-min periods per week; each Group CI child was observed for two 15-min periods per week. During the observation period, the child was watched for the first 20 sec of each 30-sec interval of time; in the remaining 10 sec, the observers recorded the behaviors that had occurred. The observation periods were randomized throughout the school day to assure an adequate time-sampling. Inter-observer reliability checks were made periodically.

Table 1 shows the categories of behavior rated. These included gross and fine motor behaviors, aggression, deviant talking, non-attending, and disobeying, thumbsucking, and relevant appropriate behaviors such as hand-raising, task-oriented behavior, and so forth. In addition, the teacher's attention to children, as well as the nature of her comments, was coded.

TEACHERS AND TRAINING SESSIONS. Three female teachers were initially informed that their behavior problem children would be observed for five weeks, at which time the investigators would again meet with them to discuss some techniques for modifying these behavior problems. None of the teachers was given any further information at this time. At no point were the teachers told that the same-class control children were being observed.

After baseline measurements had been completed, the investigators began a series of four weekly seminar-discussions with the three teachers. These sessions were devoted to discussions of behavior modification and the progress of the target children. The seminars included a general introduction to operant conditioning, reinforcement and punishment procedures, schedules of reinforcement, and selected aspects of the experimental literature relating to these and other topics (*e.g.*, Ullmann and Krasner, 1965).

It was first necessary to help teachers identify and specify deviant behaviors. Throughout the treatment phase of the study, the investigators visited the classrooms and pointed out behavior problems. Thus, rather than: "He's always bad," teachers soon learned to define inappropriate behavior in more specific terms: "He is frequently out of his seat and he blurts out without being called on." It was also necessary to indicate to teachers which behaviors were to be reinforced when. Thus, for two of the behavior problem boys, six special 30-min treatment periods were conducted, in which an experimenter-controlled signal light on the child's desk was used as a reinforcer for sustained task-relevant behavior. The main purpose of this procedure was to bring the child's behavior under experimental control and allow the experimenter to indicate to the teacher the types of behaviors to be reinforced.

The principal therapeutic tool was the contingent use of teacher attention. The teachers were instructed to extinguish deviant behaviors by ignoring them, and to strengthen task-relevant behaviors by attending to and praising them. The need for immediacy, consistency, and contingency in reinforcement therapy was stressed. That is, the teacher was instructed to give *immediate* attention in a *consistent* manner, *contingent* upon the child's exhibiting task-relevant behavior.

A fourth female teacher, from whose classroom Group CII was chosen, did not participate in the seminar-discussions; at no time was she informed of the nature of the study.

TESTS AND MEASURES. The measure of deviant classroom behavior was the direct observations described above; these included both the target behaviors and other types of deviant behavior.

In the baseline period, and again at the conclusion of the seven-week treatment period, each of the 12 children was tested individually by an independent examiner on the following battery of tests: four subtests of the WISC, the Draw-A-Person Test, and a projective

TABLE 1
Classroom Behavior Rating Schedule
(after Becker et al., 1967)

Motor Behaviors (at seat)
Rocking in chair; moving chair in place; sitting out of position; standing while *touching* chair or desk.

Gross Motor Behaviors (not at desk)
Getting out of seat; running; jumping; skipping; *not touching* desk or chair.

Aggression
Hitting; punching; kicking; slapping; striking with object; throwing object at another person; pulling hair; disturbing another's books, desk, etc.; destroying another's property. Do *not* rate unless act is committed.

Deviant Talking
Carrying on conversation with other children; blurts out answer without being called upon; making comments or remarks; crying; screaming; laughing loudly; coughing loudly, singing, whistling; any vocal noise.

Non-Attending and Disobeying
Does something different from that which he has been directed to do or is supposed to do; includes "daydreaming." *Note:* The above to be rated *only* when other classes are inappropriate (no other symbol may appear in interval). Note: Ignoring teacher's *direct* question or command may be rated in addition to other categories.

Thumb Sucking (and other objects)
Thumb or finger sucking; sucking such objects as a pencil, etc.

Relevant Behavior
Time-on-task; answering question; listening; following directions. Important: *Must* include *entire* 20-sec interval, except orienting response of less than 4-sec duration.

Hand Raising
Raises hand to ask or answer question; do *not* rate if child blurts out without being acknowledged. *Note:* May be rated with task-relevant behavior.

Teacher Attention
Teacher attends to the Subject *during* the 20-sec interval.

Positive Comments
"Good," "fine," "nice job" are said by teacher to Subject during the 20-sec interval.

General Reprimand
Teacher issues a *general* reprimand to the class or a group of students.

Negative Comments
"Shut up," "sit in your seat," "you're a bad boy," etc. are said by teacher to Subject during the 20-sec interval.

questionnaire designed to measure attitudes toward school and feelings about self.

The Comprehension, Mazes, Digit Span, and Block Design subtests of the WISC were used to reflect the child's ability to pay attention to a task, and his general scholastic functioning. In the DAP Test, the child was asked to draw a picture of a person, using standard art paper and crayons provided by the tester. Such drawings have been used as measures of a child's adjustment, maturity, and self-image. Finally, the child was shown a photograph of a Negro child of the same sex and comparable age; the facial expressions in these pictures were judged by the authors to be "neutral." Twenty questions were asked about this child's feelings toward himself and toward school (*e.g.*, "Is his teacher nice to him?" "Do the other kids in school like him?" "Does he like school?").

All children were given both sets of tests by the same examiner, who was not informed of experimental conditions.

Results

Classroom Behavior

RELIABILITY OF OBSERVATIONS. Inter-observer reliability of the observation periods was determined by the percentage of intervals in which the observers agreed perfectly as to whether deviant behavior had occurred. The mean percentage perfect agreement of the 31 reliability checks was 81% (SD = 21.6).

BEHAVIOR OBSERVATIONS. Figure 1 shows the amount of deviant behavior in the behavior problem children and their same-class controls during baseline and during treatment. In the five-week baseline period, the Group E children showed 74% deviant behavior, while the Group CI children showed 37% deviant behavior, a difference significant at $p = 0.002$ ($t = 5.14$; $df = 6$).[1] There was no overlap among subjects in the two groups.

For the last five weeks of treatment, Group E showed 57% deviant behavior, a decrease from baseline significant at $p = 0.03$ ($t = 3.91$; $df = 3$). During this same period, Group CI showed 41% deviant behavior, a slight, though not significant increase from baseline ($t = 0.32$; $df = 3$). The groups no longer differed significantly, although the deviant behavior in the target children was not decreased to the level of their controls by the end of school.

None of the specific categories of deviant behavior showed an increase in either Group E or Group CI, nor did teachers report any new behavior problems. Hence, the reduction in the target disruptive behavior was not followed by an increase in other classroom deviance.

---

1. All statistical tests of significance are two-tailed.

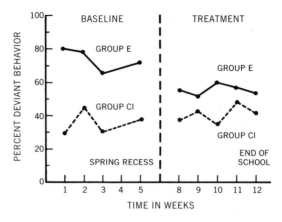

Fig. 1. Deviant behavior of Group E and Group CI

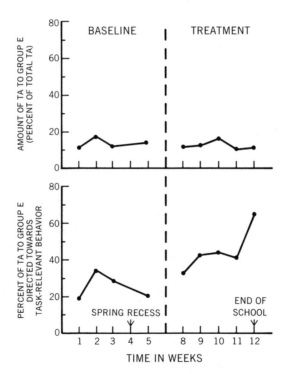

Fig. 2. Teacher attention to Group E: Amount of TA directed towards Group E and percent of attention to Group E directed towards task-relevant behavior

TEACHER ATTENTION. The principal therapeutic intervention used in the experiment was teacher attention to task-relevant behavior. However, as shown in Fig. 2, the observed improvement in the experimental children cannot be attributed simply to increased teacher attention, since there was no significant change from baseline to treatment in the *amount* of attention to target children (t = 0.07; df = 3). Teachers did increase significantly from baseline to treatment in the *proportion* of their attention to target children that was directed towards task-relevant behavior (t = 3.46; df = 3; p = 0.04).

Nevertheless, it appears that the teachers did not thoroughly master the contingent use of their attention to task-relevant behavior, and that further improvement in the target children might have been possible. For instance, the change in deviant behavior for Group E reported above did not include observations taken during the special treatment sessions with two children. For these two experimental children, the deviant behavior during the special signal-light reinforcement periods decreased dramatically to an average of 18%. Yet there was apparently little generalization to other times.

Although the teachers did not increase their attention to target children, the data suggested that they decreased their attention somewhat to Group CI children; there was a slight, but not significant decrease in the amount of teacher attention from baseline to treatment (t = 2.49; df = 3, p = 0.09). The proportion of teachers' attention directed toward task-relevant behavior did not change from baseline to treatment for Group CI (t = 0.11; df = 3).

Psychological Tests

On the pre-treatment WISC, the behavior problem children were significantly lower than the controls on the Mazes subtest (t = 2.71; df = 10; p < 0.03); the groups did not differ on the other sub-scales. The changes in WISC scores after treatment were minimal and did not significantly differentiate the groups, although Group E tended to decrease on the Comprehension subtest relative to Group CII (t = 2.14; df = 6, p = 0.08).

The pre-treatment DAP drawings of the behavior problem children were generally like those of the control children, except that the Group E drawings were significantly smaller in size (t = 2.85; df = 10, p < 0.02). This variable has been considered an indicator of anxiety (Ward, 1968).

The pre- and post-treatment drawings were scored on all those variables considered in the drawing literature to be suggestive of adjustment or maturity. No significant differences between groups in change scores were found on any single variable or on a combination score. Emotional adjustment, rated by two judges uninformed as to the order and conditions in which the drawings were produced, showed no consistent effects. Similarly, changes on the projective questionnaire did not differentiate the groups.

Discussion

One focus of the present study was to ascertain the generalized effects on the target child of treating a specific behavior; especially studied were the deleterious effects on the child's classroom behavior and psychological test functioning. The data provide no evidence for adverse changes in the children as a consequence of teachers' employing reinforcement techniques or as a result of specific deviant behaviors being reduced.

On the other hand, the target children did not show the generalized improvement in psychological test functioning found by Baker (1968) with enuretic children treated by conditioning. Yet, the present treatment did not produce the distinctive cure which results with enuretics. Also, enuresis is usually an "involuntary" behavior, the alleviation of which is a considerable relief for the child. Deviant classroom behavior is in some sense "voluntary"; it is emitted for environmental gains, such as the teacher's attention, and may be more a discomfort to others than to the child himself. If attention is withdrawn from such an operant, the child will attempt other behaviors to regain attention. Whether the end result is new maladaptive behavior or generalized improvement may depend on what the teacher now reinforces.

A second focus was the generalized effects of reinforcement therapy on the class. No support was found for the argument that behavior of other pupils in a class deteriorates when the teacher's attention is somehow diverted from them in treating behavior problem children. Although teachers did slightly decrease the amount of attention given to control children, there was no significant increase in the control children's deviant behavior. This is particularly encouraging since the treatment was carried out in the last weeks of the school year when, according to teachers, disruption in the classroom typically rises. It appears, nonetheless, that in future treatment programs, more stress should be placed on the teacher maintaining normal relations with non-target children.

The principal reinforcer employed was contingent teacher attention. It is assumed that the decrease in deviant behavior in the target children resulted from the greater proportion of attention that teachers paid to these children's task-relevant behavior. It is recognized that the observed relationship between an increase in the proportion of teacher's attention to task-relevant behavior and an increase in such task-relevant behavior may have been artifactual; that is, if task-relevant behavior increased for some other undetermined reason and amount of teacher attention remained the same, then an increase in proportion of attention to task-relevant behavior would have also been found. Yet, it seems most likely that modified use of teacher attention was primary, especially in view of other reports indicating the functional role of teacher praise in increasing appropriate behavior in the classroom (Madsen, Becker, and Thomas, 1968).

The treatment procedures were not uniformly successful with all target children. Most notably, the withdrawn and inattentive behavior of one child changed very little. This behavior seems less under the control of teacher attention than more acting out behaviors; also, the latter are easier for the teacher to define, to notice, and to respond to correctly. Treating withdrawn behaviors may require better training in behavior shaping. In general it seems possible that more behavioral improvement could have been effected in all of the target children if the teachers had been more thoroughly trained. It is clear from the results of the special treatment sessions, in which the deviant behavior of two of the children dropped to 18%, that the full effectiveness of the reinforcement techniques was not realized at all times. It is likewise possible that a longer treatment period would have provided more time for the teachers' therapeutic skills to take effect.

Yet, the significant decrease in disruptive behavior in the target children, and the absence of adverse changes in these or other pupils, indicate that teachers can be trained as effective "therapists," using reinforcement techniques in the classroom. This finding, consistent with the conclusion reached by Becker *et al.* (1967), has important implications for in-classroom management of behavior problems. First, the availability to teachers of a set of techniques for controlling the disruptive behavior of students is of obvious advantage in terms of smoother classroom functioning. In addition, being taught to manifest productive task-relevant classroom behavior is worthwhile to the child himself. A child who is hyperactive or otherwise deviant in school necessarily misses many of the learning experiences which normally accrue to an attentive, actively participating pupil. A final consideration is that *in situ* amelioration of maladaptive behavior somewhat obviates the educational and financial disadvantages involved in removing a child from the classroom in order to attempt therapeutic rehabilitation.

While the results of this limited study are themselves encouraging, future research should continue to look beyond the specific behaviors being treated, and consider the generalized effects of reinforcement therapy.

REFERENCES

Baker, B. L. Symptom treatment and symptom substitution in enuresis. *Journal of Abnormal Psychology*, in press.

Becker, W. C., Madsen, C. H., Jr., Arnold, Carol, and Thomas, D. R. The contingent use of teacher attention and praise in reducing classroom behavior problems. *Journal of Special Education*, 1967, 1, 287–307.

Clarizo, H. F., and Yelon, S. L. Learning theory approaches to classroom management: rationale and intervention techniques. *Journal of Special Education*, 1967, 1, 267–274.

Hall, R. V., Lund, Diane, and Jackson, Deloris. Effects of teacher attention on study behavior. *Journal of Applied Behavior Analysis*, 1968, 1, 1–12.

Krasner, L., and Ullmann, L. P. (Eds.) *Research in behavior modification.* New York: Holt, Rinehart & Winston, 1965.

Madsen, C. H., Jr., Becker, W. C., and Thomas, D. R. Rules, praise, and ignoring: elements of elementary classroom control. *Journal of Applied Behavior Analysis*, 1968, 1, 139–150.

Patterson, G. R. An application of conditioning techniques to the control of a hyperactive child. In L. P. Ullmann and L. Krasner (Eds.), *Case studies in behavior modification.* New York: Holt, Rinehart & Winston, 1965. Pp. 370–375.

Quay, H. C., Werry, J. S., McQueen, Marjorie, and Sprague, R. L. Remediation of the conduct problem child in the special class setting. *Exceptional Children*, 1966, 32, 509–515.

Ullmann, L. P., and Krasner, L. *Case studies in behavior modification.* New York: Holt, Rinehart & Winston, 1965.

Ward, Janet. *Integration and racial identification: a study of Negro children's drawings.* Unpublished bachelor honor's thesis, Radcliffe College, 1968.

Woody, R. H. Behavior therapy and school psychology. *Journal of Social Psychology*, 1966, 4, 1–14.

Zimmerman, Elaine H., and Zimmerman, J. The alteration of behavior in a special classroom situation. *Journal of Experimental Analysis of Behavior*, 1962, 5, 59–60.

When Social Reinforcers Fail

18

Preparing "Uncontrollable" Retarded Children for Group Instruction

J. S. Birnbrauer
University of North Carolina at Chapel Hill

Too often children whose behavior does not conform to the requirement of group instruction must be expelled from school. Because of
their behavior, another large group of children never gain entry to
school. The work that I shall describe centers around the notion of a
socialization teacher — an individual whose function is to teach self-
control and the other social skills necessary for children to start and
remain in school. She specializes in establishing typical teacher
incentives — praise, being right, and scores as powerful conditioned
reinforcers and in shaping direction following, waiting quietly, listening, working alone until finished, and so on. The measure of her
success is the number of children who are enrolled and stay in school
as a result of her work.

It has been argued that behavior problems would occur significantly less often if teachers were skilled in applying reinforcement
principles and teachers could handle their own classroom management problems. On the other hand, conducting classes according to
reinforcement principles is taxing, and regardless of a teacher's
skill, problem students will continue to require a disproportionate

Paper read at American Educational Research Association Convention, New York, Feb-
ruary 1967. The demonstration discussed is part of a project conducted at Murdoch
Center, Butner, N.C. (J. F. Elliott, superintendent), and supported in part by NIMH
Project Grant MH2130.

amount of the teacher's time and attention. Furthermore, many children learn from teachers who do not apply reinforcement principles consistently. Therefore, instead of reforming all teachers at a time when behavioral psychologists must admit to ignorance about many practical questions, the tack we have followed is to prepare children for the kind of instruction they are apt to receive. In other words—can behavioral principles be used to teach children to learn something and to not emit the kinds of responses that will result in dismissal from school even though the children will enter classes which vary quite a bit—even though their teachers often will violate reinforcement principles? It is impossible to create model pupils unless one has control over future environments. Even Watson (1930, p. 104) recognized this. But somehow most of us learn enough self-control to survive in most situations. Most children learn, for example, not to throw a chair at the teacher when things do not go to their liking.

The procedures I shall outline are based on our experiences in the programmed learning classroom for pre-educable pupils and in particular Julia Lawler's classes for very difficult severely and profoundly retarded children at Rainier School (Bijou, Birnbrauer, Kidder & Tague, 1966; Birnbrauer & Lawler, 1964).

Twenty boys attended the socialization classes for some period of time, i.e., a few days to eight months. All lived on a training and research ward for moderately to profoundly retarded problem children at Murdoch Center. Their chronological ages were 8 to 14, mental ages ranged from not testable to 5 years 3 months, and IW's were below 44. Their clinical diagnoses included mongoloid, cultural-familial, brain damaged, and emotionally disturbed.

Preparing children for classroom instruction presumes that we know how teachers teach and what the underlying prerequisites are. To begin with, it was not necessary for us to enumerate the prerequisites for group instruction, because most of the children were unteachable no matter how one went about it, short of putting them in a harness and requiring them to work for their meals. The milder children were those who would tantrum when the teacher asked them to participate in another task. Others would do *that* when you asked them to do *this*. Some could not be counted on to sit down when told. A partial list of the objectives agreed upon appears below.

The boys were assigned to groups on the basis of their demonstrated ability to perform preacademic and manipulative tasks and their response to verbal instructions. IQ, MA, CA and diagnostic categories were ignored; they did not correlate highly with our evaluations of level of competence and cooperation in a group setting. Because these classes were outside the regular school program and conducted in a room adjacent to the ward, pupils were reassigned quickly when they caught up with a higher group or were not keeping up with their group and class duration varied from 20 minutes to 3½ hours as the pupils progressed.

The general strategy was to start with conditions which differed as little as possible from typical special education procedures and limitations. The teacher conducted the classes with no helpers and used only materials that are available to any teacher or that any teacher could make. (Although she had aides later on, the pupil-to-teacher ratio was never out of line.) Also, the teacher, Miss Susan F. Moore, at first used only *social* reinforcement and opportunities to engage in preferred activities. The changes were how she dispensed these and using extinction rather than punishment. That is, she reacted immediately and quite often to responses which approximated the kinds of behavior that would be necessary in school with approval, praise, and pats on the head. She ignored behavior which was incompatible with performance in a group situation except when behavior became destructive or dangerous to the child or to others. Then, the teacher interfered physically, held the child, or if it were necessary, removed the child temporarily from the classroom. Such punitive actions were preceded by a sharp, clear "No" or calling the boy's name. (After tangible reinforcers were introduced, these were taken away from some pupils immediately after misbehaving, but the pupils had ample opportunity to earn them again.)

We were not surprised by little progress in most of the children under the circumstances. Praise was not a powerful reinforcer for several children. While attention may have been a reinforcer, controlling teacher *attention* is very difficult.

The next step was to introduce tangible reinforcers. Fortunately, most of the children in the group would work for bits of cracker, M & M's and other edibles. Miss Moore carried a variety and dispensed an edible together with praise for appropriate behavior. Dispensing edibles immediately contingent upon responses requires that the teacher be close to the children. So the children's desks were arranged in a small semi-circle around Miss Moore. (An incidental benefit of this was that she and the desks were between the children and her supplies.)

Since the world and classrooms are not conducted with immediate delivery of individually selected edibles, the second step was to establish a symbolic but tangible reinforcer. We chose poker chips for this purpose; these and praise were dispensed contingently for appropriate behavior instead of edibles. Somewhat later the chips were exchanged for candy or a toy.

The third step for those who worked well for poker chips was to replace the poker chips with a checkmark system. This system had been used successfully in the Rainier School Programmed Learning Classroom. Instead of a poker chip backed by edibles, the children received praise and a checkmark on a piece of paper contingent upon correct responses. In addition Miss Moore was doing such things as saying "You got them all correct. That means you get a hundred" and writing 100 at the top of the page. The boys were taught to recognize that ✔'s were good to have, x's were not and that all ✔'s meant 100.

In short, with regard to reinforcement we gradually made the classes more like conditions which ordinarily prevail in classrooms. The tangibles were faded out so that they were only being dispensed at the end of the class. Furthermore, the time between emitting the correct response and receiving *any* reinforcement was extended. Finally, the boys received tangible reinforcement only after they returned to their ward.

After about eight months, seven boys worked fairly well for about 3½ hours, for the receipt of white poker chips which they exchanged for toys or candy about one hour after class. These boys were then given report cards which they carried back to their ward. Thus, they were working entirely for symbolic reinforcement in school.

Meanwhile, with the aid of interviews and observation we had constructed a list of common requirements for attending school. This list included such items as: entering class at the appropriate time, picking up the necessary materials and sitting down at a particular desk, going to and from the little boys' room, going to and from recess, hand raising, talking only when given permission, watching and listening to the teacher, working at a task while the teacher was occupied with other children until it was finished or assistance was needed, "accepting" criticism, i.e., following the teacher's instructions to correct the work or whatever she chose to do when mistakes were made, and giving up an activity for another when it was time. (The socialization teacher concentrates on classroom behavior without feeling obligated to also teach the children to read, write and so on. However, reading and writing may be the vehicles for teaching self-control and these were started as the boys indicated they were ready. All the boys who graduated were at least taught to select their own names, to identify colors, and to do some counting. One boy became a refreshing sort of problem to Miss Moore. She had difficulty giving him enough work and work that was advanced enough.)

One of the first steps in teaching the children to persist in activities and to delay reinforcement was to find repetitive and not uninstructive tasks which they could do alone, for example, matching pictures and sorting objects. At first only a small amount of work was given and the teacher responded quickly with reinforcement when that was completed. Later, she programmed in delays by acknowledging a raised hand but approaching the pupil say 30 seconds later. The time was extended until she felt confident that the pupil would wait until she had time to assist or go over the work. That is, we did not extend the time to some arbitrary figure.

I shall give just one other example of what took place in class. Most primary teachers use workbooks. Whatever one may think about most workbooks, the fact is teachers use them and the pupil who does not follow the instructions and answer correctly is a burden. Therefore, Miss Moore made a variety of workbook-like pages. The simplest exercises taught the children to find a row, the top (bottom) of the page. For example, the instruction, "Put your finger (pencil) on the top of the page" was given and each pupil who responded correctly was praised and reinforced in turn. Those who did not attend or made no move to comply were bypassed. Those who complied incorrectly were assisted. More advanced sheets included items that required a different response from row to row, matching words with pictures, matching quantities with numbers and so on.

Exercises such as the above also taught the children to listen. Another simple activity to accomplish that end involved instructions like: "Put your finger on the blue cup," "pick up the blue cup," "give the blue cup to Johnny." The pupils were reinforced only if they precisely followed the instructions. That is, if asked to pick it up, pupils were not reinforced if they pointed or gave it to Johnny.

In September, 6 of the 20 children were assigned to educable or trainable classes in the Murdoch Center School and transferred to a ward for more capable children. Six others were assigned to "regular" classes but were not transferred and one was sent to another institution. His transfer was also a promotion. One of the boys who stayed in our ward was expelled almost immediately. We have received no complaints from either the principal or their teachers about the behavior of the others. An assistant recently interviewed the boys' teachers. By and large these boys do not stand out either negatively or positively. Although on one hand the teachers have much lower standards then we would set, their reports do correlate highly with our expectations. The one boy rated negatively on practically every question has not been transferred from the training ward because he continues to be a problem. That most of the boys have not been expelled and their classrooms are still intact are about the only claims we can make at this point.

The results indicate that something about our procedures was effective in enabling many pupils to at least stay in the school program. Others clearly needed more intensive and individual work before being taught in a group. The results show that children can be started on an unnatural reinforcement system, i.e., one that involves edibles and tangibles immediately presented, and subsequently be taught to work for intangibles, more remote and inconsistently delivered reinforcers — the kind of reinforcement system that teachers often practice.

The work to date in no way qualifies as research. Rather, it was a learning experience for us. The next steps are to replicate the procedures and to systematically evaluate the function of various aspects of them with the aim of building a socialization program made up of tested components.

In conclusion the notion of a socialization teacher is one worth serious consideration and does not need to be limited to retarded or disturbed children. Most problem behavior in school stems from the use of inappropriate reinforcers or the noncontingent or unsystematic use of events and, in particular, attention that could be used as reinforcers. There are two approaches. One is to use reinforcers appropriate to the pupil with whom you are working no matter what that reinforcer might be such as edibles. A second is to concentrate upon establishing preferably in the young child, the conditioned reinforcers that society is accustomed to offering. This, supplemented by the already evident trend for making education more immediately pertinent to the life condition of the children being educated has merit. The work Sue Moore did demonstrates that children can be so prepared and is replicable work. Now, we need the replication and systematic analyses of the procedures.

REFERENCES

Bijou, S. W., Birnbrauer, J. S., Kidder, J. D. and Tague, Cecilia, "Programmed instruction as an approach to the teaching of reading, writing, and arithmetic to retarded children." *The Psychological Record*, 1966, 16, 505–522.
Birnbrauer, J. S., and Lawler, Julia, "Token reinforcement for learning." *Mental Retardation*, 1964, 2, 275–279.
Watson, John B., *Behaviorism*. Chicago: University of Chicago Press, Revised Edition, 1930.

19

A Token Reinforcement Program in a Public School: A Replication and Systematic Analysis

K. D. O'Leary, *State University of New York at Stony Brook*
W. C. Becker, *University of Oregon*
M. B. Evans, *University of Illinois*
R. A. Saudargas, *Florida State University*

A base rate of disruptive behavior was obtained for seven children in a second-grade class of 21 children. Rules, Educational Structure, and Praising Appropriate Behavior while Ignoring Disruptive Behavior were introduced successively; none of these procedures consistently reduced disruptive behavior. However, a combination of Rules, Educational Structure, and Praise and Ignoring nearly eliminated disruptive behavior of one child. When the Token Reinforcement Program was introduced, the frequency of disruptive behavior declined in five of the six remaining children. Withdrawal of the Token Reinforcement Program increased disruptive behavior in these five chil-

From *Journal of Applied Behavior Analysis*, 1969, **2** (1), 3–13. Portions of this paper were presented to the American Psychological Association, September, 1968, San Francisco, California. This research was supported primarily by Research Grant HD 00881-05 to Wesley C. Becker from the National Institutes of Health and secondarily by a Biomedical Science Grant 31-8200 to K. Daniel O'Leary from the State University of New York at Stony Brook. The authors are grateful to Nancy Brown, Connie Dockterman, Pearl Dorfmann, Jeanne Kappauf, Margery Lewy, Stanley Madsen, and Darlene Zientarski who were the major observers in this study. Appreciation for support of this study is expressed to Dr. Lowell Johnson, Director of Instruction, Urbana Public Schools, and to Mr. Richard Sturgeon, elementary school principal. The greatest thanks goes to Mrs. Linda Alsberg, the teacher who executed the Token Reinforcement Program and tolerated the presence of observers both morning and afternoon for eight months. Her patience and self-control during the Praise and Withdrawal Phases of the program were especially appreciated. Reprints may be obtained from K. Daniel O'Leary, Dept. of Psychology, State University of New York at Stony Brook, Stony Brook, N.Y. 11790.

dren, and reinstatement of the Token Reinforcement Program reduced disruptive behavior in four of these five. Follow-up data indicated that the teacher was able to transfer control from the token and back-up reinforcers to the reinforcers existing within the educational setting, such as stars and occasional pieces of candy. Improvements in academic achievement during the year may have been related to the Token Program and attendance records appeared to be enhanced during the Token phases. The Token Program was utilized only in the afternoon, and the data did not indicate any generalization of appropriate behavior from the afternoon to the morning.

Praise and other social stimuli connected with the teacher's behavior have been established as effective controllers of children's behavior (Allen, Hart, Buell, Harris, and Wolf, 1964; Becker, Madsen, Arnold, and Thomas, 1967; Brown and Elliot, 1965; Hall, Lund, and Jackson, 1968; Harris, Johnston, Kelley, and Wolf, 1964; Harris, Wolf, and Baer, 1964; Scott, Burton, and Yarrow, 1967; Zimmerman and Zimmerman, 1962). When the teacher's use of praise and social censure is not effective, token reinforcement programs are often successful in controlling children (Birnbrauer, Wolf, Kidder, and Tague, 1965; Kuypers, Becker, and O'Leary, 1968; O'Leary and Becker, 1967; Quay, Werry, McQueen, and Sprague, 1966; Wolf, Giles, and Hall, 1968).

The token reinforcement program utilized by O'Leary and Becker (1967) in a third-grade adjustment class dramatically reduced disruptive behavior. In order to maximize the possibility of reducing the disruptive behavior of the children, O'Leary and Becker used several major variables simultaneously. The first objective of the present study was to analyze the separate effects of some of the variables utilized in the former study. More specifically, the aim was to examine the separate effects of Classroom Rules, Educational Structure, Teacher Praise, and a Token Reinforcement Program on children's disruptive behavior. Rules consisted of a list of appropriate behaviors that were reviewed daily. Educational Structure was the organization of an academic program into specified 30-min lessons such as spelling and arithmetic. The second objective was to assess whether a Token Reinforcement Program used only in the afternoon had any effect on the children's behavior in the morning. Third, the present study sought to examine the extent to which the effects of the Token Reinforcement Program persisted when the Token Program was discontinued.

Method

Subjects

Seven members of a second-grade class of 21 children from lower-middle class homes served. At the beginning of the school year, the class had a mean age of 7 yr, 5 months, a mean IQ score of 95 (range

80 to 115) on the California Test of Mental Maturity, and a mean grade level of 1.5 on the California Achievement Test. The class was very heterogeneous with regard to social behaviors. According to the teacher, three of the children were quite well behaved but at least eight exhibited a great deal of undesirable behavior. The teacher, Mrs. A., had a master's degree in counseling but had only student teaching experience. She was invited to participate in a research project involving her class and received four graduate credits for participating in the project.

Observation

CHILDREN. Mrs. A. selected seven children for observation. All seven children were observed in the afternoon and four of the seven (S1, S2, S4, and S6) were also observed in the morning. Morning observations were made by a regular observer and a reliability checker from 9:30 to 11:30 every Monday, Wednesday, and Friday. Afternoon observations were made by two regular observers and a reliability checker from 12:30 to 2:30 every Monday, Wednesday, and Friday. Observations were made by undergraduate students who were instructed never to talk to the children or to make any differential responses to them in order to minimize the effect of the observers on the children's behavior. Before Base Period data were collected, the undergraduates were trained to observe the children over a three-week period in the classroom, and attention-seeking behaviors of the children directed at the observers were effectively eliminated before the Base Period.

Each child was observed for 20 min each day. The observers watched the children in a random order. Observations were made on a 20-sec observe, 10-sec record basis; *i.e.*, the observer would watch the child for 20 sec and then take 10 sec to record the disruptive behaviors which had occurred during that 20-sec period. The categories of behavior selected for observation were identical to those used by O'Leary and Becker (1967). Briefly, the seven general categories of disruptive behavior were as follows: (1) *motor behaviors:* wandering around the room; (2) *aggressive behaviors:* hitting, kicking, stricking another child with an object; (3) *disturbing another's property:* grabbing another's book, tearing up another's paper; (4) *disruptive noise:* clapping, stamping feet; (5) *turning around:* turning to the person behind or looking to the rear of the room when Mrs. A. was in the front of the class; (6) *verbalization:* talking to others when not permitted by teacher, blurting out answers, name-calling; and (7) *inappropriate tasks:* doing arithmetic during the spelling lesson.

The present study was a systematic replication of O'Leary and Becker (1967). To facilitate comparison of the two studies, the dependent measure reported is the percentage of intervals in which one or more disruptive behaviors was recorded. Percentages rather than frequencies were used because the length of the observations varied due to unavoidable circumstances such as assemblies and snow storms. Nonetheless, most observations lasted the full 20 min, and no observation lasting less than 15 min was included.

TEACHER. In order to estimate the degree to which the teacher followed the experimental instructions, Mrs. A. was observed by two undergraduates for 90 min on Tuesday and Thursday afternoons. Teacher behavior was not observed on Monday, Wednesday, and Friday when the children were observed because Mrs. A. understandably did not wish to have as many as five observers in the room at one time. Furthermore, because Mrs. A. was somewhat reluctant to have three regular observers and one or two graduate students in the room at most times, she was informed of the need for this observational intrusion and the mechanics thereof. This explanation made it impossible to assess the teacher's behavior without her knowledge, but it was felt that deception about teacher observation could have been harmful both to this project and future projects in the school. Nonetheless, frequent teacher observations by two graduate students who were often in the room the entire week ensured some uniformity of her behavior throughout the week. The graduate students frequently met with Mrs. A. to alert her to any deviations from the experimental instructions, and equally important, to reinforce her "appropriate" behavior. Observations of the teacher's behavior were made on a 20-sec observe, 10-sec record basis. The categories of teacher behavior selected for observation were as follows:

I. Comments *preceding* responses.
   A. *Academic instruction:* "Now we will do arithmetic"; "Put everything in your desk"; "Sound out the words."
   B. *Social instruction:* "I'd like you to say 'please' and 'thank you'"; "Let me see a quiet hand"; "Let's sit up."

II. Comments *following* responses.
   A. *Praise:* "Good"; "Fine"; "You're right"; "I like the way I have your attention."
   B. *Criticism:* "Don't do that"; "Be quiet"; "Sit in your seat!"
   C. *Threats:* "If you're not quiet by the time I count three. . . ."; "If you don't get to work you will stay after school"; "Do you want to stay in this group?"

The teacher's praise, criticism, and threats to individual children were differentiated from praise, criticism, and threats to the class as a whole. For example, "Johnny, be quiet!" was differentiated from "Class, be quiet!" Thus, eight different classes of teacher behavior were recorded: two classes of comments preceding responses and six classes following responses.

Procedure

The eight phases of the study were as follows: (1) Base Period, (2) Classroom Rules, (3) Educational Structure, (4) Praising Appropriate Behavior and Ignoring Disruptive Behavior, (5) Tokens and Back-up Reinforcement, (6) Praising Appropriate Behavior and Ignoring Disruptive Behavior (Withdrawal), (7) Tokens and Back-up Reinforcement, and (8) Follow-up. Three procedures, Educational Structure and both of the Token Reinforcement Phases, were instituted for a 2-hr period during the afternoon. The remainder of the procedures were in effect for the entire day. The eight procedures were in effect for all 21 children. The first four conditions were instituted in the order of hypothesized increasing effectiveness. For example, it was thought that Rules would have less effect on the children's behavior then the use of Praise. In addition, it was thought that the combination of Rules and Praise would have less effect than the Tokens and Back-up Reinforcers.

BASE PERIOD. After the initial three-week observer training period, the children were observed on eight days over a six-week Base Period to estimate the frequency of disruptive pupil behavior under usual classroom conditions.[2] The teacher was asked to handle the children in whatever way she felt appropriate. During the Base Period, Mrs. A. instructed all the children in subjects like science and arithmetic or took several students to small reading groups in the back of the room while the rest of the class engaged in independent work at their seats. Neither the particular type of activity nor the duration was the same each day. Stars and various forms of peer pressure were sporadically used as classroom control techniques, but they usually had little effect and were discontinued until experimentally reintroduced during the Follow-up Phase.

CLASSROOM RULES. There were seven observations over a three-week period during the second phase of the study. The following rules or instructions were placed on the blackboard by the teacher: "We sit in our seats; we raise our hands to talk; we do not talk out of turn; we keep our desks clear; we face the front of the room; we will work very hard; we do not talk in the hall; we do not run; and, we do not disturb reading groups." Mrs. A. was asked to review the rules at least once every morning and afternoon, and frequent observations and discussions with Mrs. A. guaranteed that this was done on most occasions. The classroom activities again consisted of reading groups and independent seat work.

EDUCATIONAL STRUCTURE. It has been stated that a great deal of the success in token reinforcement programs may be a function

---

2. Ten of the 18 observations during the Base Period were eliminated because movies were shown on those days, and disruptive behavior on those days was significantly less than on days when movies were not shown. Although movies were seldom used after Base Period, the seven subsequent observations when movies occurred were eliminated.

of the highly structured regimen of the program and not a function of reinforcement contingencies. Since the Token Phase of the program was designed to be used during structured activities that the teacher directed, Mrs. A. was asked to reorganize her program into four 30-min sessions in the afternoon in which the whole class participated, *e.g.*, spelling, reading, arithmetic, and science. Thus, the purpose of the Educational Structure Phase was to assess the importance of structure *per se*. Mrs. A. continued to review the rules twice a day during this phase and all succeeding phases. During this phase there were five observations over a two-week period.

PRAISE AND IGNORE. In addition to Rules and Educational Structure, Mrs. A. was asked to praise appropriate behavior and to ignore disruptive behavior as much as possible. For example, she was asked to ignore children who did not raise their hands before answering questions and to praise children who raised their hands before speaking. In addition, she was asked to discontinue her use of threats. During this phase there were five observations over a two-week period.

TOKEN I. Classroom Rules, Educational Structure, and Praise and Ignoring remained in effect. The experimenter told the children that they would receive points or ratings four times each afternoon. The points which the children received on these four occasions ranged from 1 to 10, and the children were told that the points would reflect the extent to which they followed the rules placed on the blackboard by Mrs. A. Where possible, these points also reflected the quality of the children's participation in class discussion and the accuracy of their arithmetic or spelling. The children's behavior in the morning did not influence their ratings in the afternoon. If a child was absent, he received no points. The points or tokens were placed in small booklets on each child's desk. The points were exchangeable for back-up reinforcers such as candy, pennants, dolls, comics, barrettes, and toy trucks, ranging in value from 2 to 30 cents. The variety of prizes made it likely that at least one of the items would be a reinforcer for each child. The prizes were on display every afternoon, and the teacher asked each child to select the prize he wished to earn before the rating period started.

During the initial four days, the children were eligible for prizes just after their fourth rating at approximately 2:30. Thereafter, all prizes were distributed at the end of the day. For the first 10 school days the children could receive prizes each day. There were always two levels of prizes. During the first 10 days, a child had to receive at least 25 points to receive a 2 to 5¢ prize (level one prize) or 35 points to receive a 10¢ prize (level two prize). For the next six days, points were accumulated for two days and exchanged at the end of the second day. When children saved their points for two days, a child had to receive 55 points to receive a 10¢ prize or 70 points to receive a 20¢ prize. Then, a six-day period occurred in which points were accumulated for three days and exchanged at the end of the third day. During this period, a child had to receive 85 points to receive a 20¢ prize or 105 points to receive a 30¢ prize. Whenever the prizes were distributed, the children relinquished all their points. During Token I, there were 13 observations over a five-week period.

For the first week, the experimenter repeated the instructions to the class at the beginning of each afternoon session. Both the experimenter and Mrs. A. rated the children each day for the first week in order to teach Mrs. A. how to rate the children. The experimenter sat in the back of the room and handed his ratings to Mrs. A. in a surreptitious manner after each rating period. Mrs. A. utilized both ratings in arriving at a final rating which she put in the children's booklets at the end of each lesson period. The method of arriving at a number or rating to be placed in the child's booklet was to be based on the child's improvement in behavior. That is, if a child showed any daily improvement he could receive a rating of approximately 5 to 7 so that he could usually earn at least a small prize. Marked improvement in behavior or repeated displays of relatively good behavior usually warranted ratings from 8 to 10. Ratings from 1 to 5 were given when a child was disruptive and did not evidence any daily improvement. Although such a rating system involves much subjective judgment on the part of the teacher, it is relatively easy to implement, and a subsidiary aim of the study was to assess whether a token system could be implemented by one teacher in a class of average size. After the first week, the teacher administered the Token Program herself, and the experimenter was never present when the children were being observed. If the experimenter had been present during the Token Phases but not during Withdrawal, any effects of the Token Program would have been confounded by the experimenter's presence.

WITHDRAWAL. To demonstrate that the token and back-up reinforcers and not other factors, such as the changes that ordinarily occur during the school year, accounted for the observed reduction in disruptive behavior, the token and back-up reinforcers were withdrawn during this phase. There were seven observations over a five-week period. When the prizes and the booklets were removed from the room, Mrs. A. told the children that she still hoped that they would behave as well as they had during the Token Period and emphasized how happy she was with their recent improvement. Rules, Educational Structure, and Praise and Ignoring remained in effect.

TOKEN II. When the tokens and back-up reinforcers were reinstated, the children obtained a prize on the first day if they received 25 to 35 points. For the next four days there was a one-day delay between token and back-up reinforcement; the remainder of the Token Reinstatement Period involved a two-day delay of reinforcement. The prize and point system was identical to that during Token

I. During this phase, there were five observations over a two-week period.

Follow-up. The token and back-up reinforcers were again withdrawn in order to see if the appropriate behavior could be maintained under more normal classroom conditions. In addition to the continued use of Praise, Rules, and Educational Structure, it was suggested that Mrs. A. initiate the use of a systematic star system. Children could receive from one to three stars for good behavior twice during the morning and once during the afternoon. In addition, the children received extra stars for better behavior during the morning restroom break and for displaying appropriate behavior upon entering the room at 9:15 and 12:30. At times, extra stars were given to the best behaved row of children. The children counted their stars at the end of the day; if they had 10 or more stars, they received a gold star that was placed on a permanent wall chart. If a child received 7 to 9 stars, he received a green star that was placed on the chart. The boys' gold stars and the girls' gold stars were counted each day; and each member of the group with the greater number of gold stars at the end of the week received a piece of candy. In addition, any child who received an entire week of gold stars received a piece of candy. All children began the day without stars so that, with the exception of the stars placed on the wall chart, everyone entered the program at the same level.

Such a procedure was a form of a token reinforcement program, but there were important procedural differences between the experimental phases designated Token and Follow-up. The back-up reinforcers used during the Token Phases were more expensive than the two pieces of candy a child could earn each week during the Follow-up Phase. In addition, four daily ratings occurred at half-hour intervals in the afternoons during the Token Phases but not during Follow-up. On the other hand, stars, peer pressure, and a very small amount of candy were used in the Follow-up Phase. As mentioned previously, both stars and peer pressure had been used sporadically in the Base Period with little effect. Most importantly, it was felt that the procedures used in the Follow-up Phase could be implemented by any teacher. During this phase there were six observations over a four-week period.

Reliability of Observations

The reliabilities of child observations were calculated according to the following procedure: an agreement was scored if both observers recorded one or more disruptive behaviors within the same 20-sec interval; a disagreement was scored if one observer recorded a disruptive behavior and the other observer recorded none. The reliability of the measure of disruptive behavior was calculated for each child each day by dividing the number of intervals in which there was agreement that one or more disruptive behaviors occurred by the total number of agreements plus disagreements. An agreement was scored if both observers recorded the same behavior within the same 20-sec interval. A disagreement was scored if one observer recorded the behavior and the other did not. The reliability of a particular class of teacher behavior on any one day was calculated by dividing the total number of agreements for that class of behaviors by the total number of agreements plus disagreements for that class of behaviors. Reliabilities were calculated differently for child behaviors and teacher behaviors because different types of dependent measures were utilized for children and the teacher, and it was felt that reliability measures should be reported for the specific dependent measures used.

At least one reliability check was made during the afternoon on every child during the Base Period, and one child had three.[3] The average reliability of the measure of disruptive behavior during the afternoons of the Base Period for each of the seven children ranged from 88 to 100%. The following figures represent the number of reliability checks and the average of those reliability checks after the Base Period through the first Token Period for each child: S1: 6, 86%; S2: 7, 94%; S3: 6, 94%; S4: 6, 93%; S5: 6, 87%; S6: 6, 84%; S7: 6, 97%. Because of the repeated high reliabilities, reliability checks were discontinued when the token and back-up reinforcers were reinstated; i.e., no reliability checks were made during or after the Withdrawal Phase.

Adequate morning reliabilities were not obtained until the Rules Phase of the study. The following figures represent the number of reliability checks and the average of those reliability checks during the Rules Phase: S1: 3, 93%; S2: 4, 68%; S4: 3, 91%; S6: 3, 88%. Morning reliability checks after the Rules Phase were made approximately every three observations (approximately seven occasions) through the first Token Period. Average reliabilities of the four children during the Rules, Educational Structure, Praise and Ignore, and Token I Phases ranged from 92 to 99%.

Eleven reliability checks for the various classes of teacher behavior before the Praise and Ignore Phase was introduced yielded average reliabilities as follows: academic instruction, 75%; social instruction, 77%; praise to individuals, 77%; praise to the class, 94%; criticism to individuals, 73%; criticism to the class, 72%; threats to individuals, 83%; and threats to the class, 83%.

---

3. Before 10 of the 18 observation days during the Base Period were eliminated because movies were shown on those days, at least three reliability checks had been made during the afternoon on each child.

Results

Child Behavior

Figures 1 and 2 present morning and afternoon data; some of the variability within conditions can be seen. Figure 3 presents data of individual children as well as an average of seven children across afternoon conditions. An analysis of variance was performed on the percentages of combined disruptive behavior, averaged within the eight afternoon experimental conditions, for the seven subjects (see Fig. 3). The analysis of variance for repeated measures (Winer, 1962, p. 111) indicated differences among the eight experimental conditions ($F = 7.3$; $df = 7$, 42; $p < 0.001$). On the other hand, the percentages of combined disruptive behavior of the four children observed in the morning, averaged within conditions, did not change during Rules, Educational Structure, Praise and Ignore, or Token I ($F = 1.0$; $df = 4$, 12). Differences among afternoon conditions were assessed by t-tests. Significant and nonsignificant differences are grouped individually in Table 1.[4]

It should be emphasized that comparisons between Follow-up and Praise and Ignore are more meaningful than comparisons between Follow-up and Base, Rules, or Educational Structure. Praise and Follow-up were similar procedures; both included Rules, Educational Structure, and Praise and Ignore. The Base Period did not include any of these. Furthermore, after Rules and Educational Structure were initiated, Mrs. A. stated that she required more academic work from the children than during Base Period. A statistical analysis of the group data suggests that a token reinforcement program can reduce disruptive behavior and that a token reinforcement program can be replaced with a variant of a token program without an increase in disruptive behavior. However, a more detailed analysis of the data for individual children indicated that the Token Reinforcement Program was more effective for some children than others.

The introduction of Rules, Educational Structure, and Praise and Ignore did not have any consistent effects on behavior (see Fig. 3). Praising Appropriate Behavior and Ignoring Disruptive Behavior deserve special mention. Although Mrs. A. used criticism occasionally during the Praise and Ignore Phase, she generally ignored disruptive behavior and used praise frequently. Initially, a number of children responded well to Mrs. A.'s praise, but two boys (S2 and S4) who had been disruptive all year became progressively more unruly during the Praise and Ignore Phase. Other children appeared to observe these boys being disruptive, with little or no aversive consequences, and soon became disruptive themselves. Relay races

---

4. Two-tailed tests.

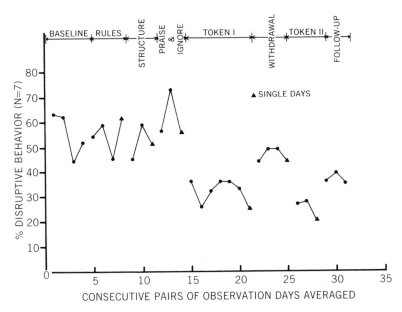

Fig. 1. Average percentage of combined disruptive behavior of seven children during the afternoon over the eight conditions: Base, Rules, Educational Structure, Praise and Ignore, Token I, Withdrawal, Token II, Follow-up

and hiding under a table contributed to the pandemonium. Several children were so disruptive that the academic pursuits of the rest of the class became impossible. The situation became intolerable, and the Praise and Ignore Phase had to be discontinued much earlier than had been planned.

The disruptive behavior of S7 was reduced to a very low level of 15% by a combination of Rules, Educational Structure, and Praise and Ignore. In the previous token program (O'Leary and Becker, 1967), in which a number of variables including rules, praise, educational structure, and a token program were simultaneously introduced, disruptive behavior during the token period was reduced to a level of 10%. Thus, the present Token Reinforcement Program probably would not be expected further to reduce disruptive behavior in this child.

During Token I, there was a marked reduction ($\geq 18\%$) in the disruptive behavior of five children (S1, S2, S3, S4, and S6) and a reduction of 3% in S5. Withdrawal of the Token Program increased disruptive behavior from 5% to 45% in these six children. Reinstatement of the Token Program led to a decrease in five of these six children (S1, S2, S3, S4, S5). The disruptive behavior of five children (S1, S2, S4, S5, and S6) ranged from 8% to 39% lower during the Follow-up than during the Praise and Ignore Phase of the study. Since on no occasion did the Follow-up procedures precede Token

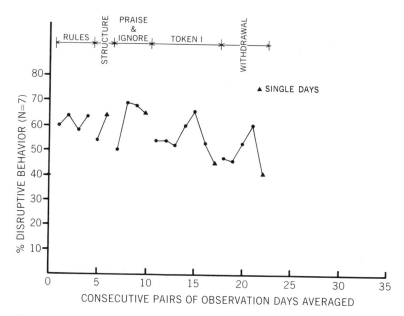

Fig. 2. Average percentage of combined disruptive behavior of four children during the morning over five conditions: Base, Rules, Educational Structure, Praise and Ignore, Token I, Withdrawal, Token II, Follow-up

I and/or Token II, this study did not demonstrate that Token I and/or Token II were necessary conditions for the success of the Follow-up procedures.

In summary, Token I and Token II were definitely associated with a reduction of disruptive behavior, *and* the Follow-up procedure was effective with three of the six children (S1, S2, and S4) who had more than 15% disruptive behavior during the Praise and Ignore Phase (S7 had 15% disruptive behavior during the Praise and Ignore Phase). Token I and Token II were associated with marked reductions of disruptive behavior of S3, but the frequency of disruptive

TABLE 1

Significant		Non-Significant	
Token I *vs.* Withdrawal	$t=3.3^{**}$	Rules *vs.* Educational Structure	$t=0.8$
Token II *vs.* Withdrawal	$t=2.9^{*}$	Educational Structure *vs.* Praise	$t=1.0$
Token I *vs.* Praise	$t=3.4^{**}$	Base *vs.* Withdrawal	$t=1.2$
Token II *vs.* Praise	$t=3.0^{*}$	Token I *vs.* Follow-up	$t=1.1$
Base *vs.* Follow-up	$t=3.2^{**}$	Token II *vs.* Follow-up	$t=1.5$
Praise *vs.* Follow-up	$t=3.3^{**}$		
Withdrawal *vs.* Follow-up	$t=3.2^{**}$		

$^{**}p < 0.02, df = 6$
$^{*}p < 0.05, df = 6$

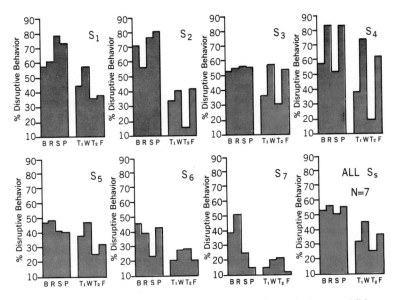

Fig. 3. Percentage of combined disruptive behavior for each of seven children during the eight conditions: Base, Rules, Educational Structure, Praise and Ignore, Token I, Withdrawal, Token II, Follow-up

behavior during the Follow-up was not substantially lower than during the Praise and Ignore Phase. Definitive conclusions concerning the effects of the Token Program cannot be drawn for S5 and S6, although some reduction of disruptive behavior was associated with either Token I and Token II for both of these children. In addition, the disruptive behavior of S5 and S6 was 8% and 20% less respectively during Follow-up than during the Praise and Ignore Phase.

Teacher Behavior

On any one day, the percentage of each of the eight classes of teacher behavior was calculated by dividing the number of intervals in which a particular class of behavior occurred by the total number of intervals observed on that day. Percentages rather than frequencies were used because of slight variations from the usual 90-min time base.

The percentages of different classes of teacher behavior were averaged within two major conditions: (1) data before Praise and Ignore Phase, and (2) data in the Praise and Ignore and succeeding Phases. The data in Fig. 4 show that in the Praise and Ignore Phase, Mrs. A. increased use of praise to individual children from 12% to 31% and decreased use of criticism to individuals from 22% to 10%. Mrs. A. also increased use of praise to the class from 1% to 7% and decreased criticism directed to the class from 11% to 3%. Because the frequency of threats was quite low, threats to individuals and threats to the class were combined in one measure. Using this com-

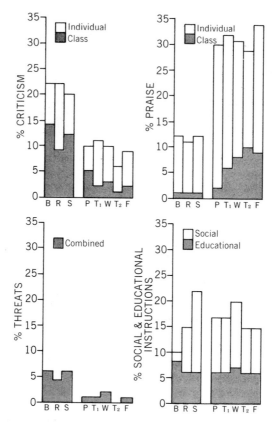

Fig. 4. Percentage of various teacher behaviors to individuals and to the class during the eight conditions: Base, Rules, Educational Structure, Praise and Ignore, Token I, Withdrawal, Token II, Follow-up

bined measure, Mrs. A.'s use of threats decreased from 5% to 1%. There were no differences in Mrs. A.'s use of academic or social instruction. Consequently, the changes in the children's disruptive behavior can probably be attributed to contingencies and not to Mrs. A.'s use of cues concerning the desired behaviors.

Discussion

Although a Token Reinforcement Program was a significant variable in reducing disruptive behavior in the present study, the results are less dramatic than those obtained by O'Leary and Becker, (1967). A number of factors probably contributed to the difference in effectiveness of the programs. The average of disruptive behavior during the Base Period in the 1967 study was 76%; in the present study it was 53%. The gradual introduction of the various phases of the program was probably less effective than a simultaneous introduction of all the procedures, as in the previous study. In the earlier study, the children received more frequent ratings. Five ratings were made each day at the introduction of the 1.5-hr token program, and they were gradually reduced to three ratings per day. In the present study, the children received four ratings per day during a 2-hr period. In the 1967 study, the class could earn points for popsicles by being quiet while the teacher placed ratings in the children's booklets; in the present study, group points were not incorporated into the general reinforcement program. In the 1967 study, the teacher attended a weekly psychology seminar where teachers discussed various applications of learning principles to classroom management. An *esprit de corps* was generated from that seminar that probably increased the teacher's commitment to change the children's behavior. Although Mrs. A. received graduate credits for her extensive participation in the project, she did not attend a seminar in classroom management. A number of children in the present study had an abundance of toys at home and it was difficult to obtain inexpensive prizes which would serve as reinforcers; in the earlier study, selection of reinforcers was not a difficult problem, since the children were from disadvantaged homes.

Related Gains

ACADEMIC. The 14 children for whom there were both pre- and post-measures on the California Achievement Test (including S1, S4, S5, S6, and S7) gained an average of 1.5 yr from October to June. The mean CAT score in October was 1.5 while the mean score in June was 3.0. Although there was no matched control group, such gains are greater than those usually obtained (Tiegs and Clark, 1963). While such gains are promising, conclusions about the effects of a token system on academic performance must await a more systematic analysis.

ATTENDANCE. Comparisons of the attendance records of the seven children during the observational days of the token and non-token phases yielded the following results: the average attendance percentage during the 45 observation days of Base, Rules, Educational Structure, Praise and Ignore, and Withdrawal was 86%. The average attendance percentage during the 20 observation days of Token I and Token II was 98%; the average attendance percentage during the 26 observation days of Token I, Token II, and Follow-up (a variant of a token program) was 99%. These attendance records are very encouraging, but because of the usual seasonal variations in attendance and the small sample of children, more definitive evidence is needed before conclusions about the effects of a token program on attendance can be made.

Cost of Program

The cost of the reinforcers in the present study was approximately $125.00. It is estimated that 3 hr of consulting time per week would be essential to operate a token reinforcement program effectively for one class in a public school. The cost of such a program and the amount of consulting time seem relatively small when compared to the hours psychologists spend in therapy with children, often without producing significant behavioral changes (Levitt, 1963). Furthermore, as evidenced in the present study, control of behavior may be shifted from reinforcers, such as toys, to reinforcers existing within the natural educational setting, such as stars and peer prestige.

Generalization

During the morning, the majority of the children were engaged in independent seat work, while four or five children were in a reading group with the teacher in the back of the room. Although there were rules and frequent instructions during the morning, there was little reinforcement for appropriate behavior, since Mrs. A. felt that it would be disruptive to the rest of the class to interrupt reading groups to praise children who were doing independent work at their seats. Ayllon and Azrin (1964) found that instructions without reinforcement had little effect on the behavior of mental patients. Similarly, Rules (instructions) without reinforcement did not influence the behavior of the children in this study.

Mrs. A. was instructed to praise appropriate behavior and ignore disruptive behavior in the morning as well as the afternoon. However, Mrs. A.'s criteria of appropriate behavior in the morning differed from her criteria in the afternoon. For example, in the morning she often answered questions when a child failed to raise his hand before speaking. In the afternoon, on the other hand, she generally ignored a child unless he raised his hand. In order to achieve "generalization" of appropriate behavior in a Token Program such as this one, the teacher's response to disruptive behavior must remain constant throughout the day. The percentage of disruptive behavior was reduced during the morning of the first few days of Token I, but the children presumably learned to discriminate that their appropriate behavior was reinforced only in the afternoon. The differences in the children's behavior between the morning and the afternoon help to stress the point that "generalization" is no magical process, but rather a behavioral change which must be engineered like any other change.

References

Allen, K. Eileen, Hart, Betty M., Buell, Joan S., Harris, Florence R., and Wolf, M. M. Effects of social reinforcement on isolate behavior of a nursery school child. *Child Development*, 1964, **35**, 511–518.

Ayllon, T., and Azrin, N. H. Reinforcement and instructions with mental patients. *Journal of the Experimental Analysis of Behavior*, 1964, **7**, 327–331.

Becker, W. C., Madsen, C. H., Arnold, Carole R., and Thomas, D. R. The contingent use of teacher attention and praise in reducing classroom behavior problems. *Journal of Special Education*, 1967, **1**, (3), 287–307.

Birnbrauer, J. S., Wolf, M. M., Kidder, J. D., and Tague, Celia. Classroom behavior of retarded pupils with token reinforcement. *Journal of Experimental Child Psychology*, 1965, **2**, 219–235.

Brown, P., and Elliot, R. Control of aggression in a nursery school class. *Journal of Experimental Child Psychology*, 1965, **2**, 103–107.

Hall, R. V., Lund, Diane, and Jackson, Deloris. Effects of teacher attention on study behavior. *Journal of Applied Behavior Analysis*, 1968, **1**, 1–12.

Harris, Florence R., Johnston, Margaret K., Kelley, C. Susan, and Wolf, M. M. Effects of positive social reinforcement on regressed crawling of a nursery school child. *Journal of Educational Psychology*, 1964, **55**, 35–41.

Harris, Florence R., Wolf, M. M., and Baer, D. M. Effects of social reinforcement on child behavior. *Young Children*, 1964, **20**, 8–17.

Kuypers, D. S., Becker, W. C., and O'Leary, K. D. How to make a token system fail. *Exceptional Children*, 1968, **35**, 101–109.

Levitt, E. E. Psychotherapy with children: A further evaluation. *Behaviour Research and Therapy*, 1963, **1**, 45–51.

O'Leary, K. D., and Becker, W. C. Behavior modification of an adjustment class: A token reinforcement program. *Exceptional Children*, 1967, **33**, 637–642.

Quay, H. C., Werry, J. S., McQueen, Marjorie, and Sprague, R. L. Remediation of the conduct problem child in a special class setting. *Exceptional Children*, 1966, **32**, 509–515.

Scott, Phyllis M., Burton, R. V., and Yarrow, Marian R. Social reinforcement under natural conditions. *Child Development*, 1967, **38**, 53–63.

Tiegs, E. V., and Clark, W. W. Manual, California Achievement Tests, Complete Battery. 1963 Norms. California Test Bureau, Monterey, California.

Winer, B. J. *Statistical principles in experimental design*. New York: McGraw-Hill, 1962.

Wolf, M. M., Giles, D. K., and Hall, R. V. Experiments with token reinforcement in a remedial classroom. *Behavior Research and Therapy*, 1968, **6**, 51–64.

Zimmerman, Elaine H., and Zimmerman, J. The alteration of behavior in a special classroom situation. *Journal of the Experimental Analysis of Behavior*, 1962, **5**, 59–60.

20

The Functional Analysis of Behavior within an Experimental Class Setting

Hill M. Walker
Robert H. Mattson
Nancy K. Buckley

Department of Special Education
University of Oregon

The functional relationships that exist between treatment and behavioral variables in behavior modification technology have been most clearly validated through applications of learning theory principles with individuals. In group applications of learning theory, especially in classroom settings, it has been assumed that modifications in behavior are due to the manipulation of a group of treatment variables such as reinforcement schedules, antecedent events, academic consequences and so forth. However, there is little empirical data which clearly validates this assumption. Also, there is very little data on the *differential* effects or weight of treatment variables such as token reinforcement, aversive control, and social reinforcement in producing behavior change within the context of the classroom setting.

The decision to attempt modification of deviant behavior within special educational settings as opposed to regular educational settings should be weighed carefully in view of advantages and dis-

This paper is a revision of an article which originally appeared in *Modifying Deviant Social Behaviors in Various Classroom Settings*, edited by A. M. Benson, University of Oregon, Department of Special Education, College of Education, Monograph 1, 1969, pp. 49–80. This research was supported by USOE Grant #OEG 4-6-061308-0571: Assessment and Treatment of Deviant Behavior in Children. Bureau of Education for the Handicapped, Division of Research.

advantages for the children involved. As a general rule, special classes should be considered only for children whose academic and social behaviors cannot be feasibly or effectively modified within the regular classroom setting. Such placement might be required for children with extremely high rates of deviant behavior and/or severe deficits in their academic skill repertoires. The ultimate goal of any special class for treatment of deviant behavior should be the reintroduction of its subjects into the regular classroom as soon as it is behaviorally possible.

This paper describes a replication study of the validity of a treatment model (Mattos, Mattson, Walker, Buckley, 1969) which was designed to provide efficient modification of one class of deviant behavior: hyperactive, disruptive, acting-out behavior in the classroom. The data presented here were generated by an inter-subject replication of the design, procedures, and results of the treatment model and by an evaluation of the components of this model. Attention is also given to the persistence of treatment effects across time and across settings. The goal of this research was the development of a workable treatment model, adapted to the school setting, which can be implemented by regular school personnel.

Method

Subjects

During the academic year, twelve subjects were admitted to the experimental classroom. The subjects, all males in grades four, five, and six, were enrolled in two groups of six each.[1] Selection criteria used average or above average intellectual ability, inadequate academic performance, and socially deviant behavior occurring within the regular classroom setting. All subjects possessed a number of behaviors which made them poor candidates for learning. Teacher defiance, distractibility, hyperactivity, and tantrum behavior were attributed to the group as a whole. Individual behaviors exhibited were physical and verbal abuse of peers, pre-delinquent behaviors (stealing, smoking, glue-sniffing) rejection of peer interaction, and excessive verbal outbursts (swearing, loud noises, etc.). These behaviors were identified as most annoying to the regular classroom teacher; yet the subjects exhibited many additional behaviors illustrative of inadequate social and academic adjustment. All candidates for the experimental classroom were screened by the Walker Problem Behavior Identification Checklist,[2] a behavior rating scale

---

1. One subject dropped out of Group 2.
2. Copyright and publication by *Western Psychological Services, Inc.* 12031 Wilshire Blvd., Los Angeles, California.

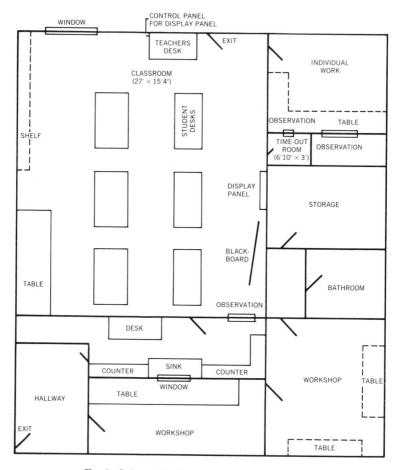

Fig. 1. Schematic diagram of treatment setting

(Walker, 1969) and baseline observations of attending behavior taken within the regular classroom.

All subjects scored average or above on standardized intelligence tests (WISC; Stanford-Binet), but had educational deficits in the basic skill areas of from 4 months to 5.1 years (Gray's Oral Reading and Wide Range Achievement Tests). None of the subjects displayed any physical or sensory deficits as measured by standard auditory, visual, and general health tests. A more extensive neurologic examination suggested that one S had evidence of minor brain damage. Another S was on mild tranquilizers prescribed by the family physician for his hyperactive behavior. He had been on the drugs for approximately one year before entering the class and continued throughout the course of treatment.

One group of subjects was used in Experiment I, and one group in Experiment II.

Setting

The classroom facilities were adjoining and affiliated with a public elementary school in the Eugene School District. The primary area for academic activities contained six double desks (approximately 20″ x 45″ work surface), the teacher's desk, and shelves and tables for the display of high interest materials. Adjoining rooms provided sink and table facilities for science and art projects, a carpentry room with a variety of tools and wood, and the necessary observation facilities. Space was also available for individual testing, tutoring, and remedial instruction. A small isolation room (time-out) containing a chair and desk adjoined the classroom (Figure I). The children used the same playground and lunch facilities as the regularly enrolled students in the school.

Academic materials used in the classroom were designed to meet the individual instructional requirements of each child. Since the subjects were academically retarded in math, reading, language, and/or spelling, instructional attention was focused on these basic skill areas. Specific educational programing was based upon diagnostic tests administered during the first week the subjects were enrolled in the experimental classroom. Materials used in the classroom included programed texts, books from the subjects' regular classrooms, and teacher prepared materials. The programed materials used were based on evaluations of materials conducted during the previous academic year (Mattson and Walker, 1967). Programed materials used included: (a) Sullivan Associates Programed Reading Series (McGraw-Hill), (b) Classroom Reading Clinic (Webster Co.), (c) Geography of the U. S. (Programed, McGraw and Williams), (d) Lessons in Self-Instruction in Basic Skills (California Test Bureau), and (e) T.M.I. Grolier Program (Teaching Machines, Inc.). The regular educational and remedial materials used included: (a) Conquests in Reading (Kottmeyer and Ware, McGraw-Hill), (b) Dr. Spello (Kottmeyer and Ware, McGraw-Hill), (c) Science Research Associates, Reading Series and Math Series, and (d) Continental Press mimeographed materials. In addition, four of the subjects received individual instruction from a graduate assistant in the Hegge-Kirk and Kirk drills.

Apparatus

Individual sixty-minute timers, placed on each child's desk, were used in a variety of ways to meet the specific behavioral requirements of each child. The timers were particularly effective in controlling high rate distractibility. When a subject produced distractive behavior (attending to non-task stimuli), he was placed on a timer for a specified period of time. The instructions to the S were that he was to attend to his task during that interval in order to receive points (reinforcers). The schedule was increased gradually from a time interval the subject could originally accommodate to one compatible with regular classroom requirements. This technique is based on the assumption that introducing a stimulus incompatible with distractions, which functions as an S^D for a reinforcing event, will lead to the response of academic production.

An electric, Universal interval timer with an eight-inch diameter face was used to record and monitor group attending behavior. The hands of the sixty-minute timer were placed on a VI schedule of thirty minutes during an academic activity. If the entire group was task-oriented during the time specified (using the same criteria as for individuals) they received a group point and the timer was reset for another interval. If at any time during the interval, one or more of the children was not task-oriented, the timer hands were placed back on the starting point and not restarted until the deviant behavior was terminated. The group points were recorded on a large cardboard "thermometer" in the front of the room. As each point was earned the red marker was moved up an additional notch. When the marker reached the top (twenty-five points) the children exchanged their group points for a reinforcement activity of their choice. These included slot car racing, pool, bowling, swimming, or museum trips. The group reinforcing climate was particularly potent since it incorporated positive stimuli (trips) and aversive consequences (peer disapproval) into the same procedure.

The project staff designed an electronic display board for recording reinforcing events and providing subjects with discriminative stimuli for appropriate and inappropriate behavior. The device was also designed to provide for a more systematic presentation and removal of points than can be accomplished with teacher marks on point sheets.

The display board contains a unit for each subject with name, stimulus light, three-digit plus and three-digit minus counters. A similar unit set apart from the rest and containing a larger light was used for recording and regulating the group reinforcing climate. Each subject was required to be in his seat ready to begin the assignment before his light came on. When the stimulus light was on, it signified that the child was behaving appropriately and that he had gained access to a schedule of reinforcement. When a child received a point, his light flashed, there was an audible click, and the cumulative counter recorded the event. If the child was behaving inappropriately, his light was extinguished and a buzzer sounded which signalled the occurrence of deviant behavior. The subject had ten seconds in which to modify his behavior. If he did not modify

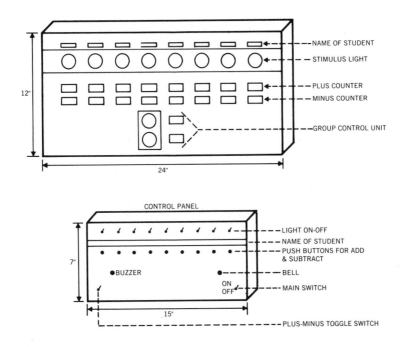

Fig. 2. Electronic display board

his behavior within this time period, one point was subtracted for every five seconds that the deviant behavior persisted. If it became necessary for a child to be placed in the time-out room or to be suspended from the experimental classroom, his stimulus light remained off, as did the group light, until he returned to the classroom.

Reinforcing System

The reinforcing system within the experimental classroom consisted of both social and non-social reinforcers. Subjects were able to earn points for appropriate social and academic behaviors which could later be exchanged for such tangible, back-up reinforcers as model cars, airplanes, games, books, paints, baseballs, and footballs. The advantage of using a large number of back-up reinforcers increases the probability that at least one of the stimuli will be relevant to the deprivation conditions of the various subjects (Ferster and DeMayer, 1962). These stimuli were grouped according to the number of points necessary to earn each item. The minimum interval of time necessary to earn the minimum stimulus (lowest point value) was approximately two days assuming the child was task-oriented during this period. Points were awarded on a combined interval-ratio basis.

Subjects also had the option of exchanging their points for free time which they could use to engage in a number of high frequency activities such as building models, playing chess, working on science and art projects, or reading. (One point was equal to one minute of free time.) The use of free time as a reinforcing alternative had several pragmatic advantages. It allowed each child to choose the free time activity that was most reinforcing for him. Free time, as a reinforcing event, can easily be used in the regular classroom to strengthen weak academic and social behaviors. In addition, teachers appear to be more amenable to consequating appropriate behavior with free time than with such contrived reinforcers as toys, trinkets, candy, etc. Finally, the use of reinforcing events available in the regular classroom can facilitate transfer of treatment effects back to full-time, regular class placement.

Observation and Recording

Graduate students in education, interested in working with deviant children, served as observers throughout the various special and regular class phases. Observers used a time-sampling technique with behavior recorded at the end of each ten-second unit during randomly selected ten-minute intervals. Interval timers that emitted a soft "bleep" through an earphone were used to insure accurate time estimation and made it unnecessary to divert attention from the subject's behavior during recording.

Although several behavior categories were recorded simultaneously, the primary criterion was the proportion of time each child spent in appropriate, task-oriented behavior. These same observation categories were used: (a) in the regular class prior to enrollment in the experimental classroom to determine the level of functioning with the use of traditional educational procedure, (b) during experimental class treatment to assess behavior change, and (c) after the child was returned to the regular classroom to assess how well modified behavior maintained within that setting.

In addition, during the time (2:00 to 3:30 P.M.) that the subjects were in their regular classes each day while enrolled in the token economy, observers recorded their behavior as well as the behavior of the "normal" children in their classroom. From these data, comparisons were made between: (a) the amount of task-oriented behavior of the deviant subjects and the classroom as a unit, and (b) the behavior of the deviant subjects in the regular classroom in relation to their concurrent behavior in the experimental class. During placement in the special class, from two to three ten-minute observations were obtained for each child per day. The amount of time spent in

Name_____Date_____Observer_____
                         Indiv._____
Activity_____Group_____ Time_____ To_____
                         Treatment Period
Baseline_____ELP Class_____Regular Class_____,Follow-up_____
                         Individual_____
Controls Operating: Group_____

TOI															
TOD															
TRD															
HTD															
H															
D															

TOI = TASK ORIENTED INDEPENDENT — Student completely involved in task independently of the teacher and is working on the task assigned to him by same.

TOD = TASK ORIENTED DEPENDENT — Teacher or teacher aid is directly assisting the student with the assigned task, includes repeating or further explaining directions.

TRD = TASK RELATED DEVIANCY — Inappropriate peer interaction and/or inappropriate classroom behavior in the course of doing or completing a task — talking to peers re: task, interrupting others in the course of completing a task (shouting out answers, etc.).

NTD = NON-TASK RELATED DEVIANCY — Behaviors disruptive of a learning climate, fighting, talking, facial grimaces, non-verbal signals between peers, loud tapping of pencils, slamming books on desk, wandering around room, etc.

H = HAND — Seeking teacher assistance, sharpening pencils, going to lavatory, getting a drink.

D = DISTRACTION — (Non-task oriented; non-deviant) — Looking into space, looking around room, looking at someone entering the room, distracting to a specific noise or event, attending to a stimulus other than the education task (fiddling with a pencil, self-stimulation, playing with erasers, etc.).

Fig. 3. Observation form and description of behavioral categories

task-oriented behavior for a ten-minute observation (600 seconds) was determined by dividing the total seconds task-oriented by 600. The observers were trained by using a video-tape recording of deviant classroom behaviors. Staff members recorded simultaneous observations with the observer trainees until reliability between the sets of observation was .90 or above. The reliabilities were calculated by a percent agreement method where number of agreements were divided by the total number of symbols. With the relatively small number of behavior categories (six) and with their precise definitions, it was possible to obtain very high (.90 and above) interobserver reliabilities within a relatively short period of time. Checks on intra-observer reliability based on repeated viewings of the videotape were also high. Once the observers were in the classroom setting, periodic checks were made to determine that inter-observer reliability remained at an acceptable level.

EXPERIMENT I. Evaluation of Treatment Model

Procedures

One of the two groups of children was used to provide a replication study of the validity of the treatment model as originally reported by Mattos, et al. (1969). As in the original study, a staging technique was used to introduce subjects into the treatment setting. Two subjects were phased into the classroom at a time. The behavior of the admitted subjects was brought under manageable control before another group was introduced. This procedure allowed for careful control of subject behaviors during the initial phases of treatment thus effecting a smoother adjustment to the treatment process. In addition, the first subjects were helpful in explaining classroom procedures to the new children. This facilitated acceptance of the program as well as providing a "review" for the initial group of subjects.

The children attended the special class from 9:15 A.M. to 1:45 P.M. At 1:45, the students were bussed to their regular schools to attend classes until 3:30 P.M. The procedure of returning the children to their regular classes served three purposes: (a) it allowed the child to remain integrated with his regular classroom peers both socially and academically, (b) it facilitated communication between the project staff and the regular classroom teacher, (c) it made possible the collection of data from the regular classroom so that the performance of subjects in the two settings could be directly compared and analyzed.

The contingencies and classroom procedures, operating within the treatment setting, were verbally specified to the subjects as they entered the special class. These rules specified consequences for both deviant and non-deviant behaviors. Figure 4 describes the consequences that were applied to the various classes of subject behavior. Individual points could be earned for appropriate behavior (task completion, correct answers on tasks, completion of specified

I. Consequences of Deviant Behaviors
  A. Immediate removal from ELP building for the following behaviors—
    (If expelled during a.m. the S will stay out for the remainder of the day
    and return the following morning. If expelled during p.m. will remain
    home following day.)
    1. Disobedience and/or defying teacher
    2. Fighting
    3. Leaving building without permission
    4. Foul language, lewd gestures
    5. Creating a disturbance during isolation period (time-out)
  B. Immediate exclusion from the classroom area for 10 minutes (mini-
    mum) for the following operants: (S decides when he will return to
    classroom area.)
    1. Talking out of turn
    2. Unauthorized standing or walking
    3. Talking or standing without raising hand and securing permission
    4. Throwing objects
    5. Other, non-tolerated operants falling within this class of behaviors
II. Reinforcement
  A. Individual basis
    1. Social:
        — raising hand
        — not talking
        — remaining in seat
        — beginning work without talking upon entering room
    2. Academic:
        — task-oriented
        — completion of tasks
        — correct answers on assignments
  B. Group Basis
    1. Clock timer will be set at preselected time intervals each day pro-
    vided all S's are present in the classroom area and are engaged in
    task-oriented behavior.
    2. A group payoff will be instituted when the group accumulates a
    preselected number of points.
III. Behaviors to Be Ignored
    — asking for help without raising hand
    — irrelevant questions
    — tapping pencils (unless disturbing class)
    — pouting and crying

Fig. 4. Program for coping with deviant classroom behaviors
ELP experimental class

units of academic work in relation to time) or for appropriate student
behavior (raising hand, beginning work without talking, task attending). During the initial stages of treatment, subjects were reinforced for minor approximations to these appropriate behaviors on
a nearly continuous basis. As treatment progressed and these behav-

iors came under control of the response-reinforcement conditions operating in the treatment setting, the frequency of reinforcement was reduced and the ratio between amount of academic production and amount of reinforcement was gradually changed until the subjects were producing large amounts of work for small amounts of tangible reinforcement. Toward the end of treatment, the subjects' academic and social behavior was reinforced on a variable interval basis. Reducing the amount *and* frequency of reinforcement and shifting to a variable interval schedule near the end of treatment was designed to facilitate the persistence of treatment effects in the regular classroom setting following treatment.

Points could be exchanged at 1:00 P.M. each day for individual stimulus items. There were six levels of point value for the items, ranging from 25 points to 200 points with occasional special items for 500 points. The values for these reinforcers were selected to approximate their purchase price; e.g., 25 points would be needed for toys costing 20¢ to 39¢; 50 points for toys costing 40¢ to 65¢; etc. The subjects were free to exchange their points for an inexpensive item or to accumulate them for a more expensive one. There was no evidence of an inability to delay gratification and save for higher prizes. Their academic production remained relatively constant whether receiving immediate exchange for toys or saving them.

Each child kept a bar graph recording on his desk of the number of points earned each day. If on any day he received more points than the previous day, he was awarded a bonus point. Points were awarded on the basis of concurrent schedules (Morse, 1966). Subjects could receive points on both a variable interval ten-minute schedule of reinforcement (VI:10) for task-oriented behavior and a fixed ration (FR:1) for completion of assignments. Social reinforcement in the form of attention, approval, praise, interest, and affection was paired with token reinforcement in order to transfer control from contrived reinforcers to those reinforcers more often available in the regular classroom and to build up responsiveness to social reinforcement through the process of generalization. Social reinforcement was also systematically applied in the regular classroom by specifying that the regular classroom teacher reinforce appropriate behavior a certain number of times per day.

Group points were effective in making a highly desirable reinforcer (trips) available while simultaneously providing aversive control in the form of group peer pressure against individual deviant behavior. Deviant behavior in the classroom setting is sometimes reinforced by approval and recognition from peers (giggles, comments, gestures). A group reinforcing climate controls this source of reinforcement by making it more desirable for peers to encourage each other to behave appropriately than inappropriately. Initially, all members of the group were required to produce appropriate social and academic behavior for an interval of five minutes in order to earn one point. The interval was gradually expanded until the subjects were working for as much as 45 minutes for one point. Group points were earned on a VI:30 schedule during academic production. Thus, approximately five points could be earned daily. However, even with a quiet, highly structured classroom, the subjects rarely earned more than two or three points a day. It usually took two to four weeks to earn the points necessary for a group reinforcement.

Reinforcement procedures used in the treatment setting were supplemented by aversive consequences applied to several classes of deviant behavior. Time-out from a reinforcing climate was used to consequate such behaviors as talking out, throwing objects, out-of-seat and inappropriate verbal behavior. Subjects were placed in time-out for a minimum of ten minutes. During time-out, subjects were unable to receive points, attend to the class, or work on an assignment. The group reinforcing climate was immediately terminated when a subject was placed in time-out and remained suspended until he re-entered the class. Time-out proved especially effective in terminating deviant behaviors before they became disruptive (Tyler and Brown, 1967).

For disruptive behaviors such as fighting, leaving the building without permission, foul language and gestures, defying the teacher, creating a disturbance during time-out, or accumulating three time-outs in one day, the child was suspended from school for the remainder of that day or the following one, depending on the time in which the incident occurred. Readmission to the classroom was made contingent upon the subject's successful completion of all regularly assigned academic tasks at home. The alleged potency of this technique rests on the assumption that its application is aversive for the child. The "cost" to the child resulting from this consequence was usually quite high. It required that all regular academic assignments for the suspension period be completed successfully; all individual points were lost for the same period; the group reinforcing climate could not operate during this time, and parents were instructed to prohibit recreational activity and television viewing while the subject was absent from school. Suspension was normally used three or four times during the first few weeks of treatment and then rarely, if ever, used for the remaining two to two and one-half months of treatment. The technique appeared to be quite effective in suppressing such behaviors as teacher defiance, verbal abuse, fighting, and tantrum behavior.

In addition to the deviant behavior exhibited by most of the group members, some behaviors unique to individual children were present which also proved amenable to reinforcement procedures and/ or aversive controls. Points and peer reinforcement were used to strengthen behaviors incompatible with distractibility, and to control such behaviors as crying, hyperactivity in seat, frontal lisp, and inappropriate verbal behavior. They were also used successfully to strengthen such behaviors as athletic coordination and positive playground interaction.

Once the target behaviors for the experimental class had been altered and observations in the regular classroom indicated the child was functioning on a level at or above the class mean in task-oriented performance, arrangements were made to place the child back in his regular classroom. Before the child was returned to the classroom, points were given only once a day, assignments were made longer, the amount of group work was increased, teacher attention was reduced, and the frequency of social reinforcement was increased. The climate of the special class was programed to more nearly approximate that of an ordinary classroom. Before returning the child to his regular classroom, the project staff members prepared an individual program for each child's teacher to follow. The program specified academic and social consequences for appropriate and inappropriate behavior so as to adapt the special class contingencies to the individual child in the regular classroom and to facilitate transfer and persistence of modified behavior across the two settings. A staging technique was again used to phase the subjects back into the regular classroom and to introduce a new group of deviant subjects into the special class.

Results and Discussion

The data in Figures 5A and 5B provide a graphic record of the attending behaviors of subjects in Experiment I during both baseline and treatment conditions. These data successfully replicate the design, procedure, and results of the treatment model applied to the behavior of a group of subjects (all males) in grades four, five, and six during the previous academic year (Mattos, et al., 1969). The primary difference(s) between the two applications of the treatment model were in the area of reinforcement control. The behavior of subjects in the replication group came under more rapid reinforcement control, maintained at a higher level of such control, and was less variable, during the treatment process, than the behavior of subjects in the initial group. It is assumed that a more efficient operation of the treatment model accounted for this result; however, it is conceivable that variability among the subjects in their responsiveness to the treatment procedures could account for the same results.

An inspection of the data in Figures 5A and 5B indicates that attending behavior of all six subjects stabilized at very high rates during treatment. The baseline data show the characteristic patterns of variability of attending behavior in such natural settings as the regular classroom. When these subjects were brought into a highly controlled, highly structured setting where the contingencies operating were verbally specified to them, their behavior was brought under almost immediate reinforcement control. Verbally specifying con-

249

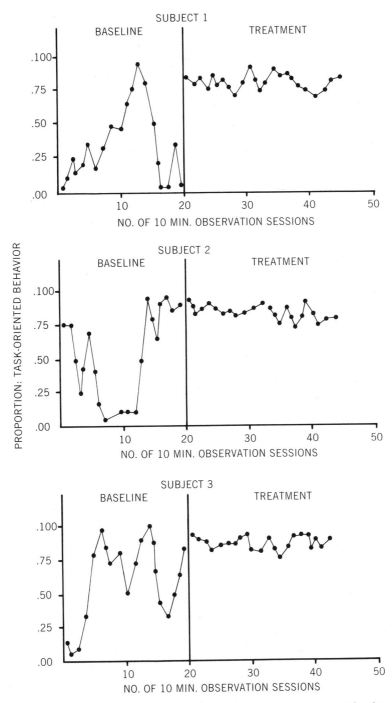

Fig. 5A. Experimental Group 1: Proportions of task-oriented behavior for deviant subjects one, two, and three during baseline and treatment conditions

250

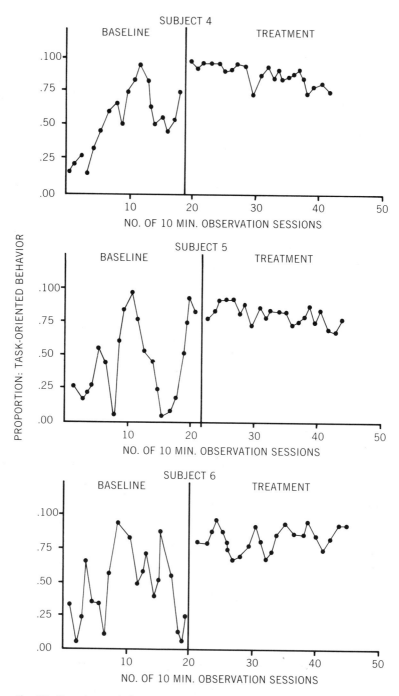

Fig. 5B. Experimental Group I: Proportions of task-oriented behavior for deviant subjects four, five, and six during baseline and treatment conditions

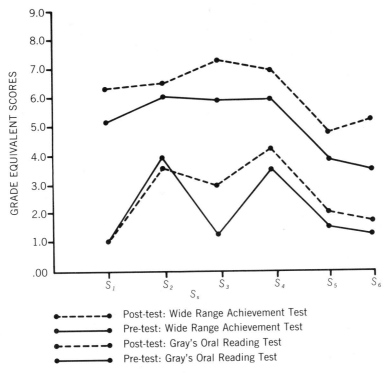

Fig. 6. Academic gains during treatment as measured by the Wide Range Achievement Test and the Gray's Oral Reading Test

tingencies and then implementing these same contingencies within a special setting appears to alter the acquisition rates of behaviors incompatible with non-attending behavior. In the usual treatment setting, acquisition rates gradually accelerate through an adaptation period and then become more stable as intervention progresses. However, the attending behavior of the above subjects is as stable during adaptation as during any other point in the treatment process.

The treatment model was very effective in producing behavior change among the subjects in Experiment I. This group produced appropriate attending behavior an average of 39 percent of the time during baseline and 90 percent of the time during treatment. The mean difference of 51 percent between the two conditions was statistically significant beyond .001.

All subjects were given the Wide Range Achievement Test and Gray's Oral Reading Test upon entry and just prior to exit from the experimental classroom (Figure 6). A span of approximately 2.5 months separated the two samples of academic behavior. All subjects improved on either one or both tests. Subject 3 made the largest

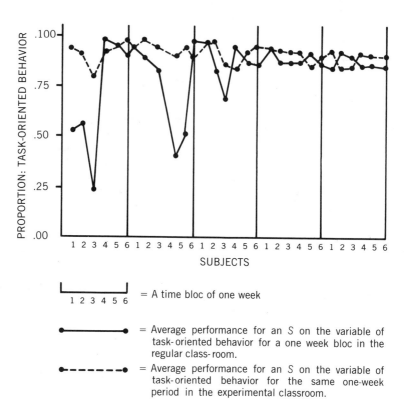

1 2 3 4 5 6 = A time bloc of one week

●━━━━━━━━● = Average performance for an *S* on the variable of task-oriented behavior for a one week bloc in the regular class-room.

●━ ━ ━ ━ ━● = Average performance for an *S* on the variable of task-oriented behavior for the same one-week period in the experimental classroom.

Fig. 7. Related changes on task-oriented behavior between treatment and non-treatment settings

academic improvement (6.0–7.8 WRAT; 1.2–3.0 Gray's Oral) while subject 1 showed the least gain (1.0–1.0 WRAT; 5.5–6.4 Gray's Oral). Subject 2's loss of a month on the Gray's Oral Reading Test was attributed to testing error. The impressive academic gains of the subjects in the basic skills area reflects an intensive emphasis upon reading, math, language, spelling, and vocabulary during the treatment period. It is assumed the improved academic and attending skills of the subjects stimulates the operation of such natural reinforcers as task completion, academic success, and acquisition of new knowledge which in turn reinforce and maintain subsequent attempts at successful academic behavior.

As mentioned earlier, all six subjects returned to their regular classrooms from 2:00 until 3:30 each day. Observation data were taken on their behavior during this period so their performance in the treatment and non-treatment settings could be compared.

The data in Figure 7 illustrate the mean performance of each subject on the variable of attending behavior during successive one week blocs. During bloc one, there is a pronounced discrepancy between the performances of subjects in the experimental and regular classroom settings. During the second and third blocs, this discrepancy gradually decreases until by the fourth week of treatment, the behavior of all six subjects is indistinguishable within the two settings. As a group, the subjects' attending behavior followed a fairly typical acquisition pattern. However, some variability was present for individual subjects. No attempts were made to reprogram the regular classroom environment in order to facilitate transfer either before or during the period in which these data were recorded.

After determining that transfer of modified behaviors between the experimental and regular classrooms did occur during treatment, procedures were established for measuring the maintenance of effects after treatment in the special setting was terminated. Procedures were also established to determine how well a "treated" subject's behavior maintained in relation to the behavior of his peer group in the regular classroom.

In Figures 8A and 8B, each datum point on the dotted axis represents twenty minutes of randomized observation data taken on one of the subject's peers in the regular classroom. Each datum point on the solid axis represents ten minutes of randomized observation data taken on the "treated" subject in his regular classroom following treatment. Observers recorded ten minutes of observation data on the experimental subject and then randomly selected one of his peers for observation. Two ten minute observations were completed on the peer. Observers then returned to the experimental subject and completed a second ten minute observation. A second peer was then randomly selected for observation. The procedure was repeated until twenty minutes of observation data were obtained on each of the subject's peers. This allowed for simultaneous monitoring of the experimental subject's behavior as well as the classroom in which he was placed. From these data, it was possible to compute ratios between a subject's treatment and post-treatment performance and between the subject's post-treatment behavior and the behavior of his peer group.

The ratio of *treatment attending* to *post-treatment attending* was .97, .76, .84, .67, .39, and .72 for subjects 1 to 6 respectively. The behavior of the group was being maintained at .72 value three months after treatment. Ratios of post-treatment attending for problem children relative to their peer group were 1.02, .90, 1.27, .75, .49, and .85 respectively. Relative to peer behavior, these data speak well for a persistence of treatment effects. It appeared that the academically more skilled children (achievement relative to grade level) maintained better over time.

254

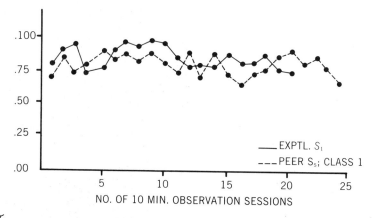

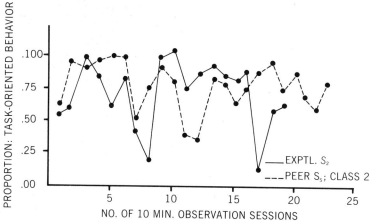

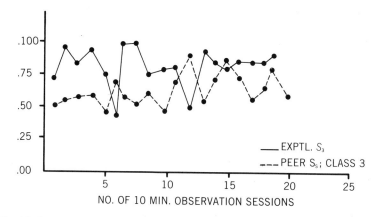

Fig. 8A. Post-treatment comparisons of deviant subjects one, two, and three with their respective peer group subjects on the variable of task-oriented behavior

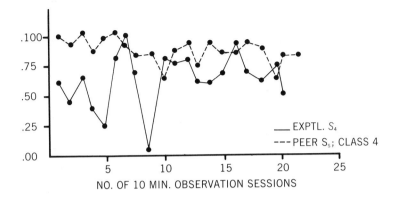

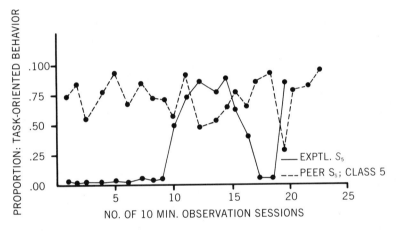

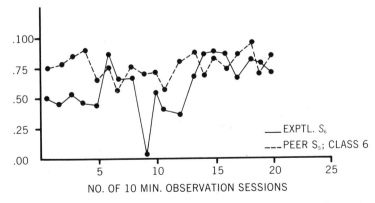

Fig. 8B. Experimental Group I: Post-treatment comparisons of deviant subjects four, five, and six with their respective peer group subjects on the variable of task-oriented behavior

EXPERIMENT II. Experimental Evaluation of Treatment Model Components

Results of the initial application of the treatment model (Mattos, et al., 1969) (the experiment just reported) indicate this model was very effective in producing behavior change and modifying deviant behavior. However, these data do not provide information about which components of the treatment model produced the behavior change. It is possible that only one or two variables are accounting for the major portion of variance in the treatment outcome(s). It is also conceivable the behavior change depends upon the interaction of these variables or that behavior change is due to other than treatment variables such as stimuli specific to the treatment setting. (Reduced teacher-student ratios, individual attention, teacher-skill, special materials, novel stimulation, change in setting, etc.) The specification, control, and evaluation of all variables which could possibly affect treatment outcome in an applied setting would be practically impossible. However, it is possible to specify those variables which have been manipulated in the treatment process and which can logically be assumed to have a causal relationship to treatment outcome.

Procedures

A probe technique (Sidman, 1960) was used to evaluate the effects of five treatment model components upon the academic and social behavior of an additional group of subjects. This experiment was designed to provide data on the influence or weight of a series of independent variables upon the dependent variable of attending behavior. The specific question investigated was the extent to which these variables controlled or accounted for variance in behavioral rates.

The components which were controlled and manipulated during the experiment were:

1. *Individual Reinforcing Climate.* Positive reinforcement for social and academic behavior was administered on an individual basis in the form of points that could be exchanged for tangible, back-up reinforcers.
2. *Group Reinforcing Climate.* Subjects "cooperated" in securing group reinforcement by producing appropriate social and academic behaviors for predetermined intervals of time. These group points were exchanged for special trips and activities.
3. *Social Reinforcement.* Social reinforcers in the form of interest, praise, attention, approval, and feedback from the teacher, were consistently paired with the administration of points. As treatment progressed, these reinforcers were gradually substituted for points.

4. *Time-out from a Reinforcing Climate.* Deviant behaviors such as talking out of turn, throwing objects, unauthorized standing or walking, inappropriate verbal behavior and other, non-tolerated operants within this class of behaviors were consequated by immediate exclusion from the classroom area for a minimum of ten minutes.

5. *Suspension from a Reinforcing Climate.* The following behaviors were consequated by immediate removal from the treatment setting: fighting, foul language, lewd gestures, tantrum behavior, defying teacher and leaving building without permission. If the S was suspended during the morning he remained home the remainder of the day; if suspension occurred in the afternoon he remained home the following day.

The design of the experiment required that stable baseline rates of behavior be achieved for all subjects before the effects of any one variable or combination of variables could be measured. The subjects were placed in the classroom with all treatment components operating. The controls were kept in operation until the subjects' behavior stabilized at values ranging from .80 to 1.00 (proportions: task-oriented behavior) across all academic activities. This criterion was reached after three weeks of treatment. The experiment was divided into seven phases. The schedule for manipulating treatment components was as follows:

TABLE 1
Schedule of Manipulating Treatment Components — Group II

Control Variables	Phases						
	I	II	III	IV	V	VI	VII
Individual token	X		X	X	X	X	X
Group token	X		X	X	X	X	X
Social	X	X	X		X	X	X
Time-out	X	X	X	X	X		X
Suspension	X	X	X	X	X		X

X = Control variables operating

There were four baseline and three experimental phases. The phases were altered without any explanation to the subjects. During Phase I (baseline) task-oriented behavior was stabilized with all controls in operation. During Phase II, all token reinforcement was abruptly withdrawn. Removal of the individual and group reinforcing climates simply involved not administering points for appropriate social and academic behaviors. The display board remained off. The point record forms were removed from the subjects' desks and the back-up reinforcers (on display) were removed from the classroom area. When effects of the withdrawal had been determined, the variables were reinstated during Phase III (baseline 2) and the behavior returned to baseline levels.

When the behavior had stabilized, Phase IV was introduced in which all social reinforcement was controlled in the classroom setting. Both positive (praise, gestures, physical contact, feedback, etc.) and negative (reprimands, glares, warnings, gestures, etc.) teacher-student interactions were considered under social reinforcement. The social component of the reinforcement was defined as non-tangible stimuli dispensed by a human agent in the process of interaction. In the process of implementing Phase IV, the following instructions were given to the teacher:

1. "No instructions will be given that anything is being changed. The children will *not* be told that social reinforcement is being changed or controlled.
2. No comments are to be placed on papers other than the number wrong.
3. No praise of any kind will be given.
4. Each child will be limited to five questions per day. Approximately one minute of time will be allowed to answer each question. When 5 questions have been asked and answered, ignore any attempts by children to ask additional questions . . . Don't say "I can't answer," etc.
5. No physical contact such as gestures of approval, pats on the back, etc.
6. *No warnings or reprimands. If a child is not working, ignore him.*
7. Time-out and suspension plus points will be used."

The teacher was continuously supervised by the project staff during this phase to insure that specific instructions were carried out. Social reinforcement was reinstated in Phase V (baseline 3) and stable rates were achieved before beginning Phase VI.

In Phase VI, it was necessary to tell the subjects that they would no longer be suspended or placed in time-out for deviant behavior. This change in procedure was due to the low frequency at which it was necessary to use either control. The subjects could have gone the entire two-week period without exhibiting behavior deviant enough to warrant use of either control. When these controls were reinstated in Phase VII they were simply placed into effect with no accompanying verbal instruction to the subjects. The final phase, Phase VII (baseline 4) involved the permanent reinstatement of all treatment variables.

Results and Discussion

The data in Figure 9 contain the results of Experiment II. The data in Phase I record the performance of the subjects with all controls

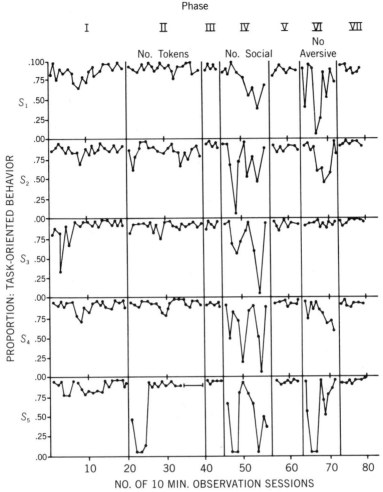

Fig. 9. Experimental analysis of the effects of three treatment variables upon the task-oriented behavior of deviant subjects in grades 4, 5, and 6

operating. This phase lasted until the behavior of all subjects stabilized at high rates. During Phase II all token reinforcement dispensed through both individual and group reinforcing climates was withdrawn. This procedure had very little effect upon the attending behavior of subjects one, three, and four. It had an initially substantial impact on subject two's behavior and a very dramatic impact on the behavior of subject five. However, the behavior of both subjects returned to its original level after several days and remained there until Phase II was terminated. Token reinforcement was reintroduced during Phase III. This phase was designed to return the behavior to its original, pre-intervention level of stability.

During Phase IV all social reinforcement was controlled within the classroom environment. Effects of the withdrawal of this component were not immediately reflected within the data; perhaps because it took the subjects some time to discover that the social reinforcement had, in fact, been withdrawn. The withdrawal produced a marked increase in the variability of the behavior of all subjects, indicating that this variable exercised powerful control over the subjects' attending behavior. This phase was terminated at the end of two weeks when it became obvious that the subjects' behavior was not going to return to its original level or stability (as in Phase I) with this variable withdrawn. When social reinforcement was reinstated, the attending behavior of all subjects immediately returned to its original level of stability and remained there until the beginning of Phase VI where all aversive controls were withdrawn. The removal of time-out and suspension, as aversive controls, had differential effects upon the subjects' behavior. Subject three's attending behavior was apparently not under the control of these aversive stimuli. In fact, his behavior during this period was slightly more stable than at any other time during the experiment. Though less pronounced than the effect of removing social reinforcement, the withdrawal of all aversive controls indicated that these components accounted for large amounts of variance in behavioral rates and were very effective in controlling the behavior of subjects in this experiment. The aversive controls were reinstated after a two-week period and the experiment was terminated at this point. The remainder of the treatment period consisted of preparing the subjects for full-time entry into their regular classrooms.

TABLE 2

Summary Data on the Effects of Experimental Manipulation
in Phases I through VII (N=5)

Phases													
I		II		III		IV		V		VI		VII	
M	SD	M	SD	M	SD	M	SD	M	SD	M	SD	M	SD
86	2.40	80	10.44	90	2.12	59	10.77	88	3.03	68	12.96	88	3.42

Table 2 contains the mean scores and standard deviations for the group of subjects during baseline and experimental phases. Although slightly more variable after the experimental interventions, the behavior of all subjects was very stable during Phases I and VII. The group's attending behavior was most variable during Phase VI and lowest, in terms of mean score, during Phase IV. This inter-subject variability, however, is very misleading when used to evaluate the effects of experimental intervention. The inter-subject variability in Phases II, IV and VI is approximately the same; yet Figure 9 indicates that very differential effects were produced in the subjects' attending behavior. For example, in Phase II, the variance in the data was attributable to the behavior of only two subjects. The data in Phase IV show the same inter-subject variability as those in Phase II; yet inspection of Figure 9 indicates the intra-subject variability of these same data clearly establishes social reinforcement as the most potent component of the treatment model in controlling attending behavior.

Although conclusions based upon the data generated by this experiment must be regarded as less than conclusive until an exact replication has been successfully completed, the results are nevertheless worthy of discussion and speculation. The effects of withdrawing token reinforcement was rather unexpected. Token reinforcement was apparently exercising much weaker control over the social and academic behaviors of the subjects, at this point in the experiment, than the authors had estimated. If all token reinforcement had been withdrawn during the initial stages of treatment, the authors suspect that its effect upon the subjects' behavior would have been much more marked. The subjects' appropriate behavior was apparently under the control of such intrinsic reinforcers as academic success, social approval, individual attention, task mastery, and positive feedback by the time token reinforcement was removed.

The data appear to be in contrast to evidence provided by Levin and Simmons (1962) which suggests that adult praise did not exercise control over the behavior of fifteen emotionally disturbed males between the ages of 7.2 and 11.9. There was evidence suggesting that adult praise was actually aversive for some of the subjects.

Praise, in addition to expressions of positive and negative feedback approval, attention, affection, and interest by the teacher were controlled in Phase IV of the present study. These stimuli were not aversive for this group of subjects. They were, in fact, highly reinforcing and functioned as very powerful controls of their appropriate social and academic behavior. This result is consistent with findings of other experimenters who have used social reinforcement effectively in controlling the social and academic behaviors of children, in the classroom, laboratory, and clinic setting (Allen, Hart, Buell, Harris, Wolf, 1964; Harris, Johnston, Kelley, Wolf, 1964; Harris, Wolf, Baer, 1964; Becker, Madsen, Arnold, Thomas, 1967; Hall and Broden, 1967; Hall, Lund, Jackson, 1968; Thomas, Becker, Armstrong, 1968).

Time-out from a reinforcing climate (the experimental class setting) contingent upon the production of deviant behavior proved to be a powerful treatment variable in this study. This finding is also consistent with results of other studies on time-out reported in the literature (Tyler and Brown, 1967; Wahler, 1969). Time-out used in combination with positive reinforcement procedures appears to be more effective than either one in isolation.

This experiment provided only a gross evaluation of the treatment model's components. It should be carefully replicated before its results are generalized and applied to the response class of acting-out, disruptive behavior in children. In addition, differential effects may be associated with individual versus group reinforcing climates and time-out versus suspension in the control and modification of behavior. The interaction between various combinations of these variables may also be a crucial factor in producing behavior change. Additional experiments will have to evaluate these interactions before the functional relationships which exist between such behavioral and treatment variables are clearly established and precisely described.

Summary

Two experiments were discussed. The first experiment provided an inter-subject replication of the design, procedure, and results of an earlier application of a treatment model to the behavior of male subjects in grades four, five, and six. The model was very effective in producing changes in both attending behavior and academic proficiency. Follow-up data indicated that the behavior of the six subjects was maintaining at a 72 percent level of efficiency at three months after the termination of treatment. Three components of the treatment model, token reinforcement, social reinforcement, and aversive controls were evaluated in terms of their efficiency or potency in controlling the behavior of a second group of five subjects. The results indicated that social reinforcement exercised the greatest control over the subjects' behavior while aversive controls were slightly less effective in controlling the same behavior. Token reinforcement exercised surprisingly little control over the subjects' attending behavior.

REFERENCES

Allen, K. E., Hart, B. M., Buell, J. S., Harris, F. R., and Wolf, M. M. Effects of social reinforcement on isolate behavior of a nursery school child. *Child Development*, 1964, **35**, 511–518.

Becker, W. C., Madsen, C. H., Arnold, C. R., and Thomas, D. R. The contingent use of teacher attention and praise in reducing classroom behavior problems. *Journal of Special Education*, 1967, **1**, 287–307.

Ferster, C., and DeMayer, M. K. A method for the experimental analysis of the behavior of autistic children. *The American Journal of Orthopsychiatry*, 1962, **32**, 89–98.

Hall, R. V., and Broden, M. Behavior changes in brain-injured children through social reinforcement. *Journal of Experimental Child Psychology*, 1967, **5**, 463–479.

Hall, R. V., Lund, D., and Jackson, D. Effects of teacher attention on study behavior. *Journal of Applied Behavior Analysis*, 1968, **1**, 1–12.

Harris, F. R., Johnston, M. K., Kelley, C. S., and Wolf, M. M. Effects of positive social reinforcement on regressed crawling of a nursery school child. *Journal of Educational Psychology,* 1964, **55,** 35–41.

Harris, F. R., Wolf, M. M., and Baer, D. M. Effects of adult social reinforcement on child behavior. *Young Children,* 1964, **20,** 8–17.

Levine, G. R., and Simmons, J. T. Response to food and praise by emotionally disturbed boys. *Psychology Reports,* 1962, **11,** 539–546.

Mattos, R. L., Mattson, R. H., Walker, H. M., and Buckley, N. K. Reinforcement and aversive control in the modification of behavior. *Academic Therapy Quarterly,* Fall 1969, **5,** 37–52.

Mattson, R. H., and Walker, H. M. Identification and treatment of social-emotional problems, Interim Report, May 1967. Division of Research, Bureau of Education for Handicapped Children, U.S. Office of Education.

Morse, W. H., in Honig, W. K., *Operant Behavior: Areas of Research and Application.* New York: Appleton-Century-Crofts, 1966, p. 59.

Sidman, M. *Tactics of Scientific Research,* New York: Basic Books, 1960.

Thomas, D. R., Becker, W. C., and Armstrong, M. Production and elimination of disruptive classroom behavior by systematically varying teacher's behavior. *Journal of Applied Behavior Analysis,* 1968, **1,** 35–45.

Tyler, V. O., and Brown, G. D. The use of swift, brief, isolation as a group control device for institutionalized delinquents. *Behavior Research and Therapy,* 1967, 3, 1–9.

Wahler, R. G. Oppositional Children: A quest for parental reinforcement control. *Journal of Applied Behavior Analysis,* 1969, **2,** 159–170.

Walker, H. M. Empirical assessment of deviant behavior in children. *Psychology in the Schools,* January 1969, 93–97.

21

Human Motivation and Environment

Lloyd E. Homme

One way to get behavior executed is by the use of punishment or threats of punishment. "Do X or else . . ." appears to be the most popular behavioral contingency in our culture. But control of behavior by aversive stimulation is not the topic of this paper. I will assume that we are in agreement concerning the undesirable side effects of control through aversive stimulation and that what is needed is a system for control through positive reinforcement.

The Conventional Motivation Concept

Conventional motivation concepts appear to be quite satisfactory as long as one stays in the laboratory. The deprivation operations one performs are said to induce a drive or need state which in turn is reflected by a number of physiological and behavioral changes. According to this conception, one change is that the drive state makes a reinforcer available. The reinforcer, of course, is that of which the subject was deprived. For example, when an animal is deprived of water, a thirst drive is induced which can be reduced by the presen-

From Symposium in Education Series, Kansas Studies in Education, University of Kansas. The research reported here was partially supported by Contract OE 4-16-033 with the U.S. Office of Education.

tation of water. This is often said to explain why water is a reinforcer, under these circumstances.

The conventional conception of operations and drive can be summarized in the diagram:

deprivation ————→ drive ————→ physiological and
operations   state   behavioral changes

Drive is thus a logically impeccable intervening variable firmly anchored in observables at both ends. Drive is said to be a useful construct to summarize the changes which occur as a result of the antecedent operations. This may be true. And, as I mentioned, no particular problem arises from this formulation as long as one remains in the laboratory.

I believe it to be a fact, however, that what is really wanted from the motivation concept is more than is supplied by this intervening variable construct. Evidence for this is found in elementary psychology textbooks. "A motive is whatever moves or incites to action" is a typical introduction to the topic of motivation. The fact that after this introduction the textbook author quickly moves on to the drive construct should not obscure the fact that he really has larger things in mind. One author gives himself away in this fashion: " . . . a drive is an impetus to behavior."

The point is that, as soon as one gets away from the operational laboratory definition of the drive construct, good as it sounds at first, it becomes quite useless. As soon as it is generalized to everyday situations, the necessity for specifying the antecedent operations said to produce it are commonly forgotten. Thus one is left with a topic of conversation rather than a means of manipulating or controlling behavior.

This shows up in its clearest light when motivation constructs are invoked to explain some lack of control of behavior. "Why doesn't Johnny learn?" Explanation: "He just isn't motivated." This explanation for the lack of control of behavior is rejected on the same grounds that other fictional causes of behavior are rejected. This everyday motivation concept implicitly places the cause for the present behavior inside the organism somewhere. Since it is quite clear that the explainer cannot get at the inside of the organism to fix this, he is freed of the responsibility for control. Through no fault of his, some prior operation hasn't been performed, or the organism's history is somehow deficient.

This objection is only a special case of a general objection to this sort of an explanation. It leads nowhere. It has no consequences in the sense that it does not specify any manipulable variables to control the behavior now.

Further, this tendency to look to the past for variables to control behavior obscures the search for manipulable variables which may exist in the present.

Reversal of a Concept

Usually the motivation problem is conceptualized as follows. If you have a motivated organism, you have a reinforcer. I suggest that we reverse this conceptualization of the relationship between reinforcers and motivation to be: If you have a reinforcer, you can motivate an organism. This formulation has the happy effect of causing one to search for reinforcers rather than bemoaning the lack of motivation. Happily, too, laboratory developments of the last few years tell us where to look.

Premack's P-hypothesis

As we have seen, the usual formulation of motivation involves the drive construct. David Premack, of the University of Missouri, however, has a different formulation which he calls the differential probability hypothesis, or P-hypothesis. He hypothesizes, and is finding considerable laboratory evidence in support, that any higher probability behavior will reinforce any lower probability behavior upon which it is contingent. From this standpoint, there is no need to invoke a drive concept to account for the reinforcing properties of water for a water-deprived animal. The experimenter has arranged matters through deprivation so that drinking is a higher probability behavior than the barpressing behavior which the experimenter wishes to reinforce.

In typical laboratory operant conditioning experiments, matters are arranged so that a single behavior remains at a high probability throughout the experimental session. Thus the same reinforcer can be used again and again. Taking David Premack (1959; 1965) literally, there is no reason to impose this constraint. *Any* behavior can be used as a reinforcer of *any* lower probability behavior *at the instant* it is a higher probability behavior.

Humans and Deprived Laboratory Animals

Nondeprived humans behave differently from deprived laboratory animals. Their behavior differs in many ways, but what is of interest to us now is the wide fluctuation in behavior probabilities. Rather than having one behavior, such as water-drinking or food-eating, which remains a high probability behavior throughout an extended period of time, just the opposite is the case. With the nondeprived human, specific behavior probabilities vary from very high to very low from one instant to the next. At one moment, getting a cup of coffee may be a high probability behavior. A moment later, taking a sip of it is a high probability behavior; a moment after that, taking a puff of a cigarette is a high probability behavior, and at that instant, taking a sip of coffee may be close to zero probability. Immediately after the puff of a cigarette, the probability of smoking may be near zero and taking a sip of coffee may be quite high again. And so it goes with other responses throughout the day. In general, a response may at one moment be a high probability behavior, then once executed, the probability of immediately repeating it is close to zero. The reason for dwelling on the obvious — that the probabilities of any one behavior typically vary from high to very low from moment to moment — is that, if Premack's P-hypothesis is taken literally, *each* high probability behavior is potentially as good a reinforcer as any other *for the instant* that it remains a high probability behavior.

If the P-hypothesis continues to be confirmed and turns out to be one of the fundamental laws of nature, we have to assume that it is older than man himself. Indeed, once one starts examining the matter, one can see that every one has known about the differential probability principle all along. Grandma knew all about it, for example, when she said, "Clean up your room; then you may go out and play." Grandma, the Contingency Manager, is saying, in effect, "Run off an amount of low probability behavior; then you may execute some higher probability behavior for a while." However, Grandma was the worst conceivable Contingency Manager when she said, "All right, play one game of cards; then you've *got* to do your homework." Things are exactly reversed here. She is permitting some high probability behavior to occur (playing cards), and then following it with some lower probability behavior (doing homework). A Contingency Manager who knew what he was doing would have these two activities in exactly the opposite order. I hope this one example illustrates the point that it is really quite difficult, at first, to take a scientific behavior principle literally enough to be systematic in applying it.

Contingency Management in the Nursery

As I have previously reported (Homme, et al., 1963), it was the differential behavior probability concept which, when taken literally, enabled us to transform bedlam into a highly controlled nursery school situation. For those of you who have not seen our brief report, I will summarize what happened.

We were faced with the task of controlling the behavior of three three-year-olds without the use of punishment or threats of punishment, implied or otherwise. Furthermore, we had an additional constraint that we not use candy or trinkets as reinforcers. The amount of control exercised on the first day can be summarized: none. One child was running and screaming, another was pushing a chair across the floor (rather a noisy chair), and the other was playing with a jigsaw puzzle. Once our scholars discriminated that punishment did not follow these activities (the rate at which this discrimination was made must have set a new indoor record), the response to the verbal instruction, "Come and sit down now," was to continue the running and screaming, chair-pushing, and so forth.

I have a recurring fantasy about what happens next. I am running alongside the child who is running and screaming and I am screaming too. I am screaming in her ear, "A motive is whatever moves or incites to action!" and "A drive is an impetus to behavior!" Then the child asks, "Is the drive firmly anchored to observables?" I answer, "Yes, certainly." The child continues, "Good. I have a running and screaming drive right now which needs reducing. Let's run and scream."

Back to reality.

Almost in desperation, we took Premack's P-hypothesis seriously, and labeled, as high probability behaviors for the children, those behaviors which were aversive to us. We made engaging in these behaviors contingent on the subject's doing a small amount—very small at first—of whatever we wanted them to do. A typical early contingency was merely for them to sit quietly in chairs and look at the blackboard. This was followed almost immediately by the command, "Everybody, run and scream, now." This kind of contingency management put us in immediate control of the situation. We were in control to the extent that we were able to teach everything in about one month that we could discover was ordinarily taught in first grade.

Our Contingency Management in the nursery study was quite artistic in that the Contingency Manager (the experimenter who decided what behavior was going to be contingent upon what behavior) made his decisions on the spot. Following this, we were forced to get less artistic, more specific.

The First HEW-Contract Group

Under contract to the Office of Education, Department of Health, Education, and Welfare, we were given the chance to teach literacy to 26 school dropouts, or potential dropouts. Since each student (S) had different high probability behaviors, we were forced to specify in advance what the contingencies were going to be for each S. This evolved into what we now call Contingency Contracting.

Each day when S arrived, he found a Contingency Contract awaiting him. The Contingency Contract specified a series of pairs of behavior, each pair consisting of an amount of lower probability (task) behavior leading to a set time of a higher probability (reinforcing) behavior. Besides the left-to-right or within-pairs progression of probabilities, there was a general progression between pairs from lower to higher probabilities. The S started each day's work, ideally, with the lowest probability behavior and ended it with his highest. For example, if the S "hated spelling," the first pair of activities for the day might have been: three pages of spelling leading to five minutes of the higher probability behavior (HPB) of a coffee break. Toward the end of this contract, the task of a pair of activities would be something he "didn't mind doing too much." For example, it might have been five pages of reading followed by the higher probability behavior of ten minutes' discussion of what was read.

We were quite impressed with our motivation results. To appreciate our enthusiasm, one must realize that these S's had, like other dropouts, or potential dropouts, histories of punishment for absenteeism and other nonacceptable behavior, for failure, and for other aversive events associated with school. What is more, they looked and acted the tough teenager role. Some of them wore dark glasses throughout the six-weeks' experiment even though they worked indoors. We discovered some were carrying knives.

During the first week, while we were still gearing up to utilize Contingency Contracting, we had three dropouts out of the 26 students enrolled; following that first week, there were zero dropouts. Attendance was virtually perfect. Even more impressive, but difficult to document, was the emotional change observed. Smiles became more frequent. Tasks (short ratios which led to a high probability behavior) were attacked eagerly. Just as impressive and easily documented was that, despite the fact that S's came from neighborhoods in which a special kind of diplomacy—fighting—is used to settle disagreements, there were no fights on our project. So far as we know, there were not even any arguments among the students. A remarkably serene atmosphere prevailed.

The academic gain achieved over the six weeks' period was disappointing to us. We effected, according to the California Achievement Test, a mean gain of .5 grade level in six weeks' time. Part of the reason for this showing was a lack of control of the quality of the lower probability behaviors. To correct this, we now have more Progress Checks, miniature tests which are part of the lower probability behaviors. These are now routinely included in task assignments. For example, a spelling task assignment does not read "Five pages of spelling," but "Five pages of spelling plus Progress Check."

Another reason for getting only an average of .5 grade level gain in six weeks was that several S's scored lower on the posttest than on the pretest. Incredible as it may seem, they apparently lost ground while working so hard. When it was all over, we learned how it happened that some Ss' scores went down, rather than up. They had cheated on the pretest and not on the posttest.

The Second HEW-Contract Group

In our enthusiasm for the success of Contingency Contracting, we assumed that teachers would be eager to adopt the system, and that it would be simple to teach them how to use it. As we look back, we can see that we were incredibly naive, that we grossly underestimated not only the inertia but the active resistance to change on the part of at least some teachers. Our plan was to have the teachers read eight or ten pages of material (Homme, 1964). Nobody read them. Then this was to be followed by three half-hour sessions of lecture and discussion of the system. Nobody listened. They had "had all this stuff in college psychology class." Besides, they had been working with juvenile delinquents for some time. (How long had *we* been working with juvenile delinquents?) They knew that what was required was punishment, not this positive reinforcement stuff.

To sum up the results with the second group of students, the system was so compromised and misused that no posttesting was done on the grounds that the results would have meant nothing.

That is not to say that nothing was gained from Group 2. On the contrary, we learned that our plans for communicating with the teacher were entirely inadequate. We had planned to write a small manual based on the three lecture-discussion sessions we had with the teachers and on the material we had previously written. This was going to constitute the teacher's manual. This experience with Group 2 quickly and thoroughly convinced us that our plan simply would not work. In its stead, we prepared a detailed, step-by-step utilization manual (Homme, 1965) written in the style of "This is the way it's done. Do not deviate from this plan."

The Third HEW-Contract Group

A manual such as the one described has been prepared and is currently in use in a Special Education class. Contingency Contracting is being used, and things appear to be going quite well. The teacher is quite enthusiastic about what is happening, but there is an assistant principal who is giving off some portentous signals. She is looking into the project. What this will mean for the project's future, and whether some administrative reason will be discovered to disrupt the present smoothly-running operation, only time will tell.

The Learning Center

In addition to the rest of our activities, we are also taking individual referrals from local guidance counselors, psychologists, and the like. We have students ranging from borderline retardates to those of superior intelligence. At one end of the achievement scale are those students having trouble in school; at the other end are the bright students who want to get even farther ahead. Mostly, however, our clients are students who are having trouble in school.

Across the board, with the exception of the superior students, our main job is to motivate the client. We motivate students in a somewhat peculiar way. In analyzing the circumstances under which a person will or will not say another human is motivated, we have concluded that his reaction will depend largely upon the display of three factors by the S: (1) the speed with which he works (or the latency of task attack); (2) the frequency with which he smiles; (3) certain other verbal behaviors (e.g., "I'm learning a lot." "I like it here.").

With Contingency Management, we deliberately condition these symptoms of high motivation. To get speed, we superimpose a differential reinforcement of high rate (DRH) schedule on the fixed ratio task schedule. This simply means that we say, "Do 25 frames of spelling. If you do them in less than 20 minutes and pass your Progress Check, some good contingency will befall you." After this kind of conditioning, the subjects appear to be highly motivated humans. We have no idea whether they "really" are or not. Furthermore, if they continue to display these symptoms, we don't care.

I have always been impressed with the operant conditioner's control over the attention span of an ordinary pigeon. I don't know what would happen, exactly, if educators were asked to measure a pigeon's attention span, but I suppose they would conclude it was quite short. I also suspect that the operant conditioner wouldn't pay any attention to it. He would hold the pigeon's attention as long as necessary—up to 15 hours or so if he wanted to.

To see whether we could come anywhere near approximating this with humans, we have, on two occasions, kept an S responding for a full working day, from 9:00 A.M. till 5:00 P.M. with time out for lunch. (The latter was, of course, contingent on executing some lower probability behavior.) Both of these sessions produced gains of better than a year's grade equivalent. We are certain that we can routinely do *at least* this well. We have started referring to this, incidentally, as the "one-day fix." We don't do this oftener because of the manpower it requires—one human contingency manager per S.

Westinghouse's SLATE, the Computized Contingency Manager

The manpower requirement I mentioned will soon get remedied. It will get remedied by SLATE,[1] the first real teaching machine I have ever seen. Each student (S) will be seated at a console containing a keyboard, a microphone, earphones, and a cathode ray tube for output display. The cathode ray tube also serves as a stimulus area to which the S can respond by means of the keyboard or by means of an electronic pencil with which he can be asked to point at various objects displayed on the tube or various areas of the display. I could go on talking about SLATE all day without exhausting the topic of what this almost magical machine can do, but I will sum-

---

1. This equipment is called SLATE, an acronym for Sensitive to Learner Automated Teaching Equipment.

marize: everything. Specify the function you want, and I can guarantee that SLATE can do it. That is not quite true. It cannot dice carrots, and it does not have an auditory discrimination capability — that is, it cannot read human speech. But, allowing for these restrictions, I'm convinced it can do everything.

Here is how the classroom of the future will work. The student will sit down at his console and will announce his arrival by typing his name. (If he is too unskilled to do that, we can have a monitor do it, or arrange for some easier signal to be given.) After that, SLATE will take over. It will remember what contingencies work best, with what latencies S responds, and what concepts he had trouble with yesterday (or last month, if you like). When you consider that a single computer can handle a hundred student consoles simultaneously, each presenting a different program, you get some idea of the power of this educational tool.

SLATE Simulators

While awaiting the completion of a final SLATE model, we have been preparing for it by writing programs especially for SLATE using humans to simulate computer operations. Let me tell you that humans generate only a poor approximation.

A simulator in action might proceed something like the following. He might say, "Puh," and S would respond simply by using a pencil (rather than an electronic pointer) to point to a P. The simulator then would arrange a new display, utter another sound, and so on. This sort of simulation is not too bad, but it is far from perfect. It is far too slow for us to learn anything about maximum rate, for one thing. Recently we have been working with two pre-school slum kids, supposedly difficult organisms to motivate. We find this is simply not so. These S's learn like all other organisms. They are being run only about three hours a day at present, and the reason for not running them for a greater period of time is interesting. It is not that the S's get fatigued; it is the SLATE simulators who wear out.

The High Probability Behavior Area (HPB Area)

As I have indicated, many high probability behaviors involve considerable action and generate a good deal of noise. This being the case, we have found it necessary to set aside a special area for HPB's to take place. As you may suspect, a supervisor is needed in this area; we call the supervisor the HPB Administrator.

The way the system works is this. The S, interacting with the SLATE simulator, runs off the ratio specified by the contract, e.g., pointing to the letters appropriate for a half-dozen sounds. At the end of this ratio, S is handed a card which specifies an amount of contingent time, say two minutes. S grasps this card and runs to the HPB area, hands his card to the HPB Administrator and sets his timer. He then begins his coloring, dart throwing, talking with the HPB Administrator, or whaever else the HPB Administrator specifies.

When the bell on the timer rings, signifying that contingent time has elapsed, the subject races back to the task area, and begins working again. If it seems surprising that the subject races to return to the task area, let me assure you that it was not always thus. When we first started on this project, the S's would run to get to the high probability area all right, but they would dawdle for what seemed an interminable time in returning to the task area. Laboratory animals on a fixed ratio schedule often show a similar behavioral phenomenon. After a reinforcement, they pause for varying lengths of time, depending on the richness of the schedule. Undue pausing is common enough so that it is said to reflect "ratio strain." This pause after reinforcement can be eliminated by shifting to a variable ratio schedule. This is what we did with our subjects, in effect. After returning to the task area, they would intermittently be presented with the instruction to return immediately to the high probability area. A further contingency was superimposed on this schedule: The instruction to return to the high probability area was given only if the return to the task area was prompt. With these contingencies, our subjects are now running so fast, rounding corners with such lightning speed, that we are in some fear that they might hurt themselves by their excited slipping and sliding and bumping into SLATE simulators' chairs.

The Future

No one can say with any certainty what the future will bring, of course. Nevertheless, guesses about the future are entertaining and sometimes more.

I think it is quite obvious from what has already occurred that an area which is going to yield exciting and important results is that of self-management of contingencies. A corollary of this is that it will be necessary to develop a technology for teaching the self-management of contingencies. It is not known how young this teaching may begin, but there are some encouraging signs. At least one five-year-old in the world, whose mother has been playing the Contingency Management game with her, is now beginning to play the game by herself. One day the five-year-old was observed opening the door of the freezer and beginning to reach for a popsicle when she suddenly paused. "Whoops!" she said. "I have to make my bed first." At this she dashed off, made her bed, and dashed back to the freezer. "Now I may have my popsicle," she said.

No one has yet seen an adult human who started life early as a self-contingency manager. But the chances are the results will be better than anticipated.

There is very little doubt that self-management of contingencies can be taught. Questions which remain are how early it can be taught, how much of it can be taught, and how fast it can be learned.[2]

One thing remains certain. No one knows how fast a human being can learn *anything;* we have not yet begun to approach the limits of the human's capacity to learn. And we will never begin to approach them until a computerized contingency manager such as Westinghouse's SLATE is properly programed and used.

BIBLIOGRAPHY

Homme, L. E. Perspectives in psychology: XXIV Control of coverants, the operants of the mind. *Psychol. Rec.*, 1965, **15**, 201–511.

Homme, L. E. Technical progress report no. 1: A demonstration of the use of self-instructional and other teaching techniques for remedial instruction of low-achieving adolescents in reading and mathematics, submitted to U.S. Office of Education under Contract No. OE-4-16-033 October 1, 1964.

Homme, L. E. Technical progress report no. 2: A demonstration of the use of self-instructional and other teaching techniques for remedial instruction of low-achieving adolescents in reading and mathematics, submitted to U.S. Office of Education under Contract No. OE-4-16-033 January 1, 1965.

Homme, L. E., deBaca, C. P., Devine, J. V., Steinhorst, R., and Rickert, E. J. Use of the Premack principle in controlling the behavior of nursery school children. *J. Exp. Anal. Behav.*, 1963, **6**, 544.

Premack, D. Reinforcement theory. In Levine, D., (Ed.), *Nebraska symposium on motivation 1965*. Lincoln: U. of Nebraska Press, 1965.

Premack, D. Toward empirical behavior laws: I. positive reinforcement. *Psychol. Rev.*, 1959, **66**, 219–233.

---

2. In a paper published since this symposium was held, the principles of self-management have been extended to control the frequency of events ordinarily called mental (coverants). Preliminary indications are that this kind of control can be learned without difficulty by young children.

22

An Application of Conditioning Techniques to the Control of a Hyperactive Child

Gerald R. Patterson
University of Oregon

This report describes a technique for controlling the behavior of a hyperactive child in the classroom setting. Social and nonsocial reinforcers were used to increase the rate of occurrence of a broad class of behaviors appropriate to a classroom setting. The data show that this procedure was effective in reducing the rate of occurrence of behaviors inappropriate to the classroom.

The ubiquitous presence of an activity variable is shown in the earlier factor analytic work of Baldwin (1948), Walker's (1962) observation of nursery school behaviors, and both Patterson (1964) and Dreger and Dreger's analysis (1962) of children's disturbed behavior. High rates of activity in the behavior of children are one of the most frequent complaints made by adults in referring children to child outpatient clinics, Patterson (1955). This would suggest that hyperactive behavior represents a highly aversive state of affairs to the adult. Taken together, these findings indicate that the control of

From L. P. Ullmann and L. Krasner (eds.), *Case Studies in Behavior Modification* (New York: Holt, Rinehart and Winston, 1965).

The writer gratefully acknowledges the patient cooperation of the staff at the Malabon School for permitting the introduction of these rather unusual procedures into the classroom setting. Many of the actual procedures were worked out and modified as a result of discussions with I. Hunter, Dr. J. Straughan, and R. Lane; Hunter and Lane also served as experimenters.

hyperactive behavior in children should be a problem of major concern to the child psychologist.

Extreme variations in activity level are of further interest because of its association with both anoxic births, Parmellee (1962), Graham, Ernhart, Thurston, and Croft (1962) and with premature births, Shirely (1939), Knobloch and Pasamanick (1962), Dunn, Levine, and New (1958). For these children, the assumption has been that the high rate of activity is a function of some unspecified neurological damage. In the presence of these antecedents, the suggested techniques for controlling hyperactive behavior have been either the administration of drugs or reducing the amount of external stimulation presented to the child.

This latter approach is best summarized in the publication by Strauss and Lehtinen (1950). Their dual approach of reducing sensory input and "educating the child in self control" is also reflected in the contemporary writings of Stone (1960), Bradley (1957), and Hareng and Phillips (1962).

Many of the responses that characterize the hyperactive child are not, in and of themselves, aversive. The aversive characteristic, however, is inherent in the extremely high rate of emission of these behaviors. The conditioning procedures described below are based upon the assumption that, regardless of etiology, hyperactive behaviors can be controlled by the application of general principles from learning theories outlined by Skinner (1958), and by Guthrie (1935). In this application, it is assumed that both environmental and internal stimuli have become conditioned elicitors of such behaviors as: squirming, looking "around," pinching, tapping, and walking about the room. Theoretically, it should be possible to condition a set of responses to these same stimulus matrices that would interfere with the occurrence of these "hyperactive behaviors." In the classroom setting, such interference could be achieved by strengthening any one of a number of appropriate "attending" responses such as: looking at the book, looking at the arithmetic problem, or listening to the teacher. Because of the relatively high strength of the "hyperactive" behaviors, it is necessary to introduce a procedure for strengthening the associations among the stimuli present in the classroom setting and the "interfering" responses. Skinner (1958) and other theorists would place particular emphasis upon the necessity of making reinforcing stimuli contingent upon the occurrence of these responses. In addition, the latency between the occurrence of one of these desirable responses and the occurrence of the reinforcing stimulus must be very short. For the present application, the reinforcer must also be dispensed in such a way as to provide the least amount of disruption for the other children in the classroom. The apparatus and procedure for providing these contingencies are described below. Data is also presented showing the effect of this procedure in controlling the behavior of a hyperactive boy.

Method

The Subject

Earl was a nine-year-old boy in the second grade. He was referred to the University Psychology Clinic because of marked hyperactive behavior and academic retardation. He was described as being in almost continuous motion in the classroom and impossible to control unless he was in the immediate presence of the teacher. Easily distracted, he would work upon his lessons for only short periods of time and then leave his desk to wander about the classroom. Occasionally he would literally move his desk "through" the classroom, scattering children and desks as he did so. Frequently his behavior was aggressive. For no apparent reason he would hit, pinch, or hurtle himself into a group of children and as a consequence demolish the group. Although the other children occasionally found these behaviors amusing, by and large they avoided him.

Previous to his adoption, at the age of three, he had been treated with extreme brutality by his natural parents, and later by the grandparents. His medical records show a skull fracture received when he was less than one year of age. At the age of four he was referred for a neurological examination because of reoccurring convulsions and some minor incoordination. The subsequent medical report indicated an abnormal EEG and pneumoencephalogram; these taken in conjunction with other neurological signs led to the diagnosis of minimal brain damage. Psychological tests given to Earl when he was eight showed him to be of borderline intelligence and also indicated some significant perceptual motor impairments on the Bender Gestalt.

His parents, by adoption, were dedicated in their care of this child and eventually achieved some control over his behavior when he was in the home. This was achieved by the mother's constant surveillance and by her ability to anticipate situations that would elicit uncontrolled behavior.

Procedures

After several hours of observing Earl's behavior both at home and in the school, it was decided that most of his "hyperactivity" could be described by the inappropriate occurrence of the following behaviors: talking, pushing, hitting, pinching, looking about the room, looking out of the window, moving out of location (walking or moving desk), and moving in location (tapping, squirming, handling objects).

The frequency of occurrence of each of these responses was tabulated for each thirty second interval. During this interval, a tabulation was made for each second during which a response persisted. For example, if Earl were walking about the room (when he was supposed to be studying) he received one check for each second during which he was walking.

Prior to each conditioning session, Earl was observed for twenty minutes to establish a baseline rate of estimate for the occurrence of the undesirable behaviors. The estimate of rate was calculated by dividing the total number of tabulations by the number of minutes during which the observations were made.

Following the tabulation of the baseline observations, a conditioning session was initiated. The amount of time directly involved in the conditioning sessions varied somewhat from one day to the next. The first conditioning trial lasted five minutes. By the end of the fifteen sessions, the time interval had been extended to twenty or thirty minutes. The observation data described above were also tabulated during the conditioning session. The data were collected by three experimenters who worked on alternate days, and were collected at roughly the same time on each day (10:30) over a four week period.

The apparatus consisted of a small box six by eight by five inches. A small flashlight bulb was mounted on top of the box; the dial of an electric counter could also be observed in the top of the box. The light and counter were controlled by the experimenter who sat across the room from Earl. Before the conditioning trials began, Earl was given several short trial runs with the apparatus. During the pre-training sessions, Earl was given a book to look at. During each ten second interval when only "attending" behaviors occurred, the light would flash on, the counter click, and the experimenter deposited one M&M candy on the desk. It was explained to Earl that each time the light went on in the trials that would follow it meant he had "earned" one candy or one penny. The counter would keep score for him and he would get the candy or pennies at the end of each "lesson."

At the beginning of the first conditioning trial the following instructions were given to the class, in Earl's presence.

Earl has some trouble in learning things here in school because he is always moving around. This is a magic teaching machine that is going to teach Earl to sit still so that he can learn like other children. Each time that the light flashes on it means that Earl has been sitting still. It also means that he has earned one piece of candy (penny). The counter here will keep score. At the end of the lesson we will take the candy (pennies) and divide it up among all of you. If you want to help Earl earn the candy you can do so by not paying any attention to him when he is 'working.'

The classroom situations during which the conditioning was carried out varied from silent reading and art work at the desk, reading or arithmetic in small groups, and class recitation.

During the conditioning sessions, an average of 60 to 100 reinforcers were dispensed by the experimenter. During the initial conditioning sessions, M&M candies were used; during later sessions the candy was alternated with pennies as reinforcers.

It should be noted, however, that the peer group proved to be a source of social reinforcers that undoubtedly had some effect upon Earl's behavior. For example, at the end of each conditioning session when the score was announced to the class, they would typically applaud Earl for his performance earnings. They also frequently walked by his desk and peered at the counter to see how well he was doing. During breaks in the classroom routine, for example at recess, the experimenters overheard frequent comments such as, "You sure are doing good; you get better every day." There seems little reason to deny that these reinforcers had some effect; in fact, the procedure was structured in such a way as to maximize the possibility of their occurrence.

Results

There was a significant decrease in the number of responses per minute when comparing the base operant with the conditioning scores. The average drop of 8.4 responses per minute was significant at p less than .01 level.

It was, of course, of prime importance to show that Earl's behavior was affected during the conditioning trials. It is of even greater interest to note that some of the stimuli associated with the conditioning procedure acquired the status of a discriminative stimulus. In this case, the presence of the experimenter in the classroom served to elicit attending behaviors. In the initial conditioning trials, there would be a brief reduction in the overall rate of activity during the first few minutes of the experimenter's entering the classroom and making his baseline observations. As the trials progressed, the duration of these periods increased as shown in Figure 1 below.

These data show that the presence of the experimenter is operating as a discriminative stimulus that elicits attending (non-hyperactive) behaviors. Toward the end of the experiment, the writer observed Earl for a two hour period in which he was the "best behaved child in the class." Observations of three other boys (twenty minutes each) showed a mean of 3.2 responses per minute (same behaviors being recorded for each). Earl's behavior toward the end of the conditioning compares very well with this figure.

Because of the fact that school had closed it was not possible to continue this experiment. At the end of the series of trials, the teacher reported that he was not as hyperactive and destructive on the playground and that he seemed to actually "play with other children" rather than hurtle himself at them. She felt that there was some minor reduction in his overall behavior rate in the classroom, but

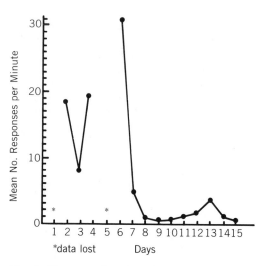

Fig. 1. The experimenter as a discriminative stimulus

at this point she was much more concerned with his continued diffi-culty in learning than with his classroom adjustment. Her report could not be taken as support for the hope that the behavior control manifest in the presence of the experimenter characterized his be-havior during the remainder of the day.

A telephone call to the parents four months after the study indi-cated that the teachers in the school reported him to be much "quieter." For the first time, other children come to his home to play, and he is making progress in a remedial reading program.

Discussion

These data offer support for the hypothesis that it is in fact possible to manipulate "high rate" behaviors occurring in the classroom setting. There is little doubt that, however effective they are, the present procedures are rather crude. Our preliminary experience with the procedure suggests several changes that would make the application more efficient.

The major problem in this (all) application of conditioning pro-cedures is to ensure generalization from the conditioning periods to behavior occurring outside of the conditioning sessions. The con-cept of stimulus generalization would suggest that the conditioning sessions should occur in as wide a variety of stimulus settings as possible. Presumably such a sampling of settings would ensure a wider range of stimuli which would be conditioned to the "attending behaviors." In Earl's case, the conditioning periods occurred at the same time of day and typically involved his participation in only a limited number of activities. Generalization would have been more likely to occur if the conditioning sessions were distributed throughout the day.

The "teaching machine" used in the present study also introduces some severe limitations upon the settings in which conditioning can be carried out. It was necessary, because of these limitations, to carry out the conditioning procedures only when Earl was seated at his desk. This would mean that none of the settings in which free movement can occur, that is, recess, can be used for conditioning purposes. Because of the undoubted importance of sampling social stimuli arising from this type of interaction, a new apparatus has been developed for research now underway. This is a radio control device which can dispense an auditory stimulus through a microphone in the child's ear even though he is sixty yards distant from the experimenter. With this improved apparatus, conditioning can take place in almost any social setting; presumably this greater flexibility will enhance the generalization.

In the last two conditioning trials, a procedure was introduced which would also tend to increase the spread of effect. This procedure involved the introduction of a type of discrimination learning paradigm. It was assumed that greater behavior change would occur if the child were first taught to use appropriate labels in describing behaviors inappropriate to the classroom setting. As a second step he was to be taught the contingencies holding between the occurrence of these behaviors and reinforcers. Earl was presented with a clip board and told to observe his classmates. Whenever he observed any of the following behaviors he was to first identify it (verbally) and then make a check upon the data sheet: talking, walking around, not listening to the teacher, squirming, tapping, or staring out the window. On each occasion in which he correctly labeled such behavior the light on the teaching machine was activated. Of all of the procedures attempted, Earl was undoubtedly most enthusiastic about this one. His dedication to locating behavioral sins made the policeman, Javert, of *Les Miserables* apathetic by comparison. Because the experiment was terminated, there is no way of knowing whether this process generalized to Earl's labeling his own behavior or to his learning to discriminate among behaviors that lead to rewards.

It is quite clear that the present procedure seriously confounds the effect of several experimental variables. There is no way of identifying which of the following variables produced the effect: candy and pennies as reinforcer, social approval dispensed by the peer group as a reinforcer, preliminary attempts at discrimination training.

Better controlled studies, now under way, will attempt to identify the relative contribution of each of these variables. For the present, however, these preliminary results seem to encourage further investigation.

References

Baldwin, A. L. Socialization and the parent child relationship. *Child Develpm.*, 1948, **19**, 127–136.

Bradley, C. Characteristics and management of children with behavior problems associated with organic brain damage. *Pediatr. clin. N. Amer.*, 1957, **4**, 1019–1060.

Dreger, R., and Georgia E. Dreger. Behavior classification project: Report #1, 1962.

Dunn, M., S. Levine, and E. New. The development of prematurely born children with birth weights or minimal postnatal weights of 1000 grams or less. *Pediatrics*, 1958, **22**, 1037–1053.

Graham, F. K., Claire B. Ernhart, D. Thurston, and Marguerite Croft. Development three years after perinatal anoxia and other potentially damaging newborn experiences. *Psychol. Monogr.*, 1962, **76** (3, Whole No. 522).

Guthrie, E. R. *The psychology of learning.* New York: Harper & Row, 1935.

Hareng, N., and E. L. Phillips. *Educating emotionally disturbed children.* New York: McGraw-Hill, 1962.

Knobloch, Hilda, and B. Pasamanick. The developmental behavioral approach to the neurologic examination in infancy. *Child Develpm.*, 1962, **33**, 181–198.

Parmellee, A. H. European neurological studies of the newborn. *Child Develpm.*, 1962, **33**, 169–180.

Patterson, G. R. A tentative approach to the classification of children's behavior problems. Unpublished doctoral dissertation. University of Minnesota, 1955.

Patterson, G. R. An empirical approach to the classification of disturbed children. *J. clin. Psychol.*, 1964, **20**, 326–337.

Shirely, May. A behavior syndrome characterizing prematurely-born children. *Child Develpm.*, 1939, **10**, 115–128.

Skinner, B. F. *Science and human behavior.* New York: Macmillan, 1958.

Stone, F. H. Psychodynamics of brain-damaged children: A preliminary report. *J. child psychol. Psychiatr.*, 1960, **1**, 203–214.

Strauss, A. A., and L. Lehtinen. *Psychopathology and education of the brain-injured child.* New York: Grune & Stratton, 1950.

Walker, R. N. Body build and behavior in young children. *Monogr. Soc. Res. Child Develpm.*, 1962, **27**, No. 3.

A Learning Theory Approach to the Treatment of the School Phobic Child

Gerald R. Patterson
University of Oregon

Most attempts to apply learning theory to the practice of psychotherapy seem as much oriented to confirming the status of a particular learning theory as to changing the behavior of the patient. Within this tradition, Salter (1950) outlined procedures that fit within the model of classic conditioning; Eysenck (1960) within Hullian theory; and Wolpe (1958) made an unacknowledged application of Guthrie's theory. However admirable the faith that these writers have in the theories that they have espoused, it would seem more reasonable for the practicing clinician to select principles from any of these theories that fit the needs of the individual case. The present report outlines procedures for application of Guthrie's concept (1935) of interference and Skinner's concept (1953) of conditioning via approximations. Standard clinical procedures were modified to provide

From L. P. Ullmann and L. Krasner (eds.), *Case Studies in Behavior Modification* (New York: Holt, Rinehart & Winston, 1965). Part of this material was presented in a paper at the annual convention of the American Association for Mental Deficiency, 1961, Portland, Oregon. The research was carried out as part of USPH grant M-5429, which provides support for investigating the application of learning principles to the socialization of the child. The writer gratefully acknowledges the cooperation of Mrs. Becktolt, Director of Special Education, and her staff, who did much to make the approach successful. The writer also acknowledges the clinical labors of Ivan Ruly, J. Wishart, and F. Miles, who carried out much of the contact with the children.

procedures for applying these principles to change the behavior of a "school phobic" child and the child's parents.

The term "school phobia" was introduced by Johnson, Falstein, Szurek, and Svendsen (1941) to describe an anxiety reaction in children that results in their persistent absence from school. Most writers agree with Estes, Haylett, and Johnson (1956), who pointed out that the stimulus that elicits the anxiety reaction is not the school per se but rather any situation that represents separation from the parent. Although these writers very properly suggested the term "separation anxiety" as a label, the term school phobia remains in currency and will be used in this paper.

A general formulation for school phobic behavior would be as follows: separation from the parent functions as an eliciting stimulus (ES)→ anxiety reaction→ escape or avoidance behaviors. According to the interference concept (Guthrie, 1935), extinction will occur if new responses can be associated with the ES. If these new responses are incompatible with the anxiety reaction, the new associations will result in gradual extinction of the escape and avoidance responses and in a diminution of the anxiety reaction. This general formulation was anticipated by the now classic work of Jones (1924). In her study, the interfering responses, eating, when associated with the feared object resulted in extinction of the escape behaviors and a marked reduction in anxiety reactions.

In pairing the interfering responses with the ES, it was decided to strengthen this association by creating a contingency between these responses and a variety of reinforcing stimuli. To determine the kind of reinforcing stimulus appropriate for the patient, he was tested in a laboratory procedure described by Patterson, Littman, and Hinsey (1963). It was found that in the early stage of treatment he was less responsive to social reinforcers dispensed by his therapist than were a hundred other children who had been reinforced by a variety of social agents. This nonresponsiveness to social reinforcers is in keeping with the findings by Levine and Simmons (1962), who showed that emotionally disturbed boys are less responsive to social reinforcers than are normal boys. For this reason, M&M candies were used in the present study as reinforcers in conjunction with social approval. It was assumed that this pairing of M&Ms and social reinforcers would increase the incentive value of social approval, resulting in a wider range of possibilities for behavior control.

In keeping with the suggestions by Jones (1924) and Wolpe (1962), the ES was presented on a graduate series so that initially only low intensity escape and anxiety reactions were evoked. As the trials progressed, the intensity of the ES was increased. In all situations, the ESs used in the conditioning trials matched as closely as possible situational cues from the child's environment.

Doll play, structured by the experimenter, was the procedure used in the conditioning trials. These sessions occurred four days a week and lasted fifteen minutes; the sessions are described in detail below. Following each conditioning session, both the child and the parents were interviewed. During the early interviews, the procedure was explained in detail to the family. The nature of the specific interfering response being conditioned was discussed with particular emphasis upon the parents' being alert to its occurrence in the home. When these behaviors occurred, they were instructed to reinforce them immediately and then to describe them in the interview on the following day. Particular emphasis was placed upon reinforcing the appropriate behaviors and ignoring behaviors associated with reactions to separation anxiety. It is felt that these highly structured interviews with the parents are of particular importance in insuring generalization of conditioning effects from the laboratory to the home.

The Patient

Karl was seven-years-old when referred to the University Clinic by the school nurse. In his first few days of attendance in the first grade, he had shown increasing reluctance to stay in school. In the second week of school, he would stay in the classroom only as long as one of his parents remained in the room with him.

Karl had similar difficulties in attending a nursery school during the previous year, even though the school was only a few blocks from his home. For the past few years, he found it necessary to play only in the immediate vicinity of his home. He would frequently interrupt his play to go into the house and "check" to see if his mother was still there. If the mother were going to the store, a short distance away, Karl would insist upon accompanying her. Attempts to use punishment, bribes, or cajoling had failed to keep him in school.

In the clinic, Karl was observed to be an attractive child, rather immature in his behavior and having a severe articulation defect. Testing at the end of treatment revealed a low reading readiness score and an above average intelligence quotient. Extensive intake interviewing with the parents revealed no marked pathology in the parents or in the family; this impression was in agreement with the essentially normal MMPI profiles of both parents.

Session 1

In his first appointment at the clinic, Karl refused to go to the playroom without his mother. Teeth chattering, he clenched one fist, while with the other he maintained a firm hold upon his mother's coat. Karl was seated at a table just inside the door of the playroom while the mother sat across from him in the doorway. The experimenter proceeded to set up a doll play situation in which a little boy, "Henry," was being taken by the mother to see a doctor. Karl divided his attention between the experimenter and his mother. The first reinforcing contingency was one M&M for each thirty-second interval during which Karl did not look at his mother. After five minutes, the mother left the room and sat outside the closed door.

The doll play was restructured so that Henry was inside the doctor's office. When Karl was asked where Henry's mother was, he replied, "Outside," and received one M&M. In the procedure that followed, the mother doll left the boy in the doctor's office for increasingly long periods of time; on each occasion Karl was queried as to how the boy felt and what he was going to do. If he replied that the boy was not afraid or that he would stay in the doctor's office, he received both praise and one M&M. Similar situations were structured in which the boy remained at home while the mother went shopping or the mother remained at home while the boy walked toward the school building.

In the interview with the mother that followed this session, she was encouraged to praise Karl for staying in the playroom without her. She was further instructed to keep track of Karl's "checking" behavior at home; if he stayed outside for longer than thirty minutes without coming inside, she was to make an announcement at the dinner table to the whole family. Karl seemed obviously pleased with his success on this first contact and listened very closely to the interchange between the mother and the experimenter.

Session 2

The mother seated herself in a chair outside the playroom. When Karl acquiesced to the experimenter's closing the door, he immediately received two M&Ms and praise from the experimenter. The doll play was repeated with the boy in the doctor's office and the mother's leaving him there for increasing periods of time. As in the previous session, if Karl said that the boy was not afraid or that the boy would stay in the situation, he was reinforced by both candy and social approval. At the end of this sequence of doll play, Karl was asked if he would, on the next visit, allow his mother to stay in the reception room rather than sitting outside the door of the playroom. He readily agreed to this and was reinforced for his bravery with both praise and several M&Ms. For any given session, there were generally thirty or forty of these reinforcers dispensed by the experimenter.

The structured play relating to the school was again initiated; on this occasion, Karl specified the reaction of the boy to saying goodbye to the mother, getting upon his bicycle, walking into the school, sitting at the desk, and reading aloud from a book.

A third play theme was introduced in this session concerning Karl's anxiety about physical injury as being the outcome of playing with his peers. Doll play was initiated involving "Little Henry's" playing with his peers and receiving minor injuries; in each case Karl reported the boy was not afraid, did not return to the mother, and he showed how Little Henry would place a band aid upon his own leg.

In the interview with the father, he reported that Karl had actually stayed outside for an hour and that they had made an announcement at the dinner table. He was told about Karl's decision to allow his parents to remain in the reception room, and he responded with approval. He was encouraged to continue to reinforce Karl for independent behavior in the home and to be particularly careful not to overreact to small injuries that he might receive while playing. It was also suggested that they obtain some preprimers from the school and reinforce Karl whenever he indicated an interest in the books or in returning to school.

Sessions 3 through 9

Karl continued to allow his parents to remain in the reception room while he "worked" in the playroom. On each occasion he was reinforced for saying that he was not afraid; he began to boast that the parents would not have to remain in the clinic at all. Karl gave a brief report of his activities at the beginning of each conditioning session and was reinforced for reports indicating attempts to read, climbing trees without being afraid of injuring himself, playing some distance from home, and not checking on his mother. The structured play sessions were expanded to include two new areas. Karl expressed some further anxiety about being attacked by members of the peer group. In the play sessions he was reinforced for counteraggressing to such attacks and heavily reinforced for attempts to initiate play activity with the peer group. Karl was also reinforced for making discriminations between behaviors appropriate for Little Henry and those appropriate for a new and more mature "Big Henry." Both of these areas had been brought up in the interviews with the parents, and they had been encouraged to reinforce him for playing with children his own age and ignoring any expression of fear of the aggression of other children. The mother particularly had been instructed to label those aspects of Karl's behavior that were immature and to respond, if possible, only when he acted maturely. As before, the parents were required to bring examples of their attempts to reinforce Karl. Arrangements were also made for a visiting teacher to assist Karl in the development of reading skills.

Session 10

The material which follows is a brief excerpt from this session and illustrates in detail the procedures used throughout the sessions.

E: What shall we have Henry do today?

K: Well, we could have him go to school.

E: Yeah, I think that is a good idea, to have some work on going to school again today. That probably is the hardest thing for him to do. O.K., here he is (picking up the Henry doll). Where is mamma, oh here she is (sets up blocks and furniture). Ah, maybe we had better have Little Henry start off from home; when he does go to school, we won't have him go into the classroom today; he'll just run errands for the principal; no reading or writing this time. So Little Henry is talking to his mother and he says, "Mom, I think I'll go to school for a little while today." What does mom say?

K: O.K.

E: Is he afraid when he is right there talking to mamma?

K: No. (one M&M)

E: And so he gets on his bike and says bye-bye mamma. He stops half way to school. What does he think now that mamma is not there?

K: Ma-amma (laughs).

E: Yeah, but what does he do? Does he go back or go on to school?

K: Goes to school. (one M&M)

E: Yeah, that's right, he goes to school; Little Henry would go back and look but Big Henry would go on to school . . . and he goes to the principal's office and says, "Hi, Mr. Principal. I though I would come back to school for a little while. Can I run some errands for you . . . ?" Henry gives the note to the teacher, then he is coming back to the principal's office. He stops. What is he thinking about now?

K: Mamma is not there again.

E: Yeah, he is scaring himself again. Now, does he go back to the principal's office or does he go home?

K: He goes back to the office. (one M&M)

E: Yeah, that is right, he does. At least Big Henry would do that; Little Henry would get scareder and more scareder; but Big Henry feels pretty good. "I am back, Mr. Principal." The principal says, "Why don't you go down to the cafeteria and get a glass of milk. I don't have any more errands for you to run right now." So he goes and is sitting here drinking his milk. What does he think about now? Every time he is alone he thinks about this.

K: Mamma again.

E: That's right, he always thinks about mamma. Does he go home?

K: No. (one M&M)

E: That's right, he doesn't. Big Henry doesn't go home.

K: (laughs) He sure is big.

—a few moments later—

E: . . . and he is lying there on the sleeping mat. What is he thinking about?

K: Mamma. No, I don't think so because he got a nice neighbor (child) next to him.

E: So, he is not thinking about mamma.

K: Nope. (E was too surprised to get reinforcement in on time.)
— about five minutes later —

E: Well, Karl what have you been doing at home like Big Henry?

K: Well, ah, yesterday I done some numbers (very excited) and I went up to a hundred. (one M&M)

E: You did! Good (with emphasis). What else did you do like Big Henry?

K: I made a cake . . .

E: Were you outside playing yesterday? Of course it was stormy yesterday.

K: Yes, I was outside playing.

E: Did you think about mamma when you were outside?

K: Uh-uh. I wasn't thinking about mamma. (one M&M) I'm not thinking about her now either. (one M&M)

In the past few sessions, several play sequences had been devoted to Little Henry's return to school for an hour or so with his visiting teacher. The possibility of Karl's actually doing this had also been discussed with him.

Sessions 11 through 23

Karl made his first trip to the school with the special teacher with him at all times. On the following day, he returned and the teacher left him alone in the room for a few minutes. On each of the days following this, the teacher left him for longer periods of time. This sequence at school was accompanied by conditioning sequences in the playroom and a good deal of praise and approval by his family. After a week of this, he announced at home that he would not be afraid to ride to school and stay by himself for one hour. He carried this out on the following day amid applause and acclaim for his singular act of bravery. He then announced that he would return to school full time within the week, which he did.

On the last week of the treatment program, Karl and the writer returned to the procedure for testing his reaction to social reinforcers. On this second trial, the reinforcers were effective in changing his position preference on the marble box game. Social reinforcers had no effect on a second disturbed boy tested at the same time as Karl but not receiving treatment. An important implication of this finding for Karl is that his behavior is now under the control of social reinforcers dispensed by a wide variety of social agents.

On a follow-up of Karl's classroom adjustment three months after termination of treatment, the school reported dramatic improvement in his general adjustment as well as no further evidence of fearfulness. The Department of Special Education is continuing their program of remedial reading and speech.

Discussion

At the cost of twenty bags of M&Ms and ten hours of staff time, Karl
returned to school. This, of course, does not constitute a record for
the "cure" of school phobia in the amount of time necessary for the
return to school (Sperling, 1961), nor is it the first time that learning
theories have been applied in treating this type of problem behavior
(Lazarus, 1960). The implication is that the present modification of
standard clinical practices is at least as effective as traditional procedures.

Since terminating the treatment program with Karl, the same
procedures have been followed in conditioning a second child whose
presenting symptoms were very similar to Karl's. The second case
responded dramatically in less than six hours of staff time. These
two cases are not offered as constituting confirmation for the efficacy
of this procedure; however, the apparent success of the procedure
has encouraged the author to apply a similar procedure to dealing
with behavior problems that are ordinarily resistive to traditional
clinical manipulations. In this third case, application of simple
operant procedures was very successful in extinguishing hyperactive behaviors in the classroom setting (Patterson, 1963). Taken
together, the successes strongly suggest that modifications of clinical
procedures in accord with principles from learning theories will be
a powerful tool in effecting behavior change in the clinical setting.

In retrospect, there is little doubt that one of the crucial variables
involved in this procedure is the reinforcement contingencies being
used by social agents other than the experimenter. Although it may
very well be true that the same effect could be achieved by relying
only upon the conditioning-play sessions, there is little doubt on
both the theoretical and the practical levels that the parents and
the teacher enhanced the generalization from behavior change in
the natural setting. Although the clinician has been concerned
traditionally with enhancing generalization from play therapy, the
present procedure does not assume that the parents are emotionally
disturbed but simply that they have been reinforcing the wrong
behaviors. This being the case, it is not necessary for the parents
to be involved in intensive psychotherapy, but it is necessary for
the parents to be given specific instructions as to what to reinforce
and how to reinforce child behaviors. In our extensive practice, with
three cases, we have been impressed with the general lack of awareness displayed by these parents as to what it is that they are reinforcing and the effect of this reinforcement upon the behavior of
the child. The procedure described here should be appropriate for
a variety of child behavior problems and for parents who do not show
obvious signs of pathology. This latter statement assumes of course
that the reinforcing contingencies adopted by any particular parents
are not necessarily determined by the intensity or kind of emotional conflict in the parents. It is hypothesized here that many

parents have been conditioned rather than "driven" to adopt their idiosyncratic schedules of reinforcement.

The research by Levine & Simmons (1962), Patterson, Littman, and Hinsey (1963) agree in identifying the child with behavior problems as being unresponsive to social approval; the research by Patterson (1963) suggests that these children might be overly responsive to disapproval. Although satisfactory empirical evidence is lacking at the present time, it seems highly probable that the child with behavior problems is responsive to only a limited aspect of his social environment. In Karl's case, for example, it seemed as if he was responsive only to the approval of his mother (and father perhaps). This restriction in responsiveness to one or two social agents would mean that his behavior was not being conditioned to the normal extent by other agents, such as the peer group or adults outside of the family circle. In such a situation, if the parental programing of reinforcers was not in accord with contingencies adopted by the remainder of the culture, it would not be surprising to observe that the child displayed some rather deviant behavior patterns.

If such a child were brought into the clinic, it would be predicted that much of his behavior would not be under the control of the therapist. One of the first functions of the therapist was to change the incentive value of social stimuli; once this was achieved, the therapist could potentially have some effect in changing the behavior of the child. It is of interest to note that Anna Freud strongly urged the pairing of primary reinforcers as food with the presence of the therapist in order to create a "relationship" with the child (Freud, 1946). It is hypothesized here that whatever such pairing might do for the "relationship" the *effect* is to increase the status of the therapist as a secondary reinforcer as witnessed by Karl's increased responsiveness to social reinforcers at termination of treatment. This would suggest either that nonsocial reinforcers be used in the earlier phases of conditioning with these children or that the therapist make it a point to become associated with a wide range of pleasant stimuli before attempting any behavior manipulation.

Summary

A procedure was described for applying the principles of interference and reinforcement to the treatment of a school phobic child. A series of twenty-three 20-minute conditioning sessions with the child followed by highly structured ten-minute interviews with the parents resulted in dramatic changes in behavior.

REFERENCES

Estes, H. R., Clarice H. Haylett, and Adelaide M. Johnson. Separation anxiety. *Amer. J. Orthopsychiat.*, 1956, **10**, 682–695.

Eysenck, H. J. (Ed.) *Behavior therapy and the neurosis*. New York: Pergamon, 1960.

Freud, A. *The psycho-analytical treatment of children*. New York: International Universities, 1946.

Guthrie, E. R. *The psychology of learning*. New York: Harper and Row, 1935.

Johnson, Adelaide M., E. J. Falstein, S. A. Szurek, and Margaret Svendsen. School phobia. *Amer. J. Orthopsychiat.*, 1941, 11, 702–711.

Jones, Mary C. The elimination of children's fears. *J. exp. Psychol.*, 1924. 7, 382–390.

Lazarus, A. A. The elimination of children's phobias by deconditioning. In H. J. Eysenck (Ed.), *Behavior therapy and the neurosis*. New York: Pergamon, 1960. Pp. 116–119.

Levine, G. R., and J. T. Simmons. Response to praise by emotionally disturbed boys. *Psychol. Rep.*, 1962, 11, 10.

Patterson, G. R. Parents as dispensers of aversive stimuli. Unpublished manuscript, 1963.

Patterson, G. R., R. Littman, and C. Hinsey. Parents as social stimuli. Unpublished manuscript, 1963.

Salter, A. *Conditioned reflex therapy*. New York: Creative Age Press, Inc., 1950.

Skinner, B. F. *Science and human behavior*. New York: Macmillan, 1953.

Sperling, Melitta. Analytic first aid in school phobias. *Psychoanal. Quart.*, 1961, 30, 504–518.

Wolpe, J. *Psychotherapy by reciprocal inhibition*. Stanford, Calif.: Stanford University Press, 1958.

24

The Elimination of
Tantrum Behavior of a Child in
an Elementary Classroom

Constance S. Carlson
Carole R. Arnold
Wesley C. Becker
Charles H. Madsen

TEMPER TANTRUMS in children produce considerable distress for parents and other adults responsible for their training. Informal observation has suggested that such tantrums are maintained by attention and other forms of reinforcement which typically follow them. Williams (1959) has described an extinction procedure he used with a 21-month-old child who tantrumed when left at bedtime. The procedure essentially involved placing the child in bed and not responding to his outburst. Tantrums were readily eliminated in seven days. Wolf, Risley and Mees (1964) have reported a related procedure. A 3½-yr-old autistic child was placed in a room by himself when he tantrumed, and was allowed to come out only after the tantrum ceased. This particular procedure combined extinction with mild punishment (time out from positive reinforcement). In the case to be reported, no facilities were available for isolating an 8-yr-old when she had a tantrum in the classroom, and an alternative procedure was devised.

Case Report

Diane was an 8-yr-old Negro child from a family of five children. An older sister died with sicle-cell anemia and a younger sister has the same difficulty. Both parents work and were in debt because of

Behav. Res. & Therapy, 6 (1968), 117–19. Pergamon Press. Printed in England.

high medical bills. Diane attended a neighborhood school which was 95 per cent Negro. Her IQ was average on the Stanford-Binet (LM). On the Wide Range Achievement Test given in January 1966 (mid-second grade) Diane scored 1.8 grades in reading, 1.2 in spelling, and 1.5 in oral math.

She began the year in one adjustment class (16 children), but was moved at Christmas to another class in an attempt by the school to establish better social relationships. She was described as being quite fearful and timid, and the children in the first grade disliked her and fought with her frequently. In her new class (Mrs. C.'s) she displayed no unusual behavior at first, perhaps because she was frequently ill and had little chance to interact with the children. Then, in February, severe tantrums started and occurred as often as three a week. When the first few tantrums occurred, Diane was taken to the office. Although Diane was isolated from her peers, she received immediate attention from her teacher, the secretaries, the social worker, the principal, and on two occasions, from her mother when she was summoned to the school. Mother reported that tantrums were quite frequent at home and that the younger siblings were isolated from Diane when a tantrum was in progress. Diane received her mother's undivided attention.

On March 1, 1966, Mrs. C. let a tantrum run its course in the room. The tantrum was actually too long and too intense to be handled in the room. Such behavior as profane screaming, running wildly from place to place, picking up chairs, and actually throwing them, attacking other children, etc. were displayed. At this point, Mrs. C., who was attending a seminar on behavior modification with the co-authors, requested help.

Procedures

The following program was established.

(1) It was explained to Diane and the class that when Diane was behaving badly, Mr. Z., a teacher aide, would hold her down in her chair. Diane resented being touched or held, so holding served as punishment.

(2) Diane's chair was placed in the back of the room so that the other children could not see her.

(3) It was explained to the other children that everyone who did not turn around at all to watch Diane would receive a candy treat. A treat was passed out to demonstrate what would happen as the explanation was given. The aim was to withdraw peer attention from the tantrum behavior. To prevent the children from provoking tantrums to get a treat, candy was given intermittently at times when Diane was not tantruming.

(4) A positive incentive for non-tantrum behavior was established. Her teacher decided that an obtainable goal would be to give Diane a star (on the board) for each half-day of non-tantrum behavior. When

four stars *in a row* were received there would be a little class party, with Diane passing out the treats. The latter provision was designed with the thought of increasing Diane's acceptance by her peers.

The program was begun on March 14th and continued through June 10th. On May 9th, Mrs. C. suggested extending the required stars to six, but Diane said "Let me try for ten." Ten became the new goal.

Results

Diane had a tantrum on Monday, March 14th, the morning the program was explained to the class. There were none the rest of the week. She earned the treat for the class and had a chance to "feel important."

During the next week, tantrums occurred on Monday, Thursday, and three times on Friday. Two of the tantrums on Friday were recorded by two observers whose notes are summarized below.

First Tantrum

1:35 P.M. Apparently it started in the hall while the class was returning from the bathroom. Mrs. C. was restraining Diane as the class came back. Mr. Z. took Diane to her seat and sat her down while continuing to hold her. Diane struggled and shouted repeatedly, "let me go," "stinking rat, you let me go." She attempted to hit Mr. Z. Mrs. C. passed out candy to those who were not turning, and took candy away from a child who turned to look after receiving candy. Yelling continued at a high volume. "Black dog, let me go." Objects were thrown at a neighboring girl. The rest of the class was very good at ignoring her. Finally she started crying and shouting, "stinking rat, black dog, let me go, can't you hear?" "Let me go. You hate me and I hate you" (repeated).

1:43 P.M. Lesson started for rest of class. Diane was shaking her desk and screaming. She kicked herself out of her chair on to the floor. Mr. Z. set her back in the chair and continued to hold her. "Stinking rat." She tried to spit on teacher.

1:46 P.M. Diane was quiet and the restraint was stopped. She started looking in her desk, rattling papers. Mrs. C. put a *Weekly Reader* in front of her. She threw it off her desk.

1:48 P.M. Mr. Z. was not holding her. In a low voice she said to him "let me go." She got her glue and some papers. Mr. Z. moved to the back of the room. This activity continued for 5–10 minutes. She ignored the class activity.

Second Tantrum

2:10 P.M. The class started out to recess, which Diane was denied. She went out with the class and Mr. Z. had to go after her and bring her back.

2:25 P.M. Mr. Z. brought her in and blocked the door. She got her glue and said "if you don't let me go, I'll throw glue on you." She tried to push through. Mr. Z. took her to her seat and told her he would have to hold her until she was quiet. "I'll throw glue on you." Mr. Z. told her he would have to take the glue away from her. "I don't care. I'll have my father buy more. You black bitch, let me go." Threw several objects from desk. "You black bitch, you let me go." Threw books. Mr. Z. said, "Sit still." "I'm gonna drop everything in my desk on this floor. I ain't gonna pick none of it up."

2:28 P.M. Tried to bite Mr. Z. several times. "I'll bite the shit out of you." She turned the desk over with her feet. "I can do so much with my foot that you will be surprised." She called for mother, "Oh, Mama," and in a half cry, "You let me go." "I'm gonna turn everybody's desk over." "Let me go." . . . "I'll make all the racket I can."

2:32 P.M. "You black dog, you don't have to hold me." She settled down and Mr. Z. turned her loose. "I'm getting my desk." She turned her desk up on its legs. "I'm getting me something to clean it with." She went to the sink and brought back a wet sponge and started washing the inside of her desk.

2:36 P.M. The rest of the class returned from recess. She ignored the rest of the class and continued to wash her desk. She then started to put the items from the floor neatly back into her desk. Diane received no attention from other students. By 2:45 things were all cleaned up and Diane was walking around the room quietly.

The observers felt that the "peak of the extinction curve" had been reached. No tantrums occurred the following week. Diane's reactions were notably changed. At first, she covered her ears so that she could not hear the children enjoying the candy (given periodically for ignoring Diane). Then she was very sullen and expressed a desire to change schools, move away, etc. During periods when no tantrums occurred, she looked noticeably happier. She began to play and take part in group activities with the girls on the playground.

During the next week she had one tantrum (Tuesday, April 14th). Her attitude seemed to be continually improving. More and more chances to praise her for success were found. On April 15th, Mrs. C. added a new component to the program. At noon, before coming in the building for the afternoon session, Diane went after Hope. In Mrs. C.'s words:

"I could see that this behavior would continue if Diane came in so I told her that she'd really goofed. She had 3 x's in a row and all she needed was four, and if she was going to act like that, she couldn't come in the building. Previously she would have reacted to this by saying "I'm going home." This time, however, she stayed outside by the fence for a while, then entered the building and stood outside our classroom door. We ignored her. After the class's bathroom break, I said, "Come on in, Diane." She broke into tears and said, 'I'm sorry, Mrs. C., I won't do it again.' I now knew that the room and the school were positive for her."

On April 18th in the presence of observers, Diane was called on in math. She did not answer correctly and a moment later spoke out saying "Hope, don't you dare call me stupid." From her tone and actions it looked like a tantrum was coming. Mrs. C. ignored Diane's speaking out and praised her neighbor for not speaking out of turn. By the careful use of praise of other children for appropriate behavior, Diane was drawn back to the class and Hope was led to turn around and ignore Diane. Both girls were then praised for properly answering questions about the lesson.

Mild tantrums, requiring Mr. Z.'s aid occurred on April 19th and 29th. They consisted mainly of crying, without profanity, and lasted less than 5 min. A mild eruption occurred on May 2nd, but was controlled by comments such as "Oh dear, I hope we don't lose our x," or "I'll be glad when everyone is in his seat."

School was out June 10th. Between May 2nd and the end of the school year, no other tantrums occurred. During the final month of school, Diane's attitudes continued to improve. She learned to make friends and to react to the school and her teacher in positive ways. Mrs. C. described her as a happy, cheerful child during the last month.

Sequel

In the fall Diane was moved to another school. With the changed situation, tantrums re-occurred. They were handled by sending Diane to the principal's office. This often required the principal to remain in the office through lunch until he could return her to class. In the middle of the year, Diane was "staffed" at the new school. Mrs. C. attended the staffing and described the procedures used to control Diane the previous year. Both the principal and the new teacher were convinced that some "deep-down disturbance" was causing the tantrums and that talking about "how she feels" would help. They could not see the behavior as being maintained by the attention it received or by escape from the classroom. An attempt was made to place Diane in a special research classroom for emotionally disturbed children, but she was not accepted. She was placed on daily tranquillizers. A report from the school social worker in April, 1967 indicated that Diane's behavior had "deteriorated to a level worse than it had ever been the previous year." Diane was re-staffed and was scheduled to enter the special research class for emotionally disturbed children in September.

On May 22, 1967, Diane came back to visit Mrs. C. at her old school. She chatted for about five minutes and gave Mrs. C. a piece of gum "for being such a nice teacher last year." She was smiling and happy, and had several friends with her. Mrs. C. commented, pointedly, that she saw "no signs of inner conflict."

25

Behavior Modification Techniques: New Tools for Probation Officers

Gaylord L. Thorne
Roland G. Tharp
Ralph J. Wetzel

University of Arizona

Probation work with juvenile delinquents, as the authors have viewed it, has not been very rewarding to the probation officers and not very helpful to the youngsters. Far too many youngsters fail probation by committing further offenses and, unfortunately, a significant percentage move on to adult crime. Probation officers frequently point to their large caseloads and lack of professional training as causes for low success rates. The former certainly warrants concern, whereas the latter is probably overemphasized. The position of this article[1] is that juvenile probation officers could be considerably more effective than they are presently even with large caseloads and no graduate training.

Such a position is based on the burgeoning evidence that has become available recently in the field of mental health. Great changes are underway. The importance of the following is diminishing in modern treatment approaches: Talking therapies as a major curative

From *Federal Probation*, June 1967. Dr. Thorne is director of the Behavioral Research Project of the Southern Arizona Mental Health Center. Dr. Tharp is director of the Psychology Department at the Center and co-investigator for the Behavioral Research Project. Dr. Wetzel is associate professor at the University of Arizona and consultant for the project.

1. This article is based on data gathered from the Behavioral Research Project which is supported by the Office of Juvenile Delinquency and Youth Development, Welfare Administration, Department of Health, Education and Welfare.

method; the medical disease model; primary reliance on highly trained therapists; institutions operating as quasi-psychiatric centers; and the emphasis on "psychiatric" causation (particularly psychoanalytic) for antisocial behavior. The abandonment or severe curtailment of these traditional approaches has led to some badly needed changes.

The application of *behavior modification* techniques is certainly one of the most exciting and refreshing of the new treatment innovations. The techniques follow from operant learning theory—a theory that is elegantly simple, easily taught, dramatically effective, and useful in an almost unlimited number of settings (Grossberg, 1964; Schwitzgebel, 1964; Ullmann and Krasner, 1965; Wolpe, et al., 1964). The juvenile probation officer is in a key position to take advantage of these new techniques. This was recently pointed out by Judge Ronald B. Jamieson (1965) in his recommendation of the use of conditioning principles in probation work.

> Judges can keep learning theory and conditioning principles in mind in drafting conditions of probation. They can require the probationer to do things (1) which will tend to break habits and associations which led him into crime and (2) which will tend to create new habits and associations which will tend to lead him into constructive, non-criminal activity (p. 7).[2]

Behavior Modification Techniques

What are behavior modification techniques? Briefly, they represent the systematic application of a reinforcement learning theory largely developed by B. F. Skinner and his associates. The basic premise is: *Behavior is governed by its consequences.* Only observable behavior is dealt with; fantasies, dreams, the unconscious, ego, etc., are not considered legitimate data. The goal or modifying behavior is accomplished by altering consequences. One technique of such an approach involves the determination of these consequences (or more technically *reinforcers*) and applying them when a desired behavior is approximated.

A child's reinforcers can be determined by carefully observing his behavior. Each child has an idiosyncratic list of reinforcers which one can rank from most to least important. Aside from candy for young children, and money for all others, it is seldom that reinforcers can be accurately specified without observation and inquiry. In working with predelinquent children, the authors determine a "reinforcement hierarchy" by inquiring directly from the child and from his parents as to what motivates him—the people, things, or events which he seeks.

---

2. Ronald B. Jamieson, "Can Conditioning Principles Be Applied to Probation?" *Trial Judges' Journal*, 1965, 4, No. 1.

There are two general types of reinforcement schedules used to modify behavior. The first is a "positive schedule of reinforcement," and is characterized by such reinforcers as praise, attention, privileges, money, food, TV, use of the car, etc. Changes in behavior promoted by such a schedule tend to be relatively rapid and durable. The second is an "aversive schedule of reinforcement," and is characterized by such reinforcers as threats, physical punishment, confinement, withdrawal of rewards and privileges, ridicule, ostracism, etc. Psychologists have shown that behavior changes promoted on the latter kind of schedule tend to be relatively limited and temporary.

In actual practice the type of schedule used to modify behavior is usually mixed, i.e., both positive and aversive. The key to modifying behavior lies with that which is given the major emphasis. Many delinquent and predelinquent children are being raised primarily on an aversive schedule and, unfortunately, the steps usually taken by public agencies to correct such behavior are also very likely to be aversive—e.g., being expelled from school, incarcerated, etc. The challenge, from a behavior modification viewpoint, is how to get the youngster onto a more balanced schedule of reinforcement.

The Concepts of Shaping and Contingency

Two more concepts are needed to round out the general description of operant principles before dealing with specific procedures to change behavior. The first is *shaping*, a term used to describe steps or approximations to a desired goal. When a behavior is selected as a goal, then all responses that approximate this goal are reinforced and all other responses are not reinforced. For example, when an otherwise very capable youngster is getting all failing grades in school one should not immediately ask for A's on his work. Instead, he should be shaped toward A's by rewarding D's and all behaviors approximating those needed for academic success (attending, opening book, completing some of the assignments). Once D's are attained the reward criterion can be gradually increased to C's, then B's, and finally A's. The same process would be used for antisocial behaviors. To illustrate, a boy who habitually fights could be rewarded for going a full day without a fight, then 2 days, then 5 days, until it was felt that he had learned new non-aggressive ways of relating to peers.

The second is the concept of *contingency* and it is absolutely essential in understanding operant principles. Contingency means that the consequences of an event are made dependent upon whether the event occurs. For example, telling a child he may have an ice cream cone only if he behaves means that ice cream is contingent upon good behavior; or, if parole depends upon acceptable prison behavior, then acting-out prevents parole. It is a very simple and straightforward concept that we deal with in a variety of ways during our daily lives. However, failure to understand the importance of rewarding or punishing *on contingency* is commonplace and can utterly destroy learning.

Alternatives to Traditional Therapy

The possible use of probation officers as agents to implement behavior modification would be highly consistent with some current outlooks on treating problem children. The traditional use of highly trained psychotherapists has not been particularly successful with children. The creation of an artificial relationship between a youngster and a caseworker, psychologist or other individual, takes considerable time and skill, yet its effectiveness can be questioned. However, the use of natural relationships (e.g., parents, friends, relatives, teachers) for bringing about changes in a youngster can be efficient and powerful. Parents have the primary responsibility for their children, and if they even display a modicum of cooperation there is a potential for bringing about behavior changes of a meaningful and durable nature.

The agents used on the Behavioral Research Project of the Southern Arizona Mental Health Center to teach new child management techniques to parents and teachers are all subprofessionals — bachelor's degrees or less. They were trained and are supervised by the authors. The training techniques could easily be taught to probation officers to improve their effectiveness.

The typical probation officer's effectiveness with youngsters could be improved with operant techniques because of the ways they usually fulfill their present roles. When a probation officer enters a child's life, his "treatment" plan is traditionally built around points of law, the prestige of the judge, threats of incarceration, the punishments and restrictions he can create in the home and community, lectures on bad behavior and society's right of revenge, lists of "Do Not" rules to follow, and the use of his presence in the home or school to prevent certain misbehaviors. Psychologists would describe this as an aversive schedule of reinforcement — only unpleasant or punishing consequences are used. They would also predict that such a reinforcement schedule will only produce circumscribed learning (Bandura, 1962; Skinner, 1953). The latter is further complicated by the fact that additional contacts with the child's parents rarely occur (while he behaves), so the changes in their behavior are not reinforced by the probation officer and thus not maintained. This represents a considerable waste of effort in a large percentage of cases, i.e., one instance of threat from the juvenile court motivates only a small number of parents to change their ways.

The error of focusing one's attention on misbehavior is certainly not unique to probation officers. It is a commonplace occurrence in schools and homes. School teachers particularly tend toward this, seldom realizing that the use of attention in this manner actually *stimulates* and *maintains* misbehavior in a large number of youngsters. It is, of course, only logical that probation officers must focus their initial attention on misbehavior since they have almost no other occasion for being in contact with a child. However, this does not justify the continuation of such a focus.

Probation officers should make use of their aversive controls, which can temporarily reduce misbehavior, and then build a treatment or rehabilitation plan around positive controls that would teach new socially acceptable behaviors. The whole purpose of behavior modification techniques is to introduce reinforcement contingencies that will encourage the emergence of nondeviant behaviors. The latter can rarely be done without teaching parents new child management techniques; juvenile probation officers are usually very remiss about doing this.

Some Case Examples

Perhaps several cases from the Behavioral Research Project will illustrate some of the alternatives available in working with the teachers and families of misbehaving children. All of this work was carried out by subprofessional staff, so in every case a juvenile probation officer (trained in operant techniques, of course) could have done the same.

Case 1

Claire is a bright, moderately attractive 16-year-old who was referred to the project for truancy, poor grades, and incorrigibility at home. The parents were divorced 6 years ago and the mother now supports the two of them as a maid. The father is out of state, as is Claire's older married sister.

When the referral came from a local high school, it stated that Claire was going to be expelled for truancy. The staff persuaded them to hold up expulsion for several days, which they were willing to do.

The mother was eager for help, although she lacked the physical or emotional resources to assist very much. Claire had been staying home from school for days and was now threatening to run away, Her mother had withdrawn all money, the use of the telephone, and dating privileges. These were all very powerful reinforcers to Claire but, unfortunately, her mother had not provided any clear way for Claire to earn them back.

Obviously, the most pressing problem was Claire's truancy and it was imperative that an intervention plan be prepared immediately to prevent suspension from school. Also, Claire's attending school would be very reinforcing to mother who was, at this time, somewhat dubious that a "noncounseling" approach would be successful. By winning her confidence it would be possible to begin shaping her to regard Claire in a more positive perspective, which would be necessary before a more amicable relationship could be worked out between them.

An intervention plan was agreed upon by mother, Claire, and a staff member. Telephone privileges and weekend dates were contingent on attending school all day. The school attendance officer would dispense a note to Claire at the end of each day if she had attended all of her classes. On presenting the note to mother, Claire earned telephone usage (receiving and calling out) for that day. If she received four out of five notes during the week she earned one weekend date night, and five out of five notes earned two weekend date nights. Phone usage on the weekend was not included in this plan.

Much to mother's astonishment Claire accepted the plan. Mother herself felt the plan "childish" and was apprehensive about Claire complying with it. Staff emphasized the necessity and benefit of praising Claire whenever she brought a note home. This would be difficult for mother, who was inconsistent, ineffectual, and emotional in all her relations with Claire. However, she was given support through several brief phone calls every week.

Despite frequent family upsets Claire attended school regularly from the first day of intervention. The plan was altered (in technical terms the schedule was "thinned") after a month so that Claire would receive only two notes a week. A note on Wednesdays would mean she attended all her classes on Monday, Tuesday, and Wednesday. This was backed up by the privilege of one weekend night out. A second note on Friday meant full attendance on Thursday and Friday, which was backed up by a second weekend night out. The telephone privileges were taken off contingency. About 7 weeks later the notes were stopped entirely.

The results were quite impressive. During the first 46 days of school (baseline period) Claire missed 30 days of school (65.2 percent absent). While working with the project for less than 3 months she was illegally absent twice (6.6 percent). She was *never* illegally absent again following termination, which covers the entire second semester of school. Grades were beyond redemption during the first semester mainly because of absences, thus causing her to fail two subjects. This dropped to one failure during the second semester.

According to her counselor at school, Claire continued to experience a poor relationship with her mother but did begin expressing positive attitudes and interests in her classes. Thus, the project was successful in preventing this girl from being expelled from school and probably running away. This was accomplished with a very modest expenditure of staff time.

Case 2

Mark is a 7th grade boy referred by the local juvenile court for (1) incorrigibility—refusing to do chores, disobedient, defiant; (2) destructiveness—toys and family property were often impulsively destroyed; (3) stealing—both at school and at home; and (4) poor peer relations—he has few friends and frequently fights with his siblings. He lives with his natural parents and two younger sisters.

The case is particularly interesting because of the great difficulty the staff had in gaining parental cooperation. The mother and father seemed to be people who derived little from experience. The father handled all discipline problems with a combination of extended lectures and punishment. His whippings were commonly followed by some destructive act by Mark, but the father still would not reduce his corporal punishment. The mother was also prone to lecture Mark, as well as being quite vague and inconsistent in her expectations of him. The destructive acts around home were serious enough to require immediate attention. Money, praise (especially from father), and a new bicycle were found to be highly reinforcing to Mark. His allowance had been placed entirely contingent on report card grades at school, which meant long periods of non-reinforcement.

The parents were persuaded to reinstate the allowance contingent on daily nondestructive behavior at home. If he did destroy or damage something, he would lose money for that day, plus having to pay for repairs. In addition, Mark could earn points each day for the successful completion of chores at home, points that would accumulate toward the purchase of a bicycle in about 6 months. Regular assignments were encouraged from school so that Mark could be rewarded for studying at least 30 minutes after school. When father would arrive home from work he praised Mark for studying. Should he study each day of the week father would "bonus" him with an extra allowance or special weekend outings together. Father was to ignore Mark on any day that he did not study. The parents kept daily records on these behaviors. The records were collected every other week.

At the end of 7 weeks Mark had not committed a single destructive act, there had been no reports of stealing, he rarely missed completing a day of his chores, and he was studying at least one-half hour 6 nights a week. The parents were pleased but informed the project that Mark did not need to be praised and rewarded for appropriate acts—this was just "bribery." It was so alien to the nature of these parents to use rewards to shape behavior that they were seriously considering dropping the plan despite its considerable success. Fortunately, report cards came out at this time and Mark showed improvement in both academic and behavior grades. Therefore, it was possible to persuade them to continue.

A disaster did occur several weeks later, though. Mark broke his eyeglasses. This prevented any studying for a week, but worse still it precipitated an infuriated reaction in his father because of the expense. Mark was castigated and the bicycle point-chart was indefinitely suspended.

Some 6 weeks passed before any consistent plan of action was reinstated. School work, intermittently reinforced with father's praise, was maintained at its prior high level. Two minor acts of destructiveness occurred at home (he broke some bathroom tile and a toy) and he exhibited some defiant behaviors toward his mother. Completion of chores began dropping again, and probably was most responsible for the parents again accepting the suggestion to make a chart for the chores and reward completion of them. The "back-up" (reward) would be interaction with father plus his praise. Earning money and the bicycle were still not allowed by the parents.

About five weeks were spent in keeping a daily chart on Mark's completion of chores. He would place a star on the chart and then the parents would praise him. The frequency of chore completion soon rose to 100 percent and this so pleased the father he decided to reinstate the bicycle point-chart. Completion of chores and obedient behaviors would then earn points, and when an arbitrary total was accumulated he would get a new bicycle. Mark got the new bicycle in 34 days. In this period he had 170 individual behaviors that could earn points, and he was reinforced on 168 of them.

The parents are fully persuaded as to the importance of making rewards contingent, and the efficacy of shaping behavior with positive reinforcement. No daily charts are now kept on Mark. A 6-week followup shows no return to previous misbehaviors. Originally, he had earned two D's and an F in eight subjects on the midterm report card. His final report card had no mark below a C.

Case 3

Blaine is a 14-year-old boy whose limited ability (IQ in low 80's) had contributed to a number of adjustment problems at home and at school. His father referred him to the project because he had been setting fires in and around his home, and frequently messing up the home. The school complained of his antagonism toward peers and general incorrigibility. The father had tried occasional spankings, lectures, and restriction of TV (the most effective). The school had tried paddling, scolding, restriction of playground privileges, plus the principal inviting him to the gym to put on the boxing gloves!

The mother had died 2 years previously in an airplane crash. Blaine and his 12-year-old brother were cared for during the day by a neighbor, while the father worked as a policeman. The neighbor lady was capable of setting limits on Blaine, but was not a source of much reinforcement. The father was quite reinforcing and capable of using his reinforcers on contingency.

The most urgent matter of business was to stop the playing with matches. Several minor fires had been started by Blaine, and his father realistically feared a serious one. A daily chart was kept by the father and the babysitter. A star was put up each day that Blaine refrained from playing with matches. This was backed up daily by praise from his father and access to evening TV. A week of success also gained him 25 cents. If on any day he was caught playing with matches, he did not get his star, he lost his TV privileges, and his quarter on the weekend. A second chart was simultaneously begun for the completion of chores (the details are unimportant here). No intervention was begun at school.

In the 2 weeks prior to intervention, Blaine had been caught playing with matches four times. Blaine continued on the chart system for nearly 6 months. He had 161 opportunities for reinforcement (no playing with matches) and he missed only one of them. Equally interesting, though, were the side effects that occurred after he was put on a positive schedule of reinforcement. Both Blaine and his brother began doing their chores regularly, thus receiving attention, praise, and money. The school reported a steady improvement in Blaine's attitude and behavior. No misbehavior incident was reported on him at school from the time following intervention. Recent followup showed no changes—the school was full of praise for his behavior and playing with matches had not recurred.

Case 4

The final case is particularly instructive because it demonstrates some of the strengths and limitations of behavior modification techniques. Loren is a 16-year-old boy who lives with his stepfather, mother, and two younger brothers. He was referred for (1) assaultive behavior—threatening to shoot his stepfather and trying to fist fight with both parents; (2) defiance of nearly all parental requests (coming home early at night, completing his household chores, mowing the lawn, not taking the car without permission); and (3) habitual truancy. Police had been called for several of these incidents, and referral was made from the local juvenile court.

Assessment of the family revealed that Loren was on an entirely aversive reinforcement schedule. He was denied allowance, restricted to the house, restricted from the car, continually threatened with the police, and verbally abused. None of these was effective. Money, use of the car, and nights-out were considered positively reinforcing, but the parents were so angry with Loren they provided no clear way for him to earn these. An interview with Loren confirmed the latter.

Loren's parents were where many are at the point of referral — desperate. They had been meeting each infraction with punishment until a point of no return was reached. The thought of rewarding Loren for approximations of "good" behavior had not occurred to them and the suggestion was met with great skepticism. However, since they had exhausted their own repertoire of controls, the project staff member was able to persuade them to at least give his suggestions a try.

Two points in the family assessment were quite important. First, Loren apparently had never been given a clear idea of his parents' expectations. For example, instructions such as, "Be in at a decent hour," made for much uncertainty. Second, it became obvious that his stepfather wanted the boy out of the home and was trying to accomplish this through unrealistic and vacillating demands.

The intervention plan consisted of a carefully devised schedule — more nearly a contract — which would allow Loren to earn money for completion of chores and being obedient (e.g., on a weekend night he must be in by midnight). Failures brought not only a loss of money but also carried a fine in the form of 15-minute blocks of restricted time from use of the family car. For the first time he knew exactly how to earn money and time away from home, and exactly what the consequences would be for not conforming. The parents were not to hedge on the contingencies, and biweekly phone calls from our staff plus a posted copy of the "contract" were used to prevent this.

Rapid changes subsequently occurred in Loren's behavior. In the first 35 days, he was rewarded an average of 81 percent of the time in each of four areas of responsibility (range 75 to 89 percent). Prior to intervention he met these obligations rarely (0 to 10 percent).

At this point a second contract was drawn up because Loren's stepfather was continuing to nag him despite tremendous improvement and because Loren's car insurance had expired and his stepfather refused to renew it. The new contract was negotiated in the presence of both parents, Loren, and a project staff member. It allowed for points to be earned for chores and responsibilities which could be applied to the car insurance premium (stepfather agreed finally to this). Loren could earn a maximum of 50 points a week, and needed 250 for the premium. The first week he earned 22 points and then the full 50 on each week thereafter.

Loren began driving the car again, but only by meeting specific contingencies agreed to by his parents, himself, and staff. In addition, he re-entered high school, achieved satisfactorily, was not truant, and had applied for an after-school job. The case was maintained at this level of success for 24 days, requiring only one phone call to the parents and two brief home visits. Loren's stepfather and mother expressed satisfaction over the changes and felt that he was doing so well that the "contract" should be abandoned. Our staff member vigorously tried to discourage this, feeling that such a drastic change was premature. However, the parents persevered and abruptly ceased abiding by the agreements and contingencies.

Events following the parents' return to preintervention conditions illustrate an unfortunate collapse of environmental controls. Loren was truant for the succeeding 7 school days, and was arrested 11 days later for burglary. His parents refused to visit him during his 2 days at a detention home. In addition, they told the probation officer that Loren was "hopelessly" bad despite all the good things they had done for him. The court placed Loren on probation and reluctantly allowed him to return to his home. The project had recommended foster placement but none was available. His adjustment remains exceedingly tenuous at home, but the parents have refused further help.

Loren's case demonstrates the validity of behavior modification techniques — behavior can be changed by altering environmental consequences, while simultaneously exhibiting its limitations, and uncooperative parents can defeat productive change. Probation officers adopting operant techniques will thus have to accept a shortcoming common to all known forms of helping children, namely, bad parents yield bad results.

Behavior Modification and Juvenile Probation Officers

What are the possible applications probation officers could make from these cases? The amount of time spent in devising intervention plans such as those used on the Behavioral Research Project of the Southern Arizona Mental Health Center probably would not burden court staff (all of these were arranged in 3 or less interviews). Once the intervention plan is underway staff contacts (by phone when possible) decrease steadily to three or four a month. Most importantly, though, the behavior modification techniques frequently *work* and the probation officer can begin experiencing positive changes in behavior rather than just suppression of misbehavior.

The authors see juvenile probation officers as having the potential for becoming experts in behavior modification. They could continue to approach their delinquent charges as representatives of the courts, and as such they would still be dispensers of aversive control. The real change, though, would be that aversive methods would no longer be their only source of control. They could also be skilled in teaching parents how to put powerful positive rewards on contingency. The combination, in the hands of a trained person, is most effective. Psychologists are increasingly available to teach operant theory and its application, and thereafter can be available on a consultative basis to juvenile courts and field offices. The time has never been more right for the people in probation work to reach out for new techniques.

REFERENCES

A. Bandura, "Punishment Revisited," *Journal of Consulting Psychology,* 1962, **26,** pp. 298–301.
J. M. Grossberg, "Behavior Therapy: A Review," *Psychological Bulletin,* 1964.
R. B. Jamieson, "Can Conditioning Principles Be Applied to Probation?" *Trial Judges' Journal,* 1965, **4,** No. 1.
F. S. Keller, *Learning: Reinforcement Theory.* New York: Random House, Inc., 1954.
R. Schwitzgebel, *Street Corner Research.* Cambridge: Harvard University Press, 1964.
B. F. Skinner, *Science and Human Behavior.* New York: Macmillan Co., 1953.
L. Ullmann and L. Krasner (editors), *Case Studies in Behavior Modification.* New York: Holt, Rinehart and Winston, 1965.
J. Wolpe, A. Salter, and L. J. Reyna, *The Conditioning Therapies: The Challenge in Psychotherapy.* New York: Holt, Rinehart and Winston, 1964.

Treatment of Nonreading in a Culturally Deprived Juvenile Delinquent: An Application of Reinforcement Principles

Arthur W. Staats, *University of Hawaii*
William H. Butterfield, *University of Michigan*

Staats has previously discussed behavior problems and their treatment in terms of learning principles (1964c, 1963). In doing so it was indicated that problem behaviors can arise in part (1) because behavior that is necessary for adjustment in our society is absent from the individual's repertoire, (2) because behaviors considered undesirable by the society are present in the individual's repertoire, or (3) because the individual's motivational (reinforcement) system was inappropriate in some respects.

Although a complete account is not relevant here, several points pertinent to the above conceptions will be made in introducing the present study. The notion that many behavior problems consist of deficits in behavior is important in the study of child development.

From *Child Development* **36** (1965), 925–42.

The present methods of reading training were formulated, and the present paper written, by the first author as part of a long-term project applying learning principles and procedures to the experimental study of language-learning and reading. The methods were applied by the second author in his position as an officer of the Maricopa County Juvenile Probation Department. The second author also collected and tabulated the data and aided in its graphic presentation. Appreciation is expressed to Chief Probation Officer John H. Walker for lending cooperation in the conduct of the study. In addition, Mary J. Butterfield made important contributions in the preparation of the reading materials used in the study, Brenda Shields typed the materials, and Janet Munir typed the present manuscript.

Behaviorally speaking, a child is considered to be a problem when he does not acquire behaviors as other children do. It is conceivable that a deficit in behavior could arise because the child simply cannot acquire the behavior involved, even though the conditions of learning have been entirely adequate.

It would be expected, however, that behavioral deficits would also arise in cases where the conditions of learning have been defective. Learning conditions can be defective in different ways. For example, the child may never have received training in the behavior he must later exhibit. Or the training may be poor, even though the "trainers," parents or teachers, and so on, have the best intentions.

In addition, however, a child may be exposed to learning conditions that are appropriate for most children but, due to the particular child's past history of learning, are not appropriate for him. It is especially in these cases that people are most likely to conclude erroneously that since other children learn in the same circumstances, the child's deficit must be because of some personal defect. For example, in cases where the training is long term, adequate reinforcement must be available to maintain the attentional and work behaviors necessary for learning. As Staats has indicated (1964c, 1963, 1962), the reinforcers present in the traditional schoolroom are inadequate for many children. Their attentional behaviors are not maintained, and they do not learn. Thus, a deficit in an individual's behavioral repertoire may arise although he has been presented with the "same" training circumstances from which other children profit. Learning does not take place because the child's previous experience has not provided, in this example, the necessary reinforcer (motivational) system to maintain good learning behaviors. It would seem that in such a circumstance the assumption that the child has a personal defect would be unwarranted and ineffective.

However, after a few years of school attendance where the conditions of learning are not appropriate for the child, he will not have acquired the behavioral repertoires acquired by more fortunate members of the class — whose previous experiences have established an adequate motivational system. Then, lack of skilled behavior is likely to be treated aversively. That is, in the present case, the child with a reading deficit (or other evidence of underachievement) is likely to be gibed at and teased when he is still young, and ignored, avoided, and looked down upon when he is older. Although the individuals doing this may not intend to be aversive, such actions constitute the presentation of aversive stimuli. Furthermore, this presentation of aversive stimuli by other "successful" children, and perhaps by a teacher, would be expected to result in further learning, but learning of an undesirable nature. These successful children, teachers, academic materials, and the total school situation can in this way become learned negative reinforcers, which may be translated to say the child acquires negative attitudes toward school (see Staats, 1964b).

At this point, the child is likely to begin to escape the school situation in various ways (daydreaming, poor attendance, and so on) and to behave aversively in turn to the school and its inhabitants (vandalism, fighting, baiting teachers and students, and the like). Thus, a deficit in behavior, resulting from an inappropriate motivational system, can lead to the further development of inappropriate reinforcers and inappropriate behaviors.

The foregoing is by no means intended as a complete analysis of delinquency, dropouts, and the like. However, it does indicate some of the problems of learning that may occur in school. In addition, it does suggest that an analysis in terms of laboratory-established learning principles, when applied to problems such as in classroom learning of the above type, can yield new research and applied hypotheses. It was with this general strategy that the study of reading acquisition employing learning principles and reinforcement procedures were commenced (Staats, 1964a, 1964d, 1964c, 1962). The present study is a replication and an extension of these various findings to the development of a program for training nonreaders to read. The program, which adapts standard reading materials, is based upon the principle of the reinforcer system employed in the previous studies with the younger children, thus testing the principles of reinforcement in the context of remedial reading training, as well as the feasibility of using the type of reinforcement system with a new type of subject. As such, the study has implications for the study of nonreading children of pre-adolescent, adolescent, and young adult ages. In the present case, the subject was also a culturally deprived delinquent child — and the study thus involves additional information and implications for the special problems associated with education in this population of children.

Methods

Subject

The subject was fourteen years and three months old. He was the fifth child in a Mexican-American family of eleven children and the mother and father. The parental techniques for controlling their children's behavior consisted of physical and verbal abuse. Both parents described their own childhood conditions as primitive. The father was taken out of school after completing the fifth grade to help with his father's work. Each of the subject's four older brothers had been referred to the juvenile court for misbehavior. The parents appeared to be at loss as to how to provide effective control for family members.

The subject had a history of various miscreant behaviors, having been referred to the juvenile department nine times for such things as running away, burglary, incorrigibility, and truancy. During the course of the study the subject was again referred (with three other boys) on a complaint of malicious mischief for shooting light bulbs and windows in a school building with a BB gun. He associated with a group of boys who had been in marked difficulty with the law. The subject smoked and on occasion he drank excessively.

The study commenced when the subject was residing with his family. However, after the complaint on malicious mischief he was sent to a juvenile detention home. During his stay there he was allowed to attend school in the daytime. The study was finally concluded when he was committed to an industrial school for juvenile delinquent boys. This occurred because he baited the attendants at the detention home and caused disturbances which, although not serious, were very unpleasant and disruptive.

On the Wechsler Bellevue Form I, given when the subject was 13-10, he received Verbal and Performance IQ's of 77 and 106, respectively, for a Full Scale IQ of 90. The examiner concluded that the subject was probably within the normal range for this test. On the basis of this test and HTP Projective Drawings, the subject was characterized as having a poor attention span and poorly integrated thought processes and as lacking intellectual ambitiousness. He was also described as seeking satisfaction in fantasy and as having good conventional judgment.

The subject had continually received failing grades in all subjects in school. He was described as having "been incorrigible since he came here in the second grade. He has no respect for teachers, steals and lies habitually and uses extremely foul language." The subject had been promoted throughout his school career simply to move him on or to "get rid of him." He was disliked by the teachers and administrators in grade school because of his troublesome behavior and was described by the principal as mentally retarded even though one of the tests taken there indicated a score within the normal range. Another test taken there gave him an IQ of 75. During the study the subject was attending a local high school and taking classes for low-level students.

Reinforcer System

In previous studies (Staats, 1966, 1964d, 1964e), a reinforcer system was demonstrated that was capable of maintaining attention and work behaviors for long term experimental studies. This system worked well with preschool children of ages 2 to 6 and with educable and trainable retardates of ages 8 to 11. The principle of the system was based upon token reinforcers. The tokens were presented contingent upon correct responses and could be exchanged for items the child could keep. In the previous studies toys of various values could be obtained when a sufficient number of tokens had been accrued in visible containers.

This system was adapted for use with the adolescent of the present study. In the adaptation there were three types of token, distinquished by color. The tokens were of different value in terms of the items for which the tokens could be exchanged. A blue token was valued at $\frac{1}{10}$ of one cent. A white token was valued at $\frac{1}{5}$ of a cent. A red token was worth $\frac{1}{2}$ of a cent.

The child's acquisition of tokens was plotted so that visual evidence of the reinforcers was available. The tokens could be used to purchase a variety of items. These items, chosen by the subject, could range in value from pennies to whatever the subject wished to work for. Records were kept of the tokens earned by the subject and of the manner in which the tokens were used.

Reading Materials

The reading material used was taken from the Science Research Associates reading-kit materials. The SRA kits consist of stories developed for and grouped into grade levels. Each story includes a series of questions which can be used to assess the reader's comprehension of the story. The reading training program was adapted from the materials as follows:

Vocabulary words. A running list was made of the new words that appeared in the series of stories. The list finally included each different word that appeared in the stories that were presented. From this list, the new vocabulary for each story was selected, and each word was typed on a separate 3 × 5 card.

Oral reading materials. Each paragraph in the stories was typed on a 5 × 8 card. Each story could thus be presented to the subject paragraph by paragraph.

Silent reading and comprehensive-question materials. Each story, with its comprehensive questions, was typed on an 8½ × 13 sheet of white paper.

Procedure

Vocabulary presentation. The procedure for each story in the series commenced with the presentation of the new words introduced in that story. The words were presented individually on the cards, and the subject was asked to pronounce them. A correct response to a word-stimulus card was reinforced with a mid-value token. After a correct response to a word, the card was dropped from the group of cards yet to be presented. The subject was instructed to indicate words that he did not know the meaning of, and this information was provided in such cases.

When an incorrect response to a word stimulus occurred, or when the subject gave no response, the instructional technician gave the correct response. The subject then repeated the word while looking at the stimulus word. However, the word card involved was returned to the group of cards still to be presented. A card was not dropped from the group until it was read correctly without prompting. After an error on a word stimulus, only a low-value token was given on the next trial when the word was read correctly without prompting. The vocabulary-presentation phase of the training was continued until each word was read correctly without prompting.

Oral reading. Upon completion of the vocabulary materials, each paragraph was individually presented to the subject in the order in which the paragraph occurred in the story. When correct reading responses were made to each word in the paragraph, a high-value token was given upon completion of the paragraph. When a paragraph contained errors, the subject was corrected, and he repeated the word correctly while looking at the word. The paragraph was put aside, and when the other paragraphs had been completed, the paragraph containing errors was again presented. The paragraph was repeated until it was done correctly in its entirety — at which time a mid-value token was presented. When all paragraphs in a story had been completed correctly, the next phase of the training was begun.

Silent reading and comprehensive questions. Following the oral reading the subject was given the sheet containing the story and questions. He was instructed to read the story silently and to answer the questions beneath the story. He was also instructed that it was important to read to understand the story so that he could answer the questions.

Reinforcement was given on a variable interval schedule for attentive behavior during the silent-reading phase. That is, as long as he appropriately scanned the material he was given a low-value reinforcer an average of every fifteen seconds. The exact time for reinforcement was determined by a table of random numbers varying from one to thirty seconds. Whenever he did anything else than peruse the material, no reinforcement was given. The next interval was then timed from the moment he returned to the silent reading, with the stipulation that no reinforcement be given sooner than five seconds after he returned to the reading. If the interval was less than five seconds, a token was not given until the next interval had also occurred. Timing was done by a continuously running stop-watch. The subject was also given an extra mid-value token at the end of the silently read story on those occasions where he read without moving his lips.

Upon completion of the story, the subject wrote his answers to the questions typed below the story and gave his answers to the technician. For each correct answer, the subject received a high-value token. For an answer with a spelling error, he was reinforced with a mid-value token when he had corrected the answer. For incorrect answers the subject had to reread the appropriate paragraph, correct his answer, and he then received a mid-value token.

Vocabulary review. Some of the vocabulary words presented to the subject in the first phase of training were words he already could read. Many others, however, were words that the procedure was set up to teach. The oral reading phase performance indicated the level of the subject's retention of the words he had learned—and also provided further training trials on the words not already learned. A further assessment of the subject's retention of the words that he did not know in the vocabulary training was made after each twenty stories of the SRA materials had been read. This test of individually presented words for each story was started about three days after completion of the twenty stories and constituted fairly long-term retention.

This test was also used as a review for the subject, and further training on the words was given. This was first done by reinforcing with a low-value token for every word he read correctly. However, the subject's attention was not well maintained by this reinforcement, and the procedure was changed to provide a mid-value token for correctly read words. When he could not read a word, or missed one, he was prompted and had to correctly repeat the name of the word while looking at the word. This word card was then put aside and presented later, at which time the subject was reinforced with a low-value token if he read it correctly. If not, the procedure was repeated until a correct unprompted trial occurred.

Achievement tests. Prior to the commencement of the training, the subject was tested to assess his reading performance, and during the period of experimental training he was given two additional reading-achievement tests. The first one given was the Developmental Reading Test. (At this time his vision and hearing were also tested and found to be normal.) After forty-five training sessions another reading test was given, this time the California Reading Test, Form BB, for grades 1, 2, 3 and L-4. Twenty-five sessions later, just before the termination of the study, the subject was given the California Reading Test, Form BB, for grades 4, 5, and 6. His performance on the three reading tests constituted one of the measures of his progress. The tests were given at the Arizona State University Reading Center.

Training sessions. The training sessions would ordinarily last for one hour or less, although a few sessions were as short as thirty minutes or as long as two hours. Not all of this time was spent in reading, however. A good deal of time was spent in arranging the materials, recording performance, keeping count of the reinforcers, plotting the reinforcers accrued, and so on. The time spent actually reading was tabulated. During the 4½-month experimental period seventy training sessions were conducted, with an average of about thirty-five minutes spent per session, or a total of forty hours of reading training.

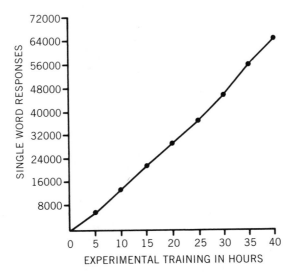

Fig. 1. Number of single-word reading responses as a function of the time in experimental reading training

During the period of training the subject made many reading responses. Figure 1 shows the number of single-word reading responses the subject made as a function of the hours of time spent in training. An estimate of the number of single-word reading responses was obtained from tabulating each presentation of a word card, the number of words in the stories, and the reading comprehension questions at the end of each story, as well as the words presented in the later single-word retention test. Actually, the number of words in the stories is an estimate obtained from the mean number of words in two out of each five stories. Thus, rather than giving the true absolute number of reading responses made, the figure gives an estimate. However, the most important aspect of the figure is to indicate the rate of this single-word reading-response measure as a function of time in experimental training. As can be seen, as the training progressed the subject covered the reading material at a slightly more rapid rate, as is shown by the slight positive acceleration in the curve. The importance of this result is to indicate that the child's behavior of attending to the task and making the appropriate reading responses did not diminish throughout the period of training. Thus, the reinforcement system employed was capable of maintaining the behavior for a long period of time. During this time the attentional and cooperative behaviors instigated resulted in many, many learning trials — *sine qua non* for the acquisition of achievement in any skill.

Before reading each story the subject was presented with individual cards for all the words included in that story which had not been presented in a previous story. When these words were presented, the subject would read a certain proportion correctly on first presentation, the other words being missed on the first presentation. The ones missed were considered to be new words, words that he had not previously learned. These words were tabulated separately. The cumulative number of these new words as a function of every five stories read is shown by the top curve of Figure 2. (The data for the first ten stories are not presented since they were not available for all three curves.) As this curve indicates, 761 new words were presented during the training.

Thus, the subject missed 761 words when they were first presented to him. However, he was given training trials on these words, and then he read them again in the oral reading of the paragraph. The number of these words that he missed in this oral reading phase is plotted in the bottom curve of Figure 2. This curve then indicates the number of errors made on the second reading test of the words that had been previously learned. Thus, only 176 words out of 761 (about 23 percent) were missed in the oral reading phase — showing retention for 585 words. The results indicate that the criterion of one correct unprompted reading trial in the original vocabulary-learning phase produced considerable learning when the words were read in context.

The middle curve in Figure 2 involves a measure of long-term retention of the words that had been learned. This measure was obtained by testing the subject on the words, presented singly, that had been learned in the preceding twenty stories. This test was given 10 to 15 days after the training occurred. The training thus included the previous single-word presentations of the words, as well as those same words read orally and silently. In addition, however, the subject had also learned a considerable number of other words by the time of this test. As the middle curve shows, when tested 10 to 15 days later, he read 430 of the 761 words correctly, or, conversely, 331 words (about 43 percent) were missed. Thus, the procedures produced retention when the words were later presented out of context after a considerable intervening period.

The results appearing in Figure 2 indicate that the child covered a considerable amount of reading material, that he learned to read a number of new words when presented individually or in context, and that he retained a good proportion of what he had learned. The results also indicate that the child improved during the training in his retention. That is, his rate of getting new words in the first-presentation phase continued at a high rate throughout the study. (This supports the results shown in Figure 1 indicating that the child's behavior did not weaken during the training.) However, his "rate" of missing the new words on the second and third presentations decreased; that is,

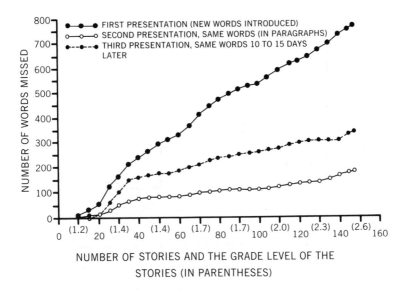

NUMBER OF STORIES AND THE GRADE LEVEL OF THE
STORIES (IN PARENTHESES)

Fig. 2. Number of words missed on first, second, and third presentations for the 150 stories

he retained more of the words he had learned. Thus, tabulation indicated that for the first thirty-five stories only about 33 percent of the words learned were retained 10 to 15 days later, whereas the subject's subsequent retention increased to about 55 percent. It should be noted that this improvement occurred even though the difficulty of the words (as shown in Figure 2 by the numbers in parentheses) became progressively greater during the training, moving from the 1.2 grade level of difficulty to the 2.6 grade level.

These results receive support from the data presented in Figure 3. As already indicated, on the first presentation of the vocabulary of a story, some words were missed out of the total presented—and the subject was then presented with training on these words. Figure 3 shows the number of the words presented and missed in ratio to the total number presented as this ratio is related to the number and difficulty of the stories presented. A smaller ratio indicates that the subject missed fewer of the total vocabulary words when they were presented for the first time. As can be seen in Figure 3, as the child read more stories in his training (even though they became more difficult), he missed fewer and fewer words that were presented to him. It should be stressed that he was thus improving in the extent to which he correctly responded to new words on *first* presentation. This improvement appeared to be correlated with other observations that indicated the subject was also beginning to learn to sound out words as a function of the training. For example, he remarked

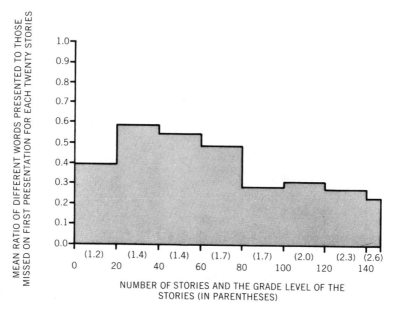

Fig. 3. Ratio of words presented to those missed on first presentation for the 150 stories

that when in the judge's office he thought a sign said "information" because he could read the "in" and the "for" and the "mation." In addition, he reported a number of times that the training was helping him in school, that reading was getting easier for him in school, that he liked the reading training better as he went along, and so on. It would be expected (as will be supported by other data) that as the reading training improved his reading in school, the things he learned in school would also improve his performance in the reading training. It is this effect that may also be reflected in his increasing ability to read the new words presented to him.

In addition to this direct evidence of the child's progress in reading training, and the foregoing indirect evidence that the reading training was having general effects upon the child's behavior, the study was formulated to obtain other sources of information concerning the child's progress. One means of doing this was to give the child reading achievement tests before beginning the reading training as well as during the training. The results of these tests are shown in Figure 4. The first point on the curve is a measurement obtained by use of the Developmental Reading Test giving a total score of reading achievement showing that the subject was performing at the grade 2 level. After forty-five reading-training sessions, the subject's performance on the California Reading Test shows a gain to the 3.8 grade level. By the end of the training, after twenty-

CHILD DEVELOPMENT

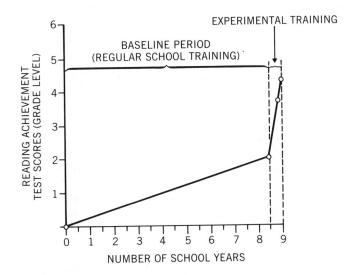

Fig. 4. Reading-achievement test scores as a function of 8½ years of school training and 4½ months of experimental training

five more training sessions, he had advanced to the 4.3 grade level on the California Reading Test.

Another indication of the general effect of the reading training came from the child's performance in school, both in school achievement and deportment. The period of reading training coincided with a school term. The boy received passing grades in all subjects: C in Physical Education, D in General Shop, D in English, and D in Mathematics. It should be emphasized that these grades represent the first courses that this child had ever passed, and thus his finest academic performance.

Furthermore, the subject began to behave better while in school. The boy had always been a behavior problem in school, and this continued into the period during which he received reading training. As Figure 5 shows, during the first month of the training he committed ten misbehaviors that resulted in the receipt of demerits. The behaviors were as follows: disturbance in class (two times), disobedience in class (five times), loitering (two times), and tardiness. In the second month he was given demerits for scuffling on the school grounds and also for creating a disturbance. In the third month he was given demerits for cutting a math class and for profanity in class. As the figure shows, however, no misbehaviors occurred in the fourth month or in the half month before the conclusion of the school term.

The subject requested that the tokens be exchanged for items that he wanted in sessions 12, 17, 25, 31, 35, 43, 49, 55, and in the last session he was given the value of the remaining tokens in cash. Items included were a pair of "Beatle" shoes, hair pomade, a phonograph record, an ice cream sundae, a ticket to a school function, money for his brother who was going to reform school, and so on. Further information regarding the reinforcement system is given in Figure 6. The vertical axis of the graph represents the ratio of the number of tokens obtained by the subject relative to the number of single-word reading responses which he emitted. Lesser ratios thus indicate more reading responses per reinforcer. This ratio was plotted as a function of the progress made in the training program, as given by the number of SRA stories he had completed. As the training progressed the subject gradually made an increasingly greater number of reading responses per reinforcer. This effect was not accomplished by changing the rules by which the reinforcers were administered. The effect, which was planned in the training program, resulted from the fact that the stories became longer as the grade level was raised. Since, for example, paragraph reading was reinforced by the paragraph, the longer the paragraph, the greater the number of reading responses that had to be emitted before reinforcement was obtained. Thus, at the end of training the subject was getting about half as much reinforcement per response as at the beginning of training. It should also be indicated that the stories were more difficult as the training progressed, so the effort involved in reading was increasing — although reinforcement for the reading was decreasing.

During the 4½ months of training, which involved forty hours of reading training and the emission of an estimated 64,307 single-word reading responses, the subject received $20.31.

Discussion

In this section the various aspects of the reading training procedures will first be discussed. Then the implications of the results and analysis will be outlined both for further studies of remedial reading training as well as for a learning conception of certain aspects of cultural deprivation and delinquency.

The method of reading training used in the present study was derived from previous studies (Staats, 1964a; 1962) with preschool children in which words were first presented singly, then in sentences, and finally in short stories. The present study indicated that SRA materials can be adapted for a similar type of presentation in conjunction with the type of reinforcer system previously developed. From the SRA materials it was possible to present single-word training trials and oral-reading training and to develop a silent reading training procedure, all involving reinforcement.

When the training of reading, at least in part, is considered as

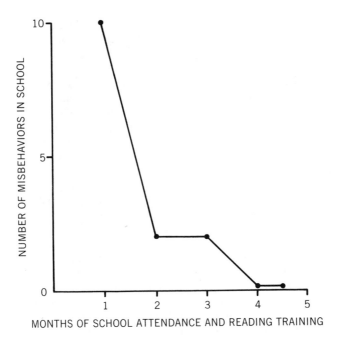

Fig. 5. Number of official misbehaviors in school as a function of time in the experimental training

instrumental (operant) discrimination learning, the learning task consists of having the subject emit the correct speech response while looking at the verbal stimulus — this process being followed by reinforcement. This basic procedure was elaborated in the present study to include two levels of reinforcement. An unprompted reading response on the first trial was reinforced more heavily than one that had been previously missed. This procedure appeared to produce learning that was retained very well when the child later read the words orally in a paragraph, with considerable retention also occurring when the child was tested on the individual words 10 to 15 days later.

It may seem incongruous at first to attempt to reinforce silent reading since this behavior is not observable. However, it should be remembered that the subject actually has two types of behavior in the silent reading act. He looks at the verbal stimuli — that is, attends — and he makes "reading" verbal responses to the verbal stimuli. While the reading responses cannot be monitored when they are covert, the attending behavior can be. Of course, there is a danger involved in reinforcing the behavior of just looking at something. Perhaps the child will do nothing else. If he is heavily reinforced for sitting and looking at a page, and the actual reading responses are effortful, he may not emit the reading responses. The present procedure was set up to eliminate this possibility by using a double contingency. The child was reinforced for simple attention, but the reinforcement was low in value. The opportunity for a greater amount of reinforcement came during the answering of the questions. Thus, although simple attention was reinforced lightly, attention and reading responses were reinforced much more heavily. In this way it was possible to use reinforcement in a procedure designed to maintain reading for understanding, in addition to simple "word-naming." (These results could be generalized to other types of learning.) Furthermore, this procedure provided an opportunity to train the subject to read silently. Although he had a tendency to make vocal or lip responses while reading, it was possible to strengthen reading without these other responses through differentially reinforcing the correct silent reading.

Thus, it may be concluded that the reading program increased the child's reading vocabulary as shown by the various measures of retention used in the study, the tests of reading achievement, as well as the child's improved school performance and his verbal description of improved attitude toward and performance in reading in school. There were also suggestions that the child was acquiring a "unit reading repertoire," that is, the general ability to sound out words through making the correct response to single letters and syllables. Thus, for example, the child made errors on fewer and fewer of the new words presented as the training progressed, even though the words were of greater difficulty. In addition, he retained a greater proportion of the words he learned as he went on. Further research of the present type must be conducted to test the possibilities for using a more phonic system of remedial reading training with the present type of subject.

A final point should be made concerning the training procedures used in the present study. The procedures are very specific and relatively simple. Thus it was not necessary to have a person highly trained in education to administer the training. In the present case the instructional technician was a probation officer. It might also be suggested that anyone with a high school education and the ability to read could have administered the training. This has implications for the practical application of the present methods, since one of the questions that arises in this context concerns the economy of the procedures. The procedures as described involved a ratio of one trainer to one student as many remedial teaching procedures do. But the simplicity of the procedures used in this case suggests the possibility that savings may be effected because the instructional technician need not be so highly trained. Thus, the procedures could be widely applied or adapted by various professionals; for example, social workers, prison officials, remedial teachers, tutors, and so on.

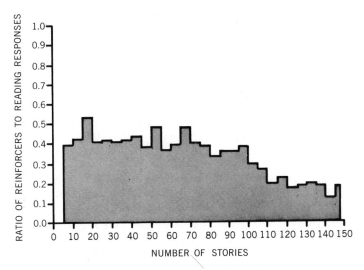

Fig. 6. Ratio of the number of tokens received divided by the number of reading responses made as a function of the number of stories read

In an even more economical application, helpers of professionals could be used to actually administer the procedures; for example, selected delinquents (or prisoners) could administer the procedures to other delinquents. Thus, the procedures could be utilized in various situations, such as settlement houses, homes for juvenile delinquents, prison training programs, parts of adult education, and so on. All that is needed is a suitable system of reinforcers to back up the tokens.

It is relevant to add here that the type of token-reinforcer system employed in the present study was first developed by Staats in 1959 in the context of an exploratory study of remedial reading. Communication of the efficacy of the token-reinforcer system to Jack Michael at the University of Houston began its use there in work with retarded. Further communication with Ayllon led to adoption of the token-reinforcer system in the psychiatric ward (Ayllon and Azrin, 1968). The token-reinforcer system has since been widely employed in various forms in educational and clinical behavior modification studies (for example, see Wolf, Giles, and Hall, 1968; and Ullmann and Krasner, 1969). After the initial development of the token-reinforcement system, Staats also adapted it for work with preschool children in a series of basic and behavior modification studies of various types of complex learning (see Staats, 1968; Staats, Finley, Minke, Wolf, and Brooks, 1964; Staats, Minke, Finley, and Wolf, 1964; Staats, Staats, Schutz, and Wolf, 1962).

Furthermore, additional studies have been conducted in the present project to further substantiate the general efficacy of the reinforcer system and the reading procedures, with various types of subjects. Thus, the present training procedures have been employed successfully in a study involving eighteen additional children (including seven educable retardates as well as several emotionally disturbed children) of junior high school age in Madison, Wisconsin. The instructional technicians were nine average high school students and nine adult volunteers (Staats, et al., 1967).

In a later study (Staats, Minke, and Butts, 1970) thirty-two Negro ghetto children with behavior problems were given the treatment in Milwaukee. The instructional technicians were literate Negro high school children from ghetto schools and two formerly unemployed Negro adults employed on the project in full-time positions. The treatment was conducted for a semester, and the results were again successful. Increases were shown in achievement tests, grades, attendance, and deportment, in comparison to a control group of thirty-two children. In addition, Staats (1968) has conducted a long term project with young children in the study and treatment of cognitive deficits in such areas as first reading acquisition, number skill learning, and writing acquisition. The present methods and principles receive strong support as being generally applicable from these various studies.

In the present study, it may be worth pointing out that the results indicated that the child advanced as many years in reading achievement, as measured by the tests, during the experimental training as he had in his previous school history. A comparison of the relative costs — in the present case about forty hours of time of a person not necessarily trained in teaching and $20.31 for the reinforcers versus 8½ years of trained teachers' time, albeit in a group situation — suggests that the procedure introduced in the present study may not be uneconomical, even without improvements in the method. And, as will be further described, the child's failure in school may in many cases be considered as a contributor to the child's delinquency — which also carries a high cost to society. The present results, in suggesting that the training procedures may also effect general improvements in behavior, including misbehaviors in school, thus have further implications concerning the economy of the procedures.

The present study, among other things, tests the feasibility of using the type of reinforcing system previously applied successfully to younger children to the study of learning in older children — in this case a fourteen-year-old juvenile delinquent. The reinforcer system worked very well with the present subject, maintaining his attention and working behaviors in good strength for a long period of time. And there was every reason to expect that the study could have been continued for a much longer period, probably as long as it would have taken to train the child to read normally.

It should be noted that although the amount of reinforcement given decreases during the training, as shown in Figure 6, the reading behavior is maintained in good strength throughout the study, as shown in Figures 1 and 2; thus, less and less reinforcement is needed to maintain the behavior even though the material increases in difficulty. As already described, this occurred because a progressively greater number of reading responses was necessary per reinforcer. This is analogous to gradually raising the ratio of responses to the reinforcers as considered in terms of ratio schedules of reinforcement. Staats has suggested that this type of gradual increase must occur to produce good work behaviors in humans (Staats, 1963).

This result in the present study is in part an answer to the question of whether the use of extrinsic reinforcers in training will produce a child who is dependent upon these reinforcers. It is not possible to discuss this topic fully now. However, it may be said that the extrinsic reinforcement can be gradually decreased until, as was happening with the present child, reading becomes reinforcing itself, or other sources of reinforcement maintain the behavior.

A word should be said concerning the relevance of reinforcement variables in the treatment of non-learning in culturally deprived children. Typically, as in the present case, such children do not, as a result of their home experiences, acquire "reinforcer systems" appropriate for maintaining learning in the traditional classroom. Rosen (1956) has shown that, in the present terminology, lower class children do not have experiences that make school involvement and learning itself positively reinforcing. This deficit, among others that affect the reinforcer system, can be expected to lead to poor school learning and other behavioral deficits. In such cases, there are increased opportunities for other poor social attitudes and undesirable behaviors to develop, as suggested in the introduction and exemplified in the present case.

The present study suggests that these conditions can be reversed through the application of learning principles and reinforcement variables to the task of repairing the child's behavioral-achievement deficit. There were indications that this treatment resulted in improvement in the reinforcement value of (attitudes toward) school for this child and consequently in the decrease in incidence of misbehaviors in school. The results thus suggest that under appropriate conditions the deficit in behavior stemming from the child's inadequate reinforcing system may be, at least in part, repaired by a properly administered, effective reinforcement system, resulting in a decrease in undesirable behaviors.

A comment should be made about the possibility of a Hawthorne effect; that is, that the social reinforcement provided by the instructional technician and possible extraexperimental reinforcement contributed to the results in the present study. It would be expected that such reinforcers could contribute to the overall effect—and in the present case the expenditure for the material reinforcers was small. In general, it can be expected that individuals will vary in the extent to which social reinforcers will be effective. For example, in preschool children social reinforcement is ineffective for long term training (Staats, 1964c, 1962), and the same would be expected for many individuals with behavior problems. Ordinarily, it might be expected that the weaker other sources of reinforcement are for the individual, the stronger must be the reinforcer system of the treatment procedure.

In conclusion, the present study helps support and replicate the previous findings and extends the general procedures and principles to the study of an adolescent child who is culturally deprived and is also a juvenile delinquent. The various sources of data used suggest that the present procedures and principles are applicable to this population also. Based upon these suggestions, further studies will be conducted on culturally deprived children, delinquent and non-delinquent, as well as studies of other types of nonachieving or underachieving readers.

It should also be indicated that the present study indicates the possibility for developing procedures for the objective application and testing of laboratory-derived learning principles within the context of an actual problem of behavior. As previously indicated (Staats, 1968, 1964a), verification of learning principles in the context of a problem of human behavior constitutes one way to further the generality of the principles themselves. It may thus be suggested that such studies have two types of implication: they have implications for people interested in dealing with the problems of human behavior, as well as for those interested in the extension and verification of the basic science.

REFERENCES

Ayllon, T., and Azrin, N. H. *The Token Economy*. New York: Appleton-Century-Crofts, 1968.

Ellson, D. G., Barber, L., Engle, T. L., and Kampaerth, L. "Programmed Tutoring: A Teaching Aid and a Research Tool," *Reading Research Quarterly*, 1965, 1.

Rosen, B. C. "The Achievement Syndrome: A Psychocultural Dimension of Social Stratification," *American Sociological Review*, 1956, 21, 203–211.

Staats, A. W. "A Case in and a Strategy for the Extension of Learning Principles to Problems of Human Behavior," in A. W. Staats (ed.), *Human Learning*. New York: Holt, Rinehart and Winston, 1964. (a)

Staats, A. W. "Conditioned Stimuli, Conditioned Reinforcers, and Word Meaning," in A. W. Staats (ed.), *Human Learning*. New York: Holt, Rinehart and Winston, 1964. (b)

Staats, A. W. (ed.) *Human Learning*. New York: Holt, Rinehart and Winston, 1964. (c)

Staats, A. W. "An Integrated-functional Learning Approach to Complex Human Behavior," in B. Kleinmuntz (ed.), *Problem Solving: Research, Method and Theory*. New York: Wiley, 1966.

Staats, A. W. *Learning, Language, and Cognition*. New York: Holt, Rinehart and Winston, 1968.

Staats, A. W., Finley, J. R., Minke, K. A., and Wolf, M. "Reinforcement Variables in the Control of Unit Reading Responses," *Journal of the Experimental Analysis of Behavior*, 1964, 7, 139–149. (d)

Staats, A. W., Minke, K. A., and Butts, P. "A Token-Reinforcement Remedial Reading Program Administered by Black Therapy-Technicians to Problem Black Children," *Behavior Therapy*, 1970, 1, 331–353.

Staats, A. W., Minke, K. A., Finley, J. R., Wolf, M., and Brooks, L. O. "A Reinforcer System and Experimental Procedure for the Laboratory Study of Reading Acquisition," *Child Development*, 1964, 35, 209–231. (e)

Staats, A. W., Minke, K. A., Goodwin, W., and Landeen, J. "Cognitive Behavior Modification: 'Motivated Learning' Reading Treatment with Subprofessional Therapy-Technicians," *Behavior Research and Therapy*, 1967, 5, 283–299.

Staats, A. W. with contributions by Staats, C. K. *Complex Human Behavior*. New York: Holt, Rinehart and Winston, 1963.

Staats, A. W., Staats, C. K., Schutz, R. E., and Wolf, M. "The Conditioning of Textual Responses Utilizing 'Extrinsic' Reinforcers," *Journal of the Experimental Analysis of Behavior*, 1962, 5, 33–40.

Ullmann, L. P., and Krasner, L. *A Psychological Approach to Abnormal Behavior*. New York: Prentice-Hall, 1969.

Wolf, M. M., Giles, E. K., and Hall, R. V. "Experiment with Token-Reinforcement in a Remedial Classroom," *Behavior Research and Therapy*, 1968, 6, 51–64.

D.

Programs and Examples for Teachers and by Teachers

Application of Behavioral Principles to Classroom Settings

David Phillips

Seven studies completed by elementary teachers on the effective use of behavioral principles are presented. These studies were conducted by the teachers named as part of a class requirement. They were taking an in-service graduate course on Behavior Management offered by the University of Illinois Educational Psychology Department. Dr. Wesley Becker and David Phillips were the instructors. Studies by two teachers are not reported here. In one case, it was unclear exactly what behaviors were being counted. In the other, the write-up was too lengthy to be included although the study was executed well.

The studies are presented as they were prepared by the teachers, and reflect their attempt to systematically apply behavioral principles to a classroom setting. The teachers involved had no prior knowledge of behavioral principles and thus are representative of most teachers. The course was a fourteen week seminar and the project was the culmination of the techniques and theory learned.

A wide variety of problems were approached and dealt with using behavioral principles. No attempt was made to produce "experimentally elegant" studies with careful controls. Rather a more pragmatic approach was taken whereby the teachers involved tackled the problems they faced in the classroom as efficiently as possible.

A brief outline of typical procedures used in dealing with behavior

This paper is an outgrowth of the Prairie School Title III Project and the In-Service Teacher Training Course connected with it. Some of the procedures used have been adapted with permission from a program developed by W. Scott Wood, Western Michigan University.

problems is presented. One of the purposes of this paper is to acquaint the reader with the kinds of problems faced and the techniques used in dealing with them.

Behavior and Its Consequences

Most all of the behavior teachers deal with is controlled by its consequences. Whatever immediately follows a given behavior will
have a definite effect on the probability of that behavior occurring
again. If you say, "Please pass the salt," and the salt is passed to
you, you have been rewarded for asking, by receiving the salt. You
are more likely to ask for it that way in the future. If you say, "Thanks,"
to the passer you reward his passing the salt and he is more likely to
pass it in the future because of the reward. Similarly, if a child ex-
hibits deviant behavior and the teacher attends to it (by nagging,
scolding, reprimanding, etc.,) the child is very likely going to do it
more in the future. Her attention is reinforcing the very behavior she
wishes to eliminate. The best way to eliminate this behavior is to
remove the attention (reinforcement) by ignoring the behavior and
reinforce some other behavior which is incompatible with the undesirable behavior. That is, praise the child when he is behaving
properly and ignore the deviant behavior.

This may seem very trivial, but in general most of our behavior
is controlled in the same way. The basic principle is: *Behavior is a
function of its consequences.* Thus, if we want to change behavior,
we must change the consequences.

Essentially, we can either *increase, decrease,* or *maintain* behavior. Behavior strengthening and maintenance is a result of reinforcement.

Behavior weakening is the result of either *extinction* or *punishment.* Extinction is the procedure of withholding reinforcement
from a particular behavior. For example, a child is teasing someone
and no one pays any attention to his teasing. This withholding of
attention (reinforcer) is going to weaken the teasing until it ceases.
Punishment is the procedure of following a specific behavior with
an unpleasant (aversive) event, like spanking a child following his
running into the street. Punishment may take the form of removing
some valued reinforcer from the individual following a specific behavior, like removing the person from the presence of other people
who may reinforce him with their attention, or taking away privileges, money, etc.

Behavior Modification — The Basic Steps

I. Definition

    A. Specifically state the problem behaviors which have been
       observed, i.e., *the child is out of his seat* or says, *"I don't like*

school," etc. Do not generalize, such as the kid fools around too much or has a bad attitude. You cannot effectively deal with these generalizations, you *can* however, deal with specific behaviors.

  B. What do you want the child to do? How does this differ from the current behavior, i.e., is this a problem of more, less, or different behavior?

II. *Measurement*

  A. In order to assess any treatment, we must know the strength of the behavior before the treatment. Observe and record systematically. *Measurement Techniques:* frequency counts and durational measures in most cases. How many times does the behavior occur in a minute, hour, etc., or how long does it last after it begins?

  B. *Data Recording:* graphs of rates and frequencies. Draw a simple graph depicting the frequency or duration for each observation period.

III. *Consequence*

Behavior is a function of its consequences. If you want to change the behavior, change the consequence.

  A. *Identify a likely reinforcer, punisher or extinction procedure.* If you want to increase a behavior, reinforce it. If you want to weaken a behavior, punish it or withhold reinforcement (extinction).

   1. *Likely pitfall: misidentified reinforcers.* We all too often assume what reinforces us will reinforce others; this is not always the case. Also what reinforces us at one time may not be a reinforcer at another time, e.g., food may be a good reinforcer before a meal, but not directly after a meal.

  B. *Set a behavioral criterion for the consequence.* Specifically what must the person do before he gets reinforced, punished, or placed on extinction.

   1. *Likely pitfall: initial criterion too high.* When increasing a behavior, begin with small steps toward the terminal performance. Don't demand too much too soon. Reinforce approximations to the desired final performance. Individualize the standards for reinforcement. Reinforce for improvement, not one standard or performance.

  C. *Arrange the details of the consequence.* How is the consequence presented? By whom and how?

   1. A *direct* consequence: immediately follow the behavior with the consequences. A child gets a problem correct; you consequate it by saying, "Good."

2. An *indirect* consequence: a "token" or "point" system whereby some symbol signifying reinforcement is given, with the actual consequence delivered at some later time. A child gets a problem correct; you consequate it by giving a token which will be exchanged for some reward at a later time.

IV. Evaluation

A. *The importance of continued measurement.* Without continued measurement, you cannot assess the effectiveness of your consequences. Some estimate of the frequency of the behavior must be made or it is likely that you will be unable to determine if your plan is effective or not. A subjective judgement can be very misleading.

B. *What to do if the consequence appears to be ineffective.* This can be established by measurement of the behavior.
   1. May be an error in consequence identification. Perhaps the consequence chosen is not an effective reinforcer or punisher. If not, change it.
   2. The initial criterion for reinforcement may be too high. You may be asking for too much too soon. Reinforce approximations to the desired behavior.
   3. The time delay between the behavior and the consequence may be too long. Delayed reinforcement or punishment will most likely be ineffective. To be effective the consequence must immediately follow the behavior.

Behavior Management in the Classroom

I. *Most classroom problems are of two general types: academic problems and problems of classroom management.*

A. *Problems of Inadequate Academic Performance.*
   1. Students who have the necessary academic skills but sometimes do not participate.
      a. Example: On the basis of achievement, you feel reasonably sure the child is capable but puts out no effort.
      b. Example: The difficulty in obtaining class participation when the material is too difficult or uninteresting.
   2. Students whose poor academic achievement results from a lack of prerequisite academic skills.
      a. Example: The student who lacks a specific skill, i.e., can't multiply because he can't add.
      b. Example: The student who lacks more general skills, i.e., hasn't learned to read because he hasn't learned how to pay attention.

B. *Problems Involving Classroom Management.*
  1. Relatively weak behaviors which should be strengthened.
     a. Example: The student who is withdrawn and generally non-communicative. Class participation behaviors should be strengthened.
  2. Students with strong undesirable or disruptive behaviors which should be weakened and/or eliminated entirely.
     a. Example: The student who is "deliberately" disruptive. These disruptive behaviors should be eliminated.
     b. Example: The noisy classroom. The noise level should be lowered by reinforcing more quiet behavior.

II. Strategies for solving academic and classroom management problems.

  A. *Consequences Designed to Strengthen Desirable Academic or Classroom Behaviors.*
     1. Have you specified the behavior of interest in terms of observable behavior?
     2. Do you have an accurate estimate of the current behavior? That is, have you measured? This must be done in order to determine the effectiveness of any program to change behavior.
     3. How to find a reinforcer. On the basis of past experience, advance knowledge or simply ask the children what they like.
        a. Will grades work? To some children grades are too far removed in time to be effective.
        b. Other reinforcers — ask your subjects. What do you like or what would you work for? (e.g., privileges, activities, or goodies)
     4. Which behavior are you going to start with, what behavior must occur before I reinforce the child? (i.e., some approximation of the desired behavior which currently is emitted with some measurable frequency)
        a. Are all the necessary prerequisite skills well learned or is some remediation necessary? Don't demand some performance the child simply cannot do because no one has taught him. Teach the skill if necessary.
        b. Be sure to make your first criterion for reinforcement something that the student can do relatively easily. If you ask for a difficult performance initially, you may readily get failure. Reinforce for a correct performance.
     5. Is the consequence going to be direct or indirect (a point system)?
        a. Example: an academic strengthening problem involving the shaping of prerequisite behaviors: reading readi-

ness skills. Reinforce these behaviors with praise or other direct reinforcer.

b. Example: classroom motivational systems in public schools: a token reinforcement system. The tokens are turned in later for a variety of reinforcers.

c. The teacher's standards keep increasing as the student's performance improves. You are succeeding but may not notice it. As the student's behavior improves, it is easy to forget the improvement you have made.

B. *Consequences Designed to Weaken Undesirable Behavior.*

  1. Specify the behavior in terms of observable behavior.
  2. Do you have an accurate estimate of the current behavior? i.e., have you measured its frequency or duration.
  3. Deciding on the consequences—three ways to weaken behavior.

  a. Extinction—this amounts to withholding the reinforcement that is maintaining the behavior.

  b. The reinforcement of incompatible behavior strengthens behaviors that are incompatible with the undesirable behavior, e.g., sitting down is incompatible with standing up.

  c. Punishment—removing a reinforcer (e.g., taking away a privilege) or presenting an aversive stimulus (e.g., spanking). These procedures when made contingent on a specified response will weaken it.

  Punishment isn't necessarily the best procedure even though it may be the fastest. It may produce side effects such as avoidance and escape behavior and may result in the increase of aggressive behavior, i.e., the person will tend to avoid a situation in which he is punished, e.g., a classroom or school.

C. *How Do You Know if You Have Succeeded?*

  1. The importance of continued measurement. The only way you can really determine how your program is working is to measure the frequency of the behavior or interest. Is it increasing or decreasing as you had planned? Casual observation can be very misleading and lead to incorrect decisions about the program.

D. *Relativity of the Consequences.*

  1. The behavior you have either strengthened or weakened is not permanent. This is true of *all* behavior. We behave according to the consequences. For example: if you reinforce and increase "on task" behavior in a child and the next year he goes into a class where the teacher gives him attention for "fooling around" he will come under the control of these new consequences and begin to "fool around" more. Most of our behavior is like this.

Summary

1. Identify and define behavior.
2. Measure.
3. Place consequence on the behavior.
4. Evaluation based on continued measurement.
5. Try again if not achieving anticipated results.

Observation Techniques

The following material is concerned with observation and graphing. Graphing is a convenient way to summarize your results. Included are: General Observation Techniques; Instructions to Observers; Coding Categories and Symbols which have been used (you need not limit yourself to these), Observation Sheet and a Summary Graph Card.

Steps to Take

Specify the behavior you are going to observe very precisely, always in terms of observable behaviors. A general class of behavior may be used such as "on task" or "off task" in so far as you have defined "on task" so that it may be reliably observed.

Behavior which is of a single response nature may be recorded with a frequency tally over a measured period of time, e.g., hitting, pinching, etc. Other types of behaviors which are composed of many separate responses and endure over an extended period of time should be recorded in short 10-15 second intervals. Behaviors in this class are such things as "on task", thumb sucking, talking, etc. This type of recording may be done as follows: take a sheet of paper, draw a series of cells on it (like large graph paper). Use this to record on. Observe for 10 seconds. If the person emits the behavior of interest place a mark in the cell. This recording is done for 10 seconds. So, you are observing for 10 seconds and recording for 10, then observe again and so on. Do not record during the 10 second observing period. This technique calls for the use of a stop watch taped to a clip board, or some similar arrangement.

The frequency of observations will vary according to many things like practicality, etc. However, be consistent and observe under the same conditions every observation period. For example, you might observe every morning from 9:30 to 10:00. This assumes the same teacher, kids and classroom each time.

After observation we end up with the percentage of intervals during which the behaviors of interest has occurred.

Examine Figures 1, 2, and 3.

Symbols	Classes	
X	Gross Motor Behaviors	Getting out of seat; standing up; running; hopping; skipping; jumping; walking around; rocking in chair; disruptive movement without noise; moves chair to neighbor; knees on chair is rated.
N	Disruptive Noise	Tapping pencil or other objects; clapping; tapping feet; rattling or tearing paper; throwing book on desk; slamming desk. (Be conservative, only rate if could hear noise when eyes closed.) Do not include accidental dropping of objects or if noise made while performing X above.)
$\wedge$	Disturbing Others Directly	Grabbing objects or work; knocking neighbor's books off desk; destroying another's property; pushing with desk.
$\longrightarrow$	Aggression (Contact)	Hitting; kicking; shoving; pinching; slapping; striking with object; throwing object at another person; poking with object; attempts to strike; biting; pulling hair.
	Orienting Responses (90° seated)	Turning head or head and body to look at another person, showing objects to another child, attending to another child. (Must be 4 seconds duration; not rated unless seated, or more than 90° using the desk as a reference.)
$\vee$	Verbalizations	Carrying on conversations with other children when it is not permitted. Answers teacher without raising hand or without being called on; making comments or calling out remarks when no question has been asked; calling teacher's name to get her attention; crying; screaming; singing; whistling; laughing loudly; coughing or blowing loudly. (May be directed to teacher or children.)
$//$	Other Tasks	Ignores teacher's question or command; does something different from that directed to do; includes minor

Fig. 1. Child behavior observation coding cateogries

Symbols	Classes	
		motor behavior such as playing with pencil eraser when supposed to be writing; coloring while the record is on; doing spelling during the arithmetic lesson; playing with objects; eating; chewing gum. *The child involves himself in a task that is not appropriate.*
———	Relevant Behavior	Time on task; e.g., answers question, listening, raises hand, writing assignment. (Must include whole 20″ interval except for orienting responses of less than 4 seconds duration.)
⊗ ⊘	Teacher Behavior	Teacher attends to a particular child at any time during the 10″ interval; gives attention by praising, disciplining. (The teacher can help the child at desk, talk to, etc.) The circle indicates the teacher attended to the behavior symbolized inside the circle.

Fig. 1. Child behavior observation coding categories (*cont'd.*)

General Instructions for Observers

1. Do not talk to any children at any time; in school room, hall, or yard, including before and after actual school hours.
2. Do not let children either see or hear you talking to their teacher or another observer. Questions on recording can be written and discussed later.
3. Do not make any differential responses to children. Do not laugh at children, answer children, or change position of head or eyes, if addressed. Do not turn and look at any child when you hear a noise. Make the minimal response necessary to see the child you are recording.
4. When observing sit silently and as immobile as possible in the most convenient observer chair. Change location quietly only when absolutely necessary.
5. Do not engage in any social behavior with children either on entering or leaving school or classroom. Do not respond to children in halls.
6. The goal is to become a piece of furniture. You are not to be a variable with reference to the children's behavior. "Neither discriminative nor reinforcing be."

342

OBSERVER_____TEACHER_____
SUBJECT_____DATE_____
TIME_____SCHOOL_____
OBSERVATION INTERVAL LENGTH: 10″, 20″, 30″, etc._____
OBSERVED BEHAVIOR_____

S#	OBSERVATIONS						COMMENTS	CODE SYMBOLS USED:

Fig. 2. Sample observation record sheet

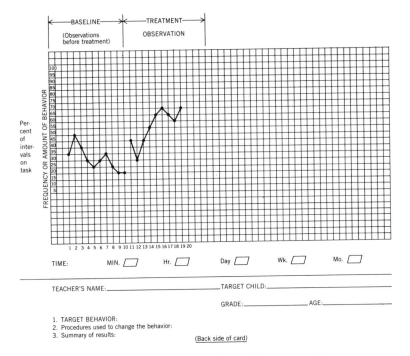

Fig. 3. Sample graph

A STUDY IN BEHAVIOR MODIFICATION
by Barbara Hernon

Steve, a ten year old 4th grader, tests at average ability. He was chosen for this study because he exhibited many behaviors incompatible with good work habits. During morning reading period he disturbed others at his groups by talking and leaning over their desks. Much of his time was also spent in daydreaming or working at something other than reading such as coloring a sheet of paper. Daily reading assignments were never completed.

The target behavior, in this case, therefore, is that Steve not disturb others or daydream but rather *work continuously on his reading.* To keep a record of Steve's behavior an observer came to the room for thirty minutes per day for nine days. Behavior was recorded in ten second intervals; observe for ten seconds, record for ten seconds. The observer recorded *time on task;* not talking and working on assigned reading task. The nine day observation period was divided into five days baseline, and four days experimental. Following five days of baseline, Steve and I visited and discussed his poor work habits. Steve expressed a desire to improve. We set up a *point*

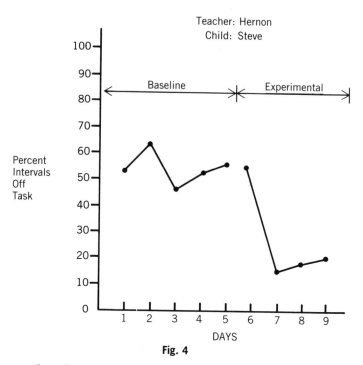

Fig. 4

system based on a set of positively stated rules for the reading period. The rules set up were working quietly and independently, and only on the reading assignment until the given assignment was completed. I explained that points would be contingent on compliance with these rules. The points would earn a mutually agreed upon reward.

I began reinforcement by rewarding with praise comments and points during a specified interval. When deviant behavior occurred it was ignored and no points were given.

Figure I shows the data gathered during observation. For the first five days of baseline, Steve shows a high rate of deviant behavior— off task as much as sixty-five per cent of the time. Reinforcement began on day six and as the figure shows his deviant behavior was just as high as on the previous days. I analyzed these data and came to the conclusion that perhaps too long a work period was being required before reinforcement occurred. I was reinforcing every fifteen-minutes. Therefore, on days seven, eight, and nine, I gave points each five minutes. As the figure shows, the deviant behavior showed a marked decline. Steve was now off task only eighteen per cent of the time. As I changed no other aspects of the program, I attributed the results to the changed schedule of reinforcement.

On days seven, eight, and nine, Steve's behavior showed improvement. He was more attentive to the task at hand, worked more quietly and independently. His mother reported to me that there has been a change in attitude. He is greatly encouraged by the feeling that someone cares about him.

Steve is a long way from the desired end behavior; however, the improvement shown is encouraging. I intend to continue the program and reinforce successive approximations of the desired terminal behavior. Eventually the interval of reinforcement will be increased and more work will be required for reinforcement. I plan to work for completion of assignments as a next step. Since Steve responds favorably to praise, I intend to continue this form of reinforcement and fade out material rewards.

A PROJECT IN BEHAVIOR MODIFICATION
by Anne Manton

The subject for this project was an eight year old fourth grade boy. He and a third grade girl come daily to my room for forty minutes of Type A tutoring in arithmetic.*

The behavior to be modified was the *utterance of words or noises not relevant to the arithmetic tasks assigned.* Acceptable verbalization, as defined for the observer, was questions about work or saying answers and problems aloud. Unacceptable verbalization was grunts and various other guttural sounds, giggles, whistles, sobbing, humming and comments such as "goodie" and "yah." Target behavior was silence or acceptable verbalization 80% of the time.

The observer sat behind the subject. She observed for ten seconds, then recorded for ten seconds using a stop watch and clip board. Data were gathered for thirty minutes each day.

Five days of baseline observation was done during which time I continued my previous practice of ignoring the deviant behavior of the subject. On the sixth day the experimental program was initiated. Both children were given copies of a chart (Figure 5). The three rules were discussed with them. It was explained that for each five minutes they followed the rules, an X would be placed in the box on the clock representing that time interval, and these points could be used to earn rewards. The reinforcers were then shown to them and consisted of things they had suggested, such as play dough, darts, a toy truck, a ring, coloring books, a doll, and candy. A chart showing the points needed to earn each reward was included.

On the third day of the experimental period I began to give additional points for work completed. They could earn two points for a perfect paper and one point for not more than two errors. A point was also given for five correct responses to flash cards. These points were recorded in the boxes to the left of the clock. Each day the

---

*Type A is a term used to designate children diagnosed as socially maladjusted.

RULES

1. No talking unless it is about arithmetic.
2. Sit in seats unless asked to come to board.
3. Raise hands in group discussions.

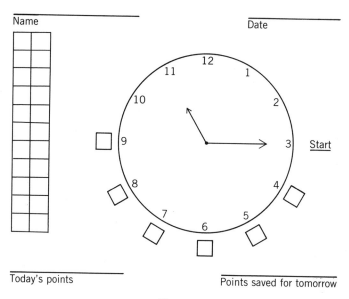

Fig. 5

points were totaled and the children chose whether to use them or save them for a reward that required more points.

The graph (Figure 6) shows the effect of the experimental program on the child. As his deviant behavior decreased his time on task increased and his work output increased from one-half paper to two or three papers completed daily.

EFFECTS OF POSITIVE REINFORCEMENT ON THUMBSUCKING
by Beatrice Marro

Procedure

The target child for this study was a five year old Kindergarten girl named Mattie. She was chosen for this study because her thumbsucking often interfered with her ability to communicate verbally.

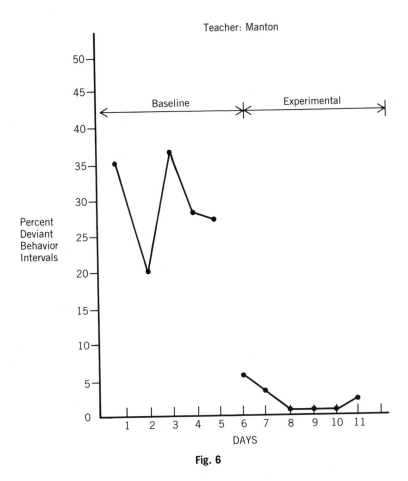

Fig. 6

BASELINE. During the baseline and experimental periods, an observer watched Mattie for ten seconds, then recorded her observations for ten seconds, then observed again, etc. The criterion for scoring was that the thumb be in Mattie's mouth at least up to the knuckle for the entire ten second observation period in order to be scored as thumbsucking. During baseline, the teacher tried to discourage thumbsucking by frowning at Mattie when she had her thumb in her mouth or by physically removing the thumb from Mattie's mouth by pulling her hand away.

EXPERIMENTAL PERIOD. Thumbsucking appears to be self reinforcing and it was felt that praise alone would not be a strong enough reinforcer in extinguishing the behavior. To determine what material reinforcers would be most effective, the teacher asked Mattie to help select them. Mattie said she liked toys such as balls, clay, small dolls and doll baby bottles. She could receive these prizes by earning points (at least five points per toy) which she could exchange for a prize.

The teacher set a timer which would ring on the average each three minutes the first day of the experimental period. This time was gradually increased to a ten minutes average. Mattie could earn one point every time she did not have her thumb in her mouth when the bell rang. Points were recorded by filling in one block on a piece of graph paper every time Mattie was exhibiting appropriate behavior (not sucking her thumb) when the bell rang. The rest of the class was instructed to ignore the bell, and everyone, the teacher included, was to ignore the thumbsucking. If Mattie had earned at least five points by dismissal, she could choose a prize or save her points until the next day and try to earn more points toward a larger prize.

Results

The results of this study are presented in Figures 7 and 8. The average incidents of thumbsucking during the instructional period of the day was 64% during baseline and 2% during the experimental period — a decrease of 62% (Figure 7). During rest period thumbsucking went from an average of 81% for baseline to 7% during the experimental period — a decrease of 74% (Figure 8). It was noted that thumbsucking was highest on day #1 for baseline and day #7 for the experimental period (Figure 7). Both of these peaks occurred during a televised phonics lesson.

On the eighth day Mattie decided to work toward a doll in a bath tub. She did not earn the needed ten points that day, so she decided to take a lesser prize instead of waiting until the next day to earn more points.

BEHAVIOR MODIFICATION PROJECT
by Wanda J. Miller

Description of Target Behavior

Selection of a target behavior was difficult, as I have one of those rare classes, a first grade, in which it is almost impossible to find undesirable behavior. I chose David, whose problem was different from usual deviant behavior. By licking, touching, and rubbing, David irritated his lips and surrounding areas with such frequency that his mouth area was constantly red and raw-looking. He frequently complained that his mouth hurt, asking that I put some medicine on it. Though I had suggested that his refraining from licking and touching would help, I did not pursue correction of the problem. The terminal behavior I sought was *cessation of the irritating behaviors* that resulted in David's sore mouth.

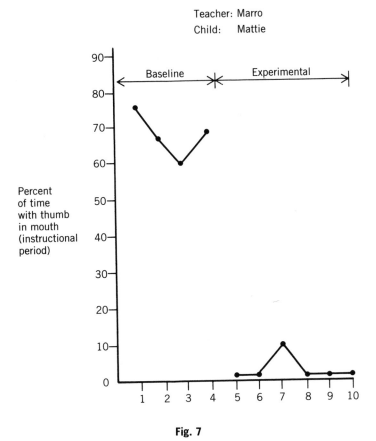

Teacher: Marro
Child: Mattie

Fig. 7

Time Span of Experiment

I was pressed for time with only thirteen possible observation days before Christmas vacation. Therefore, I limited my observation to one solid block of time before the holiday break. I realize this short time is not ideal and may cast some doubt on the results; however, this was a practical limitation.

Observation Personnel

At the time of the experiment I had a junior participant from the University of Illinois in my classroom preparing for student teaching. She was the only observer available in our building. After my discussing the principles of this course, she was extremely interested and eager to serve as my observer.

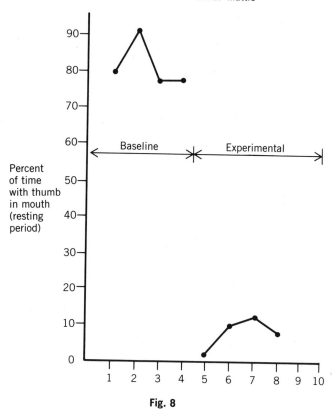

Fig. 8

Recording Procedure

Time plan:
   Three days baseline, ten days extinction
   Thirty minutes each day, same time and class activity
   Ten seconds observing—ten seconds recording Code categories:

Symbol	Definition
l	licking lips and surrounding area
p	pencil in or on mouth and surrounding area
f	fingers in or on mouth and surrounding area
a	arm or sleeve rubbing mouth area

Procedure to Weaken Target Behavior

Explanation to target child of the experiment and terminal behavior desired.

Vocal praise when undesirable behavior was absent: i.e., "Your mouth is looking better, David." "You are remembering very well." Etc.

My facial expressions of a smile, a hug, or wink when he was refraining.

Vocal praise, to the whole class, of David's positive efforts.

Getting the class to help David accomplish his goal through their praise.

Results

In three days of baseline observation the undesirable behavior registered 82%, 81% and 68% at the observed time. At the introduction of experimental procedure on the fourth day, the percentage dropped to 29%; fifth day to 18%; and the sixth day to 4%. Illness of both teacher and observer prevented data collection on days seven and eight. Post checks on days eleven and thirteen showed 5% and 2% of undesired behavior. The percentage dropped so quickly that contingent reinforcement, beyond praise, was unnecessary in order to effect weakening the undesirable behavior.

After a two-week Christmas vacation, I observed David's mouth area to be normal. His reward is a normal mouth, which he is most happy about. He is proud of our cooperative effort and says he is determined it won't happen again. The class and I continue to reinforce David's desirable behavior. My terminal objective has been reached.

A PROJECT IN BEHAVIOR MODIFICATION
by Edith Paterson

Choosing a target child presented a problem in my case. My class is a high achieving group of middle primary students. Therefore, the group has no serious problems.

Lucy is a six year old child who scores well above 150 on the California Test of Mental Maturity. Her achievement scores also place her far above the average middle primary student. She was chosen as a target child because she seldom completes assignments. Her time is usually spent staring off into space, doodling on her paper, or wiggling in her seat. Therefore, the target behavior in this case is for Lucy to *sit still, face forward, eyes on paper, and complete the assigned task.*

Lucy was observed for approximately twenty minutes a day for

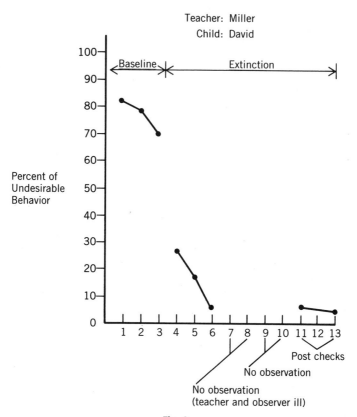

Fig. 9

eight days. Behavior was observed for ten seconds and then re-corded for ten seconds. The behavior which was observed was *time on task*. Time on task behavior was defined as: sitting appro-priately in seat, eyes on paper, and apparently working on the as-signed task. The data also indicated gross physical movement. The observations occurred during reading period. This is a time when Lucy has a specific set of tasks to complete. Previously, Lucy dis-played much deviant behavior during this period and seldom com-pleted the assigned task during the time allotted.

After four days of baseline, I changed my daily program. I opened each day with a discussion of good work habits. I praised the chil-dren by describing correct behavior in a concise, positive manner. I also began giving Lucy praise and attention contingent on the target behavior; I ignored all behaviors incompatible with good work habits.

Since the baseline data had made me aware of the extremely high rate of gross physical movement, I felt this was probably the most

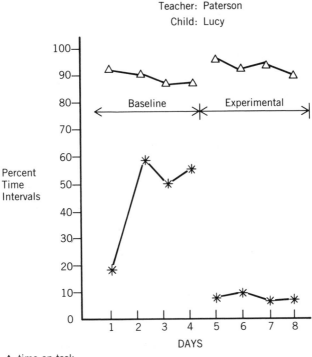

Teacher: Paterson
Child: Lucy

△ time on task

✳ gross physical behavior

Fig. 10

seriously interfering behavior. Therefore, I directed many of my praise comments toward reinforcement of sitting still.

Figure 10 presents the per cent of time spent in gross physical movement. As this figure indicates the subject responded immediately to differential reinforcement. She began to display excellent work habits. Especially noticable was the marked decrease in gross physical movement. Occasionally, she would revert to her old patterns of behavior. At that time, I used a simple comment, such as "I like the way Susie is sitting and working." Lucy would immediately begin working well again.

Lucy's work habits have improved a great deal, especially in reducing her gross physical movement. In addition to her increased time on task the work produced has been more accurate. Although there is no data to illustrate an attitude change, Lucy has expressed more of an interest in reading.

BEHAVIOR SHAPING PROJECT
by Mary V. Thornton

Subject: Tim, Grade 2.

Target Behavior: For Tim to read, or do whatever task he is given to do without arguments as to which book he should be in, or without comments concerning Darrin, a classmate with whom I also work.

Behavior to be modified or eliminated is the almost constant queries or comments concerning Darrin. Tim's preoccupation with "which book Darrin is in," "which pencil Darrin uses," "which chair Darrin sits in," "which side of the table Darrin sits on," etc. was extremely disruptive to any learning situation.

Recording Procedure: A trained observer using a stop watch and clipboard observed 10 seconds and recorded 10 seconds for approximately 30 minutes per day. A check mark was used for any comment or question about Darrin or other students that I work with which had no connection with the lessons we were doing. Such comments as "Is this the book Darrin is in?" or "Is this the story Darrin is on?" were not acceptable and received a check mark.

Experimental Procedure: Tim was told the 'Rules of my Room' were:
1. Each person works in the books he is given.
2. He doesn't worry or ask about other people's work.
3. He does the best he can.

I tried to explain to Tim how some people were stronger and could run faster, while perhaps other people could read faster or in harder books, but all we wanted was for each person to do his best and not be concerned with what others were doing. My project was a little different from the regular classroom situation since I work with the children one at a time. I could not praise others to shape Tim's behavior since this preoccupation with others was the very behavior I was attempting to eliminate.

Praise was used as a positive reinforcer for any work done right. To weaken the unwanted behavior of questions and comments about Darrin, they were ignored (as much as possible) or answered with a very short answer and a displeased look when he insisted on an answer. Reinforcing comments such as "good," "fine," "very good," and "you're doing very well" were made whenever possible.

Statement as to results: This procedure has been very effective. Tim has reached target behavior with only an occasional query concerning Darrin. His Home Room Teacher stated that he is also more cooperative in his home room.

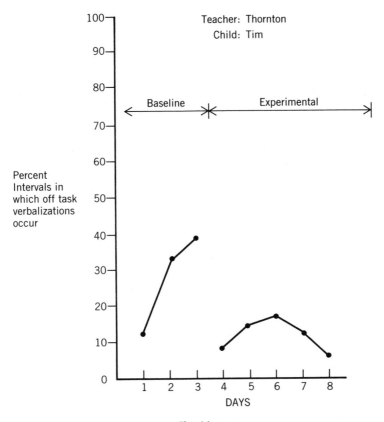

Fig. 11

CLASSROOM PROJECT IN BEHAVIOR MODIFICATION
by Judy Wieting

Target Behavior: To decrease blurting out.

Recording Procedure Used: My observer recorded the number of "blurts" (undesirable verbalizations) occurring within 30 minute periods, each day for thirteen days.

Procedures Used to Modify the Behavior: I ignored any comments which were blurted out. I praised hand raising and talking only when called on.

My subject was Louis, nine years old, a second grader.

Those verbalizations by Louis which I considered to be undesirable, i.e., blurting out behavior, were comments which he made aloud to himself, classmates, or the teacher without having first been called on. I did not count as "blurts" whispered conversations with a neighbor; but, rather, only his random remarks, often only one or two words, which were audible to all in the room.

During the four-day baseline period, I continued to treat Louis as I had all year. I felt it would render the results of the experiment invalid if I instituted any of the behavior modification procedures before baseline data had been gathered. Therefore, I at times reminded Louis, either privately or in front of the class, not to talk without being called on. On occasion I responded to Louis' blurts, especially when he had given a comment or answer that I had been seeking. Therefore, on Day 5, when the time came to begin extinction of Louis' blurting out behavior, I had to discipline myself to be sure that at all times I ignored his blurts and gave attention only to the desired behavior.

On the first of the nine experimental days (Day 5), I posted a chart in the front of the room, enumerating the following three rules:

1. Raise your hand if you wish to talk.
2. Wait to be called on.
3. Listen while others talk.

I purposely listed as few rules as possible while still managing to cover the essentials. I felt that the task might seem easier to master if it did not involve numerous rules.

The entire class read the rules together and discussed each rule, being careful to follow the rules during our discussion. Louis seemed especially anxious to please me and had his hand up constantly. On this first day and for a few days following, I called on Louis every time he raised his hand and as soon as possible after he raised it. After Day 7, I found that by stressing rules 2 and 3, I could lengthen the interval between the time Louis raised his hand and the time I called on him, and still maintain the reduction of blurts.

At first I praised Louis' slightest hand-raising movement. However, not much shaping was required. Louis was eager to receive positive attention. I praised Louis (and others) whenever they applied the rules, and referred to the rules in my reinforcing comments. Aside from the usual "goods" I used such comments as, "I called on ____ because he had his hand up" or "I like the way ____ always listens while others are talking." Whenever possible I named Louis in the comments. I praised good raisers, good waiters, and good listeners. In regards to the effectiveness of vicarious reinforcement on Louis, I found that it worked best if I could praise someone for an incompatible behavior at the *exact* moment when Louis was blurting out.

The whole class cooperated, too, by not responding to any comments blurted out by classmates. For example, during show and tell, if a classmate had a comment or question, the "shower" would not acknowledge it unless he had first called on that classmate. We recited the rules each morning, and when necessary or applicable, we reviewed the reasons for the rules and evaluated our class progress.

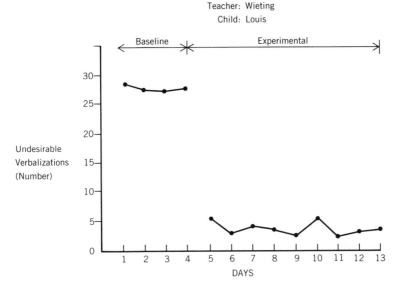

Fig. 12

Results of the Experiment: I feel that I learned and accomplished much through this first project. Not only was my target behavior realized, proving to me the effectiveness of the ignore-and-praise combination, but fringe benefits were gained also. I became accustomed to giving praise freely and sincerely. And I am training myself not to acknowledge deviant behavior by means of any verbal, facial, or physical response. Although my primary goal was to stop Louis' blurting out and to get him to raise his hand if he wished to speak, good listening habits for the whole class resulted from this experiment. Toward the end of the thirteen days, after the basics of raising-hand-to-talk had been mastered, I pursued the skills further by branching off into connecting areas. All children learned to listen while classmates or teachers were talking. If a comment was made which repeated what another had just finished saying, I ignored it. I employed such questions as "What do you think of what ____ said?" or "Please tell me what ____ just said."

The graph vividly illustrates the results of my application of principles of behavior modification. By ignoring the undesirable behavior and giving positive reinforcement to behaviors incompatible with it, the blurting out behavior was drastically reduced from a high frequency of occurrence. Perhaps over a longer period of time, the blurting out behavior can be totally extinguished.

The Lincoln Elementary School Projects: Some Results of an In-Service Training Course in Behavioral Psychology

W. Scott Wood
Western Michigan University

In the spring of 1968, I conducted an in-service training course for several of the teachers at Lincoln Elementary School in Kalamazoo, Michigan. The title of the course was Psychology 517, Psychology of Education and Learning for Teachers. Arrangements to have the course taught were made by the Principal of the Elementary School, Mr. Jack Blanke. The course was part of a more general in-service training program, jointly funded by the Michigan Department of Mental Health and the Kalamazoo Valley Intermediate School District. Dr. Roger Ulrich, Western Michigan University, is the director of this program. There were two objectives for this course: (1) to introduce the teachers to the basic principles of behavior which comprise the foundation of the modern field of behavior modification, and (2) to help the teachers adapt these same principles into techniques of classroom behavior management that would have practical value for the elementary school teachers.

To help meet this latter objective, the teachers were each assigned to carry out a classroom behavior modification project.

Behavior Modification Monographs, 1 (2), 1970, Roger Ulrich, ed. Kalamazoo, Michigan: Behavior Development Corporation. The author would like to express his appreciation to the Behavior Research Laboratory, Western Michigan University, for the help with the figures, and to Eric Haughton, Precision Teaching Center, Eugene, Oregon, for his many helpful suggestions for the organization of this course.

The project required that the teacher be able to objectively measure and record the behavior of either an individual student or the class as a whole, and then selectively modify that behavior toward some desired behavioral goal. These projects required each teacher to be familiar with standard behavior modification procedures, such as recording devices and graphing techniques, as well as required considerable creativity with respect to the application of the various principles of behavior.

Many of these projects developed practical techniques of considerable merit, so I have summarized several of these. They are presented in the remainder of this paper. Hopefully, readers may be able to see how some of these same principles and techniques can be used in other similar settings.

In conclusion, I believe that these projects demonstrate that practical behavior theory can be taught in a course of this type, and that classroom teachers are an interested and well-motivated audience for this approach.

CLASSROOM DISCIPLINE
by Stella Baker, 5th-Grade Teacher

Problem

I began my project by measuring the talking-out-of-turn episodes of a single talkative student in my class. The average number of these incidents was from ten to twelve times per day. However, during the week that I made these observations, I was forced to conclude that he really was no more talkative than some of the others in the class. So I decided to measure this behavior in the entire class.

Method

I recorded (on a golf counter) the number of verbal outbursts for the entire class for nine days. At the end of this period, I told the class what I was doing and that in the future, if the combined total for the class went over 25 in a single day, they would lose the gym period. A few days later, I indicated that if they continued to be successful on holding the outbursts down, they would be given surprises. On the 16th day, they received cookies.

After having missed two gym periods, the rate of unacceptable behavior dropped considerably. I then lowered the criterion from 25 to 15, and began to let the class have the last 15 minutes of the class to engage in activities of their own choice if the daily quota stayed under 15. Some of the activities that we decided upon were:

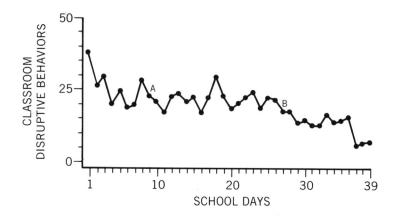

Fig. 1. Reduction in the frequency of classroom disruptive behaviors of a 5th-grade class

(1) play games, (2) play outside, (3) chew gum (which they all liked to do), (4) tell jokes and riddles (in good taste), and (5) work on projects of their own choice.

In addition, I began to record the name of the individual who was talking out of turn on the blackboard with a check by his name. A total of three checks in a day resulted in that person having to sit at the back of the room in isolation for the remainder of the day.

Results and Discussion

The results of this project are shown on the following graph. Point A indicates the beginning of the time that the gym period would be withdrawn for excessive outbursts. Point B indicates the lowering of the contingency from 25 to 15 and the addition of the reinforcing activities for remaining under 15.

As you can see, the outbursts dropped from 38 to a low of one for a single day. The children enjoy their work so much more now that sometimes they would rather use their free time on another day.

MY TOKEN SYSTEM
by James Black, 3rd-Grade Teacher

Problem

I started my project around one 3rd-grade boy, who constantly stayed out of his seat, which, to say the least, was annoying. The first six-hour session that I systematically observed his behavior, he was out

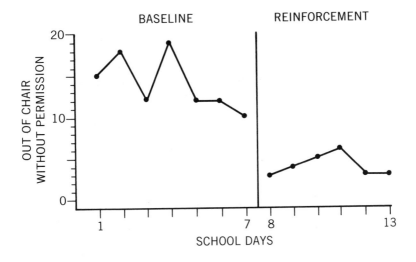

Fig. 2. The interruptive behavior of a 3rd-grader

of his chair fifteen times. I continued this observation for a total of eight classes.

Method

I decided to give the whole class stars as tokens for staying in their seats and doing their work. The stars are exchangeable for penny candy, candy bars, or they may trade in their stars if they want to sit with a friend. There is a regular price list set up for the exchange rate. They may also earn stars in other ways. When leaving the room as a group, the boys and girls compete against each other to get a star for the best behaved line. I have carried the rewards into the spelling area so that the best must get at least eleven out of fourteen words correct to get a star and the poorer spellers must get at least one more than the previous week to qualify for a star.

They may also lose stars. If they are out of their seats when they shouldn't be or if there are loud outbursts, they lose a star.

Results and Discussion

The chart shows the dramatic effect that the token system has had on the one boy's behavior. After the ninth session, when the tokens were introduced, the boy has been out of his seat no more than six times in one six-hour session. In addition, the entire class behaves much better, even when going out of the room to various parts of the school.

I've had generally good success with my projects, but some of the

children give up too easily and throw their tokens away or sometimes give them to a friend.

IMPROVING THE BEHAVIOR OF A 2nd GRADER
by Eleanor Chase, Special Education Teacher

Problem

Tommy is a sturdily built, hyperactive, very verbal, borderline
mentally handicapped boy. He is eight years old and in a special
education class. He had several disturbing behavior patterns. He
would blurt out in class whenever a question needed answering,
never giving a thought to the other members of his class. Tommy
also would move about the classroom whenever he wished. These
are behaviors that needed to be changed for the sake of everyone
involved, so these are the behaviors I attempted to modify.

Method

I began to record Tommy's behavior the week of February the 14th.
The average class time was forty minutes. The average number of
outbursts for the first sixteen days was seventeen times per day.
At the end of the sixteenth day, I explained to Tommy how I had
been using a golf counter to record the frequency of his undesirable
behavior. We came up with a plan for his improvement—the first
thing Tommy said after he found out what I had been doing was,
"I'll bet you a bottle of pop that you won't have to click that counter
for the rest of the week." This bottle of pop became the reward, or
reinforcer, for the behavioral change. It proved to be a very good one.
First of all, he had set the rules and the reward himself. Tommy
won his bottle of pop and was very proud of it.

The next week, we decided together that at the beginning of each
hour his name would be put on the board. If he did any of the things
we had discussed as undesirable, then I would put a check after
his name. When he received three checks, he was to move to the
back of the room with his back to the class for the remainder of the
period. However, if he had less than three checks, he could leave
the class five minutes early to enable him to go down and pick up
his little sister when she got out of class. At the end of the week,
he would also receive a bottle of pop if he had received less than a
total of fifteen checks.

Results and Discussion

The effects of these procedures are shown on the graph. Since the
sixth day of March, Tommy has only a total of five checks.

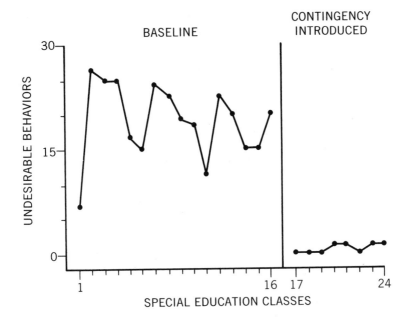

Fig. 3. The frequency of undesirable behavior in a 2nd grader

The change in Tommy's behavior has been good for all concerned, but it will still take a lot of hard work on Tommy's part to continue this new behavior pattern.

HELPING BILLY CONTROL HIS TEMPER
by Elaine Josephs, 4th-Grade Teacher

Problem

Billy is a young man who has trouble controlling his temper. He speaks right out if he is not called upon, and these outbursts often contain profanity. I decided to do something about the strength of this behavior. I wanted to weaken it.

Method

I began to record the frequency of these outbursts of temper on the week of February the 14th. Billy did not know I was taking this count. On the fifth day of my recording, Billy was expelled from school for cursing a teacher. On the day that Billy returned to the classroom, I explained to him that there were going to be some new

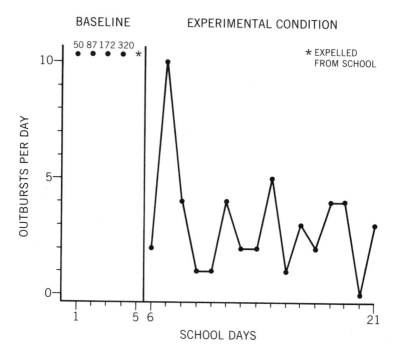

Fig. 4. The frequency of Billy's disruptive outbursts

rules in the classroom. I told him that I was going to keep track of his outbursts and that each time he went over 25 for a given day, there would be a penalty. He would have to sit in the corner, in a small desk away from everyone and would not be noticed by the teacher or the children. He indicated that he would not like this. However, he then asked me if he could try to stay under five outbursts instead of 25. We discussed the consequences, and he said that he would like to try it. He has and it has been at five ever since. There have been times when he did exceed the limit of five. Each time that this occurred, he went to the corner. In addition, each time Billy stays under five for the day, he receives some small treat or privilege. Sometimes he stays and helps me after class cleaning up the classroom, sometimes it's a special privilege such as going out to recess early or getting out of class ahead of time.

Results and Discussion

The success of these procedures are demonstrated in the following graph.

There has been a great improvement in Billy's behavior, even the children in the room noticed it and commented. Billy only has had to go to the corner two days and afterwards said that he would not go again. He has not gone to the corner since.

A SOLUTION TO AN ANNOYING PROBLEM
by Kathleen Marks, 4th-Grade Teacher

Problem

Last September the children in my class began to order milk, 12 to 18 cartons a day. Since they usually drank the milk during story time, the children were directed to quietly place the cartons on the floor when they had finished. After the story, the children whose job it had been to pass out the milk, would collect the empty cartons. I became aware that there was an occasional stomping on a carton, or someone would smash a carton with his hand on his desk lid. As the weeks went on, there seemed to be much more mutilation of milk cartons, even though the children were frequently reminded of what was expected of them. Not only was the noise annoying, but usually a broken carton meant a messy desk top or floor or milk spilled on some child's clothing. So this behavior of stomping or squashing milk cartons was the one I wanted to modify — by eliminating it!

Method

For a three-week period, I refrained from giving any direction as to how to take care of the milk cartons, and unobtrusively counted how many cartons were crushed each morning. During the first week, the percent of the milk cartons that were mutilated varied from 15 to 80 percent, but the second week showed a little more consistency.

During a conference with the instructor, we discussed several possibilities for lessening this rate: (1) Taking away the gym period. However, this involved another teacher about half the time. (2) Lining the offending child or children up at the back of the line at dismissal time. Unfortunately, this would have interfered with an already established method of leaving the classroom. (3) Keeping the child five extra minutes at noon. This seemed the most feasible.

The next day, after the milk had been passed out, I told the children there was to be no crushing or mutilation of milk cartons. If anyone did crush his carton, I would write his name on the board and he would stay after school for five minutes.

Results and Discussion

The first day, one of that day's 13 milk drinkers finished drinking his milk, crushed the carton between his hands, and then immediately

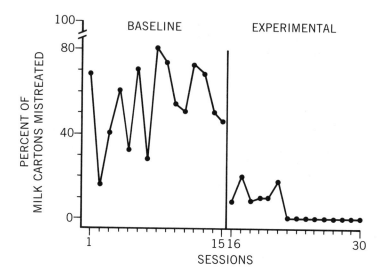

Fig. 5. Reduction in percent of milk cartons mistreated

tried to straighten the carton to its original shape. He stayed after school. The second day, I again reminded the children of the consequences for crushing cartons. Three out of fourteen crushed their cartons; they stayed after school. On the succeeding days, no reminders were given. The rate varied from zero to eighteen percent. Although it has been six weeks since this project ended, only two children have had to stay after school.

I was very pleased with the results of this behavior modification project. Participating in this work has shown me how important it is to identify the behavior one wants to modify. When one must count and calculate the rate of an identifiable behavior, I believe that one may be surprised to find that the behavior was really more or less in need of modification than previously had been thought.

SOME WAYS TO WORK WITH KINDERGARTEN CHILDREN
by Margaret Null, Kindergarten Teacher

Problem

Since I am working in Kindergarten, for many of my students this is their first experience in a classroom. As is to be expected, some children adapt to the situation with no difficulty while others find adjustment to the classroom very difficult. Though my study did not start until January, I still had some discipline problems that I had held to a minimum, but had not resolved.

For the most part, during play, milk time, and work at their tables, I expected the children to talk freely except when I call their attention to say something. But when we are sitting on the rug for instruction, I expect the children to be quiet and attentive for a reasonable period of time. I found that the children crowded together toward the front of the rug and that most of our problems occurred there.

Method

I began by sectioning off the rug into squares. The children could sit wherever they wished but were to stay within their own square. I found that this in itself solved several of my problems because each child had enough room and did not feel it necessary to push, shove, pinch, etc. I recorded the incidences of discipline problems occurring in each spot on the rug and found that there were no more discipline problems at the back or edges of the rug than at the front. I feel that this is valid because the children, of their own volition, rotated on the rug.

I then decided that I might try to work the rug squares into a game period. I used several ideas. I put colored papers on the squares and then had the children find the square that I named. I would say a number and have the children count to find their square. I put the children's name cards on the squares and they had to find the square that had their name card in it.

At the same time, I began working on some of my more serious discipline problems when the children were off the rug. I had always used a great deal of praise and edibles as rewards for good behavior, but I had also spent much of my time giving attention to those who were misbehaving. This attention might have functioned as a reinforcer for the misbehavior. I began ignoring the misbehavior as much as possible. Instead of a word to the child who was out of order, I would praise one of the children who was acting correctly. I found this method to be much more effective and permanent in behavior modification.

Results and Discussion

Both the methods I used to modify the crowding and shoving behavior on the rug, as well as the attempts to increase the amount of praise I gave for good behavior and decrease the amount of attention I gave for misbehavior, have had positive results. I feel that the experiment has been very successful and would recomment these sorts of procedures to any kindergarten teacher.

A TOKEN SYSTEM IN THE 3rd GRADE
by Lois Ostrowski, 3rd-Grade Teacher

Problem

I teach a class of 28 third graders, 16 boys and 12 girls. This group had had three teachers in the second grade, and the results were a group of very emotionally insecure children. My first concern was to give each child a secure relationship with me, confidence in their own ability, and a good self-concept. I wanted to establish positive behavior in as many children as possible.

The first area I set out to improve was the way the children came into the room. They would run around, fight, go to my desk, sharpen pencils, go out into the hall, and do anything but take their seats. I established a baseline measurement by counting those children who took their seats. At the beginning, only two or three sat down. I took data for five days. The number of children out of their seats was almost overwhelming.

Method

The children and I decided we had some work to do. We discussed how we could earn stars, which were used as tokens. Each time a child came in and sat down promptly, a star was placed on his card. As their behavior improved, we decided we could be rewarded for staying in our seats, working quietly, cooperating with special teachers, etc.

The star tokens were accumulated and traded for certain things. The price list was like this: 15 stars for a sucker, 15 stars for bubble gum, 150 stars for being taken out to lunch, 75 stars for a ride home, 10 stars to wash the blackboards. In addition, the children are always praised for good positive behavior.

Results and Discussion

In general, the results have been very good, only two children have not responded to our token and reward system. Both are very emotionally disturbed and need more help than I can give them in a short year. However, all the other children are responding very well. However, it is important to keep the situation very well structured so that they know exactly what they're supposed to do and what they will receive for it, or they seem to soon forget.

MEASURING AND SHAPING THE BEHAVIOR OF SUSAN
by Vonda Powell, Pre-1st-Grade Teacher

Problem

I chose to weaken a behavior consisting of loud outbursts by a six-year old girl in my class, Susan. Susan does not live with her parents, but was instead given to her present guardian by her mother. The foster mother worries about Susan's real mother coming to take her back. She admits to spoiling Susan and letting her have her own way most of the time. She is the only child in the home and is well-dressed and well cared for. Susan is of average intelligence.

When I started to measure Susan's behavior, she was blurting out of turn without regard to anyone else in the classroom. She once did this for a total of 45 times in a single day. I recorded this data on a golf counter obtained in my in-service training class, which I could simply wear on my wrist while teaching.

After five weeks of recording Susan's outbursts, I told her what I was doing. On this day I told her that if she could remain under 10 outbursts a day, she would receive a reward at the end of the day. I then fixed a box containing slips of paper with various rewards written on them, most of which Susan had suggested herself. At about 3:15 each day, if she had earned it, I let her draw out a slip and she could do whatever it said. These slips that were drawn out were then left out for the rest of the week so that she would not draw out the same ones over many times. Some of the rewarding activities consisted of "clean erasers," "wash boards," "have a candy bar," "go to the tape recorder," "take home some paper and old crayons," "be the teacher for ten minutes," "color in a coloring book," "paint alone at the easel," etc. However, if Susan did not stay under the maximum number of acceptable outbursts, she had to go to the back of the room to an isolated desk to do her work, and, of course would receive no reward that day.

An additional method that I used to record Susan's behavior was to mark an "X" on the board each time that I clicked the golf counter. This was done to enable Susan to see how many marks she was getting. After a week of recording in this manner, I let her have a paper taped on her desk that was marked off in squares, and she had to mark an "X" in each square if I put one on the board. She seemed to like this method and worked hard to keep from having to record any marks. The class was most interested in this recording too. They seemed to want to help Susan and never appeared to resent any extra attention she was receiving. Some even remarked about her quietness now.

Results and Discussion

The results of this project are depicted on the following graph. The first vertical line shows where Susan was first told about the new method. The second line indicates where the number of acceptable outbursts was reduced from ten to five. As the chart shows, she is doing very well and rarely has to go to the back of the room for exceeding her daily number.

I have been most pleased with the results of this experiment, and

A = BASELINE

B = EXPERIMENTAL I

C = EXPERIMENTAL II

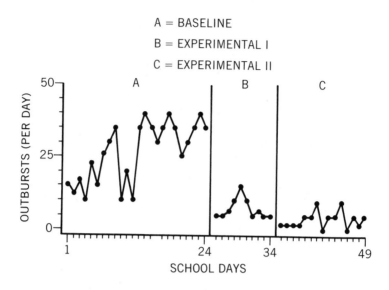

Fig. 6. The frequency of Susan's undesirable behavior in class

most of all, Susan is proud of herself. I am still using the reinforcers, but of course, do not know what will happen next year in another situation. I do know this year that our room is much more pleasant and the class is happier because of Susan's improved behavior. I feel that she has a much better self-concept because of the success of our attempt to modify her behavior, and this is most important. I would like to think there will be some carry-over the next year and that she will maintain some of the good behavior she has worked so hard to obtain.

HOW TO BEGIN A CLASS PROMPTLY
by Jill Stiltner, 2nd-Grade Teacher

Problem

The children in my class had some difficulty in settling down when they came into the classroom. Frequently many were still out of their seats when the last bell rang. I decided to attempt to change this situation by arranging things a little differently in the classroom.

Method

I began by simply counting the number of children not in their seats at the last bell both at the beginning of the morning and afternoon

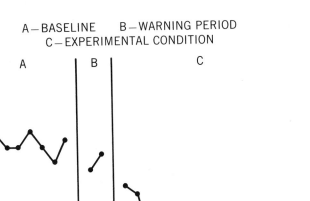

Fig. 7. The number of children who failed to be seated at the final bell for class

school sessions. In my class of 21, frequently as many as half of the children were not seated at the last bell. I kept this record without letting the children know that I was doing it for a total of eight days. On the ninth day, I told the children what I was doing and what would happen to them if they were not in their seats when the last bell rang. The punishment was that each child who was not in his seat would miss five minutes of Physical Education time. He would go to the Physical Education class but would have to remain standing at the back of the room for five minutes before he could enter into the games. I issued this warning both on the ninth and tenth day, with no appreciable effect on their behavior. On the eleventh day, the contingency went into effect.

Results and Discussion

As you can see by the graph, the number of children out of their seats at the last bell has decreased considerably. This has proven to be an effective way to lessen the confusion and increase the instruction time at the beginning of school.

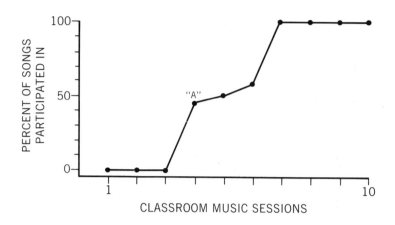

Fig. 8. The effect of social reinforcement on a girl's singing in a music class

REINFORCING A SHY GIRL'S SINGING
by Pat Sonneville, Music Educator

Problem

It has always been a problem with music educators to find a solution
to the shy child who is simply afraid and lacks the self-confidence to
sing. Discipline, in these cases, is not the answer. Punishing a shy
child for being shy simply puts him further into his shell.

I first noticed Nancy because she chose to sit in front of the piano
in our music class. When the class would sing, she would simply sit
there without attempting to participate. I would look at her and she
would quickly look away.

Method

I began recording Nancy's participation in the group singing, and for
the first two weeks there was no participation. At the conclusion of
these two weeks, I invited Nancy to come into the music room twice
a week after school along with a few other children who frequent
my room at this time to "just fool around." She came, and I let her
play the bell sets, the piano, and if she wanted to, she could sing
along with the rest of us.

During the first week of the after school meetings, she still did
not sing, and her class participation remained at zero. During the
second week, however, she did join in the singing after school. I
immediately praised her and told her that she had a nice singing
voice (which she did). This was done to reward or "reinforce" her
singing and thereby strengthen that behavior. At this point, her class

participation began to improve. We kept on with the after school get-togethers, and I kept up the constant praise for her singing.

Results and Discussion

Nancy's progress is recorded in the following graph. Point A indicates the day that Nancy first began to sing in class after I had reinforced her singing in the previous after-school session.

The week before the Spring Music Festival, Nancy worked hard on the songs. She even went so far as to take copies of the songs home so that she could practice on them. The day of the Festival, Nancy came up and told me how excited she was. From then on, Nancy has participated one hundred percent in our music activities.

IMPROVING MANNERS IN THE LIBRARY
by Sue Wilson, Education Resources Teacher

Problem

Children who take advantage of the Educational Resources Center often have undesirable methods of gaining my attention. This behavior frequently takes the form of tapping or tugging on my arm, interrupting other children, or saying "Get me this!" or "I want that." I decided to attempt to reinforce more desirable behaviors such as "excuse me," "please," or "thank you," or waiting in turn for my attention. I chose as a subject for this attempt a pre-1st-grade class with 18 children in it.

Method

Since I only saw the class once a week, for four weeks I recorded the frequency of what I considered to be desirable behavior. During these four sessions, only once did a child say "please." At the end of this period of time I talked with the children and told them that I would be looking for "good manners" and the "magic word." Both terms were familiar to the class. I did not mention that there would be any treat. This continued for two weeks. If an example of the desirable behavior had occurred during this period of time, as a reward or reinforcer, I would have given the child who made the response a treat. During the third week I told them that if I heard the magic word or saw good manners they would receive a treat.

Results and Discussion

As the graph demonstrates, there was a decided increase in the number of desirable behaviors. However, it did not represent a large increase in the overall frequency of these behaviors. Some of the

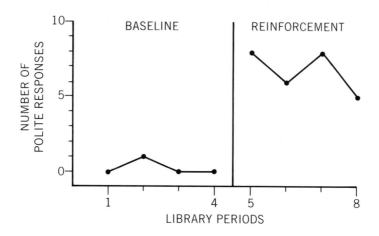

Fig. 9. The frequency of polite behaviors in a pre-1st-grade class

reasons why the change was not great are possibly (1) that there was too much time between the visits to the library, and (2) that there were too many uncontrolled factors, such as the choice of books might have been improving and, therefore, fewer children needed my attention. In addition, this was a very young class and the method might have been more successful had the children been a little older.

29

An In-Service Teacher Training Program in Contingency Management

Howard N. Sloane, Jr.
John E. Allen

University of Utah

Background

Current findings concerning learning and methods of applying laboratory findings concerning the learning process are very slow to find their way into the public school system (Skinner, 1954, 1968; Cohen, 1966, 1967). Many procedures have been attempted to remedy this, including university classes, workshops, lectures, and other similar approaches.

We have currently been operating an in-service training workshop designed to develop classroom behaviors in teachers based upon operant conditioning concepts. Our approach has been atypical, and consists of a series of written programs given one at a time to the teachers. Each is designed to help the teacher improve the behavior of a child in the classroom. The first is concerned with the child who frequently leaves his seat when it is inappropriate. Other programs are concerned with such things as children who do not complete work assignments or who do not attend to class presentations made by the teacher.

A teacher in the workshop tries all the programs, completing one before starting the next. The initial programs are extremely concrete and "cookbook," and do not rely upon technical terms or general concepts. As the units progress, communalities among programs are pointed out, technical terms are introduced, and more and

This paper was presented at the National Society for Programmed Instruction, 1968.

more demands are placed upon the teacher to design aspects of the program or to make decisions as to what should be done.

No lectures or academic exercises are included. Unlike most training attempts, which start with general concepts and proceed to specifics, this program starts with the specific and proceeds to the general. The teacher actually engages in the behavior referred to by a general idea or concept before discovering it is a general idea or concept.

Program One: To teach a child to remain in his seat

The original idea for this program was suggested by Montrose Wolf in a paper presented at AERA. In determining which program would be given to teachers first, we took the following factors into consideration:

1. We desired to start by modifying some behavior which teachers found aversive, regardless of our estimate of the seriousness of the behavior in question. This was to insure that the teachers would be reinforced for following the program if it was successful.
2. To insure success, we desired to start with a program which required very simple and unambiguous behavior from the teacher, which could be specified very simply.
3. We desired to start with a program which did not resemble too closely the procedures currently used by the teachers to modify the child behavior of concern.

Experience with teachers in the schools under consideration indicated that the teachers were quite upset by children who were out-of-seat during periods when they had been instructed otherwise. The major behaviors required of the teacher in following this program are setting a kitchen timer according to a chart, looking at a child when the bell rings, nodding at the child if he is sitting when the bell rings, and making a mark on a chart. These seemed to meet the requirements for simplicity and lack of ambiguity. The procedures typically used by most teachers to attempt modification of out-of-seat behavior can best be described as repeated instructions and reprimands; these were quite dissimilar from the behaviors required by the program. It was felt that these considerations would increase the probability that a teacher would successfully follow the program and modify the child-behavior under consideration, and it was also felt that the selection of teacher and child behaviors made it likely that the modification would reinforce the teacher for following the program.

Selected portions of the program follow.

Selection of Child for Project One

General

This project applied to children who frequently leave their seats or desks at times when they have been instructed not to do so.

Specifics

1. The child does not remain in his seat or desk at times when he has been instructed to stay seated.
2. The frequency of getting up and, perhaps, wandering around, is clearly much higher than that of most children in the class.
3. The child actually leaves his seat; he does not merely turn around in his seat, or remain in his seat while engaging in undesirable activities, sleeping, or other indications of inattentiveness. Actual physical absence from the seat or desk, with a frequency high enough to be a disturbance to the teacher or class, is required.

Do Not Consider

1. Diagnostic considerations of any sort, such as the fact that the child is said or assumed to be retarded, disturbed, brain injured, etc. Selection should not depend upon whether the child is, or is not, considered "normal" with reference to these diagnostic labels.
2. Assumptions or data concerning the development of the problem should not be considered. Even though you believe that certain specific events or circumstances did, or did not, lead to the development of the seat-leaving behavior, these factors should not be considered in selecting the child.
3. Do not consider factors which you feel may, or may not, maintain the behavior in selecting the child. Ignore considerations such as the possibility that the behavior is maintained by attention from other children, a physical problem, escape from work requirements which other children must meet, and so forth.

Summary

The child for this project should be selected on the basis of visible, objective seat-leaving behavior only.

Program to Teach Child to Stay in His Seat

This is a program to teach an elementary school child to stay in his seat. It is a remedial program, designed for the child who leaves his desk an inordinate number of times during the school day at times when he is supposed to remain seated.

Materials

1. Instructions. This sheet is the first page of the instructions.
2. Time interval sheets. These are the sheets with lists of time intervals on them. Their use will be explained later.
3. Child's graphs. These are the bar-like graphs. They are divided into sections. Their use will be explained later.
4. Timer.
5. List of possible reinforcers.

The individual school must provide the reinforcers. In addition to the materials included for the teacher, the Principal has also received a graph for record-keeping.

General Instructions

1. Read all the instructions before starting the program. Make sure you can identify all the materials and know how to use them before starting this program.
2. Collect all the possible reinforcers before starting the program.
3. If you have any questions, consult your Principal before starting the program.

Preparing the Reinforcers and the List

You will note the list of possible reinforcers. Attend only to the 5-minute average interval column at this point. We have suggested relative point values for different possible rewards. We have tentatively equated, for example, a 5¢ candy bar with 24 M&M's, and have suggested that being allowed to select the desk you will sit at (and thus your neighbors) is worth a little more than four times as much as a 5¢ candy bar. On a blank piece of paper, based upon your knowledge of this particular child, make a list of reinforcers which you feel might be attractive to him. You may talk this over with the child. You might remember to consider: (a) things he can eat, (b) small toys or trinkets, (c) comic books, (d) activities, such as favorite recess or physical education activity, leading an activity or game, and so forth, (e) social events, such as choosing own desk, being allowed a brief period (say 5 minutes) in which he may talk to some or all other students, (f) being allowed to choose a book for free reading or report, or a report topic, rather than having one assigned, (g) being allowed to leave school, class, or a specific activity a few minutes early (so many points per minute), and (h) being able to select a number of the previous items for the entire class, as well as for himself, or (i) other privileges. Possible reinforcers are limited only by your ingenuity and knowledge of the particular child.

On the separate sheet, list about 5–10 reinforcers you feel might be effective for this child. Assign point exchange values to them, using our sample as a guide. If, after a time, the points do not seem correct, or you wish to drop or add items from the list, just make the change. If the child comments, just tell him you decided that this will be "fairer." Such changes should be infrequent.

Make sure that you have these reinforcers available. Reinforcers must be delivered as soon as possible—candies and other physical items at the end of the day when the child adds up his points, other items as soon afterwards as possible, preferably the next morning.

Instructions Given to the Child

1. Give these instructions to the child whose behavior you wish to change on the first day of the program.
2. Tell the child that you are starting a game with him to help him learn to stay in his seat more by making staying in his seat more fun.
3. Tape one of the child's graphs which has a numeral "1" on the front to the left side of the child's desk top. See picture below.

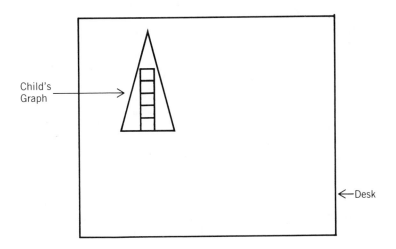

4. Tell the child that this is his chart. Tell him that he will get the number of points indicated by the number on his chart for each "x" he can fill in during the day. Tell him that you will ring a bell frequently during the day, and that each time he is sitting

down when the bell rings, you will let him fill in one more "x." Show him where to fill in his marks, one in each space. Explain to him to fill the bottom one in first, then the next, and so on. Tell him not to make any marks on the graph except when you tell him to do so, and that you are also keeping track of how many points he earns.

5. In the schematic sample drawn below, the child has earned the points indicated. This sample should *not* be shown to the child.

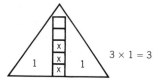
$3 \times 1 = 3$

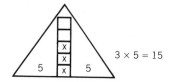
$3 \times 5 = 15$

6. Make sure the child is in his seat, and then ring the bell once by turning the timer dial past zero and then forcing it back to zero. Say, "You are in your seat and the bell just rang. Make one 'x' mark." Then guide the child to fill an "x" in the lowest space.

7. Tell the child that at the end of each day, you will see how many "x" marks he has earned. At this point, show him the list of reinforcers you have prepared, and describe to him how he can trade points for these reinforcers each day. Ask him if he has any ideas for additional reinforcers.

8. You may vary the wording of these instructions and answer any questions the child has. Do not add anything to or omit anything from the instructions. If you vary them, do it merely to make the presentation more natural and more clear to the particular child you are working with.

INSTRUCTIONS TO THE CLASS

After you have spoken to the individual child, speak to the class. Tell them that you have started a project to help _____ (child's name) learn to stay in his seat more. Tell them they can help you and _____ (child's name) by (a) ignoring the bell, (b) ignoring _____ (child's name) when he is supposed to be in his seat but is not, by not talking to him, answering him, or looking at him, and (c) by telling him how well he is doing as he gets better at staying in his seat.

STARTING THE PROGRAM

1. Start with a list of five minute average intervals. You should have already given the child and the class instructions, prepared the reinforcer list and gone over it with the child when you gave him instructions, and have the reinforcers available.

2. Place the time interval sheet on your desk, and also the timer. Look up the *first* interval, and set the timer for that time.

3. When the timer rings, immediately look at the child. If he is sitting in his seat, tell him to give himself an "x." On the time interval sheet, place a check mark in the first column to the right of the number to indicate that the child earned a point. If the child is not in his seat, say nothing to him, but place a cross on your record, rather than a check. Reset the timer for the *next* interval on the sheet.

4. Repeat the procedure for the next interval. After each interval, reset the timer for the following interval.

5. Ignore completely (do not look, comment, or frown) when the child is out of his seat. Praise him frequently, as much as you desire, when he is in his seat. You may praise other children if they ignore him when he is out of his seat or if they praise him as he improves.

6. Continue the procedure with the timer and time interval sheet at *all* times during the day when the child should be in his seat. Do not use it at other times. Make clear to the child that he *may* leave his seat at times when the class is allowed to do so.

7. At the end of the day, add up all the check marks you recorded. Add up the "x" marks the child has on his graph. Give the child his reinforcer based upon *his* check marks. He may accumulate credits toward a reinforcer over several days. If the "x" marks earned by the child do not agree within 2 points with yours, tell your Principal. He will come to your class to observe, and to see if you or the child is missing or adding points, and to help you straighten out this problem, unless you can easily correct it.

8. Record on the time interval sheet the date and the total points you have recorded on it. Your Principal will come to record this.

9. If the child has improved, praise him. If he has not, in a matter-of-fact way give him whatever he has earned, without comment on his poor performance.

10. Glue or tape the tip of the child's graph on the chart provided. Each day you will glue the child's charts on this paper, one day next to the previous day so that improvement can be noted just by glancing at this sheet. An example is drawn below. Show the child his improvements.

11. You will note that now, while you are on the shortest interval, the program requires you to attend to the child on the average of *once* every five minutes for a few seconds, plus about 5 minutes at the end of the day. This is the *most* time the program will require. As it progresses, it will require *less*.

12. Continue this procedure each day, using a new time interval sheet, until the child has three times as many checks on your

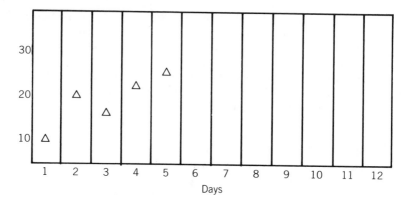

Days

record as crosses for three days in a row. Then switch to the ten-minute interval sheet.

13. Each time the child gets three times as many checks as crosses for three consecutive days, move to the next larger time interval. Each time (if at all) he gets three times as many crosses as checks, move down again to the next smaller time interval.

14. When your child is getting three times as many checks as crosses on the 60-minute interval, your Principal will give you the next program. This slowly fades out the aspects of the current program which are atypical of the classroom setting.

Time Interval Sheet
10 Minute Average

Each time the child is in his seat when the timer rings, place a check by the time. If he is not, place a cross by the time. On this schedule, he gets 3 points for each check he earns. For periods less than five minutes, turn the dial beyond five minutes to wind the spring, and then back to the time. For 30 second intervals, return pointer to halfway between 0 and 1 minute. More than one interval sheet may be used per day.

.30	11.00
12.00	.30
1.00	14.00
16.00	7.00
12.00	.30
12.00	15.00
10.00	15.00
5.00	13.00
16.00	2.00
11.00	16.00
6.00	5.00
9.00	4.00
10.00	11.00

CHILD'S GRAPHS

To Be Cut Out and Taped on Child's Desk

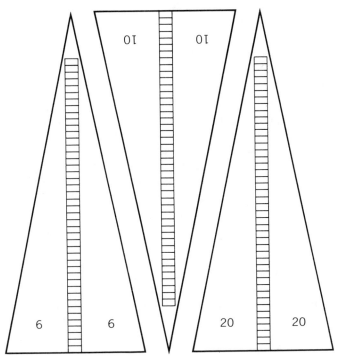

Program Two: Transition from Program One

Program Two was written as many teachers stated that although Program One was successful, success was contingent upon the use of unusual reinforcers and "mechanical" aids, and said that they doubted that the behavior could be maintained without these. In a series of steps this program (1) discontinued the use of the chart, (2) discontinued the use of the timer (3) made the reinforcement more intermittent, and (4) discontinued the use of atypical classroom reinforcers.

Program Three: Work Completion

In this program, the teacher modified the behavior of a child who did not complete his seatwork assignments. Our goals in designing this program were:

1. To train teachers to accurately assess the actual current performance of a child.
2. To train the teacher to reinforce successive approximations, starting with a child's current performance.

3. To train the teacher to use response—contingent praise, and other reinforcers typically available in the classroom.

Selected pages from this program follow:

Work Completion Program

SELECTION OF THE CHILD

This program is designed to help the child who does not complete the assignments given to him to do in class. It is not designed to help a teacher get children to complete "homework." A child should be selected who starts his class assignments, but never completes them. He may finish only a small percentage of the work, or he may complete the majority of an assignment. A follow-up program will indicate how to adapt this program to the child who does not start his work at all.

DIAGNOSIS

Before starting this program, a bit of diagnostic work is required. Some of this diagnosis is designed to evaluate the child in question; some is to evaluate the materials which will be used.

1. Variation in assignments. Children get many different kinds of assignments. For purposes of this program, the teacher should write down the different types of assignments given children in his class under the following categories:

    a. assignments which consist of a series of discrete units, such as arithmetic problems, where a set amount is to be completed each day.

    b. assignments which consist of a series of discrete units, such as arithmetic problems, but where the child is not given a specific number to do each day.

    c. assignments which do not consist of discrete units, but where the child is to complete a certain amount in a day. Examples might be to read certain material, or to draw a house.

    d. assignments which do not consist of discrete units, and where a specific task is not given each day.

    In addition, underline those assignments where the child is given a workbook or hand-out sheet on which the problems are printed. Do not underline assignments where the child is just given instructions or a list, as in "do problems 1-10 in the text" or "read the following pages: 1, 2, 3, 7, 8 . . ."

2. In this program, you will start by working with the child on only one type of material. Select as this first kind of assignment, if possible, one which is in category (a), and where each assignment has about the same number of problems or units.

3. For one week, continue using your usual procedures. However, each day collect this child's assignment and record the number of units or problems which he completed. Compute the average number completed per day for the week: i.e., Monday, 5; Tuesday, 6; Wednesday, 4; Thursday, 5; Friday, 2; Total for the week, 22 divided by 5 days gives an average of 4.4 units per day.

4. Go over the assignments the child has handed in for the week a second time. Make sure that he is not failing to complete the assignments because he lacks one or more specific academic skills. *If the child does not complete assignments because he lacks the academic skills, this program will not be of benefit.* If this is the case, the problem is due to a failure to adequately diagnose the child's educational status and/or a failure to prescribe the correct educational program for the child. Obviously, a child may be deficient in one or more circumscribed areas without assuming that these limited skill lacks account for his failure to complete assignments. However, if this is the case, these deficits should also be noted. Ideally, specific remedial attention should be given to these areas. Do not overlook the possibility that reading ability may account for difficulty in science, math, etc.

At this point, you have determined the kinds of assignments which will first be worked with, and have also evaluated the amount of each assignment which the child currently completes. You should also have identified any specific skill deficits which may create problems.

PREPARING MATERIALS

Each assignment which is to be given the child must be individually prepared in advance. However, this preparation requires only a few seconds. If the assignment is given in a workbook or hand-out (one you underlined), you must cross out items until those remaining are equal to the amount you have determined that the child usually completes. If you prefer, instead of crossing out these items, you can write the correct answers in the answer spaces for these items. If the assignment is one which you did not underline, just give the child a smaller assignment—one which contains the amount of work you found he typically completes; this may be as little as one part of a single problem.

In determining which items to omit from the child's assignment, either by crossing them out, completing them for him in advance, or leaving them off his assignment sheet, use the following guidelines:

1. Make sure you *do not omit* an item where either the specific data in the problem or answer, or the skill gained, is required to do some item you are not omitting.

2. *Do omit* those items which your diagnosis indicates the child lacks the skill to do. When your remedial program has corrected this deficit, you need no longer omit these problems.
3. As the goal is for the child to successfully complete assignments, *leave in* those items which you feel he is most likely to do.

The result of all this work, which in actuality takes a minute or two, should be an assignment each day which it is highly probable that the child will complete.

Reinforcement for Working and for Completion

1. Once you have given the child the assignment, do not continue to instruct him to work. Leave him entirely alone, unless he requests aid with some aspect he does not understand, *Do not give attention for not working.*
2. Instruct the child to let you know the minute he finishes his assignment. Make sure he does this by checking frequently in the first three days. The minute the child tells you he has completed his assignment, check to see if he has. Ignore correctness at this point; attend merely to completion. If he has finished, immediately praise the child for completing the work, and give him a choice of some enjoyable task, favored activity, or privilege in any time remaining of this assignment period. DO NOT ALLOW HIM TO DO MORE OF THE SAME TYPE OF WORK.

Increasing the Size of the Assignment

1. After the child has successfully completed the assignment five days in a row, or three days in a row during which he has spontaneously requested a longer assignment but has not received it, increase the assignment length by 25% or one unit, i.e., one math problem.
2. When the child meets the success criteria on the new and longer assignment for three days, again increase its length by 25%.
3. When the child meets these success criteria on this new and even longer assignment, increase the assignment length by 50%.
4. Each time the child meets the success criteria, increase the assignment by 50%. Continue this process until the child is finishing the same length assignment as others in his group or class.
5. For the first two 25% increases, round upward to the nearest problem or unit. For the 50% increases, round downwards to the nearest problem or unit.

6. If the child has three consecutive failures before reaching the point where he is up with the rest of the class, decrease the assignment to the previous length. If this occurs with the initial length assignments, reduce them by about one-third.

Starting Work on Other Assignments

When the child is doing at least half as large an assignment as the rest of his group or class, and at least double the number of units or problems he initially did in this program, you may start the same program for other assignments given him. If you like, you may start the program for all other assignments at the same time, or you may start gradually, adding one or more as you see fit. Samples of how to break up various kinds of assignments into units are attached.

Record and Graphs

On a sheet of paper you should keep track of each kind of assignment given the child as part of this program, the number of problems or units in each assignment, and the number of problems or units completed. For *each* kind of assignment you should keep a daily cumulative graph of success or failure. A sample is attached. You should also write in the space provided the type of assignment; and in the spaces provided for each day, indicate how many units or problems were in the assignment. Also indicate what per cent of the regular class assignment this represents. Each Friday give your principal a carbon copy or photocopy of this graph. The principal will check this and return it to us.

Program Termination

When the child finishes this program, he should be completing the majority of his assignments regularly. At this point your only special task will be praising him when he finishes and letting him use any remaining assignment time for some preferred activity. We suggest you continue this procedure indefinitely, not only with this student, but with all students, as a way of reinforcing work completion.

Programs Four and Five: Developing Verbal Responding and Attending Behavior

These programs were designed with the following objectives in mind:
1. To further reinforce the behaviors taught in the previous papers.
2. To develop appropriate prompting behavior in teachers.
3. To teach teachers to intermittently provide opportunities to respond to all students in a class.
4. To introduce to teachers some technical terminology.

5. To superficially expose teachers to the behavioral analysis of complex chains. It is hoped that future programs will further develop such behavior analysis repertoires in the teachers.

Selected parts of these two programs follow:

Program to Develop Acceptable Verbal Responding

PURPOSE

The first purpose of this program is to bring a child, who is not verbally responding at an adequate level in the classroom, under the control of the teacher, and to increase the frequency of his verbal responses to the teacher to a level equal to the average level of the class.

A second purpose is to demonstrate to the teacher that he can maintain desired levels of verbal responding without the use of reinforcers other than his own attention and praise.

An additional objective is to demonstrate that the teacher can work on a single specific child in his class while he is at the same time working in content areas with the entire class.

IDENTIFICATION OF THE CHILD

The type of child with whom to use this program does not have a speech handicap. He may or may not talk with his peers. He behaves in one or more of the following ways.
  a. He answers questions, but the answers are not related to the question.
  b. He does not answer questions with more than one word.
  c. He makes no verbal response to the teacher nor does he initiate verbal interaction.
  d. He responds to the teacher with sound not identifiable as words.

This program is not designed to get a child to learn new material, but simply to get a child to respond to the teacher when called upon to recite information already learned. This program is not to be used with a child who has a severe speech handicap.

INFORMATION NEEDED BEFORE BEGINNING THIS PROGRAM

Before starting this program for three days you should record the number of words contained in a typical response. This is to determine what level (in terms of quantity) of responding you are now accepting from the class. Using the chart "Typical Response Rate for Class," make a check for each word in the appropriate box each time a child responds to a question from you. At the end of the three days take the three charts and total the frequency for each word count, and obtain the average number of words given in response to a question. This becomes the goal for the subject in this program.

The "Typical Response Rate Chart" may also be analyzed for classroom patterns. For example (1) Do all your children respond with one or two word answers? (2) Is there a relationship between the time of day and the length of response? (3) How frequently do you ask the children to respond?

PROGRAM

As a general procedure, the teacher should reinforce any appropriate responding (verbal or nonverbal) by the child. Use attention and statements such as "good," "Yes, you are right," "That is helpful," etc. Be especially on the lookout for nonverbal responses to reinforce for the child who is not making any verbal responses, for example; raising his hand, shaking his head, pointing, etc.

One problem with verbal statements such as "That is a good job" is that we often use a different statement or tone depending on the child and the quality of his response. An example of this is that when a bright child responds we say with enthusiasm, "excellent," but when a problem child responds we say "good." Children learn to discriminate such differences and the effect may be that the statement thought to be reinforcing is in fact punishing to the child. In light of this, when using a verbal statement as a reinforcer use it consistently for all children, based on progress toward a goal you have set for them individually.

Distribute to each child in the class a set of five cards with numbers on them. Each card will have a different number from one to five. To answer a question, a child may hold up one of the cards. For example: If the question may be answered by a "yes" or a "no," a child may hold up card number one for "yes" or card number two for "no." If the question is multiple choice in form a child may hold up a card indicating a number or letter for his choice. The teacher can then quickly survey the room to see how many children have the right answer, how many are wrong, and what the wrong choices are.

When the children hold up their cards be sure to note the target child and reinforce any appropriate response. Be sure to reinforce him even though he does no more than touch the appropriate card. You might say "Bobby, that is the right answer." On the second day if he is still not holding up his card then say "Yes, Bobby, that is right. Please hold your card up so that the others can check to see if they are right."

First Day of Program. Explain to the class how the cards work and then at least eight times at random intervals throughout the day ask the class to respond to questions. All questions must be ones that you are sure the child in the program can answer, thereby increasing the probability that he will respond. Do not ask the subject questions outside of this situation, i.e. without a card response. Be sure to reinforce all of the subject's responses on this and all subsequent days until the child is off the program. Do *not* reinforce him if he makes *no* response at all.

Second Day of Program. Continue to ask questions using the response cards. Ask eight questions spaced at random intervals on material which you are sure the subject knows. Continue to reinforce him for responding.

Third Day of Program. Continue as on the second day.

Be sure to reinforce any acceptable response.

After Three Days Start Choral Responding. As soon as the child has successfully made some response 75% of the time, for three consecutive days you should start asking the class to repeat orally the right answer after you have modeled it for them. For example, "What was the name of the boy in the story (1) Tom (2) Sam (3) Jack. The class, including the subject, holds up the correct card and you say, "Yes, the name of the boy in the story is Sam. Let's all say it together, Sam." Be sure to note the response of the subject. When he makes any verbal response whatsoever reinforce this, i.e., "Yes, you got it right and *said* it right." Do this even though his response was not clearly audible to you, if you did see some approximation to a response.

Continue asking eight questions per day.

Continue reinforcing the subject when he makes appropriate responses.

Continue this until the target child has been making choral responses for three consecutive days on at least 75% of the questions asked.

After Regular Choral Responding Start Sequenced Responses. On the day after the target child has met the criterion for choral responding, 6-8 times per day, ask the class for sequenced responses. Arrange this so that the target child will be asked to provide the last answer in the sequence, thereby allowing you to reinforce his response. Examples of sequences are counting, reading a list of words, saying their own names, naming colors, objects, events or sequences of instructions. In every case you must be sure that the answer is not difficult for the child in question, keeping in mind that you are working on responding, not on learning content.

The first time you start the sequence task have the whole class respond in unison to a sequence, i.e., naming the colors of objects while you point to them. Then go over the same sequence, having each child in a row name one color as you point. In one of these sequences have the target child make the last response. After each group finishes responding praise them. Go through this rapidly so the child in question does not have time to think about the fact that he will have to respond.

Continue this sequencing procedure until the target child responds correctly 5 times out of 6 in a single day. Continue to reinforce correct responses.

If on any two consecutive days he misses approximately ¾ of the time, drop back to the choral stage.

Alternating Responding. When the child has reached criterion for sequence responding begin calling for alternating responding. Now ask a set of questions which can be answered by either "yes" or "no." Ask the questions rapidly, including the subject in the third or fourth spot. Do this for two days. On the second day ask the questions at about half the speed of the first day. Ask 6 to 8 questions each day. On the second day include the subject in the second or first spot. An example of these questions would be: "Is this a bird?" showing a picture of a bird. "Is this a car?" showing a picture of an airplane. When the child has successfully responded to the yes-no questions for two consecutive days proceed to the next stage.

Single Word Responses from Subject. By now you should be able to obtain individual responses from the child. Ask two questions of other class members and then a single direct question of the subject, calling for a response you know he is able to make, preferably one which he has made earlier in this program. You may ask him for a response whose answer you have just given. For example, after describing a picture you can then ask what the picture is about.

From this point on ask the subject for at least 6 responses each day. These may include any interaction which requires a verbal response from the child. You should accept a one-word response and reinforce this.

When the child is responding correctly more than approximately 75% of the time for three days, move to the next stage.

Expanding the Responses. From this point on the criterion for success will still be approximately 75% or better for three consecutive days at each unit of expansion.

Now the child is responding regularly with at least one word statements. After each response (at least 6 per day) ask for an additional response. For example "John, what do we mean by the word container?" He says, "holds things." "Please name one container." He says, "bottle." "That is very good, John." Another example: "What do you see in this picture?" He says, "A boy." "Tell me something about him." He says, "He has a red shirt." Reinforce after the second response, but *not* after the first.

As he responds with more than one word answers to your first question for three days ask him one more additional question or for expansion of his first comments until in three day steps he is responding at a rate similar to the average for the class.

Developing Class Attending Behavior
(Takes approximately 6 weeks)

PURPOSE

1. The first purpose of this program is to help the teacher develop good attending behaviors in students.
2. The second purpose of this program is to help teachers see the similarities or common concepts which are part of all the programs.
3. The third purpose of this program is to reinforce teachers for sticking with the procedures by exposing the teacher to the differential consequences, in terms of children's behavior, of different teacher behaviors. This program hopes to demonstrate that the behavior of the teacher controls the behavior of the children.

DEFINITION OF TARGET CHILDREN'S BEHAVIORS

This program is concerned with the behavior of each child during periods when the teacher is presenting material, either verbally, on the board, or through some other medium to the children in a group situation. By "attending" is meant children's looking and listening to the teacher presentation, children's *not* engaging in competing behaviors during the teacher presentation, and the children's performance in making responses based upon the teacher presentation.

RATIONALE

Why should a child attend to teacher presentations? That is, what factors are there which can maintain attending, and in whose absence attending will not be maintained? If a child listens to what the teacher says, what consequences happen as a function of listening? Very simply, if the child listens, he hears what the teacher said. Is this, all by itself, reinforcing and likely to maintain the behavior of listening? Probably not. How can it be made reinforcing? Suppose the child is given some opportunity to respond, either right after the teacher presents some information, or at some later time. Assume further that the child can only respond *correctly* if he has heard the material presented by the teacher. Further assume that the teacher reinforces the child in some manner for correct, but not for incorrect, responses. Now we have a complex chain of events which may maintain attending.

Attend—hear material—make correct response—teacher reinforces. Don't attend—don't hear material—make incorrect response —no reinforcement.

Note some of the things required here to maintain good attending:
1. If the child attends he hears or sees something.
2. Child is frequently given some opportunity to make responses —to answer questions, respond on quizzes or assignments, or in discussion.
3. Child is able to make correct response if he has heard or seen the teacher's presentation. For example, the material must not be "too difficult" so that a child cannot respond correctly even if he has attended.
4. The child is unable to respond correctly if he has not attended to the teacher's presentation. For example, if the child already is familiar with what the teacher is presenting, and can already answer the questions which may be asked, he does not have to attend to respond correctly and be reinforced. He thus may become "bored."
5. The teacher does reinforce correct responses, and not incorrect responses. Some teachers respond in the same manner to correct and incorrect responses. They may matter-of-factly go on to the next question or child regardless of the correctness of a child's response (no reinforcement for correct or incorrect answers) or they may give social reinforcement for correct *and* for incorrect responses, for example, "that's a good try."

PREPARATION

1. List all the students in the class, dividing them into 3 categories as follows:
   A. Good attenders—students who appear to attend to teacher presentations well, and who usually are able to answer questions or engage in discussion related to the presentation.
   B. Students intermediate between the first group (A) and the last group (C).
   C. Poor attenders—who do not appear to attend to teacher presentations and who usually are unable to answer questions or engage in discussion related to the presentation.

The assignment to categories should be checked informally for several days. Keep your list with you as you make presentations, and casually note if the assignments seem correct. Make changes as indicated. If the assignment is approximately correct no problems will arise. No serious errors will occur due to putting a child in the "wrong" categories.

2. When you feel that the assignments are essentially correct, get some white 3 x 5 cards. Each group will have their names listed on cards. Use a different color ink for each group to help you identify the kind of question you will ask.
   A. Write the name of each child in group A on *one* card.

B. Write the name of each child in group B on *two* cards.

C. Write the name of each child in group C on *three* cards.

The cards for each group should be written in a different color ink, that is, the child's membership in groups A, B, or C should be color-coded. For example if you had 10 good attenders, 7 intermediate and 11 poor attenders you would have a deck of 10 red ink cards with one card for each child in the good group, 14 blue ink cards — two each for the children in the intermediate group and 33 black ink cards, three for each child in the poor group or a total of 57 cards.

PROGRAM

1. Before a period during which you will make some presentation before all or part of the class, shuffle *all* your cards together. All the group A cards should be one color ink, the group B cards another color ink, and group C a third color ink. Each individual in group C should have his name on 3 separate cards, group B members should each have their name on two different cards, and members of group A should have their name on one card.

2. Before you make the presentation, tell the students that they should *not* volunteer answers to questions, but that you will call on the student you wish to answer a question. Ignore any volunteered responses.

3. As you make your presentation, periodically select the top card, and ask that student a question about the presentation. If he answers it correctly, praise him, place a + (plus) mark on his card, and place his card on the bottom of the pack. If he is incorrect, tell him so matter-of-factly and briefly (e.g. "NO, John"). Place a − (minus) mark on his card. Tell him the answer, make him repeat it, and place his card on the bottom of the pack.

4. Your questions should be frequent enough so that you call on each student *at least once* for every 45 minutes that you present.

5. Students in group A should be asked questions calling for information presented during any part of the day's activities.

6. Ask group B questions that come from the previous 3 minutes of material.

7. Students in group C should be asked very concrete simple questions. These questions should *not* relate to material you covered more than 60 seconds previously (and shorter in lower grades). The questions should not require that the student integrate material from your presentation with any other material. Many of the questions asked group C should be answerable merely by mimicking what you have just said, or written on the board. Examples are:

Today I am going to tell you a story about a piggy.
John, what is the story about?

Giraffes and elephants live in Africa.
John, name an animal that lives in Africa.

Decimals are like fractions in many ways.
John, what are decimals like?

ALL GAUL IS DIVIDED INTO THREE PARTS (written on board).
John, how many parts was Gaul divided into?

The goal with group C is to ask a question which the child cannot help but get correct, so you can reinforce him for attending.

8. At the end of each day transfer all the pluses and minuses for groups B and C onto one of the cards for the child, crossing out the other marks, so all the child's marks will be on one of his cards. Write the marks in order so you can tell which are most recent. Then reshuffle.
9. Keep track of the total time spent in presenting each day. This is called the "time."
10. If a child is absent record this on his card.

RECORDS

1. At the end of each day, on the data sheet record how many children were present in each group. From the cards add up the number of questions you asked each group, and the number which were scored "plus." Record these on the data sheet, and compute the "% correct" for each group. Then add up the total questions asked all three groups, and record this, along with the total presentation time at the bottom of the data sheet.
2. The above data sheet will be used to make the daily graph. Each day, on the daily graph record the date, total presentation time, and number of questions asked at the bottom. Then graph the percent correct for each of the groups.
3. Your principal will examine the graph weekly. From the relationship betwen the total questions asked and the total presentation time he will obtain one major indication of how well the program is going.

CHANGING CHILDREN FROM ONE GROUP TO ANOTHER

When a child in group B or group C has gotten a plus on 8 out of the most recent 10 questions asked him, move him to the next group. This means you must do the following:
a. eliminate one of his cards from the deck and check remaining cards in appropriate color ink

b. indicate on the data sheet and graph that he has been changed
c. change the count of how many are in each group
If a child in a group misses half of the most recent 10 questions asked him, move him down a group by adding one card to the deck. Make the necessary changes as when moving a child up.

Demonstrations

One of the original purposes of this program, described on the first page, was to demonstrate to teachers the role which their behavior plays in determining the behavior of the children. The following procedures should be tried starting at any point after the program has been in effect for two weeks.

1. For two days do not ask any questions but give presentations as usual. Then resume the procedure and note the "% plus" scores for each group for the first presentation after this. Before going on to the next step, spend at least two days on the attending program.
2. For three days give presentations as usual. However, regardless of the quality of the answer given by a child, make no remark but continue your presentation. After a correct response just start presenting again; after an incorrect response you may start presenting again, or ask a second child the question without commenting on the first child's response. Resume the program for two days before going on to the next step.
3. For three days praise every child who responds, regardless of the quality of his answer. You need not untruthfully claim that an incorrect answer is correct. For all responses, though, you can thank the child for answering, or something similar. Then resume the program for two days.
4. For three days, only call on children in group A. Then resume the program, and note the percent correct for groups B and C after this.
5. Resume the regular program.

Your graphs and data sheets should indicate the periods during which you are trying these special demonstrations.

Program Termination

We would suggest that you maintain essentially the same procedure as you did during the program during presentations after you complete the program. Stay on the program until all children are in group B, and most in group A. If a few children do not progress, consult your principal as to the cause. Consider as possibilities factors such as a vision or hearing problem, gross misplacement of the child as far as ability or academic skills, or the possibility that the social responses you have made to the child's answers are not reinforcing. If you suspect the latter you might attempt the program with this child using some other reinforcer.

After program termination, if most children are in group A or B, you can probably discontinue using cards and still maintain approximately the same approach. It is probably worthwhile for any teacher to occasionally check to see that all children are frequently being given an opportunity to respond, and are reinforced for appropriate responding.

Although this program used answering questions as the pupil response, the same principles would hold for written responses or for discussion based upon presentations.

FUTURE PLANS

1. Additional programs will be developed aimed at giving teachers the skills necessary to design procedures for novel situations.
2. An evaluation of the programs will be made which stress assessment of changes in teacher behavior, and the success of the teachers in changing pupil behavior.

PROGRAMING EDUCATIONAL SEQUENCES

Part III. *Programing Educational Sequences*

The most important payoff for education from the growing knowledge of behavior theory is the ability to teach children more usable knowledge more efficiently. Educational researchers are currently designing and testing hundreds of possible new procedures. Several volumes could be devoted to describing them.

The selections presented in this final section detail concepts and procedures that offer a basis for a complete revamping of educational programs at all levels. In the opening paper, a behavioral concept of a concept is discussed, as well as Engelmann's contribution to the experimental work on concept teaching. This analysis is then extended to the building of response systems (operations) that generate new responses under specifiable conditions. The analysis has clear implications for how to make children smarter. In the next paper, Baer, Peterson, and Sherman show how to go about building the important operation called *generalized imitation*. After a certain amount of training on specific tasks, imitation occurs on first presentation of new tasks. The procedures used in this training have important implications for the teaching of concepts and operations that can be generalized. Lovaas provides another illustration of how to teach children to imitate.

The papers by Engelmann describe programing sequences and strategies that have been especially effective in teaching children who often fail when typical methods are used. It would seem that procedures that work for hard-to-teach children ought to be effective with all children.

The final three papers illustrate instructional systems based on technologies of teaching: linear programing for self-instruction; individually prescribed instruction; and a self-paced, unit-progress approach to the teaching of college courses. It is very likely that before too long, all texts other than programed texts will be outdated.

30

Teaching Concepts and Operations, or How to Make Kids Smart

Wesley C. Becker
University of Oregon

In the first Banff International Conference on Behavior Modification, Dr. Richard Stuart, who is back again this year, presented a pointed and scholarly analysis of a host of current problems in the field of mental health. (Stuart, 1969). His analysis of the role of poverty in "mental illness" pointed at deficiencies in basic life resources and in education as providing the clearest account of the development of behavior patterns that are rejected and punished by the middle-class establishment.

A corrective approach to such problems is to provide the basic necessities to all in one way or another and to change the educational institutions in directions that insure that all children, not just the privileged, learn or are taught. Dr. Stuart suggested the possible value of using TV to teach young children. *Sesame Street* is a current experiment in this direction, which has at least turned on a lot of adults. Dr. Stuart also suggested Community Centers for teaching parents basic literacy and to provide for other needs. But primarily,

Adapted from Becker, Engelmann, and Thomas, *Teaching: A Course in Applied Psychology*. Palo Alto, Calif.: Science Research Associates, 1971. No part of this paper may be reproduced without permission of the authors and publisher. This paper was first presented at the Banff International Conference on Behavior Modification, Alberta, Canada, May 1970. My thanks to Jim Sherman and Dick Stuart for their helpful critiques of earlier drafts of this paper.

Stuart emphasized, and I must agree, that the major change has to occur in schools themselves. Schools historically designed for the advantaged have been adapted for the poor by adding the various special remedial programs after the children have already failed. In many cases not even special remedial programs are available. It is no secret that many remedial programs do little more than classify children as being retarded, emotionally disturbed, or socially maladjusted, or having a learning disability. Nor is it a secret that more often than not the label given a child leads to a self-fulfilling prophecy. The "stupid" child is presumed to learn at a "slower rate." Thus, less is required of him. He is taught at a slower rate and the early prediction of retardation is confirmed. The emotionally disturbed child is presumed not to be able to learn until his emotional disturbances are treated. Too often he too is prepared by the school to fail in mainstream society. Socially maladjusted children are placed in groups with a special teacher, and, whether they are raising hell or not, are often given understanding and kindness as long as the teacher can take it, but are not taught the basic skills in language concepts and reading needed to get back into an ordinary classroom. The "learning disability" child is often found to function delightfully in a one-to-one situation with his special teacher, but still fails to perform in the classroom. Current remedial programs make it possible for nearly all *teaching failures* to be blamed on the child and for nearly all of these children to be shipped out of the classroom.

For those who see education as playing a major role in breaking the poverty cycle, Stuart correctly identifies two major changes required in current educational practices. The first is to provide more effective instruction; the second is the massive use of positive reinforcers to motivate children to behave and learn in school. I wholeheartedly agree, although the better the instruction, the less the need for unusual reinforcers. A third approach is to begin to teach children of the poor earlier.

During the past two years Siegfried Engelmann and I and a very valuable staff have been working with some five thousand poor children in eighteen parts of the United States under a program called Follow Through. This is a sequel to Head Start. We have also been teaching children labeled "educable retarded" by the public schools. Our uniform experience is that these children can be taught readily when effective reinforcers and teaching strategies are utilized. We see no reason why the mass of special labels and classes for problem children are needed except for those with very obvious impairments in vision, hearing, and motor functioning.

While it is too early to present final data, the Follow Through program is probably the most significant experiment in educational change ever attempted, and therefore merits mention in my introductory remarks. Follow Through uses funds from Title II of the Economic Opportunity Act and is administered by the Office of Education.

Engelmann and I are among fifteen to twenty sponsors selected to provide experimental programs to school districts with high percentages of children of the poor. Based on Engelmann's work with Bereiter (Bereiter and Engelmann, 1966) in teaching the disadvantaged, and our own work in using behavior modification to motivate and teach disadvantaged children (Becker, Thomas, Carnine, 1969), we teamed together to structure a Kindergarten-through-third-grade program for poor children. The program has the following key features:

1. Classroom structure:	One teacher and two aides for each 25 children. (Aides from the parent group where possible.) Small group instruction in groups of 3 to 8. Academic goals given priority, but not exclusively.
2. Teaching formats:	Daily programed lessons for direct instruction in language concepts, reading, and arithmetic by teachers and aides using prepared materials.[1] Science and social science added at level 2. Art and music designed to reinforce language program. Daily "take home" sheets of skills learned in each area with instructions for parents.
3. Continuous monitoring:	Progress of the children is monitored by testing (on the tasks taught) each month, by weekly reports of teaching, and by video tapes. Progress of the teachers and aides are monitored by video tape and consultants who supervise in-service training.
4. Parent involvement:	Parents are provided with instructions on classroom teaching methods. Parents are provided with daily lessons to practice at home with their children. A course in child management based on behavior modification procedures is available to most parents.[2] Parents are hired as testers, aides, and video clerks.

----

1. Science Research Associates is publishing these materials under the trade name Distar[TM].

2. Wesley C. Becker, *Parents Are Teachers. A Child Management Program* (Champaign, Ill.: Research Press, 1971).

The key assumptions underlying the program are that children learn if they are taught, and that the only way to help disadvantaged children catch up is to teach them at a faster than normal rate, *and to continue to do so.*

To insure that children are taught at a faster than normal rate it is first necessary to have more manpower in the classroom. Aides are used because of cost considerations and because parents who have become teacher aides are likely to be better parents. The added manpower is needed because, if children cannot read well, they can be taught best by a person who can talk to them. By using daily lessons that program the teachers' and aides' behavior (about 30 minutes a day for each subject for each child), aides and teachers can be taught to start teaching our way with a week's pre-service training. Continuing in-service training for about 2 hours a week is also required. The use of well-programed materials makes it not only possible to use paraprofessionals, but also makes the teacher's use of her time more efficient. She is provided with programing sequences that work. She is taught how to *get* and *hold* attention (looking and listening), how to correct, and how to reinforce. The programed materials help her to teach more in less time. The children proceed at a faster than normal rate. Efficiency is achieved in the moment-by-moment teacher-child interactions that constitute teaching. Engelmann, Thomas, and I have detailed a theory of teaching that encompasses behavior modification and spells out the details involved in efficient teaching interactions.[3]

However, in my opinion, the most important aspect of what we are doing involves the programing strategies embedded in Engelmann's programs. During the past year I have attempted to determine what it is that Engelmann does better than other people and place his procedures within a general framework of behavior theory. It is my major task today to try to share with you some outcomes of this continuing analysis.

There are two focal points to this presentation. The first is a discussion of concepts and operations. The second is a discussion of some implications of Engelmann's viewpoint for programing.

Concepts

For many, the explanation of a concept presented here will seem simple and obvious. At least we hope that will be the case *after* the presentation.

We begin with an operational test for the teaching of a concept. Consider the following diagram:

---

3. In W. C. Becker, S. Englemann, and D. R. Thomas, *Teaching: A Course in Applied Psychology* (Palo Alto, Calif.: Science Research Associates, 1971).

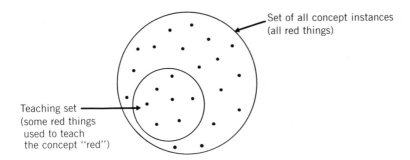

We have taught a concept when any or all members of the concept set are correctly identified (responded to), even though some were not in the teaching set. What is required to do this?

A Behavioral View

There is an area in the experimental analysis of behavior that provides some basis for specifying how stimulus events that precede a response can come to reliably control that response. The area is called *stimulus control of behavior* (control by preceding stimuli).

The basic paradigm is this:

a. In the presence of concept instances, reinforce one response consistently.

b. In the presence of not-instances, reinforce some other response or no response.

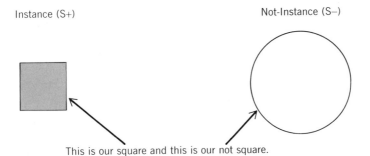

This is our square and this is our not square.

We present the square and circle many times until the child always responds one way to the square and another way to the circle.

Have we taught a concept? How can we tell? We can't look inside the head, so we must present some other stimuli and see how the organism responds.

Some tests: New members of the class and not-class are presented.

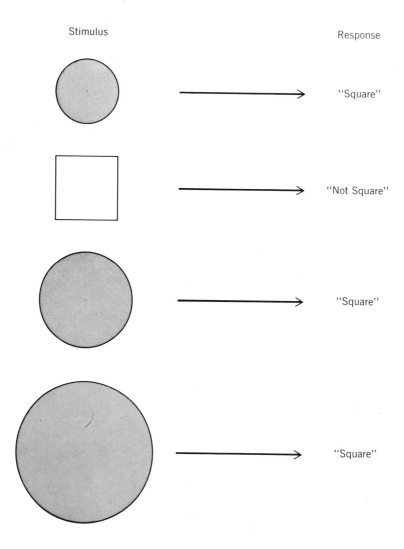

Stimulus   Response

⟶   "Square"

⟶   "Not Square"

⟶   "Square"

⟶   "Square"

We appear to have taught a brightness discrimination. We thought we were teaching squareness, but the child *could* respond correctly on the basis of size, brightness, *or* shape, and he responded to color. The teaching has to insure responding to critical concept characteristics. Let's correct that.

We make S+ and S− so that they differ only in shape. We again train until there is consistent response to S+ and not to S−. Have we taught a concept? Let's test:

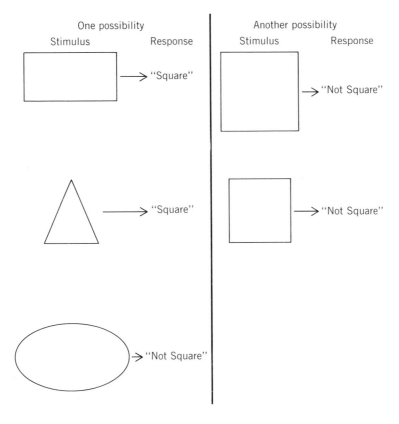

In the first case, the child learned a rule about corners, but not about equal 90-degree corners and equal length sides.

The second case was puzzling, so we asked the child what he was doing. He was responding to a smudge on the corner of the display square that wasn't on the display circle. The new squares did not have these cues.

Implication: To teach a concept it is necessary to insure that responding is controlled *only* by the *essential characteristics* of the concept. How do we do this?

1. It is not possible to teach a concept through one instance and one not-instance. A set of instances and not-instances is required.

2. The set should be constructed so that all instances share all essential concept characteristics, and not-instances possess none of or only some of these characteristics.

3. Within the set of instances or not-instances, it is necessary to vary stimulus characteristics that are not essential to instances or not-instances.

Concept learning involves a double discrimination: (1) the discrimination of relevant characteristics of instances (S+) from relevant characteristics of not-instances (S−); (2) the discrimination of relevant from irrelevant characteristics (Si) within instances or not-instances.

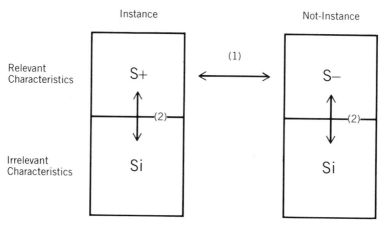

Note: S+, S−, and Si may be one characteristic or a set of characteristics.

Now what does all of this mean? Essentially it means, we *can not teach a concept without teaching the relevant characteristics of other concepts from which the given concept is to be discriminated.* In other words, we cannot teach red without teaching not-red by including orange, blue, violet, and so forth in the not-set. We do not have to teach the discrimination of orange from blue to teach red. We only have to teach the discrimination of red from not-red colors.

Furthermore, we cannot teach red without teaching that surface textures or patterns are not colors, that brightness differences or

differences in shape or size of objects do not matter when we talk
about red or any color. At some point in the teaching, *colors* as a set
of concepts, or *color* as a higher order concept, have to be discriminated from patterns, textures, size, shape, brightness differences,
materials, and positions. Even a concept as simple as red involves
the teaching of a lot of discriminations.

The above ideas can be gleaned from the literature on stimulus
control. However, in that literature

$$S+ = S^D \text{ (Discriminative Stimulus)}$$
$$S- = S^\Delta \text{ (S } - \text{ Delta)}$$
$$\text{Si is not labeled or is confused with } S^\Delta.$$

Also, the literature fails to explicitly recognize the double discrimination problem.

In my opinion Engelmann adds significantly to this view.

Engelmann's Definition of a Concept

In his book *Conceptual Learning*, Engelmann defines a concept as
*the set of characteristics shared by a set of instances in a given uni-
verse of concepts and not shared by other instances in that universe.*

Shared characteristics refer to physically definable stimulus properties. *Instances* are the basic units the teacher would have to present to give examples of the concept. The *universe of concepts* is the
set of concepts from which a given concept is to be discriminated.
The universe includes concepts whose characteristics can occur in
the same instance with concept under consideration, as well as concepts whose characteristics cannot occur in the same instance.

Engelmann's definition is procedural rather than functional. That
is, a concept is defined in terms of the operations or procedures
people would go through in identifying a concept in a given universe, rather than in terms of how stimulus events control the behavior of a person. From this approach, the first step is to determine
logically (using induction and deduction) which characteristics are
shared by a group of instances and *are not* shared by other instances
in a given universe. The procedure required to identify essential
concept characteristics is called *concept analysis*, or the logical analysis of concept characteristics. This approach should be familiar to
every behaviorist. He uses logical analysis to determine his experimental design and specify the procedures to be followed (what is to
be measured under what conditions). He uses functional definitions
in talking about the generalizations that can be induced from his
outcomes. In general, the experimental behaviorist, the teacher,
and the programer all use logical analysis of available information
and procedural definitions in *designing* new experiments or programs; they use functional definitions in *evaluating* the outcomes of
their efforts. The process of design requires the logical use of what
is known; the process of evaluation requires an openness to the

empirical facts to determine if the design was appropriate. Engelmann's definition of a concept is geared to the needs of the teacher or programer who must look at concepts from the point of view of what has to be done to design efficient teaching programs. These programs are still subject to empirical evaluation of adequacy, but with a proper use of known knowledge from the start we will more quickly develop good programs.

Let's look at some of the implications of Engelmann's definition. This definition is important because it leads the teacher and programer to look at *sets of concepts* and their structure in designing teaching strategies, rather than looking at *single concepts* one-by-one (as in the case of most other definitions of concept).

Engelmann's definition of a concept implies that a concept changes as the universe changes. Suppose we make up a universe that contains only dogs and horses. Our concept instances are dogs and the not-instances are horses. For S+ we note that dogs have *paws, small size, light weight, a bark,* and a *dog-like configuration.* For S— we note that the not-instances have *hoofs, large size, heavy weight, a whinney,* and a *horse-like configuration.* According to Engelmann's definition of a concept, we can change the concept of dog by changing the universe of concepts. For example, if we add mice to the universe, our concept of dog changes. Now *small size* and *light weight* are not characteristics that are shared only by all dogs (S+). If we add lions to the universe, our concept of dog changes again. Paws are no longer S+. If we include all known animals in the set of instances, our concept of dog would be quite different from the one obtained when the set of instances included only dogs and horses.

This definition of a concept allows the teacher or programer to specify the essential discriminations that must be taught to avoid confusing concept instances with not-instances. These discriminations can be determined by a logical analysis of concepts within a given universe. (If the universe is not explicitly defined, the discriminations to be taught have to be based on estimates by the teacher or programer as to what is most likely to be useful in an average child's environment. Logical analysis of essential characteristics is only possible within a defined universe of concepts.)

Concept Analysis of Squareness

We want to teach the concept of squareness within a universe of concepts that contains all *closed geometric figures* (circles, triangles, rectangles, and irregular closed figures, and so forth). All of the figures can vary in size, color, position, and texture.

Concept instances and not-instances have the following characteristics:

	INSTANCES (S+)	NOT-INSTANCES (S−)
Relevant in (S+ and S−) Characteristics	Closed geometric figures with: a. 90-degree angles, and b. equal sides, and c. straight sides.	Closed geometric figures with: a. any other angle, or b. unequal sides c. curved lines, or irregular lines
	S+ ← ＿＿＿ → S− Si	Si
Irrelevant (Si) Characteristics	size color position surface texture	size color position surface texture

To teach the concept of squareness in this universe it is necessary to teach the discrimination of S+ from S− characteristics, and S+ from Si characteristics. It is probably also important to teach the discrimination of S− from Si as a part of teaching the discrimination of S−.

To test whether or not we have taught the concept of squareness within the defined universe, we would use items like these:

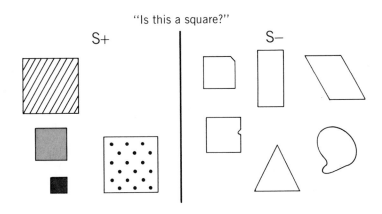

"Is this a square?"

S+   S−

Instead of trying to write programs adapted to each student's needs, it is possible to determine the essential discriminations that must be learned in a given universe to be sure a concept has been taught, and then program the teaching of those discriminations. If a child already knows some of the discriminations, the program simply functions as a test and the teacher moves on.

Engelmann's definition also calls attention to the fact that the teaching universe is a growing one. Initially, the programer does not have to be concerned with all possible discriminations, but just those concerning concepts already introduced. For example, in teaching sounds, we start with a universe of letters and their sounds. We select one letter (m) and a not-letter and start. "This is mmmmmm. This is not mmmmm." Then we add a second letter (a). A basic principle guides the selection of new sounds. We start with letters and sounds that are least similar to each other—that have the fewest common properties. If two letters (like m and n, or d and b) are very similar in shape or sound, the introduction of *one of them* is delayed as long as possible.

In deciding if two concepts are similar or not, we determine whether any properties are shared. For example, squares and rectangles are similar in that they are both closed figures that have four 90-degree angles and straight sides. Therefore, rectangles are more likely to be confused with squares than are circles. It is more important in teaching the concept "square" to be sure that the child is taught to discriminate rectangles from squares than circles from squares. This teaches an essential property of squares—namely, that squares have equal sides. Some concept differences are categorical, as above, and some concept differences are dimensional, as in the difference between the following a and d:

$$ \mathsf{d} \quad \mathsf{d} $$

These letters differ only in the height of the stem. When analysis reveals that two concepts differ only in very small ways, we know we have to do something to be sure the discrimination gets taught. The alternatives are: (1) we can focus directly on the difference in our program; or (2) we can exaggerate the difference by adding cues [for example, make the stem of the d especially long or make

the a this way (a); and the d this way (d)]. Once the most basic discriminations have been mastered, we can introduce the more conventional discrimination requirements without overburdening the child.

Concepts and Operations

I want to pursue next the implications of this definition of a concept for teaching and talking about response mechanisms. The definition of an operation we are going to introduce is directly related to the concept of a *generalized response class* introduced by Baer and Sherman (1964). Both terms refer to operant behavior that functions beyond the situation in which it was taught.

Concepts are essential *stimulus* characteristics shared by a set of instances and not shared by other instances in a given universe of concepts. *Operations* are the essential *response* characteristics shared by a set of responses in a given universe of operations. *Instances* are to a *concept* as *individual responses* are to an *operation.*

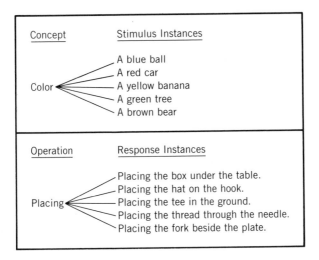

Just as concepts are ordered into hierarchies, so are operations. The following illustrate lower-order concepts and operations than those just presented.

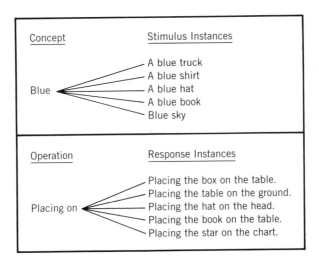

The following illustrate higher-order concepts and operations than those presented first.

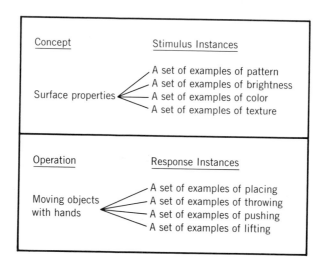

Concept　　　　　　　　Stimulus Instances

Surface properties
- A set of examples of pattern
- A set of examples of brightness
- A set of examples of color
- A set of examples of texture

Operation　　　　　　　Response Instances

Moving objects with hands
- A set of examples of placing
- A set of examples of throwing
- A set of examples of pushing
- A set of examples of lifting

Concepts are taught through a set of instances (a program) designed to teach the range of instances, the range of not-instances, and the range of irrelevant stimulus characteristics. One response is reinforced in the presence of instances and another response in the presence of not-instances. Similarly, operations are taught through a set of tasks designed to teach the essential characteristics of the operation, the essential characteristics of not-operations, and the irrelevant response characteristics. Correctly performed tasks are reinforced. Incorrectly performed tasks are not reinforced.

When we teach with properly designed sets of tasks, we have the basis for teaching both concepts and operations at the same time. For example, take the general task: *Move this object in relation to that object.* From this statement we can generate an endless series of tasks for teaching operations on objects, *or* concepts about operations on objects, *or* concepts about objects. For example:

Put the cup in the box.
Throw the ball at the desk.
Lift the dog up to the bed.

Usually, we would teach the object concepts prior to teaching the operations. If we require a child to perform many task responses on objects under conditions where the operations, the distance cues, the location of objects, and the objects themselves are varied, generalized response operations will be learned.

The significance of this analysis is that if we approach the teaching of operations as outlined above, we have the basis for building response systems that transcend our teaching. Task responses are instances of operations. If we teach a number of tasks for the same operation, there will come a point at which new tasks involving that operation are correctly responded to on first presentation. This means that the operation has been taught. This analysis directly parallels that for concepts. In concept teaching, we teach some instances in the concept set, and the rest are responded to correctly, if we have taught in the right way. In teaching operations, we teach some tasks involving that operation and the rest are responded to correctly on the test, if our teaching really teaches the operation.

It is important to discriminate between an operation and a concept about an operation. For example, when a child learns to plus (increase the members in a group), he is taught an operation. The teacher observing the behavior of a child who is plussing or not-plussing is observing instances or not-instances of the concept of plussing. What is an operation for the doer is concept for the observer. We have concepts of running and operations of running.

The paper by Baer, Peterson, and Sherman illustrated the process of teaching an operation called imitation, or looking at what someone else does and doing (approximately) the same thing.

Imitating, following instructions, paying attention, responding on signal, and working for periods of time (persistence) are operations that are very important to the teacher. When children do not respond to the concept signals controlling such operations with the appropriate operations, the operations have to be taught, if the children are to succeed in school activities.

Essentially I am postulating that operations are established by a procedure equivalent to that used to establish concept control over behavior.

In the case of concepts, the response is arbitrary.

Concept

A variety of stimulus instances sharing characteristics lead to ⟩ ⟶ one arbitrary R.

In the case of operations, the controlling concept stimulus is arbitrary.

Operation

One arbitrary S cues ⟶ { a variety of task responses sharing characteristics.

As in the case of the term *concept*, the term *operation* is defined procedurally rather than functionally. On the basis of a logical analysis of the responses to be taught, a set of procedures that will very likely lead to teaching a given operation in a given universe is specified. This is done without testing to see whether or not the operation has been taught by presenting new instances of the class. In the behavioral-analysis literature, a "response" or a "generalized response class" is defined by the fact that more behavior is controlled by a given set of cues than that specifically taught. A generalized response class is defined functionally in terms of *the effects* of certain training procedures on behavior. The difference in these two positions is more one of emphasis than anything else. When Baer and Sherman *plan* a set of procedures that they believe will produce a generalized response class, they are talking about the procedures for defining an operation. When Becker and Engelmann talk about *testing* for having taught an operation, they are talking about a test for a functional generalized response class. In each case, one set of procedures is used for designing or planning, and another in evaluating or testing. Design is procedural; evaluation is functional. There is no reason that the term operation (or generalized response class) cannot be used both procedurally and functionally. In fact, there may be very good reasons for doing so, as long as one is clear in communication.

Our preference for the term operation rather than generalized response class, or just *operant response,* arises from the communication difficulties we have encountered in using the terms generalized response class or response. People do not readily see that you are not dealing with a given response, but with what is common to a set of responses. The term operation more directly allows one to focus on those response characteristics shared by a set of responses. Also, use of the term operation may facilitate communication between Piagetians and behaviorists. We believe that the concept of an operation used by Piaget in his theory of development is entirely compatible with the one proposed here.

Habits and Operations

Concept teaching makes what is being taught relevant beyond the immediate classroom. Responses are tied not to specific stimulus instances as in simple discrimination training, but to essential concept characteristics that go across instances. The teaching of operations has the same kind of power. The response mechanisms are not restricted to specific task signals or to specific task responses. They are response mechanisms under the control of concepts that can be used in large sets of tasks. Furthermore, operations can be combined in an infinite number of new ways to produce new task responses. All that is required is that each operation going into a new combination be under the control of a separate signal. When we have established such control, we can teach all sorts of skills by instruction. We can teach driving, flying, golfing, writing, and so forth. When we say "Turn left," or "Lift your foot off the gas," these tasks can be executed even if they have never been performed before.

Our language behavior illustrates the ways in which we can combine operations (in this case words) into new statements. The constraints on the ways in which we can put words together into statements—that is, the rules of grammar—are cross-statement concepts controlling operations, such as "Say nouns before verbs in declarative statements," or "A plural noun requires a plural verb."

Contrast these flexible response systems with habits. Many things are done more efficiently if they are done the same way each time. We all learn a variety of habits about how we brush our teeth, where we put our keys, how we eat, and so forth. A response gets "grooved" and we do it the same way each time. The trouble with habits is that if the conditions change, current habits must be unlearned and new ones established.

Arithmetic

Let's take the habit or simple discrimination approach to teaching arithmetic. We have to teach number concepts, number names, and number symbols in some way. Now we are ready to teach addition facts. It is possible to teach addition as a series of specific problems of this form:

Stimulus		Response
$9 + 1$	$=$	10
$4 + 5$	$=$	9
$7 + 2$	$=$	9
$2 + 5$	$=$	7

We can have the children practice their addition facts (with sums up to 10) until they have learned all problems of this form. Then we can move up to higher numbers and practice some more. We are teaching habits. In the presence of a particular stimulus instance, a particular response should be made.

Alternatively, we could break the task down into a series of concepts and operations, as Engelmann does in Distar, and teach the general case so that the child could solve any of 40 problems (with sums up to 10) in the form $2 + 7 = \Box$.

1. We teach the child to count to a number. This is a rote chain.
2. We teach him to use this chain to count objects. Counting objects is an operation for determining how many are in a group.
3. Symbol identification is taught using concept teaching rules.
4. Given a numeral, the child is taught to make as many lines as the numeral stands for. This is also an operation.
5. The concepts of plus and equality are taught. Plussing is getting some more. Equality is a rule: "As many as we have on this side of the equal sign we have to have on the other side of the equal sign." The operation of counting is used to verify the equality rule.

Now when a child is presented with a problem like this

$$4 + 5 = \square$$

he can solve it by putting five lines under the 5, and counting "four — five, six, seven, eight, nine." He touches each line as he counts it.

6. A little later, the lines are dropped and fingers are used in the operation. "We have four and we plus five." (The children put out five fingers on the cue "and we plus five." Then they count, "Fouuurrr, five, six, seven, eight, nine," touching each of the five fingers as they count.

7. Still later the children are taught to count from a number to a number. They can now handle forty new problems like this:

$$4 + \square = 9$$

They just need to draw a line, or stick out a finger for each number they count after four until they get to nine, and they can produce the answer. With a slight variation on counting from a number to a number, they can also do forty problems of this form:

$$9 = 4 + \square$$

While this approach may take a little more time in building up the basic operations, the dividends are great, since the children can solve whole sets of new problems after going through just a few of them with the teacher. The basis has also been laid for solving algebraic equations. Note too that each example gives the child practice on the rote facts. At the end of each example he is trained to say the whole statement, "Four plus five equals nine."

Reading

Let's compare a hypothetical sight-reading program with the Distar reading-by-sound program. There is no doubt that we can teach a child to give responses to ten words faster than we can teach responses to ten symbols for sounds. It is easier to find words and word sounds that are markedly different from each other than it is to find ten letters and sounds that differ in many ways. However, by the time we have taught ten sounds and blending skills, we have the potential basis for reading-by-sound some 720 three-sound words, 4,320 four-sound words, and 21,600 five-sound words. Not all of these "words" would be real words, but the number of permutations of ten sounds is illustrated. By the time we have taught forty sounds, a basis has been established for reading a large percentage of the English language. Irregularities still need to be taught, but the child has skills with which to attack any new word. He has the basic operations for reading.

The strategy of teaching concepts and operations is a powerful one. Component operations are taught that can be *recombined* in any number of ways. In the Distar reading program, some of the operations taught are holding continuous sounds, switching to a new sound with no pause (sssssssssaaaaaaammmmmmmm), speeding up the sounds *(sam)*, and blending a stop sound *(t, p, b)* in with the next continuous sound *(taaaaaannnnnnn)*. Also, the child is taught to produce the sounds for any order of letters, even nonsense words. The combination of these operations is reading, for reading is a complex *operation* in which letters in space are converted to sounds in time.

It should be evident that Engelmann's view of concepts and operations leads to considerable power in programing, since it leads one to look for sets of concepts and operations that can be taught using a common format.

Problem-Solving Behavior

Problem-solving behavior involves the *operations* that can be used to solve sets of problem tasks. When a child is taught to read-by-sounds, he has been taught several problem-solving operations. The test for this teaching is the ability to solve problems that have not been taught. New combinations of the sounds that have been taught are read on first presentation. Similarly, to test whether we have taught the operation of adding two numbers with sums up to 10, we present number combinations that have not been taught to see whether the operation is correctly performed.

Problem-solving behavior involves using *operations* that have been taught, often in *new* combinations or orderings, to solve problems that have not been seen before. All that is required is that *each operation in a new combination be under the control of a separate signal* that is available in the new context.

Problem-solving behavior also involves applying *strategies* for analyzing the nature of a problem to help determine which operations in which sequence will produce a solution. Strategies are rules for systematizing behavior in the face of a problem. Strategies will vary with different types of problems. For strategies to be useful, it is necessary that the *classes of problems* requiring different strategies be specified, or that the child be trained to test out a series of strategies for a new problem until he finds one that works.

If children are given training in a variety of problems and their solutions, the solutions become instances for deriving general procedures for operating on classes of problems. It is at this point in the educational process that a case can be made for teaching that uses the "discovery method." In teaching operations for *finding out something the child does not know,* the discovery method offers the possibility of *programing* repeated instances of various strategies to teach problem-solving operations.

At present a comprehensive analysis of problem-solving strategies has not been made. We can currently only illustrate the directions such an analysis might take.

Consider the following concept identification task. The universe of possible concepts is restricted to groups of three geometric figures, each of which is a circle, triangle, or square. Concept instances and not-instances can vary in the type of figure found in any of the three positions. The problem is to find out, from as few instances as possible, what concept this is an example of:

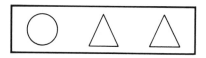

You are to select instances one at a time from the following test. After each selection, check the key below to find out if you have picked an instance or not-instance of this concept. Try to figure out the concept as you go along.

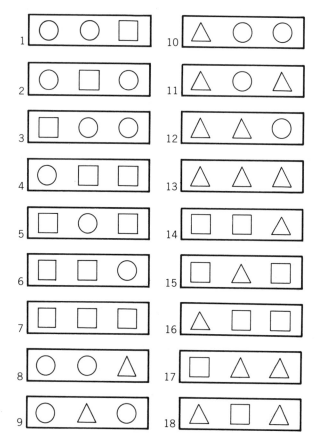

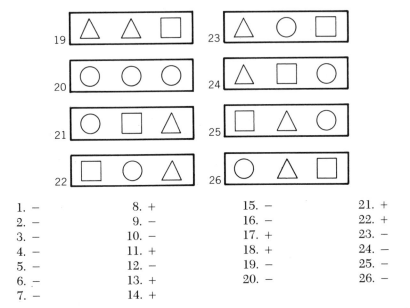

1. −	8. +	15. −	21. +
2. −	9. −	16. −	22. +
3. −	10. −	17. +	23. −
4. −	11. +	18. +	24. −
5. −	12. −	19. −	25. −
6. −	13. +	20. −	26. −
7. −	14. +		

The smart way to go about it is to select instances that change only one characteristic at a time (Bruner, Goodnow, and Austin, 1956). This will tell you what is essential to instances and not-instances. For example:

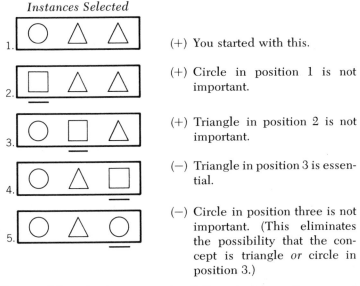

Instances Selected

1. (+) You started with this.

2. (+) Circle in position 1 is not important.

3. (+) Triangle in position 2 is not important.

4. (−) Triangle in position 3 is essential.

5. (−) Circle in position three is not important. (This eliminates the possibility that the concept is triangle *or* circle in position 3.)

Since nothing else is common to all three instances, the concept must be "triangle (only) in position three."

Note carefully the problem-solving strategy: change only one thing at a time to identify the critical elements and to eliminate alternatives systematically.

The principle involved in finding the solution to our concept-identification problem is the same as the one used in teaching concepts. To find out (or show) what is essential to some thing or process, change only one thing at a time. This same problem-solving strategy is the essence of the experimental method in science. To find out about causes, change one thing and check its effect, then change another, and so on.

We can teach this strategy by presenting a number of concept-identification problems and various solution strategies, and allowing the children (with guidance) to compare strategies to determine the essential features. The strategy can then be extended to new sets of related problems.

There are a number of such rules for solving problems that can be taught to children through the programed presentation of sets of problem tasks that require common solution operations. Becker, Engelmann, and Thomas (1969) discuss some of these possibilities.

Intelligent Behavior

Intelligent behavior involves various combinations of operations under the control of concepts. If we know how to teach concepts and operations, we know how to make people more intelligent. This is not to say that some people are not more readily taught than others, or that genetics makes no difference. It is quite evident that genetics exerts control over the development of organisms as they constantly interact with an environment. The point to be made is that intelligent behavior does not come with the baby; it is learned. It is the produce of *interactions* with an environment. If we as teachers know how to induce behavior that is considered intelligent, we know how to make people smarter than they were when they came to us.

Summary

We have attempted to illustrate some of the potential gains to be derived from placing Engelmann's view of concepts and operations into the framework of general behavior theory. Concepts and operations are seen to be induced by quite analogous teaching processes. The primary difference is that in teaching concepts we are concerned primarily with stimulus events. The response forms are not essential. In teaching operations we are concerned with response events. The form of the stimulus events controlling the operations are not essential. Concept teaching involves a double discrimination problem. Relevant characteristics of *instances* have to be discriminated from relevant characteristics of *not-instances*, and, within instances, *relevant* characteristics have to be discriminated from *irrelevant* characteristics. Restricting the definition of a concept to a given *teaching universe* leads to the specification of the discriminations that have to be taught by the teacher and programer. Finally, we have suggested that intelligent behavior is essentially comprised of concepts and operations. Since we know how to teach such behavior, we know how to make kids smart.

Nowhere in this report have we attempted to deal with the rules for specific teaching strategies. Instead, we have focused our efforts on key concepts and rationales underlying Engelmann's approach. To know *how* to make kids smart, it would also be important to explore in detail what Engelmann has to say about teaching interactions (Engelmann, 1969; Becker, Engelmann, and Thomas, 1971).

REFERENCES

Baer, D. M., and Sherman, J. A. Reinforcement control of generalized imitation in young children. *Journal of Experimental Child Psychology,* 1964, 1, 37–49.

Becker, W. C., Engelmann, S., and Thomas, D. R. *Teaching: A Course in Applied Psychology,* Palo Alto, Calif.: Science Research Associates, 1971.

Becker, W. C., Thomas, D. R., and Carnine, D. *Reducing Behavior Problems: An Operant Conditioning Guide for Teachers* (monograph). Urbana, Ill.: Educational Research Information Center (ERIC), 1969.

Bereiter, C., and Engelmann, S. *Teaching Disadvantaged Children in the Preschool.* Englewood Cliffs, N.J.: Prentice-Hall, 1966.

Engelmann, S., *Conceptual learning.* San Rafael, Calif.: Dimensions Publishing Co., 1969.

Stuart, Richard B., "Critical Reappraisal and Reformulation of Selected 'Mental Health' Programs," in L. A. Hamerlynck, P. O. Davidson, and L. E. Acker (eds.), *Behavior Modification and Ideal Mental Health Services.* Calgary, Alberta, Canada: Proceedings of the 1st Banff Conference on Behavior Modification, University of Calgary, 1969.

31

The Development of Imitation by Reinforcing Behavioral Similarity to a Model

Donald M. Baer, *University of Kansas*
Robert F. Peterson, *University of Illinois*
James A. Sherman, *University of Kansas*

This research demonstrated some of the conditions under which retarded children can be taught to imitate the actions of adults. Before the experiment, the subjects were without spontaneous imitative behavior, either vocal or motor. Each subject was taught, with food as reinforcement, a series of responses identical to responses demonstrated by an experimenter; *i.e.*, each response was reinforced only if it was identical to a prior demonstration by an experimenter. Initially, intensive shaping was required to establish matching responses by the subjects. In the course of acquiring a variety of such responses, the subjects' probability of immediate imitation of each new demonstration, before direct training, greatly increased. Later in the study, certain new imitations, even though perfect, were never rein-

From *Journal of the Experimental Analysis of Behavior,* 1967, **10**, 405–16.

A portion of this research was presented at the biennial meeting of the Society for Research in Child Development, Minneapolis, Minnesota, March, 1965. This research was supported by PHS grant MH-02208, National Institute of Mental Health, entitled An Experimental Analysis of Social Motivation. Mr. Frank Junkin, Superintendent, Dr. Ralph Hayden, Medical Director, and other members of the staff of the Fircrest School, Seattle, Washington, made space and subjects available. We wish to thank Mrs. Joan Beavers for her help as a "new" experimenter in the tests of generalization and for assistance in the preparation of this manuscript. Reprints may be obtained from Donald M. Baer, Department of Human Development, University of Kansas, Lawrence, Kansas 66044.

forced; yet as long as some imitative responses were reinforced, all remained at high strength. This imitativeness was then used to establish initial verbal repertoires in two subjects.

CONTENTS

The development of a class of behaviors which may fairly be called "imitation" is an interesting task, partly because of its relevance to the process of socialization in general and language development in particular, and partly because of its potential value as a training technique for children who require special methods of instruction. Imitation is not a specific set of behaviors that can be exhaustively listed. Any behavior may be considered imitative if it temporally follows behavior demonstrated by someone else, called a model, and if its topography is functionally controlled by the topography of the model's behavior. Specifically, this control is such that an observer will note a close similarity between the topography of the model's behavior and that of the imitator. Furthermore, this similarity to the model's behavior will be characteristic of the imitator in responding to a wide variety of the model's behaviors. Such control could result, for example, if topographical similarity to a model's behavior were a reinforcing stimulus dimension for the imitator.

There are, of course, other conditions which can produce similar behaviors from two organisms on the same occasion, or on similar occasions at different times. One possibility is that both organisms independently have been taught the same responses to the same cues; thus, all children recite the multiplication tables in very similar ways. This similarity does not deserve the label imitation, and hardly ever receives it; one child's recitation is not usually a cue to another's, and the similarity of their behavior is not usually a reinforcer for the children. Nevertheless, the children of this example have similar behaviors.

The fact that the world teaches many children similar lessons can lead to an arrangement of their behaviors which comes closer to a useful meaning of imitation. Two children may both have learned similar responses; one child, however, may respond at appropriate times whereas the other does not. In that case, the undiscriminating child may learn to use this response when the discriminating one does. The term imitation still need not be applied, since the similarity between the two children's responses is not functional for either of them; in particular, the second child is not affected by the fact that his behavior is similar to that of the first. This arrangement approaches one which Miller and Dollard (1941) call "matched-dependent" behavior. One organism responds to the behavior of another merely as a discriminative stimulus with respect to the timing of his own behavior; many times, these behaviors will happen to be alike, because both organisms will typically use the most efficient response, given enough experience.

It should be possible, however, to arrange the behavior of two organisms so that one of them will, in a variety of ways, produce precise topographical similarity to the other, but nothing else. A study by Baer and Sherman (1964) seemingly showed the result of such prior learning in several young children. In that study, reinforcements were arranged for children's imitations of three activities of an animated, talking puppet, which served both as a model and a source of social reinforcement for imitating. As a result of this reinforcement, a fourth response of the puppet was spontaneously imitated by the children, although that imitation had never before been reinforced. When reinforcement of the other three imitations was discontinued, the fourth, never-reinforced imitation also decreased in strength; when reinforcement of the original imitations was resumed, imitation of the fourth response again rose in rate, although it still was never reinforced. In short, these children apparently generalized along a stimulus dimension of similarity between their behaviors and the behaviors of a model: when similarity to the model in three different ways was reinforced, they thereupon displayed a fourth way of achieving similarity to the model. Thus, similarity between their behavior and the model's was a functional stimulus in their behavior.

Metz (1965) demonstrated the development of some imitative behavior in two autistic children who initially showed little or no imitative response. In this study, responses similar in topography to demonstrations by the experimenter were reinforced with "Good" and food. Metz found that, after intensive training, several imitative responses could be maintained in strength even when not reinforced with food, and that the subjects had a higher probability of imitating new responses after training than before. However, in one of the conditions used to evaluate the subjects' imitative repertoire before and after imitative training, "Good" was still said contingent upon correct new imitations. Thus, for one subject who initially showed a non-zero rate of imitation, it could be argued that the increased imitation in the test after training was due to an experimentally developed reinforcing property of "Good," rather than to the imitation training as such. Further, in the Metz study, due to a lack of extinction or other manipulation of the behavior, it is difficult to specify that the higher probability of imitating new responses, and the maintenance of unreinforced imitative responses, were in fact due to the reinforcement of the initial imitative responses during training.

Lovaas, Berberich, Perloff, and Schaeffer (1966) used shaping and fading procedures to establish imitative speech in two autistic children. They reported that as training progressed and more vocal behavior came under the control of a model's prior vocalization, it became progressively easier to obtain new imitative vocalizations. When reinforcement was shifted from an imitative-contingent schedule to a basically non-contingent schedule, imitative behavior deteriorated. In an additional manipulation, the model presented Norwegian words interspersed with English words for the children to imitate. Initially, the children did not reproduce the Norwegian words perfectly. However, the authors judged that the subjects gradually improved their imitations of the Norwegian words even though these imitations were not reinforced.

The studies by Baer and Sherman (1964), Metz (1965), Lovaas et al (1966), and other reports (Bandura, 1962) suggest that for children with truly imitative repertoires, induction has occurred, such that (1) relatively novel behaviors can be developed before direct shaping, merely by providing an appropriate demonstration by a model, and (2) some imitative responses can be maintained, although unreinforced, as long as other imitative responses are reinforced.

The purpose of the present study was to extend the generality of the above findings and to demonstrate a method of producing a truly imitative repertoire in children initially lacking one.

Method

Subjects

Three children, 9 to 12 years of age, were selected from several groups of severely and profoundly retarded children in a state school. They were chosen not because they were retarded, but because they seemed to be the only children available of a practical age who apparently showed no imitation whatsoever. (The success of the method to be described suggests that it may have considerable practical value for the training of such children.) The subjects were without language, but made occasional grunting vocalizations, and responded to a few simple verbal commands ("Come here," "Sit down," *etc.*). They were ambulatory (but typically had developed walking behavior relatively late in their development, in the sixth or seventh year), could dress themselves, were reasonably well toilet trained, and could feed themselves. Fair eye-hand coordination was evident, and simple manipulatory skills were present.

The subjects were chosen from groups of children initially observed in their wards from a distance over a period of several days. No instances of possible imitation were noted in the subjects finally selected. (That is, on no occasion did any subject display behavior similar to that of another person, except in instances where a common stimulus appeared to be controlling the behaviors of both persons, *e.g.*, both going to the dining area when food was displayed on the table.) Subsequently, an experimenter approached and engaged the subjects in extended play. In the course of this play, he would repeatedly ask them to imitate some simple response that he demonstrated, such as clapping his hands, or waving. The children failed to imitate any of these responses, although they clearly were capable of at least some of them. Finally, during the training itself, every sample of behavior was initially presented to the child as a demonstration accompanied by the command, "Do this"; at first, none of these samples was imitated, despite extensive repetition.

First Training Procedures

Each subject was seen at mealtimes, once or twice a day, three to five times a week. The subject's food was used as a reinforcer. It was delivered a spoonful at a time by the experimenter, who always said "Good" just before putting the spoon into the subject's mouth. The subject and experimenter faced each other across the corner of a small table, on which were placed the food tray and the experimenter's records. Elsewhere in the room was another small table on which were placed some materials used later in the study, a desk with a telephone on it, a coat rack holding one or more coats, a wastebasket, and a few other chairs.

The basic procedure was to teach such subject a series of discriminated operants. Each discriminated operant consisted of three elements: a discriminative stimulus (S^D) presented by the experimenter, a correct response by the subject, and reinforcement after a correct response. The S^D was the experimenter's command, "Do this," followed by his demonstration of some behavior. The response required was one similar to the experimenter's. Thus, the operant learned was always topographically imitative of the experimenter's demonstration. The reinforcement was food, preceded by the word "Good."

Since none of the subjects was imitative, none of the initial S^D's was followed by any behavior which resembled that demonstrated by the experimenter. This was true even for those behaviors which the subjects were clearly capable of performing. Subject 1, for example, would sit down when told to, but did not imitate the experimenter when he said "Do this," sat down, and then offered her the chair. Hence, the initial imitative training for all subjects was accomplished with a combination of shaping (Skinner, 1953) and fading (Terrace, 1963a, 1963b) or "putting through" procedures (Konorski and Miller, 1937).

The first response of the program for Subject 1 was to raise an arm after the experimenter had raised his. The subject was presented with a series of arm-raising demonstrations by the experimenter, each accompanied by "Do this," to which she made no response. The experimenter then repeated the demonstration, reached out, took the subject's hand and raised it for her, and then immediately reinforced her response. After several trials of this sort, the experimenter began gradually to fade out his assistance by raising the subject's arm only part way and shaping the completion of the response. Gradually, the experimenter's assistance was faded until the subject made an unassisted arm-raising response whenever the experimenter raised his arm. The initial responses for all subjects were taught in this manner whenever necessary.

Occasionally during the very early training periods a subject would resist being guided through a response. For example, with a response involving arm raising, Subject 3 at first pulled his arm downward whenever the experimenter attempted to raise it. In this case, the experimenter merely waited and tried again until the arm could be at least partially raised without great resistance; then the response was reinforced. After subjects had received a few reinforcements following the experimenter's assistance in performing a response, they no longer resisted. As the number of responses in the subjects' repertoire increased, the experimenter discontinued the guiding procedure and relied only on shaping procedures when a response did not match the demonstration.

A number of responses, each topographically similar to a demonstration by the experimenter, was taught to each subject. Training of most responses was continued until its demonstration was reliably matched by the subject. The purpose of these initial training procedures was to program reinforcement, in as many and diverse ways as practical, whenever a subject's behavior was topographically similar to that demonstrated by the experimenter.

Further Training Procedures

PROBES FOR IMITATION. As the initial training procedures progressed, and the subjects began to come under the control of the
experimenter's demonstrations, certain responses were demonstrated which, if imitated perfectly on their first presentation, were
deliberately not reinforced on the first or any future occasion. These
responses served as probes for the developing imitative nature of the
subject's repertoire. A list of the responses demonstrated, including
the reinforced ones for the initial training procedure and the unreinforced probe demonstrations, is given in Table 1 for Subject 1. These
responses are listed in the order of first demonstration. Subject 1
had 95 reinforced and 35 unreinforced responses. Similar responses
were used with Subjects 2 and 3. Subject 2 had 125 reinforced and
five unreinforced probes; Subject 3 had eight reinforced responses
and one unreinforced probe.

During the probes, the experimenter continued to present S^D's
for imitation. If the response demonstrated belonged to the group
of reinforced responses and the subject imitated within 10 sec, reinforcement ("Good" and food) was delivered and the next response
was demonstrated. If the subject did not imitate within 10 sec, no
reinforcement was delivered and the experimenter demonstrated
the next response. If it belonged to the unreinforced group of responses (probes), and if the subject imitated it, there were no programmed consequences and the experimenter demonstrated the
next response no sooner than 10 sec after the subject's imitation.
If it was not imitated, the experimenter performed the next demonstration 10 sec later. The purpose of the 10-sec delay was to minimize
the possibility that the subjects' unreinforced imitations were being
maintained by the possible reinforcing effects of the presentation
of an S^D for a to-be-reinforced imitative response. Demonstrations
for reinforced and unreinforced responses were presented to subjects in any unsystematic order.

NON-REINFORCEMENT OF ALL IMITATION. After the probe phase,
and after stable performances of reinforced and unreinforced imitative responses were established, non-reinforcement of all imitative
behavior was programmed. The purpose of this procedure was to
show the dependence of the imitative repertoire on the food reinforcement which was apparently responsible for its development.

Non-reinforcement of imitation was instituted in the form of reinforcement for any behavior other than imitation. Differential reinforcement of other behavior is abbreviated DRO (Reynolds, 1961).
The experimenter continued saying "Good" and feeding the subject, but not contingent on imitations. Instead, the experimenter
delivered reinforcement at least 20 sec after the subject's last imitation had taken place. Thus, for the group of previously reinforced
responses, the only change between reinforcement and non-rein-

TABLE 1

The Sequence of Responses Demonstrated to Subject 1

(*Asterisks indicate unreinforced responses.*)

1. Raise left arm	48. Put hat in chair
2. Tap table with left hand	49. Tap wall
3. Tap chest with left hand	50. Move waste basket
4. Tap head with left hand	51. Move paper from desk to table
5. Tap left knee with left hand	52. Stand in corner
6. Tap right knee with left hand	53. Pull window shade
7. Tap nose	54. Place box in chair
°8. Tap arm of chair	55. Walk around desk
9. Tap leg of table	56. Smile
10. Tap leg with left hand	57. Protrude tongue
11. Extend left arm	58. Put head on desk
°12. Make circular motion with arm	°59. Ring bell
13. Stand up	60. Nest two boxes
14. Both hands on ears	61. Crawl on floor
15. Flex arm	°62. Walk with arms above head
16. Nod yes	63. Sit on floor
17. Tap chair seat	64. Put arm behind back (standing)
18. Extend both arms	65. Walk with right arm held up
19. Put feet on chair	66. Throw box
20. Walk around	°67. Walk to telephone
21. Make vocal response	°68. Extend both arms (sitting)
22. Extend right arm sideways	69. Walk and tap head with
23. Tap shoulder	left hand
24. Tap head with right hand	70. Walk and tap head with
25. Tap right knee with right hand	right hand
26. Tap leg with right hand	°71. Walk and clap hands
27. Tap left knee with right hand	°72. Open mouth
28. Raise right arm overhead	73. Jump
29. Tap chest with right hand	74. Pat radiator
30. Tap table with right hand	°75. Nod no
31. Move chair	76. Pick up phone
32. Sit in chair	77. Pull drawer
33. Throw paper in basket	78. Pet coat
34. Pull up socks	79. Tear Kleenex
35. Tap desk	80. Nest four boxes
36. Climb on chair	81. Point gun and say "Bang"
37. Open door	°82. Put towel over face
38. Move ash tray	°83. Put hands over eyes
39. Put paper in chair	°84. Tap floor
40. Sit in two chairs (chained)	°85. Scribble
41. Tap chair with right hand	°86. Move toy car on table
42. Move paper from basket to desk	87. Place circle in form board
43. Move box from shelf to desk	88. Place circle, square, and
44. Put on hat	triangle in form board
45. Move hat from table to desk	°89. Crawl under table
46. Move box from shelf to desk	°90. Walk and clap sides
47. Nest three boxes	°91. Lie on floor

TABLE 1 (*Continued*)

°92. Kick box	°112. Push large car
°93. Put foot over table rung	113. Put beads on doorknob
°94. Fly airplane	°114. Put hat on hobby horse
°95. Rock doll	115. Sweep block with broom
°96. Burp doll	116. Place box inside ring of beads
°97. Tap chair with bat	117. Put glove in pocket of lab coat
°98. Open and close book	118. Push button on tape recorder
99. Work egg beater	°119. Bang spoon on desk
100. Put arm through hoop	120. Lift cup
101. Build three block towers	121. Use whisk broom on a wall
°102. Stab self with rubber knife	°122. Put a cube in a cup
103. Put blocks in ring	123. Rattle a spoon in a cup
104. Walk and hold book on head	°124. Throw paper on the floor
105. Ride kiddie car	°125. Hug a pillow
106. Sweep with broom	126. Tap pegs into pegboard with
107. Place beads around neck	hammer
108. Ride hobby horse	°127. Wave a piece of paper
°109. Put on glove	°128. Shake a rattle
110. Use whisk broom on table	°129. Hit two spoons together
111. Work rolling pin	130. Shake a tambourine

forcement periods was a shift in the contingency. For the group of unreinforced or probe responses there was no change; food reinforcement still did not follow either the occurrence or non-occurrence of an imitative response. This procedure involved simultaneously the extinction of imitation and also the reinforcement of whatever other responses may have been taking place at the moment of reinforcement.

For Subject 1, the DRO period was 30 sec. For Subject 2, DRO periods were 30, 60, and 0 sec. (DRO 0-sec meant reinforcement was delivered immediately after the S^D, before an imitative response could occur.) This sequence of DRO intervals was used because, as displayed in the Results section, Subject 2 maintained stable imitation under the initial DRO procedures, unlike the other subjects. For Subject 3, the DRO period was 20 sec. After the DRO procedure for each subject, contingent reinforcement of imitation was resumed and the procedures described below were instituted.

IMITATIVE CHAINS. After reinforcement for imitative behavior was resumed with Subjects 1 and 2, the procedure of chaining together old and new imitations was begun. At first only two-response chains were demonstrated; then three-response chains, after two-response chains were successfully achieved; and so on. During chaining, the experimenter demonstrated the responses the subject was to imitate as an unbroken series. In all cases, the demonstrated chain contained both responses previously learned by the subject and relatively new ones. Walking from one locale to another in the process of performing these behaviors was not considered part of the imitative chain and was not judged for imitative accuracy.

VERBAL IMITATIONS. Late in the training program for Subjects 1 and 3, when virtually any new motor performance by the experimenter was almost certain to be imitated, vocal performances were begun with simple sounds. The experimenter, as usual, said "Do this," but instead of making some motor response made a vocal one, for example, "Ah." Subjects 1 and 3 repeatedly failed to imitate such demonstrations. Different procedures were then employed to obtain vocal imitations. For Subject 1, the vocal response to be imitated was set into a chain of non-vocal responses. For example, the experimenter would say, "Do this," rise from his chair and walk to the center of the room, turn towards the subject, say "Ah," and return to his seat. To such a demonstration Subject 1 responded by leaving her seat, walking toward the center of the room, turning toward the experimenter, and then beginning a series of facial and vocal responses out of which eventually emerged an "Ah" sufficiently similar to the experimenter's to merit reinforcement. This coupling of motor and vocal performances was maintained for several more demonstrations, during which the motor performance was made successively shorter and more economical of motion; finally, the experimenter was able to remain seated, say "Do this," say "Ah," and immediately evoke an imitation from the subject. Proceeding in this manner, simple sounds were shaped and then combined into longer or more complex sounds and finally into useable words.

Subject 3, like Subject 1, initially failed to imitate vocalizations. In his case, the experimenter proceeded to demonstrate a set of motor performances which moved successively closer to vocalizations. At first the experimenter obtained imitative blowing out of a lighted match, then blowing without the match, then more vigorous blowing which included an initial plosive "p," then added a voiced component to the blowing which was shaped into a "Pah" sound. Proceeding in this manner, a number of vocalizations were produced, all as reliable imitations.

GENERALIZATION TO OTHER EXPERIMENTERS. When the imitative repertoire of Subject 1 had developed to a high level, new experimenters were presented to her, of the opposite or the same sex as the original male experimenter. These novel experimenters gave the same demonstrations as the original experimenter in the immediately preceding session. The purpose of this procedure was to investigate whether the subject's imitative repertoire was limited to demonstrations by the original male experimenter. During this procedure, the new experimenters delivered reinforcement in the same manner as the original experimenter; i.e., previously reinforced imitations were reinforced and probes were not.

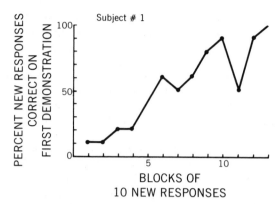

Fig. 1. The development of imitation in Subject 1

Results

Reliability of Scoring Imitative Responses

Checks on the reliability of the experimenter's scoring of any response as imitative were made at scattered points throughout the study for Subjects 1 and 2. The percentage of agreement between the experimenter's scoring and the independent records of a second observer exceeded 98%.

First Training Procedures

The initial training procedure contained occasions when the extent of the developing imitative repertoire of each subject could be seen. These were occasions when behavior was demonstrated by the experimenter to the subject for the first time. Any attempt by the subject to imitate such new behavior before direct training or shaping could be attributed to the history of reinforcement for matching other behavior of the experimenter. Thus, it was possible to examine the sequence of initial presentations to each subject to discover any increasing probability that new behavior would be imitated on its first presentation.

The sequence of 130 responses in Subject 1's program was sufficient to increase her probability of imitating new responses from zero at the beginning of the program to 100% at the end. This was demonstrated by grouping the 130 responses into 13 successive blocks of 10 each. As shown in Fig. 1, the proportion imitated on the first presentation within each block rose, not too steadily, but nonetheless clearly, to 100% by the 13th block.

The proportion of new responses successfully imitated by Subject 2 upon their first presentation rose from 0% to 80%, through a sequence of 130 new responses, as shown in Fig. 2.

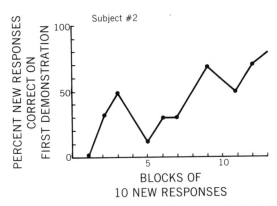

Fig. 2. The development of imitation in Subject 2

Subject 2 displayed both more variable and less thorough imitation of new responses on their first presentation than did Subject 1, although the general form of the data is similar.

Subject 3 was taught only eight discriminated operants of imitative topography, which he acquired much more rapidly than did either Subject 1 or 2. He imitated the ninth spontaneously on its first presentation, although he had not imitated it before training.

The progressive development of imitation was apparent in other aspects of the data as well. The number of training sessions required to establish new imitations was displayed by plotting this number of sessions for each successive block of 10 new responses. The criterion for establishment of a new imitative response was that, for one trial, a subject displayed the response demonstrated by the experimenter with no shaping or fading procedures required for that trial. This is shown in Fig. 3 for Subject 1 and in Fig. 4 for Subject 2, as solid lines. Both graphs show a systematically decreasing number of sessions required to establish successive new imitations. The dotted portions of each graph represent deviations from the usual type of training procedure and thus are plotted differently. For Subject 1 the dotted portion represents a period in which verbal responses were introduced (not plotted as part of Fig. 3, but discussed later in this report). For Subject 2 the dotted portion represents a sequence of sessions in which few new imitative responses were introduced. Rather, two previously established imitative responses of similar topography, which the subject no longer clearly displayed, were worked on intensively.

DRO Procedures

For all subjects, both reinforced and unreinforced imitative behavior was maintained over continuing experimental sessions as

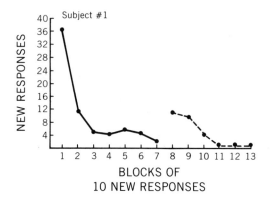

Fig. 3. The rate of development of imitation in Subject I

long as food reinforcement was contingent upon at least some imitative behavior. When reinforcement was no longer contingent upon imitative behavior during the DRO periods, both the previously reinforced imitations and the never-reinforced probe imitations decreased markedly in strength.

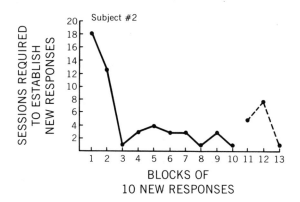

Fig. 4. The rate of development of imitation in Subject 2

Figure 5 is a plot of the percentages of each type of imitative response by Subject 1. It shows that her probability of imitating the 35 probes varied between 80 and 100%, as long as the other 95 imitations, within which the probes were interspersed, were reinforced. The application of the DRO 30-sec procedure extinguished

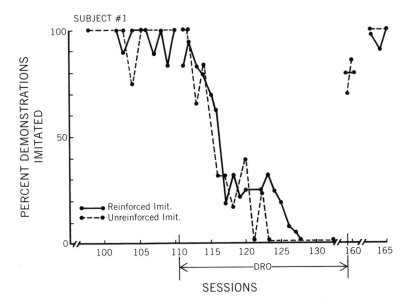

Fig. 5. The maintenance and extinction of reinforced and unreinforced imitation in Subject 1 (The breaks in the data before and after session 160 represent periods of experimentation aimed at other problems.)

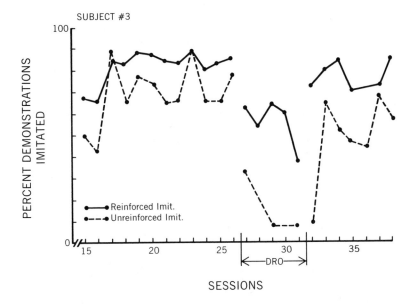

Fig. 6. The maintenance and extinction of reinforced and unreinforced imitation in Subject 3

virtually all imitative behavior within about 20 hr. The previously reinforced imitations and the probe imitations extinguished alike in rate and degree. All imitative behavior recovered when, with a small amount of shaping, reinforcement was again made contingent upon imitative behavior.

Figure 6 is a similar plot of the imitative behavior of Subject 3. It shows the maintenance of the one probe imitation and eight reinforced imitations during reinforcement of imitation, a marked decrease in both types of imitative behavior during the DRO 20-sec period, and a recovery when contingent reinforcement of imitations was resumed.

Figure 7 is a plot of the imitative behavior of Subject 2. Her results were similar to those obtained for Subjects 1 and 3, in terms of the maintenance of 125 reinforced and five probe imitations, under conditions of reinforcement of imitations. However, her data depart from the others' during the DRO period. Initially, this subject showed no reliable signs of extinction after four sessions of DRO with a 30-sec delay. Next, DRO 60-sec was instituted for four sessions, still without any reliable effect. At that point, a procedure of DRO 0-sec was begun, meaning that the experimenter demonstrated some behavior, and instantly, before the subject could respond, said "Good" and delivered the food to her mouth. Thus, reinforcement served to forestall the durable imitative responses this subject was displaying. Figure 7 demonstrates the immediacy of effect of this procedure. After four sessions of DRO 0-sec, it was possible to resume the procedures of DRO 30-sec and produce only a brief and partial recovery of the rate of imitation, which then declined to zero. A return to contingent reinforcement, with a small amount of shaping, quickly reinstated the high rate of imitation previously displayed.

In all cases, then, it is clear that the imitative repertoire depended on reinforcement of at least some of its members. It is noteworthy that those responses which had developed and been maintained previously without direct reinforcement could not survive extinction applied to the entire class of behaviors.

Imitative Chains

Subjects 1 and 2 were exposed to the procedure of chaining together old and new imitative responses. At the end of 10 hr of the procedure for Subject 1, lengthy chains containing already established and new imitative responses became practical. It was possible to obtain perfect imitation on 90% of the chains, some of which involved as many as five responses. Subject 2 received only 2 hr of training on chains. At the end of this time, she would imitate 50% of the three-response chains demonstrated to her, and 80% of the two-response chains.

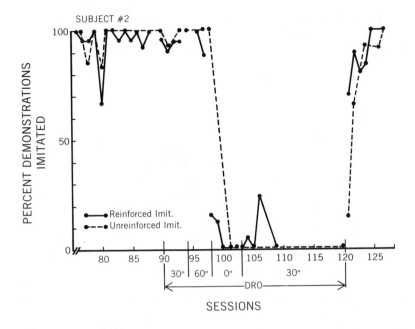

Fig. 7. The maintenance and extinction of reinforced and unreinforced imitation in Subject 2

Verbal Behavior

Subjects 1 and 3 were used in the procedures for the development of verbal imitation. Verbal imitations were established for Subject 1 by chaining together motor and vocal behaviors and then fading out the motor components. Twenty hours of training resulted in 10 words which were reliably imitated such as, "Hi," "Okay," the subject's name, and the names of some objects. Subject 3's training in vocal imitations was accomplished by evoking a set of motor imitations which moved successively closer to vocalizations. Approximately 10 hr of training produced the reliable imitative vocalizations of seven vowel and consonant sounds.

Generalization to Other Experimenters

When Subject 1 was presented with new experimenters, of both the opposite and same sex as the original male experimenter, she showed approximately the same degree of imitation displayed to the original experimenter. That is, she imitated all of the three probe demonstrations given by one new male experimenter and imitated 12 of 15 reinforced demonstrations by a second new male experimented on the first demonstration and the remaining three by the third demonstration. On another occasion, the second new male experimenter re-presented the 15 demonstrations; all were imitated on their first demonstration. The subject also imitated all of a series of demonstrations by a female experimenter.

Discussion

The procedures of this study were sufficient to produce highly developed imitation in the experimental subjects. However, a noteworthy point is the relative difficulty experienced in obtaining initial matching responses from a subject even when the response required (*e.g.*, arm raising) clearly was in the subject's current repertoire. This suggests that the subjects were not so much learning specific responses as learning the instruction, "Do as the experimenter does." Initially, then, the procedures of this study seem to have involved bringing a number of the subjects' responses under the instructional control of the experimenter's demonstration.[1] To establish this type of instructional control by demonstration requires that the subjects either have or develop responses of observing their own behavior as well as the experimenter's behavior.

As an increasing number of the subjects' behaviors came under the instructional control of demonstration, additional behavior, not previously observed in the subjects' repertoires, became increasingly probable, merely as a result of presenting an appropriate demonstration by a model. In the terminology suggested by Miller and Dollard (1941), a sufficiently extensive arrangement of one child's behavior into matched-dependent response with a model's behavior was sufficient to induce a tendency to achieve similarity in more ways than were originally taught.

The development of imitative repertoires, including the unreinforced imitation of probe demonstrations, could be accounted for by the effects of conditioned reinforcement. Conditioned reinforcement may have operated in the present study in the following way: the basic procedure was that of teaching the subject a series of responses, each of which was topographically similar to a demonstration just given by a model. Initially, each response had to be established separately. When established, such responses were imitative only topographically and would better be called matched-dependent behavior; the fact that a subject's response was similar to the experimenter's behavior at that point had no functional significance for any of the subject's other responses. Nevertheless, topographical similarity between child and experimenter was there to be attended to by the child, and this similarity was potentially discriminative with

---

1. The authors are indebted to Israel Goldiamond for his suggestions in clarifying this point.

respect to the only reinforcement delivered in the experimental situation. One of the most effective ways of giving a stimulus a reinforcing function is to make it discriminative with respect to reinforcement. In these applications, the stimulus class of behavioral similarity was, in numerous examples, made discriminative with respect to positive reinforcement. Hence, similarity could be expected to take on a positive reinforcing function as well as a discriminative function. As a positive reinforcer, it should strengthen any new behavior that produced or achieved it. Behaviors that achieve similarity between one's self and a model are, of course, imitative behaviors; furthermore, they are imitative by function and not by coincidence.

This analysis is simple only at first inspection. In particular, it should be noted that "similarity" is not a simple stimulus dimension like the frequency of sound or the intensity of light. Similarity must mean a correspondence of some sort between the stimulus output of the child's behavior and the stimulus output of the model's. A correspondence between two stimuli is not too esoteric a stimulus to consider as functional in controlling behavior. However, for an imitative repertoire to develop, a class of correspondences must become functional as stimuli. The child must learn to discriminate a correspondence between the appearance of his hand and the model's hand, his arm and the model's arm, his leg and the model's leg, his voice and the model's voice, *etc.* It would seem reasonable that each of these kinds of difference must require some prior experience on the child's part to appreciate. A scantiness of such experience may well be characteristic of retarded children, and makes them intriguing subjects for such studies. The ability to generalize similarities among a considerable variety of stimuli, which the children of these studies evidence, suggests that the training they were subjected to was adequate to the problem. An immediate next problem, it would seem, is the detailed analysis of those procedures to find out which of them accomplished what part of this generalization. That analysis might yield a fair understanding of imitative behavior.

REFERENCES

Baer, D. M., and Sherman, J. A. Reinforcement control of generalized imitation in young children. *J. exp. Child Psychol.*, 1964, 1, 37–49.

Bandura, A. Social learning through imitation. In M. R. Jones (Ed.), *Nebraska symposium on motivation.* Lincoln: University of Nebraska Press, 1962, pp. 211–269.

Konorski, J., and Miller, S. On two types of conditioned reflex. *J. gen. Psychol.*, 1937, 16, 264–272.

Lovaas, O. I., Berberich, J. P., Perloff, B. F., and Schaeffer, B. Acquisition of imitative speech by schizophrenic children. *Science*, 1966, 151, 705–707.

Metz, J. R. Conditioning generalized imitation in autistic children. *J. exp. Child Psychol.*, 1965, **2**, 389–399.

Miller, N. E., and Dollard, J. *Social learning and imitation.* New Haven: Yale University Press, 1941.

Reynolds, G. S. Behavioral contrast. *J. exp. Anal. Behav.*, 1961, 4, 57–71.

Skinner, B. F. *Science and human behavior.* New York: Macmillan, 1953.

Terrace, H. S. Discrimination learning with and without "errors." *J. exp. Anal. Behav.*, 1963, **6**, 1–27. *(a)*

Terrace, H. S. Errorless transfer of a discrimination across two continua. *J. exp. Anal. Behav.*, 1963, **6**, 223–232.*(b)*

32

Acquisition of Imitative Speech by Schizophrenic Children

O. Ivar Lovaas
John P. Berberich
Bernard F. Perloff
Benson Schaeffer

Department of Psychology
University of California, Los Angeles

Abstract: Two mute schizophrenic children were taught imitative speech within an operant conditioning framework. The training procedure consisted of a series of increasingly fine verbal discriminations; the children were rewarded for closer and closer reproductions of the attending adults' speech. We found that reward delivered contingent upon imitation was necessary development of imitation. Furthermore, the newly established imitation was shown to have acquired rewarding properties for the children.

With the great majority of children, the problem of teaching speech never arises. Speech develops within each child's particular environment without parents and teachers having to know a great deal about how it occurs. Yet, in some children, because of deviations in organic structure or prior experience, speech fails to develop. Children with diagnosis of childhood schizophrenia, especially autistic children, often show little in the way of speech development.[1] The literature on childhood schizophrenia suggests two conclusions

From *Science*, **151**, February 11, 1966, 705–7. This study was supported by grants from Margaret Sabl of Los Angeles. We express appreciation to James Q. Simmons and the staff at the Children's Unit, Neuropsychiatric Institute, University of California, Los Angeles.
1. Rimland, *Infantile Autism* (Appleton-Century-Crofts, New York, 1964).

regarding speech in such children: first, that the usual treatment setting (psychotherapy) in which these children are placed might not be conducive to speech development; and second, that a child failing to develop speech by the age of 5 years remains withdrawn and does not improve clinically.[2] That is, the presence or absence of speech is an important prognostic indicator. It is perhaps obvious that a child who can speak can engage in a much more therapeutic interchange with his environment than the child who has no speech.

The failure of some children to develop speech as a "natural" consequence of growing up poses the need for an increased knowledge of how language is acquired. A procedure for the development of speech in previously mute children would not only be of practical importance but might also illuminate the development of speech in normal children. Although several theoretical attempts have been made to account for language development, the empirical basis for these theoretical formulations is probably inadequate. In fact, there are no published, systematic studies on how to go about developing speech in a person who has never spoken. We now outline a procedure by which speech can be made to occur. Undoubtedly there are or will be other ways by which speech can be acquired. Furthermore, our procedure centers on the acquisition of only one aspect of speech, the acquisition of vocal responses. The development of speech also requires the acquisition of a context for the occurrence of such responses ("meaning").

Casual observation suggests that normal children acquire words by hearing speech; that is, children learn to speak by imitation. The mute schizophrenic children with whom we worked were not imitative. Thus the establishment of imitation in these children appeared to be the most beneficial and practical starting point for building speech. The first step in creating speech, then, was to establish conditions in which imitation of vocal sounds would be learned.

The method that we eventually found most feasible for establishing verbal imitation involved a discrimination training procedure. Early in training the child was rewarded only if he emitted a sound within a certain time after an adult had emitted a sound. Next he was rewarded only if the sound he emitted within the prescribed interval resembled the adult's sound. Toward the end of training, he was rewarded only if his vocalization very closely matched the adult's vocalization—that is, if it was, in effect, imitative. Thus verbal imitation was taught through the development of a series of increasingly fine discriminations.

The first two children exposed to this program are discussed here. Chuck and Billy were 6-year-old in-patients at the Neuropsychiatric Institute at UCLA. These children were selected for the program

---

2. Brown, *Amer. J. Orthopsychiat.* **30**, 382 (1960).

because they did not speak. At the onset of the program, vocal behavior in both children was restricted to occasional vowel productions with no discernible communicative intent. These vowel sounds occurred infrequently, except when the children were tantrumous, and did not resemble the pre-speech babbling of infants. In addition, the children evidenced no appropriate play (for example, they would spin toys or mouth them). They engaged in a considerable amount of self-stimulatory behavior such as rocking and twirling. They did not initiate social contacts and became tantrumous when such contact was initiated by others. They evidenced occasional self-destructive behavior (biting self, head-banging and so forth). Symbolic rewards such as social approval were inoperative, so biological rewards such as food were substituted. In short, they were profoundly schizophrenic.

Training was conducted 6 days a week, 7 hours a day, with a 15-minute rest period accompanying each hour of training. During the training sessions the child and the adult sat facing each other, their heads about 30 cm apart. The adult physically prevented the child from leaving the training situation by holding the child's legs between his own legs. Rewards in the form of single spoonsful of the child's meal, were delivered immediately after correct responses. Punishment (spanking, shouting by the adult) was delivered for inattentive, self-destructive, and tantrumous behavior which interfered with the training, and most of these behaviors were thereby suppressed within 1 week. Incorrect vocal behavior was never punished.

Four distinct steps were required to establish verbal imitation. In step 1, the child was rewarded for all vocalizations. We frequently would fondle the child and we avoided aversive stimulation. This was done in order to increase the frequency of vocal responses. During this stage in training the child was also rewarded for visually fixating on the adult's mouth. When the child reached an achievement level of about one verbal response every 5 seconds and was visually fixating on the adult's mouth more than 50 percent of the time, step 2 of training was introduced.

Step 2 marked our initial attempt to bring the child's verbal behavior under our verbal control in such a manner that our speech would ultimately stimulate speech in the child. Mastery of this second step involved acquisition of a temporal discrimination by the child. The adult emitted a vocal response—for example, "baby"—about once on the average of every 10th second. The child was rewarded only if he vocalized within 6 seconds after the adult's vocalization. However, any vocal response of the child would be rewarded in that time interval. Step 3 was introduced when the frequency of the child's vocal responses within the 6-second interval was three times what it had been initially.

Step 3 was structurally similar to the preceding step, but it in-

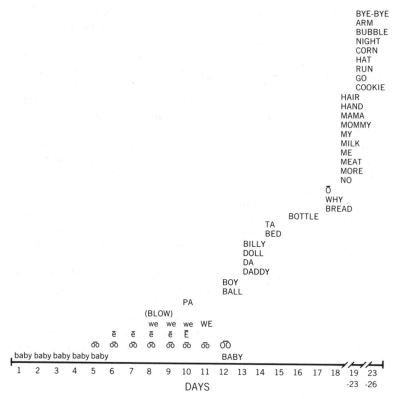

Fig. 1. Acquisition of verbal imitation by Billy. The abscissa denotes training days. Words and sounds are printed in lower case letters on the days they were introduced, and in capital letters on the days they were mastered.

cluded the additional requirement that the child actually match the adult's vocalization before receiving the reward. In this and in following steps the adult selected the verbalization to be placed in imitative training for a pool of possible verbalizations that had met one or more of the following criteria. First, we selected vocal behaviors that could be prompted, that is, vocal behaviors that could be elicited by a cue prior to any experimental training, such as by manually moving the child through the behavior.

An example of training with the use of a prompt is afforded in teaching the sound "b." The training would proceed in three stages: (i) the adult emitted "b" and simultaneously prompted the child to emit "b" by holding the child's lips closed with his fingers and quickly removing them when the child exhaled; (ii) the prompt would be gradually faded, by the adult's moving his fingers away from the child's mouth, to his cheek, and finally gently touching the child's jaw; (iii) the adult emitted the vocalization "b" only, withholding all prompts. The rate of fading was determined by the child; the sooner the child's verbal behavior came under control of the adult's without the use of the prompt, the better. The second criterion for selection of words or sounds in the early stages of training centered on their concomitant visual components (which we exaggerated when we pronounced them), such as those of the labial consonant "m" and of open-mouthed vowels like "a." We selected such sounds after having previously found that the children could discriminate words with visual components more easily than those with only auditory components (the guttural consonants, "k" and "g" proved extremely difficult and, like "l" and "s," were mastered later than other sounds). Third, we selected for training sounds which the child emitted most frequently in step 1.

Step 4 was a recycling of step 3, with the addition of a new sound. We selected a sound that was very different from those presented in step 3, so that the child could discriminate between the new and old sounds more easily. To make certain that the child was in fact imitating, we randomly interspersed the sounds of step 3 with the sound of step 4, in a randomized ratio of about 1 to 3. This random presentation "forced" (or enabled) the child to discriminate the particular sounds involved, in order to be rewarded. There was no requirement placed upon the child in step 3 to discriminate specific aspects such as vowels, consonants, and order of the adult's speech: a child might master step 3 without attending to the specific properties of the adult's speech. Each new introduction of sounds and words required increasingly fine discrimination by the child and hence provided evidence that the child was in fact matching the adult's speech. All steps beyond step 4 consisted of replications of step 3, but new sounds, words, and phrases were used. In each new step the previously mastered words and sounds were rehearsed on a randomized ratio of 1 to 3. The next step was introduced when the child had mastered the previous steps—that is, when he had made ten consecutive correct replications of the adult's utterances.

One hour of each day's training was tape-recorded. Two independent observers scored the child's correct vocal responses from these sessions. A correct response was defined as a recognizable reproduction of the adult's utterance. The observers showed better than 90 percent agreement over sessions. When the child's correct responses are plotted against days of training, and the resulting function is positively accelerated, it can be said that the child has learned to imitate.

The results of the first 26 days of imitation training, starting from introduction of step 3, have been plotted for Billy (Fig. 1). The abscissa denotes training days. The words and sounds are printed in lower case letters on the days they were introduced and in capital letters on the days they were mastered. It can be seen that as training progressed the rate of mastery increased. Billy took several days to learn a single word during the first 2 weeks of the program, but a single day to master several words during the last 2 weeks. Chuck's performance was very similar to Billy's.

After 26 days of training both children had learned to imitate new words with such ease and rapidity that merely adding verbal responses to their imitative repertoire seemed pointless. Hence the children were then introduced to the second part of the language training program, wherein they were taught to use language appropriately.

The imitation training took place in a rather complex environment, with many events happening concurrently. We hypothesized that it was the reward, given for imitative behavior, which was crucial to the learning. To test this hypothesis, the adult uttered the sounds as during the training and the children received the same number of rewards as before. However, the rewards were contingent upon time elapsed since the last reward, regardless of the child's behavior.

The data show a deterioration in imitation behavior whenever rewards are shifted from response-contingent to time-contingent delivery. It is concluded, therefore, that reward immediately following correct, imitative behavior (and withholding of reward following incorrect responding) is a crucial variable in maintaining imitative behavior in these children. The same finding has been reported by Baer and Sherman[3] who worked with imitative behavior in normal children.

Since the child was rewarded whenever he responded like the adult, *similarity* was consistently associated with food. Because of such association, similarity should become symbolic of reward. In other words, imitative behavior, being symbolic of reward, should eventually provide its own reward.[4] To test this hypothesis, both children were exposed to Norwegian words which they were unable to reproduce perfectly when first presented. The adult simply stated the Norwegian word and the child always attempted to repeat it; no extrinsic rewards were delivered. However, occasionally the child was presented with English words which the adult rewarded when correctly imitated. This procedure was necessary to maintain the hypothesize symbolic (learned) reward function of imitation.

The children improved in the imitation of the Norwegian words over time. It is as if they were rewarded for correct behavior. In view of the data pointing to the need for rewards in maintaining imitative behavior, and in the absence of extrinsic rewards we would argue that the reward was intrinsic and a function of the prior imitation training. There is one implication of this finding which is of particular interest for therapeutic reasons; children may be able to acquire new behaviors on their own. (This finding contrasts with the

---

3. D. Baer and J. Sherman. *J. Exp. Child Psychol.* 1, 37 (1964).
4. Ibid.

frequent stereotype of a conditioning product, namely, that of an automaton unable to function independently.)

Currently, three new schizophrenic children are undergoing the same speech training program as Billy and Chuck. After 3 days of training, one of these children achieved a level of imitative behavior similar to that shown by Bill and Chuck after 26 days. It should be pointed out that schizophrenic children are a very heterogeneous group with respect to their speech histories and symptomatology in general, and that Billy and Chuck had failed in development to a profound degree. Insofar as one works with such a diverse population, it is likely that numerous procedures could be helpful in establishing speech.

33

Teaching Reading to Children with Low Mental Ages

Siegfried Engelmann
University of Oregon

Little progress has been made in developing effective reading instruction for children with low mental ages, i.e., below six and one-half years. In fact, little progress has been made in developing effective approaches for school age children with average mental ages (MA's). Although the average child learns to read, he does not usually learn very quickly; some average children have extreme difficulties, although they are intelligent and seem to have the mental equipment necessary to read.

Why does this situation exist? The answer seems to be that the authors of reading programs have typically approached in an awkward way the problem of teaching children to read. They have worked with average children of about six and one-half years. These children are relatively sophisticated. They have a pretty good idea of what reading is and they know what they are supposed to do in a new learning situation. They know how to treat words as sounds and not merely as signals that convey content. They play word games; they rhyme and alliterate. They probably know letter names and have a fair idea of some letter sounds. These children are able to learn to read from a variety of approaches, so they are thus able to compensate for gaps in an instructional program. They often learn in spite of the program. If the program does not provide adequate

From *Education and Training of Mentally Retarded*, 1967, **2**(4), 193–201.

instruction for a particular subskill such as rhyming or blending, the children usually learn anyhow.

When the author of a beginning reading approach works with such children, he cannot clearly see the relationship between the effectiveness of his program and the children's reading performance. He cannot clearly see which skills he has successfully taught, which skills were taught before the child began the program, and which were obliquely induced through instruction. In other words, the author cannot refer to the performance of the children after they have received instruction and specify how much of it he is responsible for and how much of it is accounted for by home and previous training. Typically, he presumes that he is responsible for a great deal more than he deserves credit for. But since most of the children learn to read, it is difficult to discredit his presumption. For example, he may introduce exercises that are supposed to teach comprehension. He can refer to most of the children in the class who have received the instruction and note that they do comprehend. He may then conclude that his exercises were a success. But it is quite possible that these children would have comprehended well without the instruction he provided; it may be that their performance is not clearly a function of the instruction they have received. The author may justify readiness exercises in a similar manner, noting that the children who received the instruction are ready to read. However, much of the readiness training may be quite irrelevant to the problems associated with learning to read. If one provides a broad enough scope of tasks, one will undoubtedly hit upon some tasks that actually do prepare the child. In the process, however, one may provide many tasks that accomplish little.

When the author works with children who may have mastered skills that are necessary to read, there are relatively few checks on his imagination. He may identify skills that are basically irrelevant to the act of translating those clusters of squiggles on the printed page into word sounds, and he may fail to identify sub-skills that are crucial to the translation process. It might be difficult for us to demonstrate possible weaknesses in his program for the simple reason that most of the children who receive instruction perform well. It can be pointed out that a certain number of children who receive the instruction do not perform well, but the author is not usually compelled to take responsibility for these children. These children can be viewed in two ways: as children who fail because they have not received adequate instruction, or as children who fail because they lack aptitude, readiness, or intelligence. By attributing their failure to a lack of aptitude rather than a lack of appropriate instruction, the author can write them off, maintaining that his program is designed for "average" children. There is a certain appeal to this argument. Children do vary in aptitude, as any teacher knows, and it seems reasonable that not all can learn from a given approach. The

danger in this argument, however, is that it leaves the author un-
bridled. He is provided with a floating standard. If the children
succeed, the program is responsible; if they fail, the children are
responsible. The instruction is exonerated from all responsibility
for failure. Obviously, this situation is not healthy and does not
promote better instruction. Rather, it encourages post hoc justification of what happened, with no fixed standard against which to
measure the effectiveness of various approaches.

There have been comparisons of different reading approaches, but
such comparisons do not tell us precisely in what areas a given
program is strong or weak, and they do not effectively discredit the
approach that is relatively poor in comparison with others. The author of an approach that does not do well in comparative studies may
contend that his program achieves objectives that are not measured
or taken into consideration in the comparison, such as an appreciation of reading. The act of reading is so broad and involved that it
may be difficult to demonstrate that he is mistaken.

Solving the Problem

To solve the problem of providing better reading instruction for
children who may have trouble with traditional approaches (including preschool and mentally retarded children), we must identify
the various trouble spots encountered by those children in learning
to read. Obviously, we cannot do this by working with children who
are more sophisticated than those with reading trouble, because
more sophisticated children often do not encounter the severe difficulties that the children with less reading aptitude encounter.
Therefore, children that are more sophisticated don't provide the
kind of feedback that is necessary to identify the primary problems
in learning to read. An analysis of the reading code provides important information about what is involved in reading, but it doesn't
tell which skills are relatively difficult to learn and which are easy.
The only way one discovers what the central problems are is to work
with children who have low MA's. These children are ideal subjects
for developing solid instructional approaches for these reasons:
(a) they learn slowly, which means that the method developer can
observe the problems they encounter in some detail; and (b) they
probably have not learned or even partially learned the key sub-
skills in reading outside of the instructional setting, which means
that if they learn to handle a particular subskill, we can credit the
instruction with their learning.

The method developer working with low MA children is less
likely to use a floating standard, less likely to say that those children
who fail lack aptitude. All of his subjects lack aptitude: therefore,
he is in a better position to accept the idea that if the children fail,

the instruction has failed, and if they learn, the instruction has succeeded. This attitude is potentially productive because it allows the method developer to look at each segment of reading behavior and see whether or not he can teach it. It is difficult to evaluate an approach by looking at it as a whole. An approach is more productively viewed as a series of components, each of which can be separately evaluated and subsequently improved. This kind of evaluation assumes that we clearly understand what the components are. The best way to find out is to work with the children who will tell us through their performance. The slow learning child does this. When he comes to a gap in instruction, he doesn't merely pause before working through the gap. He stops and he may remain stopped for weeks. His performance tells the curriculum designer when a technique works and when it doesn't work. The performance of the more sophisticated child does not.

A New Reading Program

The reading program that we are currently using in the Bereiter-Engelmann preschool certainly does not represent the ultimate in reading instruction, but it is a good start. The program was developed by working with preschool children. Some were culturally deprived (with entering Stanford-Binet IQ scores of about 91); others were middle class children (with entering IQ scores of about 113); all were four years old. After 48 hours of classroom instruction the culturally disadvantaged children read on the 1.25 grade level (Wide Range Achievement scores) and the middle class children read on the 2.3 grade level. Another group of disadvantaged children who received instruction for two school years read on the 2.6 grade level at the end of their kindergarten year. Not one child read below the 1.6 grade level, although some of these children wouldn't have been expected to read by the second or third grade if they had received traditional instruction.

While our work has been primarily focused on culturally disadvantaged children, it has implications for teaching reading to mentally retarded children for the following reasons:

1. Over one-third of the disadvantaged children we work with have entering IQ scores in the 80's, which place them on the fringe of the mentally handicapped.
2. Typically, IQ scores of four and five year old children who have IQ scores in the 80's will drop as the children get older, which means that these children are potentially mentally handicapped at age four.
3. The mental ages of these children are as low as many children in special classes. An eight year old child who has an IQ score

of 75 has a mental age of six years. The initial mental age of the disadvantaged children we work with is less than four years. This means that many of the children we have taught to read have less knowledge of the world and fewer skills than children who do not learn to read in special classes.

4. The younger child is often more difficult to teach than the older child with the same mental age because the younger child is generally more difficult to motivate, has a shorter interest span, and knows less about the type of classroom behavior that is expected of him.

Thus the approach that we use should work with all children who have MA's of four and above, whether they are classified as mentally retarded, culturally deprived, or gifted children.

The Method. Our motto in trying to work out a successful reading approach was simply to "keep the baloney out of the program." We did not analyze the reading code as the linguist or the educator typically analyzes it. We tried to determine what kind of behavior is demanded of the children, asking ourselves, What must they be able to do? Next we tried to develop tasks to teach them the appropriate behavior. And finally, we tried to remain sensitive to the children's reaction to the presentations. If they stalled and failed to learn a skill such as blending, we tried to make the rule for blending more obvious so that the children could see more clearly what they were expected to do. If various approaches seemed to make little difference in the children's progress, we used the approach that seemed most economical and manageable, but we did not close the book on the issue. We recognized that it may be possible to supplant the drill with an approach that is far superior.

The children were taught in small groups, averaging about five children each. They were grouped homogeneously, according to performance in the classroom. The method of instruction demanded a great many responses from the children, so that the teacher received maximum feedback and the children received maximum corrected practice. Each daily reading period lasted from 15 to 20 minutes. The goal of instruction was to pack as much learning into these periods as possible.

We were particularly interested in identifying the places at which the children encountered difficulties. The first stumbling block encountered by our low MA children was in learning that the letters in a word stand for sounds that are sequenced in time. When a person says the word "Batman," some of the parts occur before other parts, and the order of the parts (or sound elements) is fixed. The words "manbat" or "tabman" are not the same as "Batman," because in these words, the order of parts has been violated. The instruction must therefore teach the naive child (a) that the spoken word is composed of parts, (b) that the parts occur in a fixed order in time, and (c) that the reading code represents the passage of time through a left to right progression of symbols.

To teach the child to focus on parts of words, the teacher introduces rhyming and alliteration tasks. In rhyming, the child must hold part of the word constant—the ending—and vary the other part. "Okay, I want to hear some words that rhyme with superman. . . . Here's one: boo—perman. Here's another: foo—perman. And another: moo—. . ." To teach alliteration (in which the beginning part stays the same and the ending changes) the teacher says, "I want some words that start out the same way as SSSS-uper. Here's one: SSSS-ister. Another: SSSS-ee. Another: SSSS—. . ."

If the child has not mastered rhyming and alliteration skills, he will probably have an extremely difficult time reading. Specifically, he'll have difficulty understanding how similar words are similar. Similar words are similar because part of one word is the same (makes the same sound) as a part of the others. If the child cannot hear the way in which "car" is the same as "far," he is not in a very good position to look for the sameness in the orthography of the two words.

To teach the children the rule for mapping the passing of time from left to right, the teacher begins by demonstrating how to sequence events from left to right. The teacher claps her hands together and follows this action by tapping herself on the head with one hand. "I'm doing it the right way," she says, and invites the children to do it with her, pausing between each trial. After the children have produced the pair of actions a number of times, the teacher says, "My turn. Watch me and tell me if I'm doing it the right way." She then produces the actions either in the correct or the reverse order. "Did I do it the right way?" Not all children will be able to see the difference. Some will insist that the sequence head tap-hand clap is the right way.

After the teacher has made the children aware of the right way using a variety of examples, she symbolizes the actions and presents them on the chalkboard from left to right. For the hand clap she uses this symbol: "----" (demonstrating how it is formed by holding her hands at the ends of the line and bringing them together in a clap); for the head tap, she introduces this symbol: "O." She draws an arrow on the board pointing from left to right. She claps her hands and makes the corresponding symbol at the tail of the arrow. "I'm drawing a picture of what I did." She then follows with the head tap, and makes the symbol for it near the head of the arrow. She asks the children to read what happened. "Start here and go with the arrow." After demonstrating how the code works, she presents a series of examples in which the children are asked to do what the symbols tell them to do. For example, she may present the following series and have the children read it and do what it says. As the children become increasingly proficient in working with the

Fig. 1 Sample code series

code, she can introduce other symbols and introduce more difficult tasks, such as having a child symbolize a series of events that is produced either by the teacher or by another child.

As the children learn the rules for translating events that occur in time onto space, they are also introduced to the conventional sound symbols used in reading. Initially, the following sounds are presented: "ă," "ŏ," "e," "m," "f," "r," "s," and "n." There is no particular difficulty involved in teaching these. Young disadvantaged and retarded children learn the symbol slowly, but they succeed in time. The teacher should be careful not to overload the children by presenting too many examples. She must also be careful not to present the same objects unless she wants to induce mislearning. She must present many different examples of each letter, as it appears on cards and on the chalkboard in different colors and different sizes. All letters are presented as sounds; "a" is identified as the short "a" sound ("and"); "f" is the unvoiced sound that occurs at the beginning of such words as "fan."

These initial letters are selected not on the basis of frequency of occurrence or on the basis of linguistic considerations, but on the basis of specific difficulties the low MA child has in learning to read. Stated differently, they are selected because they allow for the most precise demonstration of the relationship between the unblended word and the blended word. Typically, the disadvantaged child and the retarded child have trouble learning to blend. One can walk into virtually any third grade class for disadvantaged children and note many children making the same type of error. They can sound out a word such as "cat," saying, "cu-ah-tu." But they cannot put the pieces together to form a word. When asked, "What word is that?" they either shrug or repeat, "cu-ah-tu." Their failure to see the similarity between "cu-ah-tu," and "cat" is not without cause. The relationship between "cu-ah-tu" and "cat" is not particularly obvious. The parts of the unblended word are separated by pauses in time; the parts of the blended word are not. There are sounds in the unblended word that do not appear in the blended word. The relationship between blended and unblended words can be made more obvious by the following method:

First, the teacher introduces only those words that begin with a continuous sound, not a stop sound. Such words as "cat" are not introduced. Such words as "fan" and "ran" are introduced. Next, the teacher teaches the children to blend without pausing between letters. The child is taught the convention that one sound is held until the next one is produced. When the child attempts to sound out the word "ran," he says, "rrraaannn." In this unblended word there are no pauses; there are no extra sounds. Its relationship to "ran" is therefore quite obvious.

After the child has learned to process simple two and three letter words composed of continuous sound letters, he is introduced to words that contain stop sounds. The stop sounds are first introduced at the end of three sound words — "rat," "rag," and "rab."

The stop sounds are then moved to the beginning. To demonstrate how they work, the teacher begins a series of familiar endings, such as: "an," "an," and "an." She introduces familiar continuous sound beginnings: "fan," "ran," and "man." She then erases these beginnings and introduces stop sound beginnings: "can," "gan," and "tan." Before attacking a word she calls attention to the vowel. "What does this say? Yes: ă. So this word is că — n." By calling attention to the vowel, the teacher allows the child to produce the sounds of the first and second letter together — "că" — thereby eliminating some of the difficulties associated with stop sounds.

The conventions introduced to demonstrate blending make a significant difference in the performance of the children.

The teacher next introduces a long vowel convention. A long line drawn over a vowel changes the sound to the letter names, "a," "e," "i," "o," and "u." The teacher proceeds quickly to exercises in which the children first sound out and identify a familiar word, such as "rat." The teacher then draws a line over the vowel, "rat," and the children sound out the new word, "rate."

The children now have a large enough repertoire of sounds to begin reading small stories. Initially, the teacher avoids any of the vowel sounds that have not been introduced (such as the vowel sounds in the words "all," "foil," etc.) and she avoids such combinations as "th" and "ch."

She limits herself to those sounds the child has learned and she spells all words phonetically. For example, she spells the word "said" as "sed," and the word "have," "hav." The following is an example of the kind of story the teacher might introduce:

A cat līks mēt.

Hē ēts mēt and he runs.

Hē has fun.

These stories familiarize the children with the conventions involved in moving from one line of text to the next.

The teacher then introduces new sound combinations — "th," "ch," "oo," "ee," "oi," and "oy" — and expands the scope of her stories.

The final step, which is actually taken in gradual stages starting when the children begin reading stories, is to introduce irregularly spelled words. These are presented as "funny words," that is, words that are spelled a sound at a time, the way any other word is spelled, but that are pronounced as if they were spelled differently. Handling irregulars in this way is extremely important. The child must learn that the spelling of words is not arbitrary. The word "have" is always spelled the same way; however, it is pronounced as if it were spelled differently, without the final "e." It looks like 'hav-ĕ,' but we don't say 'hav-ĕ,' we say, 'hav.'" Unless irregulars are handled this way, a certain number of children will abandon any kind of phonetic attack, trying to remember individual words and making wild guesses such as calling the word "have," "got."

Some irregular words are introduced early so that the child doesn't get the idea that the reading code is perfectly regular. The initial irregular words the teacher introduces are: "he," "she," "we," "me," "go," "so," and "no." These are presented by erasing the diacritical marks over the vowel. To prompt the children on how to sound out these words, the teacher simply indicates with her finger (drawing an imaginary line over the vowel) that the vowel should be treated as a long vowel.

After the children have become reasonably familiar with the initial set of irregulars, the teacher introduces other common words that are not as neat as the originals: "to," "want," "like," "was," "were," etc. These are carefully programed so that the child receives sufficient exposure on one or two of them every day until these are mastered. Then, the next pair is introduced while the previous pair is continued as a fairly regular schedule.

Implications

The major implication of our work seems to be that children with relatively low mental ages (initially less than four years) can learn to read if the instruction is adequately geared to give them instruction on all of the subskills demanded by the complex behavior we call reading. Furthermore, virtually all children with mental ages of four or over can learn to read. Their progress is relatively slow, but all can progress from one subskill to the next until they are reading. With the emphasis on subskills, the teacher is in a position to know precisely what skills a child has not learned. She therefore knows which skills to work on. When a child masters a given skill, the teacher can proceed to the next one.

If a child has a mental age of four to six years, the chances are overwhelming that he can learn to read, if the instructional program is adequate. Such programs are not commercially available, however, and the teacher of the mentally retarded child is therefore faced with a dilemma. Should she continue to use material that has been proven to be inadequate to teach mentally retarded children to read, or should she wait until programs are commercially available? She should not wait, because the children she is teaching cannot wait. They cannot place themselves in a state of suspended animation for several years, at which time adequate programs will probably be on the market. She must do the best she can. Specifically, this means:

1. She should recognize that the most difficult skills the child must learn are not gross comprehension or experiential skills, but skills in learning how to translate a written word into a series of sounds and putting these sounds together to form a spoken word.
2. She should be extremely skeptical of published materials that do not concentrate on these skills; she should not use a given method merely because it works on normal children; she should not introduce whole words.
3. She should be cautious about assuming that different children "learn in a different way" and must be treated differently. If the criterion of performance is the same for all children, the steps they must take to arrive at that criterion must be the same; therefore, the instruction should be basically the same, in that it should concentrate on the skills that the children must learn in order to achieve the desired criterion of performance (which is to be able to translate clusters of symbols into words).
4. She should work with i.t.a. if possible, recognizing that the program as published is inadequate, but also recognizing that it provides the children with clear demonstrations of the relationship between sounds and symbols, since one symbol stands for one and only one sound.
5. She should not try to teach all of the symbols, but merely enough of them to allow for word building; she should not initially program stop sound consonants ("b," "d," "c," "g," "h," "k," "p," and "t") but only those consonants which can be blended continuously ("f," "j," "l," "m," "n," "r," and "s").
6. She should introduce word blends early with the continuous sound convention.
7. She should simultaneously teach the children the verbal skills of saying words fast, saying words slowly, rhyming, and alliterating. Saying words fast is a blending task; the teacher says a word such as "ta−ble" and asks the children to "Say it fast−'table.'" Saying words slowly is an unblending task in which the teacher says words and asks children to say it slowly, a sound at a time. ("Listen: 'man.' Say it slowly−'mmmaaannn.'"). The focus of rhyming should be a task in which the children are assigned an ending, the teacher says various beginnings, and the children say the ending and identify the word. ("Here are some words that rhyme with table: 'table,' 'ra-ble,' 'ma−,' 'ca−,' 'sta−.'") The focus of alliteration should be a task in

which the children are assigned a beginning to which the teacher attaches various endings; the children must then identify the word. (Children say "sss." Teacher follows with "'and' —What word is that?" Children say, "ssss." Teacher follows with "'eee'—What word is that?"

8. She should introduce stop sounds only after the children have learned to handle continuous sound blends.

9. She should introduce irregulars very cautiously (but relatively early); she should treat these as "funny words," pointing out that they are sounded out in the same way other words are, but aren't pronounced that way.

Teaching reading to children with low mental ages is not easy because these children must learn a great deal before they can hope to read. Their progress is much slower than that of children with higher mental ages. But they can and should be taught if the aim of education is to educate. There is nothing unique about the problems encountered by mentally handicapped children. The problems are the same as those encountered by any child with a relatively low mental age. To read, all children must learn the set of skills. The child with a higher mental age has already been taught many of these before he steps into the classroom. By focusing on these skills and forgetting about such empty labels as "dyslexia" and "perceptually handicapped," a teacher can succeed with children who have mental ages of four or over. The secret of success is simply to provide the children with adequate instruction.

34

The Effectiveness of Direct Verbal Instruction on IQ Performance and Achievement in Reading and Arithmetic

Siegfried Engelmann
University of Oregon

Introduction

The performance of a child on an IQ test is taken by some as an indication of the child's intelligence. It is suggested that the child's performance indicates something about the child's ability to learn and retain information and skills. On the surface, this interpretation has a certain face-value appeal; however, if it is analyzed more carefully, it becomes something of an absurd position. There is no learning in the abstract. The child who is learning is always taught. He is provided with models of behavior; he is corrected if his performance is incorrect; he is reinforced for appropriate behavior. In other words, the term "learning" is not a very accurate description of what happens in a "learning situation," since the child is always being taught. Even if he is working alone, with no "teacher" present, he is still being taught by the physical environment. The physical environment provides rather clear demonstrations of what can be done and what can't.

Since there can be no learning (except in trivial, autistic instances) without teaching, we can categorically assert that if a child performs appropriately on an IQ item, he has been taught the skills needed to handle that item. This does not mean that the item on which he is

From Jerome Hellmuth (ed.), *Disadvantaged Child*, vol. 3 (New York: Brunner/Mazel, 1968).

tested has been presented to the child. It means, however, that he has learned the words, the operations, and concepts that would allow him to handle that item or similar items dealing with the problem (assuming that the words used in the item are within the child's repertoire). The amount of teaching that has been required for two different children to achieve a particular criterion of performance on an IQ item may vary considerably. One child may have required only a minimum of "teaching" while another child may have required a considerable amount of instruction. The performance on the item provides for no inference about the amount of teaching that has been provided; therefore, the item cannot be seriously considered as an indicator of the child's innate capacity or genetic endowment. Two six-year-old children may score correctly on the same set of IQ items. One child may have received three times the amount of instruction that the other child received. Yet, the IQ score tells us nothing about the environment. Therefore, the IQ test can in no way be a very reliable indicator of the genetic composition of these children.

It may be argued that the children who respond to an IQ test appropriately are not actually taught the skills that would lead to correct performance. Such would be an ill-conceived argument. We could test the limits to see what the child had been taught. If we were to present the same item using a foreign language, such as Pali, the chances are that the child who responded appropriately when the task was presented in English would not respond appropriately. We could therefore conclude that successful performance on the item is contingent upon an understanding of the English language. How does a child acquire an understanding of this language? He is taught. To say that he learns it begs the question. The language is not a whole. It is the sum of various meanings and operations. He does not acquire the "language" as a whole. He acquires it as he is taught it, a meaning and operation at a time.

What if we were to change the IQ item so that it involved English, but a very anfractuous English. Would the child perform on the item? Probably not, simply because he has not been taught the meanings we refer to with the revised item. On the other hand, we could construct a number of items that are similar to the original that do not involve "difficult" language, but do involve different responses. (We may require the child to produce a verbal response, in which he answers a what question, a response to a yes-no question, a pointing response, etc.) We could also change the examples used in the original item. Through these procedures, we would be able to make some kind of strong statement about what the child has been taught about the operation being tested. Again, however, it would tell us precisely nothing about the child's genetic endowment, merely about the *effective* instruction that he has received.

It may be that some children are taught analogies, for example, through very oblique teaching demonstrations. It is quite probable that the teacher demonstrations of analogies that are effective for some children would not be effective for others. Unless, however, there are precise statements about the type of instruction that has been provided to teach the operations that underlie basic analogies, it is impossible to make precise statements about the nature of the child's genetic capacity. Two children may exhibit the same successful performance on Stanford-Binet analogies; yet, they may have received rather drastically different degrees of instruction. To attempt to derive conclusions about their genetic endowment, therefore, would be something verging on the absurd.

The work that has been conducted at the University of Illinois (formerly under the direction of Carl Bereiter, and currently under the direction of Wesley Becker) was based on the simple proposition that if disadvantaged or "normal" children are taught a wide variety of concepts at a faster-than-normal rate, they will become relatively "smart." Their smartness should be reflected in both performances on IQ tests and on achievement tests that deal with the specific skills taught in the program. These measures are admittedly poor, since they do not articulate precisely what has been taught. At best, they sample, and the sampling is sometimes obscured by items that test operations that the children have been taught but involve language that may not have been taught.

Note that the goal of the program is to teach specifics. The notion of non-specific operations is rejected. An operation is applicable only to certain concrete problems. The subject must somehow be able to see that certain aspects of the problem imply a particular operation. Without this assumption, the operation would be used either universally or randomly. If it is used in a discriminated manner, there must be a basis for discrimination, which means that the operation is specific to a certain set of cues. The operation can be applied to a wide variety of situations, but the operation still remains quite specific.

Also note that the idea of long-range effects of the program is rejected as a legitimate measure of the program's effectiveness. Granted, it is quite possible, even probable, that if children who receive an intensive preschool and kindergarten instruction are tested four years later, there should be a *tendency* for the children in the experimental program to perform better than the children who received no such intensive training. However, the argument is based on the idea that all things are equal. And when we deal with questions of intellectual growth, the question becomes a very troublesome one at best. It is one thing if we mean by "all things are equal" that the children are allowed to progress from the point at which they are and are taught according to the skills that they have at any given time. The "all things are equal" means something quite different if the children, regardless of the skills that they have at the time, are put through a lockstep program, which may in fact attempt to teach skills that have been taught or skills for which adequate preparation has not been provided. One would expect that the differences between the experimental children and the controls would be lessened — either because the experimental children are being relatively held back and are not receiving the opportunity to "develop" at an accelerated rate, or because both the controls and the experimental children would have an "equally" inadequate base for performing or "developing."

The measure of the "long range" effectiveness of an approach, unfortunately, is not a clean test of the program. It is a test of the program plus a host of intervening variables. Unless the nature of these variable is clearly specified, one would be at a loss to make strong inferential statements about the effectiveness of the experimental program. The results may lead the investigator to a number of spurious conclusions, such as: "The program shows a slight tendency to be better than the traditional program. . . ." "The gains that are realized through the program do not hold up over time. . . ." These conclusions may be spurious in the sense that different programs that intervene between the termination of the experimental program and the test of long-range effectiveness may change the outcomes astronomically, even if the same program is provided for both the control and experimental children.

In short, the position is this. Children get relatively smart if you teach more than they would be expected to be taught under "normal" conditions during a given period of time. Similarly children become relatively less smart if the rate of effective instruction is slowed. When children begin to regress, it means only one thing. They are not being taught at relatively the same rate that they had been taught before. It can mean nothing else. This is not to say that all of the instruction a child receives goes on in school. But it is axiomatic that if his performance begins to slow, he is not being taught at the rate that he had been taught. No statement of the child's genetic composition or capacity is implied. This statement is strictly one about what he is taught.

As an indication of what can be done with middle-class and disadvantaged children, I refer to the disadvantaged and middle-class children who graduated from the Bereiter-Engelmann kindergarten program in 1967. In one sense, this group received the most concerted instruction of any experimental classes from 1965-1969. Our best teachers were assigned to these children. We had no trainees working with the children (the instruction of whom tends to reduce by about one-third the rate at which the children are taught). Finally, there was a concerted attempt to make sure that the lowest performing children were taught. Program improvements were introduced. These were based on the performance of the low-performing children who had graduated the preceding year. Also during the school years of 1966–1967 a continuous program of program revision was adopted, based on the difficulties the lowest performing children were having.

The hypotheses investigated were:

1) effective instruction can dramatically increase the rate at which children are taught new behaviors that are relevant both to specific achievement tests (such as reading achievement) and more general achievement tests (such as the Stanford-Binet);

2) the children will achieve gains both in the first and second year of instruction if the instruction continues to teach skills at a faster-than-expected rate. The IQ drop noted during the second year of many preschool programs (after a 4–8 point first-year gain) is a function of poor instruction, not of the genetic capacity of the children;

3) any child can be accelerated to at least "average" if the instruction is effective.

The goal of the program was not to achieve mere statistical differences between experimental and control groups, while demonstrating no obvious differences in performance between the groups. Rather it was to achieve changes of such magnitude that there could be little doubt (statistically or otherwise) that the changes were a function of instruction. The basic goal was to bring all of the children to "average" on some of the more common measures of achievement, such as IQ measures.

Method

Subjects

The disadvantaged subjects for the present experiment were four-year-old culturally disadvantaged children who would be eligible for Head Start. The selection criteria were:

1) according to Warner ratings of occupations (1949) and housing ratings obtained through the City Planning Commissioner's office, subjects were from low socioeconomic homes (mean weighted S.E.S. in the low 40's);

2) subjects were four years old by December 1, in keeping with public school's entrance policies;

3) subjects did not have previous preschool experience;

4) children with gross physical handicaps and severely retarded children were excluded.

Subjects received Stanford-Binet tests and were divided into three groups—high intelligence, middle intelligence, and low intelligence. Children were assigned to the experimental and comparison classes, each class receiving the same proportion of highs, middles, and lows. Adjustments were made so that each class had approximately the same proportion of Negro-whites, and a nearly equal

TABLE 1
Characteristics of Disadvantaged Subjects

Subjects	Mean CA	Mean Binet IQ	White	Negro	Male	Female	Mean Weighted S.E.S.
Experimental N=15	4-3	95.33	6	9	8	7	41.93
Comparison N=15	4-3	94.50	11	17	15	13	42.50

number of male and female subjects. Fifteen children were assigned to the experimental group and twenty-eight to the comparison group. The composition of both groups is summarized in Table 1.

In addition to the disadvantaged subjects, eighteen middle-class four-year-old children were selected for a two-year program. These subjects were not given IQ tests upon entrance. They were introduced into the experiment to demonstrate the differential effects of the experimental program on children who might be considered developmentally impaired and those considered normal. The control for the middle-class children was a group of middle-class four-year-olds in a Montessori preschool. The middle-class subjects in the experimental program were referred by parents of the Montessori children as children whose parents would be interested in a Montessori type of education (or a relatively intensive preschool education). Some of the experimental children were on the Montessori waiting list. The selection criterion was adequate, it was felt, to identify children who should be roughly comparable to the Montessori children. The Montessori controls were the same age as the experimental children although the Montessori children had already had one year of schooling at the time the experimental children began their program.

Evaluation of Performance

The disadvantaged children were given Stanford-Binet IQ tests after the first and second year of instruction. The middle-class children received Stanford-Binets only after the second year of instruction. These tests were taken as a measure of "general achievement," primarily in language concepts. The disadvantaged and middle class subjects in the experimental program were also tested on reading, arithmetic, and spelling achievement with the Wide-Range Achievement Test (1965). This test was selected for evaluating the subjects because:

1) There are fewer potential sources of extraneous difficulty. The instructions are uncomplicated, and the tests are clearly tests of relevant content. For a child to achieve a given score in reading, he has to read—not circle words or follow complicated instructions.

2) No multiple-choice items appear in the Wide Range, which means that the children cannot receive a spuriously high score because they happened to guess correctly.
3) The Wide Range is capable of measuring achievement below the first grade level.

The disadvantaged children in the comparison group were not given achievement tests, because they were not taught skills in reading, arithmetic, or spelling. The Montessori group was given the Wide Range Test once, after they had finished their pre-kindergarten year.

Procedure

The subjects in the disadvantaged comparison class received a traditional preschool education. During the first year, they attended a two-hour-a-day preschool based as closely as possible on the recommendations of child development authorities. The emphasis of the program was on play, self-expression, developing a positive self image through role playing, and typical nursery-school activities. The preschool was outfitted with a sand table, dress-up corner, and a variety of toys. The child to teacher ratio was about 5 to 1. During the second year, comparison subjects went to public-school kindergartens.

The middle-class comparison group attended a Montessori program which operated for three hours a day. The emphasis of the program was on non-verbal manipulative activity. The child to teacher ratio was about 10 to 1.

During the first year (1965–1966) 15 disadvantaged children and 19 middle-class children were enrolled in experimental programs for two hours a day. Three of the disadvantaged children were not continued in the program the second year, and 12 middle-class children were not continued. The 12 remaining disadvantaged children and 7 middle-class children were integrated in a single class and received a second year of two-hours-a-day instruction. Throughout the two-year treatment, the child to teacher ratio was about 5 to 1.

The Experimental Program

The emphasis of the experimental program was on rapid attainment of basic academic concepts. The children attended three twenty-minute classes daily—a language concept class, an arithmetic class, and a reading class. For these classes, the children were divided into small (4–7 children) relatively homogeneous groups (based on performance in the classroom). For the remaining hour the children engaged in a period of semi-structured activities (writing, drawing, working reading-readiness problems), a music period (in which the songs were geared to the concepts presented in the language-concepts program), and a juice-and-toilet period.

Both the content and the style of teacher presentation used in the language, arithmetic, and reading sessions derived from a relatively simple principle: teach in the fastest, most economical manner possible. In language, the children were taught how to use a "minimum" instructional language. The language derived from the requirements of future teaching situations. In future teaching situations, the teacher would present physical objects of some kind and call the children's attention to some aspect of the objects—perhaps the color, perhaps the relative size, perhaps the position in relation to another object. The teacher would also "test" the children, primarily by asking a child (or the group) questions. The basic language that is needed for all such instructional situations is one that adequately describes the objects presented, that adequately calls attention to the conceptual dimension to which the teacher is directing the children, and that allows for unambiguous "tests" or questions.

The language that satisfies the requirements of the teaching situation consists of the two statement forms,

This is a ....

This .... is ....

with plural and *not* variations (This is not a ....), with *yes-no* questions (Is this a ball?), and with the *what* question (What is this?).

The basic language of instruction was taught during the first year. The language teachers did not use a rich variety of expressions; rather, they confined themselves to the basic patterns noted above until the children had demonstrated through performance that they understood the statements and the relationships between statements and questions.

The content that was taught in connection with the basic language consisted of names of common objects, polars (hot-cold, wet-dry, big-little, long-short, etc.), colors, prepositions, and hierarchical classes (vehicles, buildings, tools, clothing, weapons, etc.). After the children mastered the basic language they were introduced to tense variations, action verbs, conditional statements, *and, or, if-then,* and *only.* Finally, during the second year, the children were taught methods for defining words (through genera and differentia), and for describing complex figures and events.

In arithmetic, the children were taught how to count both objects and events (Tell me how many times I clap). They were then shown how addition, subtraction, and multiplication reduce to counting operations. For example, the children were shown how to translate such a problem as

$$5 + 3 = b$$

into the counting operation: start out with five; get more; get three more; and you end up with ....; we have to count them to find out.

All addition problems were reduced to this operation. The children were taught some rote facts, such as the series

$$1 + 1 = 2$$
$$2 + 1 = 3$$
$$3 + 1 = 4$$
$$\text{etc.,}$$

which articulates the relationship between counting and adding. There was, however, no attempt to teach the children an exhaustive set of arithmetic facts. Rather, the emphasis was on the operations that would lead to a correct solution.

The children were introduced to algebra and story problems early. To work algebra problems, the children used a variation of the translation they were taught for handling regular problems. For example, the operation for handling the problem

$$5 + b = 8$$

was: start out with five; get more; we don't know how many more, but we know we end up with 8. By starting out with five and getting more until he ends up with eight, the child discovers how many more he has to get.

The initial story problems were quite similar to the statement operations taught in connection with each type of problem. For example: a man starts out with five balls; then he gets more; he gets three more; how many does he end up with? The problem translates directly into the arithmetic statement:

$$5 + 3 = b$$

Problems were then systematically de-structured. That is, synonymous expressions were systematically introduced. After the children had learned to handle the basic story problems, the children were introduced to problems in which a man *has* so many balls, in which he *finds* so many balls, in which he *makes* so many balls.

The children were taught to read according to a modified ITA approach (the first version of DISTAR reading, 1969). The innovations which were introduced into the experimental program (primarily with the low performing children) had to do with the formation of long-vowel sounds and the convention for blending words. The following symbols were introduced to designate long-vowel sounds: $\bar{a}, \bar{e}, \bar{\imath}, \bar{o}$. The rationale for these symbols was that they could be introduced to help the child "spell" or sound out a variety of long-vowel words; after the children learned these words ($\bar{so}, \bar{go}, \bar{no}, \bar{he}$, $\bar{she}, \bar{me}, \bar{save}, \bar{fine}$, etc.), the diacritical mark could be dropped without grossly changing the total configuration of the word.

To help the children learn how to blend words, a skill disadvantaged children often fail to master after years of reading instruction, only continuous-sound words (*fan*, not *ban* or *tan*) were introduced initially. The children were taught how to proceed from letter to letter *without pausing.* In sounding out words in this manner, the children were actually saying the words slowly and could see the relationship between the slowly produced word and the word as it is normally produced. To assure adequate performance in blending, the children were given say-it-fast drills with spoken words. "Say it fast and I'll show you the picture: te-le-phone."

As early as possible, the children were introduced to controlled-vocabulary stories. After reading the stories, the children took them home. Taking stories home functioned as an incentive.

In each of the three study areas, the teachers proceeded as quickly as possible, but only after the children had demonstrated through performance that they had mastered the skills that they would be expected to use on higher-level tasks.

The above description of the curriculum is very rough. In each of the major subject areas, there are many sub-tasks. To teach each of the sub-tasks, the teacher had to take a number of steps. For example, to teach the children to blend words that are presented orally (a sub-task reading), the teacher first presented two-part words, each part of which is a word—ice-cream, motor-boat, snow-man. Next, the teacher introduced relatively long words the parts of which were not "words," sit-ting, shov-el, mon-ey, etc. Next, the teacher broke the words that had been presented into more than one part—mo-tor-boat, snow-ma-n, sh-ov-el. The teacher then introduced shorter words, broken into two parts: si-t, bea-t, c-ream, m-an. Finally, the teacher introduced short words that were divided into individual phonemes—m-a-n, s-i-t, sh-o-v-e-l. (A more detailed description of the arithmetic and language programs is contained in, *Teaching Disadvantaged Children in the Preschool* [1966].)

The Teacher's Behavior

The teacher had three primary roles in the experimental program:

1) she managed the group of children, keeping them on task;
2) she taught concepts;
3) she tested the children's knowledge of concepts before either providing a remedy or proceeding to the next task.

The general rules that guided her behavior in all three areas were:

1) don't assume that the children know anything unless they have demonstrated that they do;
2) get as many correct responses and as few incorrect responses out of the children during the alloted time as possible.
3) teach the behaviors necessary for successful classroom performance.

Since the goal of the program was to induce learning at an above average rate, procedures that induce learning at a normal rate were rejected. The teacher did not first "shape" behavior and then introduce academic content. She simultaneously introduced academic content and the rules of behavior associated with the content. The focus was always on the behavior related to the task, never on behavior in the abstract. The sanctions that were used were:

Negative:

Loss of food reinforcers (raisins, juice);

Additional work ("If you keep that up, you'll have to work when the other children are singing. You're here to work.");

Physical manipulation (tugging on an arm to secure attention, tapping leg, physically turning children around in seat, turning face toward presentation);

Scolding, usually in loud voice ("Cut that out! Sidney! Look here!");

Repetition of task, "Do it again . . . Again . . . Again . . . Again. Now, after this when I tell you to do it, you do it.").

Positive:

The use of reinforcing objects in presentations ("Look at that silly number. That's 7. I can't stand a 7. I have to erase it. Oh, there's another 7. I can't stand a 7 . . .");

The use of personalization ("Here's a story about, guess who! Sidney!");

The use of mock shock ("Everybody knew the answer. And I just said nobody will know the answer. You guys really fooled me.");

The use of praise ("Now, did you hear Sidney? He's a smart boy. Let's clap for him. He is smart and he's working hard.");

Dramatic change of pace (After having the children repeat a series of statements in unison, the teacher stops. The room is dead silent. The children look at each other and smile. Then they laugh. The teacher interrupts in a loud voice, "Okay, let's hear it: four plus zero equals four.");

A dynamic presentation of objects (During a two-minute segment, the teacher may present as many as 30 objects — some repeated — and as many questions. "Tell me about this . . . What about this . . . And this . . . And this . . .");

Positive speculations ("Boy, will your mother ever be surprised when she finds out that you can read. She'll say, 'I never knew you were so smart.' That's what she'll say.");

Exercises with a reinforcing pay-off ("Everybody likes to erase numbers, right? So I'll point to it and you can erase it.");

Relating positive comments of others — both real and fictitious ("Do you know what the man who watched you read said to me? He said, 'These are the smartest kids I've ever seen in my life.' And you want to know something? He's right.");

Food rewards ("If you do a good job on this problem, I'll give you some raisins. So work hard.");

Fooler games (The children say that when they add 3 to 4, they end up with seven. The teacher says, "So I write a 7." She writes a 4. The children object and the teacher pouts, "I guess I just can't fool you guys." The children laugh.);

Hand shakes ("Sidney did such a good job that I'm going to shake his hand. Good boy, Sidney.");

Special privileges ("Sidney is working so hard I'm going to let him be the teacher.");

Singling out a member of the group for praise ("Debby did it that time. I didn't hear the rest of you guys, but I sure heard Debby. Let's do it again; see if anybody else can say it like Debby does.");

Presenting take-homes ("Tell me this sound and you can take it home.").

The teacher had a full range of social and physical reinforcers at her disposal to use as the situation demanded. Some of the reinforcers listed as positive reinforcers are "acquired." Once taught, however, they proved to be quite effective in influencing behavior, increasing attention, and maintaining the kind of concerted participation that might be called "working hard."

Note that the primary reinforcing emphasis was on positive reinforcement. The teacher used herself as a model, "I'm smart. I can do this stuff." She used other children in the group as models. "Did you hear Sidney? He and I are the only ones who can do this. We're smart." She always tried to acknowledge the correct responses of every child in the group. "Hey, everybody did it that time. Boy you are smart kids. Good work, Tyrone. You too, Lisa."

Whenever the teacher taught, she utilized some of the reinforcing techniques noted above. She moved quickly so that the children were not confronted with a static presentation. She spoke loudly one moment, softly the next. She presented interesting examples of the concept, when the interesting aspects of the objects did not interfere with the concept being taught. She structured the presentation so that the children had a pay-off—perhaps playing a fooler game, perhaps a hand-out for correct responses.

In addition to the reinforcing aspects of the presentation, however, the teacher followed a basic rule in presenting any new concept: *The presentation must be consistent with one and only one concept.* When the teacher presented the concept big, for example, she used the statement forms, "This .... is big," and "This .... is not big," to describe a variety of object pairs—cups, circles, figures, men. Each of the objects in the pair was identical except for size. Through this type of presentation, the teacher demonstrated what the invariant *big* means. She further demonstrated the type of statement that is used to describe the invariant. "This cup is big; this ball is big; this man is big . . ."

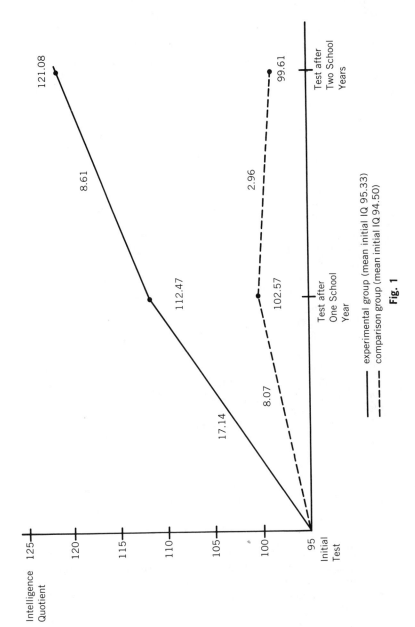

Intelligence Quotient

125 — 120 — 115 — 110 — 105 — 100 — 95 —

Initial Test

Test after One School Year

Test after Two School Years

121.08

8.61

112.47

17.14

8.07

2.96

102.57

99.61

experimental group (mean initial IQ 95.33)
comparison group (mean initial IQ 94.50)

Fig. 1

Because of the presentational requirements necessary to demonstrate a concept, the teacher presented a great many examples, usually 10-15 times more than are used by the average classroom teacher (a judgment based on the presentational suggestions of instructional programs designed for children in the early primary grades).

The teacher tested the children on various levels of performance. The first test of a concept was whether the children could find (or point to) the appropriate example. "Find the man that is big."

The next test was whether the children could answer *yes-no* questions about an object the teacher pointed to. "Is this ball big? . . . Is this ball big?"

The next test was whether the children could answer *what* questions. These are more difficult than *yes-no* questions because the children must supply the content word. "This ball is what? . . . Yes, this ball is *big.*"

The teacher usually introduced the various tests rapid fire, in no particular order. However, if the children had difficulty with a *what* question, the teacher would re-structure the tasks, starting with the *finding* task and working up to the *what* task. "Sidney, find the ball that is big . . . Good. This ball is big. Is this ball big? . . . Yes, this ball is big. This ball is what? . . . Yes, this ball is big."

While the rate at which questions are presented to the group and to individuals in the group varied with the tasks, the teacher often introduced as many as 20 questions a minute. She used the children's responses to these questions as indications of whether or not they had learned the concepts she was presenting. She geared her presentation *to the lowest performer in the group,* because the goal of instruction was to teach every child each criterion skill. (If a child consistently lagged behind the others in the group, he was moved to a slower group in which his performance was more consistent with that of the other members.)

Results

IQ Performance of Disadvantaged Subjects

The disadvantaged subjects in the experimental program achieved significantly greater Stanford-Binet IQ gains than the subjects in the comparison program. More important, the mean IQ of the experimental subjects after two years of instruction was 121.08, well above the mean of normal, middle-class children. The mean of the comparison group was 99.61 after two years of instruction.

Figure 1 shows the IQ performance of the experimental and comparison groups after one and two years of instruction. The comparison group achieved an 8.07 gain after the first year of instruction,

TABLE 2

Stanford-Binet IQ Performance of Disadvantaged Experimental
Subjects after One and Two Years of Training

Subject*	Entering IQ	IQ after One Year	First-Year Gain	IQ after Two Years	Second-Year Gain	Total Gain
MA	92	113	+21	123	+10	+31
TA	93	94	+1	103	+9	+10
TB	105	112	+7	121	+9	+16
MB	89	101	+12	131	+30	+42
(DB)	(82)	(112)	(+30)	——	——	(+30)
RC	99	116	+17	119	+3	+20
MC	86	105	+19	112	+7	+26
(NC)	(70)	(89)	(+19)	–	–	(+19)
BG	119	130	+11	139	+9	+20
BP	90	107	+17	112	+5	+32
SV	85	101	+16	108	+7	+23
RV	109	127	+18	138	+11	+29
DD	99	118	+19	129	+11	+30
DW	101	123	+22	118	−5	+17
(BW)	(111)	(139)	(+28)	——	——	(+28)
X Total	95.33	112.47	17.14	–	–	24.20
X One-Year Subjects	87.66	113.33	25.67	–	–	25.67
X Two-Year Subjects	97.25	112.25	15.00	121.08	8.83	23.83

*One-year subjects in parentheses

but had a loss of 2.96 points after the second year (which is typical of early compensatory programs). The experimental group showed a 17.14 gain after the first year and an 8.61 gain after the second year.

Table 2 shows the performance of the individual disadvantaged subjects after one and two years of instruction. The mean first year gain of those children who were retained in the program for two years was 15.00 (IQ 112.25). The mean gain of those who were not continued a second year was 25.67 (IQ 113.33). The total mean gain for the two-year subjects after the second year of instruction was 23.83.

There was only one instance of an IQ loss in either the first or second year of the experimental program. Subject DW had a second-year loss of 5 IQ points. None of the experimental subjects experienced an overall loss. The lowest gain was 10 points. The largest total gain was 42. The lowest IQ score after two years of instruction was 103 (subject TA). The highest IQ score after two years of instruction was 139 (subject BG).

Table 3 shows the IQ performance of the disadvantaged children in the comparison group after two years of instruction. Only 12 of the 28 control subjects scored higher than 103, the score of the lowest

TABLE 3

IQ Performance of Disadvantaged Comparison Subjects

Subject	Entering IQ	IQ after Two Years Training	Change
AB	94	115	+21
AC	118	115	−3
AD	83	94	+11
BA	90	92	+2
BB	88	74	−14
BC	76	93	+17
BD	92	90	−2
CR	101	87	−14
CS	82	95	+13
DB	85	100	+15
BC	79	83	+4
DF	107	97	−10
DJ	113	114	+1
DK	107	120	+13
EA	97	109	+12
EE	97	88	−9
EM	89	94	+5
EP	93	93	0
MA	92	107	+15
MB	88	87	−1
MC	79	87	+8
MR	93	89	−4
NB	94	104	+10
NS	91	106	+15
NT	101	109	+8
PA	109	127	+18
PB	111	117	+6
PR	97	103	+6
X	94.50	99.61	+5.11

IQ performer in the experimental group. Eight control subjects had overall IQ losses compared to no IQ losses for the experimental group. The highest IQ gain for the control group was 21 points, whereas the *mean* gain for the experimental group was 24 points.

Achievement Performance of Experimental Disadvantaged Subjects

Table 4 shows the achievement performance in reading, arithmetic, and spelling of the 12 subjects who finished two years of the experimental program. The mean reading achievement was grade level 2.60 with a range of 1.6–3.7. The mean arithmetic performance was 2.51 with a range of 1.4–3.3. The mean spelling performance was 1.87 with a range of 1.0–2.3. As Table 4 indicates, the correspondence between IQ scores and achievement scores is not perfect. Subject MC had the second highest reading achievement score and the highest spelling achievement score; yet, he had an IQ of only

TABLE 4

Achievement of Disadvantaged Experimental Subjects after
Two Years of Instruction

Subject	Grade Level on Wide Range Achievement Test			
	IQ	Reading	Arithmetic	Spelling
MA	123	2.7	2.2	1.8
TA	103	1.6	2.3	1.7
TB	121	3.1	3.3	2.2
MB	131	3.7	3.1	2.1
RC	119	2.7	2.9	2.0
MC	112	3.6	2.5	2.3
BG	139	3.1	3.3	2.1
BP	112	1.6	1.4	1.0
SV	108	2.0	2.2	1.7
RV	138	3.1	2.7	2.0
DD	129	1.7	2.2	1.9
DW	118	2.3	2.0	1.6
	121.08	2.60	2.51	1.57

112. Similarly, subject TB had achievement scores of 3.1, 3.3, and 2.2 in reading, arithmetic, and spelling; however, TB's IQ was only "average" for the group — 121.

The Middle-Class Subjects

Table 5 summarizes the performance of the middle-class experimental subjects. After the end of the first year of instruction, the mean achievements of the middle-class subjects in reading and spelling had nearly reached the level that was achieved by the disadvantaged subjects after two years of instruction. The middle-class children had achieved a mean grade level of 2.43 in reading and 1.72 in spelling (compared to 2.60 and 1.87 for the disadvantaged children after two years of instruction). At the end of the first year, the achievements of the seven children who continued in the program for two years was below the mean of those who did not continue for a second year in all achievement areas, but most noticeably in reading achievement. The mean reading achievement for the continuing children was 2.03 (compared to 2.68 for the one-year subjects); however, during the second year, continuing subjects progressed a full year and a half in reading achievement, terminating the program with a mean reading achievement score of 3.41 (eight tenths of a year above the mean of the disadvantaged children).

Interestingly enough, the IQ performance of the middle-class children was only about 2 points higher than that of the disadvantaged subjects, after two years of instruction. Both middle-class

TABLE 5

Achievement and IQ Scores of Middle-Class Subjects after
One and Two Years of Instruction

Subject	First-Year Achievement on Wide Range			Second-Year Achievement on Wide Range						IQ Stanford-Binet
	Read.	Ar.	Sp.	Read.	Gain	Ar.	Gain	Sp.	Gain	
MC	2.0	1.4	1.8							
M	3.5	2.0	2.0							
G	1.4	1.2	1.0	3.3	+1.9	2.2	+1.0	2.2	+1.2	113
H	2.0	1.2	1.9							
H	2.7	1.4	1.8							
H	2.7	1.2	1.9	3.9	+1.2	3.9	+2.7	2.3	+1.4	125
H	1.7	1.6	1.6	3.0	+1.3	2.9	+1.3	1.9	+.3	118
SK	2.7	1.2	1.9							
VK	3.4	2.0	2.1							
JL	1.8	1.4	1.5	3.4	+1.6	2.7	+1.3	1.8	+.3	121
KM	2.0	1.5	1.6							
BO	2.6	1.4	2.2							
CP	1.9	1.4	1.5	2.9	+1.0	3.1	+1.7	2.1	+.6	140
MP	2.2	1.4	1.8							
GS	1.7	1.4	1.2	3.5	+1.8	2.5	+1.1	2.0	+.8	110
KT	2.7	1.5	1.8							
T	3.0	1.4	2.1	3.9	+.9	3.1	+1.7	2.1	—	137
SW	3.7	1.6	1.3							
M of Two yr. sub.	2.03	1.37	1.54	3.41	+1.4	2.91	+1.5	2.06	+.66	123.43
M of One yr. sub.	2.68	1.51	1.84							
M of Total	2.43	1.46	1.72							

and disadvantaged subjects seem to be regressing toward a mean, but this mean is not IQ 100; it is considerably higher than that. This mean would be an operational indicator of the effective rate of "cognitive development" induced by the program in which these subjects were placed.

Table 6 shows the achievement scores of the middle-class comparison children after they had two years of instruction (having finished pre-kindergarten). The mean grade levels of achievement for the Montessori-trained children in reading and arithmetic (1.04 and 1.21) were well below the means of the middle-class experimental children after one year of Bereiter-Engelmann training (2.43 and 1.46). Significantly the Montessori-trained children did not "burst into reading."

Discussion

Performance of the Disadvantaged Children

The performance difference between the experimental and control disadvantaged children is most economically explained as a function

TABLE 6

Performance of Middle-Class Comparison Five-Year-Olds on
Wide Range Achievement Test after Two Years of Instruction

(Test, May 1966)

Subject	Reading	Arithmetic
DA	1.1	.7
SA	2.6	2.3
JD	.9	1.2
KD	.3	1.4
CE	1.3	1.0
CG	.5	1.0
MH	1.8	1.6
FJ	1.5	1.2
MK	1.3	1.4
EL	1.2	1.5
RM	1.2	1.5
JP	0	.3
LS	.9	1.2
AS	1.3	1.4
DV	.9	1.4
MV	.7	1.1
MW	.3	.6
X	1.04	1.21

of different training. The experimental children were taught new skills at a much higher rate than the children in the comparison program. The children in the comparison group were taught at a rate only slightly higher than the rate at which they would have been taught if they had not attended the preschool-kindergarten program. The experimental children, on the other hand, were taught at a rate substantially higher than they would have been taught if they had not been enrolled in the program.

There is a tendency in evaluating the effectiveness of instructional programs to look at the long-range effects of the program. While such effects are relevant, they are not of primary concern. The primary issue is: Can a program meet the educational objectives to which it addresses itself? In the case of the present experiment, can the program teach disadvantaged preschool and kindergarten children basic skills in reading, arithmetic, and the logical use of language? The IQ scores of the children reflects the effectiveness of the language program. The achievement scores in reading, arithmetic, and spelling indicate the effectiveness of the arithmetic and reading programs. Not one experimental child scored below 100 in IQ after two years of instruction (compared with 14 children in the comparison group who scored below 100). Not one experimental child scored below 1.6 grade level in reading or below 1.4 grade level in arithmetic. In other words, there were no instructional failures.

All of the children were taught. The mean performance in arithmetic and reading indicates that the experimental subjects, after finishing their kindergarten year, performed as well as "average" disadvantaged children two or three years older. Mean achievement scores of 2.5 in reading and arithmetic are not unusual for fourth grade disadvantaged children. If children can be accelerated by 3 years (as the present experiment indicates), the general failure in the public schools is not necessarily a result of the children's innate inferiority or lack of aptitude. It is a function of inadequate instruction.

Middle-Class Children

At the end of the first year of reading instruction, the middle-class children performed on the 2.43 grade level, which means that they had progressed nearly a year and a half during the first year. Those children who continued for a second year in the program had progressed one year (achieving a mean reading score of 2.03 at the end of the first year). During the second year, however, the children who continued gained nearly a year and a half in reading. These children, in other words, were progressing at a faster rate than older children in the public schools.

By the end of the second year, two disadvantaged children scored above grade 3.4 in reading, the mean of the middle-class children, and interestingly, both of these children were Negroes who entered with IQ's in the 80's (MB and MC). Four disadvantaged children scored on or above the middle-class mean in arithmetic. By the end of the second year, there were disadvantaged children in the top-performing study group and there were middle-class children in the B and C groups.

The middle-class children did not have to be taught many of the sub-skills that had to be programmed for the disadvantaged children, especially in reading. For example, the middle-class children did not have to be taught how to blend the letters of a word. The disadvantaged children required a great deal of practice in this skill. By the end of the second year, the advantaged children were almost a full year ahead of the disadvantaged children in reading, although the disadvantaged children made more than one year's progress during the second year.

The reading performance of the middle-class and disadvantaged children was achieved with only about 96 hours of classroom instruction. The amount of time devoted to reading in the regular school program during the first two years of instruction is probably 3–6 times greater. It seems evident, in terms of the performance of children, that the public schools do not utilize their available time to good advantage.

The performance of the experimental children may be viewed as an example of the "hawthorn" effect. However, in the program there was very little interaction with the parents and correspondingly little attempt to change the patterns of behavior in the home. There was a total of three parent meetings over a two-year period. During these meetings, the staff members emphasized the good performance of the children and tried to persuade the parents that their children were smart. Beyond this, however, nothing was done to change the conditions which affected the outside-school learning of the children. The changes that took place in these children were changes that resulted primarily from the experimental treatment in the classroom.

The Effects of "Pressure" on Younger Children

One of the traditional encumbrances to early formal education is the belief that the pressure resulting from such instruction will developmentally malform the children. While it is difficult to evaluate the effects of the present program on the children's personality, interviews with parents and observations of the children disclosed no ill effect. In the program there were virtually no tantrums or behavior problems beyond the second week, although at least two of the disadvantaged children were considered emotionally disturbed. The children participated, and they seemed to enjoy participation. All children engaged in the music period. All complied with the rules—but not as automatons. If the program failed in any respect, it did not adequately prepare the children for the kind of behavior-for-behavior-sake rules which they would encounter in school. During free time or semi-structured activities, the children talked freely to each other. They made observations and asked questions. When given the slightest opportunity, they would relate personal experiences and engage in conversations that were sophisticated for four and five-year-old children. In short, they showed no engrams from the "pressure" of the program. They worked hard; but the parents noted no regressive behavior, bed wetting, thumb sucking, nightmares, etc. In fact, if the parents' reports are to be taken seriously, the children had fewer emotional problems than any sample of "unpressured" children.

Perhaps the most noticeable characteristic of the children after two years of instruction was their confidence. The easiest way for the teacher to capture their interest was to announce a difficult task. "This is so hard I shouldn't even be giving it to little kids like you. You'll never be able to do it." The children would respond to this type of challenge by insisting, "We can do it! You'll see." Their confidence had been programmed through fooler games in which the children proved to be "smarter" than the teacher. The children exhibited confidence because they had received many demonstrations that they were competent and could succeed in challenging situations. They had surprised—even crushed—the teacher with their smartness. This is not to say that the children would be con-

fident in *all* situations or even all instructional situations. But they
had firm and realistically based confidence about their capacity to
perform in new-learning situations of the type presented in the
B-E program.

Summary

A group of disadvantaged four-year-olds and a group of middle-
class four-year-old children were taught intensively in the Bereiter-
Engelmann program for two years (the preschool and kindergarten
years). The group of disadvantaged children was comparable in
IQ and race-sex composition to a group of 28 children assigned to
a traditional nursery-school and kindergarten program. The middle-
class children were roughly comparable to a group of Montessori
trained four-year-olds. The major hypothesis tested by the program
was that children are taught at different rates; if the effective rate
at which disadvantaged and middle-class children are taught is
increased substantially, these children will perform at an above-
normal level, which means that the disadvantaged subjects may
become "superior" in specific areas of achievement.

The hypothesis was confirmed. The disadvantaged children in
the comparison group showed no particular advantage over children in similar compensatory programs, such as Head Start programs. The program failed to bring half of the children up to an IQ
of 100. The mean for the group was 99.6. The experimental program,
however, brought the IQ's of every child to above 100. The mean
IQ after two years of instruction was 121, with a range from 103 to
139. The mean achievements of the experimental group were:
reading, 2.6; arithmetic, 2.5; and spelling, 1.9. The scores are what
one would expect from 8-10-year-old disadvantaged children; the
experimental subjects, however, were six years old at the end of
the program.

After one year of instruction, the middle-class subjects had achievement scores of 2.4 in reading, 1.5 in arithmetic, and 1.7 in spelling.
The comparison group did not score as well in any of these achievement areas, although the comparison children had been in a Montessori program for two years at the time of testing. By the end of the
second year, those middle-class children who continued in the program scored 3.4 in reading, 2.9 in arithmetic, and 2.1 in spelling.
The mean IQ of the group after the second year was 123, only several
IQ points higher than the mean IQ of the disadvantaged experimental children.

The present experiments seem to indicate, rather strongly, that
the reason disadvantaged children fail in public schools is not necessarily that they are genetically inferior or developmentally impaired
but that they receive poor instruction. If younger children with
initially lower mental ages can achieve at an above-normal rate,

school-age disadvantaged children (who usually learn more rapidly) should have little trouble achieving at the rate of normal children in specific achievement areas if instruction is adequate.

The results of the experiment cast rather serious doubt on the validity of IQ measures as indicators of genetic endowment. The children in the experimental program were changed rather dramatically during the two years of instruction. Unless one knew what went on in the environment during these two years, one would be at something of a loss to describe these children. If we were to take their terminal IQ scores as indications of genetic endowment, then we would be faced with the difficult problem of explaining how the genetic composition of the children changed over the two year period. Was it something that they ate?

The fact that some of the children made relatively little progress compared to others may be taken as an indication of differential genetic influence. But again, this conclusion would be quite hasty. Before we can intelligently discuss what happened to individuals, we would have to know what went on in that individual's environment (his total waking environment and not merely the 2½ hours a day that he was in school) before we could presume to talk about the relative influence of the "environment" on intelligence. Probably everyone would agree that genetic endowment makes a difference, but the extent of that difference is far from obvious. At best, genetic influence seems to be a minor factor among the overwhelming majority of children.

35

Self-Instruction on How to Pick a Lock

How to Take this Program

"How To Pick A Lock" is a new kind of instructional book called a "program." It is so called because it is an example of the new training technique, "programmed instruction," which is founded on recent scientific breakthroughs in learning theory.

The subject matter is arranged in a number of small steps, called "frames," each of which presents a small part of the total information to be learned. Each frame builds on the information that has preceded it, and prepares you for the information that follows. Most of the frames present new information. Some review important facts or concepts that have been introduced earlier in the program.

Every frame provides a unit of learning to which you respond by writing the answer to a question, completing a sentence, or labeling a diagram. Although none of the questions is very difficult (because previous frames have prepared you to answer them), it does little harm if you get some of them wrong. However, if you read each frame carefully, paying close attention and following instructions, you will probably make very few errors.

Remember these Procedures as You Go Through the Program:

1. Be sure to actually *write in* the answers to each frame. Avoid the temptation to race ahead without writing in an answer even though you feel that you are sure of it and *could* write it in correctly.

Courtesy of Xerox Learning Systems, 600 Madison Avenue, New York.

2. As you are reading a frame and answering the question, keep the correct answer (which appears in the box just to the right) covered with the mask provided. Expose the correct answer only *after* you have written your answer.
3. Some frames provide review or repeat material that you may feel you already know. Answering the review questions may seem pointless or tedious. Nevertheless, these review questions are important to the learning process. It is necessary that you write in your answers as required.

1

This program will teach you to open certain locks without a key.

It is designed to teach you to:
(CHECK ONE)

☐ pick a fight

☐ pick a lock

☐ pick a pocket

> pick a lock

2

A self-instructional program is the result of a concerted effort by two groups of people: one group, the "programming staff," collaborates with another group, the "subject matter specialists."

Since there is little normal opportunity to become expert in the questionable art of lock-picking, which of the following would be most qualified as subject-matter specialists:

☐ chorus girls

☐ burglars

☐ pickpockets

> burglars

3
Old Fagin taught Oliver Twist to pick _____.

> pockets
> (or equivalent response)

This program will teach you to pick a(n) _____.

lock
(Don't laugh. It might come in handy when you are technologically unemployed.)

4

In order to pick a lock efficiently, quietly and with a minimum number of tools, you must first learn something about:

☐ the way locks are constructed

☐ the way nits are constructed

the way locks are constructed

(Remember, this is a program on lock picking, NOT nit-picking.)

5

Most locks consist of two cylinders, one inside the other. The outer cylinder is called the "barrel." The inner cylinder is called the "plug." Using this information, LABEL the diagram below.

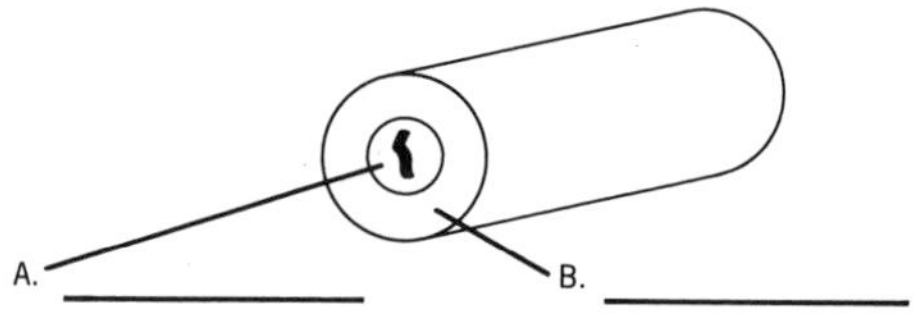

A. _____   B. _____

A. _____   B. _____

If a key is inserted into the lock and turned, it will cause the (☐ barrel ☐ plug) to rotate.

A. plug
B. barrel
   plug

6

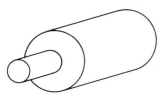

In the illustration above, which cylinder
is shown pulled forward from the
other? _____

What is the other cylinder
called? _____

the plug

the barrel

7

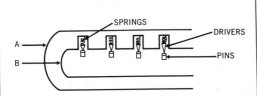

Above is a cross-sectional drawing of a lock.

Arrow A points to the _____.

Arrow B points to the _____.

In addition, other parts of the lock are
shown. As the key is inserted, it pushes
first against the _____.
In turn, there is a push against the
_____ directly above, and
thirdly, there is a push against
the _____.

barrel

plug

pins

drivers

springs

8

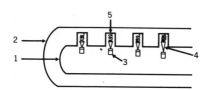

MATCH each part shown in the
illustration with its correct name.

A. barrel	1. _____	1. D
B. drivers	2. _____	2. A
C. pins	3. _____	3. C
D. plug	4. _____	4. B
E. springs	5. _____	5. E

9

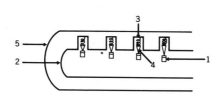

NAME the parts of the lock.

1. _____	1. pins
2. _____	2. plug
3. _____	3. springs
4. _____	4. drivers
5. _____	5. barrel

10

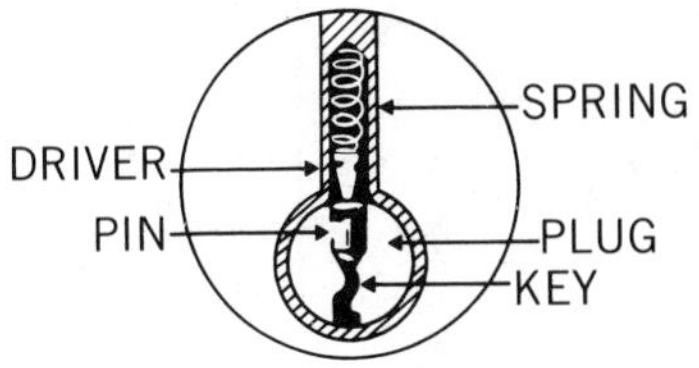

As shown in the illustration above, when the correct key is inserted into a lock, it applies just enough pressure to push which of the following into the barrel?

☐ the driver

☐ the pin

Which of the following remains in the plug and is free to move with it as the key is turned?

☐ the driver

☐ the pin

the driver

the pin

11

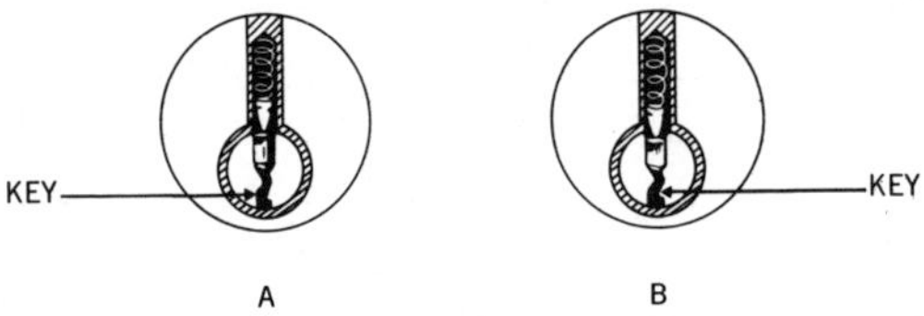

In which of the drawings above is the key applying too little pressure to push the driver all the way into the barrel?

☐ A ☐ B

B

12

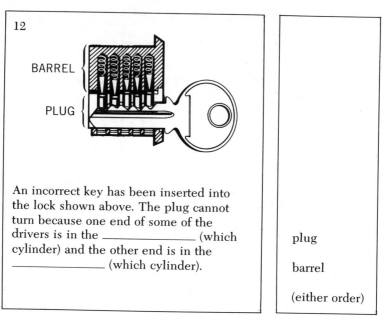

An incorrect key has been inserted into the lock shown above. The plug cannot turn because one end of some of the drivers is in the _____ (which cylinder) and the other end is in the _____ (which cylinder).

plug

barrel

(either order)

13

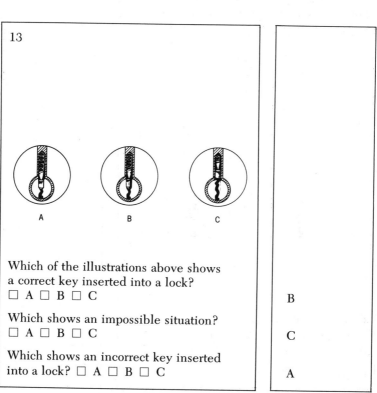

Which of the illustrations above shows a correct key inserted into a lock?
☐ A ☐ B ☐ C

B

Which shows an impossible situation?
☐ A ☐ B ☐ C

C

Which shows an incorrect key inserted into a lock? ☐ A ☐ B ☐ C

A

14

In order for a key to lift the pins inside a lock, its dimensions must be such that it can pass into the _____.

plug

The key above is wrong for the lock shown. It strikes against the _____ and cannot pass into the _____.

barrel
plug

15

BARREL

PLUG

The lock above can be opened, since the plug is free to turn. The plug can be turned because at the intersection of plug and barrel, the bottom edge of each (☐ driver ☐ pin) and the top edge of each (☐ driver ☐ pin) meet.

driver
pin

16

A   B

Which plug is not free to turn? ☐ A ☐ B

EXPLAIN your answer.

B

The plug is not free to turn because one driver remains in the plug.

(or equivalent response)

17

You have now, inadvertently, learned the fundamentals involved in picking a lock.

In order for a lock to open, what must turn? _____

the plug

In order for the above to occur, the lower edge of all the _____ must be lined up with the upper edge of all the _____ right at the outer edge of the _____.

drivers

pins
plug

The normal tool for lining up the internal parts of a lock is a(n) _____.

key

18

PREVIEW FRAME

In order to successfully pick a lock, one must align the lower edge of each
_____ and the upper edge of each _____ with the edge of _____.

driver
pin
the plug

Of course, all of the above must be done without the use of a(n) _____.

key

The following frames will teach you how to do this.

19

A   B

In diagram A, the plug has been given a slight turn. It is prevented from turning any further by the position of the _____.

Driver

How far up could the pin be pushed?

Until it hits the inside wall of the barrel.

In diagram B, the pin has been pushed up until it hits against the inside wall of the barrel. In this position, the plug

☐ is free to turn.

is free to turn.

☐ is not free to turn.

Which diagram above represents the goal of a lock-picker?

B

20

When a lock-picker, utilizing a hairpin, pushes the pin up, it will stop at the edge of the plug providing that the plug has been turned exactly enough. You can guess that the real artistry involved in successfully picking a lock lies in

☐ inserting the hairpin

☐ turning the plug just enough

turning the plug just enough

21

A lock-picker can use a hairpin to push the pins up to the lip of the barrel, providing that he has first given the plug a slight twist.

NUMBER the following events in the order in which a successful lock-picker would carry them out.

_____ push up the first pin

_____ push up the second pin

_____ push up the third pin

_____ push up the last pin

_____ twist the plug slightly

2

3

4

5

1

22

Once the lock-picker has lined up the tops of all the pins with the edge of the plug, what can he do to the plug?

He can turn the plug and open the lock.

(or equivalent response)

23

DESCRIBE the three steps involved in picking a lock.

Your response should include the following points:

1. Insert the hairpin and turn the plug slightly.

2. Push up the pins one by one until they are all lined up with the edge of the barrel.

3. Turn the plug to open the lock.

24

You have just taught yourself: (CHECK ONE)

☐ the legality of picking a lock

☐ the technique of picking a lock

☐ the risk involved in picking a lock

the technique of picking a lock

Individually Prescribed Instruction

Robert G. Scanlon

History of Individualization

A survey of the history of instruction indicates that formal learning began very much as an individual affair—that is, pupils came to school to receive instruction individually from the teacher. Education was generally for a select few; therefore, fewer pupils attended school. This made possible the provision of individualized instruction for those students. For example, in the one-room school, pupils proceeded on an individual basis rather than as intact groups. As educational advantages were offered to a larger proportion of the population, it became necessary to deal with pupils in grade-level groups, and individualized instruction diminished. Since then, however, as awareness of individual differences among pupils increased, many efforts were made to individualize instruction even within the context of schools offering mass education.

Individually Prescribed Instruction consists of planning and conducting with each student a program of studies that is tailored to his learning needs and to his characteristics as a learner. Team teaching, non-graded classrooms, programmed instruction, grouping, etc., all have attempted to administratively accommodate within the classroom these differences among individuals. Individually

Abridged from brochure issued by Research for Better Schools, Inc., Philadelphia.

Prescribed Instruction takes a new direction in this continuing search for ways to adapt instruction to the individual. In it, there have been taken into account such parameters of individual differences as rate of learning, amount of practice and, to some extent, preference for mode of instruction.

The Individually Prescribed Instruction at the Learning Research and Development Center, University of Pittsburgh, has currently adopted instructional materials in elementary mathematics and reading that are designed for the individual student.

(1) the rate of speed at which each child progresses depends upon his own capacities. He places himself on the continuum by taking both placement tests and pre-tests.
(2) the curriculum material is arranged in a sequential order called continuum. The assignments are given by a prescription to fit his individual needs. (A prescription is an individual lesson plan for each student each day.)
(3) the student's mastery of the curriculum is judged by curriculum-embedded tests and post-tests. He is required to perform at a level of 85%.
(4) the child works independently in most cases, thus building up his sense of responsibility and also his confidence in his own knowledge. He begins to realize that learning is a process that is dependent on his own participation and initiative.

Background Information

The Learning Research and Development Center

The Learning Research and Development Center at the University of Pittsburgh is the creator of Individually Prescribed Instruction and specializes in the research and basic design of new educational technology.

Individually Prescribed Instruction was developed by Drs. Glaser, Bolvin and Lindvall with the cooperation of the University of Pittsburgh and the Baldwin-Whitehall Public Schools of suburban Pittsburgh, Dr. W. R. Paynter, Superintendent of Schools.

During the school year of 1963–64, the Learning Research and Development Center and the Baldwin-Whitehall Public Schools of suburban Pittsburgh initiated an experimental project to investigate the feasibility of a system of individualized instruction in an entire K-6 school. This came about as a result of a series of prior exploratory studies, begun in 1961–62, designed to test preliminary notions on a smaller scale in single classrooms. The work started with the use of programmed instruction in an intact classroom. "Intact classroom" being defined as a classroom unit in which the teaching practices were oriented around the conventional grade-by-grade progression of learning.

As work proceeded, it soon became apparent that the significant individualization feature of programmed instruction could not be manifested unless the intact classroom changed its organization to permit a more flexible progression.

As a result, a second set of studies was instituted, using programmed instruction and other materials in a more flexible context. Out of this experience grew the Individually Prescribed Instruction project currently in progress, in which various combinations of instructional materials — including programmed materials, special workbook and test procedures — and teacher practices are being used for the purpose of adapting them to individual student requirements.

Distinguishing Fundamentals

1. Individually Prescribed Instruction must be based on a carefully sequenced and detailed listing of behaviorally stated instructional objectives. Such listings must be used in planning most other aspects of the program and should have the following characteristics:

   (a) Each objective should tell exactly what a pupil should be able to do to exhibit his mastery of the given content and skill. This should typically be something that the average student can master in such a relatively short time as one class period. Objectives should involve such action verbs as solve, state, explain, list, describe, etc. rather than general terms such as understand, appreciate, know, and comprehend.

   (b) Objectives should be grouped in meaningful streams of content. For example, in arithmetic the objectives will typically be grouped into such areas a numeration, place value, addition, subtraction, etc. Such grouping aids in the meaningful development of instructional materials and in the diagnosis of pupil achievement. At the same time, this grouping does not preclude the possibility of having objectives that cut across areas.

   (c) Within each stream or area the objectives should, to the extent possible, be sequenced in such an order that each one will build on those that precede it and, in turn, be a prerequisite to those that follow. The goal here is to let the objectives constitute a "scale" of abilities.

   (d) Within the sequence of objectives in each area the objectives should be grouped into meaningful sub-sequences or units. Such units can be designated as representing different levels in progress and provide break-points so that when a student finishes a unit in one area, he may either go on to the next unit in that area or may switch to a unit in another area. (For example, upon completing Level B Addition the pupil may either go on to Level C Addition or move to Level B Subtraction.)

2. Individually Prescribed Instruction lesson materials must be geared exactly to the instructional objectives and must be such as will permit pupils to proceed quite independently and with a minimum of direct teacher instruction.

3. A basic aspect of the Individually Prescribed Instruction procedure is a rather detailed provision for diagnosis of pupil skills and abilities and continuous monitoring of pupil progress.

4. The unique feature of Individually Prescribed Instruction is its requirement that each pupil's work be guided by written prescriptions prepared to meet his individual needs and interests.

5. As is true with most types of classroom instruction, the work of the teacher is a key aspect of Individually Prescribed Instruction. Among the essential aspects of the change in teacher performance are:

    (a) Little time is spent in lecturing to a group.
    (b) Much time is spent in evaluating the individual pupil's record, in diagnosing his needs, and preparing individual learning prescriptions for each child.
    (c) Most time is spent in helping individual pupils.
    (d) Frequent and regular staff conferences are held to discuss individual pupils, to evaluate and adapt materials and procedures, and to make future plans for each child on an integrated part of the system.

6. The success of any type of educational curriculum will rest ultimately on the quality of the experiences that the pupils have. Individually Prescribed Instruction is pupil-oriented instruction and differs from other procedures in terms of activities in which pupils are engaged.

Four Types of Diagnostic Instruments are Used in the Individually Prescribed Instruction

Type I—Placement Instruments

Placement instruments are used to assess mastery of units of work along the learning continuum. The placement instrument permits a general diagnostic evaluation of levels of work mastered for each unit of the learning continuum. The placement instrument has the following characteristics:

1. It measures mastery for each unit of work.
2. It measures the mastery level within each unit of work.
3. It provides a gross profile for any student along the learning continuum.
4. It is an indicator of strengths and weaknesses of a student.
5. It focuses on the area or areas that need further exploration for proper diagnosis.

Type II — Pre-Test Instruments

Since several specific objectives are assigned to each unit and level of work, an instrument is needed to discover which specific objective within the unit and level a student knows or does not know. The pre-test instrument is designed to measure the specific objectives within a specific unit and level of the learning continuum. The following functions of the pre-test should be noted:

1. A pre-test is needed for each unit and level of the continuum.
2. Determination of the proper pre-test to administer is based on the placement profile of each student.
3. The pre-test measures each specific objective within the one level and unit.
4. Pre-tests are assigned prior to any teaching within the unit.
5. Information as to strengths and weaknesses of each objective within the level and unit of work helps to determine the learning tasks.
6. The pre-test score can be considered the entering behavior of the student for each objective within a level and unit of work.

Type III — Post-Test Instruments

The post-test is an alternate form of the pre-test and is assigned at the end of each unit of work to determine the pupil's mastery of the unit. The post-test score also indicates growth in total behavior for each student of that level and unit.

Type IV — Curriculum-Embedded Test

The curriculum-embedded test is a short test of a student's progress toward a particular objective within a level and unit of work. It has two parts, the first part measures his progress toward a particular objective, and the second part serves as a short pre-test of his ability to achieve the next objective within the unit and level of work.

Research for Better Schools, Inc. Evaluation

Research for Better Schools, unlike the Learning Research and Development Center which operates in an experimental and research environment, functions in the world of the day-to-day problems of helping children learn. Its role is to test and perfect new innovations in the field and bring better education to the attention, and within reach, of the public schools of America. This of course means that considerable efforts must be made in testing, evaluating, and modifying educational innovations.

For Individually Prescribed Instruction, five major kinds of data are collected to answer the question — "How does this innovation work in the pilot schools?" These are information about:

(1) the materials
(2) the pupils
(3) the teaching staff
(4) the community setting
(5) the Individually Prescribed Instruction concept as an educational system.

How well the materials do the job of helping pupils learn, how adaptable they are to the varying requirements of each pupil, how the individual pupil responds to this different approach, how the teacher's role changes, what happens to the pattern of staffing the school, what the effects are on the community and its expectations of the "system," and the variations in cost are all carefully monitored and compared with other schools not using Individually Prescribed Instruction.

In this manner, Research for Better Schools is able to feed back to the Learning Research and Development Center information needed to improve the system (or, in some cases, Research for Better Schools makes the improvements itself) and to determine generally how effective this change in the school pattern really is under as differing circumstances as possible. Does Johnny really learn more? Quicker? Faster? Are there side effects that are undesirable? Do we need to retrain teachers? Is it possible to lower the cost of Individually Prescribed Instruction? The job of the laboratory only starts there, however. When these questions have been satisfactorily answered, the laboratory then changes its field-testing role to a dissemination role and sets up demonstration centers in a number of typical schools in a variety of typical communities. Other schools in other communities are invited to examine the program in action in a real setting much like their own school.

It is obvious that it takes time to answer the questions raised about how good a new program is. When these questions have been satisfactorily answered, the laboratory is then ready to respond in a different role. It is now the role of the laboratory to figure out strategies for diffusing the product to the public schools as rapidly as possible.

Research for Better Schools is currently field-testing the Individually Prescribed Instruction project in elementary mathematics and reading in four elementary schools located in Quakertown and Harrisburg, Pa., Trenton, N.J., and Dover, Delaware. It has also established the McAnnulty School in Baldwin-Whitehall Twp., Pa. as its demonstration and teacher-training school.

Obviously several years will be required before Research for Better Schools can say Individually Prescribed Instruction is ready for adoption and use.

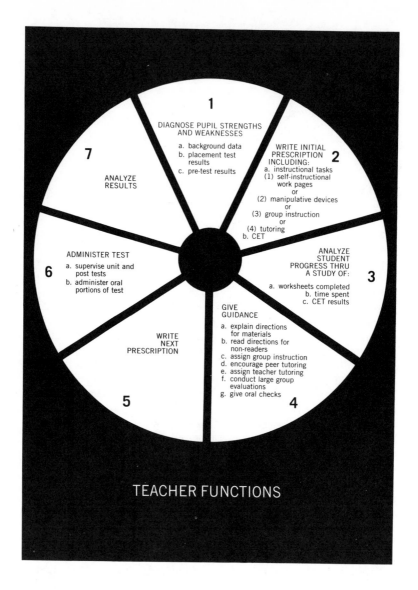

1

DIAGNOSE PUPIL STRENGTHS
AND WEAKNESSES

a. background data
b. placement test
   results
c. pre-test results

7

ANALYZE
RESULTS

2

WRITE INITIAL
PRESCRIPTION
INCLUDING:
a. instructional tasks
(1) self-instructional
   work pages
   or
(2) manipulative devices
   or
(3) group instruction
   or
(4) tutoring
b. CET

3

ANALYZE
STUDENT
PROGRESS THRU
A STUDY OF:

a. worksheets completed
b. time spent
c. CET results

6

ADMINISTER TEST

a. supervise unit and
   post tests
b. administer oral
   portions of test

4

GIVE
GUIDANCE

a. explain directions
   for materials
b. read directions for
   non-readers
c. assign group instruction
d. encourage peer tutoring
e. assign teacher tutoring
f. conduct large group
   evaluations
g. give oral checks

5

WRITE
NEXT
PRESCRIPTION

TEACHER FUNCTIONS

Math & Reading Curriculum

The mathematics curriculum includes thirteen specific areas—numeration, place value, addition, subtraction, multiplication, division, combination of processes, money, time, system of measurements, geometry, fractions, and special topics. A total of 400 specific objectives have been established as part of the mathematics

Mathematics Continuum

level C	level D
Numeration	
1. Reads, writes numerals 1-200. Sequence from any starting point. 2. Supplies number 1 more, or less, or in between—1 to 200. 3. Skip counts 2's, 5's, 10's to 200.	1. Reads, writes to 1,000. Any point. 2. Skip counts, by 3's, 4's from any point. 3. (a) Identifies and reads decimal fractions to hundredths. (b) Converts decimal numbers to fractions and other forms. (c) Fills in missing single decimals.
Place Value	
1. Identifies place value of the units, 10's, 100's to 200. Indicates >, <. 2. Writes numbers, columns 100's, 10's, units.	1. Identifies units, 10's, 100's, 1000's. Uses >, <. Writes number before, after to 1,000. 2. Writes numerals, expanded notation, to 1,000. Regroups, renames. 3. Uses number families, bridging, to work addition, subtraction problems. 4. (a) Gives place value of decimal fractions in fractional or other form. (b) Makes place value chart.
Addition	
1. Use of associative principle. 2. Adds 2 numbers—sum of 20. 3. Sums of 2 or 3 numbers, no carrying. 4. Uses >, <, =. Equations, 2 step, combining add-subtract. 5. Works column addition—3 or more addends, sums to 20.	1. Demonstrates mastery, sums thru 20. 2. Does column addition—no carrying. 3. Finds missing addends—3 single digits. 4. Uses words, sum, addend—labels part. 5. Adds, carrying to 10's using 2 digit numerals, 2 or more addends. 6. Adds, carrying to 10's, 100's, using 3 digit numerals, 2 or more addends. 7. Adds, carry 10's, 100's, using 3 digit numerals, 2 or more addends. 8. Finds sums, column addition. Using 2 or more addends of 1 digit.
Subtraction	
1. Subt. problems—numbers to 18. 2. Subt. 2 digit—no borrowing. 3. Finds missing addend—2 single digits.	1. Mastery subtraction facts, numbers to 20. 2. Subtraction no borrowing—3 or more digits. 3. Subtraction borrowing 10's place—2 digits. 4. Subtraction borrowing 10's, 100's—3 digits. 5. Subtraction borrowing 10's, 100's—3 digits.

continuum. The reading curriculum has been developed by sequencing the specific reading skills that need to be mastered by each youngster. The skills are worked into units and levels of work much the same as in the mathematics continuum. The beginning reading program is built around the first fourteen programmed texts by Sullivan Associates. This material is supplemented by Center-prepared records and special work sheets. A second phase of the reading program is built around paperback published materials. The third phase of reading is the independent reading program, in which children select their reading material from the school's library. During the independent phase of the reading program, students are also working on prescribed skills material.

Glossary of IPI Terms

1. Individually prescribed instruction
   An instructional system which attempts to adapt learning to the needs of the individual.
2. Continuum
   The sequence of behavioral objectives outlining the curriculum.
3. Units
   Subdivisions of the mathematics, reading, or science program. For example, there are thirteen specific units comprising the mathematics continuum. These include numeration, place value, addition, subtraction, multiplication, division, combination of processes, fractions, money, time, systems of measurement, geometry, and special topics.
4. Behavioral objectives
   Stated instructional goals in terms of the behavior that one desires the learner to demonstrate.
5. Placement tests
   The diagnostic instruments which assess mastery for each unit of work and provide a gross profile of any student along the learning continuum.
6. Pre-test
   The diagnostic instrument which measures the student's strengths and weaknesses in his progress toward each objective within the level and unit of work. It can be considered the entering behavior of the student for each objective and helps to determine the learning tasks.
7. Post-test
   This instrument is an alternative form of the pre-test and is assigned at the end of each unit of work to determine mastery.
8. Curriculum-embedded test
   This short test provides specific data on mastery of each specific objective within the learning continuum. It provides a limited pre-test of the following objective within a level and unit of work.

9. LEVELS

A way of categorizing the difficulty of the objectives within the continuum with A being the simplest and I the most difficult.

10. PRESCRIPTION

A plan for an individual to improve and master a particular objective or skill on the learning continuum.

11. RATE OF LEARNING

The time it takes a student to master each objective or unit.

37

A Programmed System of Instruction

Fred S. Keller
Western Michigan University

No one needs to be told today that the requirements for survival in the modern world are getting more complex, or that better education is needed everywhere. Our old ways are no longer good enough, and we all know it. The pressure on us to improve matters in this country, in our own schools, and at every level of instruction, is mounting daily.

From *Behavior Modification Monographs*, 1(3), 1970, Roger Ulrich, ed. Kalamazoo, Michigan: Behavior Development Corporation.

This paper was originally presented, with minor changes, as an invited address to the Autumn Conference of the Pacific Northwest Association for College Physics, at the University of Washington, Seattle, on October 25, 1968. The system of instruction described by Professor Keller in this Monograph is now being used at a number of educational institutions in this country, mainly in psychology courses at the college-freshman level. It should be apparent, however, that an enterprising teacher, with sufficient freedom and administrative support, might extend its application to other subject matters and at other educational levels. Indeed, the first known anticipation of this procedure was in the teaching of arithmetic to children by practice teachers of the San Francisco State Normal School in 1912. More recently, the method was adapted successfully by Professor J. L. Michael of Western Michigan University in teaching behavior principles to high school juniors.

With carefully written work units, study questions, and alternate test forms; with proctors selected from the superior-student group and rewarded by Honor Society status or something comparable, it should be possible for a qualified teacher to try out a go-at-your-own-pace course with little or no extra expense, for students of widely differing backgrounds and capacities.

The problem that we face will not, I think, be solved by increasing the salaries of the teachers, by raising the standards of their education, or by bearing down upon their pupils. I don't think it will be solved by imitating the procedures of a few prestigious institutions, by publicizing the methods and achievements of earlier times, or even by an appeal to Yankee ingenuity in the fields of automation and visual aids. These things have all been tried, and are not without value, but we need something more, and the continued existence of our jobs may depend upon our finding it.

The system of college instruction that I will here describe is one of a number of current attempts being made in this country to apply our knowledge of learning process to the problem of effective education. I don't offer it as the best of all programs. But, in comparison with the kind of system it was designed to replace, I think it merits the consideration of any teacher of science who seriously desires to improve his efficiency, his professional status, and the pleasure he gets from his work.

In earlier accounts of this system, it has been called *personalized, programmed,* and *proctorial.* No one of these names is quite satisfactory, but they all apply in some degree, for reasons that will soon be clear. (I prefer *personalized,* although it suggests monograms on bathroom towels). The system originated in 1963, as a result of some brain-storming by two Brazilian and two American psychologists[1] who had been asked to set up a department of psychology at the new University of Brasilia and had been given a free hand in the design of curriculum and teaching procedures. It was first tried out at Brasilia in 1964 and, a few months later, in this country, at Arizona State University. The Brasilia project was terminated in its second semester because of a political upheaval within the University, but has since been revived in part at several other institutions in that country. The method is still in use at Arizona State and has been adopted, or is being tested, in a growing number of educational programs in the United States.

The way the system operates can best be understood, perhaps, if you will try to imagine for a moment that you are once again a college freshman. Assume that you have just arrived, along with about a hundred other students, at the first meeting of a course in elementary psychology, with laboratory. This is a one-term course, with 75-minute class meetings scheduled for Tuesday and Thursday mornings (a Wednesday afternoon and Saturday morning period will soon be added in response to student demand).

Since this is the first meeting of the class, you probably arrived late and missed some of the Professor's opening remarks (and a little cup of coffee, if you're in Brazil), but one of the assistants greets you

---

1. J. G. Sherman, professor of psychology at Arizona State University, was one of the two Americans involved in this venture.

pleasantly and gives you a mimeographed hand-out, from which I shall now quote:

> This is a course through which you may move, from start to finish, at your own pace. You will not be held back by other students or forced to go ahead before you are ready. At best, you may meet all the course requirements in less than one semester; at worst, you may not complete the job within that time. How fast you go is up to you.
>
> The work of this course will be divided into 30 units of content which correspond roughly to a series of homework assignments and laboratory exercises. These units will come in a definite numerical order, and you must show your mastery of each unit, by passing a "readiness test" or carrying out an experiment, before moving on to the next.
>
> A good share of your *reading* for this course may be done in the classroom, at those times when no lectures, demonstrations, or other activities are taking place. Your classroom, that is, will sometimes be a study hall.
>
> The lectures and demonstrations in this course will have a different relation to the rest of your work that is usually the rule. They will be provided only when you have demonstrated your readiness to appreciate them; no examination will be based upon them; and you need not attend them if you do not wish. When a certain percentage of the class has reached a certain point in the course, a lecture or a demonstration will be available at a stated time, but it will not be compulsory.
>
> The teaching staff of your course will include proctors, assistants, and an instructor. A *proctor* is an undergraduate who has been chosen for his mastery of the course content and orientation, for his maturity of judgment, for his understanding of the special problems that confront you as a beginner, and for his willingness to assist. It is he who will pass upon your readiness tests as satisfactory or unsatisfactory. His decision will ordinarily be law, but if he is ever in serious doubt, he can appeal to the classroom assistant or even the instructor, for a ruling. Failure to pass a test on the first try, the second, the third, or even later, will not be held against you. It is better that you get too much testing than not enough, if your final success in the course is to be assured.
>
> Your work in the laboratory will be carried out under the direct supervision of a graduate laboratory assistant, whose detailed duties cannot be listed here. . . . There will also be a graduate classroom assistant, upon whom your proctor will depend for various course materials (assignments, study questions, special readings, and so on), and who will keep up to date all progress records for course members. The classroom assistant will confer with the instructor daily, aid the proctors on occasion, and act in a variety of ways to further the smooth operation of the course machinery.
>
> The instructor will have as his principal responsibilities:

(a) the selection of all study material used in the course; (b) the organization and the mode of presenting this material; (c) the construction of tests and examinations; and (d) the final evaluation of each student's progress. It will be his duty also to provide lectures, demonstrations, and discussion opportunities for all students who have earned the privilege; to act as a clearinghouse for requests and complaints; and to arbitrate in any case of disagreement between students and proctors or assistants. . . . .

All students in the course are expected to take a final examination, in which the entire term's work will be represented. With certain exceptions, this examination will come at the same time for all students—at the end of the term. . . . The examination will consist of questions which, in large part, you have already answered on your readiness tests. Twenty-five percent of your course grade will be based on this examination; the remaining 75 percent will be based on the number of units of reading and laboratory work that you have successfully completed during the term. . . . .[2]

Together with this description and a few items of information concerning course machinery, staffing, and study materials, you are handed your first work unit—your first assignment—and listen to a few inspiring words from your instructor. He outlines the rules of the game once more, for those who didn't read them or didn't believe them; he expresses his complete faith in your maturity and willingness to work for what you get; he promises you a square deal; he tells you of his great expectations; and he ends by suggesting that you drop the course at once if the prospects don't appeal.

Along with the unit assignment, you receive a set of *study questions* and some advice on how to use them. These questions will vary in number with the degree of their generality and the type of reading that they cover, but they are designed to include every point that your instructor thinks essential in the reading assignment (and to exclude, perhaps, some items that he thinks are of lesser merit).

You are now on your own in the course, although you may not really believe it. You are somewhat disturbed by your "freedom," the amount of testing that you see ahead, the talk about "excellence" and "perfection," the apparent absence of lectures to clarify your reading, and the general strangeness of everything. On the other hand, there are the positive features of non-compulsory lecture attendance, going at your own speed, and of getting your first A or B. You decide to hang on, at least until the drop-out dead-line.

The course description tells you exactly what steps to take from this day on. First, you are to study your assignment until it is fully

---

2. This quotation is also to be found in F. S. Keller, "Good-bye, Teacher. . . ." *Journal of Applied Behavior Analysis*, 1968, 1, 79–89 (Copyright 1968, Society for the Experimental Analysis of Behavior).

mastered—until you are sure that you can cope successfully with all the study questions of the unit. You can do this work at home, in your dormitory, or in the classroom (which was recommended by the instructor). Others will be studying in the classroom, and the study-hall proctor will always be on hand to help if you have trouble with any part of the assignment. Besides, the study hall will be the source of announcements and new materials for the course. You decide to work at home.

When you are ready for testing, you report to your study-hall proctor, who doesn't seem surprised to see you, or ask you where you have been. He sends you immediately to the testing room or asks you to wait a moment until a place is ready. (The number of students to be tested at one time will depend upon the current availability of proctors for grading, and a pile-up of students waiting to be tested is preferable to a pile-up waiting to be graded).

When you get to the testing proctor, you will receive one of the four or more test forms for the unit on which you have been working. He will also hand you your blue book, one or two pages of which you will use in answering your test questions. In ten or fifteen minutes, when you have completed your answers, you will return your test form to the testing proctor. He will record the event and send you, with your blue book, into the proctor's room next door, for grading. There you will find, in a special cubicle or at a special table, the grading proctor to whom you have been assigned for the duration of the course, to whom you will always report except on those occasions when a substitute may be necessary.

The next step is the important one. The proctor, with you seated beside him, will grade your readiness test. First, he scans the test quickly, checking each wrong answer with his pen. If there are too many of these, the grading operation stops right there and you are advised to study further before coming to be tested and graded; this test won't be counted. (You will also be told not to come back until a certain time has elapsed—say at least 30 minutes. This is not only to encourage studying, but also to keep you from "shopping around" among test forms or gaining familiarity with all the available questions).

However, if you have made but two or three errors, you will be given a chance to defend your answers. If your defense is impressive and if a restatement of the questions evokes satisfactory replies, your proctor will add an O.K. to his earlier check marks to indicate a change of grade. If your defense turns out to be inadequate, he will discuss the matter with you, recommend the restudy of certain points, and send you away with the promise that your failure will not weigh against you, either then or in the future. In case all the answers were initially correct or deserve an O.K., he will probably congratulate you, record your success, and send you back to the study hall for your next assignment. If time permits, he may ask you why you answered one or two questions as you did, just to probe the depth of your understanding or to get acquainted. He keeps your blue book when you leave, and will pass it along to the assistant or the instructor at the end of the period, for inspection and recording.

This sequence of events will be repeated for the remaining units of the course, with review assignments and laboratory exercises introduced at appropriate times along the way. The number of tests that you will require for each unit may vary considerably, but the average may be no more than two. When the last one has been passed, you can arrange the date of your final examination. Beyond that, you are free to turn to other matters or, ideally, to begin another course of study under a similar program of advancement.

This learning situation is in some respects similar to that which one meets in the field of programmed textbooks, teaching machines, and computer-based instruction. There is an initial analysis and organization of subject matter; there is great concern for the terminal behavior aimed at in each student; there's the provision for individualized progression, as each basic step is mastered; and there is a feedback to the instructor which enables him to improve the program.

In this case, however, the steps are not "frames" in a "set"; they are more inclusive, and better described as homework or laboratory assignments. The "response" is not simply the completion of a prepared statement by filling in a work or phrase; it is the resultant, you might say, of many such responses, and better described as the understanding of a principle, a formula, a concept, or a technique. Advance within the program is not based simply upon the appearance of a confirming word or presentation of the next frame, but involves a *personal interchange between the student and his peer or his better.*

The use of a programmed text, a teaching machine, closed-circuit television, or a computer is quite possible within such a system. It may even be desirable. (One of the textbooks was programmed in the course I've just described). But such devices are not at present to be equated with the course itself.

As I mentioned before, a relatively minor role is given to lectures and demonstrations in such a system as this. Their purpose here is primarily motivational. They are not central to the educational process and they could be eliminated entirely without serious damage. Yet they are not useless. They permit an instructor to appear at his inspirational best before an unusually receptive and well-prepared audience. He is free to speak about some favorite topic, some newly-discovered fact, some experiment in which he is engaged, or almost anything he wishes, without feeling that he should be doing something more useful or significant. Also, they permit the students to see their instructor in action, to sample his style and get the flavor of his thought, under the best of circumstances. No threat of future quizzing hangs over their heads, nothing important rides on

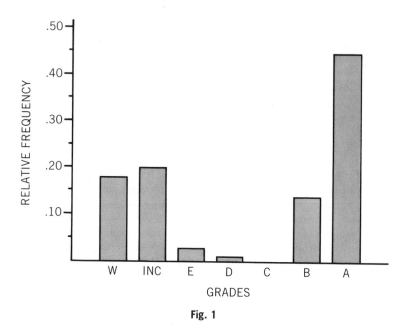

Fig. 1

their failure to catch every detail of his message, and no struggle with note-taking distracts them from the flow of the instructor's words or the sequence of events in the show that is going on.

By ordinary standards, lectures, demonstrations, and the like within a programmed course are short in duration (perhaps 20 or 30 minutes) and few in number (eight or ten in a semester). If a lecture or a demonstration, no matter how interesting, competes with an opportunity to pass a test, or even to prepare for one in study hall, it will attract only a handful of students who have earned the right to come, and even these may not repeat. If a lecture is announced in advance, with a catchy title, it may encourage a flurry of test-taking to qualify for the event—which may then be unattended. By increasing the available hours per week in which tests can be taken and graded, by placing a ban upon test-taking while the speech or demonstration is in progress, and by making each performance as interesting as possible, an instructor may come to draw a modest crowd. In the process, however, he is likely to conclude that other features of the course are more important, and that the lure of the lecture has been vastly overrated.

Optimally, in a well-programmed course, every student should come out with an A. In practice, however, this is never fully realized. Some students may fail to withdraw from the course when they should have; others may have put off their final examination too

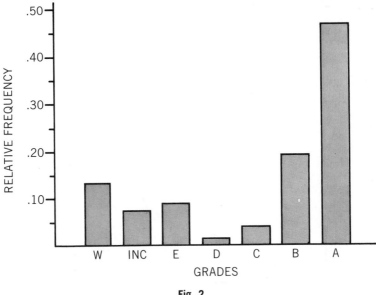

Fig. 2

long and done insufficient reviewing, thus bringing their course grade down to a *B*; and a less-than-*A* grade may also be given when a student fails to complete his course units within the term and does not wish to use the Incomplete.

These factors have the effect of producing distributions like that shown in Figure 1. This is based upon data from a class of 94 students at Arizona State University, in the Winter Term of 1966–67. In this course, *Withdrawals* were possible at a very late date, because of excessive enrollment in the course, and the rating of *Incomplete* was easily obtained. (About half of these Incompletes were later removed.)

Figure 2 represents the grade distribution for 208 students in the Spring Term of 1966–67 at the same institution. *Withdrawal* was not especially encouraged, hence there was an increase in the number of course failures (*E*'s); and *Incompletes* were possible only after a review by the instructional staff of each individual petition.

Figure 3 (darkened bars) gives the grade distribution for a class of students at Queens College of the University of the City of New York. Essentially the same course material was covered and the same quality of performance was demanded as in the Arizona State classes, but no *Incompletes* were used and the category of *Failure* includes some cases that would ordinarily be counted as *Withdrawals*. In quality of performance, this class is perhaps the best of any that has yet been taught by our present method.

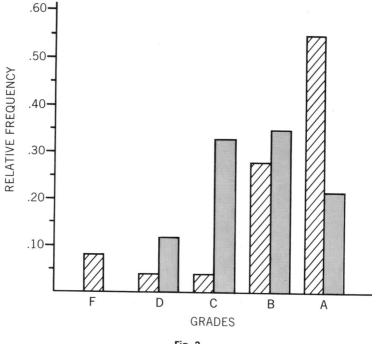

Fig. 3

In this connection, I would like to say something about the *In-complete*. There are many reasons why a student's work in any course of study may be interrupted or slowed down. *Illness* has traditionally been a good one, and *"outside work"* has been grudgingly accepted on occasion. But there are others that deserve recognition in any educational institution that pretends to an awareness of the individual needs of its students, or which sponsors activities that conflict with fulltime devotion to the academic ideal. *Extra-curricular* activities of one kind or another—glee club, dramatics, publications, athletics, recognized social functions, even the demands of married life and other personal-social relationships—these ought also to be considered. They should not jeopardize the grades of all but a favored few who are able to handle them and get Phi Beta Kappa too.

In a programmed system of instruction, many of these slow-downs and interruptions may be offset by a little extra effort when the critical season has passed, but some of them may leave the student in arrears when the term comes to its end. He must then settle for a final grade that represents neither his ability nor his motivation; or he must be given an *Incomplete*. Until the day when letters and numbers are no longer employed as they are now and when a course of study is terminated whenever its requirements are met, the

Incomplete has value. Properly administered, it need not be abused, and the bookkeeping problems it may generate will not be serious.

Related to the question of when a course *ends* is when it *begins.* Modern academic practice asks students to line up together at some starting point to await the same starting gun. In a programmed system, wherein each student moves at his own speed, with no premium placed on group activity or group assembly, there is little reason to select one time for starting a course in preference to another. More latitude in this respect might also give instructors freedom from the requirement that all courses be of the same duration, or a multiple thereof. It might even relieve the university or college of peak pressures of registration and record-keeping.

Ours is an interlocking system of instruction. Each person involved gets his rewards from the behavior of the others. Each one's work produces the task for the next in line. The student provides work for the proctor; the proctor and the student give the assistant his data; the assistant provides feedback from the proctor and the student for the instructor; and the instructor starts the cycle all over again. It is a system of "mutual reinforcement" and, in my opinion, no system is a good one unless it is just that—mutually rewarding for all participants.

The proctor is the new link in this chain. He is the focus of critical attention and the object of suspicion. Perhaps I ought to say a few more words about him—about what he should do, and should not do, in performing his function.

First, his principal job is that of decreasing the gap of understanding between the student and the assistant or the instructor—a gap that is sometimes very wide. He can do this because he has a repertory of behavior that is intermediate between the two with respect to the subject matter of the course. He may find logic in an answer that an instructor would never have perceived; he may restate a question in a way that brings out real knowledge; he may, by example or parallel statement strengthen a student's grasp of a concept. He provides individualized consideration that a student may never have had before.

He is not a teacher or a coach, in the usual sense of these words. He should not give lectures, nor should he try to drill students in the "one right answer." But he may check on test responses that clearly hit or miss the target; he may raise objections to other answers and he may evaluate their defense (an evaluation that will be in turn evaluated by the assistant or instructor); he may clarify points on which he is well informed; and he may direct students to certain reading, or to consultation with staff members.

He is helped in his work by (1) his experience with a similar course in which he was recently successful; (2) a weekly proctors' meeting in which every question on every test may be discussed; (3) a handy list of acceptable answers to these questions, often coupled with a brief discussion of the point involved; and, usually, (4) relevant knowledge from advanced courses within the same subject-matter field.

His work is well rewarded. There is recognition from his superiors, especially his instructor; respect from his friends and family; satisfaction from his increased grasp of the course material; and perhaps a couple of points of academic credit. But his principle satisfactions come from his daily interaction with his students. With them he enjoys a status which is commonly denied to graduate assistants and faculty members. From them he receives close attention, respect, even affection, as the course goes on. Every step ahead for them becomes a source of pleasure for him. It is no wonder that proctors will often work overtime without complaint, that they will volunteer for a second term of duty, or that they will work without pay — either in terms of money or academic credit.

I have been speaking of the *grading* proctors, ten or more of which would be needed for a class of 100 students. There is also a *testing* proctor and a *study hall* proctor. The former is not a proctor at all, in the sense of furthering instruction. His work could be done by any reliable clerk with a grade school education. If no such clerk is available, grading proctors may take their turn as testing proctors in regular rotation, each carrying a bit of this noneducational load.

The study hall proctor is more important. He is the one who stands between the textbook and the student, in the same way that the grading proctor stands between the student and the instructor. He clarifies obscure passages, difficult operations, unintelligible references, and the like. His work load will depend on the adequacy of the textbook and the study questions, but it will not be overwhelming. He serves a small percentage of the class, usually the weakest members, and the number of cries for help will decrease as the course gets under way and the students gain in self-reliance.

The study hall proctor may be selected on the basis of course history, achievement, or special aptitude. Or he may be drawn from the larger group in regular rotation, regardless of special qualifications. The first procedure would seem to be preferable, but we have no good data for deciding. The study hall proctor who "acts like a teacher" in his tendencies to talk, to clarify, or simply to "help," is not necessarily the most effective promoter of learning, in the classroom or elsewhere.

The work of the *classroom assistant* (the *laboratory assistant's* duties cannot be treated here) is subject to a good deal of variation. Early in the course, when the instructor is developing his materials and organization, he may be no more than a clerk and errand boy. Once the course is under way, however, his duties would include the distribution of assignments, study questions, and other material to the proctors; the regulation of student flow from place to place; the assignment of students to substitute proctors; the checking of supplies; the maintenance of progress charts; and helping out in demonstrations and proctors' meetings.

Still later, if given some clerical aid, the classroom assistant may preside at proctors' meetings, evaluate proctors' ratings, prepare demonstrations, or give an occasional lecture. He may become practically indistinguishable from the teacher of the course. This is as it should be, in terms of his own growth and the instructor's need for time in which to change the content or procedures of the course, but it should never be permitted unless the assistant fully understands the system of rewards upon which the course depends. The classical role of the assistant as a boss or martinet is out of place within a programmed course. The whip is never needed in such a system; motivation grows with every unit passed, even for students who are well behind; additional pressure would only be disruptive.

The *instructor* in this system is a manager of learning. He selects and analyzes the material to be learned, he decides on how to present it, he constructs the various questions based upon it, and he arranges the contingencies of reward essential to the learning process.

The *textbook*, to begin with, must be carefully read before it is selected, to determine its suitability for students who will be questioned upon it in detail, and who will be given the opportunity to defend their answers. Errors, confusions, and contradictions that might go unnoticed or unremarked within a conventional system may stand out as unsightly blemishes in a programmed-course assignment. Study questions must skirt around them, proctors must be schooled to deal with them, test questions must take them into account, and supplementary material may have to be written to avoid the damage they might do.

The breakdown of material into *study units* is also a task of some magnitude. The textbook chapters may or may not be of suitable size. Their complete mastery has never before been required of all his pupils, and the amount of material assigned may have less than a perfect relation to the amount that a student learns. Difficulty of a unit can only be estimated roughly in advance of an actual tryout, and the instructor in such a course may be in for some surprises.

In writing *study questions*, he must avoid the extremes of over-generality and over-specificity. If his questions are too detailed, they may delay the grasp of major concepts and broad principles—the student won't see the woods for the trees. If too general, they will foster confusion, and they will restrict the number and variety of later test questions that can be based upon them.

(Study questions help the inexperienced or inefficient reader to do what the well-trained reader can do for himself, and they are more important at the beginning of a course than at the end. It is likely that they could be systematically eliminated in successive units, in a manner that would bring the study habits of the initially inferior student to a comparable level with that of the initially superior.)

Test questions are harder to compose than study questions. Ideally, the forms for each unit should be clearly different from each other, but should sample all the basic material of the assignment. They should minimize the role of guessing and they should be suitable for proctors' grading, without encouraging drill in single verbal responses. Wherever possible, they should encourage concept formation, thinking, and reference to affairs that lie beyond the purely academic.

The instructor in such a course has detailed feedback on every question he constructs. As a result, many test questions will have to be rewritten or discarded. Others will cause him to revise the study questions or write supplements to his reading assignments. If this supplementation is on a large enough scale, it can give him a chance to develop original assignments, testing them out on his students as he goes along. Unit by unit, he may even write his own text, as part of his daily teaching function, rather than at times which might better be devoted to research or recreation.

In the spring of 1965, near the end of the semester, I asked the members of my class in elementary psychology to register their reactions to our programmed system, on an unsigned questionnaire. The results of this inquiry suggest that, in comparison with that of the usual lecture or lecture-and-laboratory course, the new method requires a *greater mastery of work assignments* (46 percent of the group said *much greater,* 38 percent said *greater,* and 9 percent said *about the same*). It requires *as much or more memorizing* of detail (19 percent said *much greater,* 38 percent said *greater,* and 22 percent said *about the same*). It involves *greater understanding of basic principles* (44 percent said *much greater,* 41 percent said *greater,* and 14 percent said *about the same*). It generates a *greater feeling of achievement* (33 percent said *much greater,* 46 percent said *greater,* and 13 percent said *about the same*). It gives *greater recognition to the student as an individual* (55 percent said *much greater,* 36 percent said *greater,* and 7 percent said *about the same*). And it is *enjoyed to a greater extent* (48 percent said *much greater,* 32 percent said *greater,* and 17 percent said *about the same*).

It appeared also, from this questionnaire, that, as the course progressed, there was an improvement in study habits, increased confidence in ability to master assignments, an increase in the desire to hear lectures, and a positive change in attitude toward test-taking. The percentage values for the first three categories of the five-point scale are almost as convincing as the ones already mentioned.

With respect to the student-proctor relationship, 94 percent of the class reported that the discussion of tests with the proctors was helpful or very helpful; 79 percent said that the proctor's nonacademic, personal relation to them was important or very important; and 94 percent felt that the use of proctors in the grading and discussion of

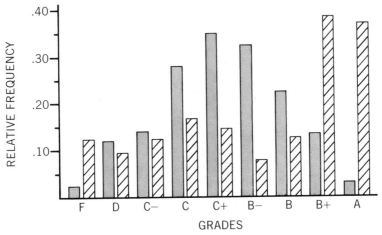

Fig. 4

tests was desirable (64 percent said very desirable).

(A recent study at Queens College, in New York, by Professor John Farmer and associates, gives strong support to the conclusion that student-proctor interaction is directly related to speed of progress through a programmed course. Their data show that the greater the percentage of course units discussed by the student with his proctor the lower the number of tests required to pass each unit. There was no discernible effect of the amount of interaction upon final examination scores).[3]

Results almost identical with these were obtained during the following term by one of my colleagues who distrusted my questionnaire and rewrote all the questions with a negative bias; and similar, but less impressive, data were collected last year by Professor Gary Tolman at Morehouse College in Atlanta, Georgia.

Two or three attempts have been made to compare our system with more conventional ones on the basis of examination scores or final-grade distributions. Figure 4 compares an experimental class from Arizona State with one from an eastern university on a mid-term examination having the same questions but administered to the Arizona group without warning while they were working at many different unit levels of the course. The shaded bars represent the Arizona data.[4]

Figure 3 represents a final-grade comparison of two classes of students in the same course at Queens College. One class was taught conventionally and the other employed the proctorial system

3. Reported by J. Farmer, G. D. Lachter, and J. J. Blaustein, at the 39th Annual Meeting of the Eastern Psychological Association in Washington, D.C., on April 18, 1968.
4. A more detailed description of this comparison may be found in F. S. Keller, *Engineering Personalized Instruction in the Classroom*. Revista Interamericana de Psicologia, 1967, **1**, 3, 189–97.

I've described. The shaded bars, as noted before, picture the distribution of grades under the programmed system.

Results like these point in the direction of the superiority of our system, but they should not be taken too seriously. We are still in the exploratory phase of our work, and we have a great deal to learn — about the frequency of reviews, the size of assignments, the nature of study questions, the degree of mastery desired, and so on. There is hardly an area in which changes cannot be made, to the possible advantage of the system.

A programmed system, however, is one in which the proper functioning of each part depends on the proper functioning of the others, and a change in one area may conceivably have bad effects in others. Especially sensitive in this respect are those aspects of the system which mark it as distinctive.

There is, first, the *go-at-your-own pace* feature. The teacher who places a restriction on this goes back in some degree to conventional procedures, and he must be prepared for negative repercussions.

Secondly, there is the demand for *unit perfection* as the basic condition of advance. *Perfection* is a relative term, but its value for the student should not be underestimated. To accept even a 90 percent criterion of success is to return to a numerical rating that is meaningless in describing what a student does or does not know. Not all A-students are alike in their potentiality, but they *are* alike in the requirements they have satisfied, and that is the only realistic meaning that can be given to the grade.

Thirdly, there is the *use of proctors*, which permits immediate scoring and repeated testing, which facilitates student-instructor communication, and which enhances the personal-social aspect of the educational process. This is the kind of learning situation suggested by the classic example of Mark Hopkins and his Williams student on a log together. It is not entirely different from the situation that was provided for John Stuart Mill when he learned Greek, with his father across the table from him as his only lexicon. Something like it was also found in the one-room schoolhouse of my youth; it may operate at any time when the children of a family gather in the light of a single lamp to do their homework; and it is even akin to the relationship of master to apprentice since the beginnings of civilization. I refer simply to the rewarding influence of a knowledgeable human organism upon the learning of an organism somewhat lower in the intellectual scale.

I know that learning is possible in the absence of such "live" human interaction. It may even be true that the essence of such interaction will one day be captured by computerized instruction. Until that day comes, I suggest that the well-controlled proctor, despite his human weaknesses, may simulate computer function. Any large-scale attempt to replace him in the system should be made with caution.

Finally, there is the use of *lectures and demonstrations as motiva-*

tional devices, rather than sources of information. The tendency today is strong within most teachers to give speeches which students are compelled to attend and upon which they will be examined. The role of the teacher in the history of mass education has been, unfortunately, that of the talker; and when one comes to direct a programmed course he may find it hard to resist his old behavior patterns. They should, however, be resisted, or given very limited opportunity for expression.

Generally speaking, no change should be introduced within a programmed system without carefully considering its possible effect upon everyone involved. It is not enough to think only of the student's welfare; the proctor, the assistant, and the instructor must also be looked after, if their optimal interaction is to be maintained, and if the system itself is to survive. What is meat for one must not be poison for another.

There are pitfalls for the operator of a programmed course, even when he is most successful. A couple of illustrations from an earlier address may be useful at this point:

> When one finds that some of the members of his class (I'm speaking of a programmed course) complete their assignments, without apparent effect, five weeks before the end of the semester, he begins to wonder if the course is too easy. When he sees students and proctors who are obviously enjoying themselves in their educational activity, he asks himself if something immoral isn't taking place. When he replaces an *Incomplete* with an A ten weeks after the course has officially ended, for a student who is clearly inferior in his intellectual powers to one who took but ten weeks to do the whole job, he finds himself lying awake at night wondering about the meaning of an A.
>
> Such things may lead the instructor to ask for better performance from next semester's class. The assignments get larger; the study questions are more detailed; and the proctors are told to grade more strictly. Little by little, the educational control becomes more conventional and more aversive for an increasing number of students. Disputes arise in various quarters; complaints become more common; someone discovers a student trying to cheat; proctors are more often absent from their work; and, ultimately, a pleasant query may come to the Departmental Chairman from the Office of the Dean.
>
> Another and more serious pitfall lies in the premature acceptance of the challenge to teach large numbers. The pressure today is great in this direction, but what begins as flattering testimony to the success of a method could easily end in its destruction. A naive observer might be tempted to conclude that one instructor could teach a class of a thousand students as easily as he teaches fifty, assuming that he had sufficient space, facilities, assistants, and proctors. Actually, however, the maximal number may be [no more than] a hundred, within a single course of study. To add more might remove the instructor from effective

contact, not only with his students but with his proctors. If the assistants were made into teachers and the teachers were given assistants, the outcome [would] be different; but one ought to approach very gingerly any other proposal to multiply his function. A semester is a long time in which to live with an educational mistake; and the quality of teaching is more important than its quantity, even in a population explosion.[5]

About a week ago I received a letter from a young professor of psychology in a well-known eastern college. It reads in part as follows:

> Thanks for putting me on to your course format. I'm much too busy to write, but it sure is exciting: 240 students, 11 proctors, and myself; we also have labs—I've never worked so hard in my life.
>
> I was skeptical of your optimism last Spring, but no longer. We had a student finish the course today, and he's now reading Galanter's chapter on Contemporary Psychophysics in Newcomb's book, *New Directions in Psychology* . . . Not bad for a freshman.

My friend fell into both of the traps I just mentioned. First, he overreached in the number of students he attempted to serve. He should have about 15 more proctors and at least one more assistant, to whom he should now be able to turn over half of his students and proctors. Secondly, he probably should not have put his Number 1 boy to work on psychophysics at this time or under these conditions of study. He might rather have set him free, or even broken him in as a next term proctor. As for overwork, next year will be better, and so will the remainder of this term. His course logistics must now be well arranged and his first man has finished the course, which means that all the unit assignments and study questions have been prepared for the rest of the class, together with at least one round of readiness tests for every unit.

Letters like this, however, brighten my days. Without people who are willing to break with tradition, to try out new procedures, and to undergo fire, perhaps, from many quarters, the best teaching system in the world will never find acceptance.

And the system I've described is surely *not* the best one. It is not even the only one, as I noted at the outset of this paper. I can think of others—at Bucknell, at Georgetown, at Palomar, at Purdue, at Western Michigan, and elsewhere—in each of which a serious attempt is being made to overhaul our teaching methods in the light of what we know about the learning process; and there will be more.

---

5. This quotation is from F. S. Keller, *Neglected Rewards in the Educational Process,* Proc. 23d American Conference of Academy Deans, Los Angeles, January 1967, pp. 9–22.

The text of this book was set Linofilm in 9 point Caledonia. This versatile typeface was designed by William Addison Dwiggins and was cut by the Mergenthaler Linotype Company in 1938. Display heads were set in Clearface Bold, and most figures and tables in Trade Gothic.

Composition was done by Applied Typographic Systems of Mountain View, California.

Printing and binding were done by Kingsport Press, Inc., Kingsport, Tennessee.

12345/987654321